PERGAMON GENERAL PSYCHOLOGY SERIES
EDITORS
Arnold P. Goldstein, Syracuse University
Leonard Krasner, Stanford University & SUNY at Stony Brook

THE PRACTICE OF CHILD THERAPY

(PGPS-124)

Pergamon Titles of Related Interest

Hersen/Last HANDBOOK OF CHILD AND ADULT
PSYCHOPATHOLOGY: A Longitudinal Perspective
Johnson/Rasbury/Siegel APPROACHES TO CHILD TREATMENT:
Introduction to Theory, Research and Practice
Kazdin CHILD PSYCHOTHERAPY: Developing and Identifying
Effective Treatments
Roberts PEDIATRIC PSYCHOLOGY: Psychological Interventions and
Strategies for Pediatric Problems
Schwartz/Johnson PSYCHOPATHOLOGY OF CHILDHOOD: A
Clinical-Experimental Approach, Second Edition
White THE TROUBLED ADOLESCENT

Related Journals
(Free sample copies available on request.)

CLINICAL PSYCHOLOGY REVIEW
JOURNAL OF CHILD PSYCHOLOGY AND PSYCHIATRY
JOURNAL OF SCHOOL PSYCHOLOGY
RESEARCH IN DEVELOPMENTAL DISABILITIES

THE PRACTICE OF CHILD THERAPY

Second Edition

Edited by

THOMAS R. KRATOCHWILL
University of Wisconsin–Madison

RICHARD J. MORRIS
University of Arizona

PERGAMON PRESS

Member of Maxwell Macmillan Pergamon Publishing Corporation
New York • Oxford • Beijing • Frankfurt
São Paulo • Sydney • Tokyo • Toronto

Pergamon Press Offices:

U.S.A.	Pergamon Press, Inc., Maxwell House, Fairview Park, Elmsford, New York 10523, U.S.A.
U.K.	Pergamon Press plc, Headington Hill Hall, Oxford OX3 0BW, England
PEOPLE'S REPUBLIC OF CHINA	Pergamon Press, 0909 China World Tower, No. 1 Jian Guo Men Wai Avenue, Beijing 100004, People's Republic of China
FEDERAL REPUBLIC OF GERMANY	Pergamon Press GmbH, Hammerweg 6, D-6242 Kronberg, Federal Republic of Germany
BRAZIL	Pergamon Editora Ltda, Rua Eça de Queiros, 346, CEP 04011, Paraiso, São Paulo, Brazil
AUSTRALIA	Pergamon Press Australia Pty Ltd., P.O. Box 544, Potts Point, NSW 2011, Australia
JAPAN	Pergamon Press, 8th Floor, Matsuoka Central Building, 1-7-1 Nishishinjuku, Shinjuku-ku, Tokyo 160, Japan
CANADA	Pergamon Press Canada Ltd., Suite 271, 253 College Street, Toronto, Ontario M5T 1R5, Canada

Library of Congress Cataloging in Publication Data

The Practice of child therapy / edited by Thomas R. Kratochwill,
   Richard J. Morris. -- 2nd ed.
      p.   cm. -- (Pergamon general psychology series ; 124)
     Includes bibliographical references.
     ISBN 0-08-036430-6 : -- ISBN 0-08-036429-2 (pbk.) :
     1. Child psychotherapy. I. Kratochwill, Thomas R. II. Morris,
   Richard J. III. Series.
   RJ504.P68   1990
   618.92′8914--dc20   89-78238
                                                           CIP

Printing   2 3 4 5 6 7 8 9   Year: 1 2 3 4 5 6 7 8 9

Printed in the United States of America

The paper used in this publication meets the minimum requirements of American National Standard for Information Sciences—Permanence of Paper for Printed Library Materials, ANSI Z39.48-1984

To
Tyler Thomas Kratochwill
and
Lee Meyerson and Nancy Kerr, who have
dedicated their professional careers to helping children

CONTENTS

Part III. ISSUES AND CONCERNS REGARDING INTERVENTION

PREFACE

We are delighted to produce a second edition of *The Practice of Child Therapy*. Research, theory, and practice continue to grow rapidly in the area of treatment of childhood learning and behavior disorders. Nevertheless, there are still relatively few books that have presented a systematic review and detailed discussion of existing treatment procedures for children's learning and behavior disorders. In our volume we have tried to present a broad range of child treatment approaches in which systematic and detailed discussion of available treatment techniques takes precedence over conceptual and theoretical issues.

Our book is again intended to be a treatment-oriented reference volume for individuals who work and intend to work directly in the area of childhood learning and behavior disorders. The second edition has been enlarged and expanded. The book contains 14 chapters covering obsessive compulsive disorders, childhood depression, childhood fears and phobias, attention-deficit disorder, academic problems, aggressive behavior and conduct disorder, so-matic disorders, childhood autism, mental retardation in children, children medically at risk, psychopharmacotherapy, prevention, and professional, legal, and ethical issues in childhood treatment.

The book is designed to assemble in one volume summaries of the treatment literature and related treatment procedures on some of the more common childhood disorders. As was true in the first edition, we have not included all possible childhood disorders. On the other hand, we have attempted to sample those most often encountered by individuals who practice in applied settings (e.g., clinic and counseling centers; classroom and school settings; home, residential, and hospital settings). Each chapter is written by an individual or individuals who are well qualified to discuss the treatment practices for the specific topic under consideration. Although the authors have generally adopted a broad-based behavioral orientation in their respective chapters, the reader will also note that we have asked them to take an empirical approach toward inclusion of treatment techniques that have been applied to the disorder.

Authors were again encouraged to sample widely from existing sources in the treatment literature and to construct their presentation on the basis of empirically derived treatment techniques and procedures. Some chapters include a discussion of theoretical issues, but the primary emphasis is on intervention techniques and strategies for changing various problem behaviors. Case examples are often used to elucidate the treatment procedures presented in the chapter.

The book is intended for individuals who have entered or plan to enter mental health and related applied professions, including special education, nursing, rehabilitation, and counseling. The book will be especially useful for individuals taking child therapy and child intervention courses and practicum courses as well as for those professionals who work in applied settings, including schools, clinics, counseling psychology, special education, social work, and psychiatry.

A number of individuals made major contributions to completion of this work. Thanks are given to Jerry Frank at Pergamon Press for his support in the development of a first edition and continuing support in the preparation of this edition. In addition, we express our appreciation to Karen Kraemer for all her secretarial assistance during various phases of this project. Appreciation is also extended to Hugh Johnston for his review efforts. Primarily, we express our special thanks to our wives, Carol Kratochwill and Vinnie Morris, who have constantly served as inspirations for our professional work and our work with children.

PART I

INTRODUCTION

CHAPTER 1

INTRODUCTORY COMMENTS

Richard J. Morris
Thomas R. Kratochwill

HISTORICAL CONTEXT OF CHILD THERAPY

Although we currently find a great deal of interest in the care and treatment of behavior-disordered children, this is a relatively recent event in the mental health field. Unlike the adult treatment literature—which can be traced back to ancient civilizations, with reliance on such practices as trephining and exorcism—the child mental health treatment literature can be traced with any clarity only to the early twentieth century (Achenbach, 1974; Kanner, 1948). The one notable exception is the literature on children who were diagnosed as mentally retarded.

Concern for the systematic and organized care of mentally retarded children can be traced to Jean Itard and his attempts, beginning in 1799, to educate the "Wild Boy of Aveyron." These initial treatment approaches were continued by Edward Seguin in the mid-1800s, with research concerned with the causes, nature, and treatment of mental retardation (Achenbach, 1974). This work was followed by the building of residential schools for mentally retarded persons—

the first in Massachusetts in 1848 and the second in New York in 1851. These facilities were initially established on an experimental basis as educational institutions, almost like boarding schools, rather than as custodial asylums. The assumption here was that after receiving training to assist them in their functioning in society, these children would be returned to their homes. However, this assumption was found to lack empirical support, since few students/residents actually returned home. By the end of the nineteenth century, the state residential "educational" institution, although still typically called a "state school" for the mentally retarded (mentally deficient or idiots and feebleminded), had become a custodial treatment institution.

Other notable developments in the early twentieth century that contributed to the concern with the treatment of children were the following: (1) the mental hygiene movement, (2) the establishment of child guidance clinics, and (3) the introduction of dynamic psychiatry. Within the mental hygiene movement, Clifford Beers is credited with changing the direction of the treatment of mentally ill persons in America. Beers, a law student at Yale University, had become clinically depressed and suicidal and was hospitalized. Following his hospitalization, Beers published *A Mind That Found Itself* (1908), describing the mistreatment that he and others received while they were patients at a state mental hospital. The book gained considerable popularity and raised the level of public awareness of the terrible conditions in the state hospitals and the inadequate treatment received by mental patients. With the help of a number of prominent professionals (for example, Adolph Meyer and William James), Beers formed the National Committee for Mental Hygiene to inform the public of the conditions in state hospitals, to promote the establishment of better treatment methods, and to sponsor research on the prevention and treatment of mental illness. This led to the establishment of mental hygiene programs in schools and the beginning of the child guidance movement (Kauffman, 1981).

The child guidance movement had actually started prior to the publication of Beers's book, because of the establishment of a psychological clinic in 1896 by Lightner Witmer at the University of Pennsylvania. However, the movement gained impetus following the publication of Beers's book and the establishment, in 1909, of the Juvenile Psychopathic Institute (now called the Institute for Juvenile Research) in Chicago, under the leadership of William Healy. The institute staff worked directly with juvenile offenders and stressed an interdisciplinary approach to studying them. Psychiatrists, psychologists, and social workers worked together on particular cases, emphasizing the multiple contributing factors to any given child's behavior disorder(s).

Aided by Beers's National Committee for Mental Hygiene, other child guidance clinics developed across the country to work with a broader range of children's behavior disorders. Kanner (1948) reports that by 1930, there were about 500 such clinics in the United States.

The introduction of dynamic psychiatry in the early twentieth century also substantially contributed to our current emphasis on treatment services to children. Sigmund Freud, in Vienna, and Adolph Meyer, in the United States, are often credited with introducing the dynamic approach. Individuals affiliated with this approach maintained that the origins of behavior problems lay in the past (typically, childhood) experiences of the person (Kanner, 1948). With adult pa-

tients, these experiences were explored retrospectively by the psychiatrist, who attempted to draw causal relationships between these past experiences and the patients' present behavior. It should be emphasized that, during these early years, children were usually not seen in treatment by psychiatrists. In fact, as Kanner (1948) states, "Even Freud, who so clearly understood the influence of early experiences on emotional development, had his theory of infantile sexuality all worked out and published [in 1905] three years before he even saw one single child professionally" (p. 7). However, the retrospective search for the relationship between early childhood events and present functioning aroused sufficient interest among professionals that some began to acquaint themselves specifically with the behavior problems of children as well as with the dynamics that contribute to their difficulties.

This psychodynamic interest in children was not formally realized in the literature until the publication, in 1909, of Freud's detailed case of "Little Hans." Interestingly, although Freud formulated his etiological theory of phobias on the basis of Hans's symptoms and experiences, he did not treat Hans directly. Hans's father treated him under Freud's direction and supervision (Morris & Kratochwill, 1983).

Although Hans's problem was treated successfully, it was not until 15 to 20 years later that Freudian psychoanalytic child therapy came into existence. This was largely due to the contributions and adaptations of his treatment for children by Melanie Klein, Freud's student, and Anna Freud, his daughter. Their changes made his therapeutic approach more applicable to children and contributed to its increasing popularity in subsequent years. Some of the changes were the substitution of play activities for the technique of free association and the use of drawings and dreams to understand a child's problem more completely (Knopf, 1979). These changes and the emphasis on the child's internal dynamics from Freud's psychoanalytic theory made psychoanalytic play therapy popular and influential in the development of many later forms of child therapy.

Thus, these three major developments—and the earlier concerns by professionals for the care and treatment of children and adults who were mentally retarded—contributed substantially to our present focus on the provision of clinical services to emotionally disturbed children. Other developments also contributed to the current focus and should be mentioned briefly. The intelligence testing movement, begun by Alfred Binet at the beginning of the twentieth century, had a tremendous influence on the study of children. As a result, it became possible to learn the extent to which a particular child differed from the norm in cognitive ability. It also demonstrated clearly the diversity of children in terms of their comprehension of classroom instruction (Kanner, 1948).

The formation of three professional associations, in addition to Clifford Beers's National Committee for Mental Hygiene, also contributed to the increasing emphasis on the treatment of children. The first association was the Association of Medical Officers of American Institutions for Idiots and Feebleminded Persons, founded in 1876, which evolved into the present-day American Association on Mental Retardation. Its first president was Edward Seguin. In 1922, the second association, The Council for Exceptional Children, was formed. It consisted primarily of educators and other professionals, although parents were members too. The third early association was the American Orthopsychiatric Association, founded in 1924 and consisting primarily of psychiatrists, applied psychologists, and social workers, although educators as well as other professionals and parents were also members. Each of these groups encouraged the formulation and conduct of research with behavior-disordered children as well as the sharing of information regarding effective psychological and/or educational interventions.

Finally, following the emerging changes in the early twentieth century in the predominant and very rigid and structured philosophy surrounding the education of students, and in recognition of Alfred Binet's work, a movement to provide more individualized instruction and special education classes for mentally and emotionally handicapped students began. These classes were to be taught by teachers who had studied the particular behavior disorders and had developed specific methods for modifying them. As a result, teacher-training programs began to develop—the earliest appearing in 1914, in Michigan.

In considering all these developments, one begins to realize that concern with the treatment and care of children did not stem from one or two major activities. Rather, many events, occurring over approximately 50 years, set the stage for our present-day services for children. The authors of the remaining chapters provide a brief historical perspective on their respective topics and then present a detailed account of various therapeutic methods for helping children and adolescents change their behavior. We hope that readers will find these chapters of great interest and practical value.

REFERENCES

Achenbach, T. M. (1974). *Developmental psychopathology*. New York: Ronald Press.

Beers, C. (1908). *A mind that found itself*. New York: Longmans, Green.

Freud, S. (1963, 1909). The analysis of a phobia in a five-year-old boy. *Standard edition of the complete psychological works of Sigmund Freud* (Vol. 10). London: Hogarth Press.

Kanner, L. (1948). *Child psychiatry*. Springfield, IL: Charles C Thomas.

Kauffman, J. M. (1981). *Characteristics of children's behavior disorders*. Columbus, OH: Merrill.

Knopf, I. J. (1979). *Childhood psychopathology*. Englewood Cliffs, NJ: Prentice-Hall.

Morris, R. J., & Kratochwill, T. R. (1983). *Treating children's fears and phobias: A behavioral approach*. Elmsford, NY: Pergamon Press.

PART II

INTERVENTION STRATEGIES FOR SPECIFIC BEHAVIOR DISORDERS

CHAPTER 2

OBSESSIVE COMPULSIVE DISORDERS

Jesse B. Milby
Anna Weber

This chapter reviews research and clinical findings on obsessive compulsive disorders (OCD) in children. First, the epidemiology, etiology, and theories of OCD are briefly reviewed. Then the various assessment and treatment strategies are described and those that seem most useful and effective recommended.

HISTORICAL PERSPECTIVE

Religious and medical conceptualizations of OCD antedate Freud's postulation that obsessions stem from defensive reactions to psychosexual anxiety. The earliest concepts of obsession were probably religious, since its genesis was considered to be religious experience, specifically demonic influence (Rachman & Hodgson, 1980). Early medical conceptualization of OCD involved the role of fevers and a disordered imagination.

There has been a historical transition from religious and medical to psychoanalytic and psychological conceptualizations of OCD. Most contemporary work utilizes the medical and psychological models. Those interested in fur-

ther historical background are directed to Rachman and Hodgson (1980, chapter 3) and Hunter and MacAlpine (1963); historical sources; and Skoog (1959), who reviews the early psychiatric literature.

TERMINOLOGY PROBLEMS

The literature on OCD is confusing because there is no agreement on definitions and terminology. Terms like "obsessionality," "obsessive compulsive personality," "obsessive compulsive traits," "obsessive compulsive neurosis," and "obsessive compulsive disorder" are often used interchangeably. This complicates the search for trends in patient types. Consequently, the assumption that such terms refer to obsessive compulsive neurosis or OCD may be erroneous unless a careful description of symptoms is included. For example, in most of the inheritance studies reviewed by Rachman and Hodgson (1980), co-twins and relatives were almost always classified as having "obsessionality," without further specification. No distinction was made between the disorder and personality traits;

they were assumed to be synonymous. In order not to perpetuate this problem, we will use terms as defined by Rachman and Hodgson (1980).

KEY TERMS AND CONCEPTS

Obsession—an intrusive, repetitive thought, image, or impulse. It is unacceptable, associated with subjective resistance, and usually produces distress.

The reader should be aware that others have included, within this definition, repetitive thoughts that reduce distress (Meredith & Milby, 1980). Foa and Tillman (1978) have developed a useful taxonomy of obsessions based on their function for the individual.

Compulsion—a repetitive, stereotyped act, completely or partly unacceptable but regarded as excessive and/or exaggerated. It is accompanied by a subjective need to perform the act and often provokes long-term distress but usually reduces immediate distress.

Compulsive ritual—an act that is performed in a prescribed manner. Although the ritual is under voluntary control, the urge to perform it is strong and the performer experiences a sense of diminished volition.

Four other OCD phenomena are defined and described later, in the section on behavioral assessment issues. They are *compulsive rituals, cognitive compulsions, primary obsessional slowness,* and *obsessive doubting.*

DIAGNOSIS OF OBSESSIVE COMPULSIVE DISORDER

The diagnosis of obsessive compulsive disorder includes the following characteristics:

1. Reported occurrence of an obsession and/or a compulsion.
2. Reliable accompanying behavioral signs of the obsessions and compulsions.
3. Complaint and signs associated with at least moderate distress and impairment of functioning (i.e., in social, vocational and academic spheres).
4. The presence of three key indicators:
   a. Experience of subjective compulsions.
   b. Report of internal resistance.
   c. Presence of insight or some awareness, depending on the child's age.

The clinician also looks for a relatively intact personality outside the domain of the obsessive and compulsive symptoms, although this is not a diagnostic criterion as such.

The recent revision of the American Psychiatric Association's *Diagnostic and Statistical Manual of Mental Disorders* (APA, 1987) contains several clarifications of the diagnostic criteria for obsessive compulsive disorder that appeared in DSM-III (APA, 1980). Both editions require the presence of either obsessions or compulsions that cause distress sufficient to interfere with normal social and occupational functioning. However, DSM-III-R makes the additional requirement that the obsessions for compulsions are time-consuming—requiring more than one hour per day. DSM-III-R also subdivides and makes more explicit the individual criteria for obsessions and compulsions. The obsessions or compulsions must meet the specific criteria outlined in the following lists and the obsessions or compulsions must cause marked distress, be time-consuming, or "significantly interfere with the person's normal routine, occupational functioning, or usual social activities or relationships with others" (APA, 1987, p. 247).

There are four explicit criteria for obsessions:

1. recurrent and persistent ideas, thoughts, impulses, or images that are experienced, at least initially, as intrusive and senseless, e.g., a parent's having repeated impulses to kill a loved child, a religious person's having recurrent blasphemous thoughts;
2. the person attempts to ignore or suppress such thoughts or impulses or to neutralize them with some other thought or action;
3. the person recognizes that the obsessions are the product of his or her own mind, not imposed from without (as in thought insertion);
4. if another Axis I disorder is present, the content of the obsession is unrelated to it, e.g., the ideas, thoughts, impulses, or images are not about food in the presence of an Eating Disorder, about drugs in the presence of a Psychoactive Substance Use Disorder, or guilty thoughts in the presence of a Major Depression.

There are three explicit criteria for compulsions:

1. repetitive, purposeful, and intentional behaviors that are performed in response to an obsession, or according to certain rules or in a stereotyped fashion
2. the behavior is designed to neutralize or to prevent discomfort or some dreaded event or situation; however, either the activity is not connected in a realistic way with what it is designed to neutralize or prevent, or it is clearly excessive
3. the person recognizes that his or her behavior is excessive or unreasonable (this may not be true for young children; it may no longer be true for people whose obsessions have evolved into overvalued ideas).

These criteria thus exclude the psychotic child, who may also have troubling obsessions and rituals, and the brain-damaged child, who fails to meet the criteria. The diagnosis should not be dismissed with a brain-injured individual with a known preinjury OCD. However, OCD or obsessive compulsive personality styles may co-exist with other psychiatric syndromes. Generally, obsessive compulsive personality disorder should not be diagnosed as such in children, since the DSM-III-R criteria generally refer to "behaviors or traits that are characteristic of the person's recent (past year) and long-term functioning since early adulthood" (APA, 1987, p. 335). However, in unusual instances where the maladaptive OC pattern appears to be stable, it may be used. The clinician should understand that in such cases there is less certainty that the personality disorder will persist through adolescence and emerge relatively unchanged in adulthood.

ON THE RELATIONSHIP BETWEEN OBSESSIONS AND COMPULSIONS

There is usually a close relationship between obsessions and compulsions such that the former predisposes, if not causes, the latter. The presence of one implies the other. However, there may be exceptions. In primary obsessional slowness found in adults, there is dissociation between the ritualized behavior and identifiable obsessions (Rachman, 1974). In obsessive doubting, cognitive activities dominate the conscious state without provoking overt behavior. One adult study found that 25% of reported obsessions were not associated with compulsions (Akhtar, Pershad, & Verma, 1975). Ob-

sessions and compulsions in adults can run independent courses within the same patient, or obsessions may irrevocably lead to some compulsive activity (Milby, Meredith, & Rice, 1981).

Case Illustration

The case of Matthew, a 9-year-old white male, is given to illustrate the clinical presentation of childhood OCD. The case exemplifies the type of childhood OCD that the reader is likely to confront in daily practice. It is not presented as exemplary clinical intervention; rather, it addresses a number of clinical issues that confront those working with OCD youngsters.

Matthew was seen for evaluation with the primary presenting problems of an extremely high level of anxiety, difficulty sleeping, and various obsessive and compulsive behaviors. Matthew was the oldest of three children, having a 7-year-old brother and a 2-year-old sister. He was living with his natural mother, following his parents' divorce approximately a year prior to referral. The family situation was extremely tense, with ongoing hostility and strife between the mother and father. Matthew clearly felt divided loyalty and affection for each of his parents. In addition to this major source of stress, Matthew's family was also experiencing severe financial difficulties; they had recently moved to a new residence, which necessitated a change of school. Also, the mother was working, thus spending less time at home.

The mother's pregnancy and delivery care had been without complications. Matthew achieved developmental milestones within normal limits. His early educational experiences were generally positive; he was a diligent and successful student with no history of learning problems. Intellectually, he performed in the bright normal range.

On mental status examination, Matthew was extremely shaky and tense, preoccupied with fears of dying and that his mother or grandmother might die. He was neat in appearance and rather withdrawn but somewhat ingratiating on interview. His mood was primarily depressed, with vegetative signs of weight loss and sleep disturbance. There was no evidence of psychotic process.

His obsessive symptomatology included repetitive thoughts and fantasies of mother and grandmother dying as well as ritualistic counting, which he reportedly did to avoid harm to his family or himself. As this problem developed, he stated that odd numbers represented his father and even numbers his mother. In addition, he exhibited a number of compulsive motoric behaviors, including ritualized hand-washing to avoid contamination of himself or family members and repetitive touching of many objects (e.g., a coffee cup) in a specific manner and for a specified number of times.

Matthew was initially seen for several outpatient evaluative visits. It was soon apparent that his level of distress and discomfort was reactive to his family situation, particularly to his parents' divorce. His mother was concerned with Matthew and appeared excessively protective. She was embittered by her divorce and had achieved little resolution of her anger and hostility toward her ex-husband. This theme was pervasive throughout the interactions.

Matthew was hospitalized to remove him from some of the sources of stress impinging upon him and to allow him and his mother some relief from their rather strained interactions while each was working toward a more healthy emotional independence. He was treated medically with 50 mg of imipramine at bedtime and involved in the therapeutic milieu of the hospital setting. The separation of mother and son was difficult for both; in Matthew, an initial intensification of crying and ritualized behavior was observed. As this occurred, the mother's distress intensified and she became more indulgent and protective, to the point of demanding discharge on several occasions. She found it difficult to proceed with hospitalization and spent most of her free time with Matthew on the treatment unit or with staff members, discussing his treatment. Treatment on the hospital unit assumed the form of matter-of-fact involvement of Matthew in therapeutic activities (group therapy, occupational therapy, recreational therapy), reassurance, and gentle but firm response prevention and interruption of his rituals. He was seen daily for individual sessions over his 2½-week period of hospitalization. Discussion revolved around his parents' divorce. Themes discussed included his anger and ambivalence about his parents and guilt that he was experiencing over sexual feelings and behavior. His mother was also involved in several individual and family sessions with Matthew, with a focus on helping her adjust more effectively to the divorce and to changing her pattern of reinforcing Matthew's behavior. The mother maintained a rather hostile and resistive reaction to the identification of her part in Matthew's difficulties, choosing to project blame on the absent father.

Matthew responded with a gradual diminution of anxiety and a substantial reduction in obsessional and ritualistic behavior. Relatively symptom-free periods were, on several occasions, interrupted by visits with the mother and a resulting intensification of distress on Matthew's part. On the mother's insistence, but prematurely as viewed by the treatment team, Matthew was discharged from the hospital. His condition on discharge was much improved with respect to his concerns about death, counting and touching rituals, compulsive hand-washing, general anxiety level, sleep patterns, and return to normal appetite. Although Matthew and his mother achieved some improvement in terms of more appropriate emotional independence, less was accomplished in terms of helping the mother deal more effectively with her feelings about the divorce or to be more therapeutic with Matthew.

Matthew and his mother missed the first two scheduled outpatient visits, reportedly due to difficulty "getting Matthew to the clinic." As Matthew's symptoms were beginning to show some exacerbation with his return to the unsettled family situation, arrangements were made for Matthew and his mother to be followed more closely through a community mental health center, which provided an opportunity for more consistent involvement due to easier access for the family.

This case illustrates the development of both obsessive and compulsive behaviors as a reaction to extreme environmental stress. Obsessive compulsive symptoms functioned to reduce the discomfort generated by severe family conflict. This case also illustrates the role of family dynamics in the development and maintenance of OCD. It highlights the importance of a broad-spectrum approach to treatment, which may need to include environmental restructuring as well as specific behavioral and family interventions. It raises questions about the generalization of treatment effects as well as the selection of primary treatment targets (i.e., intrapsychic dynamic issues such as dealing with anger and sexuality, family dysfunction, and specific behavioral or cognitive excesses) and the use of hospitalization.

This case is a typical example of OCD as it presents in childhood. The remaining portions of this chapter will review what is currently known about the assessment and treatment of

OCD in children and answer some of the questions that arise when we try to treat youngsters like Matthew.

THE EPIDEMIOLOGY OF OCD

The Natural History and Course of OCD

Though descriptive data on the natural history of any disorder are useful, and there are such data on OCD, a caveat must be registered. These data are imprecise, mostly retrospective, incomplete, and lacking in minimally adequate sampling procedure. All are nonrandom and most are nonsystematic samples. Most importantly, the data are obfuscated by the unreliable application of variable diagnostic concepts and definitions. Despite this elaborate demurrer, we feel that the observations and impressions making up such works as Black's (1974), Kringlen's (1970), and Rachman and Hodgson's (1980, chapter 3) are valuable. Considering the obstacles previously mentioned, there is a surprising amount of agreement on the essential features of OCD and its course; exceptions involve reports of prognosis for improvement, where the range is 25% to 71% (Kringlen, 1965).

Goodwin, Guze, and Robins (1969) reviewed 13 follow-up studies of obsessive compulsive neurosis and concluded that it has its onset in childhood or early adult life and follows a chronic but variable course. They found a more favorable prognosis than is often reported in the literature. Their data were not consistent with opinion about prognosis generally expressed in the psychoanalytic literature. Their findings did not suggest that OCD involves increased risks of suicide, homicide, substance abuse, chronic hospitalization, or the development of other mental disorders, especially schizophrenia. Black (1974) in his review found that one third of OCD patients had a history of neurotic symptoms at early adolescence. The disorder began for most between the ages of 10 and 15 and had been initiated in more than half the cases by age 25.

In one study, 10 of 17 cases of childhood OCD treated with psychotherapy were interviewed to determine outcome (Hollingsworth, Tanguay, Grossman, & Pabst, 1980). All 10 reported serious problems with social life and peer relationships. None were married and only 30% were dating. Seven still suffered from obsessive compulsive symptoms. Though selection bias may have been operating, with only the more dysfunctional patients volunteering for follow-up, the results were telling. If one assumes that the seven uninterviewed patients were asymptomatic (an unlikely possibility), that still means 41% were symptomatic and 59% somewhat impaired.

Two investigators classified adult patients according to whether their level of dysfunction required outpatient or inpatient hospital care. They found 60% to 80% were asymptomatic or improved 1 to 5 years after diagnosis, with higher rates of improvement among outpatients (Lo, 1968; Pollit, 1957). But two other studies reported no more than 33% symptomatically improved several years after discharge (Kringlen, 1965; Ingram, 1961).

One cross-cultural review of 13 follow-up studies from six countries, involving 816 patients, classified three different courses for OCD in adults (Goodwin et al., 1969): (1) unremitting with or without social incapacity, (2) episodic, and (3) incomplete remitting that permitted normal social functioning.

Rasmussen and Tsuang (1986) described a sample of 44 patients who met DSM-III criteria for OCD. They found that 84% of these patients had a continuous course, 14% had a chronic deteriorative course, and only 2% (one patient) had an episodic course. However, until these courses can be traced from childhood OCD, it would be a mistake to assume such courses for children.

The most common complication of adult OCD is depression. However, in spite of the frequency with which self-harm is an obsessional theme, most studies show less than 1% commit suicide (Goodwin et al., 1969; Grimshaw, 1965; Ingram, 1961; Pollit, 1957). Another complication or result of OCD is failure to marry. Several investigators have noted a larger ratio of unmarried obsessionals compared to the general population (Kringlen, 1965; Lo, 1968; Pollit, 1957; Rachman & Hodgson, 1980). This has implications for childhood OCD in that development of heterosexual social interaction usually occurs in adolescence, when many OCDs first appear.

The Incidence of OCD

OCD in children is rare. The highest incidence rates seem to be less than 2% of child cases seen. Judd (1965) found 1.2% incidence in 405 children seen in inpatient and outpatient settings. Adams (1972) also found a 1.2% incidence in a pool of 2,500 children seen for evaluation or treatment. Berman (1974) described 6 cases among 3,500 patients, a rate of 0.002%. Rutter, Tizard, and Whitmore (1970) found 7 OCDs among 2,193 children 10 to 11 years of age who were screened in a nonpsychiatric population, a rate of 0.003%. This low incidence partly explains the paucity of well-controlled group research.

The most recent prevalence study (Flament et al., 1985) of an entire school population of a New Jersey county ($N = 5,000$) revealed a prevalence rate of 0.33% of the general adolescent population. This rate is considerably higher than most reported in the literature; it remains to be seen whether other recent estimates of prevalence corroborate it.

In their recent review of the prevalence rates of anxiety disorders in general, Weissman and Merikangas (1986) noted the lack of data concerning children. Clearly, there is a need here for more systematic prevalence data that use the new DSM-III-R diagnostic criteria. Until this data base is established, the prevalence data to date should be interpreted with caution.

Age of Onset

Goodwin et al. (1969) found that about 65% of people with OCD had developed their disorder by age 25. Fewer than 15% developed OCD after age 35. They found a mean onset at age 20 in both sexes, with mean age of first psychiatric contact 7 years subsequent to onset. In Beech's (1974) review of 357 cases, one third were discovered before age 15. In Kringlen's (1965) study of 91 adult cases, one half were discovered before age 20 and one fifth before puberty. Ingram's (1961) study of 89 obsessionals showed that 16% had rituals alone or rituals associated with phobias during childhood. These data suggest that between one third and one half of those with a treated OCD seek treatment before age 20. Thus, a significant proportion experience onset of symptoms during childhood and early adolescence. These figures may be conservative. All these data were collected in treatment centers, where the patient or the parents first had to recognize the disorder as one that needed treatment. Many OCD children are embarrassed about their obsessional and ritualized behaviors and carry out their rituals in a furtive manner long before their problems are recognized by others. Consequently, a higher incidence of OCD

may exist because of failure to identify the disorder and relatively low rates of referral to treatment centers.

The same limitation applies to the Rasmussen and Tsuang (1986) study. Although the mean age at onset in this sample was 19.8, there was a wide variation among individual patients, and 70% reported that the onset of obsessive symptoms occurred between the ages of 10 and 23. These investigators obtained a bimodal distribution of age at onset that peaked at ages 12 to 14 and 20 to 22. Men were significantly younger at onset than women. Thyer, Parrish, Curtis, Neese, and Cameron (1985) reported that 48% of the OCD patients they studied had onset of symptoms between the ages of 11 and 25, with 15% of those cases developing before the age of 10. These authors also pointed out that a large number of their cases had onset of OCD after the age of 25.

It should be noted that some investigators could not determine specific times of onset. Goodwin et al. (1969) and Black (1974) found that 30% and 50%, respectively, of their adult patients could give no specific onset. Accurate data are difficult to collect because they are retrospective and may be unreliable.

Childhood Precursors

Though it is usually assumed that there is a continuity between neurotic disorders in childhood and in adult life, research suggests that this may be only partially true. Rutter (1972) cites several studies supporting this view. For example, Robins (1966) did a 30-year follow-up of 500 child psychiatric patients and 100 controls. He found that neurosis in adult life was no more common in the patients than in the controls. Rutter (1972) concluded there is some continuity between child and adult neurosis, but this may be true only of a minority. Thus, in his view, most neurotic children become normal adults. Most neurotic adults manifest their neurotic behavior only in adulthood. Though there has been definite interest in describing precursors for OCD (Ingram, 1961; Kringlen, 1965; Lo, 1968; Rachman & Hodgson, 1980; Robins, 1966; Rutter, 1972), none of these investigators has really examined precursors for childhood OCD. The closest approximation to this type of investigation lies in trying to describe precipitating events and child-rearing patterns shown by the parents. These topics are covered next.

Precipitating Events

Rachman and Hodgson (1980) reviewed seven studies with a total of 655 patients, almost all adults, and found 40% to 90% with precipitating factors. One retrospective review found 17 patients with childhood OCD. In 82% of the parents, there was a significant life stress, defined as severe psychiatric or medical impairment; in 29% of the children, it was defined as serious medical illnesses (Hollingsworth et al., 1980). In 15 of the children, obsessive thoughts and phobic reactions appeared to be clearly related to realistically frightening home situations or family distress.

Although 70% of the OCD patients described in Rasmussen and Tsuang's (1986) study were unable to identify a particular precipitating stress or environmental precipitant that triggered their illness, these investigators note that almost all their patients experienced a worsening of symptoms in times of stressful life events. It would seem that if there were a sudden onset of OCD in a child, search for precipitating stress factors should be thorough, and the meaning to the child of such stress factors should be pursued. However, search for precipitating factors does not imply that they are causal, since an underlying and largely unnoticed pattern of OC adjustment may be exacerbated by current stressors.

Sex Ratio

Goodwin et al. (1969) found that although sex ratios differed among 13 studies they reviewed, the ratio for the combined sample approached unity. Thus, it appears that sex ratios for incidence of adult OCD are about the same. Not as much evidence has been accumulated on sex ratios of OCD in childhood, and reviewers have been more reluctant to formulate conclusions (Templer, 1972). With our present knowledge, it seems premature to formulate a conclusion regarding sex ratio in childhood OCD.

Birth Order

The only quasi-controlled study of birth-order effects known to the authors was done by Kayton and Borge (1967). They studied 40 obsessive compulsive children and compared them with 40 controls. Thirty-one of the 40 obsessive compulsive children were firstborn or only children, compared with 11 of 40 controls. This difference is statistically significant. Twenty-six of 30 males in the group were firstborn, a statistically significant difference, but birth order was not found to be significant in the females. These results are interesting in view of Toman's (1969) theory that firstborn and only children are more performance- and achievement-oriented.

Intelligence

None of the studies we reviewed have reported consistently low measured intelligence for obsessive compulsive children. Generally, the literature shows intelligence to be average or above, with most of the evidence supporting higher than average intelligence. However, it is noteworthy that most of these studies involved adult OCD. Templer (1972) found impressive evidence that obsessive compulsive adults were usually of above-average intelligence. Rachman and Hodgson (1980) see the matter as settled. We agree with regard to adults but feel that the evidence on children is inconsistent with this conclusion. Further research on children is still needed.

Genetics of OCD

Genetic evidence for OCD seems to occur in three categories: (1) studies of familial incidence, (2) comparisons between monozygotic and dizygotic twins, and (3) studies of adopted parents and children (Rachman & Hodgson, 1980). These types of studies have clarified the genetic contribution to psychiatric disorders in general, especially schizophrenia. Relatively little research has been done on the genetics of OCD. This neglect is a partial function of the low incidence of the disorder. However, another problem has been the confusion in classification and failure to distinguish between OCD and obsessive personality traits.

There is some impressive animal research on selective breeding for emotional factors that has implications for inherited emotionality in humans. However, the aspects of anxiety in humans are not well known, and, except where studies have used identical twins reared apart, the role of environment, especially family practices and modeling, cannot be disentangled from genetic effects. Thus, although there are numerous studies showing a higher incidence of anxiety states in families of patients and in twins (Dilsaver & White, 1986), few exclude the effect of the family environment.

Elkins, Rapoport, and Lipsky (1980) reviewed twin studies in the literature and found four that met some reasonable criteria. These four had 30 sets of twins, of which 24 showed concordance for OCD. This high rate would be suggestive of genetic transmission, but nongenetic factors could not be ruled out. There was no comparison of monozygotic and dizygotic twins.

The best case for a genetic etiology based on twin concordance would be made by studies of adoptive twins reared together and apart, with blind and independent assessment of the twins. This strategy for genetic research on OCD has not been used. There is, however, sound evidence indicating an increased frequency of psychiatric disorders in general among close relatives of OCD patients (Templer, 1972). Thus, the best evidence available, though still meager, suggests the possibility of a nonspecific reactivity and anxiety in the neuroses generally (Shields, 1962). This notion is argued persuasively by several psychogeneticists.

Child-Rearing Practices

Rachman and Hodgson (1980) have observed that parental reactions to OCD in childhood are of two types: rejection or overindulgence of the child's fears and problems. The development of more effective parenting is a significant treatment target. It should be noted that any causal link between child-rearing practices and OCD, if there is one, may be bidirectional.

The family involved in a pattern of overindulgence of ritualistic behavioral demands may become preoccupied with the child's obsessive compulsive behavior. For example, the family may react to the child's washing and cleaning compulsions by trying to meet the child's demands for a nonthreatening environment (e.g., a clean and sterile home). These types of parental responses may influence the family's functions in other ways. For instance, others may be discouraged from visiting. Thus, with a pattern of overindulgence, children or adult OCD members can exert tyrannical influence over the lives and behavior of the rest of the family. Compliance to excessive and even bizzare rituals is often demanded, and noncompliance leads to tantrums, crying, or other aversive behavior that motivates compliance.

Cases of overt rejection are probably more common where an OCD family member is an adult. Here, the patient is isolated from other family members and asked to leave or is subtly influenced to depart from the home. This overt reaction is less likely with children. But rejection in less direct ways can take a great variety of forms.

When there is OCD in parents (as opposed to non-OCD psychiatric illness), child-rearing practices are likely to lead to widespread psychological dysfunction, but not necessarily OCD (Cooper & McNeil, 1968; Rutter, 1972). The attributes likely to contribute to the children's maladjustment are timidity, shyness, anxiety, and overdependence rather than specific obsessional preoccupations.

Family Characteristics

Because OCD is relatively rare, there have been few opportunities to study large numbers of families and draw generalizations. Child-rearing practices are also relevant for the study of family characteristics. The few studies that have attended to family variables are small, select, and therefore probably biased. Nevertheless, they are still informative.

Adams's (1973) sociopsychiatric study of 30 OCD children from a pool of 2,500 children yielded a sample of Caucasian, predominantly Protestant, highly educated, mostly affluent middle-class children with intact and geographically stable conjugal families of 4.8 persons. Family characteristics noted were the following: (1) were highly verbal; (2) placed positive emphasis on etiquette; (3) valued social isolation or withdrawal; (4) emphasized cleanliness; (5) adhered to an instrumental morality (i.e., goodness not as a goal but as a way of reaching heaven or asserting moral superiority); (6) derogated maleness; (7) practiced limited commitment in religion, politics, and social views; and (8) had a hoarding orientation toward money.

Tseng (1973) reported case studies of 10 selected Chinese males ages 18 to 30, from intact families, who had been undergoing psychotherapy for 3 months to 2 years. He found a close, intimate, and prolonged mother-son relationship, frequent absence of the father, or a distant father-son relationship. The mother-son interaction was one of overprotection, overworry, and excessive restriction of normal activities.

Manchanda and Sharma (1986) described the parents of their OCD patients in India as strict, consistent in enforcing discipline, and having high expectations. Clark and Bolton (1985) found that OCD adolescents perceived higher parental expectations than did anxious adolescents, even though this was not actually the case. These authors reported that there was no evidence of obsessive traits in the parents of their OCD adolescents.

"Fixedness" of OC Symptoms in Children

Symptomatology of OCD in children appears less stable than in adults. Although OC symptoms wax and wane in less severe forms in adults, there is usually a prevailing and apparent pattern of adjustment or obsessive compulsive personality. This underlying pattern is often not present in children showing acute obsessive compulsive symptoms. During periods of intense stress, children discover, or perhaps model, certain ritualized obsessive compulsive patterns, which provide some relief from intense and aversive arousal. Thus, patterns are repeated because they are negatively reinforced. Additional reinforcement may occur as symptoms produce reinforcing reactions in family members, school, etc.

THEORIES OF ETIOLOGY

The first models we examine suggest that there is one cause (although the logic of the models does not preclude more than one) of OCD that is biological in origin. They hypothesize an illness, disease, or biological malfunction as the cause of OCD. The models suggest that there is a particular causal agent, potentially isolatable, that exerts effects within a certain time frame. They differ with regard to the hypothesized causal agent.

Neurological Dysfunction Hypothesis

This hypothesis has not been labeled as such by any of its supporters, and they have not proposed a specific neurological deficit to account for OCD. However, such neurological dysfunction is implied. Some authors see the possible relationship between OCD and Gilles de la Tourette syndrome as support for a common neurological basis for both (Elkins et al., 1980). A recent study reported that 34 to 50 consecutive cases of Gilles de la Tourette syndrome also had obsessive compulsive behavior that met DSM-III criteria (Nee, Caine, Eldridge, & Eibert,

1980). Obsessive compulsive behavior was more common in Tourette patients who had a family history of the syndrome or of tics than it was in other Tourette patients. However, given the problems associated with defining and reliably diagnosing tics and Tourette syndrome (Harrison, 1976), it is understandable that others are skeptical about the possible relationship of obsessive compulsive behavior and Tourette syndrome (Shapiro, Shapiro, Braun, & Sweet, 1978). More research is needed that uses DSM-III-R criteria for OCD instead of looking for obsessive compulsive behavior or traits. Research must use accepted criteria for diagnosing Tourette syndrome before a compelling argument can be made for the association of these two disorders.

Some authors have maintained that brain pathology is a causal factor in obsessive compulsive neurosis, and correlational evidence is cited as supportive. Grimshaw (1965) found that 20 of 105 obsessive compulsive people had a history of previous neurological illness, contrasted with 8 non-obsessional compulsive psychiatric controls. Pacella, Polatkin, and Nagler (1944) found that 22 of 31 patients with obsessive symptoms but various diagnoses had abnormal EEGs. However, others have failed to replicate these findings (Ingram & MacAdams, 1960; Rockwell & Simmons, 1947). Templer's (1972) review concluded that although obsessive compulsive manifestations are seen frequently in organic patients, evidence for brain pathology in the majority of typical obsessive compulsive neurotics is quite slim. Almost all these studies involved adult OCD.

Because patients with OCD frequently suffer concurrently from depression or depressive symptoms (Jenike, 1981) and are often successfully treated with tricyclic antidepressants (Flament et al., 1987), it has been suggested that there is a biological link between depression and OCD (Lieberman, 1984). Several studies of the classification of patients with OCD as normal or abnormal on the dexamethasone suppression test (DST) have evaluated this possibility (Jenike et al., 1987; Lieberman et al., 1985; Monteiro, Marks, Noshirvani, & Checkley, 1986). All these investigators found that the majority of OCD patients studied suppress normally and thus provide little evidence supporting such a link.

Baxter, Phelps, Mazziotta, Guze, Schwartz, and Selin (1987) have provided the most compelling evidence to date for a neurological defect in OCD in their study—with positron emission tomography—of 14 OCD patients, 14 depressed patients, and 14 normal controls. They found that metabolic rates for glucose were significantly increased, bilaterally, in the left orbital gyrus and the caudate nucleus in their OCD patients. They also found differences between recovered OCD patients and controls in patterns of cerebral glucose metabolism. A study by Luxenberg, Swedo, Flament, Friedland, Rapaport, and Rapaport (1988) also indicated involvement of the caudate nucleus in OCD. Using computed tomography, they found that the volume of the caudate nucleus was significantly smaller in their 10 OCD patients than in 10 controls.

Serotonergic Defect Hypothesis

A serotonergic defect has been proposed as an explanatory mechanism for OCD (Yaryura-Tobia, Bebirian, Neziroglu, & Bhagavan, 1977). They argue obliquely from clinical and animal research findings. Clomipramine has been found to relieve OC symptoms in several of their previous studies. Animal research has shown this compound to be a potent and relatively selective blocker of serotonin reuptake. They hypothesize that OCD may be caused by some defect in the serotonergic system. Blood serotonin was significantly lower in drug-free OCD patients than in controls. After clomipramine therapy, OC symptoms were reduced.

Flament, Rapoport, Murphy, Berg, and Lake (1987) present clearer support for a serotonergic defect hypothesis. Their study was aimed specifically at assessing serotonergic effects of clomipramine in children and adolescents with OCD. They found that clomipramine treatment reduced obsessional symptoms. More importantly, in terms of the hypothesis, clomipramine produced a significant reduction in platelet serotonin concentration. As the authors pointed out, this change "seemed closely associated with the therapeutic response" (p. 222). They also cautioned, however, that other neuropharmacologic properties of clomipramine could account for its treatment efficacy.

The Genetic Model

Obsessive compulsive disorders are alleged to be due to some inherited defect or polygenetic abnormality. The evidence for this hypothesis has been reviewed earlier. It must be noted that even if the evidence were convincing (which is not the case), arguing genetic causality from an identified inherited defect is risky on logical grounds. Some third factor could be causally related to both the inherited defect and the OCD.

Medical and Disease Models: A Critique

Elkins et al. (1980) review several streams of evidence for a biological etiology of OCD: familial and twin studies; the possible association between Gilles de la Tourette syndrome and OCD; neuropsychological assessment implicating dysfunction in the nondominant frontal lobe; outcome data on results of stereotaxic surgery; and accounts of successful treatment with clomipramine for OCD in adults, which implicates a neurotransmitter imbalance. Each etiological hypothesis fails to account for OCD when the specific hypothesis is critically examined. For example, in spite of the fact that Elkins et al. (1980) found 50 studies of clomipramine effects on OCD, only 2 used double-blind control procedures, and those had methodological problems that could have accounted for their findings. The evidence is tantalizing but not scientifically compelling. Careful work may show a biological factor or factors that contribute to the understanding of this disorder. However, psychological treatments have proven to be efficacious; for example, exposure and response prevention (Foa, Steketee, & Milby, 1980; Rachman & Hodgson, 1980). These treatments derive from experimentally sophisticated outcome and follow-up studies. Therefore, it seems inappropriate to conceptualize OCD as a "treatment resistant disease" (Elkins et al., 1980, p. 521). There is little evidence to support OCD as a "disease" and much evidence to suggest that it is not treatment resistant in most cases. If such evidence were forthcoming, OCD would become another of many diseases that respond well to psychological treatments (i.e., asthma, hypertension, irritable bowel syndrome, etc.).

Psychological Models

Psychoanalytic Theory
According to this theory, the genesis of obsessive compulsive neurosis is the anal stage of development, during which toilet training occurs. The obsessive compulsive person allegedly had difficulties during this stage, which later led

to the characteristic rigidity, overcontrol, scheduling, and other OC traits and behaviors. In three empirical studies that tested the hypothesis of toilet-training problems in OC children, 17 of 18 cases showed no evidence of strict toilet training (Dai, 1957; Judd, 1965; Tseng, 1973).

Learning Theory and Conditioning Models

There are many learning theories (Bolles, 1979), several of which have been used to explain OCD; but two-factor learning theory (Mowrer, 1960) seems to be the one most called upon. This theory proposes that obsessive thought produces anxiety because, in experience, it has been associated with unconditioned anxiety-arousing stimuli. Obsessions then elicit conditioned anxiety, the reduction of which is reinforcing. Compulsions become established and maintained as they follow and serve to reduce anxiety. They become elaborated via response chaining. Thus, factor one is classical conditioning of the anxiety response, and factor two is instrumental conditioning of compulsive behavior reinforced by reduction of anxiety (i.e., negative reinforcement).

Rachman–Hodgson Model

Rachman and Hodgson (1980) propose four determinants of OCD: (1) a genetic component of hyperarousability, (2) mood disturbances, (3) social learning, and (4) specific learning exposures. They postulate a continuum of OC behavior with the OCD maladaptive pattern at the extreme. For them, the most important question for understanding OCD becomes the following: What generates the behavior and what maintains it? Multiple determinants are assumed instead of a particular cause. They propose that it makes no more sense to question the cause of excessive talkativeness than the cause of excessive hand-washing. In both cases, the more helpful question is: What conditions promote excessive talkativeness or compulsive hand-washing?

Observational Learning Hypothesis

This is not a well-articulated scientific hypothesis but rather one explanation considered by several researchers. Obsessive and compulsive symptoms may develop via observational learning; that is, the symptoms may be socially transmitted. However, as Rachman and Hodgson (1980) argue, if direct transmission by observational learning were the major factor in the development of OCD, then the prevalence in families with an OCD patient or close relative model should be considerably higher than has been observed. Considering the available evidence, the hypothesis of a direct social transmission of OCD has little support. However, a less stringent hypothesis regarding social transmission may still be viable. If one postulates the social transmission of OC traits and that when individuals with such traits became stressed they developed OCD, this hypothesis becomes more credible.

Family-Systems Model

Although we know of only one attempt to describe OCD specifically from a family-systems perspective (Watzlawick, Weakland, & Fisch, 1974), this approach and theoretical system is now widely used and accepted for a variety of disorders (Gurman & Kniskern, 1981). There is not one family-systems theory. However, various theories share some fundamental assumptions. Symptoms are understood as existing within a interpersonal context—that is, the person's family. Symptoms represent a dysfunction of a system. The system consists of the relationships or patterns of interaction between its members. The individual (and the symptoms) is influenced by others' actions and, in turn, influences them in a circular rather than a linear fashion. Causality is seen as a mutually causative sequence or may even be rejected as a concept in favor of describing a "coherent pattern" in a self-recursive cycle of events (Dell, 1981; Dell & Goolishian, 1979) with no real beginning or end. Therapy is primarily aimed at altering patterns of relating.

For example, a child's hand-washing rituals might represent part of a pattern in which a perfectionistic, demanding mother remains overinvolved with her problem son rather than dealing with her distancing husband. Unable to handle an important transaction, such as seeing the last child enter school and the world of its peers, the family might focus on the child's fastidious habits of cleanliness. The child's hand-washing could serve to gain him a great deal of attention and power in preventing his mother from disciplining him. She might feel helpless in disciplining a "sick" child, especially since his problem might serve to keep her husband more tied to home than to work. The father would then tend to want to escape these unhappy conditions even more, thus increasing his wife's loneliness. The symptoms of the son could be seen, therefore, as part of a pattern that ensures this family system's continuity—a "homeostatic" function—while it also pushes the family to evolve into a more functional organization (Hoffman, 1981).

OVERVIEW OF TREATMENT METHODS

The OCDs are traditionally viewed as highly resistant to treatment. Treatments from most major theoretical viewpoints are used, ranging from medical (such as psychotropic drugs, electroconvulsive treatment, and psychosurgery) to psychotherapeutically oriented approaches (for example, traditional psychoanalysis). The literature covers adult populations more than children and adolescents.

Characteristics of Research

The OCD treatment literature reveals several trends. Until the last decade, most papers have been anecdotal case reports or poorly controlled outcome studies, with a paucity of well-designed single-case studies or controlled group investigations. Most reports reflect the investigators' theoretical biases, with scant empirical documentation. The resultant quagmire of ideologies tells more about the therapist or school of thought than the components of treatment and its efficacy. We are not saying clinical approaches are of dubious value, merely that they have yet to be carefully scrutinized or evaluated. In the last 15 years, a more research-based literature has developed. Treatment advances seem to be occurring in psychological (Meredith & Milby, 1980; Rachman & Hodgson, 1980), pharmacological (Jenike, 1981; Isberg, 1981), and, with severe and recalcitrant cases, psychosurgical treatment of OCD (Mitchell-Heggs, Kelly, & Richardson, 1976).

Experimental study of treatment for childhood and adolescent OCD has yet to receive the same attention found in the adult literature. The literature is rich in clinical discussion and case illustration but weak in controlled data. Consequently, our treatment sections required some extrapolation from the adult literature as well as unique interpretation and clinical elaboration on the existing child literature. We will not review assessment and treatment of OCD with adults, although familiarity with several comprehensive reviews (Foa & Tilman, 1978; Foa, 1982; Meredith & Milby, 1980; Rachman & Hodgson, 1980; Salzman & Thaler, 1981) might be of value to the reader.

Conceptualization of Treatment Goals

Before examining treatment strategies, some comment about the conceptualization of treatment goals is required. We have noted that children and their families vary considerably in conceptualization of the problem and desired treatment outcome. Mental health practitioners also vary greatly in their criteria for successful intervention. Outcome goals reflect intrapsychic, interpersonal, and practical considerations. Outcome goal decisions reflect a sensitivity to the needs and concerns of the child and family, but they also reflect theoretical formulations of the disorder. The selection of appropriate targets for change implicitly involves a contract among therapist, child, and family. Details of such a contract influence the choice as well as the scope of treatment goals.

Adams's (1972) review of psychodynamically oriented treatment outcome alleges that the following types of change result from his comprehensive and intensive treatment model: (1) symptomatic decreases in obsessions and ritualistic behavior, (2) modification of behavior (e.g., communication style, gross motor fluidity, play, and academic progress), (3) changes in feelings concerning self, (4) changes in ego structure or strengths (e.g., willpower, initiative, decisiveness, cognitive, intellectual, and concentration skills; accuracy of perception; etc.), and (5) changes in superego (e.g., reasoning and thinking about moral issues, interpersonal honesty, self-criticism, development of a more personal set of values, etc.). Treatment approaches that generate such profound changes may not be consistent with the perception of need defined by the therapist, child, and family in consultation about treatment goals that necessitate flexibility of approach and that demand efficiency of cost and time while forfeiting other potentially desirable changes. Consequently, it is imperative that treatment goals be carefully specified, following consultation with the child and family, and that such goals realistically reflect the expectations and needs of the child and family.

These issues are relevant for other childhood disorders but are particularly germane to OCD.

Theoretical discussions about the nature of the problem and the approach to treatment are widely disparate. The more dynamic approaches essentially view obsessive compulsive behaviors as symptoms of underlying psychopathology, while family approaches view the behaviors as products of faulty family interactional patterns. Behavioral approaches view the obsessive compulsive behaviors as primary treatment targets. Consequently, it is difficult to separate theoretical issues and values from the evaluation of treatment efficacy. Examination of empirically based data to the exclusion of less rigorous but clinically meaningful literature risks omission of useful clinical formulations and procedures. The following review of treatment approaches will, therefore, be an attempt to blend our combined knowledge of clinical issues with the available clinical and empirically oriented literature. The selection of specific approaches to treatment should consider these various types of information, but it should also reflect the more practical expectations and goals of the child and family.

Continuum of Treatment Approaches

Theories and therapies dealing with OCD can be understood as varying along a continuum according to how they see the etiology of this (or any) disorder. One end views problems as lodged primarily within the individual, while the other sees problems as belonging to systems of interacting people. The intrapsychic end includes psychodynamic approaches as well as behavioral therapies that explain OCD symptoms using a conditioning paradigm. The latter imply the use of individual psychotherapy or behavioral techniques, such as response prevention, flooding (exposure), thought stopping, desensitization, modeling, and aversive procedures.

The system end of the continuum would include a number of family therapy approaches such as structural (Minuchin, 1974), strategic (Madanes, 1981), systematic (Palazzoli, 1974), Bowen systems (Bowen, 1978), and behavioral (Jacobson, 1981) family therapies. Although it may be argued persuasively that behavioral family therapy is interpersonal rather than transpersonal or systemic, that argument is beyond the scope of this chapter. Here OCD symptoms are seen as functional parts of an interpersonal behavior pattern that is itself disturbed (Haley,

1976). Rituals or compulsions may be "strategies" for human relationships that define, control, and protect. In more behavioral terms, they may be reinforced operants that meet needs in relationships. These viewpoints suggest approaches aimed at changing patterns of relating or mutually causative patterns of reinforcing.

Individual Treatment Approaches

Individual treatment approaches for children and adolescents with OCD can be categorized into psychodynamic and behavioral approaches.

Psychodynamic Treatment

The treatment literature on childhood OCD includes a wealth of fascinating and detailed case studies by psychoanalytic and psychodynamic therapists. These approaches focus on the exploration and elimination of intrapsychic conflicts through insight, corrective emotional experiences, and enhanced ego functioning. Techniques of interpretation, working through transference, free association, and ego support are used. Many therapists also include parallel counseling for parents (e.g., Adams, 1972; Furman, 1971).

Perhaps the most complete exposition of a contemporary psychodynamic approach to childhood OCD is that of Adams (1972), who advises therapists to deal with concrete examples from the patient's life, not generalized verbal formulations. He recommends searching for contemporary patterns as well as origins of conflicts; developing an "I–thou" therapeutic relationship explored with home visits, family sessions, play observation, and so on; and expressing and understanding feelings. He encourages honesty, the simplification of obsessive ramblings, risk taking, and teaching children to be more at ease. Adams's paper merits careful review by anyone seriously interested in working with obsessive compulsive youngsters. In a 1985 review article, Adams readdressed the issues involved in the treatment of childhood OCD and noted that although his basic approach has remained the same, it would now be better described in terms of a multimodal approach involving verbal therapy, medication, and behavior therapy.

Psychodynamic approaches to OCD have the support of creative clinical case reports by enthusiastic and gifted therapists. However, there is no empirical research indicating that these psychodynamic approaches, which typically involve years of time-consuming and costly therapy, are more efficacious than the other, briefer methods described (Meredith & Milby, 1980). The main usefulness of this literature is in its reflection of the clinical acumen of these therapists, who seem skilled in establishing caring, growth-facilitating relationships with children who are notoriously difficult to work with.

Behavioral Treatment
Behavioral treatment is generally derived from two specific models of OCD. The first views obsessive compulsive behaviors from a drive-reduction model, where obsessions and rituals reduce anxiety. Treatments generated from this model focus on decreasing intrusive cognitions and rituals by reducing arousal to situations that elicit anxiety. The second, an operant-conditioning model, focuses on modifying consequences of obsessions and compulsive behavior. Punishment and extinction paradigms are derived from this model.

Techniques reflecting the anxiety-reduction model include systematic desensitization, variations of modeling, and exposure and response prevention. Systematic desensitization has been widely and usefully used for anxiety-mediated conditions. Anxiety-eliciting situations are presented to the child in graded order from least to most anxiety-arousing. Presentation may be in vivo or imaginal. During presentation, an anxiety-inhibiting competing state is developed in the child. The anxiety-inhibiting state is usually some form of relaxation.

In the case of a youngster with obsessions about thunderstorms, excessive vigilance, and checking on weather conditions, the hierarchy might include reading about the development of weather conditions, visual details of cloud formations, depictions of thunder, lighting, heavy rain, and so on. No research documents the efficacy of this treatment procedure with child and adolescent populations. However, a review of treatment with adult OCD (Meredith & Milby, 1980) reveals degrees of success in four of five cases.

Modeling techniques, procedurally similar to exposure paradigms, have also received experimental attention with OCD. Two have been used: participant and passive modeling. Participant modeling has been used most. Like systematic desensitization, this approach involves a hierarchy of stimuli that elicit distress. From the lowest to the highest hierarchy item, the therapist demonstrates exposure. The patient then confronts and contacts the stimulus situation until he or she is able to complete the sequence without assistance. Passive modeling involves observing the therapist confronting the various graduated stimuli but it does not include patient contact with the stimuli. Both techniques use response prevention. In the case of a cleaning compulsion, all washing would be prevented by agreement with the therapist and/or supervision. The adult literature (Meredith & Milby, 1980) suggests that participant modeling is more effective than passive modeling. There are no data to suggest superiority of modeling over exposure. Both procedures are essentially similar. Exposure usually involves some therapist modeling, and modeling involves exposure. We found no reports where modeling has been experimentally investigated with children.

Exposure has been used increasingly in the last decade. Typically, the child is exposed, either in imagination or in vivo, to highly anxiety-arousing stimuli in a graduated fashion. The exposure is continuous and prolonged until there is an observed and reported diminution of anxiety to a comfortable level. This approach requires abandoning the typical therapy hour for sessions of 2 hours or more. Examination of published studies using exposure (flooding, flooding plus modeling, and participant modeling) plus response prevention with adults resulted in a treatment success rate of approximately 75% (Meredith & Milby, 1980). These techniques have been used with adolescents and young adults with similar results, but not with younger children. It is important to note that anxiety-eliciting stimuli need not be "horrific" to produce positive results (Foa, et al., 1977).

Response prevention has been investigated and seems to contribute to treatment efficacy beyond mere exposure (Foa et al., 1980; Steketee, Grayson, & Foa, 1981). These results suggest that exposure reduces elicited anxiety while response prevention serves the dual function of prolonging exposure to first-order (anxiety-eliciting) stimuli and disassociating second-order stimuli (stress, mood state, environmental cues) from the rituals. This allows new responses to these stimuli to appear and thus extinguishes their reinforcement and discriminative stimulus properties. Response prevention also reduces the time spent ritualizing. The combination of exposure and response prevention seems essential. Each component produces meaningful results. Response prevention, like flooding, has also been reported with adolescents and young adults.

Techniques based on an operant model include thought stopping, faradic disruption, and cognitive flooding. Thought stopping and faradic disruption via mild electric shocks have been conceptualized as aversive procedures. Cognitive flooding seems to fit an extinction model.

Thought stopping involves the presentation of an aversive event contingent on the undesired obsession. Relaxed and with eyes closed, the individual is instructed covertly to verbalize the obsession and signal its occurrence. This signal is immediately followed by an aversive stimulus (e.g., the therapist shouting "stop!" or introducing a loud noise). After repeated trials, the child both presents the obsessive thought and subvocates the aversive stimulus (thinking "stop!"). Variations of this technique have included using high-intensity notes or mild electric shock as the aversive stimulus. Imagining a reinforcing scene following successful interruption of the obsession has been used as a variant of the procedure.

Martin (1982) has used patient-selected photographs and positive self-statements as a variant. This procedure may be useful for children, because it utilizes pictures to elicit pleasant imagery instead of depending on the child's unassisted use of imagery. In addition, the positive self-statements affixed to the back of each pleasant photograph might also increase the possibility of disrupting the disturbing thoughts. To our knowledge no research on the use of this technique with children has been done.

Thought stopping has been used with reported beneficial results in children and young adults (Campbell, 1973; Kumar & Wilkinson, 1971; Yamagami, 1971). But the superiority of thought stopping over placebo factors or nonspecific therapeutic factors has not been demonstrated. Questions remain about the relative contributions of aversive stimuli, interruption of the obsessions, and repeated exposure, all of which are included in thought stopping (Meredith & Milby, 1980).

Faradic disruption is a technique similar to thought stopping (Kenny, Mowbray, & Lalani, 1978; Kenny, Solyom & Solyom, 1973). Although it seems promising with adults, it has not been used with children or adolescents. It involves asking the patient to reproduce obses-

sive ideation or imagery. This cognitive event is followed by a painful electrical shock administered until the client signals that the ideation has terminated. Four of five adults improved following this treatment, while none improved in a waiting-list control.

Cognitive flooding (Milby et al., 1981) is a relatively new treatment that avoids the punitive aspect of other operant-based treatments for obsessive ideation. The procedure involves repeated videotape presentations of the client discussing bothersome obsessive ideation. Results with a single case evaluation suggest clinical effectiveness and are consistent with the extinction or habituation of anxiety associated with obsessional thinking. This technique has not been used with obsessive children or adolescents.

Family- or Interpersonal-Based Treatment

A number of therapeutic approaches to OCD have emphasized interpersonal factors and eschewed or deemphasized purely individualistic or intrapsychic procedures. These include a pragmatic use of parents or paraprofessionals as therapists for children, adjunctive counseling with parents as part of the child's treatment, and approaches where parents or others in the child's environment are viewed as part of the problem. In the latter approaches, people other than the index patient may be seen as part of a reinforcement pattern maintaining operant rituals or compulsions. In other approaches, the family unit may be treated as the patient. In a family-systems approach, the OCD is taken as the symptomatic expression of a disturbed system and the therapist treats the relationships or patterns of interactions. Some behavioral family therapists would argue that these "family problems" are essentially patterns of mutual reinforcement, while strategic therapists question this concept of chains of causal events, preferring to see a "coherent" but noncausal "pattern" that belongs to the system as an organism.

Specific techniques corresponding to these general approaches have included the following:

1. Training parents as psychoanalytic counselors who deliver interpretations to the child or as behavioral therapists to carry out response-prevention programs (Mills, Agras, Barlow, & Mills, 1973; Zikis, 1983).
2. Parallel, ego-strengthening counseling with parents while the child is in psychodynamic

treatment (Adams, 1972) or behavior therapy (Hersen, 1968).

3. Work on family relationships as part of a multimodal behavioral therapy for the child (Bolton, Collins, & Steinberg, 1983; Scott, 1966).

4. Family communications skills training (Fine, 1973), training parents to extinguish symptoms by changing their responses to them while reinforcing desirable alternatives (Ayllon, Garber, & Allison, 1977), and training institutional staff to withdraw positive reinforcement contingent on symptoms being displayed (Wetzel, 1966).

5. Conjoint discussions on family conflicts (Scott, 1966) and strategic family therapy (Harbin, 1976; O'Conner, 1983).

Some of these interpersonal or family therapies will be examined in greater depth later in this chapter.

Hospital-Based Treatment

Sometimes it is necessary to remove highly distressed youngsters from the family environment and provide relief to family members who are overwhelmed. This is often accomplished via hospitalization. There is debate about the advisability of hospitalization. Adams (1972) is a strong opponent of it. He states:

> A child belongs with his family. . . . Naturalness can be achieved in the child's natural habitat of home, school, and neighborhood. Parents often crave hospitalization for the child and although I would not hold out stubbornly against all odds, I would try to convince them of the greater wisdom (on my side of course) of having the child relearn and release in a more homelike setting. (page 475)

It can also be argued that a richer learning environment can sometimes be provided in structured inpatient programs. Hospitalization can involve the family where this seems therapeutically beneficial. Our experience suggests that obsessive compulsive youngsters benefit enormously from an inpatient therapeutic milieu comprising supervised peer interaction, group therapy, and a structured therapeutic community. In an environment where problems can be discussed openly, where social reinforcement for improvements in target behaviors is readily available, and where emotional attachments can grow and flourish, we have frequently seen ob-

sessive compulsive behaviors decrease substantially without more direct intervention. This seems especially true where the OCD has manifested itself as a result of high family stress. Our clinical impression is that positive peer attention and emotional bonding are of primary importance. A general atmosphere of openness and reinforcement for discussions of "unacceptable" emotions in an accepting and supporting context seem important. With more severe cases, our experience suggests that there is a need for more structured behavioral contingency programs and specific techniques to decrease obsessive compulsive behaviors in the hospital environment. Concomitant with hospitalization, family therapy and individual therapy may serve to increase generalization beyond the relatively "safe" hospital environment.

Other Psychotherapeutic Treatment Approaches

Several other approaches do not clearly fall within one conceptual scheme. A social-skills training model is based on the premise that part of the child's problem may be the lack of an appropriate behavior to substitute for a symptom that satisfies needs (Lindley, Marks, Philpott, & Snowden, 1977). Treatment involves training in functional behaviors, specifically general social, assertive, and communication skills.

Weiner (1967) attempted to establish positive reasons for rituals and to construct more efficient substitute rituals. For example, a 15-year-old boy who repeatedly checked his school locker because "he might wind up in Vietnam" was helped to substitute a positive reason for checking: "protecting his belongings." He could continue to check, but in far less time. This approach seems similar to strategic (family) therapists' "reframing" or relabeling techniques (Sluzki & Vernon, 1971) and to the "whittling away" approach of famed hypnotherapist Milton H. Erickson (Haley, 1973). Erickson, too, accepted the rituals offered by his patients but suggested that they try seemingly minor variations that he felt would slowly unritualize or defuse the performances. For example, he might suggest that a hand-washer use a different soap or wash longer. These changes allow for the possibility of others until the original behavior has been eroded, all within the context of a psychotherapeutic relationship.

Paradoxical intention avoids resistance by accepting the obsessive thoughts and encouraging patients to elicit them. Developed as a technique within Frankl's logotherapy, this method has been adapted by some behavior therapists (Solyom, Garza-Perez, Ledwidge, & Solyom, 1972). It can be conceptualized as changing part of an interactional pattern that includes compulsive behaviors, reframing, preventing accustomed avoidance, altering a hopeless attitude through the experience of more control, or habituation through exposure.

The skills-training, reframing, "whittling," and paradoxical intention methods are very appealing in their simplicity, demand for therapist creativity, and ability to avoid some patient resistance, but they require empirical support, particularly for use with children. They might also be useful as part of a broader clinical armamentarium.

Chemotherapy. Chemotherapy has also been used with OCD children and adults, either in combination with their therapies or as the primary treatment. Oxazepam reportedly reduced anxiety and its somatic components in adolescent and adult phobic obsessive compulsives (Orvin, 1967), as did monoamine oxidase inhibitors (MAOIs) (Isberg, 1981; Jenike, 1981). However, Zahn, Insel, and Murphy (1984) found that the MAOI clorgyline did not produce significant improvements in ratings of obsessive behavior. Psychotherapy was not used in these studies.

Haldol has been used successfully to eliminate the obsessive compulsive symptoms of several children also treated for tics (Tapia, 1969). A word of caution about the use of benzodiazepines and neuroleptic medications is that both may cause the child to experience a loss of control due to the effect of sedation, thereby producing a paradoxical increase in subjective discomfort and distress. Perhaps the most promising and best-studied form of chemotherapy is the use of tricyclic antidepressants as an adjunctive treatment for the depressive and phobic-anxiety elements of the syndrome. Tricyclic antidepressants such as imipramine usually do not increase subjective anxiety and may not be perceived as intrusive.

The majority of drug studies have focused on the treatment of obsessive compulsive adults. There have been six double-blind (and with one exception, placebo-controlled) studies of clomipramine, a tricyclic antidepressant that is now approved for use in the United States (Ananth, Pechnold, Van Den Steen, & Engelsmann, 1981;

Insel, Murphy, et al., 1983; Marks, Stern, Mawson, Cobb, & McDonald, 1980; Montgomery, 1980; Thoren, Asberg, & Cronholm, 1980; Yaryura-Tobia, Bergman, Neziroglu, & Bhagavan, 1977). These studies have all shown clomipramine to be superior to placebo or alternative drug therapies. Flament et al. (1985), in the first controlled study of pharmacological therapy of OCD in children, extended the previous findings concerning the efficacy of the tricyclic clomipramine in the treatment of adult OCD. In their study, a double-blind crossover design, 74% (16) of 19 patients were at least slightly improved following treatment, while 10% (2) were symptom-free at the end of treatment. Improvement was measured by the authors' own obsessive compulsive rating scale, the National Institute of Mental Health's Obsessive-Compulsive Scale (Insel, Murphy, et al., 1983), and the Leyton Obsessional Inventory—Child Version (Berg et al., 1980). These authors call clomipramine "the drug of choice for OCD in children" (p. 983). However, it is important to note that several authors have reported rapid relapse when clomipramine therapy was withdrawn (Flament et al., 1985, 1987; Insel, Murphy, et al., 1983; Thoren et al., 1980; Yaryura-Tobia et al., 1977). This finding would seem to argue for clomipramine combined with behavioral or other psychotherapeutic intervention, with slow withdrawal of clomipramine while utilizing psychotherapeutic interventions to sustain improvement of symptoms.

There have also been case reports of successful treatment of OCD in adolescents with trimipramine, a tricyclic that is similar to clomipramine (Bartucci, Stewart, & Kemph, 1987); and a combination of clonidine, which has been used to treat Tourette syndrome, and clomipramine (Lipsedge & Prothero, 1987). It has been suggested that the beneficial effects of these tricyclic antidepressants in treating OCD are due to their role as inhibitors of serotonin reuptake. Lydiard (1986) reported a single case of OCD successfully treated with trazodone, which is also a serotonin-reuptake blocker. In light of this hypothesis, Perse, Greist, Jefferson, Rosenfeld, and Dar (1987) examined the treatment efficacy of fluvoxamine, an antidepressant that is structurally unrelated to the tricyclics but which also has serotonergic properties. In their double-blind, placebo-controlled crossover study, 81% (13 out of 16) of their patients showed improvement with fluvoxamine. Further research comparing tricyclics such as clomipramine with fluvoxamine is needed. It is important to note that one study with OCD adults reported side effects of such severity with trazodone and tryptophan (Mattes, 1986) that treatment had to be discontinued.

Medication is often one component of a more complete behavioral therapy approach intended to work on the affective and behavioral aspects of OCD (Lindley et al., 1977; Stern, Marks, Cobb, Jones, & Luscombe, 1977). Chemotherapy is largely unstudied with childhood OCD, but it is potentially helpful. It will most likely continue to be construed as a part of a broader treatment package including some form of psychotherapeutic intervention.

Using data from the family assessment, the clinician would do well to combine the use of medication with efforts to educate the family and to alter any pathological interaction patterns. If medication is not introduced into the family system skillfully, it may be perceived by the child as a form of punishment or an effort at control, setting the stage for noncompliance and resistance to treatment. Thus, the introduction of chemotherapy must be integrated into the total psychosocial approach to the child.

Treatment Approaches:
An Integration

Two treatments in the adult literature, behavioral therapy exposure with response prevention and clomipramine therapy, are claimed to be "treatments of choice"; however, it is interesting that there is an absence of investigations comparing drugs and behavior treatment with either adults or children. It appears that advocates of both treatment methods have overstepped their data in describing their methods as the "treatment of choice."

The overview of treatment methods for OCD suggests a number of general treatment considerations. At the onset, treatment strategies should closely follow careful idiographic assessment. This assessment should consider not only the child but also the family system. The literature suggests that a more problem-oriented assessment for specific disorders of the child, family, and interpersonal context is the most useful. Less focus is directed toward assessment of intrapsychic conflicts and more on determining what conditions generate and maintain the behavior. Discovery of multiple determinants is the expected outcome of this type of problem-oriented assessment.

The literature on OCD reflects a trend away from time-consuming and expensive psychodynamic strategies to more directive intervention. A search for underlying causes of problematic behavior may not enhance treatment efficacy. This is not to say that the clinician should avoid examining affective issues that relate directly to the clinical presentation. In fact, one therapeutic focus should be to strive toward helping the child to become more affectively oriented and expressive. Typically, problem-oriented assessment will stimulate a focus on specific target behaviors and the selection of specific strategies to attain treatment goals.

Moving toward a more directive focus can involve two risks. First, clinical efficacy may depend on addressing other treatment goals besides obsessive compulsive symptoms. The use of specific techniques may unintentionally result in a myopic focus on specific behaviors to the exclusion of seeing the child in a more complete context of individual and family dysfunction. Second, specific treatment procedures are not a substitute for the development of a therapeutic alliance with the child. Time and attention offered in a nondemanding or less structured fashion continue to be of importance. It is wise to keep in mind the child's modeling of therapist behavior, specifically that compulsive approaches by the therapist may serve to communicate nontherapeutic messages that actually bolster the child's typical form of adjustment.

Treatment for childhood OCD should also focus on family relationship issues as important contextual factors for dysfunctional communication and reinforcement patterns. The family plays an important role in the maintenance of the OCD and can often be of help in modifying the behavioral pattern and facilitating generalization to the natural environment. Generalized levels of anxiety that relate to the OCD can be diminished by a focus on sources of stress within the family. It is not always necessary or desirable to utilize more specific techniques if the obsessive compulsive symptoms are directly responsive to family intervention. For some OCD youngsters, as contrasted with OCD adults, developing more open emotional discussion and more effective problem-solving skills within the family can directly and efficiently produce results.

As a general rule, our therapeutic recommendations involve approaching the child from a comprehensive format consistent with a multimodal approach. Psychotherapeutic techniques are usually used, psychotropic medications may be utilized, but family intervention is almost always one component of the treatment package. Our work has yet to develop and probably will never develop to the point where a "cookbookish" approach to clinical decision making is possible. Our approach suggests careful and detailed assessment at several different levels, with selection of interventions based on the results of idiographic assessment. When possible, goal-oriented and directive treatment approaches are utilized to produce specific clinical results.

ASSESSMENT AND TREATMENT PRESCRIPTION

This section addresses common interventions that seem most useful with specific components of childhood OCD. Use of family-relationship and behavioral approaches will be discussed in detail. It should be understood that these usually can be accomplished in outpatient rather than inpatient settings. It should also be noted that psychotropic medications, especially tricyclic antidepressants, are common treatment components that are frequently useful in decreasing depressive symptomatology and diminishing transient phobic/anxiety reactions. These symptoms and reactions are commonly a part of the clinical picture.

Interpersonal-Systems Approaches

Here we examine assessment and treatment approaches on the interpersonal-systems side of our continuum. Parallel counseling for parents and skills training have been previously discussed. These can be useful parts of an intervention package. Inpatient residential treatments have also been covered previously.

Family-Oriented Behavioral Assessment
Operant-conditioning approaches to behavioral assessment have been reviewed by a number of authors (e.g., Diebert & Harmon, 1970). They involve systematic observation of the child's interactions and that of other family members regarding OCD symptoms. The goal is to define eliciting stimuli (i.e., time, place, preceding behaviors, cognitions, etc.), the child's "symptomatic" responses (e.g., hand-washing, checking rituals), and the responses of other family members to these behaviors. The latter responses can be seen as the factors maintaining the (symptomatic) behaviors through positive or negative reinforcement. A sophisticated technology has been developed for data collection. These include therapist observation, home recording, time sampling, self-charting, and so on. A variety of treatment strategies can then be implemented (e.g., extinction, response prevention, rewarding alternative responses) and evaluated by comparison with baseline data.

Family Behavioral Intervention
A number of behavioral therapists have attempted to modify children's OCD symptoms by changing the parents' response to them. For example, Ayllon and his associates (Ayllon et al., 1977), treated a 5-year-old child with symptoms of ritualistic sleeping with his parents, ritualistic switching on and off of electrical devices, and oppositional behavior. They instructed the parents to stop their spanking, reasoning, and asking for explanations, concluding that these were ineffective as punishers or even as positive reinforcers. Parents reinforced the child with tokens for the competing behavior of staying in his bed and charged him tokens for light-switching. A significant decrease in the undesirable behaviors was reported. It might be questioned, however, whether these were truly OCD symptoms. It is not clear whether the symptoms were ego-dystonic, because the child clearly controlled his parents with obvious rewards for himself, despite concurrent punishment.

In another case, Mills and associates (Mills et al., 1973) trained the mother of a 15-year-old boy to conduct a response-prevention program for his complex checking rituals. Home reinforcement and relaxation training were also used. This regimen worked successfully in a multiple baseline design during his inpatient admission. However, it did not generalize to his home under his mother's care until the father participated. Thus, it may be argued that the response prevention was ineffective without the alteration in the parental and father–child relationship. These well-conducted case studies suggest that further investigation of operant approaches might be productive.

A similar response-prevention program was reported in which all family members altered their responses to an 8-year-old girl's rituals. For example, the mother no longer spent 10 minutes helping her adjust her bed-cover fringe to precise length. The child gave everyone permission to stop her from rechecking and performing bedtime rituals. The parents were also helped to handle their anxiety when this regimen began. Thus, this case involves the use of response prevention (individual level), altering the reinforcement contingencies (interpersonal), and changing the family's affective stance toward the problem and patterns of interaction in which everyone had a disturbed role (family-systems level).

Family-Systems Assessment Issues

Family therapy is not a specific treatment modality but a viewpoint that stresses a level of analysis and conceptualization (i.e., the transpersonal or systems level). It is not a unitary method but a shared set of assumptions from which a myriad of techniques have been developed. Each school (e.g., structural, Bowenian, etc.) utilizes a variety of techniques. The presentation of all of these is beyond the scope of this chapter. In fact, to teach "family therapy for childhood OCD" is antithetical, because family therapists emphasize understanding the particular system of interactions within each family. OCD symptoms, like any functional symptoms, may be part of a variety of disturbed family systems. Techniques are selected from any approach (e.g., behavioral, gestalt, structural family therapy, etc.) or created on the basis of how they can facilitate the family's desired organizational change (Haley, 1976).

Assessment describes the family's patterns of interaction. Unlike therapists using medical models, family therapists see assessment as an ongoing process in which the therapist tests initial hypotheses by actively intervening to change the system. Intervention results provide information to confirm hypotheses and evaluate interventions as well as to suggest new directions for change. Thus, intervention includes both assessment and treatment procedures. It is also important to see the therapist as part of the assessment and problem definition (Haley, 1976). The therapist is part of the patients' broader social context, and he or she joins the family to form a therapeutic system.

In general, family-system therapists want to evaluate and induce change in several major areas (Minuchin, 1974):

1. Family structure, including preferred transactional patterns, especially reactions to OCD symptoms.
2. The system's flexibility and capacity for change.
3. The family members' responsiveness to each others' needs.
4. The family's life context and social support systems.
5. The family's handling of the developmental stage in their family life cycle.
6. The way OCD symptoms fit into preferred transactional patterns.

Family-Systems Intervention

Few studies have utilized a family-systems therapy approach to OCD, perhaps because many family therapists consider it less essential to understand the identified patient's symptomatology than to grasp the family system's disturbance. An early case report (Scott, 1966) described the treatment of a 10-year-old boy obsessed with schoolwork who compulsively called his teacher several times a night and repeatedly questioned his mother about lessons. The family was treated as a unit one to three times per week for a year, exploring everyone's part in the maladaptation to a grandmother's death. The mother was also treated with a tricyclic antidepressant.

The Fine (1973) cases, mentioned previously, utilized a behavioral family therapy approach. Family members stopped repeating statements demanded by the 11-year-old boy. Individual therapy, positive reinforcement for alternative behaviors, and response prevention were also used. In another case of a 9-year-old boy with bedtime rituals, Fine combined conjoint with individual sessions, marital work, and training in communication of affect. He seems to have included each family member in treatment, although he did not offer a clear systematic conceptualization of the problem beyond an interpersonal level.

Harbin (1976) described strategic family therapy (Haley, 1976) with a 16-year-old girl who had a compulsion to redo homework. She had been treated previously with an insight-oriented approach. Observed symptoms were followed by mandatory exercises for 30 minutes the next night. Within a few months she was symptom-free and, at 1-year follow-up, had maintained progress. Treatment lasted 8 months and included a change in parental discipline, antidepressants, a new job for the mother, and alteration of a hostile mother–daughter dyadic relationship that pulled in the father. Thus, a systematic formulation is implied in this case, which also illustrates use of a "paradoxical" intervention teaching increased self-control.

An unpublished case by Frey (1982) clearly illustrates a systemic conceptualization for a 13-year-old boy with ritualistic movements and obsessional repetitions of magazine titles, even though the strategic "paradoxes" were given primarily to the boy. He had been seen previously in individual therapy for school refusal, and the parents had recently received marriage counseling. He was afraid his mother would not return from work or would leave if he did not do his rituals. He was instructed "to gain self-control" by increasing his rituals, with the threat of having to perform them the entire next therapy session if he did not.

The symptoms decreased, but the parents reported that the boy was now afraid he would have to ritualize or not be able to visit a cousin he liked. Frey accepted this new "real" problem and continued his "restraint from change" injunctions, predicting a relapse of symptoms. The next "real" problem was not allowing his parents to sleep with their door closed. Next, he was afraid to spend the night at friends' houses. Each week the injunction not to change was repeated, with various predictions of doom given that addressed the systemic issues in a "paradoxical" fashion. Frey saw the previously over-enmeshed mother–son dyad (the root of the school refusal) as having been threatened by the mother's recent remarriage, especially at the time of the son's entering of adolescence, with its attendant adjustment difficulties. The stepfather had lost his job, further complicating his entry into the family. Frey's strategies allowed these difficult issues to emerge and be handled as the family passed through its transitions. The pattern of focusing on the compulsive rituals dissolved as the system evolved into a new level of organization. Therapy lasted about six sessions, with no reemergence of symptoms.

Although family therapy has been shown repeatedly to be as effective as or more effective than other therapies with a variety of other problems (see Gurman and Kniskern, 1981, for a review of outcome research), there are no controlled studies of its use with OCD patients. These case studies are intriguing, however, for their simplicity, their treatment of several people at once, and their ability to add a comprehensive level of analysis. As with the other interpersonal and at-home approaches, they also offer a methodology to make therapy generalize from the office to the natural environment.

Behavioral Approaches

Assessment Issues

Behavioral assessment with OCD children and adolescents should address four basic goals. The first is to provide a detailed definition of the problem behaviors. This is accomplished through a focused clinical interview with the child and family. An attempt should be made to develop a comprehensive list of behaviors perceived by the child and family as problematic. It is wise to examine functioning in terms of Lazarus's (1976) multimodal profile. The result should be a detailed description of performance in the cognitive, motoric, and affect modalities that addresses the specific nature of the obsessions and/or ritualized behavior. Attention should be given to the interpersonal and perceptual dimensions. It is also useful to examine the role of imagery (particularly with reference to fantasies about dire consequences or catastrophic outcomes) and to develop a clear understanding about the general level of the child's arousal. The presence of a major affective component (e.g., depression) or acute panic attacks may necessitate the use of various psychotropic medications.

The primary types of obsessive compulsive disorder requiring specific examination include the following:

1. *Compulsive rituals,* which often assume the form of washing, checking, or other forms of repetitive motoric behavior.
2. *Cognitive compulsions,* consisting of words, phrases, prayers, sequences of numbers, or other forms of counting, etc.
3. *Primary obsessional slowness,* in which simple tasks of living require excessive time to complete.
4. *Obsessive doubting* and other anxiety-elevat-

ing obsessions, in which specific cognitive patterns (e.g., questioning the adequacy of specific behaviors) increase distress or discomfort.

Compulsive rituals and cognitive compulsions are typically anxiety-reducing in that their performance decreases aversive levels of arousal. Doubting, in contrast, is anxiety-elevating and seems to be more clearly a cognitive component of a general anxiety response to specific stimuli. Primary obsessional slowness may be anxiety-decreasing in a general sense, as the various types of behaviors involved serve to avoid confrontation of more threatening stimuli. For example, excessively slow dressing and preparation for school may delay or even allow the child to avoid school completely. In most cases, the positive reinforcers that relate to primary obsessional slowness (e.g., parental attention, satisfaction with personal appearance, etc.) can be identified.

Assessment should also focus on a number of other dimensions of functioning. In the interpersonal modality, it is important to examine basic communication skills, assertion skills, heterosocial skills, and interpersonal emotional responsivity. Frequently, children and adolescents with OCD have major difficulty with basic interpersonal transactions. Their speech and interpersonal posture may be pedantic, stilted, intellectualized, and self-preoccupied. Expressions of feeling may be restricted to discussion of dysphoria or distress associated with their particular problematic behavior. The direct expression of anger and even more positive and intimate patterns of communication may not be a comfortable part of their interpersonal repertoire. Interpersonal honesty and genuineness are often avoided due to marked fears of interpersonal criticism, disapproval, or rejection. Cognitive patterns that emphasize rigidity of thought, perfectionistic demands for self and others, and external criteria for self-evaluation are almost universally present. Problem-solving styles reflect a lack of creativity and risk-taking, and there is excessive preoccupation with the selection of one proper or correct solution to problems. Associated phobic behavior is observed in most performance situations where concern with failure or rejection stimulates undue arousal, which, in turn, serves to compromise the possibility of success. Basic interpersonal fears and fears of self-expression, particularly of

strong, affectively laden issues (anger, sexual feelings) are a common component of the clinical picture.

Once problem behaviors across modalities have been specified, it is then desirable to carefully determine both antecedent and consequent events that elicit or maintain the problematic behavior.

Subjective scaling of fears using the Subjective Units of Discomfort Scale (SUDS) is often illuminating (Wolpe, 1973). This scale simply asks the child to rate anxiety-producing stimuli (distress) on a continuum from 0 (absolute calm) to 100 (absolute panic). Careful specification of antecedent events using this scale is an effective way to identify problem patterns and to develop hierarchies for use later in treatment. By carefully identifying antecedent events, it is also possible to develop a clear understanding of the relationship between obsessive compulsive behaviors and the role they play with respect to either eliciting or reducing discomfort. It is extremely important to examine other potential sources of reinforcement (in addition to anxiety reduction) that influence the obsessive-compulsive behavior. Of particular importance is the interpersonal response to others. It is wise to keep in mind that once established, obsessive compulsive behaviors can exert tremendous control over family members and significant others (e.g., schoolteachers). Obsessive compulsive behaviors may serve to promote interpersonal reinforcement by eliciting caring, sympathetic, and supportive responses from others and serve as a means to passively express anger or hostility (i.e., obsessive compulsive behavior may occasionally be analogous to passive-resistive behavior).

The assessment of the problem behaviors and examination of antecedent and consequent events is time-consuming and should not be equated with the typical clinic intake evaluation of 1 hour. For the first session, we recommend a focus on collecting relevant history regarding an overview of the problem, early development, relationships with immediate and extended family, educational history, sexual development, moral-religious development, and medical history. This more general intake evaluation is important to avoid omission of significant information (e.g., academic deficiencies, recent psychosocial stressors, medical problems, etc.) that might be of value in the overall treatment plan. The next several hours in the evaluative sequence would then address examination of family functioning as previously outlined and also address behavioral assessment issues.

The second goal of behavioral assessment is to devise behavioral objectives in concert with the child and family and to detail an intervention plan. The objectives may address specific types of changes required of the family and significant others in addition to changes in obsessive compulsive behaviors. It is essential that treatment objectives be discussed with the child and family because their expectations will directly influence the course and approach to treatment.

The third goal of behavioral assessment is to establish ongoing objective evaluation of treatment. Ongoing assessment follows directly from treatment objectives and implies detailing methods to assess relative attainment of treatment objectives. These measures may range from family ratings of success with homework assignments to specific measurement of obsessive-compulsive behaviors..

The last goal of a detailed behavioral assessment involves increasing expectations/motivation for change by the child and family members. As the child and family begin to articulate problems and controlling variables, they develop understanding of the disorder. They see the development of a specific plan and begin to experience positive effects resulting from collaborating with the therapist. Motivation is enhanced and trust in the therapeutic alliance begins to develop. Advances toward this goal occur when the therapist communicates understanding of what the child and family have been coping with and expresses hopefulness about the process of change.

Since this chapter's first addition, other assessment instruments have become available for children: the Leyton Obsessional Inventory—Child Version (Berg et al., 1980), the Obsessive-Compulsive Rating Scale (Rapoport, Elkins, & Mikkelson, 1986), the Comprehensive Psychopathological Rating Scale (Thoren, Asberg, & Cronholm, 1980), and the NIMH Self-rating Scale (Post, Korin, & Goodwin, 1983). Space does not permit a detailed review of their psychometric properties, but each is purported to provide workable and valid assessments for children (Wolff & Rapoport, 1988). The reader who wishes to use them would be wise to evaluate their reliability and validity before adopting them for clinical use.

Individual-Behavioral Intervention

Behavioral intervention may assume several different forms, depending on the results of the behavioral analysis. From our conceptualization, behavioral intervention strategies would be only one part of the treatment package. The application of behavioral programs in the family has been discussed in the section on family-interpersonal strategies. The focus of this section will be on the review and illustration of promising behavioral techniques. Most often, such techniques would be used concurrently with strategies designed to deal with the interpersonal context of OCD.

Exposure Treatment. Exposure and response prevention usually occur concurrently during treatment but will be reviewed separately for the sake of clarity of presentation. Exposure must be scheduled for prolonged time periods (usually 2 hours) to accomplish therapeutic goals. Brief periods of exposure may increase rather than diminish levels of anxiety.

The technique requires the development of a hierarchy of anxiety-eliciting stimuli. These are presented in ascending order, either in vivo or in imagination to the child. Typically, the starting point is toward the low-anxiety end of the continuum (SUDS 40). For example, in the case of compulsive hand-washing, various types of contaminants would make up the hierarchy. A contaminant in the lower SUDS range would be selected as the first item (e.g., playground dirt). The contaminant would be spread by the therapist and/or the child on the hands, face, and other body parts shown by analysis to be important. This would be done every 10 minutes or so for the duration of the session. A SUDS level would be recorded at each exposure and periodically throughout the session. Repeated exposures are provided until the SUDS range and observation of the child clearly suggested that anxiety had diminished to a comfortable level. Usually a 2-hour session will allow for intensification of anxiety and its gradual reduction. An analogous paradigm is followed in using imagery. Where anxiety-arousing stimuli are not readily available or where the anxiety-eliciting stimuli are covert (e.g., thoughts about harm occurring to a family member, eliciting ritualized behavior to avoid the anxiety produced by the cognition), exposure is to described imaginal scenes.

Homework assignments for prolonged exposure (2 to 4 hours) are made each day. Directions for response prevention are also initiated on the first day of exposure. The next therapy session involves an initial review of homework, assessment of any changes in avoidance behavior (monitoring response prevention), and the provision of support and reassurance. With younger children, parents conduct or monitor homework, modeling after the therapist.

Movement up the hierarchy requires SUDS reduction to 20 to 30 or less for an item before proceeding to the next item in the hierarchy. This process continues until the child can experience a relatively low level of distress to the highest item. The entire process may require daily sessions for as long as 2 weeks. When the exposure is complete, it may be necessary to begin other interventions for additional treatment objectives.

Although 2 hours will usually suffice to allow anxiety levels to peak and significant reduction to occur by the end of the session, the therapist should coach the child and parents to continue beyond 2 hours if needed to experience reduction in anxiety significantly below peak levels. Sessions lasting longer than 2 hours are sometimes required when high-hierarchy items are first introduced. Reduction of SUDS levels to 50 or less is a reasonable indicant for termination of the exposure session.

Response Prevention. This treatment consists of preventing the child from using any rituals or other avoidance behaviors. Although exposure and response prevention are descriptively simple, they are difficult to accomplish. Typically, the child will require supervision during treatment and homework sessions. Home treatment requires the assistance of family members, who spend considerable time supervising the child. These supervisors require detailed instructions, review of the treatment rationale, specific guidelines for supervision, and modeling by the therapist. The efficacy of treatment can be diminished greatly by ineffective supervision. Consequently, it may be necessary to utilize behavioral technicians or hospitalization to accomplish the treatment goal.

Review of a relatively straightforward case (Meredith & Milby, 1980) of OCD treated by exposure and response prevention illustrates these techniques. Although this case illustrates these specific techniques, it does not represent as well the multimodal approach that is often required

in the clinical setting. Successful treatment was conducted without the need for a more comprehensive treatment package. Although this sometimes happens, readers should not assume that these procedures alone will suffice to produce efficacious treatment.

The youngster was a 15-year-old male of above-average intelligence enrolled in a suburban Catholic high school and working part time as a busboy. He presented with excessive hand-washing and showering rituals related to a fear of contamination from feces, body fluids, and related materials. Rituals averaged 30 minutes for hand-washing and 65 minutes for showering per day. He was also obsessed about punishment from God and prayed ritualistically to allay these fears. The ritualistic praying ceased spontaneously during the pretreatment assessment. Washing rituals began 2 years prior to treatment. No precipitating events were recalled, although his uncle was described as having washed excessively because of a preoccupation with germs, especially in relation to venereal disease. The uncle had warned the patient to avoid various situations for fear of contamination.

At the time of treatment, the patient's fears and rituals had begun to interfere with his scholastic performance but not with his functioning at work. Sexual development, family relationships, and peer relationships appeared normal. No previous psychiatric treatment had been attempted.

The behavioral assessment was completed in three-and-a-half 2-hour sessions. In addition to detailed interviewing, assessment included a daily log of the number, type, and duration of ritual behaviors as well as the times at which they occurred. The antecedent and consequent events associated with the rituals were also noted. Assessment included a behavioral avoidance test using the most feared sources of contamination: human feces and urine.

The assessment revealed that ritualized washing occurred when the patient was exposed to contamination from feces, body fluids, and related items. A SUDS analysis of various types of contamination revealed the hierarchy of contamination shown in Table 2.1.

During assessment, details of the treatment plan—involving 2 weeks of exposure followed by 2 weeks of response prevention—were agreed upon. In addition, the patient signed a consent form to participate in a clinical study. This form also spelled out the major aspects of treatment.

Table 2.1. SUDS Analysis of Types of Contamination

SOURCE	SUDS
Human feces, other	100
Animal feces	95
Own feces	90
Human urine, other	85
Own urine	80
Pubic hair, other	75
Pubic hair, own	60
Bird droppings	55
Semen	50
Washing-machine water	45
Rain-sewer water	40
Shoe-sole bottom	35
Vomit	30
Bellybutton lint	25
Bathroom doorknob	20
Dirty floor	15
Fingernail dirt	10

In vivo exposure began using a moderate SUDS level contaminant: washing-machine water (SUDS = 45). After initial review of progress and problems, the 2-hour session was divided into 15-minute exposure segments. Every 15 minutes, washing-machine water was spread on the patient's hands and face. He was permitted to wash immediately after exposure but chose not to. His SUDS levels were recorded every 10 minutes throughout the session. Between exposures, discussion of progress and problems would often continue. However, an effort was made to direct conversation to topics that did not arouse anxiety and could serve to aid counterconditioning. When the patient showed clear diminution of SUDS levels during exposure, semen was added to the washing-machine water. When SUDS levels diminished to this, urine and bird droppings were added. Last, human feces were used. Homework exposure involved the same procedure and schedule of spreading contamination materials on the patient's face and hands every 15 minutes for 2 consecutive hours twice per day. Between exposures he was encouraged to engage in his normal routine. Homework also involved self-monitoring and recording of washing activities as well as any avoidance behavior. Exposure sessions were scheduled 5 days per week for 2 weeks. Homework continued 7 days per week, except that exposure homework was eliminated during the last weekend, while self-monitoring continued. Because this patient was treated as part of a research protocol, response prevention was ad-

ministered in a second 2-week period. Aside from supervised response prevention (i.e., no bathing or washing for a week at a time), this plan of treatment was essentially the same as during the first 2 weeks. During the last 5 days, therapist-supervised showers and hand-washing were introduced. Showering was limited to 10 minutes and hand-washing to 30 seconds, both without rituals. Therapist supervision was phased out over the last 3 days of treatment.

Two weekly follow-up sessions were scheduled to monitor progress, detect any rituals or other avoidance behavior, and work on a conflict situation between the patient and his mother. Additional follow-up sessions were scheduled at 1-, 2-, and 3-month intervals.

Ritual hand-washing and showering behavior are illustrated in Figure 2.1. At the start of exposure, hand-washing averaged 30 minutes and showering 65 minutes per day. As can be seen in the graph, ritualized behavior tended to increase during exposure, an understandable and predictable result when one recalls that the patient was exposed to contamination for as long as 6 hours per day. After exposure but before response prevention was introduced, ritual behavior dropped to baseline levels, although it was still above what were considered to be normal limits. With the introduction of exposure plus response prevention, ritual behavior dropped to zero and remained there until supervised normal washing and showering were introduced during the second week of treatment.

Following exposure plus response prevention and up to 3 months' follow-up, there was no ritualized behavior. The data shown in Figure 2.1 for these sessions represent the normal amount of time to wash hands (2 to 3 minutes per day) and to bathe or shower (8 to 10 minutes per day).

Behavioral-exposure test data are illustrated in Figure 2.2. In this test, the patient was asked to touch contamination materials—a combination of human feces and urine—using a glove. Then starting with eight paper towels and using fewer paper towels each time, he gradually progressed to touching the materials with his bare hand. With each progression, his SUDS levels for anxiety, contamination, and urge to wash were assessed. The first exposure test was given before treatment began. The patient did not touch the contamination materials with his bare hand but completed the rest of the progression, showing higher SUDS levels through the pro-

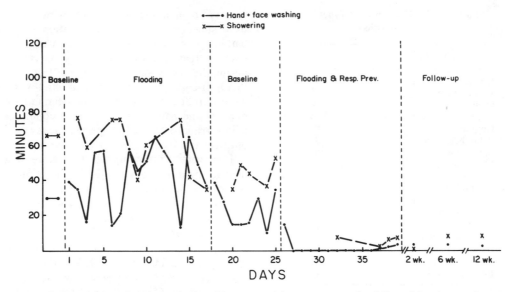

Figure 2.1. Daily washing time for a single subject treated by exposure only, followed by the combination of exposure and response prevention. From "Differential effects of exposure and response prevention in obsessive compulsive washers" by E. B. Foa, G. Steketee, and J. B. Milby, 1980, *Journal of Consulting and Clinical Psychology*, *48*, 71–79. Copyright 1980 by the American Psychological Association. Reprinted by permission of the publisher.

gression. Test 2 was conducted after flooding but before the combination treatment was given. As can be seen in Figure 2.2., SUDS levels were reduced significantly but were still above zero. In both tests 2 and 3 the patient touched contamination materials with his bare hand. In test 3, SUDS are near zero except for when materials were touched using one towel and with the bare hand. These are interpreted as normal-level reactions.

This case illustrates the treatment of OCD with individual behavioral-therapy techniques. Other examples of treatment approaches using exposure and response prevention with children or adolescents include the work of Green (1980); Mills et al. (1973); Turner, Hersen, Bellack, Andrasik, and Capparell (1980), and Stanley (1980). The Stanley article is noteworthy because of the family's involvement in the behavioral-treatment approach. The Turner et al. (1980) article examines the impact of psychotropic medication and behavioral approaches.

Other Behavioral Procedures. A number of additional treatment considerations demand attention. Treatment of the motoric and emotional aspects of compulsive behaviors should generally follow the exposure/response prevention format. With some children, the obsessional correlates of the disorder do not respond readily

to a focus on overt behavior. Specific treatment approaches may have to be scheduled to deal directly with the cognitive modality. This need also exists when the child presents with cognitive compulsions or doubting in the absence of motoric rituals.

Treatment for anxiety-decreasing cognitive compulsions should generally assume the same basic format as that used with compulsive rituals. Exposure, by necessity, involves the use of covert techniques. Anxiety-eliciting cognitions are identified and presented via exposure in imagery, using hierarchies similar to those discussed for compulsive rituals. Repeated exposure to the cognitions is demanded until anxiety diminishes. One shortcoming of this approach is the lack of control over the performance of the cognitive compulsions as a means of avoiding the anxiety associated with distressing cognitions (hierarchy items). More appropriate self-statements, verbalizing during exposure, can be substituted. For example, with a child who is frightened by sexual thoughts and exhibits repetitive covert praying to allay anxiety, more positive thoughts about sexuality can be introduced (e.g., feeling anxious about sex is okay for right now, and this will be less of a problem as I feel more comfortable talking with girls/ boys).

Although no data on efficacy presently exist,

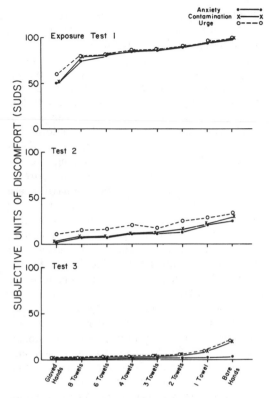

Figure 2.2. Subjective anxiety during the exposure test reported by a single subject treated by exposure only, followed by the combination of exposure and response prevention. From "Differential effects of exposure and response prevention in obsessive compulsive washers" by E. B. Foa, G. Steketee, and J. B. Milby, 1980, *Journal of Consulting and Clinical Psychology, 48,* 71–79. Copyright 1980 by the American Psychological Association. Reprinted by permission of the publisher.

homework assignments involving adaptive overt verbal behavior (discussions with family and friends) may be useful to promote these more positive cognitive patterns.

Treatment of anxiety-elevating obsessions is less well developed and has not received much research attention. At this point, no specific treatments of choice exist. The treatments described in the literature include prolonged exposure (negative practice), thought stopping, faradic disruption, and cognitive flooding. With children, procedures that minimize aversive stimulation seem more desirable. It is possible that systematic desensitization or variations of this technique (e.g., anxiety-management training) may prove to be useful. No studies used cognitively oriented behavioral approaches. These may be useful when combined with treatments

that also reduce the affective response to the anxiety-elevating cognitive pattern.

Of the techniques reviewed, modifications of the thought-stopping technique and cognitive flooding may be most promising. Campbell (1973) successfully treated a 12-year-old boy with a variation of thought stopping that creatively minimized the aversiveness commonly associated with it. The child presented with obsessions about the violent death of his sister, which he had witnessed 9 months prior to treatment. The youngster described in detail how he had watched his sister become entangled in a machine used to grind grain. Behavioral analysis revealed that he averaged 15 daily rumination periods and that these periods lasted approximately 20 minutes each. Treatment involved training the child "to evoke a negative thought and then to stop the thought pattern by loudly counting backwards from ten to zero as rapidly as possible." Following his counting, he was instructed to switch his thoughts to one of a number of pleasant scenes previously identified. Following mastery of this procedure, he was instructed to repeat the methodology utilizing the subvocal counting verbalization. Practice occurred in the therapy session, outside of therapy, whenever anxiety-arousing obsessions occurred, and prior to retiring each evening. Three-year follow-up with the mother suggested a good response to this intervention.

Cognitive flooding (Milby et al., 1981) may prove to have clinical utility with anxiety-elevating obsessions. In the treatment of an obsessive adult, repeated videotaped exposure to anxiety-arousing stimuli produced a relatively rapid response. Procedurally, the technique involves videotaping the child's own description of anxiety-producing obsessions with discussion of associated catastrophic events. These monologues are then edited. Separate tapes are then developed that repeat a particular theme every few seconds for an hour. Training involves sitting with the child and helping him or her focus attention on a television screen on which he or she repeatedly discusses a particular obsessive theme. In the case of obsessive concerns of harm befalling a family member, the child's description of his or her thoughts would be videotaped, edited, and then played back. The child would be encouraged to listen and watch the repetition of the same performance 30 to 40 times within the therapy hour. Such prolonged exposure seems to produce extinction or habituation of the emotional component of the obsessive thought. This technique seems quite promising with youngsters experiencing anxiety-elevating obsessional thinking. However, more research is needed. This technique could easily be combined with others designed to promote more adaptive cognitive patterns.

A final treatment consideration involves intervention with primary obsessional slowness. This pattern is not well researched but is commonly observed in the clinical situation. The only treatment approach isolated thus far is a combination of prompting, shaping, and pacing of responses suggested by Rachman and Hodgson (1980). After providing instructions and modeling, the therapist prompts quicker behavior while the child carries out the task. Shaping, instructions, and verbal reinforcement are used to encourage a faster pace and to discourage persistent slowness. External pacing by timing devices is used. This general approach would be easily complemented by the introduction of structured token or point programs to add more positive reinforcement to the treatment package. For example, specific numbers of points could be awarded for meeting time deadlines with respect to showering, dressing, and grooming before school. These points could later be exchanged for rewards selected from a reward menu generated by the child.

It should be understood that other presenting problems besides OCD may need to be addressed. Of particular importance are approaches to develop more effective general interpersonal and heterosocial skills. A focus on increasing "emotional freedom" through assertiveness training is also often a necessary component. As previously mentioned, more cognitively oriented strategies that deal with perfectionistic striving and problem-solving skills may also have application with OCD youngsters. These techniques and approaches are beyond the scope of this discussion but should not be omitted in the basic treatment package. Successful and lasting treatment in most cases will demand a working knowledge of these approaches.

TREATMENT GENERALIZATION

The generalization of treatment effects with OCD involves several issues. The first is how to promote generalization across settings. With the obsessive compulsive child, this involves transfer of effects from the treatment setting (clinic or hospital) to the home or school. At this point, we are not guided by firm empirical data. From our viewpoint, however, treatment generalization across settings demands treatment involvement of family members and school personnel. With the family, this may assume several forms, ranging from formal family therapy sessions to utilizing parents in administering behavioral programs in the home. School personnel also should be involved in treatment programming in cases where consent has been granted by both parents and child and the problematic behaviors are manifest in school. Practically speaking, it is usually not possible to develop elaborate behavioral programs in the school. It may be possible, however, to inform teachers, counselors, and the school psychologist of problems and of treatment goals and methods that they might utilize in the educational setting to assist treatment. Such discussions should avoid theoretical issues and emphasize practical case management (i.e., what the teachers can do to promote treatment success). Specific goals should be addressed and reviewed thoroughly. It is our experience that school personnel are extremely cooperative when this type of approach is utilized. A general premise is that to promote generalization across settings, informal involvement of representatives of these various settings is necessary.

A second issue concerns generalization across behavioral modalities. It is clear that generalization across behaviors should not be anticipated. The literature on adult OCD suggests a specific association between treatment choice and type of therapeutic change (i.e., a relative independence of treatment effects). Several examples are suggested from the literature. Milby et al. (1981) found it necessary to design a specific treatment for obsessive ideation that did not diminish after exposure/response prevention successfully decreased compulsive rituals. In a related example, Foa et al. (1980) demonstrated that response prevention had more impact on the operant response of compulsive rituals, while exposure treatment clearly had more effect on decreasing the emotional response. A third example is provided by Marks et al. (1980), who clearly demonstrated independent treatment effects for depressed OCDs in which antidepressant medication clearly decreased depressive symptoms but did not significantly influence compulsive rituals. Exposure and response-prevention techniques were also effective in alleviating the compulsive rituals but did not substantially modify depressive symptoms.

Evaluation of treatment effects must utilize multiple outcome measures to assess the impact of treatment accurately. Assessment should be sensitive to the generalization of treatment across response modalities. For example, what effect does exposure for compulsive rituals have on cognitive compulsions? It should also be sensitive to generalization of treatment from specific obsessive compulsive responses to associated problems (e.g., the impact of exposure for compulsive rituals on mood or interpersonal behavior). At this point in our clinical understanding, it makes sense to treat discrete problems (family problems or OC symptoms) and monitor the impact of this focus on remaining problems. It should be realized that most clinical cases demand multitreatment packages. In the absence of more robust techniques, this will likely continue to be the case. Clinically, the question of generalization across response modalities may be practically conceptualized as: What treatment approaches or combination of approaches will produce the desired changes in targeted problems? The answer implies the use of multiple treatment techniques and multiple measures of change. The question should also alert the clinician to the risk of a myopic focus on obsessive compulsive behaviors to the exclusion of problems in other areas (e.g., interpersonal skills, problem-solving styles, academic deficiencies, etc.).

LIMITATIONS AND PITFALLS

Because the approach we advocate is one that involves not only the child but also the family and school, there are many opportunities for problems, misunderstandings, inconsistencies, and noncompliance to arise. The best antidote for this is thorough groundwork and follow-up consultations with all who are supporting the intervention program. However, in spite of the best efforts and intentions of all concerned, the treatment may not be effective. The success rates for behavioral therapy with adult OCDs has been about 75%; thus the clinician could expect one child in four or so to not respond well to behavioral intervention. In such cases, a thorough review of the assessment data and the way in which the program was implemented may point out correctable flaws. Where none are found, another treatment approach—including the consideration of another medication—should be considered.

The side effects of medication are sometimes a limitation on treatment because these may be intolerable even though the drug does reduce OC symptomatology. Also, the medication may simply not produce the therapeutic effect desired. In both cases a trial of another medication may be in order. Often parents will have strong concerns about giving the child medication and some may even be responsible for noncompliance and the child's subsequent relapse. Of course, the concerns of parents must be assessed. If it is determined that they are unwilling to support the medication regimen prescribed, even after education and support, alternative means of treatment (i.e., behavioral and/or family-systems therapy) may be attempted.

No clinician likes to "give up" on a child even if treatment is not going well. But if systematic assessment has been followed by systematic and multimodal intervention and the child and/or family system are still unresponsive, a consultant can often add to the conceptualization of the case and make suggestions to increase treatment efficacy. Last, referral to another clinician may help treatment to get "unstuck." Although often consulted as a last resort, a new clinician, starting fresh with the child and family—especially if a more acceptable or believable treatment approach is attempted—will often be successful.

SUMMARY

This chapter reviewed the available literature on the epidemiology, theories of etiology, assessment, and treatment of OCD in children and adolescents. A continuum of treatment approaches was covered, ranging from system-level interventions to interventions focusing on modifying the behavior of the individual obsessive compulsive child. Assessment strategies were reviewed for both interpersonally oriented and behavioral treatments. The suggested treatment model incorporates a focus on idiographic assessment with prescriptive treatments that address family and interpersonal functioning, specific obsessive compulsive behaviors, and treatment for associated problems (e.g., assertiveness deficits, etc.) that are often a part of the presenting clinical picture. This chapter argues for the use of a multimodal approach to case conceptualization and treatment. The most significant aspects of effective treatment appear to be careful idiographic assessment of child and family, development of an accepting and nurturing therapeutic alliance, and active, directive interventions that focus on changing specific problems in the interpersonal system of the child while also addressing the child's individual obsessive compulsive behaviors.

This approach demands flexibility and clinical sensitivity to the given case. It also demands an understanding of several different levels of conceptualization as well as a grasp of the assessment and treatment issues associated with this multilevel approach. Technical sophistication is no substitute for clinical sensitivity. This model is an experimental approach that demands ongoing assessment to monitor the impact of treatment techniques developing from clinical hypotheses.

The empirical foundations of this model are weak, even though data are accumulating about the use of specific intervention approaches. The clinical support for it is witnessed in the day-to-day behavior of practitioners who deal with obsessive compulsive youngsters. We hope for the resolution of this schism as clinically sensitive practitioners stimulate further experimental investigation of treatment approaches to childhood OCD.

REFERENCES

Adams, J. (1972). Psychotherapy with obsessive children. *American Journal of Psychiatry, 128,* 1414–1417.

Adams, P. L. (1973). *Obsessive children.* New York: Brunner/Mazel.

Akhtar, S., Pershad, D., & Verma, S. K. (1975). A Rorschach study of obsessional neurosis. *Indian Journal of Clinical Psychology, 2,* 139–143.

American Psychiatric Association. (1980). *Diagnostic and statistical manual of mental disorders* (3rd ed.). Washington, DC: Author.

American Psychiatric Association. (1987). *Diagnostic and statistical manual of mental disorders* (3rd ed. rev.). Washington, DC: Author.

Ananth, J., Pechnold, J. C., Van Den Steen, N., & Engelsmann, F. (1981). Double-blind comparative study of clomipramine and amitriptyline in obsessive neurosis. *Progress in Neuropsychopharmacology, 5,* 257–262.

Ayllon, T., Garber, S. W., & Allison, M. G. (1977). Behavioral treatment of childhood neurosis. *Psychiatry, 40,* 315–322.

Bartucci, R. J., Stewart, J. T., & Kemph, J. P. (1987). Trimipramine in the treatment of obsessive-compulsive disorder. *American Journal of Psychiatry, 144,* 964–965.

Baxter, L. R., Jr., Phelps, M. E., Maziotta, J. C., Guze, B. H., Schwartz, J. M., & Selin, C. E. (1987). Local cerebral glucose metabolic rates in obsessive-compulsive disorder. *Archives of General Psychiatry, 44,* 211–218.

Beech, H. R. (Ed.). (1974). *Obsessional states.* London: Methuen.

Berg, C. J., Rapoport, J. L., & Flament, M. (1980). The Leyton Obsessional Inventory—Child Version. *Journal of the American Academy of Child Psychiatry, 25,* 84–91.

Berman, L. (1974). The obsessive-compulsive neurosis in children. *Journal of Nervous and Mental Disease, 95,* 26–39.

Black, A. (1974). The natural history of obsessional neurosis. In H. R. Beech (Ed.), *Obsessional states.* London: Methuen.

Bolles, R. C. (1979). *Learning theory.* New York: Holt, Rinehart, & Winston.

Bolton, D., Collins, S., & Steinberg, D. (1983). Treatment of OCD in adolescence: A report of 15 cases. *British Journal of Psychiatry, 142,* 456–464.

Bowen, M. (1978). *Family therapy in clinical practice.* New York: Jason Aronson.

Campbell, L. M. (1973). A variation of thought stopping in a twelve-year-old boy: A case report. *Journal of Behavior Therapy and Experimental Psychiatry, 4,* 69–70.

Clark, D. A., & Bolton, D. (1985). Obsessive-compulsive adolescents and their parents: A psychometric study. *Journal of Child Psychology and Psychiatry, 26,* 267–276.

Cooper, J., & McNeil, J. (1968). A study of houseproud housewives and their interaction with children. *Journal of Child Psychology and Psychiatry, 9,* 173–188.

Dai, B. (1957). Obsessive-compulsive disorders in Chinese culture. *Social Problems, 4,* 313–321.

Dell, P. F. (1981). *Beyond homeostasis: Toward a concept of coherence.* Unpublished manuscript.

Dell, P. F., & Goolishian, H. A. (1979). "*Order through fluctuation:*" An evolutionary epistemology for human systems. Paper presented at the Annual Scientific Meeting of the A. K. Rice Institute, Houston, TX.

Diebert, A. N., & Harmon, A. J. (1970). *New tools for changing behavior*. Champaign, IL: Research Press.

Dilsaver, S. C., & White, K. (1986). Affective disorders and associated psychopathology: A family history study. *Journal of Clinical Psychiatry, 47,* 162–169.

Elkins, R., Rapoport, J. L., & Lipsky, A. (1980). Obsessive-compulsive disorder of childhood and adolescence: A neurological viewpoint. *Journal of the American Academy of Child Psychiatry, 19,* 511–524.

Fine, S. (1973). Family therapy and a behavioral approach to childhood obsessive-compulsive neurosis. *Archives of General Psychiatry, 28,* 695–697.

Flament, M. F., Rapoport, J. L., Berg, C. J., Sceery, W., Kilts, C., Mellstrom, B., & Linnoila, M. (1987). Clomipramine treatment of childhood obsessive-compulsive disorder. *Archives of General Psychiatry, 44,* 219–225.

Flament, M. F., Rapoport, J. L., Murphy, D. L., Berg, C. J., & Lake, C. R. (1985). Biochemical changes during clomipramine treatment of childhood obsessive-compulsive disorders. *Archives of General Psychiatry, 42,* 977–983.

Foa, E. (1982). Treatment of obsessive-compulsive—When do we fail? In E. Foa & P. Emmelkamp, *Failure in behavior therapy.* New York: John Wiley & Sons.

Foa, E., & Tillman, N. S. (1978). The treatment of obsessive-compulsive neurosis. In A. Goldstein & E. Foa (Eds.), *The handbook of behavioral interventions* (pp. 416–500). New York: Wiley Interscience.

Foa, E. B., Steketee, G., & Milby, J. B. (1980). Differential effects of exposure and response prevention in obsessive-compulsive washers. *Journal of Consulting and Clinical Psychology, 48,* 71–79.

Furman, E. (1971, April). *Some thoughts on reconstruction in child analysis.* Paper presented at Sixth Annual Scientific Meeting of the American Association for Child Psychoanalysis, Williamsburg, VA.

Goodwin, D. W., Guze, S. B., & Robins, E. (1969). Follow-up studies in obsessional neurosis. *Archives in General Psychiatry, 20,* 182–187.

Green, D. (1980). A behavioral approach to the treatment of obsessional case study. *Journal of Adolescence, 3,* 297–306.

Grimshaw, L. (1965). The outcome of obsessional disorder III: A follow-up study of 100 cases. *British Journal of Psychiatry,* 1051–1056.

Gurman, A. S., & Kniskern, D. P. (1981). Family therapy outcome research: Knowns and unknowns. In A. S. Gurman & D. P. Kniskern (Eds.), *Handbook of family therapy* (pp. 742–775). New York: Brunner/Mazel.

Haley, J. (1973). *Uncommon therapy: The psychiatric techniques of Milton H. Erickson, M.D.* New York: Ballantine Books.

Haley, J. (1976). *Problem-solving therapy.* San Francisco: Jossey-Bass.

Harbin, H. T. (1976). Cure by ordeal: Treatment of an obsessive-compulsive neurotic. *International Journal of Family Therapy, 1,* 324–332.

Hersen, M. (1968). Treatment of a compulsive and phobic disorder through a total behavior therapy program: A case study. *Psychotherapy: Theory, Research, and Practice, 5,* 220–225.

Hoffman, L. (1981). *Foundations of family therapy.* New York: Basic Books.

Hollingsworth, C. E., Tanguay, P. E., Grossman, L., & Pabst, P. (1980). Long-term outcome of obsessive-compulsive disorder in childhood. *Journal of the American Academy of Child Psychiatry, 19,* 134–144.

Hunter, R., & MacAlpine, T. (Eds.). (1963). *Three hundred years of psychiatry.* London: Oxford University Press.

Ingram, I. M. (1961). Obsessional illness in mental patients. *Journal of Mental Science, 197,* 382–402.

Ingram, I. M., & MacAdams, W. A. (1960). The electroencephalogram, obsessive illness and obsessive personality. *Journal of Mental Science, 106,* 686–694.

Insel, R. S., Hoover, C., & Murphy, D. L. (1983). Parents of patients with obsessive-compulsive disorder. *Psychological Medicine, 13,* 807–811.

Insel, T. R., Murphy, D. L., Cohen, R. M., Alternam, I., Kiles, C., & Linnoila, M. (1983). Obsessive-compulsive disorder: A double-bind trial of clompramine and clorgyline. *Archives of General Psychiatry, 40,* 605–612.

Isberg, R. S. (1981). A comparison of phenelzine and imipramine in an obsessive-compulsive patient. *American Journal of Psychiatry, 138,* 1250–1251.

Jacobson, N. S. (1981). Behavioral marital therapy. In A. S. Gurman & D. P. Kniskern, (Eds.), *Handbook of family therapy* (pp. 556–591). New York: Brunner/Mazel.

Jenike, M. A. (1981). Rapid response of severe obsessive-compulsive disorder to tranylcypromine. *American Journal of Psychiatry, 138,* 1249–1250.

Jenike, M. A., Baer, L., Brotman, A. W., Goff, C., Minichiello, W. E., & Regan, N. J. (1987). Obsessive-compulsive disorder, depression, and the dexamethasone suppression test. *Journal of Clinical Psychopharmacology, 7,* 182–184.

Judd, L. L. (1965). Obsessive-compulsive neurosis in children. *Archives of General Psychiatry, 12,* 136–142.

Kayton, L., & Borge, G. F. (1967). Birth order and the obsessive-compulsive character. *Archives of General Psychiatry, 17,* 751–753.

Kenny, F. T., Mowbray, R. M., & Lalani, S. (1978). Faradic disruption of obsessive ideation in the treatment of obsessive neurosis. *Behavior Therapy, 9,* 209–221.

Kenny, F. T., Solyom, L., & Solyom, C. (1973). Faradic disruption of obsessive ideation in the treatment of obsessive neurosis. *Behavior Therapy, 4,* 448–457.

Kringlen, E. (1965). Obsessional neurotics: A long-term follow-up. *British Journal of Psychiatry, 111,* 709–722.

Kringlen, E. (1970). Natural history of obsessional neurosis. *Seminars in Psychiatry, 2,* 403–419.

Kumar, K., & Wilkinson, J. C. M. (1971). Thought stopping: A useful treatment in phobias of "internal stimuli." *British Journal of Psychiatry, 119,* 305–307.

Lazarus, A. A. (1976). *Multimodal behavior therapy.* New York: Springer.

Lieberman, J. (1984). Evidence for a biological hypothesis of obsessive-compulsive disorder. *Neuropsychobiology, 11,* 14–21.

Lieberman, J. A., Breener, R., Lesser, M., Coccaro, E., Borenstein, M., & Kane, J. M. (1983). Dexamethasone suppression tests in patients with panic disorder. *American Journal of Psychiatry, 140,* 917–919.

Lindley, P., Marks, I., Philpott, R., & Snowden, J. (1977). Treatment of obsessive-compulsive neurosis with history of childhood autism. *British Journal of Psychiatry, 130,* 592–597.

Lipsedge, M. S., & Prothero, W. (1987). Clonidine and clomipramine in obsessive-compulsive disorder. *American Journal of Psychiatry, 144,* 965–966.

Lo, W. (1968). A follow-up study of obsessional neurotics in Hong Kong Chinese. *British Journal of Psychiatry, 113,* 823–832.

Luxenberg, J. S., Swedo, S. E., Flament, M. F., Friedland, R. P., Rapoport, J., & Rapoport, S. I. (1988). Neuroanatomical abnormalities in obsessive-compulsive disorder detected with quantitative x-ray computed tomography. *American Journal of Psychiatry, 145,* 1089–1093.

Lydiard, R. B. (1986). Obsessive-compulsive disorder successfully treated with trazodone. *Psychosomatics, 27,* 858–859.

Madanes, C. (1981). *Strategic family therapy.* San Francisco: Jossey-Bass.

Manchanda, R., & Sharma, M. (1986). Parental discipline and obsessive-compulsive neurosis. *Canadian Journal of Psychiatry, 31,* 698.

Marks, I. M., Stern, R., Mawson, D. J., Cobb, J., & McDonald, R. (1980). Clomipramine and exposure for obsessive-compulsive rituals: I. *British Journal of Psychiatry, 136,* 1–25.

Martin, G. L. (1982). Thought-stopping and stimulus control to decrease persistent disturbing thoughts. *Journal of Behavioral Therapy and Experimental Psychiatry, 13,* 215–220.

Mattes, J. A. (1986). A pilot study of combined trazodone and tryptophan in obsessive-compulsive disorder. *International Clinical Psychopharmacology, 1,* 170–173.

Meredith, R. L., & Milby, J. B. (1980). Obsessive compulsive neurosis: Behavioral approaches to evaluation and intervention. In R. J. Daitzman (Ed.), *Clinical behavior therapy and behavior modification.* Stanford, CT: Garland Press.

Milby, J. B., Meredith, R. L., & Rice, J. (1981). Video-taped exposure: A new treatment for obsessive-compulsive disorders. *Journal of Behavioral Therapy and Experimental Psychiatry, 12,* 249–255.

Mills, H. L., Agras, W. S., Barlow, D. H., & Mills, J. R. (1973). Compulsive rituals treated by response prevention: An experimental analysis. *Archives of General Psychiatry, 28,* 524–529.

Minuchin, S. (1974). *Families and family therapy.* Cambridge, MA: Harvard University Press.

Mitchell-Heggs, N., Kelly, O., & Richardson, A. (1976). Stereotactic limbic leucotomy: A follow-up at 16 months. *British Journal of Psychiatry, 128,* 226–240.

Montgomery, S. A. (1980). Clomipramine in obsessional neurosis: A placebo controlled trial. *Pharmacological Medicine, 1,* 189–192.

Monteiro, W., Marks, I. M., Noshirvani, H., & Checkley, S. (1986). Normal dexamethasone suppression test in obsessive-compulsive disorder. *British Journal of Psychiatry, 148,* 326–329.

Mowrer, O. H. (1960). *Learning theory and behavior.* New York: John Wiley & Sons.

Nee, L. Caine, E., Eldridge, R., & Ebert, M. (1980). Gilles de la Tourette Syndrome. Read at the Tourette Syndrome Association, New York. Reported in R. Elkins, J. L. Rapoport, & A. Lipsky, Obsessive-compulsive disorder of childhood and adolescence: A neurobiological viewpoint. *Journal of the American Academy of Child Psychiatry, 19,* 511–524.

O'Conner, J. J. (1983). Why can't I get hives: Brief strategic therapy with an obsessional child. *Family Process, 22,* 201–209.

Orvin, G. S. (1967). Treatment of the phobic obsessive-compulsive patient with oxazepam, an improved benzodiazepine compound. *Psychosomatics, 8,* 278–280.

Pacella, L., Polatkin, P., & Nagler, R. (1944). Clinical and EEG studies on obsessive-compulsive states. *American Journal of Psychiatry, 100,* 830–838.

Palazzoli, M. S. (1974). *Self-starvation: From the intrapsychic to the transpersonal approach to anorexia nervosa.* Trans. Arnold Pomerans. London: Chaucer, Human Context Books.

Perse, T. L., Greist, J. H., Jefferson, J. W., Rosenfeld, R., & Dar, R. (1987). Fluvoxamine treatment of obsessive-compulsive disorder. *American Journal of Psychiatry, 144,* 1543–1548.

Pollit, J. (1957). Natural history of obsessional states: A study of 150 cases. *British Medical Journal, 1,* 194–198.

Post, R., Korin, J. V., & Goodwin, F. K. (1983). Tetrahydrocannabinol (THC) in depressed patients. *Archives of General Psychiatry, 28,* 345–352.

Rachman, S. (1974). Primary obsessional slowness. *Behavioral Research and Therapy, 12,* 9–18.

Rachman, S. J., & Hodgson, R. J. (1980). *Obsessions and compulsions.* Englewood Cliffs, NJ: Prentice-Hall.

Rapoport, J., Elkins, R., & Mikkelson, E. (1986). Clinical controlled trial of clomipramine in adolescents with obsessive compulsive disorder. *Psychopharmacology Bulletin, 16,* 61–63.

Rasmussen, S. A., & Tsuang, M. T. (1986). Clinical characteristics and family history in DSM-III obsessive-compulsive disorder. *American Journal of Psychiatry, 143,* 317–322.

Robins, L. N. (1966). *Deviant children grow up.* Baltimore: Williams & Wilkins.

Rockwell, L. F., & Simmons, D. (1947). The EEG and personality organization in the obsessive-compulsive reactions. *Archives of Neurology and Psychiatry, 57,* 71–77.

Rutter, M. L. (1972). Relationships between child and adult psychiatric disorders. *Acta Psychiatrica Scandinavia, 48,* 3–21.

Rutter, M., Tizard, J., & Whitmore, K. (Eds.). (1970). *Education, health and behavior.* London: Longmans.

Salzman, L., & Thaler, F. H. (1981). Obsessive-compulsive disorders: A review of the literature. *American Journal of Psychiatry, 138,* 286–296.

Scott, M. E. (1966, September). Treatment of obsessive behavior in a child. *Southern Medical Journal,* pp. 1087–1089.

Shapiro, A., Shapiro, E., Braun, R., & Sweet, R. (1978). *Gilles de la Tourette Syndrome.* New York: Raven Press.

Shields, J. (1962). *Monozygotic twins brought up apart and brought up together.* London: Oxford University Press.

Skoog, G. (1959). The anacastic syndrome. *Acta Psychiatrica Scandinavia, 34,* 134.

Sluzki, C. E., & Vernon, E. (1971). The double-bind as a universal pathogenic situation. *Family Process, 10,* 397–410.

Solyom, J., Garza-Perez, J., Ledwidge, B. L., & Solyom, C. (1972). Paradoxical intention in the treatment of obsessive thoughts: A pilot study. *Comprehensive Psychiatry, 13,* 291–297.

Stanley, L. (1980). Treatment of ritualistic behavior in an eight-year-old girl by response prevention: A case report. *Journal of Child Psychiatry, 21,* 85–90.

Steketee, G., Grayson, J. B., & Foa, E. B. (1981, August). *Effects of exposure and response prevention on obsessive-compulsive symptoms.* Paper presented at American Psychological Association meeting, Los Angeles, CA.

Stern, R. S., Marks, I. M., Cobb, J. P., Jones, R. B., & Luscombe, D. K. (1977). A preliminary report on clinical response and plasma levels of clomipramine and desmethylclomipramine in obsessive-compulsive neurosis. *Post-graduate Medical Journal, 53*(Supp. 4), 97–103.

Tapia, F. (1969). Haldol in the treatment of children with tics and stutters—and an incidental finding. *Psychiatric Quarterly, 3,* 648–649.

Templer, D. (1972). The obsessive-compulsive neurosis: Review of research findings. *Comprehensive Psychiatry, 13,* 375–383.

Thoren, P., Asberg, M., & Cronholm, B. (1980). Clomipramine treatment of obsessive-compulsive disorder: I. A controlled clinical trial. *Archives of General Psychiatry, 37,* 1281–1285.

Thyer, B. A., Parrish, R. T., Curtis, G. C., Neese, R. M., & Cameron, D. G. (1985). Ages of onset of DSM-III anxiety disorders. *Comprehensive Psychiatry, 26,* 113–122.

Toman, W. (1969). *Family constellation.* New York: Springer.

Tseng, W. (1973). Psychopathologic study of obsessive-compulsive neurosis in Taiwan. *Comprehensive Psychiatry, 14,* 139–140.

Turner, S., Hersen, M., Bellack, A., Andrasik, F., & Capparell, H. (1980). Behavioral and pharmacological treatment of obsessive-com-

pulsive disorders. *Journal of Nervous and Mental Disease, 168,* 651–657.

Watzlawick, P., Weakland, J., & Fisch, R. (1974). *Change: Principles of problem formation and problem resolution.* New York: W W Norton.

Weiner, I. B. (1967). Behavior therapy in obsessive-compulsive neurosis: Treatment of an adolescent boy. *Psychotherapy: Theory, Research, and Practice, 4,* 27–29.

Weissman, M. M., & Merikangas, K. R. (1986). The epidemiology of anxiety and panic disorders: An update. *Journal of Clinical Psychiatry, 47,* 11–17.

Wetzel, R. (1966). Use of behavioral techniques in a case of compulsive stealing. *Journal of Consulting Psychology, 30,* 367–374.

Wolff, R., & Rapoport, J. (1988). Behavioral treatment of childhood obsessive-compulsive disorder. *Behavior Modification, 12,* 252–266.

Wolpe, J. (1973). *The practice of behavior therapy.* Elmsford, NY: Pergamon Press.

Yamagami, T. (1971). The treatment of an obsession by thought stopping. *Journal of Behavior Therapy and Experimental Psychiatry, 2,* 133–135.

Yaryura-Tobia, J. A., Bebirian, R. J., Neziorglu, F. A., & Bhagavan, H. N. (1977). Obsessive-compulsive disorders as a serotonergic defect. *Research Communications in Psychology, Psychiatry and Behavior, 2,* 5–6.

Zahn, T. P., Insel, R. R., & Murphy, D. L. (1984). Psychophysiological changes during pharmacological treatment of patients with obsessive compulsive disorder. *British Journal of Psychiatry, 145,* 39–44.

Zikis, P. (1983). Treatment of an 11-year-old ritualizer and tiquer girl with in vivo exposure and response prevention. *Behavioral Psychotherapy, 11,* 75–81.

CHAPTER 3

CHILDHOOD DEPRESSION

Nadine J. Kaslow
Lynn P. Rehm

Cognitive-behavioral therapy for depressed children is a budding field of endeavor. Although there have been years of interest and research in cognitive-behavioral approaches to depression in adults (Rehm, 1981; Rehm & Kaslow, 1984), there are only a few outcome studies assessing the efficacy of cognitive-behavioral interventions with depressed children. However, the study of childhood depression has become increasingly popular in recent years, with particular focus on assessment and diagnostic issues, associated correlates, and the relationship between depression in parents and in children.

The purpose of this chapter is to review some of these recent developments and to outline some strategies for the conceptualization, assessment, and intervention of depression in children. In general, we will argue that current diagnostic practices identify children with a correlated set of presenting behavioral problems for whom special treatment strategies will be appropriate. Prominent among the characteristics of the population is a set of overgeneralized and maladaptive cognitive and behavioral skills

for self-management. We will make the case that these skills can be individually assessed and may be the target for intervention strategies. These targets may be modified along with other cognitive and behavioral deficits and excesses associated with depression that have already been the focus of prior work in cognitive behavior therapy with children. Finally, we will argue that the cognitive-behavioral interventions should be informed by a developmental perspective and conducted within a family context.

HISTORICAL PERSPECTIVES

Historically, little empirical work was done in the area of childhood depression because of the controversy that surrounded the very existence and nature of depression in children. A number of distinct perspectives characterized this debate. More recently, a consensus position has emerged in which depression in childhood is considered to be similar to depression in adults. The emergence of this consensus view has enabled research in the field to burgeon.

Depression Cannot Exist in Childhood

The first perspective is the classical psychoanalytic view, which states that for structural reasons, depression cannot exist in children. Clinical depression is viewed as a superego phenomenon involving aggression turned against the self. Furthermore, it is the existence of a superego conflict that arouses guilt, which is central to depression. Because a child's superego is not fully developed, clinical depression cannot exist in children (Beres, 1966; Rochlin, 1959). Rie (1966), in a review article, points out that there are psychoanalysts who conceptualize depression as low self-esteem resulting from a discrepancy between the real self and the ideal self. Because a stable self-representation does not develop until adolescence, the major dynamic elements of depression are not present in children. According to ego-analytic models of depression, which do not depend heavily on structural development (e.g., Bibring, 1953), depression is possible in children (e.g., Anthony, 1975; Bemporad, 1978). According to Bemporad (1978), depressed children's cognitive distortions are a function of problematic parent–child interactions. These interactions produce impaired self-esteem, a perceived lack of instrumentality regarding the environment, and dependence on significant others for gratification. These children's perception of their environment frequently renders them unhappy. Historically, the prominence of the classic psychoanalytic view was one factor that kept the term "depression" out of the lexicon of childhood psychopathology.

Depression in Childhood Is Masked

A second major perspective on childhood depression posits the concept of "masked" depression or "depressive equivalents." This position argues that depression exists in children in the sense of an internal, unobservable pathological entity, the external manifestations of which are depressive equivalents. The assumption is that children may be depressed but that they display this depression in the form of a variety of behavioral complaints typical of childhood (Cytryn & McKnew, 1974; Glaser, 1968; Malmquist, 1977).

Frequently cited "masking" symptoms include many of the nonpsychotic disorders of childhood: enuresis, temper tantrums, hyper-

activity, disobedience, truancy, running away, delinquency, fire setting, phobias, somatization, irritability, learning disabilities, and school failures. There are a few studies that examine the connection between a specific "depressive equivalent" and associated depression in the child or a history of depression in the child's family (e.g., Brumback & Weinberg, 1977; Gittelman-Klein & Klein, 1973; Lesse, 1974; Ling, Oftedal, & Weinberg, 1970; Zrull, McDermott, & Poznanski, 1970).

In general, the logical problems inherent in this position made it untenable. The major criticisms of it are that it is not of clinical or heuristic significance, because every possible symptom has been considered as an indication of depression, and there is no way to be certain these symptoms "mask" a depression (Rie, 1966; Welner, 1978). Furthermore, these "symptoms" may be developmentally and culturally determined ways of responding to many forms of psychological distress (Kovacs & Beck, 1977) or they may be adaptive behaviors in response to stressful life situations (Bemporad, 1978). Although this position has largely been abandoned in current usage, it does point out the important clinical observation that depression may frequently accompany other forms of childhood psychopathology, most notably anxiety disorders and conduct disorders (Kovacs, 1989). These comorbid conditions may make it more difficult to diagnose the depression. However, unless the syndrome of depression can be clearly observed, a diagnosis of childhood depression is not warranted.

Depression in Childhood Is Transitory

A third perspective is provided by Lefkowitz and Burton (1978). There are three major assumptions in their work:

1. If the behaviors that constitute the syndrome of depression are prevalent in normal children, the clinical manifestations of these symptoms are neither statistically atypical nor psychopathological. Therefore, the syndrome does not exist.
2. The putative symptoms of the syndrome of depression are transitory developmental phenomena that dissipate with time. Therefore, they cannot be considered pathological.
3. If symptoms remit spontaneously, clinical intervention is not necessary.

A number of criticisms have been made about this work (e.g., Costello, 1980). First, although single symptoms may be prevalent in a given population, it is the constellation of symptoms that defines the syndrome. The assumption of Lefkowitz and Burton (1978) relies too heavily on a purely statistical definition of pathology. The aversiveness of a particular behavior is not diminished by its frequency in the population. The second assumption is questionable when one considers the transitory nature of the developmental stage within which the child may be attempting to cope with a stressor. That the child may ultimately mature by developing new coping skills or attending to new problems does not lessen the impact of the problem in the current context. The argument that a problem is transitory within a given developmental context does not justify calling it normal—any more than the argument that because certain problems in society are transitory, they too are "normal" when seen in a historical context. The third assumption is problematic because of its functional relationship to a later, more persistent problem. The actual persistence of depressive behaviors can be determined empirically. Recent empirical studies adopting a longitudinal perspective (Kovacs, Feinberg, Crouse-Novak, Paulauskas, & Finkelstein, 1984; Kovacs & Gastonis, 1989; McGee & Williams, 1988) reveal that while the depressive episodes of most children eventually remit, they tend to be of longer duration than previously thought, they tend to recur, and the youngsters are likely to develop other psychiatric conditions as complications of the depression. On the average, the duration of an episode of major depression is 7 to 9 months, and an episode of dysthymia may exceed 3 years. These findings argue against Lefkowitz and Burton's hypothesis.

Depression in Childhood Parallels Depression in Adulthood

The proponents of the fourth view of overt depression in children describe a disorder that is similar to that seen in adults. The four sets of complaints used by Beck (1967) to characterize adult depression are evident in the classification of the pathology of childhood depression: (1) affective—e.g., dysphoria, mood change, weepiness, loneliness, apathy; (2) cognitive—e.g., low self-esteem, self-depreciation, guilt, indecision, pessimism; (3) motivational—e.g., avoidance, escape, passivity, anergia, decreased socialization; and (4) vegetative and psychomotor—e.g., sleep disturbance, appetite disturbance, and somatic complaints. In addition, developmentally appropriate complaints may exist in conjunction with the specifically depressive symptoms; they may include enuresis, encopresis, school phobia, decreased school performance, suicidal behavior, and aggressive or antisocial behavior (Kashani, Holcomb, & Orvaschel, 1986; Ryan, et al., 1987).

The most commonly held view is that depression in children is a distinct clinical entity whose defining characteristics are isomorphic with its adult counterpart (Cytryn, McKnew, & Bunney, 1980; Mitchell, McCauley, Burke, & Moss, 1988). Indeed, this is the perspective that has recently been adopted by the American Psychiatric Association's *Diagnostic and Statistical Manual of Mental Disorder* (APA, 1987). Childhood depression is not listed as a diagnosis in the section entitled "disorders usually first evident in infancy, childhood or adolescence." Rather, the DSM-III-R states that the essential features of affective disorders in children are the same as those in adults, and that therefore an adult diagnosis is appropriate. Although the DSM-III-R notes that there are differences in the associated features of depression in children as opposed to adults, these features are neither well defined nor to be considered when one is making a diagnosis.

DEVELOPMENTAL PERSPECTIVE

The basic tenet of the organismic-developmental approach is a general developmental or orthogenetic principle. According to this principle, ". . . whenever development occurs it proceeds from a state of relative globality and lack of differentiation to a state of increasing differentiation, articulation, and hierarchic integration" (Werner, 1957; p. 126). Psychopathology such as depression results when there is a lack of organization or integration of social, cognitive, or emotional competencies that influences the successful resolution of the salient developmental tasks that need to be negotiated (Cicchetti & Schneider-Rosen, 1986). The developmental perspective complements standard diagnostic classification schemas by providing a broader framework for addressing the etiology and clinical manifestations of psychopathology over the course of development and by highlighting new dimensions, variables, and parameters to be utilized in a more comprehensive, developmentally relevant nosology (Carlson & Garber, 1986). The research, which indicates that the rates of depression and suicidal behavior increases with age, argues in support of a developmental mediation of affective disorders (Rutter, 1986).

There are a number of implications of this developmental perspective for the classification of childhood depression, and the importance of utilizing a developmental perspective has been emphasized by a number of authors (e.g., Anthony, 1975; Bemporad & Wilson, 1978; Digdon & Gotlib, 1985; Malmquist, 1977; Rutter, 1986). In accordance with a developmental perspective in describing childhood depression, it is important to take into account children's cognitive, affective, and interpersonal competencies. Further, depression should be evaluated in relation to what is "normal" for a particular stage of development. Developmentally oriented writers have expressed concerns about adopting the adult, essentially unmodified DSM-III-R criteria for children (Carlson & Garber, 1986), because these criteria do not account for age-related differences in the defining attributes or manifest expressions of childhood depression (Kovacs, 1986) and because developmental advances in cognitive structures and functioning influence the manner in which children experience, interpret, and express emotions at different ages (Cicchetti & Schneider-Rosen, 1986). Future diagnostic systems need to address both the similarities and the differences in depression as manifested in children and adults. It will also be important to identify age-appropriate signs and symptoms, taking into account the level of the child's cognitive, affective, and interpersonal functioning.

DIAGNOSTIC CRITERIA AND ASSESSMENT

A review of the literature reveals compelling evidence that school-age children and adolescents experience not only the symptom of depression (dysphoric mood) but also a depressive syndrome which impairs the child's functioning and includes a characteristic symptom pattern and duration (Kovacs, 1989). The current view is that to be eligible for a diagnosis of major depression, a child must exhibit a change from previous functioning during a single 2-week

period. The child must have a prominent, relatively persistent depressed mood or a loss of interest or pleasure in almost all usual activities. Four of the following seven symptoms must be present almost daily: (1) significant weight loss or weight gain when not dieting, almost daily decrease or increase in appetite, or failure to make expected weight gains; (2) sleep disturbance, including insomnia or hypersomnia; (3) psychomotor agitation or retardation; (4) fatigue or loss of energy; (5) feeling of worthlessness or excessive or inappropriate guilt; (6) indecisiveness or diminished ability to think or concentrate; and (7) recurrent thoughts of death or recurrent suicidal ideation, threats, or attempts (APA, 1987).

Cantwell and Carlson (1979) suggested that a major obstacle to the investigation of childhood depression was the lack of a well-developed assessment methodology analogous to the techniques available for studying adult depression. Kazdin (1981) concluded his review of the assessment of childhood depression by asserting that the assessment area is underdeveloped. The past 10 years have witnessed a proliferation of assessment techniques for use in clinical and research settings. These techniques encompass a variety of types, including self-report, structured interviews, parent and clinician or staff ratings, peer nominations, and projective techniques (for reviews see Kazdin, 1981; Kazdin & Petti, 1982; Kovacs, 1981). A summary of the major scales is presented in Table 3.1.

The major self-report inventory is the Children's Depression Inventory (CDI), which is a modified form of the Beck Depression Inventory (BDI) for children (Kovacs & Beck, 1977). Other self-report scales include the Children's Depression Scale (CDS) (Lang & Tisher, 1978), Depression Self-Rating Scale (DSRS) (Birleson, 1981), Depression Adjective Checklist (CDACL) (Sokoloff & Lubin, 1983), Center for Epidemiological Studies—Depression Scale Modified for Children (CES-DC) (Weissman, Orvaschel, & Padian, 1980), Children's Depression Scale-Revised (CDS-R) (Reynolds, Anderson, & Bartell, 1985), and the Modified Zung (M-Zung) (Lefkowitz & Tesiny, 1980).

Several interviews have been developed to examine depression and its concomitant symptoms in children. The major interview schedules for children age 6 to 16 are the Kiddie-SADS-Epidemiologic Version (K-SADS-E) (Orvaschel & Puig-Antich, 1987) and the Kiddie-SADS-Present Episode (K-SADS-P) (Puig-Antich & Ryan, 1986), which are based on the Schedule for Affective Disorders and Schizophrenia (SADS) (Endicott & Spitzer, 1978). A DSM-III diagnosis is obtainable from these interviews. Additionally, DSM-III diagnoses may be based on information from the Interview Schedule for Children (ISC) (Kovacs, 1981), Diagnostic Interview Schedule for Children (DISC) (Costello, Edelbrock, Dulcan, Kales, & Klavic, 1984), and Diagnostic Interview for Children and Adolescents (DICA) (Herjanic, Herjanic, Brown, & Wheatt, 1975). Other clinician interview scales include the Bellevue Index of Depression (BID) (Petti, 1978) based on the Weinberg criteria (Ling et al., 1970; Weinberg, Rutman, Sullivan, Penick, & Dietz, 1973), the Children's Depression Rating Scale (CDRS-Revised) (Poznanski et al., 1984), the Children's Affective Rating Scale (CARS), (McKnew, Cytryn, Efron, Gershon, & Bunney, 1979) and the Child Assessment Schedule (CAS) (Hodges, McKnew, Cytryn, Stern, & Kline, 1982). Clinician ratings of dysthymia can also be made utilizing the Dsythymic Checklist (DCL) (Fine, Moretti, Haley, & Marriage, 1984).

Peer ratings have been found to be useful in assessing psychopathology among children. Lefkowitz and Tesiny (1980) developed the Peer Nomination Inventory for Depression (PNID) specifically to measure depression as reported by peers. Costello (1981) describes two questionnaires that may be filled out by parents about their child's behavior, including his or her depressive behaviors. These include the Personality Inventory for Children (PIC) (Wirt, Lachar, Klinedinst, & Seat, 1977) and the Child Behavior Checklist (CBCL) (Achenbach, 1978; Achenbach & Edelbrock, 1979).

In addition to measures of depression per se, there is a need for measures of constructs related to depression that various theories implicate as central to depression (e.g., social skills, attributional style, self-control behavior). These constructs are usually the direct targets of intervention, and changes in depression are assumed to occur secondarily. Selected relevant scales are discussed under the specific treatment strategies that might use them.

During the past decade, considerable progress has been made in the area of assessment. However, additional work must focus on the utilization of a developmental perspective to inform the design and administration of assessment devices. All these instruments are modeled after adult scales. They assess analogues of adult symptomatology and, therefore, do not take into account differences in the child's developmental level. It might be expected, for instance, that sleep disturbances or somatic complaints would vary for children in different age brackets. Future scales might be enhanced by incorporating items pertinent to different developmental levels and, perhaps, by developing relatively age-specific norms. Additionally, "it is important to recognize that age-dependent constraints on self-understanding, language, and memory organization may limit the accuracy of the assessment" (Kovacs, 1989, p. 211).

Further, the data on interinformant agreement reveal that it is essential to assess depression in children from more than one perspective. That is, a diagnosis or an assessment of severity of depression based on self-report, parental report, teacher report, clinician rating, or peer nomination alone should not be relied upon. Situational differences in depressive behavior, depressive distortions, denial, or exaggeration of complaints may render instruments from a single perspective invalid. Even clinician ratings based on interviews with the child versus interviews with the parents may not give equivalent results. Clinical evidence for depression should rest on at least two perspectives. For example, a diagnosis of depression could be based on data obtained from the Kiddie-SADS administered as an interview to both the parent or parents and the child and the child's self-report (perhaps on the CDI) of depressive complaints. Evaluations of depressive behavior in the school context should include teacher or peer evaluations in addition to a self-report. Multiple criteria should also be used to evaluate treatment outcome.

BEHAVIORAL AND COGNITIVE MODELS OF ADULTHOOD DEPRESSION

The adoption of diagnostic criteria and the development of assessment methods have increased interest among clinicians in the systematic evaluation of treatment strategies for childhood depression. One major area of interest has been in the possibility of using new antidepressant medications in treating children (Puig-Antich, 1982; Weller & Weller, 1984). A second area receiving increasing attention has been the application of innovations in the treatment of adult depression to childhood depression (Kas-

Table 3.1. Assessment Instruments

SCALE	AUTHOR	DESCRIPTIONS	SAMPLES AND PSYCHOMETRICS REPORTED
Children's Depression Inventory (CDI)	Kovacs & Beck (1977)	27-item self-report. Modified version of Beck Depression Inventory for adults. Measures severity of depression.	Psychiatric, medical, and normal children ages 6–17 Item-total correlations, internal consistency, test-retest reliability, and discriminant validity are acceptable. Correlates with clinician rating and DSM-III diagnosis.
Children's Depression Scale (CDS)	Tisher & Lang (1983)	66-item self-report. Alternate forms for parents, teachers, and siblings. Subscales for affect, social problems, self-esteem, thoughts of death and illness, guilt, pleasures.	Psychiatric and normal samples ages 9–16. Internal consistency and discriminant validity are adequate.
Depression Self-Rating Scale (DSRS)	Birleson (1981)	18-item original scale and 21-item modified scale. Self-report scale patterned after the Zung.	Psychiatric inpatients, children ages 7–13. Adequate criterion validity, concurrent validity, and internal consistency.
Depression Adjective Checklist (C-DACL)	Sokoloff & Lubin (1983)	Both forms of C-DACL self-report scale contain 34 adjectives pertaining to presence or absence of depressed mood.	Emotionally disturbed youth. Excellent internal consistency, alternate form, and split-half reliabilities. Good concurrent validity.
Center for Epidemiologic Depression Studies—Depression Scale Modified for Children (CES-DC)	Weissman, Orvaschel, & Padian (1980)	20-item self-report scale which is a derivative of the adult CES-D.	Normal sample and inpatients, ages 6–17. Adequate test-retest reliability, internal consistency, and concurrent validity.
Reynolds Adolescent Depression Scale (RADS)	Reynolds (1986)	30-item self-report scale reflecting DSM-III symptomatology for major and minor depression.	Normal samples of adolescents. Good reliability and concurrent validity.
Children's Depression Scale—Revised (CDS-R)	Reynolds, Anderson, & Bartell (1985)	30-item self-report scale with 29 items measuring depressive symptoms and 1 item being a global rating of depression.	Normal children ages 8–13. Demonstrated high internal consistency, high correlation with CDI and with teacher's global ratings.
Modified Zung (M-Zung)	Lefkowitz & Tesiny (1980)	11-item self-rating scale. Modified version of Zung for adults. Measures presence or absence of depressive symptoms.	Normal children, ages 10–11. Adequate internal consistency.
Kiddie-SADS—Epidemiologic Version (K-SADS-E)	Orvaschel & Puig-Antich (1987)	Structured interview to assess past and current episodes of depression and other forms of psychopathology. Based on the SADS interview and DSM-III-R compatible.	Psychiatric and normal samples ages 6–17. Adequate psychometrics.
Kiddie-SADS—Present Episode (K-SADS-P)	Revised by Puig-Antich & Ryan (1986)	Structured interview for depression, other diagnoses, and psychiatric history focuses on present episode. Modified version of Schedule for Affective Disorders and Schizophrenia. DSM-III-R compatible revised version. Interview administered to parent and child.	Psychiatric and normal samples ages 6–17. Interrater reliability high, good convergent validity, but low to moderate interinformant reliability.
Bellevue Index of Depression (BID)	Petti (1978)	Structured interview with 40 items under 19 headings. Assesses severity and duration of symptoms on basis of Weinberg criteria. Parent and child report used.	Inpatient and outpatient samples aged 6–12. Good interrater reliability and adequate convergent validity.

Table 3.1. Assessment Instruments (*continued*)

SCALE	AUTHOR	DESCRIPTIONS	SAMPLES AND PSYCHOMETRICS REPORTED
Interview Schedule for Children (ISC)	Kovacs (1981)	Structured interview covering mental status, behavioral observations, and DSM-III diagnoses. Child and parent administered the interview.	Psychiatric and normal samples ages 8–13. Adequate interrater reliability for most items. Correlates with CDI.
Children's Affective Rating Scale (CARS)	McKnew, Cytryn, Efron, Gershon, & Bunney (1979)	Clinical interview assessing mood behavior, verbal expression, and fantasy on 10-point scales.	Psychiatric inpatients, medical patients, normals, and children of depressed parents. Ages 5–15. Adequate interrater reliability and concurrent validity.
Children's Depression Rating Scale—Revised (CDRS-R)	Poznanski et al. (1984)	Clinician-rated instrument. The severity-of-depression scale has 17 items, 14 scored on verbal observation and 3 on nonverbal observation. Revision of Hamilton Depression Rating Scale.	Psychiatric and pediatric samples of children, ages 6–12. Scale has good test-retest reliability, interrater reliability, and concurrent validity.
School Aged Depression Listed Interview (SADLI)	Petti & Law (1982)	28-item interview to measure change in severity of depressive symptomatology.	Psychiatric inpatients ages 6–13. Psychometric properties not explored, although there is high interrater reliability on videotaped interviews.
Dysthymic Check List (DCL)	Fine, Moretti, Haley, & Marriage (1984)	Clinician rating scale to assess each criterion of dysthymia on a 3-point severity scale.	Outpatient, inpatient, and medical populations ages 8–17. Good interrater reliability.
Diagnostic Interview Schedule for Children (DISC)	Costello, Edelbrock, Dulcan, Kales, & Klavic (1984)	Clinical interview.	Children ages 6–17. Adequate test-retest and interrater reliability.
Diagnostic Interview for Children and Adolescents (DICA)	Herjanic, Herjanic, Brown, & Wheatt (1975)	Interview with parent and child forms to assess school progress, social behavior, somatic and psychiatric symptoms. Parent form also assesses early development, family history, and socioeconomic status.	Adequate psychometrics.
Personality Inventory for Children—Depression Scale (PIC)	Wirt, Lachar, Klinedinst, & Seat (1977)	600-item parent report inventory, 46-item depression scale; symptoms identified by clinicians.	Designed for ages 3–16. Good test-retest reliability. Factor analysis yields clusters directly comparable to DSM-III-associated symptoms of depression.
Child Assessment Schedule (CAS)	Hodges, McKnew, Cytryn, Stern, & Kline (1982)	Scale includes a clinical interview and clinician rating of depression and other forms of psychopathology. Administered to the child.	Outpatients, inpatients, and normal latency-age children and offspring of affectively disturbed and normal mothers. Satisfactory interrater reliability and concurrent validity.
Peer Nomination Inventory for Depression	Lefkowitz & Tesiny (1980)	Peer nomination ratings for depression (13), happiness (4), and popularity roles (2).	Given to fourth and fifth graders. Good internal consistency; good test-retest and interrater reliability; good content and concurrent validity.
Staff Nomination Inventory of Depression	Saylor, Finch, Baskin, Furey, & Kelly (1984)	20-item scale by which staff members nominate children who best fit each description.	Staff members on inpatient unit rating 7–11-year-olds. No psychometrics reported.

low & Rehm, 1985). If the concept of syndromal depression has proved useful in adults—for directing treatment efforts toward specific sets of cognitive and behavioral targets—and if these treatments have been demonstrated to be effective, might not these same treatment methods or adaptations of them also prove useful in dealing with depressive behavior in children? To answer this question, it is necessary to review those current behavioral and cognitive models of depression that have led to the development of effective treatment programs with adults.

A number of the current theoretical models of adult depression stress behavioral and cognitive variables as central to depressive symptomatology. However, it is only recently that the major behavioral or cognitive theories of adult depression have been specifically applied or adapted to children. The fact that behavioral and cognitive variables are central in theories of adult depression, and that these variables are manifest and measurable in children, suggests that they are fruitful and critical ones for the study of depression in children. Additionally, a focus on specific core behaviors and core cognitive characteristics that are postulated to occur from childhood to adulthood provides a meaningful way to examine the relationship between adult and childhood depression. An outgrowth of the behavioral cognitive theories is the development of a number of treatment intervention strategies for depression in adults, which will be discussed in the following section. These include the following: social-skills training, activity-level increase, attribution retraining, cognitive therapy, and self-control therapy.

Social-Skills Training

Depressed adults are often seen as lacking the social skills necessary to obtain reinforcement from their social environment, which results in a low rate of response-contingent positive reinforcement (Lewinsohn, 1974; Lewinsohn, Biglan, & Zeiss, 1976). Wolpe (1979) argues that one cause of depression is an inability to control interpersonal situations. According to Lewinsohn and colleagues (1976), the goal of social-skills training is to enhance skills in eliciting reinforcement from others.

Numerous studies have been conducted with depressed adults to improve their social skills. In these programs, the participants are taught appropriate assertive social skills to use in prob-lematic interpersonal situations. Skills taught vary from the specific details of voice quality and posture to the more general goals of improving the individual's interpersonal style and increasing his or her level of social activity. Methods include instruction, modeling, role play, feedback, homework practice, and situation logs. The research in this area includes case studies (Lazarus, 1968), single-subject-design studies (Hersen, Bellack, & Himmelhoch, 1980; Wells, Hersen, Bellack, & Himmelhoch, 1979), studies that compare social-skills training taught in individual therapy sessions to another form of individual treatment (Zeiss, Lewinsohn, & Munoz, 1979; Zielinski, 1979), and programs that compare social-skills training taught in a group format with another form of group therapy (Hayman & Cope, 1980; Lewinsohn, Weinstein, & Alper, 1970; Rehm, Fuchs, Roth, Kornblith, & Romano, 1979; Sanchez, Lewinsohn, & Larson, 1980; Shaw, 1977; Taylor & Marshall, 1977). A study by Hersen, Bellack, Himmelhoch, and Thase (1984) compared social-skills training combined with a tricyclic antidepressant or a placebo to the drug alone and to traditional psychotherapy combined with a placebo. The therapy program is described by Becker, Heimberg, and Bellack (1987). According to Rehm and Kaslow's (1984) review of this literature, social-skills training is marginally superior to control conditions but equivalent or inferior to the more complex cognitive and behavioral programs. However, in most of these studies, individuals did become less depressed and more assertive.

In the adult literature on depression there are several other variations on the theme of deficits in social skills as the basis for depression. Nezu, Nezu, and Perri (1989) see interpersonal problem solving as the focal deficit associated with depression and have reported a program that teaches interpersonal problem-solving skills (Nezu, 1986). Communication skills have been viewed by several authorities as central to depression, especially in marital situations. Marital communication skills have been the focus of several reports of marital therapy for depression (McLean & Hakstian, 1979; Beach & O'Leary, 1986). From a different perspective, Klerman, Weissman, Rounsaville, and Chevron (1984) describe an interpersonal approach to psychotherapy for depression that stresses identifying central relationship problems and developing approaches to resolve these difficulties.

The approach has been evaluated in studies by these researchers (e.g., Weissman, Klerman, Paykel, Prusoff, & Hanson, 1974) and has been included in a national collaborative study of therapy for depression (Elkin et al., 1986.)

Activity-Level Increase Programs

The use of programs designed to increase activity level as treatments for depression is an outgrowth of the early behavioral conceptualizations in which depression was seen as reduced activity caused by low rates of environmental reinforcement (Ferster, 1971; Lewinsohn, 1974; Lewinsohn et al., 1976). According to Lewinsohn, the etiology of depression is a lack of response-contingent positive reinforcement that may be the result of a reinforcement-poor environment or an environment that has changed, so that prior to reinforcement is no longer present. Activity-level increase programs assume that by increasing pleasant or rewarding activities, it will be possible to increase the general level of response-contingent reinforcement in a person's life and that this will produce a general reduction in symptoms of depression.

Lewinsohn and his colleagues have conducted a number of group design studies in which activity-level increase has been the major focus of at least one of the experimental conditions (Grosscup & Lewinsohn, 1980; Lewinsohn et al., 1976; Zeiss et al., 1979). Additionally, there are a number of studies that examine variants of activity-level increase with depressed adults (Anton, Dunbar, & Friedman, 1976; Barrera, 1979; Padfield, 1976; Turner, Ward, & Turner, 1979; Zielinski, 1979).

The therapeutic interventions in these programs include the following: (1) monitoring mood and activity level to obtain a baseline, (2) identifying positive activities in an individual's repertoire that correlate with daily pleasant mood, (3) instigating increases in those activities that are potentially reinforcing, (4) decreasing negative activities that correlate with negative mood, and (5) setting up environmental contingencies to reinforce increased positive activity and decreased negative activity. The activity level increase studies conducted with adults have yielded partially successful results, though many subjects are still depressed at posttesting (Rehm & Kaslow, 1984). Changes in activity level do correlate with changes in depression.

Attribution Retraining

The reformulated model of learned helplessness (Abramson, Seligman, & Teasdale, 1978) and recent elaborations (Alloy, Clements, & Kolden, 1985) postulates an insidious attributional style that filters experience in such a way as to produce the deficits in affectivity, motivation, and self-esteem associated with depression. When a person experiences an aversive event, the way in which the person attributes the cause of the event will determine whether he or she becomes helpless and hopeless, hence depressed. The person's attributional style will influence the attribution made in each specific instance. An individual makes an internal attribution in concluding that he or she was responsible for a given outcome; he or she makes an external attribution in concluding that a given outcome was determined by other people or circumstances. Stable attributions are made when the individual believes that the causes of the outcome will always be present, whereas an unstable attribution is made when the cause is viewed as transitory in nature. A global attribution is made when an individual feels that the cause of the outcome influences all areas of his or her life, whereas specific attribution is made when the cause is viewed as situation-specific. It is hypothesized that depressed individuals make more internal-stable-global attributions for failure and more external-unstable-specific attributions for success than do their nondepressed counterparts. An internal-stable-global attribution for an important aversive event will produce helpless depression.

Metalsky and Abramson (1981) assert that the concept of attributional style is of major importance to cognitive–behavioral researchers and therapists. A number of investigators (Abramson et al., 1978; Beck, Rush, Shaw, & Emery, 1979; Dweck, 1975) argue that there are individual differences in attributional patterns and that certain attributional styles increase an individual's vulnerability to various psychological problems. There are a number of studies conducted with adults that examine the relationship between attributions and depression. Mildly depressed college students (Seligman, Abramson, Semmel, & von Baeyer, 1979) and a clinical sample of unipolar depressives (Raps, Peterson, Reinhard, Abramson, & Seligman, 1982) have the attributional style predicted by the model.

Based on the attributional model of learned

helplessness, Seligman (1981) described four therapeutic strategies that should be effective in treating depression: (1) environmental enrichment—use of environmental manipulation to reduce the estimated likelihood of aversive outcomes and increase the estimated likelihood of desired outcomes, (2) personal control training—the strategy of changing expectations from uncontrollability to controllability, (3) resignation training—the strategy of making highly preferred outcomes less preferred, and (4) attribution retraining—the use of methods to change an individual's unrealistic attributions. Individuals should be retrained to attribute failure to more external, unstable, and specific factors and success to more internal, stable, and global factors.

Cognitive Therapy

In Beck's (1967) cognitive model of depression, depressive cognitions—the "negative cognitive triad"—are regarded as the essential features of the depressive syndrome. Depressed people have a systematically negative bias in their thinking, which leads them to have a negative view of *themselves,* the *world,* and the *future.* Negative cognitive schemas, the basis of the cognitive triad, develop early in life and are reactivated in response to stress (real or perceived loss). Experiences are filtered through a set of schemas that distort reality in a negative way. A number of studies provide correlational evidence that each element of the cognitive triad is associated with depression (e.g., Beck, 1967, 1976; Laxer, 1964).

Cognitive therapy, as a way of conceptualizing patients' problems and as a set of cognitive and behavioral strategies, has been described in a lengthy therapy manual (Beck et al., 1979). The techniques used are designed to help the patient identify, reality-test, and modify distorted conceptualizations and dysfunctional attitudes and beliefs. The cognitive techniques proposed include the following: (1) recognizing the connection between cognition, affect, and behavior, (2) monitoring negative automatic thoughts, (3) examining evidence for and against distorted automatic thoughts, (4) substituting more reality-oriented interpretations for distorted cognitions, and (5) learning to identify and modify dysfunctional beliefs.

The behavioral techniques utilized in cognitive therapy also have as their goal changing the patient's cognitions. Typically, these strategies are used in the initial phase of treatment or with severely depressed individuals to initiate changes in behavior that will facilitate changes in cognition. These include scheduling activities, mastery and pleasure techniques, graded task assignment, cognitive/behavioral rehearsal, assertiveness training, and role playing.

Cognitive therapy has been evaluated in a number of reports by Beck and his colleagues (Beck et al., 1985; Rush, Beck, Kovacs, & Hollon, 1977; Rush, Khatami & Beck, 1975; Rush, Shaw, & Khatami, 1980; Rush & Watkins, 1981; Shaw, 1977) and in independent evaluations (Blackburn, Bishop, Glenn, Whalley, & Christie, 1981; Murphy, Simons, Wetzel, & Lustman, 1984). A number of researchers have used modifications of Beck's therapy or other forms of cognitive therapy (Dunn, 1979; Schmickley, 1976; Taylor & Marshall, 1977; Zeiss et al., 1979). In evaluating these studies, Rehm and Kaslow (1984) concluded that, in an absolute sense, the outcome in the cognitive therapy studies is somewhat better than that found in studies using other forms of treatment. Although only partial remission is reported in a few of the studies, several studies showed high rates of remission at posttest and follow-up. Cognitive therapy has been reported to be superior to no-treatment control conditions, to tricyclic antidepressants, and to certain behavioral therapy conditions.

Self-Control Therapy

Rehm's (1977) self-control model of depression attempts to incorporate aspects of the models of Beck (1967), Lewinsohn (1974), and Seligman (1975). It derives from and expands Kanfer's self-control model (Kanfer 1970; Kanfer & Karoly, 1972). Self-control, a three-stage feedback-loop process, includes self-monitoring, self-evaluation, and self-reinforcement. Depressed individuals are hypothesized to have deficits in one or more of these phases. Symptoms of depression are considered to result from deficits in self-control behavior. Rehm characterizes the self-control deficits evidenced by depressed individuals as follows: (1) selective monitoring or attending to negative events to the exclusion of positive events, (2) selective monitoring of immediate as opposed to delayed consequences of one's behavior, (3) setting overly stringent self-evaluative criteria, (4) making negative attributions of responsibilities for one's behavior, (5) utilizing insufficient contingent self-reinforcement, and (6) administering excessive self-punishment.

There is research evidence supporting the idea that depressed individuals have deficits in self-monitoring (e.g., Buchwald, 1977; DeMonbreun & Craighead, 1977; Nelson & Craighead, 1977; Rehm & Plakosh, 1975; Roth & Rehm, 1980; Wener & Rehm, 1975), self-evaluation (e.g., Rehm, Roth, & Farmartino, 1976), and in their self-reward and/or their self-punishment behavior (e.g., Nelson & Craighead, 1977; Roth, Rehm, & Rozensky, 1980; Rozensky, Rehm, Pry, & Roth, 1977). An overall summary is provided by Rehm (1982).

On the basis of the self-control model of depression, Rehm and his colleagues have conducted six therapy studies (Fuchs & Rehm, 1977; Rehm et al., 1979; Rehm et al., 1981; Kornblith, Rehm, O'Hara, & Lamparski, 1983; Rehm, Kaslow, & Rabin, 1987). Independent replications have also been reported (e.g., Fleming & Thornton, 1980; Rude, 1986). Rehm and Kaslow (1984) conclude that the comparative outcome is fairly good in these studies. Although a significant portion of the clients remain mildly depressed at the end of treatment, a large number are nondepressed at the completion of therapy and at follow-up. Self-control therapy is found to be superior to a waiting-list control group and to assertion training. There is some evidence that suggests that self-control packages have not yielded clear-cut outcome differences corresponding to program components.

The specific techniques used in self-control therapy are designed to improve the individual's self-control skills. Participants are taught to monitor their positive activities and self-statements, and they are instructed to increase those positive behaviors and cognitions that are associated with improved mood. They are trained to identify the delayed versus immediate consequences of their behavior and are taught the importance of attending to the positive and delayed consequences that will result from performing a difficult behavior. Participants are instructed in how to set more realistic and attainable standards. They break goals down into attainable subgoals. Participants are taught to make more appropriate attributions for success and failure. Finally, they are taught to increase the contingent overt and covert self-reinforcement.

TREATMENT OF CHILDHOOD DEPRESSION

If evidence of syndromal depression is found, the first consideration should be whether or not the depressive complaints may be secondary to effects of another major childhood disorder. For instance, depression may be a consequence of enuresis, school phobia, hyperactivity, impulsivity, or aggression problems. In such cases, treatment should first be aimed at alleviating these problems. Depression should be monitored and, if it persists after these problems have been remedied, treatment strategies targeted at specific depressive behaviors should be considered. Reviews of methods for the treatment of these other childhood problems can be found elsewhere in this book. If the depression appears to be primary, the cognitive and behavioral intervention strategies described in this section should help to relieve the depressive symptoms.

Reports of treatment of depression in children have been relatively sparse. A few case studies have appeared in the literature describing traditional psychotherapeutic approaches to childhood depression (Bemporad, 1978; Beres, 1966; Boverman & French, 1979; Cohen, 1980; Furman, 1974; Gilpin, 1976; Sacks, 1977). There have also been a number of reports of treating childhood depression with antidepressant medications (for review see Campbell & Spencer, 1988; Petti, 1983; Puig-Antich, 1982). All these studies contain various methodological flaws. Taken together, however, they indicate a trend toward using tricyclic antidepressants like imipramine (Tofranil) and amitriptyline (Elavil) as a means of treating depression in children. Controversies and public concern over the use of psychotropic medications with children may restrain this trend.

Demonstrations of effective behavioral and cognitive treatments for treating childhood disorders are clearly needed. It is only recently that these techniques have begun to be utilized systematically in the treatment of depression in children. This section of the chapter reviews the behavioral and cognitive studies that have appeared in the literature (see Table 3.2) and attempts to integrate adult treatment models of depression with related behavioral and cognitive approaches for treating a myriad of problem behaviors in children. As part of the discussion of each strategy, we also suggest assessment techniques that may be applicable to the evalu-

Table 3.2. Treatment Studies

AUTHORS	SAMPLE	ASSESSMENT	TREATMENT	RESULTS	FOLLOW-UP
Calpin & Cincirpini (1978)	N = 2, depressed inpatients—10-year-old girl, 11-year-old boy.	Behavioral Assertiveness Test for Children.	Multiple baseline training of specific (e.g., eye contact) and more general (e.g., positive peer interactions) social skills including instruction, modeling, and videotape feedback.	Both demonstrated significant improvement on target behaviors.	At 1 and 3 months (N = 1), target behaviors were back to baseline levels. Continued to evidence mood swings and oppositional behavior. Suicidal ideation cleared.
Calpin & Kornblith (1977)	N = 4, inpatient boys with aggressive behavior, met modified RDC criteria for depression. Low average or borderline intelligence.	Behavioral Assertiveness Test for Children.	Target behaviors included the following: requests for new behaviors, affect expression, and overall social skills. Training consisted of instructions concerning appropriate responses, modeling behavioral rehearsal, and videotape feedback.	All four children improved on all three target behaviors.	At 1 and 3 months, three maintained gains. One returned to baseline.
Matson, Esveldt-Dawson, Andrasik, Ollendick, Petti, & Hersen (1980)	N = 4, inpatients met modified RDC criteria for depression—two boys ages 9, 11; two girls both age 11.	Assessed a number of social skills (e.g., giving compliments, giving help or assistance).	Instruction, information feedback, modeling, role playing, and social reinforcement. Verbal behavior, psychomotor behavior, affect, and eye contact were target behaviors.	Social skills in group. Treatment improved and generalized to social environment. Observing a peer was not effective. Three showed improvement.	Effects maintained at 15 weeks.

Study	Sample	Measures	Treatment	Results	Follow-up
Petti, Bornstein, Delamater, & Connors (1980)	N = 1, 10½-year-old girl.	Children's Behavior Inventory, Scale of School Age Depression, Social Skills.	Multimodal treatment including individual psychotherapy, psychoeducational intervention, creative dramatics group, imipramine, social-skills training, and supportive family therapy.	Little change until antidepressant medication was included; became less depressed and more stable. Social-skills training improved social-skills behavior.	Most gains maintained at 3 weeks, 6 weeks, 1 year, and 3 years.
Bulter, Miezitis, Friedman, & Cole (1980)	N = 56 fifth- and sixth-grade schoolchildren.	Children's Depression Inventory, Piers-Harris Children's Self-Concept Scale, Moyal-Miezitis Stimulus Appraisal Questionnaire, Nowicki-Strickland Locus of Control Scale for Children.	10-week intervention conditions; role play, cognitive restructuring, attention placebo, control.	Quantitative and qualitative improvements in role playing and cognitive restructuring condition. Greatest improvement reported in role-play condition.	None reported.
Stark, Kaslow, & Reynolds (1987)	N = 29 fourth-, fifth-, and sixth-grade schoolchildren.	Children's Depression Inventory, Child Depression Scale, Children's Depression Rating Scale—Revised, Child Behavior Checklist, Coopersmith Self-Esteem Inventory, Revised Children's Manifest Anxiety Scale.	12 sessions, self-control therapy, behavioral problem-solving intervention, waiting-list control.	S's in both active treatment reported and significant improvement in depressive symptoms while S's in the waiting-list condition reported minimum change.	Results were maintained at an 8-week follow-up.
Reynolds & Coats (1986)	N = 30 moderately depressed adolescents in high school.	Beck Depression Inventory, Reynolds Adolescent Depression Index of Depression, Rosenberg Self-Esteem Scale, Concept Scale, State-Trait Anxiety Inventory.	10 sessions, cognitive–behavioral therapy, relaxation training, waiting-list control.	S's in both active treatments reported significant decrease in depression and anxiety and improved academic self-concept. S's in waiting-list condition reported minimal change.	Results were maintained at a 5-week follow-up.

ation of the specific targeted depressive behavior. Our assumption is that when a child evidences depression according to the criteria generally applied to adults, specific potential targets should be evaluated individually. Therapeutic strategies will then be chosen based on the identification of these individual targets.

Social-Skills Strategies

Recently, some data have become available regarding the relationship between childhood depression and interpersonal functioning, including social skills. Depressed children display deficits in social functioning with their parents, peers, and siblings (Altmann & Gotlib, 1988; Blechman, McEnroe, Carella, & Audette, 1986; Kazdin, Esveldt-Dawson, Sherick, & Colbus, 1985; Puig-Antich et al., 1985a; Sacco & Graves, 1984) and these difficulties are more pronounced in children with concurrent depression and externalizing disorders (Asarnow, 1988). Some of these interpersonal deficits persist after recovery from a depressive episode (Puig-Antich et al., 1985b). Depressed children are cognizant of these interpersonal difficulties and report dissatisfaction with their interpersonal problem-solving performance (Sacco & Graves, 1984). Depressed elementary school children are rated by peers as less likable and attractive, as emitting fewer positive behaviors, and as being in greater need of therapy than are nondepressed children (Peterson, Mullins, & Ridley-Johnson, 1985). Research in a related vein reveals that unpopular and socially withdrawn children are more depressed than their popular and more sociable peers (Lefkowitz & Tesiny, 1980; Jacobsen, Lahey, & Strauss, 1983; Strauss, Forehand, Smith, & Frame, 1986; Vosk, Forehand, Parker, & Rickard, 1982). Experimental assessment techniques have begun to appear in the literature for assessing the social skills of children. Bornstein, Bellack, and Hersen (1977) describe a Behavioral Assertiveness Test for Children (BAT-C), modeled on behavioral assertiveness tests that have been used for assessing social skills in adults and which may be useful in assessing social skills in depressed children. The Social Adjustment Inventory for Children and Adolescents (SAICA) (John, Gammon, Prusoff, & Warner, 1987), a semistructured interview which can be administered to children and their parents, provides an evaluation of children's functioning in school, in spare-time activities, and with peers, siblings, and parents.

In a comprehensive review, Combs and Slaby (1977) discuss the recent trend in social-skills training as an approach to treatment with children. They define social skills as "the ability to interact with others in a given social context in specific ways that are societally acceptable or valued and at the same time personally beneficial, mutually beneficial, or beneficial primarily to others" (p. 162). They assert that social skills are among the most important skills a child must learn, and that a lack of social skills may result in problematic interpersonal interactions and difficulty in functioning effectively in school, at home, and at play with peers. Following the analogy to adults, social-skills deficits related to depression in children would involve those specific skills that are effective in eliciting consistent and enduring contingent positive reinforcement from significant others in the social environment. One of the clearest needs in the social-skills area with children is the identification of specific skills that, in natural settings, are rewarding to children at different levels of development. Research in childhood depression and in other childhood disorders would be enhanced by naturalistic study of the social skills of clinical, normal, and socially adept samples of children.

The literature on social-skills training procedures with children suggests that three main strategies have been used: (1) shaping procedures that use adult reinforcement, (2) modeling or combined modeling and reinforcement procedures, and (3) direct training procedures to make use of the child's cognitive and verbal skills. More specific strategies include instructions, modeling, role playing, rehearsal, feedback, and self-management techniques. Studies of social-skills treatment of children in general suggest that contingent adult reinforcement and modeling techniques can be useful in shaping the amount of interaction between children. While contingent adult attention is effective in shaping peer interaction, the stability of these effects is questionable. Modeling techniques appear to have dramatic effects in increasing the child's social interaction, and some stability of this behavior is reported. The more recent verbal–cognitive approaches emphasize teaching relatively specific social skills (e.g., asking a peer for help) and general problem-solving techniques. Initial results obtained from these studies indicate that they do effectively teach specific social skills.

Four studies have been reported that specifically examine social-skills training for depressed children. Frame, Matson, Sonis, Fialkov, and Kazdin (1982) described the successful treatment of a 10-year-old boy diagnosed as depressed according to DSM-III criteria. Behaviors targeted were body position, eye contact, speech characteristics, and affect expression. Calpin and Cincirpini (1978) described a multiple-baseline analysis of social-skills training for two children who were depressed inpatients. Both children were found to have social-skills deficits according to the BAT-C (Bornstein et al., 1977). The target behaviors for treatment were determined by this assessment. Both children improved following a program of instruction in appropriate interpersonal interactions, modeling of these social skills, and videotaped feedback of their own responses. Calpin and Kornblith (1977) used a social-skills training program—including instructions concerning appropriate responses, modeling, behavioral rehearsal, and videotape feedback—in treating four hospitalized depressed children. These children had shown markedly aggressive behavior, met modified RDC criteria for depression, and had deficits in their social skills as assessed by the BAT-C. At the completion of the multiple-baseline-design study, all the children had improved on the target behaviors. At follow-up, the improvement was maintained for three of the children.

In a study on the observation and generalization effects of social-skills training with four emotionally disturbed children who met modified RDC criteria for depression, Matson and colleagues (Matson et al., 1980) used instruction, information feedback, modeling, role playing, and social reinforcement. Results from the study indicated that the effects of social-skills training were immediate when taught by an adult but that peer observation of appropriate social skills was not influential. The more skilled the subject was initially, the more he improved with treatment. Booster sessions were helpful in maintaining treatment gain. Furthermore, social skills taught in groups appeared to be effective for three of the children. The children were able to use their newly acquired skills in similar social situations and in their natural environment.

One final study, which is relevant here, was done by Petti, Bornstein, Delamater, and Connors (1980). They describe the assessment and treatment of a 10½-year-old girl on an inpatient unit who was chronically depressed. They utilized a multimodal approach similar to the BASIC ID (Lazarus, 1973). The initial treatment consisted of individual therapy to help her understand her feelings, a psychoeducational intervention to help her become "turned back on to school," and a creative dramatics group to improve her peer interactions. Additionally, supportive family therapy was conducted with her foster parents. These treatments were not particularly effective in alleviating the depression; therefore imipramine treatment was begun and was credited with significantly improving her behavior. Social-skills training was conducted to help facilitate her return home. Training consisted of instructions about how to interact, behavioral rehearsal, and performance feedback. Deficient behaviors (e.g., eye contact, smiles, duration of speech, response to compliments, and request for new behavior in response to unreasonable demands) were the targets of intervention. A multiple-baseline analysis revealed that social-skills training resulted in improvement in all the target behaviors. Follow-up data suggested that most of the improvement was maintained at the 3- and 6-week posttreatment evaluations. These studies are promising and should provide the impetus for further systematic study of social-skills training with depressed children.

Strategies to Increase Activity Level

To date, no empirical work addressing activity level and depression in children has been published, although there is some evidence that depressed adolescents report more unpleasant activities than their nondepressed counterparts (Carey, Kelley, Buss, & Scott, 1986). Although it was not designed specifically for use in cases of depression, there is a children's self-report instrument that may be utilized in assessing activity level in children. Cautela (1977) published a Children's Reinforcement Survey Schedule (CRSS) to parallel the Cautela and Kastenbaum (1967) Reinforcement Survey Schedule for adults. The main purpose of the CRSS is to identify potential rewards to use in external or self-management programs for other target behaviors. The questionnaire gives information about the degree of positive valence for each behavior and the frequency with which it currently occurs. Recently, Cole, Kelley, and Carey (1988) developed the Adolescent Activities Checklist, which includes unpleasant and pleasant events. A child version of this questionnaire could readily be developed.

There are no reports of activity-increase programs as the sole treatment for depression in children. However, the monitoring and increasing of positive events was one component of the behavioral problem-solving therapy of Stark, Kaslow, and Reynolds (1987). Given empirical evidence that depressed adults have a reduced activity level and benefit from activity-increase programs—also that depressed children are socially withdrawn and that similar programs for them are efficacious (Gelfand, 1978)—it behooves clinician-researchers to evaluate activity level in depressed children and to intervene with this symptom when indicated.

The assumption underlying strategies to increase activity level is that behavior which is intrinsically reinforcing or behavior which is highly likely to be reinforced by the environment is not being produced. It is assumed that the child has the social skills to produce the behavior, but that performance is lacking. It is further assumed that performance is not being inhibited by anxiety. If it were, then desensitization of that anxiety would be the treatment of choice. Some form of extinction is the assumed reason for a low level of positive activities in children or adults. To select the targets for activity-increase programs, it is important to demonstrate that the targeted behavior is indeed intrinsically reinforcing or that it has a high probability of producing external reinforcement. This may be demonstrated in several ways. First, targeted behaviors may be those that were found to be enjoyable in the past. The observation that there had been a clear decrease in the level of a particular activity associated with the onset of depression would be supportive evidence. For example, social withdrawal in a child who had formerly enjoyed good peer relationships might suggest that certain social activities should be the target of an activity-increase program. Second, an activity might be targeted if it could be empirically shown to be associated with improved mood. Lewinsohn et al. (1976) have adult subjects monitor potential target behaviors over a period of weeks and look at the correlations between these behaviors and self-rated mood. Empirically correlated activities become the target for increase programs. Third, in the adult literature, self-report events schedules consisting of lists of potentially rewarding activities have been used to survey possible targets for

intervention. Lewinsohn's program has used the Pleasant Events Schedule (MacPhillamy & Lewinsohn, 1971). The therapy program of Rehm and his colleagues has used a relatively brief Positive Activity List (e.g., Fuchs & Rehm, 1977). As in adult activity-increase programs, the Premack principle—whereby more frequent positive behavior is used to increase the frequency of less probable behaviors—may be employed. Parallel to the adult programs, activity increases may be prompted merely by scheduling the activities, or external or self-managed reinforcement programs may be used. Initially developed for younger children, external reinforcement may be preferable to self-reinforcement. Major techniques found to be effective in increasing children's activity level include the following: modeling (O'Connor, 1972), individual and group contingencies and social reinforcement (Weinrott, Corson, & Wilchesky, 1979), and social-skills training (Bornstein et al., 1977; Rhodes, Rodd, & Berggren, 1979).

Cognitive Strategies

In line with Beck's cognitive model of depression, depressed children—as compared to their nondepressed counterparts—have lower self-esteem and perceived competence, show cognitive distortions, and feel more hopeless about their futures (Asarnow, Carlson, & Guthrie, 1987; Blechman et al., 1986; Haley, Fine, Marriage, Moretti, & Freeman, 1985; Hammen & Zupan, 1984; Kaslow, Rehm, & Siegel, 1984; Kazdin, French, Unis, Esveldt-Dawson, & Sherick, 1983; Kazdin, Rodgers, & Colbus, 1986; Layne & Berry, 1983; Leitenberg, Yost, & Carroll-Wilson, 1986; McGee, Anderson, Williams, & Silva, 1986; Windle et al., 1986). Self-report scales to assess self-esteem and perceived competence (Self-Perception Profile for Children) (Harter, 1985), cognitive distortions (Children's Negative Cognitive Error Questionnaire; CNCEQ) (Leitenberg et al., 1986), and hopelessness (Hopelessness Scale for Children; HSC) (Kazdin et al., 1986) can be found in the literature.

Some recent papers have suggested methods for adapting cognitive therapy for adult depression (Beck et al., 1979) to the treatment of nonpsychotic depressed children and adolescents (DiGiuseppe, 1986; Emery, Bedrosian, & Garber, 1983; Wilkes & Rush, 1988). These authors have enumerated a number of ways in which cognitive therapy for depressed youths differs from cognitive therapy for depressed adults. First, the therapist should be well trained in conducting child psychotherapy, as this will enable him or her to establish an effective therapeutic alliance with the patient and to be more cognizant of the meaning of his or her nonverbal and verbal communications. Second, it is important to involve the child's or adolescent's family of origin in the assessment and treatment process. The family's cognitions interact with those of the depressed child in a way that may reinforce and perpetuate the child's depression. Parents can be aided in arranging more appropriate contingencies that will extinguish the child's depressive behaviors and increase more socially adaptive behaviors. In those instances in which the family holds distorted cognitions, it is necessary to challenge and change these distortions so as to ameliorate individual depressive experiences and alter parents' child-rearing practices, which may be reinforcing and perpetuating their child's depression. Parental involvement may also facilitate the therapeutic process if the parents become involved in actively providing opportunities that will enable their child to acquire new information and test new hypotheses to modify their cognitive distortions.

Third, it is crucial for the cognitive interventions to take into account the child's or adolescent's level of cognitive development. By the time children reach the concrete-operational stage, they have the cognitive capacity to experience many of the cognitive symptoms associated with depression—such as guilt, low self-esteem, misattributions of negative events, and feelings of rejection. However, given their lack of a fully developed time perspective, they may not yet possess the cognitive capacity to experience hopelessness fully. Children at the concrete-operational stage can make inferences about concrete reality and thus distort and misinterpret reality. These concrete-operational preadolescents are cognitively capable of generating and testing propositions and can understand the technique of hypothesis testing. However, they may require help from adults in identifying alternative inferences from their reality and in modifying their reality. Although the cognitive interventions utilized with preadolescent children are similar to those used with depressed adults, their implementation and efficacy depend upon the age of the child and the child's level of cognitive functioning. By the time children reach adolescence and formal op-

erations, they are cognitively capable of experiencing all the cognitive symptoms associated with depression; they can generate hypotheses and logically deduce the relations among two or more propositions. Thus, many of the techniques that cognitive therapists utilize with adult depressives are potentially effective with depressed adolescents. However, the difficulties that adolescents sometimes encounter in communicating with a therapist as well as the key features of adolescent depression (e.g., anhedonia, self-esteem and identity issues, feelings of helplessness, rejection, and loss) call for the modification of cognitive therapy methods.

Butler and Miezitis (1980) have described an overall program for dealing with a variety of classroom behavior problems, with a central focus on cognitive techniques for dealing with depressive behavior. The program is aimed at giving practical suggestions to teachers and consultants. Empirical results for aspects of the program have been reported (Butler, Miezitis, Friedman, & Cole, 1980). As an example of this approach, these authors describe ways in which low self-esteem may be expressed by children in the classroom, including verbal self-depreciation, slouching posture and averted eyes, failure to interact interpersonally, and lack of academic effort or pride. Strategies recommended include frequent and regular approaches to the child, expressions of acceptance and affection, and the assigning of tasks that ensure success experiences. Exercises involving the entire class are also recommended for dealing with self-depreciating remarks. This includes assigning a composition in which children describe their best characteristics and those they would like to change. The intent is to demonstrate to the self-depreciating child—and to the other children as well—that all children perceive weaknesses and faults in themselves. The suggestions are given in the context of experience from a larger research program evaluating a teacher mediated-intervention program. Butler and Miezitis (1980) provide detailed recommendations, case-study examples, and a guide for classroom observation.

Another cognitively oriented general approach to core issues of depression in children is presented in the book *Self-Esteem Enhancement with Children and Adolescents* by Pope, McHale, and Craighead (1988). These authors describe treatment modules that cover topics relevant to all the approaches described in this chapter. Social problem solving, self-statements, attributional style, self-control, standard setting, social understanding and skills, communication skills, and body image are all addressed as means of enhancing self-esteem.

Helplessness Strategies

While the helplessness model is consistent with a number of models of treatment, most interest in research with children has focused on the assessment and modification of maladaptive attributions. A number of studies have been conducted that examine helpless attributions in depressed and nondepressed children. As predicted by the reformulated model of learned helplessness (Abramson et al., 1978), higher levels of depression in children are associated with an external locus of control, "contingency uncertainty," and a depressive attributional style (Blumberg & Izard, 1985; Kaslow et al., 1984; Kaslow, Rehm, Pollack, & Siegel, 1988; Lefkowitz, Tesiny, & Gordon, 1980; Leon, Kendall, & Garber, 1980; Mullins, Siegel, & Hodges, 1985; Nolen-Hoeksema, Girgus, & Seligman, 1986; Saylor, Finch, Baskin, Furey, & Kelley, 1984; Seligman, Peterson, Kaslow, Tanenbaum, Alloy, & Abramson, 1984; Tesiny & Lefkowitz, 1982; Tesiny, Lefkowitz, & Gordon, 1980; Ward, Friedlander, & Silverman, 1987; Weisz, Weiss, Wasserman, & Rintoul, 1987). Research on attributional style has been based on the KASTAN-R Children's Attributional Styles Questionnaire (Seligman et al., 1984).

Dweck and her colleagues have conducted a research program relating deficits in problem solving, helplessness, and attributions (Diener & Dweck, 1978; Dweck, 1975; Dweck & Bush, 1976; Dweck, Davidson, Nelson, & Enna, 1978; Dweck & Repucci, 1973). Dweck and Repucci (1973) found that children who persisted in the face of failure attributed helplessness to a lack of effort, whereas children whose performance deteriorated after failure attributed this to a lack of ability. Diener and Dweck (1978) found that helpless children attributed their failure to lack of ability, that their performance deteriorated after failure, and that they demonstrated negative affect about their tasks. In contrast, mastery-oriented children engaged in ways of changing failure situations and did not make causal attributions for failure; also, their performance did not deteriorate. Diener and Dweck (1978) also found that in comparison to mastery-ori-

ented children, helpless children were less likely to attribute success to ability, expected to do poorly in the future, and believed that other children would do better than they had done.

Another approach, which is akin to Seligman's (1981) attribution retraining, is described by Dweck (1975) in her work with children who had extreme reactions to failure. These children received one of two training procedures. One group was given success experiences only, which may be similar to the environmental enrichment proposed by Seligman. The second group was given attributional retraining, which taught these helpless children to take responsibility for their failure and to attribute it to lack of effort. Thus, they were taught to make an internal-unstable-specific attribution for failure. Results from this study revealed that after the training was complete, the performance of the children in the success-only condition continued to deteriorate when they were confronted with failure. However, the children in the attribution retraining group maintained or improved their performance. Furthermore, they showed an increase in the degree to which they emphasized lack of effort versus lack of ability as a determinant of their failure. It is notable that Dweck has children learn to make *internal*-unstable-specific attributions for their failure. This is appropriate to instigate greater effort on solvable problems.

Dweck's attribution retraining program demonstrates that an adaptive coping response can be taught to children as an alternative to helplessness. This lends further support to the potential utility of using attribution retraining with those depressed children with a "depressogenic" attributional style, as measured by the KASTAN-R Children's Attributional Styles Questionnaire (Seligman et al., 1984).

Depressed and helpless children appear to have a depressogenic attributional style similar to that seen in depressed adults. Attributional retraining as proposed by Seligman and/or Dweck and her colleagues may be beneficial to such children.

Self-Control Strategies

The self-control model of depression (Rehm, 1977) differs from the other models in that it postulates that a sequence of related but semi-independent behaviors are central to depression. It assumes that depression is associated with deficits at one or more stages of self-control.

The applicability of the model to depression in children would depend partly upon demonstrating these deficits in children. Assessment may be aimed at evaluating specific deficits or at obtaining an overall evaluation of self-control skills. The latter has been the case for instruments recently developed assessing self-control in children.

In accord with Rehm's self-control model, depressed children evidence deficits in self-monitoring, attribution, self-evaluation, and self-reinforcement (Cole & Rehm, 1986; Kaslow et al., 1984, 1988). The evidence reviewed, which was relevant to the cognitive and helplessness models for depression in children, also supports the self-control model. That is, evidence that depressed children have low self-esteem and depressive attributional styles may be construed as evidence for deficits in the self-evaluation and self-attribution components of self-control.

Standardized assessment methodologies for systematically evaluating the self-control deficits in depressed children have not been developed as such. Again, measures of self-esteem or attributional style may be useful for evaluating these two specific deficits postulated by the model. Specific measures of other deficits—such as negative self-monitoring or self-reinforcement behavior—have not been developed. However, two measures of overall self-control behavior in children have been developed. Kendall and Wilcox (1979) developed a rating scale for teachers to fill out concerning the self-control behavior of students. Kendall, Zupan, and Braswell (1981) describe three studies validating the scale. They conclude that their data question the existence of a single unitary construct of self-control, although they feel that the instrument does have some utility in assessing children's self-control. Humphrey (1982) developed a teacher form and a child form of a rating scale to assess self-control behavior. Initial psychometric findings are promising. The overall utility of instruments measuring self-control behavior globally has yet to be demonstrated. It may be that assessment techniques that index more specific self-control behaviors will prove superior.

During the past decade, self-control behavior in children has received considerable attention (Barth, 1986). One strategy for improving overall self-control skills in children is self-instruction training (Meichenbaum, 1977), which has received considerable attention as a training method in the literature on cognitive-behavioral therapy with children. Verbal self-regulation (self-instruction training) is one type of self-control strategy in which the individual's verbalizations are intended to increase the probability of the corresponding overt behavior. Cole and Kazdin (1980) describe self-instructional training as a multifaceted intervention technique used to teach children to monitor their progress, to compare what they are doing to what they should be doing, and to self-reinforce contingently. Self-verbalizations are developed through modeling, overt and covert rehearsal, prompts, feedback, and reinforcement. Self-instruction training has been used with children demonstrating a variety of behavior problems including impulsivity, hyperactivity, delinquency, social withdrawal (an aspect of depression), and learning disabilities.

Cole and Kazdin (1980) enumerate three major advantages of self-instruction training. First, it is a form of self-control that children can use to interrupt or inhibit a sequence of thoughts or actions. The use of self-instruction enables the child to become less dependent on external contingencies and more reliant on internal control. This facilitates generalization and maintenance of treatment effects. Second, verbal self-instruction training is a component of the natural developmental sequence in which children gain control of their verbal behavior (Vygotsky, 1962). It may be that a remedial procedure for children with self-control deficits may enhance the development of self-control skills and may lead to the growth of automatic covert verbal self-control. Third, self-instruction training provides people with the basic skills for adaptive problem solving. Such training may hold some promise as a primary prevention procedure providing children with skills for avoiding depression and other problems later in their development.

Recently, Rehm's self-control therapy was adapted for use with depressed children (Stark et al., 1987). This intervention program takes into account children's cognitive developmental capacities and requires the therapist to play a more active role in effecting the desired change by utilizing more action-oriented techniques and concrete task assignments. In a treatment-outcome study (Stark et al., 1987), a self-control intervention program for teaching children self-management skills (such as adaptive self-monitoring, self-evaluating, self-reinforcing, and appropriate causal attributions) was compared to a behavioral problem-solving therapy (education, self-monitoring of pleasant events, and group problem-solving lessons directed toward improving social behavior) and a waiting-list control condition. Postintervention and follow-up assessments found participants in both active interventions significantly improved on self-report and interview measures of depression, while members of the waiting-list condition reported minimal change. Although comparison of the self-control therapy and behavioral problem-solving therapy was equivocal, the pattern suggested that the self-control intervention was the most effective.

Reynolds and Coates (1986) examined the relative efficacy of a cognitive-behavioral therapy based primarily on Rehm's (1977) self-control model of depression. It included relaxation training and a waiting-list control condition for depressed adolescents. At both posttest and follow-up, the two active treatments were effective in reducing depression and anxiety symptoms as well as in enhancing academic self-concept. However, there were no significant differences between the active treatment groups. Overall, self-control as a model for assessing and treating depression in children seems to have promise. As with the other models, continued work is necessary.

RECOMMENDATIONS FOR CHOICE OF STRATEGY

Each of the strategies discussed is based on a different model of the nature of depression in adults and in children. Each model postulates a different core symptom or symptoms and suggests therapeutic strategies for targeting these specific behaviors. In dealing with children clinically, it is desirable to identify which of these deficits seem to be most prominent. One could approach this problem by attempting to assess all the potential deficits and then choosing specific interventions, or one might develop a very large treatment package that would attempt to cover all the potential targets systematically. Either of these strategies would most likely be cumbersome and time-consuming. A more rational strategy might be to order the potential treatments in a logical sequence and then to make sequential decisions as to which ones to use and in which order.

The flowchart shown in Figure 3.1 is an attempt to suggest such a sequential decision process. It assumes that some skills may be prerequisites to others and that some deficits may be more fundamental than others. For example, the model assumes first that depression may be a secondary consequence of the complex ramifications of the behavioral disorders of childhood. If this is the case, then it would be logical to treat the other problems first. Basic interpersonal social skills may be a necessary prerequisite to an adequate level of satisfying activity. Modifying activity per se is much more logical when there is some assurance that the child has the prerequisite minimal social skills. Targeting of overt behavioral change is placed in the flowchart prior to covert or cognitive targets on the basis of the assumption that accuracy of self-monitoring probably cannot be well evaluated unless some level of appropriate overt behavior is present. The final steps in the flowchart are ordered according to the self-control model. Cognitive and helplessness strategies are incorporated at various stages of this model. All these interventions must be adapted for use with children at different developmental levels and must take into consideration the child's level of cognitive, affective, and interpersonal functioning (Rehm & Carter, in press; Cole & Kaslow, 1988).

When discussing overall clinical strategies, it is also worth noting some special comments on the possibility of using parent-training methods to help depressed children. Parents can be involved in facilitating several of the strategies described previously. For example, parents might be incorporated into an activity-increase strategy as the managers of the external reinforcement for the program and might help the children become involved in the various activities. In self-control programs, parents may model for children the various self-management strategies; support their children in utilizing these strategies; and utilize appropriate monitoring, evaluation, attribution, and reinforcement of their children's behavior (Lewinsohn & Clarke, 1984). However, involving the parents of depressed children in the treatment program raises some special issues relatively specific to depression.

There is a substantial body of research demonstrating a relationship between depression in a child and depression in the child's parents. There is a high incidence of depression and psychopathology in the parents and extended family of depressed children (for a review see Orvaschel, Weissman, & Kidd, 1980). Further, parent–child conflict; parental death, divorce, or separation; child maltreatment or physical

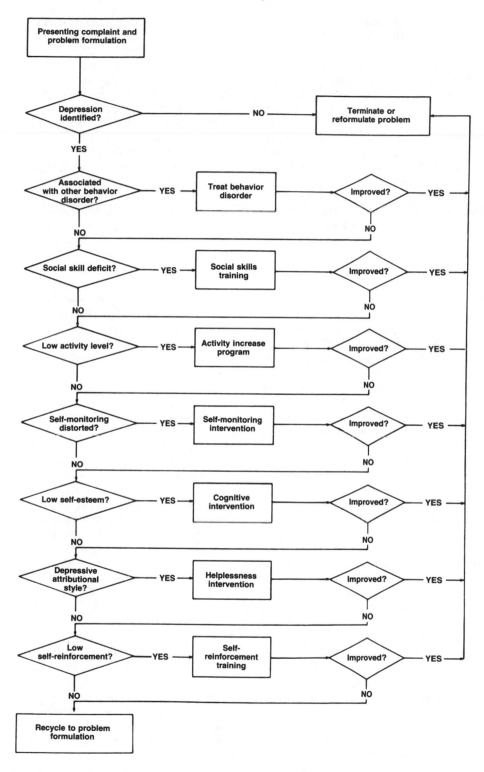

Figure 3.1. Flowchart for ordering decisions about intervention targets in treating depression in children.

abuse; marital discord; and a problematic parenting style characterized by hostility and alternating rejection and overinvolvement have been reported in the families of depressed children (Beck & Rosenberg, 1986; Bemporad & WonLee, 1984; Forehand et al., 1988; Handford, Mattison, Humphrey, & McLaughlin, 1986; Kazdin, Moser, Colbus, & Bell, 1985; Lefkowitz & Tesiny, 1984; Poznanski & Zrull, 1970; Puig-Antich-Blau, Marx, Greenhill, & Chambers, 1978; Trad, 1987). A related body of research reveals that children of parents with affective disorders have an increased incidence of childhood depression and other forms of psychopathology and have difficulties in concentration and attention, academic performance, and competent social functioning (for reviews see Beardslee, Bemporad, Keller, & Klerman, 1983; Morrison, 1983; Trad, 1987). The primary explanation for the psychological, affective, behavioral, and cognitive deficits observed in children of depressed parents is that being depressed as a parent makes it difficult to function effectively in the parenting role (McLean, 1976). Compared to their nondepressed counterparts, depressed women are less emotionally involved, have impaired communication, describe a loss of affection for their children, and report considerable hostility and resentment toward their children (Weissman & Paykel, 1974).

All these lines of evidence suggest that parental pathology, and—more specifically—parental depression may be intimately involved with a child's depression. A variety of mechanisms could easily be postulated to explain this relationship. It may be that parents model a depressive disorder that is vicariously learned by the child. Parents may also model components of depressed behavior. Parents may inadvertently reinforce depressive behaviors on the part of the child and thus develop and maintain their child's depressive behavior. Parents may also create an external environment that produces depressive behavior. For example, they may consistently monitor negative aspects of the child's behavior, set exceedingly high standards for the child's performance, use low rates of reward and high rates of punishment, or be noncontingent in their reward or punishment. Children may incorporate these behaviors into their self-management skills.

Any cognitive-behavioral approach to therapy with children—whether individual, group, or family—would suggest the careful assessment of the environmental contingencies impinging on the child. In treating depressed children, it is important to attend to family difficulties, the possibility of depression in the parents, and the implications of these factors for the child's environment. Parent training and family therapy may greatly enhance the treatment of depressed children, particularly if the parents' difficulties are also attended to.

The major alternative to cognitive-behavioral approaches to depression is pharmacotherapy. As with adults, a choice between pharmacologic and psychosocial intervention must be made. Genetics and other biomedical approaches clearly point to a biological contribution to the occurrence of depression in children (e.g., Mendels, 1975; DePue, 1979). The biological assessment of depression is, however, not yet firmly established. More heavily biologic depressions may be characterized by strong somatic symptomatology, as exemplified by DSM-III-R criteria for melancholia (APA, 1987): onset with no clear precipitating event and family history of depression. Early onset is considered as a clinical sign of a relatively severe biological disorder. Biological contributions to etiology do not necessarily imply that pharmacological approaches are the most effective, and there are no clear guidelines for determining the best approach to treatment. Caution has been traditional in administering drugs to children. Reports of the use of both tricyclic antidepressants (Puig-Antich et al., 1987) and lithium (e.g., Jefferson, 1982) have appeared in the literature, but the overall results are confusing. Although a significant percentage of children recover after receiving antidepressants, youngsters have been shown to respond equally well to and tricyclic antidepressants and placebos (Puig-Antich et al., 1987).

SUMMARY

Depression in children has been a topic of theoretical and clinical interest for the past decade. Evidence supports the idea that children may manifest the syndrome of depression and that depressive behavior is not reducible to mere transient reactions to life's situations or to other problematic behavior. Current behavioral and cognitive models of depression indicate that depressed individuals have inadequate social skills, low activity level, maladaptive attributions, distorted cognitions, and deficits in self-control behaviors. These models suggest specific intervention targets that have been the focus of successful adult treatment programs. Parallel behaviors appear to be problematic in children, and child cognitive-behavioral therapy strategies may be applicable to their assessment and modification. Studies of cognitive-behavioral therapy with depressed children are only beginning to appear, and it is a growing field of interest. We hope that this chapter will contribute to the systematic development of this field.

REFERENCES

Abramson, L. Y., Seligman, M. E. P., & Teasdale, J. (1978). Learned helplessness in humans: Critique and reformulation. *Journal of Abnormal Psychology, 87,* 49–74.

Achenbach, T. M. (1978). The child behavior profile: I. Boys aged 6–11. *Journal of Consulting and Clinical Psychology, 46,* 478–488.

Achenbach, T. M., & Edelbrock, C. S. (1979). The child behavior profile: II. Boys aged 12–16 and girls aged 6–11 and 12–16. *Journal of Consulting and Clinical Psychology, 47,* 223–233.

Alloy, L. B., Clements, C., & Kolden, G. (1985). The cognitive diathesis-stress theories of depression: Therapeutic implications. In S. Reiss and R. R. Bootzin (Eds.), *Theoretical issues in behavior therapy* (pp. 379–410). Orlando, FL: Academic Press.

Altmann, E. O., and Gotlib, I. H. (1988). The social behavior of depressed children: An observational study. *Journal of Abnormal Child Psychology, 16,* 29–44.

American Psychiatric Association. (1987). *Diagnostic and statistical manual of mental disorders* (3rd ed. rev.). Washington, DC: Author.

Anthony, E. J. (1975). Childhood depression. In E. J. Anthony & T. Benedek (Eds.), *Depression and human existence* (pp. 231–277). Boston: Little, Brown.

Anton, J. L., Dunbar, J., & Friedman, L. (1976). Anticipation training in the treatment of depression. In J. D. Krumbotlz & C. E. Thoresen (Eds.), *Counseling methods* (pp. 67–73). New York: Holt, Rinehart & Winston.

Asarnow, J. R., Carlson, G. A., & Guthrie, D. (1987). Coping strategies, self-perceptions, hopelessness, and perceived family environments in depressed and suicidal children. *Journal of Consulting and Clinical Psychology, 55,* 361–366.

Barrera, M., Jr. (1979). An evaluation of a brief group therapy for depression. *Journal of Consulting and Clinical Psychology, 47,* 413–415.

Barth, R. P. (1986). *Social and cognitive treatment of children and adolescents.* San Francisco: Jossey-Bass.

Beach, S. R. H., & O'Leary, K. D. (1986). The treatment of depression occurring in the context of marital discord. *Behavior Therapy, 17,* 43–49.

Beardslee, W. R., Bemporad, J., Keller, M. B., and Klerman, G. L. (1983). Children of parents with major affective disorder: A review. *American Journal of Psychiatry, 140,* 825–832.

Beck, A. T. (1967). *Depression: Clinical, experimental and theoretical aspects.* New York: Hoeber.

Beck, A. T. (1976). *Cognitive therapy and emotional disorders.* New York: International Universities Press.

Beck, A. T., Hollon, S. D., Young, J. E., Bedrosian, R. C., & Budenz, D. (1985). Treatment of depression with cognitive therapy and amitriptyline. *Archives of General Psychiatry, 42,* 142–152.

Beck, A. T., Rush, A. G., Shaw, B. F., & Emery, G. (1979). *Cognitive therapy of depression.* New York: Guilford Press.

Beck, S., & Rosenberg, R. (1986). Frequency, quality and impact of life events in self-rated depressed, behavioral-problem and normal children. *Journal of Consulting and Clinical Psychology, 54,* 863–864.

Becker, R. E., Heimberg, R. G., & Bellack, A. S. (1987). *Social skills training treatment for depression.* Elmsford, NY: Pergamon Press.

Bemporad, J. (1978). Psychotherapy of depression in children and adolescents. In S. Arieti & J. Bemporad (Eds.), *Severe and mild depression: A psychotherapeutic approach* (pp. 344–357). New York: Basic Books.

Bemporad, J. R., & Wilson, A. (1978). A developmental approach to depression in childhood and adolescence. *Journal of the American Academy of Psychoanalysis, 6,* 325–352.

Bemporad, J. R., & WonLee, K. (1984). Developmental and psychodynamic aspects of childhood depression. *Child Psychiatry and Human Development, 14,* 145–157.

Beres, D. (1966). Superego and depression. In

R. M. Lowenstein, L. M. Newman, M. Scherr, & A. J. Solnit (Eds.), *Psychoanalysis—a general psychology* (pp. 479–498). New York: International Universities Press.

Bibring, E. (1953). The mechanism of depression. In P. Greenacre (Ed.), *Affective disorders* (pp. 13–48). New York: International Universities Press.

Birleson, P. (1981). The validity of depressive disorder in childhood and the development of a self-rating scale: A research report. *Journal of Child Psychology and Psychiatry, 22*, 73–88.

Blackburn, I. M., Bishop, S., Glenn, A. I. M., Whalley, L. J., & Christie, J. E. (1981). The efficacy of cognitive therapy in depression: A treatment trial using cognitive therapy and pharmacotherapy each alone and in combination. *British Journal of Psychiatry, 139*, 181–189.

Blechman, E. A., McEnroe, M. J., Carella, E. T., & Audette, D. P. (1986). Childhood competence and depression. *Journal of Abnormal Psychology, 95*, 223–227.

Blumberg, S. H., & Izard, C. E. (1985). Affective and cognitive characteristics of depression in 10- and 11-year old children. *Journal of Personality and Social Psychology, 49*, 194–202.

Bornstein, M. R., Bellack, A. S., & Hersen, M. (1977). Social skills training for unassertive children: A multiple baseline analysis. *Journal of Applied Behavior Analysis, 10*, 183–195.

Boverman, H., & French, A. P. (1979). Treatment of the depressed child. In A. French & I. Berlin (Eds.), *Depression in children and adolescents* (pp. 129–139). New York: Human Sciences Press.

Brumback, R. A., & Weinberg, W. A. (1977). Relationship of hyperactivity and depression in children. *Perceptual and Motor Skills, 45*, 247–251.

Buchwald, A. M. (1977). Depressive mood and estimates of reinforcement frequency. *Journal of Abnormal Psychology, 86*, 443–446.

Butler, L., & Miezitis, S. (1980). *Releasing children from depression: A handbook for elementary teachers and consultants*. Ontario: OISE Press.

Butler, L., Miezitis, S., Friedman, R., & Cole, E. (1980). The effect of two school-based intervention programs on depressive symptoms in preadolescents. *American Educational Research Journal, 17*, 111–119.

Calpin, J. P., & Cincirpini, P. M. (1978, May). *A multiple baseline analysis of social skills training in children*. Paper presented at the meeting of the Midwestern Association for Behavior Analysis, Chicago.

Calpin, J. P., & Kornblith, S. J. (1977). *Training of aggressive children in conflict resolution skills*. Paper presented at the meeting of the Association for the Advancement of Behavior Therapy, Chicago.

Campbell, M., & Spencer, E. K. (1988). Psychopharmacology in child and adolescent psychiatry: A review of the past five years. *Journal of The American Academy of Child and Adolescent Psychiatry, 27*, 269–279.

Cantwell, D. P., & Carlson, G. A. (1979). Problems and prospects in the study of childhood depression. *Journal of Nervous and Mental Disease, 167*, 522–529.

Carey, M. P., Kelley, M. L., Buss, R. R., & Scott, W. O. N. (1986). Relationship of activity to depression in adolescents: Development of the adolescent activities checklist. *Journal of Consulting and Clinical Psychology, 54*, 320–322.

Carlson, G. A., & Garber, J. (1986). Developmental issues in the classification of depression in children. In M. Rutter, C. E. Izard, & P. B. Read (Eds.), *Depression in young people: Developmental and clinical perspectives* (pp. 399–435). New York: Guilford Press.

Cautela, J. R. (1977). Children's Reinforcement Survey Schedule (CRSS). In J. R. Cautela (Ed.), *Behavior analysis forms for clinical intervention* (pp. 45–52). Illinois: Research Press Company.

Cautela, J. R., & Kastenbaum, R. (1967). A reinforcement survey for use in therapy, training, and research. *Psychological Reports, 20*, 1115–1130.

Cicchetti, D., & Schneider-Rosen, K. (1986). An organizational approach to childhood depression. In M. Rutter, C. E. Izard, & P. B. Read (Eds.), *Depression in young people: Developmental and clinical perspectives* (pp. 71–134). New York: Guilford Press.

Cohen, D. J. (1980). Constructive and reconstructive activities in the analysis of a depressed child. In A. J. Solnit, R. Eissler, A. Freud, M. Kris, & P. B. Neubauer (Eds.), *The psychoanalytic study of the child, 35*, (237–266). New Haven: Yale University Press.

Cole, D. A., & Rehm, L. P. (1986). Family interaction patterns and childhood depression. *Journal of Abnormal Psychology, 14,* 297–314.

Cole, P. M., & Kaslow, N. J. (1988). Interactional and cognitive strategies for affect regulation: A developmental perspective on childhood depression. In L. B. Alloy (Ed.), *Cognitive processes in depression* (pp. 310–343). New York: Guilford Press.

Cole, P. M., & Kazdin, A. E. (1980). Critical issues in self-instruction training with children. *Child Behavior Therapy, 2,* 1–21.

Cole, T. L., Kelley, M. L., & Carey, M. P. (1988). The adolescent activities checklist: Reliability, standardization data, and factorial validity. *Journal of Abnormal Psychology, 16,* 475–484.

Combs, M. S., & Slaby, O. A. (1977). Social skills training with children. In B. B. Lahey & A. E. Kazdin (Eds.), *Advances in clinical child psychology* (pp. 161–201). New York: Plenum Press.

Costello, C. G. (1980). Childhood depression: Three basic but questionable assumptions in the Lefkowitz and Burton critique. *Psychological Bulletin, 87,* 185–190.

Costello, C. G. (1981). Childhood depression. In J. E. Mash & L. G. Terdal (Eds.), *Behavioral assessment of childhood disorders* (pp. 305–346). New York: Guilford Press.

Costello, A. J., Edelbrock, C. S., Dulcan, M. H., Kales, R., & Klavic, S. H. (1984). *Report on the NIMH diagnostic interview schedule for children (DISC).* Bethesda, MD: National Institute of Mental Health.

Cytryn, L., & McKnew, D. H. (1974). Factors influencing the changing clinical expression of the depressive process in children. *American Journal of Psychiatry, 131,* 879–881.

Cytryn, L., McKnew, D. H., & Bunney, W. E. (1980). Diagnosis of depression in children: A reassessment. *American Journal of Psychiatry, 137,* 22–25.

DeMonbreun, B. G., & Craighead, W. E. (1977). Distortion of perception and recall positive and neutral feedback in depression. *Cognitive Therapy and Research, 1,* 311–329.

Depue, R. A. (Ed.) (1979). *The psychopathology of the depressive disorders: Implications for the effects of stress.* New York: Academic Press.

Diener, C. I., & Dweck, C. S. (1978). An analysis of learned helplessness: Continuous changes in performance, strategy, and achievement cognitions following failure. *Journal of Personality and Social Psychology, 36,* 451–462.

Digdon, N., & Gotlib, I. H. (1985). Developmental considerations in the study of childhood depression. *Developmental Reviews, 5,* 162–199.

DiGuiseppe, R. (1986). Cognitive therapy for childhood depression. In A. Freeman, N. Epstein, & K. M. Simon (Eds.), *Depression in the family* (pp. 153–172). London: Haworth.

Dunn, R. J. (1979). Cognitive modification with depression-prone psychiatric patients. *Cognitive Therapy and Research, 3,* 307–317.

Dweck, D. S. (1975). The role of expectations and attributions in the alleviation of learned helplessness. *Journal of Personality and Social Psychology, 31,* 674–685.

Dweck, C. S., & Bush, E. S. (1976). Sex differences in learned helplessness: Differential debilitation with peer and adult evaluators. *Developmental Psychology, 12,* 147–156.

Dweck, C. S., Davidson, W., Nelson, S., & Enna, B. (1978). Sex differences in learned helplessness: II. The contingencies of evaluative feedback in the classroom and III. An experimental analysis. *Developmental Psychology, 14,* 268–276.

Dweck, C. S., & Repucci, N. D. (1973). Learned helplessness and reinforcement responsibility in children. *Journal of Personality and Social Psychology, 25,* 109–116.

Elkin, I., Shea, T., Imber, S., Pilkonis, P., Sotsky, S., Glass, Watkins, J., Leber, W., & Collins, J. (May, 1986). *NIMH treatment of depression collaborative research program: Initial outcome findings.* Paper presented at the meeting of the American Association for the Advancement of Science.

Emery, G., Bedrosian, R., & Garber, J. (1983). Cognitive therapy with depressed children and adolescents. In D. P. Cantwell & G. A. Carlson (Eds.), *Affective disorders in childhood and adolescence: An update* (pp. 445–471). New York: Spectrum Publications.

Endicott, J., & Spitzer, R. L. (1978). A diagnostic interview: The Schedule for Affective Disorders and Schizophrenia. *Archives of General Psychiatry, 35,* 837–844.

Ferster, C. B. (1971). The use of learning principles in clinical practice and training. *The Psychological Record, 21,* 353–361.

Fine, S., Moretti, M., Haley, G., & Marriage, K. (1984). Depressive disorder in children and adolescents: Dysthymic disorder and the use of self-rating scales in assessment. *Child Psychiatry and Human Development, 14,* 223–229.

Fleming, B. M., & Thorton, D. W. (1980). Coping skills training as a component in the short-term treatment of depression. *Journal of Consulting and Clinical Psychology, 48,* 652–655.

Forehand, R., Brody, G., Slotkin, J., Fauber, R., McCombs, A., & Long, N. (1988). Young adolescent and maternal depression: Assessment, interrelations, and family predictors. *Journal of Consulting and Clinical Psychology, 56,* 422–426.

Frame, C., Matson, J. L., Sonis, W. A., Fialkov, M. J., & Kazdin, A. E. (1982). Behavioral treatment of depression in a prepubertal child. *Journal of Behavior Therapy and Experimental Psychiatry, 3,* 239–243.

Fuchs, C. Z., & Rehm, L. P. (1977). A self-control behavior therapy program for depression. *Journal of Consulting and Clinical Psychology, 45,* 206–215.

Furman, E. (1974). *A child's parent dies. Studies in childhood bereavement.* New Haven: Yale University Press.

Gelfand, D. M. (1978). Social withdrawal and negative emotional states: Behavior therapy. In B. B. Wolman, J. Egan, & A. O. Boss (Eds.), *Handbook of treatment of mental disorders in childhood and adolescence* (pp. 330–353). Englewood Cliffs, NJ: Prentice-Hall.

Gilpin, D. C. (1976). Psychotherapy of the depressed child. In E. J. Anthony & D. C. Gilpin (Eds.), *Three clinical faces of childhood* (pp. 229–245). New York: Spectrum Publications.

Gittelman-Klein, R., & Klein, D. F. (1973). School phobia: Diagnostic considerations in the light of imipramine effects. *Journal of Nervous and Mental Disease, 156,* 199–215.

Glaser, K. (1968). Masked depression in children and adolescents. *Annual Progress in Child Psychiatry and Child Development, 1,* 345–355.

Grosscup, S. J., & Lewinsohn, P. M. (1980). Unpleasant and pleasant events, and mood. *Journal of Clinical Psychology, 36,* 252–259.

Haley, G. M. T., Fine, S., Marriage, K., Moretti, M. M., & Freeman, R. J. (1985). Cognitive bias and depression in psychiatrically disturbed children and adolescents. *Journal of Consulting and Clinical Psychology, 53,* 535–537.

Hammen, C., & Zupan, B. A. (1984). Self-schemas, depression, and the processing of personal information in children. *Journal of Experimental Child Psychology, 37,* 598–608.

Handford, H. A., Mattison, R., Humphrey, F. J., & McLaughlin, R. E. (1986). Depressive syndrome in children entering a residential school subsequent to parent death, divorce, or separation. *Journal of the American Academy of Child Psychiatry, 25,* 409–414.

Harter, S. (1985). *Manual for the Self-Perception Profile for Children (Revision of the Perceived Competence Scale for Children).* Unpublished manuscript, University of Denver, Denver.

Hayman, P. M., & Cope, C. S. (1980). Effects of assertion training on depression. *Journal of Clinical Psychology, 36,* 534–543.

Herjanic, B., Herjanic, M., Brown, F., & Wheatt, T. (1975). Are children reliable reporters? *Journal of Abnormal Child Psychology, 3,* 41–48.

Hersen, M., Bellack, A. S., Himmelhoch, J. M. (1980). Treatment of unipolar depression with social skills training. *Behavior Modification, 4,* 547–557.

Hersen, M., Bellack, A. S., Himmelhoch, J. M., & Thase, M. E. (1984). Effects of social skills training, amitriptyline, and psychotherapy in unipolar depressed women. *Behavior Therapy, 15,* 21–40.

Hodges, K., McKnew, D., Cytryn, L., Stern, L., & Kline, J. (1982). The Child Assessment Schedule (CAS) diagnostic interview: A report on reliability and validity. *Journal of the American Academy of Child Psychiatry, 21,* 468–473.

Humphrey, L. L. (1982). Children's and teacher's perspectives on children's self-control: The development of two rating scales. *Journal of Consulting and Clinical Psychology, 50,* 624–633.

Jacobsen, R. H., Lahey, B. B., & Strauss, C. C. (1983). Correlates of depressed mood in normal children, *Journal of Abnormal Child Psychology, 11,* 29–40.

Jefferson, J. W. (1982). The use of lithium in

childhood and adolescence: An overview. *Journal of Clinical Psychiatry, 43,* 174–177.

John, K., Gammon, D., Prusoff, B., & Warner, V. (1987). The Social Adjustment Inventory for Children and Adolescents (SAICA): Testing a new semi-structured interview. *Journal of the American Academy of Child and Adolescent Psychiatry, 26,* 898–911.

Kanfer, F. H. (1970). Self-monitoring: Methodological limitations and clinical applications. *Journal of Consulting and Clinical Psychology, 35,* 148–152.

Kanfer, F. H., & Karoly, P. (1972). Self-control: A behavioristic excursion into the lion's den. *Behavior Therapy, 3,* 398–416.

Kashani, J. H., Holcomb, W. R., & Orvaschel, H. (1986). Depression and depressive symptoms in pre-school children from the general population. *American Journal of Psychiatry, 143,* 1138–1143.

Kaslow, N. J., & Rehm, L. P. (1985). Conceptualization, assessment, and treatment of depression in children. In A. E. Kazdin & P. Bornstein (Eds.), *Handbook of clinical behavior therapy with children* (pp. 599–657). New York: Dorsey Press.

Kaslow, N. J., Rehm, L. P., Pollack, & Siegel, A. W. (1988). Attributional style and self-control behavior in depressed and nondepressed children and their parents. *Journal of Abnormal Child Psychology, 16,* 163–177.

Kaslow, N. J., Rehm, L. P., & Siegel, A. W. (1984). Social cognitive and cognitive correlates of depression in children. *Journal of Abnormal Child Psychology, 12,* 605–620.

Kazdin, A. E. (1981). Assessment techniques for childhood depression: A critical appraisal. *Journal of the American Academy of Child Psychiatry, 20,* 358–375.

Kazdin, A. E., Esveldt-Dawson, K., Sherick, R. B., & Colbus, D. (1985). Assessment of overt behavior and childhood depression among psychiatrically disturbed children. *Journal of Consulting and Clinical Psychology, 53,* 201–210.

Kazdin, A. E., French, N. H., Unis, A. S., Esveldt-Dawson, K., & Sherick, R. B. (1983). Hopelessness, depression, and suicidal intent among psychiatrically disturbed inpatient children. *Journal of Consulting and Clinical Psychology, 51,* 504–510.

Kazdin, A. E., Moser, J., Colbus, D., & Bell, R. (1985). Depressive symptoms among physically abused and psychiatrically disturbed children. *Journal of Abnormal Psychology, 94,* 298–307.

Kazdin, A. E., & Petti, T. A. (1982). Self-report and interview measures on childhood and adolescent depression. *Journal of Child Psychology and Psychiatry, 23,* 437–457.

Kazdin, A. E., Rodgers, A., & Colbus, D. (1986). The Hopelessness Scale for Children: Psychometric characteristics and concurrent validity. *Journal of Consulting and Clinical Psychology, 54,* 241–245.

Kendall, P. C., & Wilcox, L. E. (1979). Self-control in children: Development of a rating scale. *Journal of Consulting and Clinical Psychology, 47,* 1020–1029.

Kendall, P. C., Zupan, B. A., & Braswell, L. (1981). Self-control in control of children: Further analyses of the self-control rating scale. *Behavior Therapy, 12,* 667–681.

Klerman, G. L., Weissman, M. M., Rounsaville, B. J., & Chevron, E. S. (1984). *Interpersonal psychotherapy of depression.* New York: Basic Books.

Kornblith, S. J., Rehm, L. P., O'Hara, M. W., & Lamparski, D. M. (1983). The contribution of self-reinforcement training and behavioral assignments to the efficacy of self-control therapy for depression. *Cognitive Therapy and Research, 7,* 499–527.

Kovacs, M. (1981). Rating scales to assess depression in school-aged children. *Acta Paedopsychiatrica, 46,* 305–315.

Kovacs, M. (1986). A developmental perspective on methods and measures in the assessment of depressive disorders: The clinical interview. In M. Rutter, C. E. Izard, & P. B. Read (Eds.), *Depression in young people: Developmental and clinical perspectives* (pp. 435–469). New York: Guilford Press.

Kovacs, M. (1989). Affective disorders in children and adolescents. *American Psychologist, 44,* 209–215.

Kovacs, M., & Beck, A. T. (1977). An empirical-clinical approach toward a definition of childhood depression. In J. G. Schulterbrandt & A. Raskin (Eds.), *Depression in childhood: Diagnosis, treatment, and conceptual models* (pp. 1–25). New York: Raven Press.

Kovacs, M., Feinberg, T. L., Crouse-Novak, M. A., Paulauskas, S. L., & Finkelstein, R. (1984). Depressive disorders in childhood I. A longitudinal prospective study of characteristics and recovery. *Archives of General Psychiatry, 41,* 229–237.

Kovacs, M., & Gastonis, C. (1989). Stability and change in childhood onset depressive disorders: Longitudinal course as a diagnostic validator. In L. N. Robins, J. L. Fleiss, & J. E. Barrett (Eds.), *The validity of psychiatric diagnosis* (pp. 57–75). New York: Raven Press.

Lang, M., & Tisher, M. (1978). *Children's Depression Scale.* Victoria, Australia: The Australian Council for Educational Research.

Layne, C., & Berry, E. (1983). Motivational deficit in childhood depression and hyperactivity. *Journal of Clinical Psychology, 39,* 523–531.

Laxer, R. M. (1964). Self-concept changes of depressive patients in general hospital treatment. *Journal of Consulting Psychology, 28,* 214–219.

Lazarus, A. A. (1968). Learning theory and the treatment of depression. *Behavior Research and Therapy, 6,* 83–89.

Lazarus, A. A. (1973). Multimodal behavior therapy: Treating the "Basic I.D." *Journal of Nervous and Mental Disease, 156,* 404–411.

Lefkowitz, M. M. & Burton, N. (1978). Childhood depression: A critique of the concept. *Psychological Bulletin, 85,* 716–726.

Lefkowitz, M. M., & Tesiny, E. P. (1980). Assessment of childhood depression. *Journal of Consulting and Clinical Psychology, 48,* 43–50.

Lefkowitz, M. M., & Tesiny, E. P. (1984). Rejection and depression: Prospective and contemporaneous analyses. *Developmental Psychology, 20,* 776–785.

Lefkowitz, M. M., Tesiny, E. P., & Gordon, N. H. (1980). Childhood depression, family income, and locus of control. *Journal of Nervous and Mental Disease, 168,* 732–735.

Leitenberg, H., Yost, L. W., & Carroll-Wilson, M. (1986). Negative cognitive errors in children: Questionnaire development, normative data, and comparisons between children with and without self-reported symptoms of depression, low self-esteem, and evaluation anxiety. *Journal of Consulting and Clinical Psychology, 54,* 528–536.

Leon, G. R., Kendall, P. C., & Garber, J. (1980). Depression in children: Parent, teacher, and child perspectives. *Journal of Abnormal Child Psychology, 8,* 221–235.

Lesse, S. (1974). Depression masked by acting-out behavior patterns. *American Journal of Psychotherapy, 28,* 352–361.

Lewinsohn, P. M. (1974). A behavioral approach to depression. In R. M. Friedman & M. M. Katz (Eds.), *The psychology of depression: Contemporary theory and research* (pp. 157–185). New York: John Wiley & Sons.

Lewinsohn, P. M., Biglan, A., & Zeiss, A. M. (1976). Behavioral treatment of depression. In P. O. Davidson (Ed.), *Behavioral management of anxiety, depression, and pain* (pp. 91–146). New York: Brunner/Mazel.

Lewinsohn, P. M., & Clarke, G. N. (1984). *The coping with depression course, adolescent version: Instructor's manual for parent course.* Unpublished manuscript, University of Oregon, Eugene.

Lewinsohn, P. M., Weinstein, M. S., & Alper, T. (1970). A behavioral approach to the group treatment of depressed persons: Methodological contribution. *Journal of Clinical Psychology, 26,* 525–532.

Ling, W., Oftedal, G., & Weinberg, W. (1970). Depressive illness in childhood presenting as severe headache. *American Journal of Diseases in Children, 120,* 122–124.

MacPhillamy, D. J., & Lewinsohn, P. M. (1971). *Pleasant Events Schedule.* Mimeograph, University of Oregon, Eugene.

Malmquist, C. P. (1977). Childhood depression: A clinical and behavioral perspective. In J. G. Schulterbrandt & A. Raskin (Eds.), *Depression in childhood: Diagnosis, treatment, and conceptual models* (pp. 33–59). New York: Raven Press.

Matson, J. L., Esveldt-Dawson, K., Andrasik, F., Ollendik, T. H., Petti, T. A., & Hersen, M. (1980). Observation and generalization effects of social skills training and emotionally disturbed children. *Behavior Therapy, 11,* 522–531.

McGee, R., Anderson, J., Williams, S., Silva, P. A. (1986). Cognitive correlates of depressive symptoms in 11-year-old children. *Journal of Abnormal Child Psychology, 14,* 517–524.

McGee, R., & Williams, S. (1988). A longitudinal study of depression in nine-year-old children. *American Academy of Child and Adolescent Psychiatry, 27,* 342–348.

McKnew, D. H., Cytryn, L., Efron, A. M., Gershon, E. S., & Bunney, W. E. (1979).

Offspring of patients with affective disorders. *British Journal of Psychiatry, 134,* 148–152.

McLean, P. D. (1976). Parent depression: Incompatible with effective parenting. In E. J. Mash, L. E. Handy, & L. A. Hamerlynck (Eds.), *Behavior modification approaches to parenting.* New York: Brunner/Mazel.

McLean, P. D. & Hakstian, A. R. (1979). Clinical depression: Comparative efficacy of outpatient treatments. *Journal of Consulting and Clinical Psychology, 47,* 818–836.

Meichenbaum, D. (1977). *Cognitive behavior modification.* New York: Plenum Press.

Mendels, J. (1975). *The psychobiology of depression.* New York: Spectrum Publications.

Metalsky, G. I., & Abramson, L. Y. (1981). Attributional styles: Toward a framework for conceptualization and assessment. In P. C. Kendall & S. D. Hollon (Eds.), *Cognitive-behavioral interventions: Assessment methods* (pp. 13–58). New York: Academic Press.

Mitchell, J., McCauley, E., Burke, P. M., & Moss, S. J. (1988). Phenomenology of depression in children and adolescents. *American Academy of Child and Adolescent Psychiatry, 27,* 12–20.

Morrison, H. L. (Ed.) (1983). *Children of depressed parents: Risk, identification and intervention.* New York: Grune & Stratton.

Mullins, L. L., Siegel, L. J., & Hodges, K. (1985). Cognitive problem-solving and life event correlates of depressive symptoms in children. *Journal of Abnormal Child Psychology, 13,* 305–314.

Murphy, G. E., Simons, A. D., Wetzel, R. D., & Lustman, P. J. (1984). Cognitive therapy and pharmacotherapy singly and together, in the treatment of depression. *Archives of General Psychiatry, 41,* 33–41.

Nelson, R. E., & Craighead, W. E. (1977). Selective recall of positive and negative feedback, self-control behaviors, and depression. *Journal of Abnormal Psychology, 86,* 379–388.

Nezu, A. M. (1986). Efficacy of a social problem-solving therapy approach for unipolar depression. *Journal of Consulting and Clinical Psychology, 54,* 196–202.

Nezu, A. M., Nezu, C. M., & Perri, M. G. (1989). *Problem-solving therapy for depression: Theory, research and clinical guidelines.* New York: John Wiley & Sons.

Nolen-Hoeksema, S., Girgus, J. S., & Seligman, M. E. P. (1986). Learned helplessness in children: A longitudinal study of depression, achievement, and explanatory style. *Journal of Personality and Social Psychology, 51,* 435–442.

O'Connor, R. D. (1972). Relative efficacy of modeling, shaping, and the combined procedures for modification of social withdrawal. *Journal of Abnormal Psychology, 79,* 327–334.

Orvaschel, H., & Puig-Antich, J. (1987). *Schedule for Affective Disorder and Schizophrenia for School-Age Children—Epidemiologic version (Kiddie-SADS-E [K-SADS-E]).* Pittsburgh: Western Psychiatric Institute and Clinic.

Orvaschel, H., Weissman, M. M., & Kidd, K. K. (1980). Children and depression: The children of depressed parents; the childhood of patients, depression in children. *Journal of Affective Disorders, 2,* 1–6.

Padfield, M. (1976). The comparative effects of two counseling approaches on the intensity of depression among rural women of low socio-economic status. *Journal of Counseling Psychology, 23,* 209–214.

Peterson, L., Mullins, L. L., & Ridley-Johnson, R. (1985). Childhood depression: Peer reactions to depression and life stress. *Journal of Abnormal Child Psychology, 13,* 597–609.

Petti, T. A. (1978). Depression in hospitalized child psychiatry patients. *Journal of the American Academy of Child Psychiatry, 17,* 49–59.

Petti, T. A. (1983). Imipramine in the treatment of depressed children. In D. P. Cantwell & G. A. Carlson (Eds.), *Affective disorders in childhood and adolescence: An update* (pp. 375–415). New York: Spectrum Publications.

Petti, T. A., Bornstein, M., Delamater, A., & Conners, C. K. (1980). Evaluation and multimodal treatment of a depressed pre-pubertal girl. *Journal of the American Academy of Child Psychiatry, 19,* 690–702.

Petti, T. A., & Law, W. (1982). Imipramine treatment of depressed children: A double-blind pilot study. *Journal of Clinical Psychopharmacology, 2,* 107–110.

Pope, A. W., McHale, S. M., & Craighead, W. E. (1988). *Self-esteem enhancement with children and adolescents.* Elmsford, NY: Pergamon Press.

Poznanski, E. O., Grossman, J. A., Buchsbaum, Y., Banegas, M., Freeman, L., & Gibbons,

R. (1984). Preliminary studies of the reliability and validity of the Children's Depression Rating Scale. *Journal of the American Academy of Child Psychiatry, 23,* 191–197.

Poznanski, E. O., & Zrull, J. P. (1970). Childhood depression: Clinical characteristics of overtly depressed children. *Archives of General Psychiatry, 23,* 8–15.

Puig-Antich, J. (1982). Psychobiological correlates of major depressive disorder in children and adolescents. In L. Grinspoon (Ed.), *Psychiatry 1982: Annual review* (pp. 288–296). Washington, DC: American Psychiatric Press.

Puig-Antich, J., Blau, S., Marx, N., Greenhill, L. L., & Chambers, W. (1978). Prepubertal major depressive disorder. *Journal of the American Academy of Child Psychiatry, 17,* 695–707.

Puig-Antich, J., Lukens, E., Davies, M., Goetz, D., Brennan-Quattrock, J., & Todak, G. (1985a). Psychosocial functioning in prepubertal major depressive disorders. *Archives of General Psychiatry, 42,* 500–507.

Puig-Antich, J., Lukens, E., Davies, M., Goetz, D., Brennan-Quattrock, J., & Todak, G. (1985b). Psychosocial functioning in prepubertal major depressive disorders II. Interpersonal relationships after sustained recovery from affective episode. *Archives of General Psychiatry, 42,* 511–517.

Puig-Antich, J., Perel, J. M., Lupatkin, W., Chambers, W. J., Tabriz, M. A., King, J., Goetz, R., Davies, M., & Stiller, R. L. (1987). Imipramine in prepubertal major depressive disorders. *Archives of General Psychiatry, 44,* 81–89.

Puig-Antich, J., & Ryan, N. (1986). *Schedule for Affective Disorder and Schizophrenia for School-Age Children (6–18 years)—Kiddie-SADS (K-SADS).* Unpublished manuscript. Western Psychiatric Institute and Clinic, Pittsburgh.

Raps, C. S., Peterson, C., Reinhard, K. E., Abramson, L. Y., & Seligman, M. E. P. (1982). Attributional style among depressed patients. *Journal of Abnormal Psychology, 91,* 102–108.

Rehm, L. P. (1977). A self control model of depression. *Behavior Therapy, 8,* 787–804.

Rehm, L. P. (Ed.) (1981). *Behavior therapy for depression: Present status and future directions.* New York: Academic Press.

Rehm, L. P. (1982). Self-management in depression. In P. Karolly & F. H. Kanfer (Eds.), *Self-management and behavior change: From theory to practice* (pp. 522–570). Elmsford, NY: Pergamon Press.

Rehm, L. P., & Carter, A. S. (in press). Cognitive components of depression. In M. Lewis & S. M. Miller (Eds.), *Handbook of developmental psychology.* New York: Plenum Press.

Rehm, L. P., Fuchs, C. Z., Roth, D. M., Kornblith, S. J., & Romano, J. M. (1979). A comparison of self-control and assertion skills treatment of depression. *Behavior Therapy, 10,* 429–442.

Rehm, L. P., & Kaslow, N. J. (1984). Behavioral approaches to depression: Research results and clinical recommendations. In C. M. Franks (Ed.), *New developments in behavior therapy* (pp. 155–229). New York: Haworth Press.

Rehm, L. P., Kaslow, N. J., & Rabin, A. S. (1987). Cognitive and behavioral targets in a self-control therapy program for depression. *Journal of Consulting and Clinical Psychology, 55,* 60–67.

Rehm, L. P., Kornblith, S. J., O'Hara, M. W., Lamparski, D. M., Romano, J. M., & Volkin, J. (1981). An evaluation of major components in a self-control behavior therapy program for depression. *Behavior Modification, 5,* 459–489.

Rehm, L. P., & Plakosh, R. (1975). Preference for immediate reinforcement in depression. *Journal of Behavior Therapy and Experimental Psychiatry, 6,* 101–103.

Rehm, L. P., Roth, D., & Farmartino, R. (1976). Unpublished data. University of Pittsburgh.

Reynolds, W. M. (1986). *Assessment of depression in adolescents: Manual for Reynolds Adolescent Depression Scale.* Odessa: Psychological Assessment Resources.

Reynolds, W. M., Anderson, G., & Bartell, N. (1985). Measuring depression in children: A multimethod assessment investigation. *Journal of Abnormal Child Psychology, 13,* 513–526.

Reynolds, W. M., & Coats, K. I. (1986). A comparison of cognitive-behavioral therapy and relaxation training for the treatment of depression in adolescents. *Journal of Consulting and Clinical Psychology, 54,* 653–660.

Rhodes, W. A., Rodd, W. H., & Berggren, L. (1979). Social skills training for an unassertive adolescent. *Journal of Clinical Child Psychology, 8,* 18–21.

Rie, H. E. (1966). Depression in childhood: A survey of some pertinent contributions. *Journal of the Academy of Child Psychiatry, 5,* 653–685.

Rochlin, G. (1959). The loss complex. *Journal of American Psychoanalytic Association, 7,* 299–316.

Roth, D., & Rehm, L. P. (1980). Relationships between self-monitoring processes, memory and depression. *Cognitive Therapy and Research, 4,* 149–159.

Roth, D., Rehm, L. P., & Rozensky, R. A. (1980). Self-reward, self-punishment and depression. *Psychological Reports, 47,* 3–7.

Rozensky, R. A., Rehm, L. P., Pry, G., & Roth, D. (1977). Depression and self-reinforcement behavior in hospital patients. *Journal of Behavior Therapy and Experimental Psychiatry, 8,* 35–38.

Rude, S. S. (1986). Relative benefits of assertion or cognitive self-control treatment for depression as a function of proficiency in each domain. *Journal of Consulting and Clinical Psychology, 54,* 890–894.

Rush, A. J., Beck, A. T., Kovacs, M., & Hollon, S. (1977). Comparative efficacy of cognitive therapy and pharmacotherapy in the treatment of depressed outpatients. *Cognitive Therapy and Research, 1,* 17–38.

Rush, A. J., Khatami, M., & Beck, A. T. (1975). Cognitive and behavior therapy in chronic depression. *Behavior Therapy, 6,* 398–404.

Rush, A. J., Shaw, B., & Khatami, M. (1980). Cognitive therapy of depression utilizing the couples system. *Cognitive Therapy and Research, 4,* 103–114.

Rush, A. J., & Watkins, J. T. (1981). Group versus individual cognitive therapy: A pilot study. *Cognitive Therapy and Research, 5,* 95–104.

Rutter, M. (1986). The developmental psychopathology of depression: Issues and perspectives. In M. Rutter, C. E. Izard, & P. B. Read (Eds.), *Depression in young people: Developmental and clinical perspectives* (pp. 3–30). New York: Guilford Press.

Ryan, N. D., Puig-Antich, J., Ambrosini, P., Rabinovich, H., Robinson, D., Nelson, B., Iyengar, S., & Twomey, J. (1987). The clinical picture of major depression in children and adolescents. *Archives of General Psychiatry, 44,* 854–861.

Sacco, W. P., & Graves, D. J. (1984). Childhood depression, interpersonal problem-solving, and self-ratings of performance. *Journal of Clinical Child Psychology, 13,* 10–15.

Sacks, J. M. (1977). The need for subtlety: A critical session with a suicidal child. *Psychotherapy: Theory, Research, and Practice, 14,* 434–437.

Sanchez, V., Lewinsohn, P. M., & Larson, D. W. (1980). Assertion training: Effectiveness in the treatment of depression. *Journal of Clinical Psychology, 36,* 526–529.

Saylor, C. F., Finch, A. J., Baskin, C. H., Furey, W., & Kelly, M. M. (1984). Construct validity for measures of childhood depression: Application of multitrait-multimethod methodology. *Journal of Consulting and Clinical Psychology, 52,* 977–985.

Schmickley, V. G. (1976). The effects of cognitive-behavior modification upon depressed outpatients. *Dissertation Abstracts International, 37,* 987B-988B. (University Microfilms No. 76–18, 675).

Seligman, M. E. P. (1975). *Helplessness: On depression, development, and death.* San Francisco: W. H. Freeman.

Seligman, M. E. P. (1981). A learned helplessness point of view. In L. P. Rehm, (Ed.), *Behavior therapy for depression* (pp. 123–141). New York: Academic Press.

Seligman, M. E. P., Abramson, L. Y., Semmel, A., & von Baeyer, C. (1979). Depressive attributional style. *Journal of Abnormal Psychology, 88,* 242–247.

Seligman, M. E. P., Peterson, C., Kaslow, N. J., Tanenbaum, R. L., Alloy, L. B., & Abramson, L. Y. (1984). Attributional style and depressive symptoms among children. *Journal of Abnormal Psychology, 93,* 235–238.

Shaw, B. F. (1977). Comparison of cognitive therapy and behavior therapy in the treatment of depression. *Journal of Consulting and Clinical Psychology, 45,* 543–551.

Sokoloff, M. R., & Lubin, B. (1983). Depressive mood in adolescent, emotionally disturbed females: Reliability and validity of an adjective checklist (C-DACl). *Journal of Abnormal Child Psychology, 11,* 531–536.

Stark, K. D., Kaslow, N. J., & Reynolds, W. M. (1987). A comparison of the relative efficacy of self-control therapy and a behavioral problem-solving therapy for depression in children. *Journal of Abnormal Child Psychology, 15,* 91–113.

Strauss, C. C., Forehand, R., Smith, K., &

Frame, C. L. (1986). The association between social withdrawal and internalizing problems of children. *Journal of Abnormal Child Psychology, 14*, 525–535.

Taylor, F. A., & Marshall, W. L. (1977). Experimental analysis for a cognitive-behavioral therapy for depression. *Cognitive Therapy and Research, 1*, 59–72.

Tesiny, E. P., & Lefkowitz, M. M. (1982). Childhood depression: A 6-month follow-up study. *Journal of Consulting and Clinical Psychology, 50*, 778–780.

Tesiny, E. P., Lefkowitz, M. M., & Gordon, N. H. (1980). Childhood depression, locus of control, and school achievement. *Journal of Educational Psychology, 72*, 506–510.

Tisher, M., & Lang, M. (1983). The Children's Depression Scale: Review and further developments. In D. P. Cantwell & G. A. Carlson (Eds.), *Affective disorders in childhood and adolescence: An update* (pp. 375–415). New York: Spectrum.

Trad, P. V. (1987). *Infant and childhood depression*. New York: John Wiley & Sons.

Turner, R. W., Ward, M. F., & Turner, J. D. (1979). Behavioral treatment for depression: An evaluation of therapeutic components. *Journal of Clinical Psychology, 55*, 166–175.

Vosk, B., Forehand, R., Parker, J. B., & Rickard, K. (1982). A multimethod comparison of popular and unpopular children. *Developmental Psychology, 18*, 571–575.

Vygotsky, L. S. (1962). *Thought and language*. New York: John Wiley & Sons.

Ward, L. G., Friedlander, M. L., & Silverman, W. K. (1987). Children's depressive symptoms, negative self-statements, and causal attributions for success and failure. *Cognitive Therapy and Research, 11*, 215–227.

Weinberg, W. A., Rutman, J., Sullivan, L., Penick, E. C., & Dietz, S. G. (1973). Depression in children referred to an educational diagnostic center: Diagnosis and treatment. *The Journal of Pediatrics, 83*, 1065–1072.

Weinrott, M. R., Corson, J. A., & Wilchesky, M. (1979). Teacher-mediated treatment of social withdrawal. *Behavior Therapy, 10*, 281–294.

Weissman, M. M., Klerman, G. L., Paykel, E. S., Prusoff, B., & Hanson, B. (1974). Treatment effects on the social adjustment of depressed patients. *Archives of General Psychiatry, 30*, 771–778.

Weissman, M. M., Orvaschel, H., & Padian, N. (1980). Children's symptom and social functioning self-report scales: Comparison of mother's and children's reports. *Journal of Nervous and Mental Disease, 168*, 736–740.

Weissman, M. M., & Paykel, E. S. (1974). *The depressed woman: A study of social relationships*. Chicago: University of Chicago Press.

Weisz, J. R., Weiss, B., Wasserman, A. A., & Rintoul, B. (1987). Control-related beliefs and depression among clinic-referred children and adolescents. *Journal of Abnormal Psychology, 96*, 58–63.

Weller, E. B., & Weller, R. A. (Eds.) (1984). *Current perspectives on major depressive disorders in children*. Washington, DC: American Psychiatric Press.

Wells, K. C., Hersen, M., Bellock, A. S., & Himmelhoch, J. (1979). Social skills training in unipolar nonpsychotic depression. *American Journal of Psychiatry, 136*, 1131–1132.

Welner, Z. (1978). Childhood depression: An overview. *The Journal of Nervous and Mental Disease, 166*, 588–593.

Wener, A., & Rehm, L. P. (1975). Depressive affect: A test of behavioral hypotheses. *Journal of Abnormal Psychology, 84*, 221–227.

Werner, H. (1957). The concept of development from a comparative and organismic point of view. In D. Haris (Ed.), *The concept of development*. Minneapolis: University of Minnesota Press.

Wilkes, T. C. R., & Rush, A. J. (1988). Adaptations of cognitive therapy for depressed adolescents. *Journal of the American Academy of Child and Adolescent Psychiatry, 27*, 381–386.

Windle, M., Hooker, K., Lenerz, K., East, P. L., Lerner, J. V., & Lerner, R. M. (1986). Temperament, perceived competence and depression in early and late adolescents. *Development Psychology, 22*, 384–392.

Wirt, R. D., Lachar, D., Klinedinst, J. K., & Seat, P. D. (1977). *Multidimensional description of child personality: A manual for the Personality Inventory for Children*. Los Angeles: Western Psychological Services.

Wolpe, J. (1979). The experimental model and treatment of neurotic depression. *Behavior Research and Therapy, 17*, 555–566.

Zeiss, A. M., Lewinsohn, P. M., & Munoz, R. F. (1979). Nonspecific improvement effects in depression using interpersonal skills training, pleasant activity schedules, or cognitive training. *Journal of Consulting and Clinical Psychology, 47,* 427–439.

Zielinski, J. L. (1979). Behavioral treatments of depression with alcoholics receiving pharmacological aversion. *The Behavior Therapist, 2,* 25–27.

Zrull, J., McDermott, J., & Poznanski, E. (1970). Hyperkinetic syndrome: The role of depression. *Child Psychiatry and Human Development, 1,* 33–40.

CHAPTER 4

CHILDHOOD FEARS AND PHOBIAS

Richard J. Morris
Thomas R. Kratochwill

Concern with children's fears and phobias has increased tremendously on the part of mental-health professionals over the past 30 years—although it should be recognized that there has been a strong tradition in psychology of study and interest in this area (see Freud, 1909; Jones, 1924a, b; King, Hamilton, & Ollendick, 1988; Morris & Kratochwill, 1983; Watson & Rayner, 1920).

NORMATIVE AND PREVALENCE DATA

Fears are found in children from infancy through adolescence. Those fears seen in infancy typically occur as a reaction to something taking place in the infant's environment. As the child grows older, into the early school years, fears broaden and involve the dark, supernatural figures and particular persons, objects, and events. With increasing age, fears turn more toward imaginary figures, objects, and events as well as the future (e.g., schoolwork) (Jersild, 1968). These "age-related" fears are typically transitory in nature and of short duration; they vary in intensity both in any given child and from one child to another. Some typical childhood fears are listed in Table 4.1.

A number of studies have examined the incidence rates of children's fears within particular age ranges; however, much of this research is old and has numerous methodological problems. In addition, little normative research has been published on the incidence and prevalence of children's school-related fears (e.g., Morris, Kratochwill, & Aldridge, 1988). Jersild and Holmes (1935), for example, studied children ranging in age from 24 to 71 months; they found that such children had an average of 4.6 fears. In addition, they found the fading-out of some high-percentage fears (e.g., of dark rooms, large dogs, strange persons, and walking across high

The preparation of this chapter was supported, in part, by Grant #G008730074 to the first author from the U.S. Department of Education, Office of Special Education and Rehabilitation Services.

Table 4.1. Normative Data on Children's Fears

AGE	FEARS
0–6 months:	Loss of support, loud noises.
7–12 months:	Fear of strangers, fear of sudden, unexpected, and looming objects.
1 year:	Separation from parent, toilet, injury, strangers.
2 years:	A multitude of fears including loud noises (vacuum cleaners, sirens/alarms, trucks, and thunder), animals (e.g., large dogs), dark rooms, separation from parent, large objects/machines, change in personal environment.
3 years:	Masks, dark, animals, separation from parent.
4 years:	Parent separation, animals, dark, noises (including at night).
5 years:	Animals, "bad" people, dark, separation from parent, bodily harm.
6 years:	Supernatural beings (e.g., ghosts, witches, ghouls), bodily injuries, thunder, and lightning, dark, sleeping or staying along, separation from parent.
7–8 years:	Supernatural beings, dark, fears based on media events, staying alone, bodily injury.
9–12 years:	Tests and examinations in school, school performance, bodily injury, physical appearance, thunder and lightning, death, dark (low percentage).

Source: Ilg & Ames, 1955; Jersild & Holmes, 1935a; Kellerman, 1981; Lapouse & Monk, 1959; Scarr & Salapatek, 1970. From *Treating children's fears and phobias: A behavioral approach* (p. 2) by R. J. Morris, & T. R. Kratochwill, 1983, Elmsford, NY: Pergamon Press. Copyright 1983 by Pergamon Press. Reprinted by permission.

boards) as the children grew older and maintenance of other fears (e.g., snakes). Although Jersild and Holmes (1935) found that children's fears were relatively transient, some later research findings have questioned these investigators' conclusions. For example, Eme and Schmidt (1978) conducted a 1-year longitudinal study of 27 children. These authors found that the fears in these children were quite stable in type identified and number. Specifically, 83% of the fears identified by these children were still present at the end of a year. The difference in the results of these two studies may be related to the age differences of the two samples, methodological variations between the two studies, and the differing socialization factors of the 1930s as opposed to the 1970s (Harris & Ferrari, 1983). In another study, Lapouse and Monk (1959) investigated the fears and worries of 482 children between the ages of 6 and 12. They also found clear prevalence of children's fears within this older age group. For example, parents of children between the ages of 6 and 12 reported that 43% of their children experienced at least seven or more fears—and significantly more girls than boys reported having them. More recent studies by Ollendick and his colleagues (e.g., Ollendick, 1983; Ollendick, Matson, & Helsel, 1985) report an even larger average number of fears in children and youth—11 fears for children between 8 and 11 years of age and 13 for children and adolescents between 7 and 18 years of age. Moreover, Graziano and Mooney (1984) indicate from their review of the literature, that girls generally obtain higher fear scores than boys, although some findings do not support this conclusion with some age groups (e.g., Eme & Schmidt, 1978). During the adolescent years, however, it appears that girls do, in fact, report more fears, as well as different types of fears than do boys (e.g., Morris, Kratochwill, & Dodson, 1986; Ollendick et al., 1985).

With regard to phobias and/or severe fears, the literature is more sparse. For example, Miller, Barrett, and Hampe (1974) report that intense or excessive fears occurred in about 5% of their sample of children ranging in age from 7 to 12. Similarly, Graham, as cited in Marks (1969), reports that only 4% of the children referred for treatment had phobias. Rutter, Tizard, and Whitmore's (1970) prevalence data were only slightly higher (about 7%), as were those of Graziano and DeGiovanni (1979) regarding those children with clinical fears or phobias who were referred to behavior therapists for treatment. With regard to "school phobia," Kennedy (1965) reports that 17 out of 1,000 children (1.7%) experience this problem. This rate, however, has been questioned by Trueman (1984) because no source for this rate was provided by Kennedy. Other estimates of "school phobia" in those children referred to clinics have ranged from 0.04% (Eisenberg, 1958) to 8% (Kahn & Nursten, 1962) of all referrals. Even though these various incidence studies differ in their definitions of severe fear, clinical fear, phobia, and related problems, each study reports that the prevalence of intense fears (i.e., those necessitating clinical intervention) and/or phobias among children is equal to or less than 8% of the number of referrals to a clinician or in the general child population.

FEARS VERSUS PHOBIAS

Although the meaning of the terms "phobia" and "phobic reaction" might seem clear, the literature reveals a good deal of confusion between them and others, such as "fear," "anxiety," "stress," "refusal behavior," and "avoidance behavior." All these terms are used differently at different times. The term "fear," for example, is often used in the child development literature to refer to a *normal* reaction to a real or perceived threat. For instance, a child may develop a fear of dentists' offices because of actual pain experienced during a dental procedure. However, in the child behavior-disorders/psychopathology literature, the term "fear" is sometimes used within the context of a normal developmental reaction and at other times as a clinical problem (see, for example, Kessler, 1972; Lippman, 1967).

In an attempt to differentiate the terms "fear" and "phobia," Marks (1969) suggested that phobia should be considered a subcategory of fear that:

1. Is out of proportion to demands of the situation.
2. Cannot be explained or reasoned away.
3. Is beyond voluntary control.
4. Leads to avoidance of the feared situation.

To these criteria, Miller et al. (1974) add that a phobia "persists over an extended period of time . . . is unadaptive . . . [and] is not age or stage specific" (p. 90). This differentiation between fear and phobia—with the additional Miller et al. criteria—is among the most widely used definition of "phobia" (e.g., King et al., 1988). Phobias have also been referred to as *clinical fears*—usually also on the basis of the above criteria. Graziano, DeGiovanni, and Garcia

(1979), however, suggest that such fears "be defined as those with a duration of over 2 years, or an intensity that is debilitating to the client's routine life style" (p. 805).

Although phobias involve the observing of or direct involvement with a traumatic or aversive event, this is not always the case. In some instances, no observable aversive antecedent event precedes the phobic response. For example, some preadolescent children who refuse to stay alone in their homes have never had an identified negative experience associated with being alone. Similarly, many adolescent children who refuse to sleep in their bedroom at night without having a lamp on (versus having on a small night light) have never had any traumatic event associated with their bedroom lights being off. In such cases, an unpleasant fantasy/image/movie may be the antecedent factor. Again, all these fears fall into the subcategory of phobic behavior according to the Marks (1969) and Miller et al. (1974) criteria. However, controversy does exist regarding the differentiation of "fear" from "phobia." Suffice it to say that there is no unanimity among researchers and/or practitioners regarding the denotative operations associated with the definition of each term (Kratochwill & Morris, 1985).

ASSESSMENT OF FEARS AND PHOBIAS

Typically, the area of childhood fears and phobias is divided into two assessment categories: behavioral and traditional. However, this is somewhat of an oversimplification, because there is often a great deal of overlap in actual techniques and practice. Nevertheless, the major differences between these two positions emanates from the *assumptions* underlying each approach's view of human behavior (e.g., Barrios, 1988; Nelson & Hayes, 1979). For example, individuals working within the traditional view typically focus fear assessment toward identifying underlying causes. In contrast, behavioral assessors typically focus on environmental or person–environmental events as they relate to the development of a treatment program. Behavioral assessment can be further distinguished from more traditional forms of assessment on many other dimensions. For example, within the context of childhood fears and related problems, traditional assessment approaches have tended to emphasize intraorganismic variables to account for these disorders. In such assessment, traditional approaches focus more heavily on constructs where overt behavior (e.g., behavioral avoidance) is considered a *sign* of underlying pathology and the *situation* in which the client is assessed is of less or little importance. It is important to recognize, however, that traditional assessment is not a uniform approach with consistent models and techniques (Korchin & Schuldberg, 1981). For example, traditional approaches include both psychodynamic and trait models.

Because the assessment and treatment of children's fears and related problems represents a diverse set of procedures and practices, it would be beyond the scope of this chapter to discuss in detail all the various techniques that have evolved from various etiological positions. We have chosen, therefore, to focus specifically on behaviorally oriented procedures. The rationale for this focus is based on the very large number of empirical studies that have been published over the past 25 to 30 years supporting the use of this approach in the areas of assessment and treatment of children's fears and phobias (see, for example, King et al., 1988; Kratochwill, Accardi, & Morris, 1988; Morris & Kratochwill, 1983).

Behavioral Assessment: A Conceptual Framework

A diverse set of procedures and techniques characterize contemporary behavioral assessment (see, for example, Bellack & Hersen, 1988; Frame & Matson, 1987; Mash & Terdal, 1988). An increasingly popular conceptualization of fear (and/or anxiety) assessment in the child (and adult) literature was formally introduced by Lang (1968) and has been variously labeled the "triple response mode" (e.g., Cone, 1979), "multiple response components" (e.g, Nietzel & Bernstein, 1981), or "three-response system" (e.g., Kozak & Miller, 1982). The position is that fear and/or anxiety is a complex multichannel response pattern of behavior or emotion that includes motoric, cognitive, and physiological components (e.g., Barrios & Hartmann, 1988; Francis & Ollendick, 1987). These response patterns are not always highly correlated, but they are often related to some extent (e.g., Barrios & O'Dell, 1989; Hodgson & Rachman, 1974; Rachman & Hodgson, 1974). This implies that changes in one response channel may not be reflected by or lead to changes in another response channel, but also that results obtained in one channel may have important implications for the type of data one might obtain from a different channel.

A child or adolescent may therefore display his or her fear or phobia in any one or in all three channels. Therefore, a thorough behavioral assessment should tap responses in all three areas. Moreover, the clinician should be aware that the response channel that is most troublesome to a significant adult in the child's life may not necessarily be the one that is of most concern to the child. Thus, assessment data must be gathered from at least the target child and his or her parent (or, in the school setting, his or her teacher).

To provide a perspective on this approach for assessing child and adolescent fears and phobias, we briefly review the three response channels.

Cognitive Channel

One system or channel used to define anxiety is the cognitive system. This is regarded as a subjective system in that it depends upon the self-report of the client to validate its existence. The self-report may come through direct statements to another through self-monitoring data or from retrospective responses to structured questionnaire items (e.g., fear surveys).

Virtually every therapeutic approach reviewed in this chapter considers self-report as an important source of data to define the concept of fear, phobia, and anxiety. There is, however, considerable variation in the emphasis placed on this system in definition of fear within the behavior therapy field. For example, cognitive-behavioral therapists have tended to place much greater emphasis on self-report data than applied behavior analysts, who have generally been critical of the exclusive reliance on this data source. However, we regard the self-report channel as important to the definition, assessment, and treatment efforts of behaviorally oriented service providers.

Physiological Channel

The physiological channel focuses on measurement of the sympathetic portion of the autonomic nervous system (e.g., Nietzel & Bernstein, 1981). Fear in this channel is assessed by a variety of measures that focus on the autonomic nervous system (heart rate, blood pressure, galvanic skin response or GSR). Usually, more than one physiological measure is used to define fear and anxiety in this system. The reason for this is that different physiological assessment measures may not correlate highly (Haynes, 1978).

Motor Channel

The third channel is referred to as motor or overt behavior. Measurement here focuses on the client's actual overt behavior. This channel has been divided into *direct* and *indirect* measures (Paul & Bernstein, 1973). Direct measures involve the overt behavioral consequences of physiological arousal. For example, if a child was trembling in the presence of a particular stimulus (e.g., a dog, water), this would be a direct measure defining the presence of anxiety. Indirect measures include escape and/or avoidance behaviors from certain stimuli (e.g., running away from a horse).

Considerations

The three-channel perspective is gaining wide acceptance in the research on and behavioral treatment of fears and phobias (e.g., Barrios, 1988; Barrios & O'Dell, 1989). Indeed, a multiple-response framework has been suggested as one of the major characteristics of behavior therapy in general (Kazdin & Hersen, 1980). Despite the popularity of this approach, many writers have raised important questions in its use (e.g., Cone, 1979; Hugdahl, 1981; Kozak & Miller, 1982). For example, a major problem raised by the three-response system relates to the criteria used for definition. When the three systems are monitored, it cannot be assumed that they are highly correlated (Cone, 1979; Bellack & Hersen, 1977a, 1977b), and this may be especially true with clinically significant emotions such as fears. Another major concern with the three-system approach is that different writers have used different terms and meanings in defining aspects of the systems. This has particularly been the case in regard to the subjective status of the fear experience (Kozak & Miller, 1982). For example, researchers and practitioners may equate verbal expression with cognitions, but there may be great differences between what people "say and think." When verbal and cognitive behaviors are equated, cognition or emotion may be empirically untenable. Aside from this problem with variation in definitions

of certain systems, comparisons across studies become very difficult (Hugdahl, 1981).

A third problem raised by the three-system model is the limited number of dimensions for fear assessment that might be used in clinical research and practice. As Kozak and Miller (1982) note, "the *assessor* may be tempted to think that there are only three *things* to be measured and that getting a number for each system sufficiently measures fear" (p. 352). Thus, the usual methods for assessing the three channels (i.e., physiological arousal, overt behavior, and verbal reports) do not measure unitary phenomena.

A final concern with this approach relates to matching treatments to the systems. A common assumption has been that different treatments may be necessary for different levels of fear within the three-response system. For example, a child with high "cognitive" fear may be exposed to a cognitive intervention, while a person with behavioral avoidance ("motoric" fear) could be treated with reinforced practice (e.g., Leitenberg & Callahan, 1973). Yet, such a conclusion may be problematic, because avoidance behavior is usually present in all clinical phobias. Thus, one could question whether the behavioral component is a discrete system (Hugdahl, 1981). In the future, it may be possible to develop specific treatments based on certain response patterns within each system. Currently, there is a paucity of research in this area involving children and adolescents.

Assessment Methods

The assessment methods or procedures used to gather data can be ordered along a continuum of directness representing the extent to which they measure a behavior at the time and place of its natural occurrence (Cone, 1978). Within this framework, interviews, self-report questionnaires, and behavior checklists and rating scales are regarded as indirect measures because they are verbal representations of more clinically relevant activities that occur at some other time and place. However, self-monitoring observations, direct observation, and physiological recordings represent direct measures of behavior because the assessment occurs at the time of the natural occurrence of the behavior.

In using any of these assessment procedures within the three-channel system, it is important to draw a distinction between the mode of measurement and the content response channel that it is designed to assess (Barrios, Hartmann, & Shigetomi, 1981; Cone, 1978). In this regard, the three behavioral content areas can be measured by a technique or device whose mode is motor, cognitive, or physiological. For example, a child might be assessed on the motor component of a fear of water through an interview in which he or she was asked questions regarding approach behaviors toward a lake or pond. Data obtained through the interview therefore assess motor behavior indirectly. The child may also be assessed through direct observation via an in vivo behavioral avoidance test, wherein the clinician accompanies the child to a lake.

It is also important to note that many questionnaires and rating scales may actually measure more than one channel within the same instrument. Thus, a self-report scale may include items that provide a measure of the motoric response channel, but it may also include items that refer only to cognitions or physiological responses.

Finally, it is important to emphasize that some measurement strategies represent only theoretical possibilities within the framework presented by Cone (1977). For example, cognitive activities cannot be measured using ratings or direct observation by others.

FEAR REDUCTION METHODS

In recent years, there has been a rapid proliferation of research on the development and application of fear reduction methods with children (see, for example, reviews by Barrios & O'Dell, 1989; Francis & Ollendick, 1987; Graziano et al., 1979; Hatzenbuehler & Schroeder, 1978; Johnson, 1979; King et al., 1988; Kratochwill et al., 1988; Miller, Barrett, & Hampe, 1974; Morris et al., 1986, 1988; Ollendick, 1979b, 1986). The assumptions underlying these approaches have generally taken a behavioral orientation. There are currently four major behavior therapy methods of fear reduction in children; systematic desensitization (including variations of this procedure), contingency management procedures, modeling procedures, and cognitive-behavioral interventions (King et al., 1988; McReynolds, Morris, & Kratochwill, 1989; Morris & Kratochwill, 1983; Ramirez, Kratochwill, & Morris, 1987).

Systematic Desensitization

Systematic desensitization, developed in the early 1950s by Joseph Wolpe, is one of the most frequently used behavior therapy procedures for reducing children's fears and phobias (King et al., 1988; Morris & Kratochwill, 1983, 1985; Morris et al., 1988). The basic assumption of this technique is that a fear response can be inhibited by substituting an activity that is antagonistic to it. The response that is most typically inhibited by this treatment process is anxiety, and the response frequently substituted for it is relaxation and calmness.

The desensitization process involves exposing the child in small, graduated steps to the feared situation or event as she or he is performing an activity antagonistic to anxiety. The gradual exposure to the feared (or avoided) stimulus can take place either in the child's cognitions, where she or he is asked to imagine being in various target fear-related situations. Or the child may be asked to pretend that he or she is a popular superhero who approaches the feared situation while performing his or her "usual" superhero-related activities. Finally, the exposure can occur in real life (i.e., in vivo). Wolpe (1958) termed the principle that underlies the desensitization process *reciprocal inhibition*. He described this principle in the following way: "If a response inhibitory to anxiety can be made to occur in the presence of anxiety-evoking stimuli, it will weaken the connection between these stimuli and the anxiety responses" (Wolpe, 1962, p. 562).

There are essentially three phases to systematic desensitization: (1) relaxation training, (2) development of the anxiety hierarchy, and (3) systematic desensitization proper.

Relaxation Training

The first step in relaxation training is to let the child become very comfortable within the setting in which the desensitization procedure will be performed. Following this, the relaxation steps listed in Table 4.2 are initiated by the therapist. These steps represent a modified version of a technique developed by Jacobson (1938) for inducing deep muscle relaxation. The wording of each step should be adapted to each child's developmental level. The whole procedure usually takes about 20 to 25 minutes to complete, each step taking about 6 to 10 seconds, with a

Table 4.2. An Introduction to the Relaxation Training Steps of Systematic Desensitization

---

STEPS IN RELAXATION

---

1. Take a deep breath and hold it (for about 10 seconds). Hold it. Okay, let it out.
2. Raise both of your hands about halfway above the couch (or arms of the chair) and breathe normally. Now, drop your hands to the couch (or down).
3. Now hold your arms out and make a tight fist. Really tight. Feel the tension in your hands. I am going to count to three and when I say "three" I want you to drop your hands. One . . . Two . . . Three.
4. Raise your arms again, and bend your fingers back the other way (toward your body). Now drop your hands and relax.
5. Raise your arms. Now drop them and relax.
6. Now raise your arms again, but this time "flap" your hands around. Okay, relax again.
7. Raise your arms again. Now relax.
8. Raise your arms above the couch (chair) again and tense your biceps. Breathe normally, and keep your hands loose. Relax your hands. (Notice how you have a warm feeling of relaxation.)
9. Now hold your arms out to your side and tense your triceps. Make sure that you breathe normally. Relax your arms.
10. Now arch your shoulders back. Hold it. Make sure that your arms are relaxed. Now relax.
11. Hunch your shoulders forward. Hold it, and make sure that you breathe normally and keep your arms relaxed. Okay, relax. (Notice the feeling of relief from tensing and relaxing your muscles.)
12. Now turn your head to the right and tense your neck. Relax and bring your head back again to its natural position.
13. Turn your head to the left and tense your neck. Relax and bring your head back again to its natural position.
14. Now bend your head back slightly toward the chair. Hold it. Okay, now bring your head back slowly to its natural position.*
15. This time bring your head down almost to your chest. Hold it. Now relax and let your head come back to its natural resting position.
16. Now, open your mouth as much as possible. A little wider, okay, relax. (Mouth should be partly open afterwards.)
17. Now tense your lips by closing your mouth. Okay, relax.
18. Put your tongue at the roof of your mouth. Press hard. (Pause) Relax and allow your tongue to come to a comfortable position in your mouth.
19. Now put your tongue at the bottom of your mouth. Press down hard. Relax and let your tongue come to a comfortable position in your mouth.
20. Now just lie (sit) there and relax. Try not to think of anything.
21. To control self-verbalizations, I want you to go through the motions of singing a high note—not aloud! Okay, start singing to yourself. Hold that note. Okay, relax. (You are becoming more and more relaxed.)
22. Now sing a medium tone and make your vocal cords tense again. Relax.
23. Now sing a low note and make your vocal cords tense again. Relax. (Your vocal apparatus should be relaxed now. Relax your mouth.)
24. Now close your eyes. Squeeze them tight and breathe naturally. Notice the tension. Now relax. (Notice how the pain goes away when you relax.)
25. Now let your eyes relax and keep your mouth open slightly.
26. Open your eyes as much as possible. Hold it. Now relax your eyes.
27. Now wrinkle your forehead as much as possible. Hold it. Okay, relax.
28. Now take a deep breath and hold it. Relax.
29. Now exhale. Breathe all the air out . . . all of it out. Relax. (Notice the wondrous feeling of breathing again.)
30. Imagine that there are weights pulling on all your muscles making them flaccid and relaxed . . . pulling your arms and body down into the couch.
31. Pull your stomach muscles together. Tighter. Okay, relax.
32. Now extend your muscles as if you were a prizefighter. Make your stomach hard. Relax. (You are becoming more and more relaxed.)
33. Now tense your buttocks. Tighter. Hold it. Now relax.
34. Now search the upper part of your body and relax any part that is tense. First the facial muscles. (Pause 3 to 5 sec.) Then the vocal muscles. (Pause 3 to 5 sec.) The neck region. (Pause 3 to 5 sec.) Your shoulders . . relax any part that is tense. (Pause) Now the arms and fingers. Relax these. Becoming very relaxed.
35. Maintaining this relaxation, raise both your legs (about a 45° angle). Now relax. (Notice that this further relaxes you.)
36. Now bend your feet back so that your toes point toward your face. Relax your mouth. Bend them hard. Relax.
37. Bend your feet the other way . . . away from your body. Not far. Notice the tension. Okay, relax.
38. Relax. (Pause) Now curl your toes together as hard as you can. Tighter. Okay, relax. (Quiet . . . silence for about 30 seconds.)
39. This completes the formal relaxation procedure. Now explore your body from your feet up. Make sure that every muscle is relaxed. (Say slowly)—first your toes, your feet, your legs, buttocks, stomach, shoulders, neck, eyes, and finally your forehead—all should be relaxed now. (Quiet—silence for about ten seconds). Just lie there and feel very relaxed, noticing the warmness of the relaxation. (Pause) I would like you to stay this way for about one more minute, and then I am going to count to five. When I reach five, I want you to open your eyes feeling very calm and refreshed. (Quiet—silence for about one minute.) Okay, when I count to five I want you to open your eyes feeling very calm and refreshed. One . . . feeling very calm; two . . . very calm, very refreshed; three . . . very refreshed; four . . . and five.

---

*The child should not be encouraged to bend his or her neck either all the way back or forward.
NOTE: Adapted in part from Jacobson (1938), Rimm (1967, personal communication), and Wolpe and Lazarus (1966).
From *Treating children's fears and phobias: A behavioral approach* (p. 2) by R. J. Morris and T. R. Kratochwill, 1983, Elmsford, NY: Pergamon Press. Copyright 1983 by Pergamon Press. Reprinted by permission.

10- to 15-second pause between each step. During the first few relaxation training sessions, it is often helpful for the therapist to practice the relaxation procedure with the children, so that they can observe how to perform a particular step correctly. It may also be helpful, before training begins, for the therapist to explain to children what changes they will begin to experience in their bodies during relaxation training. This becomes especially important for those children the therapist feels have never (or rarely) experienced a waking "relaxed state."

The therapist may also have to guide the child physically at first in performing some of the steps, gradually letting this assistance fade out. Also, the therapist should make sure that she or he paces the presentation of each step to the child's readiness to perform each step. It may be found that certain steps will have to be presented and practiced many times before the child achieves mastery.

Once the child has gained a medium level of proficiency at relaxation training (usually after three or more sessions), the therapist should encourage the child to practice the relaxation method at home or during a quiet time at school (e.g., Bergland & Chal, 1972; King et al., 1988). The practice sessions should last 10 to 15 minutes per session and take place at least twice per day. To enhance the child's practice, some therapists record the relaxation procedure on an audio cassette tape and have the child or adolescent play the tape during each day's practice. Others (e.g., Koeppen, 1974) include fantasy play in the relaxation exercise to maintain the child's involvement in the task. For example, to help the child relax the jaw and lower facial muscles, the therapist might have the child pretend that she or he is a big tired lion who is taking "a great big yawn" because he or she is so sleepy. Some therapists also provide the child, where it seems appropriate, with a list of the muscle groups and encourage the child's parents and/or teachers to practice the relaxation procedure with the child.

Some children cannot relax using this training method. No matter how motivated they are, they just find it difficult to respond—or find the training instructions too complex to comprehend and/or carry out. A few children even avoid relaxation and/or report feeling tense when they engage in relaxation training. Some behaviors associated with children who are *not* relaxed are rapid and/or uneven breathing, hands clenching chair, finger tapping, giggling, smiling, fidgeting, repeatedly opening eyes and/or squeezing eyes closed, and frequent yawning (e.g., Luiselli, 1980; Morris & Kratochwill, 1983). To deal with a person's difficulty in learning to relax, Morris (1973) proposed a shaping procedure to teach children and adults to close their eyes for increasingly longer periods of time during the relaxation training session. Similarly, Cautela and Groden (1978) discuss the use of shaping to assist children in learning how to tense and then relax particular muscle groupings. They also suggest using various squeeze toys to help children (especially some special-needs children) in learning how to tense their arms and hands, as well as the use of certain air-flow toys (e.g., whistles, party horns, harmonicas, bubble pipes, etc.) to teach the breathing-step portions of relaxation training programs. Although adjunctive methods such as biofeedback-assisted relaxation (e.g., Javel & Denholtz, 1975; Reeves & Maelica, 1975; Tarler-Benlolo, 1978), hypnosis, or carbon dioxide-oxygen (Wolpe & Lazarus, 1966; Wolpe, 1973) and the administration of such drugs as Brevital (Brady, 1966, 1972; Friedman, 1966) have been recommended by some writers to assist adult clients in achieving relaxation, there is currently no organized body of literature that supports their use with children.

Development of the Anxiety Hierarchy

During the relaxation phase, the therapist should begin planning an anxiety hierarchy with the child (and, where appropriate, with his or her parents) for each of the target fears identified as needing to be reduced. A hierarchy is usually constructed on only those fears that the child and therapist agree upon as being in need of change during or immediately following the initial assessment and diagnosis period. The therapist should not impose treatment on a child for a fear that she or he has not agreed is in need of being reduced.

Typically, the client and/or the parents are given ten 3- by 5-inch index cards and asked to write down, on each card, a brief description of different situations regarding the fear that produces certain levels of anxiety or tension. Specifically, the child is asked to describe on the cards those situations that are related to his or her fear and that she or he feels produce increasing amounts of anxiety, tension, or discomfort. Each of the 10 cards is assigned a number that is a multiple of 10 (i.e., 10, 20, 30, 40, ..., 100), with the card having the value of 100 containing a description of the most anxiety-provoking situation.

When the child returns with the prepared hierarchy, the therapist goes through it with the child and adds intermediate items whenever it seems appropriate. Children's hierarchies often differ markedly from each other—even those having to do with the same type of fear. Hierarchies vary on such factors as the child's unique interpretation of the events occurring in the feared situations, the number and type of people present in the feared situations, temporal and/or spatial considerations, type of environment in which the fear might occur, level of embarrassment that the child might feel if placed in or exposed to the fear situation, and degree to which the child feels she or he can escape from or leave the feared situation without being noticed by others.

The final hierarchy usually takes at least part of two or three sessions to develop and should represent a slow and smooth gradation of anxiety-provoking situations, each of which the child can easily imagine. Most hierarchies contain 20 to 25 items. It is not unusual, however, for those hierarchies that represent a very specific fear (e.g., fear of becoming sick while riding in a car, fear of being alone in the house, or fear of entering a pool) to contain fewer items, while those representing a more complex fear (e.g., fear of being evaluated, fear of robbers entering the home, fear of school, fear of losing control, or fear of using a public toilet) contain more items.

While developing the final hierarchy, the therapist should also determine what the child considers to be a very relaxing situation—one that the child can easily imagine and that she or he would rate as a zero on the hierarchy. Some examples of "zero-level" scenes are:

> Reading a good novel in bed before going to sleep.
> Watching *Sesame Street* (favorite television program).
> Having my Daddy read to me when I go to bed at night.
> Playing in the swimming pool.
> Out riding my bicycle in the neighborhood.
> Playing a video game on our home computer.
> Going hiking in the woods.
> Playing with my train set.
>
> (Adapted from Morris & Kratochwill, 1983, p. 141)

Although most children who understand and master relaxation training are capable of constructing an anxiety hierarchy, on rare occasions a child does not comprehend the notion of an anxiety hierarchy, and, therefore, is not able to assist the therapist in formulating his or her hierarchy (e.g., Stedman & Murphey, 1984). In such cases, the therapist should switch to an alternative fear reduction method that is more concrete in nature.

Systematic Desensitization Proper

By the time the therapist is ready to begin the desensitization proper sessions, the child should have had sufficient time to practice relaxation and be proficient at relaxing on command. If the child has developed several hierarchies, the therapist should first work on the one that is most distressing to the child. Then, if time allows, the therapist can work on others.

The first desensitization session starts with having the child spend about 3 to 5 minutes relaxing on a couch or in a recliner. The child is also asked to indicate, by raising his or her right index finger, when a very relaxing and comfortable state has been achieved.

After the child signals, the therapist asks him or her to visualize a number of scenes from the hierarchy that the two of them have developed over the past few sessions. The therapist asks the child to imagine each scene as clearly and as vividly as possible—"As if you were really there"—while still maintaining a very relaxed state. If the child feels the least bit of anxiety or tension in imagining a particular scene, she or he is told to signal immediately with the right finger. If the child signals, the therapist presents the zero-level scene and then reviews with the child the steps in the relaxation sequence until the feeling of tension is gone.

Each hierarchy scene is presented three to four times, with a maximum exposure time of 5 seconds for the first presentation, and with a gradual increase up to 10 seconds for subsequent presentations. The hierarchy items are presented first in ascending order, starting with the least feared item with relaxation periods between each scene varying from 10 to 15 seconds. In most cases, three to four different scenes are presented per session. This means that a particular desensitization session will last between 15 and 20 minutes.

After the last scene for a particular session is presented and if the decision is not to go on to another fear hierarchy, the therapist usually asks the child to relax for a short time before ending the session.

The same general format is followed for all subsequent desensitization sessions. Each scene should be presented until the child has had three consecutive successes. If, however, the child has two consecutive failures (indications of anxiety), the therapist should go back to the previous successfully passed scene and work back up the hierarchy again. If failure occurs again, the previously successful scene should be presented again so that the child ends the session with a positive experience. Following this, it is often helpful to review with the child the problems she or he was having with the difficult scene.

Additional Considerations

Although there has been a substantial amount of clinical and "analogue" research conducted with adults on those factors that contribute to the effectiveness of systematic desensitization, relatively little controlled research of this nature has been done with children (see, for example, Barrios & O'Dell, 1989; Graziano et al., 1979; King et al., 1988; Morris & Kratochwill, 1983). Client factors that may contribute to the effectiveness of systematic desensitization therapy with children include the following: age of child receiving treatment, child's level of visual imagery, his or her ability to relax, child's and parents' motivation level regarding a desire to reduce the fear or phobia, child's ability to follow instructions, child's level of acquiescence, and child's threshold of fatigue (see, for example, Kissel, 1972). Regarding the age factor, very few studies report the successful use of systematic desensitization with children under 9 years of age. Little if any research has been conducted on the other client factors listed above (see, for example, Morris & Kratochwill, 1983; 1985).

As in the case of client variables, little research with children has studied variables involving the therapist or the setting and their effect on the outcome of systematic desensitization. Some research of this type has been conducted with adults (see, for example, Morris & Magrath, 1983; Morris & Suckerman, 1974a, 1974b, 1976), but it is not clear whether these findings can be transferred to the conduct of systematic desensitization with children and adolescents.

Supportive Research

As stated earlier in this chapter, systematic desensitization is one of the most frequently used procedures to reduce children's fears (see, for example, Barrios & O'Dell, 1989; Graziano et al., 1979; King et al., 1988). Mann and Rosenthal (1969), for example, compared direct (systematic) and vicarious (children observing other children receiving treatment) desensitization in individual and group treatment settings with a no treatment control group. The children in the treatment groups consisted of 50 seventh graders, while the children in the control group were 21 eighth-graders. Compared to the control group, the treatment groups showed a significantly greater reduction in their respective self-report test anxiety scores and a significant improvement in their performance on a reading test. No significant differences, however, were found between the individual or group, direct or vicarious desensitization methods.

With regard to other school-related fears, Taylor (1972) reported the successful use of systematic desensitization with a 15-year-old girl who was "school-phobic." The case was especially interesting since the girl engaged in excessive urination during school and in school-related activities, contributing to her avoidance of school and withdrawal from social relationships. Her anxiety hierarchies involved three themes: riding in the school bus, being in school, and participating in class activities. A 4-month follow-up evaluation indicated that she was no longer experiencing frequent urination and that she had satisfactory relationships in school.

Miller (1972) treated a 10-year-old boy who was reluctant to go to school and experienced "extreme fear" of being separated from his mother as well as a fear of his own death. Using systematic desensitization, Miller found that the child's fear of separating from his mother decreased gradually over the 11 treatment weeks. Systematic desensitization was also effective in reducing the boy's school phobia, but failed to decrease his fear of his own death. Lazarus (1960) also treated a school-phobic child with systematic desensitization. Following her ninth birthday, the girl became enuretic and afraid of the dark. She also developed "violent" abdominal pains at school, which eventually resulted in her being excused from class and her mother having to come to school. It was determined that her multiple fears were the result of her fear of being separated from her mother. Desensitization took five sessions over a 10-day period. A 15-month follow-up revealed a "very occasional" enuretic incident with no reported school-related problems.

In another case study, Kushner (1965) used systematic desensitization to reduce the fears of a 17-year-old youth who feared driving his car, being driven by others, and being around cars. After three treatment sessions, the client reported feeling better. At the sixth and last session the client felt 90% improved. At the 3-month follow-up, there was further improvement and no recurrence of his fears. MacDonald (1975) also reported the successful use of systematic desensitization with an 11-year-old boy who had a dog phobia, which had lasted for 8 years. By the sixth session, the boy reported staying outdoors without worrying about dogs, and at the fourteenth session, his parents reported that he was engaging in appropriate interactions in both benign and threatening dog encounters. In addition to the use of desensitization, MacDonald added some adjuncts to treatment: for example, dog pictures in the boy's room, asking the boy to write a happy story about himself and a dog, listening to an audiotape recording of barking dogs, providing skill training regarding interacting with dogs, and engaging in programmed outdoor activity. The results were maintained at 2-year follow-up.

An adjunct to systematic desensitization was also used in a study by Saunders (1976) involving a 13-year-old boy who developed motion sickness and vomiting during trips in cars or buses. In addition to the standard desensitization method, Saunders added an in vivo relaxation component, where the boy approached and sat in a vehicle. Treatment was completed in 11 sessions over a 4-month period. At the 19-month follow-up period, the child reported feeling no nausea, that he was able to take a long trip with his family, and that he was able to ride the bus to school.

Each of the studies described can best be described as clinical/descriptive case studies. Only a very few controlled single-subject time-series experiments have been published. For example, Van Hasselt, Hersen, Bellack, Rosenblum, and Lamparski (1979) used systematic desensitization with an 11-year-old boy who had fears of blood, heights, and taking tests. The authors measured the boy's motoric, cognitive, and physiological responses to each fear. Treatment lasted for four relaxation sessions and four

to six desensitization sessions for each fear. Although relaxation training did not appreciably change any of the dependent measures, systematic desensitization was found to effect changes on all but the physiological measure. A second controlled study by Ollendick (1979a) also demonstrated the effectiveness of systematic desensitization. Using a withdrawal design, Ollendick treated a 16-year-old anorexic youth who feared gaining weight and subsequent criticism from his peers. While the desensitization procedure was in effect, the adolescent gained weight, and when the procedure was withdrawn, he began to lose weight. When desensitization was reinstated, he began gaining weight again—thereby demonstrating experimental control of the desensitization procedure. Following the completion of the use of desensitization, an adjunctive weight-maintenance-enhancing procedure was introduced. At the 18-month follow-up, the weight gain was maintained, while at the 2-year follow-up a slight decrease in weight was found.

Systematic desensitization treatment has also been used with children and adolescents who are handicapped. For example, Obler and Terwilliger (1970) worked with a group of neurologically impaired children who had a "severe monophobic disorder" involving either dogs or the use of a public bus. The 30 children were assigned randomly either to a treatment or to a no-treatment control condition, with each condition subdivided further into retarded ("minimally aware" of treatment procedures) and non-retarded ("aware" of treatment procedures) groups. The subjects in each condition were also matched for age, sex, intelligence, and phobic diagnosis. The IQ of the retarded children ranged from 50 to 70 in the treatment condition and 57 to 73 in the control condition. The authors used a modified Wolpean systematic desensitization procedure, involving in vivo exposure plus social (and later, tangible) reinforcement for approaching the feared object. Although no formal anxiety hierarchy was constructed, Obler and Terwilliger (1970) indicated that a hierarchy "was determined arbitrarily" by the therapist. The results showed that all the children in the treatment condition were rated by parents as improved, whereas only 30% of the no-treatment children were so rated. When a more stringent success criterion was used, 53.3% of the treatment children were rated as improved, whereas none of the control children were so rated. Approximately the same result was also found, using the more stringent criterion, between the two subgroups of mentally retarded children—with the treatment subjects rated as 60% improved and the control subjects rated as 0% improved. Obler and Terwilliger (1970) concluded that the modified systematic desensitization procedure "significantly affected" the treatment outcome. Unfortunately, no follow-up or generalization data were provided.

In vivo desensitization has also been used successfully in the reduction of an "extreme toilet phobia" in a 5⅔-year-old boy who was diagnosed as autistic and borderline mentally retarded (Wilson & Jackson, 1980), in a 21-year-old moderately mentally retarded man with a long-standing mannequin phobia (Waranch, Iwata, Wohl, & Nidiffer, 1981), and in a 7½ year-old mildly retarded boy who had a fear of physical examinations (Freeman, Roy, & Hemmick, 1976). In addition, a modified systematic desensitization procedure using in vivo components was implemented successfully in the reduction of a 13-year-old borderline mentally retarded boy's phobia regarding body hair (Rivenq, 1974).

With respect to research comparing systematic desensitization to other therapeutic approaches, only a few studies have been reported. For example, Miller, Barrett, Hampe, and Noble (1972) compared the relative effectiveness of systematic desensitization and conventional psychotherapy to a waiting-list control condition with children having various phobias. The desensitization condition lasted 24 sessions and at times included assertiveness training, presence of parents at the desensitization sessions, and assistance of parents in developing alternative responses to fear and anxiety. This method, therefore, included elements that were additional to standard systematic desensitization. The conventional psychotherapy condition also lasted 24 sessions and included having the child talk out feelings and conflicts, with emphasis on affective expression of and subsequent cognitive awareness of preconditions for fear. As in the desensitization condition, parent training was involved. Parents were taught to alter their child's home environment and to remove any potential contributing factors to the child's fear. It thus appeared that the two treatment approaches contained many common elements. Outcome was assessed in terms of the clinician's ratings of the intensity and extent of each child's fear and by the ratings of parents on the Louis-

ville Behavior Check List and the Louisville Fear Survey for Children. No child's actual fear responses were systematically observed by the researchers.

The overall results for the clinicians' ratings showed that neither treatment method was superior to the waiting-list control condition; however, when age was considered, it was found that children between 6 and 10 years of age in both therapy groups significantly improved over the waiting-list control children. No differences were found between the desensitization and psychotherapy conditions for the 6- to 10-year-olds or the 11- to 15-year-olds. In addition, the level of experience of the clinician (clinician with 20 years experience versus recently graduated clinician with minimal child therapy experience) did not have a significant effect on the outcome of the study, nor did such factors as sex of child, IQ, or chronicity of fears. With respect to parent ratings, parents of children in both treatment groups and across age groups reported significantly greater improvement in their children than did parents of children in the waiting-list control condition. No significant differences, however, were found between the two treatment groups. The results on each of the dependent measures were maintained at a 6-week follow-up. A 21-month follow-up (Hampe, Noble, Miller, & Barrett, 1973) showed that the improvement found in the children had been maintained. It was also found that most of those children who were in the waiting-list control group or who did not respond to treatment also improved over the 21-month period. In some cases, however, this improvement was due to additional therapy. Given the "impure" nature of the systematic desensitization group, the fact that no overt fears were observed, and that this study has not been replicated, it is difficult to interpret the meaningfulness of these findings.

In another comparison study, Ultee, Griffiaen, and Schellekens (1982) compared over a four-session period in vitro desensitization (i.e., graduated imaginal exposure to anxiety-provoking scenes plus relaxation training) to in vivo desensitization (i.e., gradual exposure to anxiety-provoking stimuli in the actual or real situation plus relaxation training) and a no-treatment control group. Following this, the authors added an in vivo desensitization component to the previous in vitro group and compared this combination procedure (four sessions in vitro followed by four sessions of in vivo desensitization) with the in vivo and no-treatment control groups. The children in the study were 12 boys and 12 girls between 5 and 10 years of age who had a fear of water. The results showed that at the end of four sessions, the in vivo group improved significantly more than either the in vitro or no-treatment groups on at least two of the three dependent measures. At the end of eight sessions, the in vivo group was found to improve significantly more than the no-treatment group on two out of three of the dependent measures and to improve significantly more than the in vitro plus in vivo group on one out of three measures. On the other hand, the in vitro group or the in vitro plus in vivo condition did not show any significant differences from the no-treatment group on any of the three dependent measures. Ultee et al. concluded that the in vivo condition was better than the in vitro condition and that imaginal desensitization does not add significantly to the overall effectiveness of real-life exposure to a feared situation.

Although the findings from the Ultee et al. (1982) study are certainly noteworthy, it should be pointed out that no follow-up data were reported by the authors nor were any transfer of training effects assessed in other settings. In addition, a possible developmental artifact was noted by the authors that may be responsible for the findings: namely, the possible lack of anticipatory "imaginative capacity" in the children in this study, which would have prevented them from developing "a dynamic image of one's own behavior in the phobic situation" (Ultee et al., 1982, p. 66) and, thus, transferring this information to the actual feared situation. This point is also made by Morris and Kratochwill (1983), who point to research evidence suggesting that children cannot form visual images until they are approximately 9 years of age. Therefore, these authors tentatively recommend that the use of imaginal systematic desensitization be limited to children who have reached this age.

Interestingly, the only other controlled comparison study that has been published (e.g., Sheslow, Bondy, & Nelson, 1983) has also found—working with 4- and 5-year-old children who were afraid of the dark—that the only two treatment conditions that were effective in reducing children's fears were those that included in vivo exposure. The verbal-coping-alone condition did not differ from the control group on the dependent measures. Other than this suggestion (that in vivo exposure should be included in any desensitization treatment with children below 9 years of age), few conclusions can be drawn at this time from the research literature on this method. The volume of uncontrolled case studies and controlled research in this area, however, does suggest that this procedure is an effective fear-reduction method that can be used with children and adolescents who are intellectually normal, mentally retarded, or who manifest some other handicapping condition.

Variations of Systematic Desensitization

Various alternatives to individual systematic desensitization have been proposed by researchers; each involves variations of the desensitization procedure previously discussed.

Group Systematic Desensitization. This procedure involves the same basic phases as individual systematic desensitization, but the phases are adapted for group administration. Typically, groups of five to eight persons are included in this procedure. Hierarchy construction is conducted in the group, with the group rank-ordering the hierarchy items. An alternative approach involves having the therapist bring to the group a listing of potential hierarchy items. The group rank-orders them after deciding which are appropriate and/or need modification. In this variation, the desensitization proper stage is conducted in a slightly different manner from the individual approach. Here, the general rule is that desensitization proper is geared to the person in the treatment group who is progressing most slowly.

In terms of supportive research, we again find a disproportionate amount of it being conducted on group desensitization with adults as opposed to children and, in both instances, mostly in the area of school-related problems (e.g., test anxiety, speech anxiety, reading difficulties, etc.). For example, Kondas (1967) used group systematic desensitization with test-anxious (oral examination) 11- to 15-year-old students. Compared to the relaxation or hierarchy-only groups, the desensitization group showed significant decreases in self-reported fears and measures of palmar perspiration. Barabasz (1973) also studied the relative effectiveness of group desensitization with test-anxious students. He found that highly test-anxious treated subjects—as compared with highly test-anxious no-treatment control subjects—showed significant reductions on autonomic measures of anxiety and performed better on a group test. In addition, no differences were found on either dependent measure for the experimental and control low-test-anxious subjects. Other studies on test anxiety (e.g., Deffenbacher & Kemper, 1974a, 1974b; Laxer, Quarter, Kooman, & Walker, 1969), using a variety of different dependent measures, have also reported group treatment by systematic desensitization to be effective.

In Vivo Desensitization. In this method, as discussed above, the child is exposed to the items on the hierarchy in the real or actual situation rather than through his or her imagination. Relaxation training is not always used as the counterconditioned response to the feared situation. Instead, those feelings of comfort, security, and trust that the child has developed for the therapist and which have emerged from the therapeutic relationship are used as the counterconditioning agent. The therapist goes into the real-life situation with the child and encourages him or her to go through each item on the hierarchy.

In terms of corroborating research, a number of studies over the past 20 to 25 years have used in vivo desensitization either alone or in combination with some other procedure to reduce fears in children (e.g., Bentler, 1962; Craghan & Musante, 1975; Freeman, Roy, & Hemmick, 1976; Garvey & Hegrenes, 1966; Jones, 1924a; Kuroda, 1969; O'Reilly, 1971; Sheslow et al., 1983; Tasto, 1969; Ultee et al., 1982; Van der Ploeg, 1975; Wilson & Jackson, 1980). Few of these studies, however, are well controlled, and none have systematically examined the relative effectiveness of only in vivo desensitization (e.g., Sheslow et al., 1983; Ultee et al., 1982). Freeman et al. (1976), for example, presented a case study of a 7-year-old boy who had a fear of having a physical examination. The therapist was a nurse who had a good relationship with the child. The nurse took the child to the examining room and gradually exposed him to the 11-step physical examination hierarchy. Treatment lasted over a seven-session period, with the child permitting, in the last session, an examination of his entire body. Physicians were introduced gradually and, after three additional sessions, the boy permitted the physician to examine him entirely. Craghan and Musante (1975) used this method with a 7-year-old boy who had a fear of high buildings. Treatment

lasted for six sessions and involved both in vivo desensitization and game playing with the therapist (e.g., jumping over sidewalk cracks, kicking buildings, and throwing snowballs at buildings). Following treatment and at the 3-month and 1-year follow-up, the child showed no indication of being afraid of high buildings. This approach was also used by Kuroda (1969) in eliminating fears of frogs and earthworms in 3- and 4-year-old children.

In vivo desensitization approaches have also been used by parents of phobic children under the supervision of a therapist (e.g., Bentler, 1962; Stableford, 1979; Tasto, 1969). For example, Bentler (1962) reports a case involving an 11-month-old girl who was afraid of water. With the mother, he established a hierarchy involving increasing exposure to water and found that by age 12¾ months, the child "was thoroughly recovered," with no additional fears reported at either 13 months or 18 months of age.

In summary, although a number of case/descriptive studies have reported successful use of in vivo desensitization, there have been only a few well-controlled research studies on this method, and none of these has included both follow-up and transfer of training data. Furthermore, most of the case studies in the literature have used this method in combination with other procedures. Nevertheless, this procedure does appear to be potentially effective in reducing a variety of fears and phobias.

Automated Systematic Desensitization. In this procedure, the client goes through the desensitization process by listening to a series of audio tape-recorded scene presentations prepared by the therapist with the client's assistance. Developed by Lang (Wolpe, 1969), this procedure allows clients to pace themselves through the desensitization process. A variation of this automated procedure is called *self-directed desensitization* (e.g., Baker, Cohen, & Saunders, 1973; Rosen, 1976). In this procedure, patients use instructional materials typically provided by the therapist and conduct the treatment at their own pace at home. The major difference between these methods is that the automated method is structured by the therapist and uses recording devices and/or computers in the therapist's office to present treatment. In self-directed treatment, on the other hand, the client develops the treatment package at home, with minimal therapist control. Both procedures have been used mainly with adults, but a few studies have involved children. For example, Wish, Hasazi, and Jurgela (1973) report the use of a self-directed procedure with an 11-year-old boy who had a fear of loud noises. Following the construction of the hierarchy and relaxation training, a tape of the child's favorite music was made with sounds from the fear hierarchy superimposed on the music. The child was instructed to relax in a dark room at home and to listen to the tape with the volume gradually increased over the 8-day, 3-session-per-day period. By the end of treatment, the child could listen comfortably to the sounds he feared most at a loud intensity. In addition, the child did not show any fear responses to other noises (e.g., balloon pop, firecracker, etc.). The child's behavior was maintained at a 9-month follow-up. This is an interesting treatment approach and one that is in need of a good deal more research before any definitive statement can be made about its relative effectiveness in reducing children's fears.

Emotive Imagery. This method was first used by Lazarus and Abramovitz (1962) to adapt the desensitization proper phase to children. It involves the use of those anxiety-inhibiting images in children that arouse feelings of excitement associated with adventure as well as feelings of pride, mirth, and so on. It consists of the following steps:

1. As in the usual method of systematic desensitization, a graduated hierarchy is drawn up.
2. By sympathetic conversation and inquiry, the clinician establishes the nature of the child's hero images and the wish fulfillments and identifications which accompany them.
3. The child is asked to close his eyes and imagine a sequence of events which is close enough to his everyday life to be credible, within which is woven a story concerning his favorite hero or alter ego.
4. When the clinician judges that these emotions have been maximally aroused, he introduces as a natural part of the narrative, the lowest item in the hierarchy. If there is evidence that anxiety is being inhibited, the procedure is repeated as in ordinary systematic desensitization until the highest item in the hierarchy is tolerated without distress. (Wolpe & Lazarus, 1966, p. 143)

Relatively few studies have been published that have used this procedure (e.g., Boyd, 1980; Chudy, Jones, & Dickson, 1983; Jackson & King, 1981; Lazarus & Abramovitz, 1962; Stedman & Murphy, 1984). For example, Boyd (1980) used this method with a 16-year-old "school phobic" youth who was mildly retarded. After 2 weeks of therapy, the boy was able to attend school for the full day and finished the school year with no recurrence of the school phobia. In addition, Lazarus and Abramovitz (1962) report in a series of case/descriptive studies the successful use of the procedure with a dog-phobic 14-year-old, a 10-year-old who was afraid of the dark, and an 8-year-old who was enuretic and afraid of going to school. Although this approach is innovative and has some clinical support, systematic controlled research has not yet been published to support its effectiveness.

Contact Desensitization. Developed by Ritter (1968), this method has been used with children and adults and combines elements of desensitization and modeling approaches. The desensitization process is carried out by exposing the child to each step on the fear hierarchy only after each step has first been demonstrated/modeled by the therapist. Upon modeling a particular step, the therapist helps the child perform that step—touching the child to help guide him or her, encouraging the child with various motivating statements, and praising the child for making progress. The therapist then gradually removes the prompts until the child can perform each step on his or her own. Rimm and Masters (1974) and Morris (1985) have suggested a fourth component of this procedure, namely, the therapist's presence/relationship with the client, although the relative contribution of one aspect of this factor (therapist warmth) in contact desensitization treatment with adult acrophobic persons has been questioned by Morris and Magrath (1979).

In terms of supportive research, Ritter (1968) assigned 44 snake-avoidant children to one of three groups: contact desensitization, live modeling, and a no-treatment control condition. The children in the two treatment groups received two 35-minute small-group sessions. The result showed that both treatment conditions were superior to the no-treatment group on the behavior avoidance test, and that the children in the contact desensitization group showed more improvement than the children in the modeling group. In a second study with snake avoidant children, Ritter (1969) found that contact desensitization was superior to a contact desensitization treatment without a touch condition. Murphy and Bootzin (1973) discovered that the outcome of their study was not influenced by whether the children in their experiment approached a feared snake in the standard contact-desensitization manner (active condition) or whether the experimenter/therapist gradually approached the children with the snake (passive condition).

Self-Control Desensitization. In this approach, the desensitization procedure is construed as training the client in coping skills—that is, teaching the client to cope with anxiety (Goldfried, 1971; Meichenbaum, 1974; Meichenbaum & Genest, 1980). Clients are told, for example, to apply relaxation training whenever they become aware of an increase in their feelings of anxiety and tension. They are also encouraged, during the desensitization proper phase, to continue imagining a scene that produced anxiety and to "relax away" the anxiety and/or to imagine themselves becoming fearful and then seeing themselves coping with the anxiety and tenseness that they feel. This variation is based on the view that clients will not always be in a position where they can readily leave a fearful and tension-arousing situation—that they must learn to cope with the situation on their own. In this regard, it is not important for the anxiety hierarchy to be theme-oriented as in standard systematic desensitization (Goldfried & Goldfried, 1977). The hierarchy need only be composed of situations arousing increasing amounts of anxiety, independent of theme.

In terms of corroborating research, there is little that supports this approach with children (e.g., Bornstein & Knapp, 1981; DiNardo & DiNardo, 1981). Bornstein and Knapp (1981) used this procedure with a 12-year-old boy who had fears of separation, travel, and illness. Treatment effects were assessed using a multiple-baseline design across these fears. The authors report that the child's fear-related verbal comments, as well as the ratings on the *Fear Survey Schedule for Children* for each fear, showed "marked reductions" following treatment. In addition, these changes were maintained at 1-year follow-up. This is another interesting treatment approach, but one needing much more supportive research before any statement can be made regarding its relative effectiveness.

Contingency Management

The systematic use of contingency management procedures for the reduction of fears and phobias in children had its origins in the writing of Ivan Pavlov (e.g., Pavlov, 1927), B. F. Skinner (e.g., Skinner, 1938, 1953), and John B. Watson (e.g., Watson, 1913, 1919; Watson & Rayner, 1920). Each stressed the importance of the causal relationship between stimuli and behavior. In this section, we describe the most frequently used contingency management procedures for treating the children's fears and phobias.

Positive Reinforcement

Positive reinforcement is typically defined as an event or activity that immediately follows a behavior and results in an increase in the frequency of performance of that behavior. Thus, a positive reinforcer is something that *follows* a particular behavior and *strengthens* the number of times that behavior occurs. A reinforcer is defined here in terms of its effects on a child's approach behavior toward the feared stimulus.

Positive reinforcement has been used alone and in combination with other behavioral therapy procedures to reduce various fears and fear-related behaviors in children in a variety of settings (see, for example, Conger & Keane, 1981; King et al. 1988; Morris et al., 1988). For example, Leitenberg and Callahan (1973) used reinforcement to reduce children's fears of darkness. Fourteen children were each assigned to the experimental treatment and control (pretest and posttest only) conditions with four girls and three boys in each group. The average age for the experimental group was 6 years, 0 months, while for the control group it was 5 years, 4 months. The experimental group received a treatment procedure that Leitenberg called "reinforced practice." This procedure involved providing the children in the experimental group with feedback regarding the exact time they spent in the darkened room. In addition, praise reinforcement, repeated practice, and instructions were provided during each session. The results showed that the reinforced practice procedure produced significant improvement over the control condition in the length of time that the children remained in both the partially and completely darkened test rooms.

To increase the generalization of treatment effects, studies have also focused on the use of reinforcement by persons other than the therapist (Trueman, 1984). In this regard, parents and school personnel may be trained to provide the positive reinforcers. For example, a reinforcement contingency contracting system was used by Vaal (1973) to reduce the "school phobia" of a 13-year-old boy who was absent from school on 94% of the school days over the first 6 months of the school year. After a meeting with the child, school personnel, and his parents, the following criterion/target behaviors were established for him as part of his contingency contract:

1. Coming to school on time without any tantrum behavior.
2. Attending all classes on the schedule.
3. Remaining in school until dismissal time each day. (Vaal, 1973, p. 372)

If these criteria were met each day, he was allowed to engage in various privileges/activities of choice when he returned home (e.g., attending a professional basketball game, going bowling on Saturdays, and playing basketball with friends after school). If he did not meet the criteria, then these activities were withheld. The contingency contract started on the first school day of the seventh month of the school year and lasted 6 weeks. Vaal (1973) reported that for the next 3 months the boy "did not miss a single day of school . . . he came on time every day, came without any inappropriate tantrum behavior, attended all his classes, and was late for none" (p. 372). Following a 2-month summer vacation and over a 4-month period during the subsequent school year, the boy missed only one day of school.

Variations of Positive Reinforcement
Reinforcement has also been used with other contingency-management procedures for reducing fears in children. For example, Ayllon et al. (1970) used positive reinforcement, shaping–prompting, and withdrawal of social consequences to reduce the "school phobia" of an 8-year-old girl. After conducting an extensive behavior analysis to determine the factors contributing to the child's school phobia, Ayllon et al. established a five-phase treatment procedure.

The first phase consisted of prompting and shaping the child's school attendance. This was accomplished by having an assistant take the child to school near the end of the school day and sit near her in the classroom until the school day was over. She was also given candy to distribute to her siblings at the end of school and was encouraged to walk home with them. The amount of time that the child attended school in the afternoon gradually increased and the length of time that the assistant stayed with the child also decreased gradually. On the eighth day the child attended school by herself with her siblings, but this voluntary attendance behavior was not maintained the next day or for the next 6 school days. The second treatment phase was initiated when the child's mother was asked to leave for work at the same time that the child and her siblings were to leave for school. Ayllon et al. reasoned that this approach might remove the possibility of the child's receiving social rewards from the mother for staying home from school. This procedure did not result in any increase in the child's school attendance.

The third phase of treatment was then begun, involving a home-based contingent reinforcement and token-economy-like procedure for school attendance combined with the prompting-shaping procedure of phase one (this time involving the mother rather than an assistant). This procedure again resulted in the child's attending school with assistance, but it did not contribute to her voluntarily attending school. The fourth phase was then instituted. The mother met the child and her siblings at school and provided them with tangible reinforcers and social rewards. The home-based contingent reinforcement and token economy procedure for school attendance was also continued. If the child did not voluntarily go to the school with her siblings and meet her mother, her mother went home and on one occasion "firmly proceeded to take Val by the hand and with hardly any words between them, they rushed back to school." On another occasion, she "scolded Val and pushed her out of the house and literally all the way to school" (Ayllon et al., 1970, pp. 134–135). This procedure contributed to the child attending school voluntarily with her siblings.

During the fifth phase of treatment, the mother first withdrew from meeting the child and her siblings at school and subsequently withdrew the home-based positive reinforcement program. This fading procedure did not produce any disruption in the child's voluntary school attendance. Her voluntary attendance was also found to be maintained at 6- and 9-month follow-up.

Other variations on the use of positive reinforcement for reducing fears in children have been discussed by Kellerman (1980); Lazarus, Davison, and Polefka (1965); Luiselli (1977); and Patterson (1965). However, too few controlled studies have been published on any one variation of positive reinforcement to suggest that any of these procedures is a viable fear-reduction technique.

Shaping

For various reasons, some children have difficulty approaching a feared stimulus even though they have received positive reinforcement for their approach behavior. In some cases, they do not respond to positive reinforcement because the approach behavior, or the series of responses that they emit, is too complex for them to master. That is, the approach behavior to the feared stimulus involves so many steps that the children are unresponsive to the reinforcement contingency.

In such cases, the therapist might consider the use of shaping, whereby the child is taught the desired behavior in successive steps, with each step gradually approximating the desired target behavior. For example, instead of reinforcing an 8-year-old boy who is afraid to leave his home to take short rides with his parents, the therapist might reinforce him for approaching the front of the house and then reinforce him for opening the door and looking outside. Then the child would be reinforced for standing on the porch outside, and so forth, gradually prompting an increase in the time and distance the child was away from his house.

Other than the Ayllon et al. (1970) study, only a few studies have been published using the shaping procedure. For example, Luiselli (1978) used a graduated exposure/shaping procedure with a 7-year-old boy diagnosed as autistic who was afraid to ride a school bus. Initially, the child was familiarized with the bus by sitting in it with his mother while it was parked at the school. His mother also reinforced him for this behavior. The mother and the therapist then gradually removed themselves from the bus. The child was then reinforced for riding with the mother and therapist on the bus to school. This was followed by rides only with the ther-apist and then finally alone. Luiselli reports that the treatment took 7 days and that a year later, the boy continued to ride the bus alone. Tahmisian and McReynolds (1971) also used shaping to successfully reduce the "school phobia" (refusal to attend school) of a 13-year-old girl. This case was striking because the authors reported that they first tried systematic desensitization with this girl but found that it was not effective.

Stimulus Fading

In some instances, a fearful child can perform nonfearful behavior in *selected* settings or under certain conditions but not in other settings. When this occurs, some writers have proposed the use of a *stimulus-fading* procedure. This procedure involves teaching the child to perform the nonfearful response in the same manner and with the same frequency in the unsuccessful settings as she or he does in the successful settings. This fading process is accomplished by gradually shifting the characteristics of the successful setting to the unsuccessful one. For example, Neisworth, Madle, and Goeke (1975) used this procedure for the treatment of "separation anxiety" (crying, sobbing, screaming, withdrawal) in a 4-year-old preschool girl. The mother was instructed to stay in the preschool for several sessions before being faded out and to reinforce the girl for nonanxious behavior. The child was also reinforced by staff for increased involvement in school activities. Treatment lasted for 18 hours over an 8-day period. Neisworth et al. report that the procedure produced almost an immediate cessation of anxious behavior on the part of the child, and that this behavior was maintained at the 2-, 4-, and 6-month follow-up. Only a few fear-related studies have been published using this method; consequently, any statements about its effectiveness must be made with caution.

Extinction

Some children may exhibit fears and/or fear-related responses because they are (or have been) reinforced for performing them. It is therefore possible to reduce this behavior by making certain that a child is not reinforced whenever she or he performs this behavior. *Extinction* refers to the removal of those reinforcing consequences that follow a child's avoidance response. For this procedure to be effective, the therapist *must* be able to identify those consequences that are reinforcing the child's fear response and be in a position to determine (1) when those consequences will occur, (2) the relative contribution of those consequences to the frequency of the child's fear-related behavior, and (3) whether the therapist can modify the occurrence of the consequences. For example, one of the most common reinforcing consequences for a child's fear behavior is that of parents' attention. If, after a series of observations and discussions with parents, the therapist hypothesizes parental attention as a major contributing/causal factor to the child's fear behavior, she or he must determine the frequency and conditions under which that attention occurs and whether the parents are willing to modify their reactions to their child.

A number of studies have used the extinction procedure with children experiencing fears and related problems (e.g., Boer & Sipprelle, 1970; Hersen, 1970; Piersel & Kratochwill, 1981; Stableford, 1979; Waye, 1979). Many of these studies, however, have combined the extinction procedure with positive reinforcement for appropriate/nonfearful behaviors. For example, Hersen (1970) worked with a 12-year-old boy who had a school phobia. The child's case was striking in that his five other siblings also had a history of school phobic responses. Hersen also determined in the introductory (intake interview) sessions that the boy's parents inadvertently reinforced him each morning by coaxing and cajoling him for approximately 2 hours to go to school. A three-part procedure was therefore initiated over the 15 weeks of treatment. First, the child's mother was seen by the therapist and instructed, over a number of sessions, to (1) be "deaf and dumb" to the child's crying and firm about him attending school; (2) reward the child with praise for his school-related coping behaviors, such as his success in extracurricular activities; and, (3) be aware that the child might show other school-related avoidant behaviors and that these also should be placed on extinction.

Next, Hersen speculated, from the initial intake interview, that a guidance counselor at school had also been a contributing reinforcing agent to the child's phobia by paying attention to the boy's crying and anxiety. The therapist then visited the counselor at school and instructed him to see the boy for only 5 minutes per visit and to insist firmly that the child return to classes. The third part of the treatment consisted of the therapist seeing the boy in therapy to (1) give the therapist the opportunity to ver-

bally reinforce him for demonstrating proschool coping responses, (2) extinguish through nonattention inappropriate school-related responses, and (3) provide the child with an opportunity to express his views regarding such issues as the treatment program at home. Hersen reported that, following treatment, the boy was attending school normally and that his academic performance had returned to its prephobia level (above-average academic performance). A 6-month follow-up showed that the posttreatment behavior was being maintained. Waye (1979) also reports the successful use of an extinction procedure as part of a treatment package for a 5-year-old girl who had a fear that her thumbs were shrinking.

Variations of Extinction

Many of the studies that have used the extinction procedure have also included the use of positive reinforcement for appropriate and/or nonfearful behaviors. Combining the use of extinction and reinforcement in this manner is consistent with the general behavior modification approach to reducing those maladaptive behaviors that have been theorized or observed to be maintained by reinforcing consequences (see, for example, Kazdin, 1980; Kratochwill, 1981; Morris, 1985).

Another variation involving the use of extinction has been reported by Boer and Sipprelle (1970). They worked with a 4-year-old girl who avoided foods requiring chewing. Prior to treatment, she had lived on liquids for 6 months. The authors reported that her behavior apparently developed following a trip to a doctor's office for a sore throat, as well as the earlier ingestion of an overdose of aspirin. Boer and Sipprelle concluded that she had developed a strong conditioned anxiety response to doctors. Treatment lasted seven sessions and consisted of extinguishing her avoidance of doctors and reinforcing incompatible and appropriate behavior. The mother was also asked to stop paying attention to the child's noneating activities. In addition, shaping and positive reinforcement for appropriate eating took place, as well as generalization training to the home with her mother as therapy agent.

Boer and Sipprelle reported that after the fourth clinic session, the girl was eating solid foods in the clinic; after the fifth session, a "normal" eating pattern was found at home. At follow-up 13 months later, she ate solid foods at home without any restrictions.

An additional variation used by Stableford (1979) combined the use of extinction with in vivo deconditioning. The author worked with a 3-year-old girl who had a noise phobia. Treatment was carried out by her parents and involved (1) minimizing any parental attention to her fear reactions to noises and (2) exposing her to gradually increasing levels of noise at home and in the car. Telephone contact with the parents revealed that, after 2 weeks, the child responded favorably to most noises; but after five weeks, she still could not tolerate sounds from the car radio. The parents were again instructed to ignore the child's complaints/fear reactions and to distract her with toys. One month later, the child's behavior improved; and 6 months later, the child showed no signs of her noise phobia in any situation.

Supportive Research
The specific goal of contingency management treatment is to increase the rate or frequency of a child's approach behavior to the feared stimulus and to maintain it at that level over time. Treatment involves, first, an analysis of the factors that contribute to the low rate of approach behavior, followed by the manipulation of those factors to increase the frequency of the behavior and, finally, the provision of pleasant consequences to maintain the level of the approach behavior. Interestingly, few controlled experiments on contingency management procedures have been published that support the efficacy of this approach. The vast majority of studies are descriptive and/or uncontrolled case studies. In addition, most studies combine many contingency management procedures into one treatment package, making it difficult to discern which procedures are responsible for the reduction of the child's fear response.

It also becomes clear that only a narrow range of children's fears and phobias have been investigated using the contingency management approach. The overriding majority of published studies involving contingency management have been limited to school phobia—with only 5 to 10 additional case studies investigating a few other fears or phobias. An immediate issue that arises here is the generalizability of this approach to other clinical fears and phobias (see, for example, Ross, 1981). Given the restrictive nature of the literature in this area, a therapist should proceed with caution in the use of any contingency management procedure of behaviors other than those related to school phobia.

In addition, no research has been reported in the contingency management literature on the relative contribution of therapist and/or client variables on the outcome of therapy. For example, would we find the same treatment outcome for a school-phobic child using positive reinforcement, whether the therapist was male or female, young or old, experienced or inexperienced in the use of the procedure? Would the treatment outcome be influenced by the age of the child receiving treatment, the sex of the child, the chronicity of the phobia, or the number of other fears that the child has?

Modeling

Behavior change that results from the observation of another person has been typically referred to as *modeling* (e.g., Bandura, 1969; Kazdin & Wilson, 1978). Although the concept of modeling or imitation learning has been studied for almost 100 years, active interest in its application to the treatment and understanding of children's fears and phobias has been investigated only over the past 25 to 30 years (see, for example, Bandura, 1969, 1971; Bandura & Walters, 1963).

Modeling Proper
Although there are two distinct categories of modeling, *live modeling* and *symbolic modeling,* we tend to find certain factors that are common to both categories. As Bandura (1969) states:

> [Through modeling] one can acquire intricate response patterns merely by observing the performance of appropriate models; emotional responses can be conditioned observationally by witnessing the affective reactions of others undergoing painful or pleasurable experiences; fearful and avoidant behavior can be extinguished vicariously through observation of modeled approach behavior toward feared objects without any adverse consequences accruing to the performer; . . . and, finally, the expression of well-learned responses can be enhanced and socially regulated through the actions of influential models. (p. 118)

Modeling, therefore, involves learning through the observation of others and the imitative changes in a person's behaviors that may occur as a result of the observing activities. This procedure sets the occasion for the person to produce changes in his or her emotional and attitudinal responses and correlates of these behavior changes (Masters, Brush, Hollon, & Rimm, 1987).

The modeling procedure involves an individual called the *model* (e.g., a therapist, parent, teacher, peer, or sibling) and a person called the *observer* (i.e., the fearful child). The observer typically observes the model engage in the behavior that the observer has a history of avoiding; this is done within a stimulus setting and focuses on a feared object, event, or stimulus familiar to the observer. Thus, if a child is fearful of very active large dogs who are not chained or on a leash, it would not be appropriate to have a model touch and play with a small, quiet dog—unless, of course, the dog was only one in a series of gradually more active and larger dogs that the model was planning to touch and play with.

One aspect of the modeling situation that seems to be important for effecting positive behavior change in the observer is to have the child observe the model experience positive and/or safe consequences with the feared situation, event, or object (Perry & Furukawa, 1986). In addition, Bandura (1969, 1977a) has delineated four component processes that he theorizes govern modeling. Although these four processes represent a theoretical statement by Bandura regarding the components of modeling, they can, as Masters et al. (1987) suggest, relate to any direct application of the modeling procedure to such areas as the treatment of children's fears and phobias. The therapist should be certain that the child can *attend* to the various aspects of the modeling situation (e.g., the child can sit and watch the modeling event throughout its duration, the child can note the relevant contextual aspects of the event, etc.), can *retain* what has been learned from observing the modeling situation, has the physical and cognitive ability to *motorically reproduce* or match what was observed in the modeling situation, and, when necessary, has the *motivation* to perform the behavior that was observed.

Finally, with respect to the nature of the model's approach behavior toward the feared stimulus, object or event, most writers agree with Bandura (1971) that the model should perform the approach behavior in a graduated fashion. That is, as in the case of the anxiety hierarchy in in vivo desensitization, the model should approach the feared stimulus gradually—in increasing steps, with each being perceived by the client as more and more threatening.

Live Modeling. This involves the actual or live demonstration of the graduated approach behavior of the model toward the feared situation. For example, Bandura, Grusec, and Menlove (1967) studied the effect of live modeling on the fear of dogs in 48 children ranging in age from 3 to 5 years. In addition to live modeling, Bandura et al. studied the contribution of the modeling context (positive versus neutral) on the children's approach behavior. Specifically, children were assigned to one of four groups: (1) modeling, positive context—the children watched a peer model fearlessly interact with a dog within the context of a party atmosphere; (2) modeling, neutral context—the children also observed the model approach the dog, but they did so while seated at a table; (3) exposure, positive context—the children were having a party and the dog was present, but no modeling with the dog was occurring; and (4) positive context—the children were having a party with no dog present. Each group of children was exposed to eight 10-minute sessions held over 4 consecutive days. Follow-up evaluation took place 1 month later. The results showed that the live modeling conditions were superior to the other two. The children in the two modeling groups demonstrated significantly more approach behavior than the children in the dog-exposure and/or positive-context-only conditions. In looking at the performance of the most fearful children at pretest, Bandura et al. found that 55% of those in the modeling group performed the terminal step in the behavior avoidance test, whereas only 13% from the remaining two groups did so.

White and Davis (1974) studied the relative effectiveness of live modeling, observation/exposure only, and a no-treatment control condition on the dental-treatment-avoidance behavior of 8 girls ranging from 4 to 8 years of age. The live modeling condition consisted of having each of the five children sit behind a one-way screen with a dental student and observe a patient/confederate (8-year-old girl) undergo dental treatment. In the observation/exposure condition, the five children sat behind the one-way screen and the dentist and his assistant merely named and manipulated the equipment used in the modeling condition. No model was present. The children in both conditions were each exposed to six sessions over a 3-week period. The results showed that both the live modeling condition and the exposure condition were significantly more effective than the no-treatment condition in reducing the dental-treatment-avoidance behavior of the children. In addition, White and Davis (1974) state, "The behavior of the children under the modeling condition was far more adaptive and mature. . . . These subjects never required direct support from a significant other" (p. 31).

Mann and Rosenthal (1969) report a study involving seventh and eighth graders who were referred by a counselor for test anxiety. They compared direct systematic desensitization and modeled desensitization in individual and group situations. For example, some children were desensitized individually while being observed by a peer, while others were desensitized in a group and also being observed by a group of peers. There was also a condition in which a group of children observed a peer model being desensitized. The results showed that all of the treatment procedures produced significantly better self-report scores and performance on test-taking samples than did the no-treatment control condition.

Ritter (1968) compared the effects of live group modeling, contact desensitization (participant modeling), and a no-treatment control condition on the snake-avoidant behavior of 44 children who ranged from 5 to 11 years of age. Children in the live modeling condition observed several peers exhibit progressively more intimate interactions with a snake. The participant modeling group received Ritter's standard contact desensitization procedure. Children were seen for two 35-minute sessions over a 2-week period. The results showed that both live modeling and contact desensitization were more effective in reducing children's avoidance behavior than was the no-treatment condition. Further analyses revealed, however, that 53% of the children in the modeling condition completed the terminal item on the behavior avoidance test, whereas 80% of those in the guided-participation group completed the terminal item. No follow-up information was provided.

Few controlled experiments have been published on live modeling with children. A few more have been published involving both children and adults (e.g., Bandura, et al., 1969; Blanchard, 1970), but it is not clear what generalizations can be drawn from these latter studies. It should be noted further that the types of fears that have been studied with the live modeling procedure have been limited mostly to animals, test anxiety, and dental treatments. Consequently, any use of this procedure with other clinical fears and phobias in children should be viewed as speculative and the therapist should proceed with caution.

Symbolic Modeling. This involves the presentation of the model through film, videotape, or imagination. For example, Bandura and Menlove (1968) studied the effects of filmed modeling on the dog-avoidant behavior of 48 children ranging in age from 3 to 5. One group observed a fearless 5-year-old boy engage in increasingly fearful/fear provoking contact with a dog. For example, the initial film sequences showed the model looking at the dog in the playpen and occasionally petting the dog, while subsequent sequences displayed the model inside the playpen with the dog, feeding and petting it.

The second experimental group observed several male and female models interacting with a number of dogs of various sizes. The third group, a control condition, observed a film on Disneyland of equivalent length to the others (no dogs were depicted in the film). The children viewed eight different movies of 3 minutes each twice per day over four consecutive days. The results showed that children in both film modeling conditions significantly increased their approach scores at posttest and follow-up on a behavior avoidance test over that of the control condition children. No significant differences were found between the approach scores of the two modeling groups. The authors report, however, that when the incidence of terminal performances (i.e., being alone with the dog in the playpen) of the two modeling groups were compared, the multiple model condition was slightly better at posttest and significantly better at the 17-month follow-up than either the single model or control conditions. Other studies supporting the effectiveness of symbolic modeling include Hill, Liebert, and Mott (1968), Kornhaber and Schroeder (1974), and Faust and Melamed (1984).

A second illustrative experiment involving symbolic modeling was conducted by Melamed and Siegel (1975). They studied the relative effectiveness of symbolic modeling on reducing the anxiety level of children facing hospitalization and surgery. Sixty children ranging in age from 4 to 12 years were used in this study. They were hospitalized for the first time and scheduled to have elective surgery for either hernia, tonsil, or urinary-genital tract problems. Thirty children in the modeling condition arrived at the hospital one hour prior to admission and saw a 16-minute film called *Ethan Has an Operation.*

The 30 control children also arrived early at the hospital and saw a 12-minute film entitled *Living Things Are Everywhere,* about a child on a nature walk. Following the films, all children were given the hospital's standard preoperative instructions. Six measures were used in the study: three indices of trait anxiety (the Anxiety Scale of the Personality Inventory for Children, Children's Manifest Anxiety Scale, and the Human Figure Drawing Test) and situational/state anxiety (Palmar Sweat Index, Hospital Fears Rating Scale, and an Observer Rating Scale of Anxiety). The trait measures were obtained prior to the children observing the films and at a 26-day postoperative follow-up period. The situational anxiety measures were taken prefilm, the evening before the surgery, and at the 26-day follow-up period.

The results showed that the filmed modeling condition significantly reduced all measures of situational anxiety compared to the control condition and that these significant differences were maintained at follow-up. No differences, however, were found between the modeling and control conditions on the trait anxiety measures.

Melamed and her colleagues have also shown symbolic modeling to be effective in reducing children's uncooperative behavior and fears during dental treatment (e.g., Melamed, Hawes, Heigy, & Glick, 1975; Melamed, Weinstein, Hawes, & Katin-Borland, 1975; Melamed, Yurcheson, Fleece, Hutcherson, & Hawes, 1978). Similarly, Vernon and Bailey (1974) studied the relative effectiveness of a modeling film on the induction of anesthesia in children. Geidel and Gulbrandsen (as reported in Melamed & Siegel, 1980) investigated the use of a modeling videotape for preschool children coping with a physical examination.

Another form of modeling involved the combined use of filmed modeling and client participation. For example, Lewis (1974) examined the relative effectiveness of client participation plus filmed modeling with film modeling only, participation only, and a no treatment control condition in children who had a fear of swimming. There were 10 African-American children in each group. They were between 5 and 12 years of age and were attending a boys' club summer camp. In the client-participation plus modeling condition, each child saw an 8-minute film showing three children performing tasks in a swimming pool that were similar to the avoidance test items that each subject was exposed to during pretesting. Immediately following the film, an experimenter spent 10 minutes in the pool with each subject. She encouraged the children to practice the items on the avoidance test and physically assisted the child, if necessary, in trying the steps. The experimenter also gave social reinforcement for each child's attempt at or completion of an item on the avoidance test. The children in the modeling condition viewed the 8-minute film and were exposed to a 10-minute game of checkers alongside the pool. There was no participation in the water. The children in the participation group were shown an 8-minute neutral film (three short cartoons) containing no elements of water activities; they also took part in the 10-minute checkers game. Lewis found that all three treatment procedures were more effective than the no-treatment control condition and that the filmed-modeling-plus-client-participation condition was significantly better in reducing children's fears than were any of the other procedures. Similar findings regarding the relative effectiveness of client participation plus modeling have been reported by Bandura, Jeffrey, and Wright (1974) and Ross, Ross, and Evans (1971).

An interesting alternative form of symbolic modeling involves reading stories to children on topics related to their particular fear (e.g., Fassler, 1985; Mikulas, Coffman, Dayton, Frayne, & Maier, 1985). For example, Fassler (1985) studied the effects of reading the story *Tommy Goes to the Doctor* (Wolde, 1972), reading a poem about a child who wanted to give a doctor an injection, and engaging in play rehearsal on the reduction of children's fear of needles/injections. The results showed that the children in the experimental condition significantly reduced their fear of needles/injections in comparison to those in the no-treatment condition. Although there are some methodological problems with this study, it nevertheless represents an interesting alternative treatment to filmed modeling procedures for children undergoing dental or medical-related procedures.

Additional Considerations

As we mentioned earlier, Bandura (1969, 1977a, 1977b) maintains that for modeling to be effective, the observer must be able to attend to the model, retain what she or he observes, be able to reproduce the modeled behavior, and be motivated, when necessary, to demonstrate the behavior. Perry and Furukawa (1986) point out that the therapist can do a great deal to ensure that conditions facilitate the modeling process by attending to his or her choice of the model and the modeled behaviors, the characteristics of the observer, and the structuring of the manner in which the model and his or her behaviors are represented.

Supportive Research

The vast majority of studies on the use of live and symbolic modeling to reduce children's fears and phobias have been controlled between-group experiments (see, for example, reviews by Bandura, 1969, 1977a, 1977b; Barrios & O'Dell, 1989; Bryan & Schwarz, 1971; Gelfand, 1978; Graziano et al., 1979; King et al., 1988; Melamed & Siegel, 1980; Morris & Kratochwill, 1983; Richards & Siegel, 1978). Generally, these studies fall into three categories: fear of animals, fear of impending dental or other medical treatment or elective surgery, and test anxiety. Little or no research has been conducted on children's other fears and phobias, such as speech anxiety and fear of the dark, using public toilets, loud noises, heights, school, nightmares, moving vehicles, and separation from parents. One might conclude, therefore, that any generalizability of the research findings on modeling to these other fears and phobias is quite limited (see, for example, Ross, 1981). In addition, as Graziano et al. (1979) suggest, we might question the extent to which the children typically used in the various modeling studies were, in fact, "severely fearful children." Graziano et al. acknowledge that some of the children in the Bandura and Menlove (1968) study and in the dental and medical fears studies were quite fearful, but they point out that most of the children included in these studies were not chosen because of their severe and intense levels of fear and anxiety or because of the long-standing duration of their fears and phobias.

Although a fair amount of research has been conducted on the relative contribution of model characteristics, client characteristics, and modeling setting factors on the outcome of modeling (see, for example, reviews by Melamed & Siegel, 1980; Perry & Furukawa, 1986), additional research is needed on how such factors influence the outcome of the use of this procedure with children having fears and phobias. For example, one aspect of the modeling literature that has received a fair amount of attention is related to whether the model should engage in *coping* ver-sus *mastery* performance (e.g., Bandura, 1969; Bruch, 1976; McMurray, Lucas, Arbes-Duprey, & Wright, 1985; Meichenbaum, 1971; Perry & Furukawa, 1986). The difference between these two performance styles has to do with whether the model should begin performing the approach behavior towards the feared situation at a level of proficiency that (1) is similar to that of the observer and then gradually move towards competent performances (coping style) or (2) reflects a competent performance to the observer from the very beginning of the modeling activity (mastery style). Although some writers (e.g., Perry & Furukawa, 1986) maintain that the empirical research is not completely "in favor" of the coping style, they feel that this approach "should be considered, particularly for hesitant or anxious clients . . ." (p. 75). Some research (e.g, McMurray et al., 1985), however, suggests that *both* coping and mastery styles are comparably effective in reducing the "moderate to high" anxiety of dental anxious children. Clearly, more research is needed in this area before any definitive statements can be made regarding advocating either model performance style to reduce fears and phobias.

Additional research is also needed on the contribution of such factors as the age of the client/observer and the effect of the number and chronicity of client fears and phobias on the outcome of modeling. Moreover, data are needed on the contribution of the modeling facilitator (i.e., therapist, experimenter, parent, etc.) in these research studies. For example, to what extent does the modeling facilitator's behavior during treatment contribute to the outcome of these procedures?

Variations of the Modeling Procedure

In addition to live and symbolic modeling, a number of alternative procedures have been proposed (see, for example, reviews by Bandura, 1969; Barrios & O'Dell, 1989; Mahoney, 1974; Masters et al., 1987; Perry & Furukawa, 1986)—such as *covert modeling* (the child imagines a model approaching and interacting with a feared stimulus), *participant modeling* (the child observes the model participating increasingly with the feared stimulus, followed by the child practicing what the model performed as well as receiving corrective feedback and verbal information about the feared stimulus from the therapist), and *graduated modeling* (the child observes the model perform components of a complicated behavior, and after each component is mastered the entire complicated behavior is reconstructed by the model for the child to perform). Although there is little research on covert and graduated modeling, there is a fair amount on participant modeling (e.g., Masters et al., 1987; Morris & Kratochwill, 1983). This procedure is very much like contact desensitization treatment; in fact, many writers use these two terms interchangeably (Masters et al., 1987). Both procedures, for example, make use of the following components: (1) gradually exposing the child in small steps to the feared object or situation *after* each step has first been modeled by the therapist, (2) physically assisting the child in performing the modeled step, (3) verbally encouraging the child to perform the step and providing him or her with corrective feedback, and (4) providing the child with realistic verbal information about the feared stimulus or situation. In addition, each procedure is administered within the framework of a good, positive relationship (Masters et al., 1987; Morris, 1985). The commonalities between these two procedures have led some writers (e.g., Masters et al., 1987) to state, "Since there is a tendency for one or the other [procedure] to be used consistently by a particular author, the divergence may indicate personal preference for a term rather than an actual difference in procedure" (p. 157).

Participant modeling has been found to be an effective procedure in reducing the fears and phobias in children with "normal intelligence" (e.g., Esveldt-Dawson, Wisner, Unis, Matson, & Kazdin, 1982) as well as those who are mentally retarded (e.g., Matson, 1981). What is not clear at this point is whether all of the above components and subcomponents of this procedure are necessary for effecting positive behavioral change (see, Klingman, Melamed, Cuthbert, & Hermecz, 1984).

Cognitive-Behavioral Interventions

The role of cognition and dysfunctional cognitive processes in the development of fears and related anxieties in children has been well documented (e.g., Beck, 1976; Ellis & Bernard, 1983; Sarason, 1980). This has led to one of the most recent emphases in research and treatment to reduce fear: namely, cognitive-behavioral

therapy. Cognitive-behavioral approaches encompass many techniques that, despite their differences, share the following assumptions:

1. Cognitive mediational processes are involved in human learning.
2. Thoughts, feelings, and behaviors are causally interrelated (the program, thus, has a cognitive-affective-behavioral slant).
3. Cognitive activities, such as expectations, self-statements, and attributions, are important in understanding and predicting psychopathology and psychotherapeutical change.
4. Cognitions and behaviors are compatible: (a) cognitive processes can be integrated into behavioral paradigms, and (b) cognitive techniques can be combined with behavioral procedures.
5. The task of the cognitive behavioral therapist is to collaborate with the client to assess distorted or deficient cognitive processes and behaviors and to design new learning experiences to remediate the dysfunctional or deficient cognitions, behaviors, and affective patterns. (Kendall & Braswell, 1985, p. 2)

Cognitive-behavioral interventions can be divided into various subcategories (see, for example, Haaga & Davison, 1986; Mahoney & Arnkoff, 1978). In the area of children's fears and phobias, however, the subcategories appear at present to be self-control, self-instructional training, and rational-emotive therapy.

Self-Control

Self-control can be conceptualized as a process through which a person becomes the primary agent in directing and regulating those aspects of his or her behavior that lead to preplanned and specific behavioral outcomes and/or consequences (Goldfried & Merbaum, 1973; Kanfer & Gaelick, 1986; Richards & Siegel, 1978). Although the notions of self-control and related self-regulation processes have been included for some time in theoretical discussions and in the empirical literature on learning and conditioning (e.g., Bandura, 1969; Homme, 1966; Kanfer & Phillips, 1970; Skinner, 1953), it has only been since the early to mid-1970s that they have gained some popularity and become integrated into the literature of behavior therapy (see, for example, Goldfried & Goldfried, 1980; Mahoney, 1974; Meichenbaum, 1986; Morris, 1985).

Self-control encompasses several intervention methods, each of which acknowledge the contribution of cognitive processes and views the individual as capable of regulating his or her own behavior. According to Kanfer and his associates (e.g., Kanfer & Gaelick, 1986; Kanfer & Schefft, 1988), a common element between these self-control methods involves the therapist's role as the "instigator and motivator" in helping the client begin a behavior-change program. Self-control is thus a treatment strategy in which the therapist teaches the client how, when, and where to use various cognitions to facilitate the learning of a new (and/or more personally satisfying) behavior pattern (Kanfer & Gaelick, 1986; Richards & Siegel, 1978).

With regard to fear reduction, many writers maintain that an individual's self-statements may contribute significantly to his or her fear and anxiety (e.g., Goldfried & Davison, 1976; Kanfer & Gaelick, 1986). Self-control procedures focus on helping people to develop specific thinking skills and to use these skills when confronted with a particular feared stimulus, event, or object.

In applying self-control procedures to the modification of childhood and adolescent fears and related anxieties, it must first be demonstrated that the child is aware of his or her fear or anxiety to the extent that she or he is able to identify the various components of the specific fear or anxiety and the conditions under which he or she became fearful or anxious (Morris & Kratochwill, 1983).

Prior to beginning a self-control program, the child's motivation for behavior change, as well as his or her willingness to accept responsibility for changing the behavior, must be addressed (Kanfer & Gaelick, 1986; Kanfer & Schefft, 1988). In this regard, Kanfer and Gaelick (1986) maintain that when a client is concerned about his or her behavior and can anticipate that the problem will be resolved, self-control may be used more easily and effectively.

Although a number of studies have been published on self-control treatment with adult fears and related anxieties (see, for example, Deffenbacher & Michaels, 1980; Goldfried & Davison, 1976; Morris, 1986), only a small number of studies have been published using this approach with fearful children (see, for example, Genshaft, 1982; Kanfer, Karoly, & Newman, 1975; Leal, Baxter, Martin, & Marx, 1981). Most of the studies that have been reported in the literature on the use of self-control procedures with fearful children have focused on the modifying of children's fear of the dark (e.g., Graziano, Mooney, Huber, & Ignasiak, 1979; Kanfer et al., 1975), medical fears (e.g., Peterson & Shigetomi, 1981), and dental fears (e.g., Siegel & Peterson, 1980). For example, Leal et al. (1981) compared cognitive modification, systematic desensitization, and a no-treatment control condition on reducing test anxiety in a group of tenth-grade students. The desensitization approach followed Wolpe; the cognitive modification procedure involved informing the students that their anxiety during exams was due to self-statements and thoughts that took place prior to the examination. Students were further instructed that an increasing awareness of these self-statements was necessary if they were to learn incompatible positive self-statements. The results showed that systematic desensitization was more effective than either the cognitive modification or no-treatment control condition on direct observation of test anxiety, whereas the cognitive modification procedure was more effective on the self-report measures. No follow-up assessment period or test for generalization was conducted.

In another study, Kanfer, Karoly, and Newman (1975) compared the effectiveness of two types of verbal controlling responses on the reduction of children's fear of the dark. Forty-five children, 5 to 6 years of age, participated in the study. None of them could stay alone in the dark for more than 27 seconds. The children were assigned to one of three conditions: (1) competence group—the children heard and rehearsed sentences emphasizing their respective competence and active control in the fear situation (e.g., "I am a brave boy/girl: I can take care of myself in the dark."); (2) stimulus group—the children heard and rehearsed sentences emphasizing reduced aversive qualities of the fear situation (e.g., "The dark is a fun place to be. There are many good things in the dark."); (3) neutral group—the children rehearsed sentences related to "Mary Had a Little Lamb" (Kanfer et al., 1975, p. 253). Training took place in a well-lighted room and testing took place in a dark room. Pretest and posttest measures consisted of duration of darkness tolerance and terminal light intensity (degree of illumination children needed to stay in room).

The results showed that from the pretest to first posttest period, the competence and stimulus groups remained in the darkened room significantly longer than the neutral group. At the second posttest period, the competence group remained in the room significantly longer than either the stimulus or neutral groups—with no significant difference found between the stimulus and neutral groups at the second posttest period. The competence group was superior to the other two groups with regard to illumination. Kanfer et al. (1975) concluded that training effectiveness was related to the content of the learned sentences in the three respective groups. Specifically, placing an emphasis on the child's competence in dealing with the dark may be the salient component in teaching children to cope with stressful/feared situations. An interesting extension of this study was conducted by Giebenhain and O'Dell (1984), who wrote a parent training manual designed to teach parents fear-reducing skills that they could apply at home to help a child with fear of the dark. The results showed that parents can implement a treatment package at home with a child having moderate to severe fear of the dark. The results were also found to be maintained at the 1-year follow-up.

In another study, Graziano et al. (1979) used self-control instructions plus relaxation training and pleasant imagery to reduce "severe, clinical-level" nighttime fears of long duration in children. Five boys and two girls, ranging in age from 8.7 to 12.8 years, participated in the study. The children came from six families. The families were seen for 5 weeks (2 weeks for assessment and 3 weeks for instruction). The parents and children were seen in separate groups. The children were instructed to practice relaxation, imagine a pleasant scene, recite "brave" self-statements each night with their parents, and then to practice these exercises.

A token-economy program for the children was also established. They would receive tokens for doing their exercises at home and for going to bed and being brave throughout the night. The parents were instructed to initiate the children's exercises at night and to use tokens and praise. The measures included parent ratings of the number of child fears, strength of fears, and behavioral criteria (e.g., 10 consecutive fearless nights).

The results showed that it took from 3 to 19 weeks ($X = 8.7$ weeks) for all of the children to meet the behavioral criteria. Graziano et al.

further report that each child's "fear strength" steadily decreased through posttreatment and the 3-month, 6-month, and 1-year follow-up. Total number of fears also decreased, with only one of the children not completely free of fears at the 1-year follow-up. Finally, both parents and children reported that the program improved the children's fear behavior and sleeping patterns. Graziano and Mooney (1980) used this treatment program with another set of families having children with "severe, highly disruptive nighttime fears," comparing the treatment outcome with a matched no-treatment control condition. They found, in comparison with the control condition, that the treatment package was significantly effective in reducing the strength of fears in the children, the frequency of their fears, and the duration of the fearful events. According to parent ratings, the experimental treatment children were also significantly less disruptive. Thus, it appears that the training package contributed greatly to the parent ratings of improvement in their children. Follow-up information via the telephone also confirmed the effectiveness of the treatment package. At 12-month follow-up, only one child in the experimental group did not meet the behavioral criterion discussed. Follow-up data on the "no treatment" control group were not available, since the controls began receiving the treatment package after the experimental group completed the posttest.

In another variation on the self-control approach, Peterson and Shigetomi (1981) conducted a study with children who were to receive elective tonsillectomies. The 66 children (35 girls and 31 boys) ages 2.5 to 10.5 years ($X = 5.47$ years), were assigned to one of four conditions:

1. preoperative information—children were invited to a "party" four days before their surgery, informed via a story and the use of a puppet of the "typical hospital stay from admission to discharge";
2. coping procedures—children received the preoperative information plus cue-controlled muscle relaxation (using the cue "calm"), distracting mental imagery training (imagining a scene that was "quiet and made them feel happy"), and comforting self-talk (the children were encouraged to think of and repeat the phrase "I will be all better in a little while");

3. filmed modeling—the children received the preoperative information and watched Melamed and Siegel's (1975) film *Ethan Has an Operation;*
4. coping plus filmed modeling—the children were given a 15-minute hospital tour, shown the film, and spent another 15 to 20 minutes eating ice cream and cookies following the tour.

Six categories of dependent measures were used, encompassing the triple-mode response system discussed earlier.

The results showed that children receiving the two coping conditions experienced less distress during their hospital stay than the children in the modeling-only or information-only groups. Furthermore, children receiving the coping-plus-modeling procedure were more calm and cooperative during invasive procedures than the coping or modeling-alone conditions. In another study, Siegel and Peterson (1980) conducted similar research with children undergoing dental treatment. They compared the coping-skills condition with a sensory-information condition (i.e., children were told what to expect and heard audiotape recordings of the dental equipment) and a no-treatment/attention condition. The results showed that there was no significant difference between the coping and sensory information conditions on any of the measures taken during or after restorative treatment and that both treatment groups fared better on the measures than the no-treatment control children. A self-control package was also used successfully by Chiodos and Maddux (1985) with a 16-year-old-girl who was mentally retarded and had performance anxiety.

Given the paucity of research on self-control methods, we feel that no definitive statements can be made on the merits of this approach in reducing children's fears and phobias. The area is a burgeoning one and is in need of additional well-controlled research like that of Kanfer et al. (1975).

Self-Instructional Training

This cognitive-behavioral approach was initially developed by Meichenbaum and his colleagues (e.g., Meichenbaum & Goodman, 1971) in order to teach impulsive children a reflective problem-solving approach for improving academic performance. Treatment involves having the therapist model cognitive strategies for the child,

such as: "What is my problem?" "What is my plan?" "Am I using my plan?" "How did I do?" The self-instructional training package involves the following:

1. An adult model performs a task while talking to him or herself out loud (cognitive modeling).
2. The child performs the same task under the direction of the model's instruction (overt, external guidance).
3. The child performs the task while instructing him or herself aloud (overt, self-guidance).
4. The child whispers the instructions to him or herself as she or he proceeds through the task (faded, overt self-guidance).
5. The child performs the task while guiding his or her performance via inaudible or private speech or nonverbal self-directions (covert self-instruction). [Meichenbaum, 1986, p. 351.]

The aim of this approach is to have the child apply his or her self-talk whenever the child is placed in a particular anxiety-provoking situation. In other words, this approach is designed to have the child:

1. Become aware of the habits of thought and thinking styles that impede performance and that led to dysfunctional emotions that interfere with task-relevant activities.
2. Generate, in collaboration with the trainer, a set of incompatible, tasks-relevant specific behavioral and cognitive (self-statements) strategies and accompanying feelings of self-efficacy about implementing such skills.
3. Systematically implement the skills and learn from his or her mistakes. [Meichenbaum, 1986, p. 359.]

Several studies utilizing self-instructional training to treat children's fears have been reported in the literature (e.g., Foxx & Houston, 1981; Genshaft, 1982; Kelly, 1981). For example, Genshaft (1982) implemented a self-instructional training program in order to teach seventh-grade girls a strategy to control their anxiety regarding mathematics. Subjects were identified by their teachers as experiencing some degree of math anxiety and as lagging at least a year in math as compared with their reading achievement. The study compared self-instructional training plus tutoring, tutoring alone, and a no-treatment control condition in reducing math anxiety. The results showed a significant improvement in math computation for the group that had self-instructional training plus tutoring. It should be noted, however, that all three treatment groups were shown to improve on the test of math application. Unfortunately, no generalization or follow-up assessment data were provided.

As is the case with the self-control research, there is little well-controlled or case-study research on the application of self-instructional training to reduce children's fears and phobias. In addition, no information is presently available that suggests to which type of children with which types of fears or related anxieties—and under what environmental conditions—specific self-instructional procedures are appropriate.

Rational–Emotive Therapy
Rational–emotive therapy (RET) was developed about 30 years ago by Albert Ellis (e.g., Ellis, 1962, 1984) and extended to children on a systematic basis many years later (see, for example, Ellis & Bernard, 1983). Ellis has presented the view that psychological or emotional difficulties result form irrational thoughts and beliefs. Thus, an individual's thoughts or beliefs about particular events influences his or her feelings and behavior. The primary goal, therefore, of RET is to teach people to identify and change the irrational beliefs underlying their particular psychological difficulties—to train these people to the point where they can view themselves and others in a sensible and rational manner. Individuals are therefore taught to replace maladaptive thoughts such as "I can't stand it" with a more rational thought such as "It is unpleasant, but I can tolerate it."

Although at least two books on RET with children are available (e.g., Bernard & Joyce, 1984; Ellis & Bernard, 1983), supportive research for this procedure is quite sparse. In one study, Bernard, Kratochwill, and Keefauver (1983) applied RET and self-instructional training in order to reduce high-frequency chronic hair-pulling in a 17-year-old girl. From a cognitive-behavioral perspective, it was hypothesized that maladaptive thought patterns occasioned high levels of anxiety and worry during study periods and maintained the hair-pulling behavior. The results showed that RET led to a moderate reduction in hair-pulling behavior, while the introduction of self-instructional training in addition to RET produced a rapid cessation of

all hair-pulling—with this behavior being maintained at a 2- and 3-week follow-up. In another study, Van der Ploeg-Stapert and Van der Ploeg (1986) evaluated a group treatment that incorporated various aspects of RET for reducing test anxiety in adolescents. The treatment program consisted of muscle relaxation exercises, instruction in study skills, self-monitoring procedures, hypnosis, and RET for "worry." The results showed a significant reduction in anxiety, as measured by the various self-report inventories, for adolescents who received the group treatment in comparison to those who had no treatment. In addition, a 3-month follow-up evaluation showed that the reduction in reported test anxiety was maintained.

Warren, Smith, and Velten (1984) studied the effectiveness of RET with and without imagery; they compared both groups to a relationship-oriented counseling group and a waiting-list control group. The participants in this study were 59 junior high school students who were experiencing interpersonal anxiety. The results showed that both of the RET groups were independently rated as significantly less anxious than was the waiting-list control group. Interestingly, no significant differences were found between the RET groups and the relationship-oriented counseling group; however, the levels of irrational thinking were significantly more reduced in the RET groups than in the relationship-oriented group.

Although RET has been shown to be effective in the reduction of fears and related anxieties in adults (e.g., DiGiuseppe & Miller, 1977; Zettle & Hayes, 1980), its relative effectiveness with children has not been sufficiently demonstrated to permit any firm conclusions. In addition, no data are available regarding the types of fears and related anxieties that are amenable to this type of treatment. RET certainly appears to be a potentially useful procedure, but clearly more research is needed.

SUMMARY

In this chapter, we have reviewed assessment considerations regarding children's fears and phobias, as well as the five major behavior therapy approaches to fear reduction. In addition, variations of each major method were discussed, as was research supporting the relative effectiveness of these methods. Discussions concerning the use of each method with clinical populations were also presented, as were comments regarding procedural considerations for each method.

Without doubt, the most researched method of fear reduction is systematic desensitization and its variants, while the least researched method involves the use of cognitive-behavioral interventions. The next most heavily researched method is modeling and its variants. However, when one examines in detail the nature of the research supporting each method, it becomes clear that few well-controlled experimental studies have been published supporting the efficacy of any of these methods with clinically or severely fearful children. There is a good deal of controlled research that supports the use of contact desensitization and participant modeling, but this research has been largely of the analogue variety with nonclinically fearful children. On the other hand, a number of uncontrolled case studies using systematic desensitization to treat clinical fears have been published, but the conclusions to be drawn from them are limited.

The only fear-reduction method that has been associated with both controlled research and a clinically fearful target behavior is the modeling method. The problem, however, is that the clinical fear (fear of dental or medical treatment or an impending surgical operation) is very narrow in scope, and it is not at all clear that these findings can be generalized to other clinical fears.

Two of the most promising methods of fear reduction involve the use of positive reinforcement and cognitive-behavioral interventions. Since relatively few controlled studies have been published that use either of these methods with different clinical fears, no clear statement can presently be made concerning their relative effectiveness.

There are also major empirical questions regarding each of the five major procedures. First, researchers have not substantially verified the relative effectiveness of most of these procedures in a controlled experimental fashion, with both analogue and clinically relevant (in intensity, chronicity, regularity, and disruptiveness of everyday life) fears.

Second, few researchers studying these methods have been concerned with assessing therapy outcome using the triple-mode response system. The literature on symbolic modeling comes closest to meeting these two criticisms favorably. Here, Bandura and his colleagues have examined the use of this approach with mostly nonclinical fears (of snakes or dogs), while Melamed and her colleagues have studied the application of this method with children who primarily have transitory and highly situation-specific clinical fears. Once more, both Bandura and Melamed have made some use of the triple-mode response system in their evaluation of the outcome of treatment.

A third question that has not yet been answered involves identifying those conditions in which the treatments are effective—for example, which procedures are effective for which age groups, for which fears and phobias, with which type of therapist, and in which type of setting.

A fourth question has to do with the cost-efficient nature of treatment. For example, how realistic is it for a therapist living in St. Louis to purchase videotape equipment, a monitor, and videotapes and make a modeling tape for a child who became extremely fearful of driving on mountainous roads during a recent vacation in the Rocky Mountains in Colorado? Or how cost-efficient is it for a therapist to purchase videotape equipment and a "canned" videotape on hospital operations and surgical procedures when he or she may see only one or two children every few years who have this problem?

Finally, the vast majority of supportive case studies and experiments reviewed in this chapter have involved working with a child who has only one fear or phobia. Most therapists realize very quickly that it is unusual to see such a child in either a clinic or school setting. The question then arises as to the applicability—external validity—of these research findings to clinical practice. Independent of these comments, however, there has been some very active research on these procedures, and they appear to be very promising fear-reduction methods.

REFERENCES

Ayllon, T., Smith, D., & Rogers, M. (1970). Behavioral management of school phobia. *Journal of Behavior Therapy and Experimental Psychiatry, 1,* 125–138.

Baker, B. L., Cohen, D. C., & Saunders, J. T. (1973). Self-directed desensitization for acrophobic behavior. *Research Therapy, 11,* 79–89.

Bandura, A. (1969). *Principles of behavior modification.* New York: Holt, Rinehart & Winston.

Bandura, A. (1971). Psychotherapy based upon modeling principles. In A. E. Bergin & S. L. Garfield (Eds.), *Handbook of psychotherapy and behavior change* (pp. 653–708). New York: John Wiley & Sons.

Bandura, A. (1977a). *Social learning theory.* Englewood Cliffs, NJ: Prentice-Hall.

Bandura, A. (1977b). Self-efficacy: Toward a unifying theory of behavior change. *Psychological Review, 84,* 191–215.

Bandura, A., Grusec, J., & Menlove, F. (1967). Vicarious extinction of avoidance behavior. *Journal of Personality and Social Psychology, 5,* 16–23.

Bandura, A., Jeffrey, R., & Wright, C. (1974). Efficacy of participant modeling as a function of response induction aids. *Journal of Abnormal Psychology, 83,* 56–64.

Bandura, A., & Menlove, F. (1968). Factors determining vicarious extinction of avoidance behavior through symbolic modeling. *Journal of Personality and Social Psychology, 8,* 99–108.

Bandura, A., & Walters, R. H. (1963). *Social learning and personality development.* New York: Holt, Rinehart & Winston.

Barabasz, A. (1973). Group desensitization of test anxiety in elementary schools. *Journal of Psychology, 83,* 295–301.

Barrios, B. A. (1988). On the changing nature of behavioral assessment. In A. Bellack & M. Hersen (Eds.), *Behavioral assessment* (pp. 3–41). Elmsford, NY: Pergamon Press.

Barrios, B. A., Hartman, D. P., & Shigetomi, C. (1981). Fears and anxieties in children. In E. J. Mash & L. G. Terdal (Eds.), *Behavioral assessment in childhood disorders* (pp. 259–304). New York: Guilford Press.

Barrios, B. A., & Hartmann, D. P. (1988). Fears and anxieties. In E. J. Mash & L. J. Terdal (Eds.), *Behavioral assessment of disorders* (2nd ed.) (pp. 196–262). New York: Guilford Press.

Barrios, B. A., & O'Dell, S. L. (1989). Fears and anxieties. In E. J. Mash & R. A. Barkley (Eds.), *Treatment of childhood disorders* (pp. 167–221). New York: Guilford Press.

Beck, A. T. (1976). *Cognitive therapy and the emotional disorders.* New York: International Universities Press.

Bellack, A. S., & Hersen, M. (1977a). *Behavior modification: An introductory textbook.* Baltimore: Williams & Wilkins.

Bellack, A. S., & Hersen, M. (1977b). The use of self-report inventories in behavioral assessment. In J. D. Cone & R. P. Hawkins (Eds.), *Behavioral assessment: New directions in clinical psychology* (pp. 52–76). New York: Brunner/Mazel.

Bellack, A. S., & Hersen, M. (Eds.). (1988). *Behavioral assessment* (3rd ed.). Elmsford, NY: Pergamon Press.

Bentler, P. M. (1962). An infant's phobia treated with reciprocal inhibition therapy. *Journal of Child Psychology and Psychiatry, 3,* 185–189.

Bergland, B. W., & Chal, A. H. (1972). Relaxation training and a junior high behavior problem. *The School Counselor, 20,* 288–293.

Bernard, M. E., & Joyce, M. R. (1984). *Rational-emotive therapy with children and adolescents.* New York: John Wiley & Sons.

Bernard, M. E., Kratochwill, T. R., Keefauver, L. W. (1983). The effects of rational-emotive therapy and self-instructional training on chronic hair pulling. *Cognitive Therapy in Research, 7,* 273–280.

Blanchard, E. B. (1970). The relative contributions of modeling, information influences, and physical contact in the extinction of phobic behavior. *Journal of Abnormal Psychology, 76,* 55–61.

Boer, A. P., & Sipprelle, C. N. (1970). Elimination of avoidance behavior in the clinic and its transfer to the normal environment. *Journal of Behavior Therapy and Experimental Psychiatry, 1,* 169–174.

Bornstein, P. H., & Knapp, M. (1981). *Journal of Behavior Therapy and Experimental Psychiatry, 12,* 218–285.

Boyd, L. T. (1980). Emotive imagery in the behavioral management of adolescent school phobia: A case approach. *School Psychology Digest, 9,* 186–189.

Brady, J. B. (1966). Brevital relaxation treatment of frigidity. *Behaviour Research and Therapy, 4,* 71–77.

Brady, J. P. (1972). Systematic desensitization. In W. S. Agras (Ed.), *Behavior modification: Principles and clinical applications* (pp. 127–150). Boston: Little, Brown.

Bryan, J., & Schwarz, T. (1971). Effects of film material on children's behavior. *Psychological Bulletin, 75,* 50–59.

Bruch, M. A. (1976). Coping model treatments: Unresolved issues and needed research. *Behavior Therapy, 7,* 711–713.

Cautela, J. R., & Groden, J. (1978). *Relaxation:*

A comprehensive manual for adults, children, and children with special needs. Champaign, IL: Research Press.

Chiodos, J., & Maddux, J. E. (1985). A cognitive and behavioral approach to anxiety management of retarded individuals: Two case studies. *Journal of Child and Adolescent Psychotherapy, 2*, 16–20.

Chudy, J. F., Jones, G. E., & Dickson, A. L. (1983). Modified desensitization approach for the treatment of phobia behavior in children: A quasi-experimental case study. *Journal of Clinical Child Psychology, 12*, 198–201.

Cone, J. D. (1977). The relevance of reliability and validity for behavioral assessment. *Behavior Therapy, 8*, 411–426.

Cone, J. D. (1978). The behavioral assessment grid (BAG): A conceptual framework and a taxonomy. *Behavior Therapy, 9*, 882–888.

Cone, J. D. (1979). Confounded comparisons in triple response mode assessment research. *Behavioral Assessment, 1*, 85–95.

Conger, J. C., & Keane, S. P. (1981). Social skills intervention in the treatment of isolated or withdrawn children. *Psychological Bulletin, 90*, 478–495.

Costello, C. G. (1970). Dissimilarities between conditioned avoidance responses and phobias. *Psychological Review, 77*, 250–254.

Craghan, L., & Musante, G. J. (1975). The elimination of a boy's high-building phobia by *in vivo* desensitization and game-playing. *Journal of Behavior Therapy and Experimental Psychiatry, 6*, 87–88.

Deffenbacher, J. L., & Kemper, C. G. (1974a). Counseling test-anxious sixth graders. *Elementary School Guidance & Counseling, 7*, 22–29.

Deffenbacher, J. L., & Kemper, C. G. (1974b). Systematic desensitization of test anxiety in junior high students. *The School Counselor, 22*, 216–222.

Deffenbacher, J. L., & Michaels, A. (1980). Two self-control procedures in the reduction of targeted and nontargeted anxieties. A year later. *Journal of Counseling Psychology, 27*, 9–15.

Delprato, D. J. (1980). Hereditary determinants of fears and phobias: A critical review. *Behavior Therapy, 11*, 79–103.

DiGiuseppe, R. A., & Miller, N. J. (1977). A review of outcome studies on rational-emotive therapy. In A. Ellis, and R. Grieger

(Eds.), *Handbook of rational-emotive therapy* (pp. 72–95). New York: Springer.

DiNardo, P. A., & DiNardo, P. G. (1981). Self-control desensitization in the treatment of a childhood phobia. *The Behavior Therapist, 4*, 15–16.

Eisenberg, L. (1958). School phobia: A study in the communication of anxiety. *American Journal of Psychiatry, 114*, 712–718.

Ellis, A. (1962). *Reason and emotion in psychotherapy*. New York: Stuart.

Ellis, A. (1984). *Rational-emotive therapy and cognitive behavior therapy*. New York: Springer.

Ellis, A., & Bernard, M. (Eds.) (1983). *Rational-emotive approaches to the problems of childhood*. New York: Plenum Press.

Eme, R., & Schmidt, D. (1978). The stability of children's fears. *Child Development, 49*, 1277–1279.

Esveldt–Dawson, K., Wisner, K. L., Unis, A. S., Matson, J. L., Kazdin, A. E. (1982). Treatment of phobias in a hospitalized child. *Journal of Behavior Therapy and Experimental Psychiatry, 31*, 77–83.

Fassler, D. (1985). The fear of needles in children. *American Journal of Orthopsychiatry, 31*, 371–377.

Faust, J., & Melamed, B. G. (1984). Influence of arousal, previous experience, and age on surgery preparation of same day of surgery and in-hospital pediatric patients. *Journal of Consulting and Clinical Psychology, 52*, 359–365.

Fox, J., & Houston, B. (1981). Efficacy of self-instructional training for reducing children's anxiety in an evaluative situation. *Behaviour Research and Therapy, 19*, 509–515.

Frame, C. L., & Matson, J. L. (1987) (Eds.). *Handbook of assessment in childhood psychotherapy*. New York: Plenum Press.

Francis, G., & Ollendick, T. H. (1987). Anxiety disorders. In C. L. Frame & J. L. Matson (Eds.), *Handbook of assessment in childhood psychopathology* (pp. 373–400). New York: Plenum Press.

Freeman, B. T., Roy, R. R., & Hemmick, S. (1976). Extinction of a phobia of physical examination in a 7-year-old mentally retarded boy: A case study. *Behavior Research and Therapy, 14*, 63–64.

Freud, S. (1909). (1963). The analysis of a phobia in a five-year-old boy. *Standard edition of the complete psychological works of*

Sigmund Freud (Vol. 10). London: Hogarth Press.

Friedman, D. E. (1966). A new technique for the systematic desensitization of phobic symptoms. *Behaviour Research and Therapy, 4,* 139–140.

Garvey, W., & Hegrenes, J. (1966). Desensitization technique in the treatment of school phobia. *American Journal of Orthopsychiatry, 36,* 147–152.

Gelfand, D. M. (1978). Behavioral treatment of avoidance, social withdrawal and negative emotional stress. In B. B. Wolman, J. Egan, & A. O. Ross (Eds.), *Handbook of treatment of mental disorders in childhood and adolescence* (pp. 330–353). Englewood Cliffs, NJ: Prentice-Hall.

Genshaft, J. L. (1982). The use of cognitive behavior therapy for reducing math anxiety. *School Psychology Review, 11,* 32–34.

Giebenhain, J. E., & O'Dell, S. L. (1984). Evaluation of a parent training manual for reducing children's fear of the dark. *Journal of Applied Behavior Analysis, 17,* 121–125.

Goldfried, M. (1971). Systematic desensitization as training in self-control. *Journal of Consulting and Clinical Psychology, 37,* 228–234.

Goldfried, M., & Davison, G. (1976). *Clinical behavior therapy.* New York: Holt.

Goldfried, M., & Goldfried, A. P. (1977). Importance of hierarchy content in the self-control of anxiety. *Journal of Consulting and Clinical Psychology, 45,* 124–134.

Goldfried, M. R., & Goldfried, A. P. (1980). Cognitive change methods. In F. H. Kanfer & A. P. Goldstein (Eds.), *Helping people change* (2nd ed., pp. 97–130). Elmsford, NY: Pergamon Press.

Goldfried, M. R., & Merbaum, M. (1973). A perspective on self-control. In M. R. Goldfried & M. Merbaum (Eds.), *Behavior change through self-control* (pp. 3–36). New York: Holt.

Graziano, A. M., & DeGiovanni, I. S. (1979). The clinical significance of childhood phobias: A note on the proportion of child-clinical referrals for the treatment of children's fears. *Behaviour Research and Therapy, 17,* 161–162.

Graziano, A. M., & DeGiovanni, I. S., & Garcia, K. A. (1979). Behavioral treatments of children's fears: A review. *Psychological Bulletin, 86,* 804–830.

Graziano, A. M., & Mooney, K. C. (1980).

Family self-control instruction for children's nighttime fear reduction. *Journal of Consulting and Clinical Psychology, 48,* 206–213.

Graziano, A., & Mooney, K. (1984). *Children and behavior therapy.* New York: Aldine.

Graziano, A. M., Mooney, K. C., Huber, C., & Ignasiak, D. (1979). Self-control instructions for children's fear-reduction. *Journal of Behavior Therapy and Experimental Psychiatry, 10,* 221–227.

Haaga, D. A., & Davison, G. C. (1986). Cognitive change methods. In F. H. Kanfer & A. P. Goldstein (Eds.), *Helping people change* (3rd ed., pp. 236–282). Elmsford, NY: Pergamon Press.

Hampe, E., Noble, H., Miller, L. C., & Barrett, C. L. (1973). Phobic children 1 and 2 years posttreatment. *Journal of Abnormal Psychology, 82,* 446–453.

Harris, S. L., & Ferrari, M. (1983). The developmental factor in child behavior therapy. *Behavior Therapy, 14,* 54–72.

Hatzenbuehler, L. C., & Schroeder, H. E. (1978). Desensitization procedures in the treatment of childhood disorders. *Psychological Bulletin, 85,* 831–844.

Haynes, S. N. (1978). *Principles of behavioral assessment.* New York: Gardner Press.

Hersen, M. (1970). Behavior modification approach to a school-phobia case. *Journal of Clinical Psychology, 26,* 128–132.

Hill, J. H., Liebert, R. M., & Mott, D. E. W. (1968). Vicarious extinction of avoidance behavior through films: An initial test. *Psychological Reports, 22,* 192.

Hodgson, R., & Rachman, S. (1974). Desynchrony in measures of fear. *Behaviour Research and Therapy, 12,* 319–326.

Homme, L. E. (1966). Contiguity theory and contingency management. *Psychological Record, 16,* 233–241.

Hugdahl, L. (1981). The three-system model of fear and emotion. A critical examination. *Behaviour Research and Therapy, 19,* 75–85.

Ilg, F. L., & Ames, L. B. (1955). *Child behavior.* New York: Dell.

Jackson, H. J., & King, N. J. (1981). The emotive imagery treatment of a child's trauma-induced phobia. *Journal of Behavior Therapy and Experiment Psychiatry, 12,* 325–328.

Jacobson, E. (1938). *Progressive relaxation.* Chicago: University of Chicago Press.

Javel, A. F., & Denholtz, M. A. (1975). Audible GSR feedback in systematic desensitization:

A case report. *Behavior Therapy, 6,* 251–254.

Jersild, A. T. (1968). *Child psychology* (6th ed.). Englewood Cliffs, NJ: Prentice-Hall.

Jersild, A. T., & Holmes, F. B. (1935). Children's fears. *Child Development Monograph,* No. 20.

Johnson, S. B. (1979). Children's fears in the classroom setting. *School Psychology Digest, 8,* 382–396.

Jones, M. C. (1924a). The elimination of children's fears. *Journal of Experimental Psychology, 7,* 382–390.

Jones, M. C. (1924b). A laboratory study of fear: The case of Peter. *Journal of Genetic Psychology, 31,* 308–315.

Kahn, J., & Nursten, J. (1962). School refusal: A comprehensive view of school phobia and other failures of school attendance. *American Journal of Orthopsychiatry, 32,* 707–718.

Kanfer, F. H., & Gaelick, L. (1986). Self-management methods. In F. H. Kanfer and A. P. Goldstein (Eds.), *Helping people change* (3rd ed., pp. 283–345). Elmsford, NY: Pergamon Press.

Kanfer, F. H., Karoly, P., & Newman, A. (1975). Reduction of children's fear of the dark by confidence-related and situational threat-related verbal cues. *Journal of Consulting and Clinical Psychology, 43,* 251–258.

Kanfer, F. H., & Phillips, J. S. (1970). *Learning foundations of behavior therapy.* New York: John Wiley & Sons.

Kanfer, F. H., & Schefft, B. K. (1988). *The basics of therapy.* Champaign, Illinois: Search Press.

Kazdin, A. E. (1980). *Behavior modification in applied settings* (rev. ed.). Homewood, IL: Dorsey Press.

Kazdin, A. E., & Hersen, M. (1980). The current status of behavior therapy. *Behavior Modification, 4,* 283–302.

Kazdin, A. E., & Wilson, G. T. (1978). *Evaluation of behavior therapy: Issues, evidence, and research strategies.* Cambridge, MA: Ballinger.

Kellerman, J. (1980). Rapid treatment of nocturnal anxiety in children. *Journal of Behavior Therapy and Experimental Psychiatry, 11,* 9–11.

Kellerman, J. (1981). *Helping the fearful child.* New York: W. W. Norton.

Kelley, M. S. (1982). The effect of relaxation training and self-directed verbalizations on measures of anxiety and learning in learning-disabled children. *Dissertation Abstracts International, 42,* 3806B–3807B (United States International University).

Kendall, P. C., & Braswell, L. (1985). *Cognitive-behavioral therapy for impulsive children.* New York: Guilford Press.

Kennedy, W. (1965). School phobia: Rapid treatment of fifty cases. *Journal of Abnormal Psychology, 70,* 285–289.

Kessler, J. (1972). Neurosis in childhood. In B. Wolman (Ed.), *Manual of child psychopathology* (pp. 387–435). New York: McGraw-Hill.

King, N. J., Hamilton, D. I., & Ollendick, T. H. (1988). *Children's phobias: A behavioural perspective.* New York: John Wiley & Sons.

Kissel, S. (1972). Systematic desensitization therapy with children: A case study and some suggested modification. *Professional Psychology, 3,* 164–168.

Klingman, A., Melamed, B. G., Cuthbert, M. I., Hermecz, D. A. (1984). Effects of participant modeling on information acquisition and skill utilization. *Journal of Consulting and Clinical Psychology, 52,* 414–422.

Koeppen, A. S. (1974). Relaxation training for children. *Journals of Elementary School Guidance and Counseling, 9,* 14–21.

Kondas, O. (1967). Reduction of examination anxiety and "stage fright" by group desensitization and relaxation. *Behaviour Research and Therapy, 5,* 275–281.

Korchin, S. J., & Schuldberg, D. (1981). The future of clinical assessment. *American Psychologist, 36,* 1147–1148.

Kornhaber, R. C., & Schroeder, H. E. (1974). Importance of model similarity on extinction of avoidance behavior in children. *Journal of Consulting and Clinical Psychology, 43,* 601–607.

Kozak, M. J., & Miller, G. A. (1982). Hypothetical constructs vs. intervening variables: A re-appraisal of the three-systems model of anxiety assessment. *Behavioral Assessment, 49,* 309–318.

Kratochwill, T. R. (1981). *Selective mutism. Implications for research and treatment.* New York: Lawrence Erlbaum.

Kratochwill, T. R., & Morris, R. J. (1985). Conceptual and methodological issues in the behavioral assessment and treatment of children's fears and phobias. *School Psychology Review, 14,* 94–105.

Kratochwill, T. R., Accardi, A., Morris, R. J. (1988). Anxieties and phobias: Psychological therapies. In J. L. Matson (Ed.), *Handbook of treatment approaches in childhood psychopathology* (pp. 249–278). New York: Plenum Press.

Kuroda, J. (1969). Elimination of children's fears of animals by the method of experimental desensitization—An application of learning theory to child psychology. *Psychologia, 12,* 161–165.

Kushner, M. (1965). Desensitization of a post-traumatic phobia. In L. P. Ullmann & L. Krasner (Eds.), *Case studies in behavior modification* (pp. 193–195). New York: Holt, Rinehart & Winston.

Lang, P. J (1968). Fear reduction and fear behavior: Problems in treating a construct. In J. M. Shlien (Ed.), *Research in psychotherapy* (Vol. 3, pp. 90–102). Washington, DC: American Psychological Association.

Lapouse, R., & Monk, M. A. (1959). Fears and worries in a representative sample of children. *American Journal of Orthopsychiatry, 29,* 803–818.

Laxer, R. M., Quarter, J., Kooman, A., & Walker, K. (1969). Systematic desensitization and relaxation of high test-anxious secondary school students. *Journal of Counseling Psychology, 16,* 446–451.

Lazarus, A. A. (1960). The elimination of children's phobias by deconditioning. In H. J. Eysenck (Ed.), *Behaviour therapy and the neuroses* (pp. 114–122). Oxford: Pergamon Press.

Lazarus, A. A., & Abramovitz, A. (1962). The use of emotive imagery in the treatment of children's phobias. *Journal of Mental Science, 108,* 191–195.

Lazarus, A. A., Davison, G. C., & Polefka, D. A. (1965). Classical and operant factors in the treatment of school phobia. *Journal of Abnormal Psychology, 70,* 225–229.

Leal, L. L., Baxter, E. G., Martin, J., & Marx, R. W. (1981). Cognitive modification and systematic desensitization with test anxious high school students. *Journal of Counseling Psychology, 28,* 525–528.

Leitenberg, H., & Callahan, E. J. (1973). Reinforcement practice and reductions of different kinds of fears in adults and children. *Behaviour Research and Therapy, 11,* 19–30.

Lewis, S. A. (1974). A comparison of behavior therapy techniques in the reduction of fearful avoidant behavior. *Behavior Therapy, 5,* 648–655.

Lippman, H. S. (1967). The phobic child and other related anxiety states. In M. Hammer & A. M. Kaplan (Eds.), *The practice of psychotherapy with children* (pp. 72–98). Homewood, IL: Dorsey Press.

Luiselli, J. K. (1977). Case report: An attendant-administered contingency management program for the treatment of toileting phobia. *Journal of Mental Deficiency Research, 21,* 283–288.

Luiselli, J. K. (1978). Treatment of an autistic child's fear of riding a school bus through exposure and reinforcement. *Journal of Behavior Therapy and Experimental Psychiatry, 9,* 169–172.

Luiselli, J. K. (1980). Relaxation training with the developmentally disabled: A reappraisal. *Behavior Research of Severe Developmental Disabilities, 1,* 191–213.

MacDonald, M. L. (1975). Multiple impact behavior therapy in a child's dog phobia. *Journal of Behavior Therapy and Experimental Psychiatry, 6,* 317–322.

Mahoney, M. J. (1974). *Cognition and behavior modification.* Cambridge, MA: Ballinger.

Mahoney, M. J., & Arnkoff, D. (1978). Cognitive and self-control therapies. In S. J. Garfield & A. E. Bergin (Eds.), *Handbook of psychotherapy and behavior change* (2nd ed., pp. 689–722). New York: John Wiley & Sons.

Mann, J., & Rosenthal, T. L. (1969). Vicarious and direct counterconditioning of test anxiety through individual and group desensitization. *Behaviour Research and Therapy, 7,* 359–367.

Marks, I. M. (1969). *Fears and phobias.* New York: Academic Press.

Marshall, W. L., Gauthier, J., & Gordon, A. (1979). The current status of flooding therapy. In M. Hersen, R. E. Eisler, & P. M. Miller (Eds.), *Progress in behavioral modification* (Vol. 7). New York: Academic Press.

Mash, E. J., & Terdal, L. G. (Eds.) (1988). *Behavioral assessment of childhood disorders.* New York: Guilford Press.

Masters, J. C., Brush, T. G., Hollon, S. D., & Rimm, D. C. (1987). *Behavior therapy* (3rd ed.). New York: Harcourt, Brace Jovanovich.

Matson, J. L. (1981). Assessment and treatment of clinical fears in mentally retarded children.

Journal of Applied Behavior Analysis, 14, 287–294.

McMurray, N. E., Lucas, J. O., Arbes-Duprey, V., & Wright, F. A. C. (1985). The effects of mastery on dental stress in young children. *Australian Journal of Psychology, 37,* 65–70.

McReynolds, R. A., Morris, R. J., & Kratochwill, T. R. (1989). Cognitive-behavioral treatment of school-related fears and anxieties. In J. N. Hughes & R. J. Hall (Eds.), *Cognitive-behavioral psychology in the schools* (pp. 434–465). New York: Guilford Press.

Meichenbaum, D. (1971). Examination of model characteristics in reducing avoidance behavior. *Journal of Personality and Social Psychology, 17,* 298–307.

Meichenbaum, D. (1974). Self-instructional methods. In F. H. Kanfer & A. P. Goldstein (Eds.), *Helping people change* (pp. 357–392). Elmsford, NY: Pergamon Press.

Meichenbaum, D. (1986). Cognitive behavior modification. In F. H. Kanfer & A. P. Goldstein (Eds.), *Helping people change* (3rd ed., pp. 346–380). Elmsford, NY: Pergamon Press.

Meichenbaum, D., & Genest, M. (1980). Cognitive behavior modification: An integration of cognitive and behavioral methods in F. H. Kanfer & A. P. Goldstein (Ed.), *Helping people change* (2nd ed., pp. 390–422). Elmsford, NY: Pergamon Press.

Meichenbaum, D., & Goodman, J. (1971). Training impulsive children to talk to themselves: A means of developing self-control. *Journal of Abnormal Psychology, 77,* 115–126.

Melamed, B. G., Hawes, R. R., Heigy, E., & Glick, J. (1975). Use of filmed modeling to reduce uncooperative behavior of children during dental treatment. *Journal of Dental Research, 54,* 797–801.

Melamed, B., & Siegel, L. (1975). Reduction of anxiety in children facing hospitalization and surgery by use of filmed modeling. *Journal of Consulting and Clinical Psychology, 43,* 511–521.

Melamed, B. G., & Siegel, L. J. (1980). *Behavior medicine.* New York: Springer.

Melamed, B. G., Weinstein, D., Hawes, R., & Katin-Borland, M. (1975). Reduction of fear related dental management problems using filmed modeling. *Journal of American Dental Association, 90,* 822–826.

Melamed, B. G., Yurcheson, R., Fleece, E. L.,

Hutcherson, S., & Hawes, R. (1978). Effects of film modeling on the reduction of anxiety-related behaviors in individuals varying in level or previous experiment in the stress situation. *Journal of Consulting and Clinical Psychology, 46,* 1357–1367.

Mikulas, W. L., Coffman, M. G., Dayton, D., Frayne, C., & Maier, P. L. (1985). Behavioral bibliotherapy and games for treating fear of the dark. *Child and Family Behavior Therapy, 7,* 1–7.

Miller, L. C., Barrett, C. L., & Hampe, E. (1974). Phobias of childhood in a prescientific era. In A. Davids (Ed.), *Child personality and psychopathology: Current topics* (pp. 72–95). New York: John Wiley & Sons.

Miller, L. C., Barret, C. L., Hampe, E., & Noble, H. (1972). Factor structure of childhood fears. *Journal of Consulting and Clinical Psychology, 39,* 264–268.

Miller, P. M. (1972). The use of visual imagery and muscle relaxation in the counterconditioning of a phobic child: A case study. *Journal of Nervous and Mental Disease, 154,* 457–460.

Morris, R. J. (1973). Shaping relaxation in the unrelaxed client. *Journal of Behavior Therapy and Experimental Psychiatry, 4,* 343–353.

Morris, R. J. (1985). *Behavior modification with exceptional children: Principles and practices.* Glenview, IL: Scott Foresman & Company.

Morris, R. J. (1986). Fear reduction methods. In F. H. Kanfer & A. P. Goldstein (Eds.), *Helping people change* (3rd ed., pp. 145–190). Elmsford, NY: Pergamon Press.

Morris, R. J., & Kratochwill, T. R. (1983). *Treating children's fears and phobias: A behavioral approach.* Elmsford, NY: Pergamon Press.

Morris, R. J., Kratochwill, T. R., & Aldridge, K. (1988). Fear reduction methods in the school setting. In J. C. Witt, S. N. Elliott, & F. M. Gresham (Eds.), *Handbook of behavior therapy in education* (pp. 679–717). New York: Plenum Press.

Morris, R. J., Kratochwill, T. R., & Dodson, C. L. (1986). Fears and phobias in adolescence: A behavioral perspective. In R. A. Feldman & A. R. Stiffman (Eds.), *Advances in adolescent mental health* (pp. 63–117). Santa Barbara, CA: JAI Press.

Morris, R. J., & Magrath, K. (1979). Contributions of therapist warmth to the contact desensitization treatment of acrophobia. *Journal of Consulting and Clinical Psychology, 47,* 786–788.

Morris, R. J., & Magrath, K. (1983). The therapeutic relationship in behavior therapy. In M. Lambert (Ed.), *Therapeutic relations in psychotherapy* (pp. 102–128). Homewood, IL: Dow-Jones-Irwin.

Morris, R. J., & Suckerman, K. R. (1974a). The importance of the therapeutic relationship in systematic desensitization. *Journal of Consulting and Clinical Psychology, 42,* 148.

Morris, R. J., & Kratochwill, T. R. (1985). Behavioral treatment of children's fears and phobias: A review. *School Psychology Review, 14,* 84.

Morris, R. J., & Suckerman, K. R. (1974b). Therapist warmth as a factor in automated systematic desensitization. *Journal of Consulting and Clinical Psychology, 42,* 244–250.

Morris, R. J., & Suckerman, K. R. (1976). Studying therapist warmth in analogue systematic desensitization. *Journal of Consulting and Clinical Psychology, 44,* 285–89.

Murphy, C. M., & Bootzin, R. R. (1973). Active and passive participation in the contact desensitization of snake fear in children. *Behavioral Therapy, 4,* 203–211.

Neisworth, J. T., Madle, R. A., & Goeke, K. E. (1975). Errorless elimination of separation anxiety: A case study. *Journal of Behavioral Therapy and Experimental Psychiatry, 6,* 79.

Nelson, R. O., & Hayes, S. C. (1979). The nature of behavioral assessment: A commentary. *Journal of Applied Behavior Analysis, 12,* 491–500.

Nietzel, M. T., & Bernstein, D. A. (1981). Assessment of anxiety and fear. In M. Hersen & A. S. Bellack (Eds.), *Behavioral assessment: A practical handbook* (2nd ed., pp. 215–245). Elmsford, NY: Pergamon Press.

Obler, M., & Terwilliger, R. F. (1970). Test effectiveness of systematic desensitization with neurologically impaired children with phobic disorders. *Journal of Consulting and Clinical Psychology, 34,* 314–318.

Ollendick, T. H. (1979a). Behavioral treatment of anorexia nervosa: A five year study. *Behavior Modification, 3,* 124–135.

Ollendick, T. H. (1979b). Fear reduction techniques with children. In M. Hersen, R. M. Eisler, & P. M. Miller (Eds.), *Progress in behavior modification* (Vol. 8). New York: Academic Press.

Ollendick, T. H. (1983). Reliability and validity of the revised Fear Survey Schedule for Children (FSSCR-R). *Behaviour Research & Therapy, 21,* 685–692.

Ollendick, T. H. (1986). Child and adolescent behavior therapy. In S. L. Garfield & A. E. Bergin (Eds.), *Handbook of psychotherapy and behavior change* (3rd ed.) (pp. 525–564). New York: John Wiley & Sons.

Ollendick, T. H., Matson, J. L., & Helsel, W. J. (1985). Fears in children and adolescents: Normative data. *Behaviour Research & Therapy, 23,* 465–467.

O'Reilly, P. (1971). Desensitization of fire bell phobia. *Journal of School Psychology, 9,* 55–57.

Patterson, G. R. (1965). A learning theory approach to the treatment of the school phobic child. In L. P. Ullmann & L. Krasner (Eds.), *Case studies in behavior modification* (pp. 279–284). New York: Holt, Rinehart & Winston.

Paul, G. L., & Bernstein, D. A. (1973). *Anxiety and clinical problems: Systematic desensitization and related techniques.* Morristown, NJ: General Learning Press.

Pavlov, I. P. (1927). *Conditioned reflexes.* Trans. G. V. Anrep. London: Oxford University Press.

Perry, M. A., & Furukawa, M. J. (1986). Modeling methods. In F. H. Kanfer & A. P. Goldstein (Eds.), *Helping people change* (3rd ed., pp. 66–110). Elmsford, NY: Pergamon Press.

Peterson, L., & Shigetomi, C. (1981). The use of coping techniques in minimizing anxiety in hospitalized children. *Behavior Therapy, 12,* 1–14.

Piersel, W. C., & Kratochwill, T. R. (1981). A teacher-implemented contingency management package to assess and test selective mutism. *Behavioral Assessment, 3,* 371–382.

Rachman, S. J., & Hodgson, R. (1974). Synchrony and desynchrony in fear and avoidance. *Behaviour Research and Therapy, 12,* 311–318.

Reeves, J. L., & Maelica, W. L. (1975). Biofeedback—assisted cue controlled relaxation for the treatment of flight phobias. *Journal of Behavior Therapy and Experimental Psychiatry, 6,* 106–109.

Richards, C. S., & Siegel, L. J. (1978). Behavioral treatment of anxiety states and avoidance behaviors in children. In D. Marholin II (Ed.), *Child behavior therapy*. New York: Gardner Press.

Rimm, D. C., & Masters, J. C. (1974). *Behavior therapy: Techniques and empirical findings*. New York: Academic Press, Inc.

Ritter, B. (1968). The group desensitization of children's snake phobias using vicarious and contact desensitization procedures. *Behaviour Research and Therapy, 6*, 1–6.

Ritter, B. (1969). The use of contact desensitization, demonstration-plus-participation and demonstration only in the treatment of acrophobia. *Behaviour Research and Therapy, 7*, 41–45.

Rivenq, B. (1974). Behavior therapy of phobias: A case with gynecomastia with mental retardation. *Mental Retardation, 12*, 44–45.

Rosen, G. (1976). *Don't be afraid. A program for overcoming your fears and phobias*. Englewood Cliffs, NJ: Prentice-Hall.

Ross, A. O. (1981). Of rigor and relevance. *Professional Psychology, 12*, 273–279.

Ross, D. M., Ross, S. A., & Evans, T. A. (1971). The modification of extreme social withdrawal by modeling with guided participation. *Journal of Behavior Therapy and Experimental Psychiatry, 2*, 273–279.

Rutter, M., Tizard, J., & Whitmore, K. (1970). *Education, health and behavior*. New York: John Wiley & Sons.

Sarason, I. G. (1980). *Test anxiety: Theory, research and applications*. Hillsdale, NJ: Lawrence Erlbaum Associates.

Saunders, D. G. (1976). A case of motion sickness treated by systematic desensitization and *in vivo* relaxation. *Journal of Behavior Therapy and Experimental Psychiatry, 7*, 381–382.

Scarr, S., & Salapatek, P. (1970). Patterns of fear development during infancy. *Merrill–Palmer Quarterly of Behavior and Development, 16*, 53–90.

Sheslow, D. V., Bondy, A. S., & Nelson, R. O. (1983). A comparison of graduated exposure, verbal coping skills and their combination in the treatment of children's fear of the dark. *Child and Family Behavior Therapy, 4*, 33–45.

Siegel, L. J., & Peterson, L. (1980). Stress reduction in young dental patients through coping skills and sensory information. *Journal of Consulting and Clinical Psychology, 48*, 785–787.

Skinner, B. F. (1938). *The behavior of organisms*. New York: Appleton-Century.

Skinner, B. F. (1953). *Science and human behavior*. New York: Macmillan.

Stableford, W. (1979). Parental treatment of a child's noise phobia. *Journal of Behavior Therapy and Experimental Psychiatry, 10*, 159–160.

Stedman, J. M., & Murphey, J. (1984). Dealing with specific child phobias during the course of family therapy: An alternative to systematic desensitization. *Family Therapy, 11*, 55–60.

Tahmisian, J., & McReynolds, W. (1971). The use of parents as behavioral engineers in the treatment of a school phobic girl. *Journal of Counseling Psychology, 18*, 225–228.

Tarler-Benlolo, L. (1978). The role of relaxation in biofeedback training. A critical review of literature. *Psychological Bulletin, 85*, 727–755.

Tasto, D. L. (1969). Systematic desensitization, muscle relaxation and visual imagery in the counterconditioning of a 4-year-old phobic child. *Behaviour Research and Therapy, 7*, 409–411.

Taylor, D. W. (1972). Treatment of excessive frequency of urination by desensitization. *Journal of Behavior Therapy and Experimental Psychiatry, 3*, 311–313.

Trueman, D. (1984). What are the characteristics of school phobic children? *Psychological Reports, 54*, 191–202.

Ultee, C. A., Griffiaen, D., & Schellekens, J. (1982). The reduction of anxiety in children: A comparison of the effects of systematic desensitization *in vitro* and systematic desensitization *in vivo*. *Behaviour Research & Therapy, 20*, 61–67.

Vaal, J. J. (1973). Applying contingency contracting to a school phobic: A case study. *Journal of Behavior Therapy and Experimental Psychiatry, 4*, 371–373.

Van der Ploeg, H. M. (1975). Treatment of frequency of urination by stories competing with anxiety. *Journal of Behavior Therapy and Experimental Psychiatry, 6*, 165–166.

Van der Ploeg-Stapert, J. D., & Van der Ploeg, H. M. (1986). Behavioral group treatment of test-anxiety: An evaluation study. *Journal of Behavior Therapy and Experimental Psychiatry, 17*, 255–259.

Van Hasselt, B. B., Hersen, M., Bellack, A. S., Rosenblum, N. D., & Lamparski, D. (1979). Tripartite assessment of the effects of systematic desensitization in a multi-phobic child: An experimental analysis. *Journal of Behavior Therapy and Experimental Psychiatry, 10,* 51–55.

Vernon, V. T., & Bailey, W. C. (1974). The use of motion pictures in the psychological preparation of children for induction of anesthesia. *Anesthesiology, 40,* 68–72.

Waranch, H. R., Iwata, B. A., Wohl, M. K., & Nidiffer, F. D. (1981). Treatment of a retarded adults mannequin phobia through *in vivo* desensitization and shaping approach responses. *Journal of Behavior Therapy and Experimental Psychiatry, 12,* 359–362.

Warren, R., Smith, G., & Velten, E. (1984). Rational-emotive therapy and the reduction of interpersonal anxiety in junior high school students. *Adolescence, 19,* 893–902.

Watson, J. B. (1913). Psychology as the behaviorist views it. *Psychological Review, 20,* 158–177.

Watson, J. B. (1919). *Psychology from the standpoint of a behaviorist.* Philadelphia: Lippincott.

Watson, J. B., & Rayner, R. (1920). Conditioned emotional reactions. *Journal of Experimental Psychology, 3,* 1–14.

Waye, M. F. (1979). Behavioral treatment of a child displaying comic-book mediated fear of hand shrinking: A case study. *Journal of Pediatric Psychology, 4,* 43–47.

White, W. C., & Davis, M. T. (1974). Vicarious extinction of phobic behavior in early childhood. *Journal of Abnormal Child Psychology, 2,* 25–37.

Wilson, B., & Jackson, H. J. (1980). An *in vivo* approach to the desensitization of a retarded child's toilet phobia. *Australian Journal of Developmental Disabilities, 6,* 137–141.

Wish, P. A. Hasazi, J. E., & Jurgela, A. R. (1973). Automated direct deconditioning of a childhood phobia. *Journal of Behavior Therapy and Experimental Psychiatry, 4,* 279–283.

Wolde, G. (1972). *Tommy goes to the doctor.* Boston: Houghton-Mifflin.

Wolpe, J. (1958). *Reciprocal inhibition therapy.* Stanford, CA: Stanford University Press.

Wolpe, J. (1962). The experimental foundations of some new psychotherapeutic methods. In A. J. Bachrach (Ed.), *Experimental foundations of clinical psychology* (pp. 554–575). New York: Basic Books.

Wolpe, J. (1969). *The practice of behavior therapy.* Elmsford, NY: Pergamon Press.

Wolpe, J. (1973). *The practice of behavior therapy* (2nd ed.). Elmsford, N.Y.: Pergamon Press.

Wolpe, J., & Lazarus, A. A. (1966). *Behavior therapy techniques.* Elmsford, NY: Pergamon Press.

Zettle, R. D., & Hayes, S. C. (1980). Conceptual and empirical status of rational-emotive therapy. In M. Hersen, R. M. Eisler, & P. M. Miller (Eds.). *Progress in behavior modification, 9,* 125–166. New York: Academic Press.

CHAPTER 5

ATTENTION-DEFICIT HYPERACTIVITY DISORDER

George J. DuPaul
David C. Guevremont
Russell A. Barkley

Since the publication of the first edition of this text in 1983, a great deal of research has been conducted on the nature and treatment of childhood hyperactivity. Certainly hyperactivity, or more recently, attention-deficit hyperactivity disorder (ADHD; American Psychiatric Association, 1987) remains one of the most frequent referral complaints to child guidance clinics in this country. Epidemiological studies indicate that it occurs in 3% to 5% of the school-age population. As a result, ADHD continues to be one of the most heavily studied psychological disorders of childhood. Given its relatively high prevalence rate, it behooves clinicians and students of clinical child psychology to be able to assess this disorder competently and to design interventions that will effectively ameliorate both the core disorder and its associated deficits. The purpose of this chapter is to briefly review several treatment interventions that have demonstrated efficacy in the therapeutic management of ADHD and to provide an update regarding research into the salient parameters and outcomes associated with these interventions.

This chapter is not designed to be an exhaustive review of the literature on the treatment of children with ADHD, as this has already been accomplished by others (Ross & Ross, 1982). Further, because there are many problems associated with ADHD in addition to core deficits (see Table 5.1), it would be impossible to delineate all of the treatment interventions used with this population. The reader is directed to those chapters in this text that address these problems (aggressive behavior, academic problems, depression) in more detail. Alternatively, this chapter will focus on those behavioral or cognitive deficits felt to be central to ADHD: inattention, impulsivity, and poor rule-governed behavior (Barkley, 1981, 1988; Douglas, 1983; Rapport, 1987). The emphasis previously given to the overactivity or motor restlessness of these children was somewhat misplaced, as it seems to be their attentional, cognitive, and conduct problems that lead them into chronic conflict with their social environment, cause them to be referred for treatment (Barkley & Cunningham, 1979; Whalen & Henker, 1980), and underlie

Table 5.1. Problems Associated With ADHD in Children

GENERAL AREA	SPECIFIC PROBLEMS
Behavioral	Short attention span Distractibility Restlessness Poor impulse control Destructiveness/noisiness
Social	Poor peer relations Noncompliance to commands Aggression/lying/stealing Belligerent and disrespectful language Poor self-control/high risk taking Poor social problem-solving skills
Cognitive	Immature self-speech (internal language) Inattentiveness-distractibility Low average intelligence Lack of conscience Poor perspective of future consequences for behavior
Academic	Underachievement for intelligence Specific learning disabilities
Emotional	Depression Low self-esteem Excitability Immature emotional control Easily frustrated Unpredictable/variable moods
Physical	Immature physical size Immature bone growth Enuresis/encopresis Increased upper respiratory infections Increased frequency of otitis media Increased frequency of allergies Greater number of minor physical anomalies Underreactive central nervous system Short sleep cycle High pain tolerance Poor motor coordination

From *Hyperactive children: A handbook for diagnosis and treatment* by R. A. Barkley, 1981, New York: Guilford Press. Copyright 1981 by Guilford Press. Reprinted by permission.

their poor long-term adjustment (Gittelman, Mannuzza, Shenker, & Bonagura, 1985; Weiss & Hechtman, 1986).

AN OVERVIEW

History and Definition

Although Still (1902) is typically credited with first identifying the syndrome presently known as ADHD, he acknowledged references to these children dated in the 1860s. The serious student of the subject would be well advised to review this classic paper not only for its historic value but also for its lucid discussion of the "defects in moral consciousness" characteristic of these children and its prophetic description of their usual symptoms, family patterns, and preponderance among the male sex.

In subsequent years, researchers stressed the motor activity component of the disorder (Chess, 1960; Wender, 1971; Werry, 1968; Werry & Sprague, 1970), which resulted in the application of the label "hyperactivity" or "hyperkinesis" to it. At times, this emphasis on hyperactivity led to the exclusion of other identifying problems (e.g., inattention) now believed to coexist with fidgetiness, restlessness, and gross motor overactivity. Others (e.g., Clements, 1966) attempted to describe symptoms so numerous that virtually any child might be felt to exhibit at least one of them at some time in his or her development. Because the disorder was defined in this fashion, it became difficult to distinguish it from any other psychological disorder of childhood. In 1972, Douglas emphasized the need to consider the child's inattention and impulsivity as the more pervasive and chronic problems associated with ADHD, and follow-up research (Weiss & Hechtman, 1986) seems to have borne this out. For this and related reasons, the label "hyperactivity" is slowly being replaced by the term "attention-deficit hyperactivity disorder," as espoused by APA in its recent DSM-III-R (APA, 1987). Over the past decade, investigators have begun to consider deficits in behavioral self-regulation as a hallmark of ADHD. These have included hypothesized deficits in self-directed instruction (Kendall & Braswell, 1985), self-regulation of arousal to meet environmental demands (Douglas, 1983), and rule-governed behavior (Barkley, 1981, 1989).

It is clear from any historical review of this disorder that, until recently, there were few operational definitions which were useful, reliable, and valid for clinical or research purposes. Several commonalities (e.g., early onset of marked inattention, impulsivity, and overactivity) among the various historical definitions were helpful, however, in guiding the formulation of current diagnostic schemas. With these in mind, two definitions are currently available to aid the clinician or scientist in diagnosing ADHD. First, APA (1987) has recently revised the diagnostic criteria for what was formerly known as "attention deficit disorder with or without hyperactivity" (APA, 1980). As mentioned above, the revised label is attention-deficit hyperactivity disorder. The criteria for this diagnosis are set forth in Table 5.2. This definition certainly represents an advance over previous formulations, as the diagnostic criteria are relatively objective and the cutoff score of eight out of fourteen was established in a national clinical field trial.

Although these criteria are an improvement over those in previous DSM editions, they continue to have several limitations. First, no guidelines are provided as to how the symptoms are established as deviant for the child's age or how pervasive the problems must be (where and with whom) to "rule in" the diagnosis. While behavioral rating scales are increasingly used to select subjects as ADHD in research and clinical practice, more objective computerized tests of atten-

tion are being advocated by some (Gordon, 1983) as part of a diagnostic evaluation. Some acknowledgment of these available assessment methods would have been useful in helping to standardize diagnostic practices. Further, the symptom cutoff score is fixed, ignoring well-known age-related declines in these behaviors among both normal and ADHD children. Age-referenced cutoff scores would have been helpful, because the score needed to show statistical deviance may be higher for younger children than for teenagers. For instance, it may be that 10 of 14 symptoms is more indicative for preschool or early elementary-age children while 6 of 14 symptoms is more typical of ADHD in adolescents. Finally, no rationale has been established for the age-of-onset and duration criteria proposed.

Barkley (1988) has proposed a more stringent definition of the disorder, as follows:

> ADHD is a developmental disorder of attention span, impulsivity, and/or overactivity as well as rule-governed behavior, in which these deficits are significantly inappropriate for the child's mental age; have an onset in early childhood; are significantly pervasive or cross-situational in nature; are generally chronic or persistent over time; and are not the direct result of severe language delay, deafness, blindness, autism, or childhood psychosis.

The following diagnostic guidelines were proposed:

1. Parent and/or teacher complaints of inattention, impulsivity, overactivity, and poor rule-governed behavior (e.g., lack of sustained compliance, self-control, and problem solving).
2. A score or scores two standard deviations above the mean for same-age, same-sex normal children on factors labeled as "inattention" or "hyperactivity" in well-standardized child-behavior rating scales completed by parents and teachers.
3. Onset of problems by 6 years of age.
4. Duration of these problems for at least 12 months.
5. An IQ greater than 85 or, if between 70 and 85, comparison with children of the same mental age in using criterion 2 above.
6. The exclusion of significant language delay, sensory handicaps (e.g., deafness, blindness), or severe psychopathology (e.g., schizophrenia).

Table 5.2. Diagnostic Criteria for Attention-Deficit Hyperactivity Disorder

The essential features of this disorder are developmentally inappropriate degrees of inattention, impulsiveness, and hyperactivity. People with the disorder generally display some disturbance in each of these areas, but to varying degrees.

Note: Consider a criterion met only if the behavior is considerably more frequent than that of most people of the same mental age.

A. A disturbance of at least six months during which at least eight of the following are present:
    (1) often fidgets with hands or feet or squirms in seat (in adolescents, may be limited to subjective feelings of restlessness)
    (2) has difficulty remaining seated when required to do so
    (3) is easily distracted by extraneous stimuli
    (4) has difficulty awaiting turn in games or group situations
    (5) often blurts out answers to questions before they have been completed
    (6) has difficulty following through on instructions from others (not due to oppositional behavior or failure of comprehension), e.g., fails to finish chores
    (7) has difficulty sustaining attention in tasks or play activities
    (8) often shifts from one uncompleted activity to another
    (9) has difficulty playing quietly
    (10) often talks excessively
    (11) often interrupts or intrudes on others, e.g., butts into other children's games
    (12) often does not seem to listen to what is being said to him or her
    (13) often loses things necessary for tasks or activities at school or at home (e.g., toys, pencils, books, assignments)
    (14) often engages in physically dangerous activities without considering possible consequences (not for the purpose of thrill-seeking), e.g., runs into street without looking
B. Onset before the age of seven.
C. Does not meet the criteria for a pervasive developmental disorder.

From American Psychiatric Association: *Diagnostic and statistical manual of mental disorders,* third edition, revised. Washington, D.C., American Psychiatric Association, 1987. Reprinted by permission.

Several additional provisos should be kept in mind. First, the label "acquired ADHD secondary to———" should be applied in cases where the child exhibits these symptoms after the age of 6 as a result of central nervous system trauma or disease. This will distinguish such children from the more common developmental, idiopathic form of ADHD typically encountered in clinical practice or research investigations. Second, when the child presents with significant noncompliance or conduct disturbance, quite common among ADHD children, this does not preclude the diagnosis of ADHD. Rather, additional diagnoses (e.g., oppositional defiant disorder, conduct disorder) would need to be considered. Finally, the symptoms of ADHD may be viewed as lying on a continuum with normal development, wherein the diagnostic threshold has been established by using a somewhat arbitrary cutoff point (i.e., two standard deviations above the mean) along this continuum. One must be cognizant of the existence of borderline conditions lying near to but not beyond this cutoff point. While ADHD is generally chronic, with a high degree of stability over development for most children (e.g., Gittelman et al., 1985), those placed in the borderline range of the continuum may move into or out of the

ADHD category over development, because their individual scores may fluctuate as a function of situational or developmental variation.

Description and Developmental Course

In addition to the core diagnostic symptoms, children with ADHD may exhibit a variety of associated behavioral and emotional problems, as delineated in Table 5.1. Although these occur more frequently among ADHD children than in their normal counterparts, there is a great deal of individual variability regarding symptom emergence and chronicity through the course of development. Despite these individual differences, a plethora of empirical data has been gathered suggesting that difficulties of temperament and behavioral control begin in the ADHD child's early years and continue throughout life.

Infants exhibiting difficult temperament who are excessively active, have poor sleeping and eating habits, and are prone to negative moods are at greater risk for eventual ADHD than children with more normal temperaments (see Ross & Ross, 1982, for a review). Those at risk may also have a higher rate of minor physical anomalies. However, these are not specific precursors of ADHD and may be associated with other behavioral disorders (Pomeroy, Sprafkin, & Gadow, 1988; Quinn & Rappoport, 1974).

The majority of children who will be identified as having ADHD will have begun to manifest significant overactivity, noncompliance, and short attention span by 3 years of age. Typically, complaints regarding these excessive behaviors are first brought to the parent's attention by other caretakers, such as teachers, day-care personnel, or relatives. Toilet training may be difficult and may occur later than normal, presumably because of the child's frequent noncompliance (Hartsough & Lambert, 1985).

The stability of the ADHD child's behavioral excesses from the preschool years to early elementary grades has been well documented (Campbell, Schleifer, & Weiss, 1978). In fact, by the first grade (i.e., by age 6), more than 90% of children with ADHD will have been identified as problematic by their parents or teachers. The most significant difficulties during middle to late childhood (6 to 11 years of age) include short attention span, noncompliance with school and home rules, and excessive motor activity, particularly in structured situations (e.g., independent seat work). Associated concerns may emerge, including poor relationships with peers (Pelham & Bender, 1982), chronic underachievement or specific learning disabilities, conduct problems (e.g., lying, stealing), disruptive behavior in group situations, and, in later years, feelings of low self-esteem.

At home, ADHD children frequently evidence an inability to consistently complete routine chores and activities (e.g., preparing for school, completing homework, cleaning their rooms). In fact, this irresponsibility may cause parents to spend an inordinate amount of their time supervising their children's activities. Stress in the parental role as well as the risk for maternal depression may increase at this time (Breen, 1985; Mash & Johnston, 1983).

Several distinct developmental patterns begin to emerge during adolescence. Many children with ADHD will continue to present with the core symptoms of the disorder, with estimates ranging from 30% (Gittelman et al., 1985) to 70% (Lambert, Hartsough, Sassone, & Sandoval, 1987). Those children with "pure" ADHD who do not display significant aggressiveness or peer-relationship problems are likely to exhibit continued difficulties with inattention and impulsivity, which lead primarily to poor performance at school (Paternite & Loney, 1980).

Such youngsters are typically described as "underachievers." Once out of school and working, these teenagers presumably experience less trouble with their behavior than they did at school. Alternatively, those exhibiting aggression and conduct problems apparently are at risk for more significant maladjustment. Not only are school-performance problems evident, but difficulties with predelinquent or delinquent behavior in the community may emerge (Gittelman et al., 1985; Lambert et al., 1987; Satterfield, Hoppe, & Schell, 1982), and problematic peer relationships may continue or become worse. There is some evidence to suggest that adolescents with ADHD are more likely to abuse alcohol (Gittelman et al., 1985), although there are also contradictory findings (Weiss, Hechtman, Perlman, Hopkins, & Wener, 1979). In addition, these teenagers are at higher risk for automobile accidents (Weiss et al., 1979), dropping out of high school (Weiss, Hechtman, Milroy, & Perlman, 1985), experiencing feelings of low self-esteem, and poor social acceptance (Weiss, Hechtman, & Perlman, 1978).

In general, the behavior patterns described above may continue into adulthood, with most follow-up studies indicating that individuals with childhood ADHD function less adequately in a number of spheres (e.g., socially, psychologically, occupationally) than do controls or their normal siblings (Loney, Whaley-Klahn, Kosier, & Conboy, 1981; Thorley, 1984; Weiss et al., 1985). Specifically, there is a greater risk for adult antisocial personality disorder (Loney et al., 1981; Weiss et al., 1985), alcoholism, and complaints of interpersonal problems or psychological difficulties (Weiss et al., 1985). These findings would certainly indicate that there are adult disorders which are equivalent to or are residual forms of childhood ADHD (Wender, Reimherr, & Wood, 1981; Wood, Reimherr, Wender, & Johnson, 1976).

This course is not evident for all ADHD children and is apparently mediated by several factors. The research literature indicates that a number of significant variables are associated with poorer outcome in this population, including low intelligence in childhood, aggressiveness and oppositional behavior, poor peer acceptance, emotional instability, and extent of parental psychopathology (Hechtman, Weiss, Perlman, & Amsel, 1984; Loney et al., 1981; Paternite & Loney, 1980). While extensive, long-term treatment through adolescence may reduce the risk of maladjustment (Satterfield, Satterfield, & Schell, 1987), lesser degrees of treatment, including stimulant medication, have not been found to have a significant impact on adult outcome (Hechtman, Weiss, & Perlman, 1984; Paternite & Loney, 1980). Thus, we have taken the approach that ADHD is a developmental disorder of self-control and social conduct that is chronic and without cure. An attitude of "coping" rather than "curing" is frequently communicated to the family by the clinician, intimating that treatment may lead to the reduction of problems but not necessarily to their complete elimination.

Etiology

A wide variety of causative factors have been proposed to underlie ADHD, yet no single variable has been found to account for its genesis fully. In fact, it may be most prudent to view ADHD as the final common pathway of a number of possible etiological events, much as mental retardation or other developmental disabilities are conceptualized (Barkley, 1988). In general, the major causal variables that have been identified can be categorized as neurological factors, toxic reactions, genetic linkage, and environmental factors (see Anastopoulos & Barkley, 1988, for a more detailed review).

The etiological role of neurological variables has been the most heavily investigated over the years. Initially, gross brain damage resulting from head trauma or neurologic illness was presumed to be the primary cause of ADHD (Strauss & Lehtinen, 1947). In fact, for a time it was assumed that all children with ADHD had some level of structural insult even in the absence of "hard" evidence. Hence, the terms "minimal brain damage" or "minimal brain dysfunction" (MBD) were used in labeling children who presented with ADHD symptomatology. Recent investigations have refuted this assumption by indicating that less than 5% of ADHD children show hard evidence of neurological damage (Rutter, 1977) and most brain-injured children do not display symptoms of ADHD (Rutter, Chadwick, & Shaffer, 1983). Despite the lack of evidence for structural damage, there is intriguing evidence that ADHD children display diminished levels of cerebral blood flow in the frontal white matter and frontal midbrain tracts relative to dysphasic children (Lou, Henriksen, & Bruhn, 1984). Presumably, this suggests that children with ADHD exhibit decreased activity or stimulation in these regions (Fox & Raichle, 1985). In similar fashion, several studies have indicated potential neurotransmitter abnormalities in ADHD children (Shaywitz, Cohen, & Shaywitz, 1978; Shaywitz, Shaywitz, Cohen, & Young, 1983), although their results are often equivocal. Thus, there are strong indications that neurological dysfunction, perhaps related to neurotransmitter imbalances, is associated with ADHD; however, delineation of its causative role awaits more rigorous and specific investigation (Anastopoulos & Barkley, 1988).

Food additives, sugar, and lead have been the most widely studied environmental toxins or allergens proposed to cause ADHD. In fact, Feingold (1975) hypothesized that the vast majority of children with ADHD contracted the disorder as a result of allergic reactions to food additives (e.g., artificial colorings). He and others presumed that removal of these additives from a child's diet would effectively reduce ADHD symptomatology. Many well-controlled studies have been conducted examining this issue; they indicate that dietary management is ineffective in most cases (for reviews, see Conners, 1980; Mattes & Gittelman, 1981). The minority (i.e., 5%) of ADHD children who do respond to such treatment evidence minimal behavioral change and are typically under the age of 6. In similar fashion, ingestion of sugar has been proposed as causing ADHD (Smith, 1976). Once again, well-controlled studies, which included aspartame challenge conditions, have found no clinically significant increases in behaviors associated with ADHD following sucrose ingestion (Gross, 1984; Rosen et al., 1988; Milich, Wolraich, & Lindgren, 1986). Finally, conflicting results have been obtained regarding the role of lead exposure in causing ADHD (see Ross & Ross, 1982, for a review); the association between the two appears quite weak (Gittelman & Eskenazi, 1983).

Currently, the most fruitful line of etiological investigation is research into possible hereditary or genetic causes for ADHD. At a general level, it is well documented that the incidence of psychiatric disorders (e.g., antisocial personality, depression) among biological relatives of ADHD children is significantly greater than in the general population (Befera & Barkley, 1985; Biederman et al., 1987; Cantwell, 1975). More specifically, there is an increased incidence of ADHD among the biological parents and siblings of children with ADHD (Deutsch, 1984). Further, studies of monozygotic twins have found a relatively high concordance rate for activity level (Lopez, 1965; Willerman, 1973). Taken together, these indicate the causative role of two possibly interrelated factors: the natural variation of biological characteristics (Kinsbourne, 1977) and some unspecified mode of inheritance of psychopathological symptomatology (Anastopoulos & Barkley, 1988).

Environmental or behavioral causes of ADHD have received minimal attention, yet the scant evidence available would indicate a limited role for these factors. For example, Willis and Lovaas (1977) have surmised that ADHD is a result of poor stimulus control of behavior by parental commands, stemming from inconsistent child-management techniques. Certainly, mothers of ADHD children have been found to issue more commands and to use more negative statements; however, this appears to be partly a function of the task required (Tallmadge & Barkley, 1983) and the age of the children (Barkley, Karlsson, & Pollard, 1985). Further, because these negative mother–child interactions are reduced when the children are treated with stimulant medication (Barkley & Cunningham, 1980; Barkley, Karlsson, Strzelecki, & Murphy, 1984; Humphries, Kinsbourne, & Swanson, 1978), maternal behavior is more likely a reaction to than a major cause of behavioral difficulties associated with ADHD. Alternatively, environmental factors play an important role in modulating the severity of behavioral control difficulties, as will be discussed in subsequent sections reviewing behavioral interventions. Based on evidence gathered to date, ADHD appears to be related to multiple factors that may separately or in combination lead to onset of symptoms. Biological factors (neurological and genetic) seem to account for onset of the disorder in the vast majority of ADHD children studied. It is perhaps best to view ADHD in similar fashion to mental retardation, in that the disorder represents a final common pathway of a number of etiological events (Anastopoulos & Barkley, 1988).

OVERVIEW OF TREATMENT METHODS

Given the diversity, multiplicity, pervasiveness, and chronicity of behavior problems associated with ADHD, a variety of treatments implemented across settings and by different service providers will often be required. This necessitates the involvement of professionals from several different disciplines (e.g., physician, psychologist, social worker, special education teacher), each providing his or her own special expertise in dealing with specific problems. Thus, professional jealousies and antagonisms will have to be discarded to provide the services that will help both child and family cope with the myriad problems likely to arise throughout the child's development.

As has been stated, there is no cure for ADHD. Even the most effective treatments available are typically short-term in nature and symptomatic in focus. Knowledge of the etiology of the disorder, which is minimal, provides little assistance in treatment selection. While recent evidence would suggest that long-term multimodal therapy reduces the risk for poor adolescent and adult outcome (Satterfield et al., 1987), the results of most outcome studies do not indicate significant long-term improvements. Alternatively, to the extent that a short-term reduction in problem severity is obtained, it is also likely to reduce the degree of censure, criticism, ostracism, disciplining, and potential for abuse of the child. That these interventions can also provide some relief to the families and teachers of these children further supports their use. Therefore, the goal of therapy is to cope with, not cure, the ADHD, and periodic intervention will almost certainly be needed to guide the child through his or her often stormy developmental years.

The major targets of intervention to be discussed in this chapter are the child's poor attention span, impulsivity or lack of self-control, and noncompliance with authority-figure directives (i.e., poor rule-governed behavior). Associated problems may exist in any child with ADHD (see Table 5.1); their treatment is the subject of other chapters in this text and will not be addressed here. At the present time, the interventions that have shown the greatest effectiveness with ADHD children are pharmacotherapy, parent counseling and training in child-management skills, and classroom behavior-modification techniques. The combination of these approaches is frequently necessary, owing to the severity and pervasiveness of the ADHD child's difficulties. Alternative treatment methods with less well demonstrated efficacies will be briefly reviewed as well. Given the variety and complexity of all these techniques, it is not possible to describe their implementation in great detail; however, references to more thorough discussions will be made throughout the remainder of this chapter. Even when these readings are pursued, the student should remember that none are intended as shortcuts to or substitute for clinically supervised practicum experience.

PHARMACOTHERAPY

The use of stimulant medications for the treatment of ADHD and related disruptive behavior disorders is the most extensively studied intervention to date. Over 70% of children with ADHD who take these medications evidence behavioral improvements based on parent/teacher judgments, laboratory task performance, and direct observations (Barkley, 1977). While a brief overview of the use of these drugs will be provided here, the reader is referred to chapter 12 by Gadow and Pomeroy for more detailed discussions of their clinical use and associated ethical and professional issues. While the primary focus of the present discussion will be on the use of psychostimulants, several investigations have demonstrated the efficacy of antidepressant medications in ameliorating attention deficits while also modulating mood lability (Rapoport, Quinn, Bradbard, Riddle, & Brooks, 1974). In fact, there may be a subgroup of children with ADHD, characterized by anxiety or depressive symptoms, who may respond differentially to antidepressants (see Pliszka, 1987, for a review).

Stimulant Medications

The stimulant medications most commonly employed in the treatment of ADHD are listed in Table 5.3, along with their manufacturers, generic names, tablet sizes, and typical dosage ranges. Traditionally, recommended dosages for stimulant medications have been based on a child's body weight, using a milligram per kilogram formula (American Academy of Pediatrics, 1987). Recent dose-response studies indicate, however, that the behavioral effects of methylphenidate (MPH) are highly idiosyncratic and not moderated by differences in body weight (Rapport, DuPaul, & Kelly, 1989; Rapport et al., 1987). For this reason Table 5.3 presents recommended dosages in terms of fixed doses, as they are typically prescribed.

A great deal of evidence has been gathered indicating that MPH and other stimulants significantly enhance certain behavioral, cognitive, and academic processes. For example, MPH has been found to improve the performance of children with ADHD on laboratory tests of sustained attention (Barkley, Fischer, Newby, & Breen, 1988; Rapport et al., 1987), impulsive-reflective responding (Brown & Sleator, 1979; Rapport et al., 1988), short-term recall (Barkley et al., 1988; Rapport, Stoner, DuPaul, Birmingham, & Tucker, 1985), and associative learning (Vyse & Rapport, 1987). Medication-induced enhancements of children's on-task and academic accuracy rates in the classroom have also been obtained (Douglas et al., 1986; Pelham, Bender, Caddell, Booth, & Moorer, 1985; Rapport et al., 1987, 1988), along with concomitant reductions in disruptive, out-of-seat behavior (Werry & Conners, 1979). Gains in academic productivity and learning are primarily attributed to a general enhancement of attentional processes. Further behavioral effects are found with respect to increased compliance, independent play, and responsiveness to social interactions with parents, teachers, and peers (Barkley et al., 1984; Cunningham, Siegel, & Offord, 1985). In response, the volume of commands, criticism, punishment, and censure directed at the children is often reduced.

In contrast to the above, the results of several long-term follow-up studies investigating stimulant medication effects have been quite disappointing (e.g., Hechtman, Weiss, & Perlman, 1984). Children can apparently remain on these medications from 2 to 10 years with little additional improvements seen beyond that obtained at the outset of treatment. It should be pointed out, however, that there are many shortcomings to these investigations (e.g., poor outcome measures, inconsistent dosage titration procedures), thus minimizing the likelihood of obtaining more positive findings.

Side Effects

Contrary to recent media reports (e.g., Bacon, 1988), which have reported severe side effects associated with psychostimulants, such effects are quite mild relative to other classes of medications. The most frequent side effects are decreased appetite and insomnia. Several others—including somatic symptoms (e.g., headaches or stomachaches), increased tension, growth inhibition, and increases in heart rate or blood pressure—may be associated with stimulant treat-

Table 5.3. Stimulant Medications, Tablet Sizes, and Dose Ranges

BRAND NAME[a]	MANUFACTURER	TABLET SIZES	DOSE RANGE[b]
Ritalin (methylphenidate)	CIBA	5 mg 10 mg 20 mg SR 20 mg[c]	2.5 to 25 mg
Dexedrine (d-amphetamine)	Smith, Kline & French	5 mg (tablet & spansule) 10 mg (spansule)[c] 15 mg (spansule)[c] 5 mg/5 mL (elixir)	2.5 to 20 mg
Cylert[c] (pemoline)	Abbott	18.75 mg 37.5 mg 75 mg	18.75 to 112.5 mg

[a]Generic name is in parentheses.
[b]Dose range for each administration is provided.
[c]Sustained-release (SR) Ritalin, Dexedrine spansule, and Cylert are administered once per day.

ment in a minority of cases. In general, the frequency and severity of these effects are apparently dose-related and may diminish with reductions in dosage and/or the passage of time. In rare cases, symptoms of Gilles de la Tourette syndrome may appear following treatment with stimulant medication. Although the research evidence documenting the validity of this side effect is equivocal, caution is advisable before prescribing these drugs for patients with a personal or family history of motor and/or vocal tics.

When to Prescribe Drugs
There is no easy answer to this question. However, the chief indications for drug therapy are the severity of the child's problems and the degree of distress suffered by the child, the parents, or teachers. Several guidelines have been proposed by Barkley (1981) as aids to this decision. They are as follows:

1. Has the child had an adequate physical and psychological evaluation? Medications should never be prescribed if the child has not been directly and thoroughly examined.
2. How old is the child? Drug treatment is often ineffective or leads to more severe side effects among children below the age of 4. It is therefore not recommended for them.
3. Have other therapies been used? If this is the family's initial contact with the professional, prescription of medication might be postponed until alternative interventions (e.g., parent training in child-management skills) have been attempted. Alternatively,

when the child's behavior presents a severe problem and the family cannot participate in child-management training, medication may be the only possible alternative.
4. How severe is the child's current behavior? Where it is extremely unmanageable or distressing to the family, treatment with drugs may be the fastest and most effective way of dealing with the crisis until other forms of therapy can begin. Once progress with other therapies becomes evident, some effort can be made to reduce or discontinue medication
5. Can the family afford the medication and associated costs (e.g., follow-up visits)? Long-term compliance rates are typically poor (Firestone, 1982) and may be particularly problematic among families of low socioeconomic status (Brown, Borden, Wynne, Spunt, & Clingerman, 1987).
6. Are the parents sufficiently intelligent to adequately supervise the use of the medication and guard against its abuse?
7. What are the parents' attitudes toward pharmacotherapy? Some parents are simply "antidrug" and should never be coerced into agreeing to this treatment.
8. Is there a delinquent sibling or drug-abusing parent in the household? In this case, psychostimulant medication should not be prescribed, since there is a high risk of its illicit use or sale.
9. Does the child have any history of tics, psychosis, or thought disorder? If so, stimulant drugs are contraindicated.
10. Is the child highly anxious, fearful, or more likely to complain of psychosomatic distur-

bances? If so, a trial of antidepressant medication may be more fruitful than prescription of a stimulant.

11. Does the physician have time to monitor medication effects properly?

12. How does the child feel about medication and its alternatives? It is important that the use of drugs be discussed with older children and adolescents and its rationale sufficiently explained. In cases where children oppose the use of drugs, they may sabotage efforts to administer them (e.g., by not swallowing their pills).

Treatment Generalization

Of all of the interventions available in treating ADHD, pharmacotherapy produces effects across the widest variety of settings for the greatest length of time. It is typically effective for as long as the child requires it (e.g., several years), assuming minor dosage adjustments over the course of time. As would be expected, the effects of medication are limited to the active period of the drug (i.e., 3 to 7 hours, depending on the specific agent). Behaviors occurring outside this time period may not be improved and, in fact, may be worsened because of a "washout" effect when the medication is wearing off.

Behavioral control is evident across home, school, and public situations during the time that the drug is active. Alternatively, medication effects differ to some extent across settings (Barkley, 1977; Whalen et al., 1978) and appear to be most marked in situations that are highly structured or demand greater attention and self-control from the child. Further, there is a certain degree of behavioral specificity in the actions of psychostimulant medications. As summarized above, they primarily enhance sustained attention, which indirectly leads to greater academic productivity and accuracy, diminished disruptive or noncompliant behavior, and the display of more appropriate interpersonal skills. The specific doses that optimize therapeutic changes may differ across behavioral realms.

Limitations

The major limitation of drug treatment is that it must be carefully prescribed, titrated, monitored, and sometimes withdrawn under the supervision of a limited number of professionals (i.e., physicians). Thus, in certain rural areas where such medical care is scarce, pharmacotherapy may simply be unavailable. Several investigations have shown that the rate of compliance or adherence to regular administration of stimulant medications over long periods of time is alarmingly low (e.g., Firestone, 1982). Medication effects do not typically generalize to times or situations where the drug is not active; this limits long-term therapeutic benefits. Further, psychostimulants may be ineffective or inappropriate in treating certain subgroups of children with ADHD (e.g., those with anxiety symptoms), some behavioral classes (e.g., aggression), or behavior in certain settings. Finally, for some families, the expense of medication may place it beyond their means, making the efficacy of drugs irrelevant.

PARENT COUNSELING AND TRAINING

Parent Counseling

As is the case with other forms of child psychopathology, one of the most important components to the overall treatment of the ADHD child is the education and counseling of his or her parents on the nature, causes, course, prognosis, and treatment of this disorder. This component of treatment does not directly address the management of child behavior but rather those issues pertaining to the parents' understanding of the disorder and the variety of practical life circumstances for which research gives us little guidance.

Parent education may also serve as an essential prerequisite to specialized training in behavior management, because a number of procedures parents may be asked to use are predicated on their understanding of the specific deficits that their children may display (e.g., inattention). More specifically, parents may have questions about which school placements are best suited to the ADHD child's needs (e.g., public or private), whether the child should be encouraged to joined organized youth groups despite chronic problems in peer relations, how best to help the child with homework, and whether the child be required to eat despite finicky habits or medication-induced anorexia. To what text or journal is the clinician to turn for counsel on these questions? Yet it will be these issues that the clinician will confront more than any others as he or she provides supportive services to the child and family throughout the child's development.

There can be no substitute for common sense, clinical skills, and the wisdom the professional gains from the sheer quantity and variety of interactions experienced over time in serving the needs of previous patients with this disorder. Coupled with these stylistic and experiential factors is the need for specific types of information before the clinic door is opened to these children and their families. The following list is not nearly exhaustive but will offer an overview of the types of information required:

1. Copies of the federal and state laws on mandated educational services for handicapped children (Public Law 94-142 and its state equivalents). Also, awareness of laws governing the emergency placement of children in psychiatric hospitals, children's homes, or foster care. Along with these is the obvious need for an awareness of those social and educational agencies or community resources that deal with these subjects.
2. Copies of up-to-date reading material on ADHD or behavior-management skills. Several recent books by Wender (1987) and Ingersoll (1988) provide accurate and current information on ADHD for parents who can read at the high school level. For those who are less literate, an audio or videotape can be lent to parents or used in the clinic.
3. The clinician should be prepared to give advice to parents of ADHD children, particularly those with young children, on how to "childproof" their home to diminish the likelihood of accidents, injuries, or the destruction of property. Similarly, clinicians should be ready to discuss practical issues raised by the parent of an adolescent with ADHD, such as letting the child obtain an automobile license.
4. Given the greater incidence of parental psychopathology in ADHD families, an awareness of community resources for marital, sexual, or substance-abuse counseling is most useful.
5. Awareness of local support groups for parents of ADHD, learning-disabled, or behavior-disordered children will enable the clinician to provide parents with a social network that can offer the kind of help that is not provided by therapy alone.
6. The nonmedical professional must cultivate responsible medical referral sources when the total care of the ADHD child calls for

therapies, neurologic and physical exams, or medical advice. The long-term treatment of this disorder calls for a multidisciplinary approach and well-developed ties with other professionals.

Parent Training

Parent training in child behavior management is an essential component in the overall treatment of most ADHD families.

There are many programs on parent training, each differing in philosophy, method, and effectiveness. Barkley (1981) initially described a parent-training program for use specifically with ADHD children. Although it is similar to other parenting programs, it has several unique components that address the special needs of ADHD children and their families. The program was built on several theoretical and empirical foundations, the earliest being the "two-stage program" developed by Hanf (1969) and later refined and extensively researched with noncompliant children by Forehand and his associates (e.g., Forehand & McMahon, 1981; Wells & Forehand, 1985). There has been little research on its effectiveness with ADHD children in particular. Nonetheless, the early studies (Pollard, Ward, & Barkley, 1983) are promising. As used specifically with ADHD children, this program is thoroughly discussed in Barkley (1981) and in Anastopoulos and Barkley (1989).

Like other behaviorally based parent training programs, the program described by Barkley (1981) for ADHD children emphasizes the control of behavior by its consequences and, more specifically, the components of reinforcement, extinction, and punishment. Unique is the emphasis on tailoring specific parenting methods to theoretically and empirically derived notions of ADHD. An especially prominent premise taught in the program is that ADHD is largely a biologically based temperamental style (Anastopoulos & Barkley, 1988) that predisposes a youngster to be inattentive, impulsive, and restless as well as deficient in the capacity to comply with rules (Barkley, 1989). A variety of specialized parenting skills are emphasized to address these deficits. In a similar vein, data derived from years of laboratory research—showing fundamental differences in the performance of ADHD children under various reinforcement and punishment schedules—are incorporated into disciplinary strategies that parents are asked to introduce at home. Specifically, great emphasis is placed on the need for immediate consequences and "richer" reinforcement schedules for ADHD children as well as on the consistency in which consequences are delivered over time and across caregivers. The use of more intensive motivational–incentive procedures and response cost techniques is also emphasized. Implicit in these methods is the premise that a therapeutic home environment has to be developed and, more explicitly, that parents must learn to cope with, rather than cure, what is likely to be a chronic problem.

Screening Parents for Training

Education in the management of child behavior is neither possible nor desirable for all parents of ADHD children. For some, the main concern is the child's school achievement; thus, other forms of intervention are warranted. Although the ADHD child may pose problems at home for other parents, they may be unwilling or unable to invest the necessary time or effort in such a program. The clinician will readily recognize these types of parents during the evaluation and they will most likely not be asked to enter a parent training program.

But there also exists a sector of the parent population for whom parent training will prove difficult, less effective, and possibly inadvisable despite their interest in participating. An initial screening and the use of selection guidelines should be a matter of routine. In most cases, children between the ages of 2 and 11 will be responsive to the procedures that parents will learn to use. Along with age considerations, assessment should be made of other complicating diagnoses, such as severe language disorders, delays in mental development, depression with suicidal ideation, and other medical or psychiatric disabilities. Serious parental psychiatric disturbances such as substance abuse, depression, or severe marital problems will generally lead to a referral to appropriate mental health professionals before such parents can be enrolled in the parent training program. The presence of severe forms of aggressiveness, assaultiveness, or violence on the part of the child will also preclude immediate parent involvement in the program. Likewise, families whose children display conduct disorders involving fire setting, cruelty, or chronic patterns of stealing or truancy are generally not considered appropriate for this program. In such cases it may be necessary to manage the child in a residential setting in order to develop better control of serious antisocial behavior patterns. Those who are isolated from their community, engage in few social activities outside the home, or bear the burden of frequent unpleasant social contacts (Wahler, 1980) are a poor risk for parent training programs. In summary, parent training is not for everyone, and screening parents for their responsiveness to it is a necessary step if limited resources are to be applied to the best effect.

A Parent Training Program for ADHD Children

The approach that we employ in our frequent treatment of ADHD children comprises a core of nine sessions with the parents, which, once the core sequence is completed, can be extended to cover problem areas other than noncompliance. This program is similar to that discussed in detail in Forehand and McMahon (1981), except that certain core principles are given greater emphasis in response to empirical findings regarding the deficits that make up ADHD. Several additional sessions are included to deal with the particular difficulties faced by families with ADHD children. The sessions can be conducted individually or, when clinic caseloads are high, parent groups can be used. Individual training allows for greater practice time in the clinic and specific tailoring of the methods to the particular case. Still, group training can be equally effective provided that care is taken to keep the group membership relatively homogenous on important variables, such as parental ages and education, child ages, and the severity of the child's problems. Group sessions may also provide support, giving parents an opportunity to hear about the behavioral difficulties that other parents routinely encounter and also about the beneficial effect of various management strategies. Each session lasts 1.5 to 2 hours for group training and 1 to 1.5 hours for an individual family. In the latter case, the children are present for the third and later sessions and participate in the practice phases of each session.

Each session follows a similar sequence of events, including a review of the information covered in the previous week, a brief assessment of whether any critical events transpired since the previous session, and a review of homework that may have been assigned. The therapist then introduces new information with respect to particular methods the parents are to employ the next week. During sessions in which the child is included for practice, a playroom with observation facilities is used. Using a "bug-in-the-ear" telecommunications device (Farrell Instrument Co.) can greatly enhance the ability to shape parental behavior in an unobtrusive manner. The session then concludes with feedback to the parents and homework is assigned. Written handouts detailing the session's techniques and procedures are distributed to parents for review during the coming week.

Session 1

Review of ADHD. This session is not designed to train parents in a skill but to educate them about their child's disorder. Specifically, the therapist provides information on the primary symptoms and currently accepted diagnostic criteria used by professionals to derive a diagnosis. Next, the parent is informed about the prevalence of the disorder and the accepted etiologies. Such information may both alleviate unsubstantiated concerns that the child's problems are purely emotional or psychological while, at the same time, setting the stage for what is to follow: that is, therapeutic efforts to create a therapeutic home environment and an emphasis on coping with rather than curing the disorder. Next, the therapist directs attention to the features commonly associated with ADHD (see Table 5.1). Finally, a detailed discussion is conducted on the many proven and unproven therapies for ADHD, dispelling a number of myths and widely held misconceptions about effective treatments.

Session 2

Understanding Parent–Child Relations and Principles of Behavior Management. Bell's theory on reciprocity and parent–child interactions provides a useful model for educating parents (see Bell & Harper, 1977). The precise method of presenting this material to parents is discussed in detail in *Hyperactive Children: Handbook for Diagnosis and Treatment* (Barkley, 1981, chapter 8). Bell has long argued (Bell, 1968) that children have extensive effects on their caretakers, and that these effects, in turn, partly dictate the manner in which the children are treated. In this context, four major factors are discussed as contributing to child misbehavior, including characteristics of child and parents, situational consequences, and familial stressors. Thus, parents are told that while inborn characteristics and stressors may increase the risk of behavioral difficulties, it is the nature

of parent–child interactions that most reliably predict child behavior. Hence, the rationale for parent training is provided: namely, the need to modify the way parents respond to their children's behavior. The session concludes with the therapist outlining for parents the principles of general behavior management that will have to be practiced in the context of changing, ongoing interaction patterns with the child.

Session 3

Developing and Enhancing Parental Attention to Child Behavior. Patterson (1976) has demonstrated that the value of parental praise and attention in the families of children with behavioral problems is greatly diminished and unlikely to be useful in reinforcing appropriate behavior. Parents are informed that many ADHD children engage in fewer behaviors that elicit any type of positive parental response while engaging in a higher rate of behavior that elicits corrective, directive, and coercive interactional patterns. It is for this reason that Session 3 introduces procedures designed to improve both the amount and quality of parental attention to the child. This is accomplished by teaching parents the techniques of "special playtime," during which the child is allowed to select an activity to be used daily and the parent is to interact with the child only and is not to give commands or ask questions. The use of parental social reinforcement is emphasized as is the fact that punishment strategies will be grossly undermined unless the parent builds in many more reinforcing and positive interactions with the child. Naturally, this change of style must be initiated by the parent rather than the child.

Session 4

Attending to Appropriate Behavior. While Session 3 was designed to enhance parental attending skills in general and the quality of positive attention given to the child, Session 4 begins the application of these techniques to child behavior outside the realm of special playtime. Parents are now taught to become skillful at "catching" their children in instances of appropriate behavior, especially those that have proven problematic in the past. Likewise, positive attending skills are encouraged in the context of compliance with parental commands as well as with spontaneous instances of prosocial behavior or compliance with house rules. The second item on the agenda for Session 4 is generally a detailed discussion of parental command giving and its relationship to compliance in general. This includes coverage of the types, timing, and forms of commands that increase or decrease the probability of compliance.

Session 5
Establishing a Home Token System. The initiation of a structured home token system is designed to augment parental attention to appropriate and compliant child behavior while introducing highly predictable, frequent, and immediate consequences for specific behavior. Such a system is also utilized for the simple reason that positive attending and social praise from parents is often insufficient in the overall management of the ADHD child. Details of the token system as applied to ADHD children are presented in Barkley (1981; 1987). During the initial phase, children are allowed only to earn tokens and parents are encouraged to dispense bonus tokens for especially well done chores or for appropriate behavior.

Session 6
Using Response Cost and Time Out. Up until this point, parents are not given specific instructions regarding punishment tactics for noncompliance or other forms of misbehavior. This is done to make sure that positive interaction skills are well established. Also, the effects of punishment procedures are likely to be weak or short-lived without a high rate of positive attention for prosocial behaviors. This session introduces two punishment procedures to apply to misbehavior; response cost and time out. Response cost involves the removal of tokens or points, while time out involves the isolation and removal of attention from the child for specified misbehavior. Parents are instructed to begin deducting tokens or points for noncompliance with requests or violations of other household rules. A considerable amount of time is spent carefully and thoroughly detailing the mechanics of time out prior to its implementation at home.

Session 7
Extending Time Out to Other Behaviors. No new material is introduced in Session 7. Much of the session is used to review parental efforts to incorporate the response-cost and time-out strategies into the ongoing home token system. Provided that implementation of these procedures has proceeded without major problems,

parents are instructed to use time out for two or three other types of misbehavior (e.g., fighting with siblings, swearing). The use of time out is restricted to the home setting and parents are encouraged not to attempt to implement such procedures outside of the home.

Session 8
Managing Misbehavior in Public. Most ADHD children present problems for their parents in public places, such as stores, churches, restaurants or the homes of others. Assuming that parents have demonstrated competence with previously discussed material, disciplining procedures are extended to the community. All the principles already taught are presented in the context of managing public noncompliance and misbehavior. First, parental anticipation of such problems is emphasized. Parents are then encouraged to establish a plan of action for handling public displays of misbehavior. Specifically, parents are advised to increase their use of praise and positive attention for appropriate behavior, dispense tokens or points for compliance, and be prepared to introduce response cost and/or time out for infractions.

Session 9
Managing Future Misbehavior. A final session of the parent training program is used to review the essential principles of management that were incorporated into each of the methods parents were taught to employ. Examples of anticipated or hypothetical problems may be generated by the therapist and parents questioned about how they would attempt to manage the problem. Parents are reminded about the chronicity of their children's deficits and that some degree of long-term adherence to the program will be necessary to maintain appropriate behavior. It is customary to schedule a "booster" session 4 to 6 weeks after the final session, so as to assess how well the parents are continuing to manage the child. Should continued help appear warranted and desired by the parents, treatment can be renewed.

Following the child-management training portion of the program, other issues may be added to deal with particular problems of the ADHD child for whom the parent is seeking counsel. Common among these include getting homework done, addressing academic and achievement issues, developing sibling cooperation, managing enuresis or encopresis, dealing with problematic peer relations, and treating lying or stealing.

Research Findings

Despite its substantial research record in the treatment of noncompliance in children (see Forehand & McMahon, 1981), the child management program outlined above has not yet received comprehensive empirical evaluation in the treatment of ADHD (Pollard et al., 1983). Drawing from the research findings with problem children in general, a number of studies have attested to the efficacy of this training model in managing children's noncompliance, decreasing defiance, and increasing compliance and cooperation (e.g., Eyberg & Robinson, 1982; Forehand, Wells, & Griest, 1980). Long-term outcome studies have reported favorable results as well, with treatment effects persisting for as long as 4 to 5 years after training (e.g., Baum & Forehand, 1981; Forehand, Rogers, McMahon, Wells, & Griest, 1981; Webster-Stratton, 1984).

Studies examining the generalization of treatment effects across settings have also reported positive outcomes in child compliance following parent training in the clinic (e.g., Forehand et al., 1979; Peed, Roberts, & Forehand, 1977; Webster-Stratton, 1984). More pervasive generalization following treatment, however, does not appear to be a natural outcome of parent training. When teachers do not receive comparable training in behavior management procedures, little change in child compliance is observed in the school setting (e.g., Breiner & Forehand, 1981; Forehand et al., 1979). The results suggest that increases in child compliance are specific to the adult trained in management techniques and to the settings in which they are actively applied.

Although pervasive generalization across settings is an uncommon finding, significant generalization of treatment effects to deviant child behaviors that were not specifically targeted in the training program have been reported. Forehand, Wells, and Griest (1980), for example, reported that treated children showed significant declines in tantrums, destruction, and aggression even though noncompliance was the focus of treatment. Other researchers have reported similar positive outcomes of treatment (e.g., Russo, Cataldo, & Cushing, 1981). The generalization across behaviors probably resulted from

the high correlation between noncompliance and these other deviant behaviors. In a similar vein, several studies have also shown that treatment effects often generalize to untreated siblings of the clinic-referred child and that family functioning in general is viewed more positively after training (e.g., Eyberg & Robinson, 1982; Humphreys, Forehand, McMahon, & Roberts, 1978).

In summary, the management program for ADHD children, initially described by Barkley (1981) and based on the work of Hanf and Forehand, represents a behaviorally based approach that is tailored to the deficits inherent in ADHD children with emphasis on the development of a therapeutic home environment. Despite its intuitive appeal and widespread clinical use, it has not received adequate empirical evaluation with ADHD families specifically. Available pilot data and our clinical experience with this program have strongly suggested that it can result in treatment effects in the home setting comparable to those reported by Forehand and his colleagues with noncompliant children. Future research will be required to examine the durability and generalization of treatment effects with ADHD families as well as the specific components that may facilitate the efficacy of these strategies with this population.

Interventions With Adolescents

Until recently, the prevailing clinical lore held that the symptoms of ADHD diminished significantly or "disappeared" during adolescence, presumably because of maturational processes. Over the last decade, several independent prospective longitudinal investigations have refuted this belief while providing evidence for continued ADHD symptomatology among 20% to 60% of probands studied (Gittelman et al., 1985; Ackerman, Dykman, & Peters, 1977; Lambert et al., 1987; Weiss & Hechtman, 1986). Relative to their normal peers, adolescents with ADHD are at higher risk for conduct disturbance or antisocial behavior (Gittelman et al., 1985; Satterfield et al., 1982), academic underachievement (Hoy, Weiss, Minde, & Cohen, 1978), low self-esteem (Feldman, Denhoff, & Denhoff, 1979), and substance abuse (Gittelman et al., 1985). While teenagers with ADHD apparently exhibit a high rate of positive response to psychostimulant medications, similar to that of younger children (Klorman, Coons, & Borgstedt, 1987; Varley, 1985), empirical investigations of the effects of psychological interventions with this population are sorely lacking.

Application of the parent training program described above has generally been studied and applied with ADHD children between the ages of 2 and 11 years of age. Problems with attention span, impulse control, and restlessness may persist. However, by the time the typical ADHD child reaches adolescence, most significant family issues center around acceptance of responsibility (e.g., chores, homework), disagreements over rights and privileges, and permissible social activities. Thus, the target behaviors or goals included in such programs may need to be modified to account for these developmental differences. In addition, it may be important to include adolescents in therapy sessions that will motivate them to participate in the negotiation of responsibilities and privileges.

In many cases the normal striving for independence is complicated by more pronounced conduct problems and oppositional behavior, resulting in significant levels of family conflict. Arthur Robin and his associates (e.g., Foster & Robin, 1988; Robin, Kent, O'Leary, Foster, & Prinz, 1977; Robin, 1981) have developed and evaluated a treatment program specifically addressing the conflicts encountered in distressed parent–adolescent relations. As in the parent training approach employed with preadolescents, family conflict is viewed in the context of bidirectional influences in which both parents and teenagers play prominent roles. Unlike child management training, however, the adolescent is asked to take part and his or her active participation is generally required. Problem-solving communication training (PSCT) entails a highly directive skill-oriented therapy that includes an integration of behavioral, cognitive, and family system models. Four components are used in the context of a relatively short-term approach generally involving 6 to 25 sessions: (1) teaching problem-solving skills, (2) modifying problematic communication patterns, (3) modifying faulty cognitions (e.g., irrational thoughts) that may precipitate or maintain problematic interactions, and (4) altering structural patterns (e.g., triangulation, nonparticipation of a parent) within the family. Integrated throughout therapy is the imparting of information pertaining to appropriate and effective behavior management strategies such as establishing incentives, clarifying and specifying household rules, and using contingency contracting as an adjunct to other, less

formal methods. Underlying these methods is active shaping and instruction in negotiation and compromise, highlighting the bidirectional view of conflict and the developing role of the teenager as active in conflict resolution.

PSCT has been shown to be effective in reducing family conflict in distressed parent–adolescent dyads (e.g., Robin et al., 1977; Foster, Prinz, & O'Leary, 1983). These positive findings with distressed families suggest that PSCT may be an appropriate treatment approach where ADHD children are too old for or are resistant to participating in a child-management training program. The decision to use PSCT should be based upon the motivation of the adolescent and parents to enter family therapy, the level of verbal intelligence of family members, and the severity of conduct or oppositional problems. This approach may not be best suited for adolescents with severe conduct disorders. Although the effects of either PSCT or parent training procedures have not been specifically investigated with ADHD teenagers and their families, such studies are currently under way in our clinic and would indicate positive results for these treatment modalities relative to more traditional family therapy procedures.

CLASSROOM BEHAVIOR MANAGEMENT

One of the most problematic situations for children with ADHD is their classroom. It is quite evident that the requirements (e.g., sit still, remain quiet, complete work) placed upon children in educational settings are difficult for the ADHD child to meet. These children typically exhibit "out-of-seat" or "off-task" behaviors wherein they may wander about the room, disturb others, play with objects irrelevant to the assigned task, or display excessive restlessness at their desks. Hence, academic assignments are rarely completed on time or are completed in a hasty, careless fashion. Accuracy on such tasks suffers as a result. On the playground, peer interaction problems are typical, owing to the child's immature, selfish, and often aggressive behavior. Thus, the school setting taxes the child with ADHD in precisely those areas where he or she has the greatest deficits—sustained attention, impulse control, and compliance.

Numerous behavior modification procedures have been employed to enhance the classroom performance of children with ADHD, but space limitations preclude detailing them all here. Only the most salient and widely studied techniques will be discussed, including token reinforcement programs, contingency contracting, punishment procedures, and home-based contingency methods. The reader is referred to Ayllon and Rosenbaum (1977), Barkley (1981), O'Leary and Wilson (1987), and Rapport (1987) for further discussion of various behavioral techniques with this population.

Several general guidelines should be followed regardless of the specific behavior modification technique employed:

1. Children with ADHD require more frequent and specific feedback than their classmates; thus the initial stages of any program should incorporate relatively continuous contingencies.
2. Too much or too highly salient positive reinforcement may distract the child from the task at hand; thus prudent negative consequences may be necessary to maintain appropriate on-task behavior (Rosen, O'Leary, Joyce, Conway, & Pfiffner, 1984). The latter should be delivered immediately contingent upon the occurrence of disruptive behavior in a consistent, specific fashion. Further, reprimands are most effective when given so as to be audible only to the particular child.
3. Academic tasks should be assigned one at a time, with lengthier assignments broken down into smaller units so as to minimize overtaxing the child's attention span. When task instructions are presented to the child, they should not involve more than a few steps, and he or she should be asked to repeat the instructions to ensure understanding. Avoid assigning repetitive material (e.g., reassigning an erroneously completed worksheet) and, whenever possible, alternate types of assignments.
4. Employ behavioral products (e.g., task completion and accuracy) as targets of intervention rather than specific behaviors such as attention to task or staying in seat. This is not only logistically simpler for the classroom teacher to monitor but providing consequences contingent upon completion of products increases their frequency and that of the behavioral chains that produce them.
5. In general, use preferred activities (e.g., recess time, access to computer) as reinforcers rather than concrete rewards. Further, the specific rewards employed should be varied or rotated frequently so as to prevent boredom or satiation with the program.

Token Reinforcement Programs

A consistent finding in the research literature is that contingent praise and attention are not sufficient to bring about consistent increases in the ADHD child's classroom performance. Thus, these children seem to require more powerful reinforcement systems—such as token economies—which incorporate potency, immediacy, and specificity.

The procedures employed in establishing such a program are similar to those used with parents, as discussed previously in this chapter. Initially, the target behaviors are selected. These can include behavioral products (e.g., number of math problems completed in a given amount of time) or specific actions (e.g., immediate compliance with teacher commands). Next, the type of secondary reinforcer or token—such as poker chips, check marks on a card, stickers, or points on a card stand—must be chosen. Younger children prefer tangible tokens, while older youngsters generally respond more positively to points or check marks. Children under 5 years of age do not, in our experience, respond as well to token economy systems. Third, the teacher and student jointly develop a list of privileges or rewarding activities within the classroom for which the tokens can be exchanged. In some cases, the parents can collaborate on this list to make available additional home privileges in exchange for the tokens. Fourth, the teacher begins dispensing tokens frequently for the target behaviors. Tokens are then exchanged by the child for classroom privileges on at least a daily basis. After several weeks, when the efficacy of the program is evaluated, new targets may be added, old ones deleted or modified, and privileges rotated or varied as the situation dictates. Response cost procedures (as discussed below) may also be incorporated into the system.

Several teacher reactions should be anticipated when the use of token economy systems is recommended. The most common teacher complaint is that the child's classmates will become jealous of the token program and will diminish their own performances so as to receive similar treatment. It should be pointed out to the teacher that any jealous reactions that occur are usually temporary and do not lead to the deterioration of other students' performances. Some teachers have argued that these methods draw undue attention to the child with ADHD, thus creating a stigma and further alienating the child from his or her classmates. Since this system primarily involves the use of positive reinforcement procedures, it is hard to imagine how it would lead to a negative perception of the child. Finally, other educators maintain that providing tangible rewards for academic work may decrease the child's intrinsic motivation to learn and to complete assignments. This viewpoint assumes that the child should find his or her classwork intrinsically motivating and that, if this were the case, he or she would probably not require the use of a behavioral program. However, most children with ADHD do not appear to be sufficiently motivated intrinsically or by the natural contingencies associated with work completion; thus the use of external consequences becomes necessary.

Contingency Contracting

This method involves the negotiation of a contract, with the student stipulating the desired classroom behaviors and consequences contingent upon performance of these actions. A sample contract appears in Box 5.1; it shows that any type of classroom behavior (including academic productivity or achievement) can be included. The delay between meeting a behavioral goal and receiving reinforcement should be adjusted on the basis of the child's age. For instance, an 8-year-old may negotiate a contract for each school day, setting forth what he or she is to do and receive that day. Alternatively, older children may have contracts that involve a longer time span (e.g., several days) between performance and receipt of reinforcement. In either case, the consequences employed can be available at school, at home, or in the community.

Although this is a relatively straightforward technique, there are a number of factors that strongly determine its efficacy with the ADHD population. First, the age of the child must be considered. The use of contingency-contracting procedures with a child who does not possess sufficient verbal skills or is not able to defer reinforcement for long periods of time is usually unsuccessful. This is most often the case with children who are at or below age 6. Another

consideration is the length of the time delay between performance of the requisite behavior and when reinforcement is provided. For example, one cannot require an 8-year-old ADHD child to complete 80% of his or her math problems correctly each day for a 1-week period before earning a reward; such a project would be doomed to failure. It would be more effective to require that 80% be completed correctly each day, with a reward provided at the end of the math period or the conclusion of the school day.

A crucial determinant of a behavioral contract's success is the manner in which requisite behaviors are specified. Frequently, an excessive number of expected behaviors or extreme standards of quality are demanded, presenting the ADHD child with an insuperable task. In similar fashion, the behavioral goals may be too complex to let the child complete them in a timely fashion. For these reasons, it is best to delineate *very* simple behaviors or outcomes initially, so that the child can easily achieve success. More difficult or complex goals may be included in subsequent contracts. This gradual increase in the demands of a contract can be built in easily enough by an experienced therapist or teacher, so that the child will rarely fail to complete a contract yet produces a greater quantity of higher-quality work.

Other important considerations are the types of consequences employed and the manner in which they are delivered. On many occasions, the rewards included in a contract are not especially valuable or important to the child, thus limiting their motivational properties. This occurs most often when the child is not consulted about the rewards he or she would like to work for; that is, they are imposed unilaterally on the assumption that they will be highly motivating. In short, reinforcers should be negotiated with the child before the contract is implemented, and they should be changed often to avoid satiation. Another alternative would be to employ the Premack principle (Premack, 1965), wherein completion of less-preferred activities (e.g., completion of academic work) would allow access to highly preferred activities (e.g., recess, educational games).

Behavioral contracts with ADHD children are frequently more successful when they include a response cost contingency in addition to rewards. This merely involves stating what the child will lose if the contracted goals are not met. This could mean removal of a privilege,

---

BOX 5.1. SAMPLE BEHAVIOR CONTRACT

I, _____, agree to do the following:
1. Pay attention to my teacher when he or she is talking to the class.
2. Complete all my written math and phonics workbook assignments at an 80% accuracy level before lunchtime.
3. Remain quiet when lining up for recess, lunch, and physical education class.
4. Follow playground rules (no fighting or loud yelling) during recess.

If I do these things successfully, I will receive one of the following (my choice):
1. Time at the end of the schoolday to play an educational game with a classmate of my choosing.
2. Time to work quietly on the computer.
3. The opportunity to do some errands for my teacher.

If I have a successful week, I will be able to purchase a paperback book of my choosing.

If I do not do these things as I promised, then I will lose:
1. Daily recess time.
2. The opportunity to participate in daily free-time activities.

I agree to fulfill this contract to the best of my ability.

Signed:

(Signature of child/adolescent)   (Signature of teacher)

Date:

---

loss of tokens or points, or even a brief stay in a time-out location. As with the home-based behavior management system described above, it is best to delay the inclusion of response cost procedures in the contract until after some initial successes have been achieved.

As suggested above, it is very important that the child be involved in the initial and ongoing negotiations of the contract. As in adult life, both parties to a contract must participate in its formation and must frequently reach compromises if the agreement is to be successfully transacted. Rigid demands, intimidation, reneging on the promises involved, and lack of sensitivity to each other's desires can effectively ruin a contingency contract. This is especially the case when working with an older child or adolescent with ADHD.

Punishment Methods

The use of positive reinforcement procedures in isolation is rarely effective in maintaining appropriate levels of academic and social behavior among children with ADHD. Several recent in-vestigations have indicated the need for concurrent application of mild punishment contingencies following inappropriate (i.e., off-task) behavior to maintain treatment gains (Pfiffner & O'Leary, 1987; Pfiffner, Rosen, & O'Leary, 1985; Rosen et al., 1984). Several punishment methods have been found to be effective in combination with positively based procedures in managing classroom behavior, including "prudent" negative reprimands (as discussed in the introduction to classroom management above); loss or removal of attention, privileges, points, or tokens (i.e., response cost); and time out from positive reinforcement.

The contingent use of response cost has been found to lead to increased levels of on-task behavior, seat-work productivity, and academic accuracy among children with ADHD—in some cases to an equivalent degree to that obtained with stimulant medication (Rapport, Murphy, & Bailey, 1980, 1982). Typically, this has involved the provision of positive reinforcement (e.g., tokens, points) administered on a fixed-interval schedule, with point (or token) loss following instances of off-task behavior. As in the token economy system described above, any tokens or points remaining at the end of a work period are then exchanged for backup reinforcement (e.g., minutes of "free-time" activity). Since this could potentially become time-consuming and impractical for most classroom teachers, several apparatuses have been developed to reduce the time requirements for the teacher while maintaining treatment integrity. These range from handmade wooden stands with numbered cards attached all the way to commercially available electronic units that allow for "remote" contingency application by the teacher.

Other methods found useful in the classroom involve various forms of time out from positive reinforcement. As with that used at home, time out at school must be implemented swiftly and should involve a sufficiently long time period to prove aversive to the child—otherwise it is unlikely to reduce the frequency of inappropriate behavior. The teacher, not the child, determines when time out is over, and where possible the child should, once it is over, correct, amend, or compensate for the misbehavior that led to time out. Children who leave the time-out area without permission can have their time interval lengthened by a fixed amount for each violation, lose points/tokens if a token economy is being used, or be swiftly removed from class. Such a suspension from class can be served in the school's main office or at home. Obviously, this must be well specified and agreed to by the child's parents prior to implementation. A time-out chair located in a dull corner of the classroom is preferred to a separate room. Closets, cloakrooms, or hallways are to be avoided, owing to ethical and humane reasons as well as practicality (i.e., supervision of the child is hindered).

As discussed above, punishment procedures should always be used in combination with or in the context of positive reinforcement strategies. It is preferable to organize punishment contingencies in a hierarchical fashion, ranging from least to most aversive and restrictive. Thus, inappropriate behavior would initially lead to brief, prudent negative reprimands, followed by response cost, time out with head down at desk, time out in a corner of the room, or removal from the classroom as necessary if the transgression were to continue. More severe negative behaviors (e.g., physical aggression) should lead to immediate application of the most aversive procedure (i.e., time out).

Rationale for Inclusion of Punishment Procedures

The behavioral interventions outlined above for home and school use comprise a combination of positive reinforcement and mild punishment procedures. For many years, the use of punishment, particularly with children, has been criticized due to a lack of long-term maintenance of effects (Skinner, 1938); production of "unfortunate by-products" such as negative emotional reactions towards the punisher (Skinner, 1953); ineffectiveness in providing alternative responses to the organism (Epstein, 1985); and undesirable ethical considerations, as many punishing contingencies are intrusive and produce discomfort (Epstein, 1985). Certainly the ethical and empirical evidence would indicate that behavioral programs should be heavily weighted toward provision of reinforcing rather than punishing contingencies, as in the proposed parent training and classroom management programs above.

While an exclusive reliance upon punishment is ethically and empirically undesirable, there are several reasons why such contingencies should be included in behavioral programming for ADHD children. First, a plethora of investigations have demonstrated the superior effectiveness of reward–punishment treatment combinations relative to reinforcement alone, especially in terms of maintaining attentive behavior and academic performance (e.g., Pfiffner & O'Leary, 1987; Pfiffner et al., 1985; Rosen et al., 1984). While most of these studies did not specifically target the performance of ADHD children, ADHD behaviors are obviously quite problematic for most of those given this diagnosis. A second factor related to the above is the laboratory evidence documenting the insensitivity to rewards or high threshold for reinforcement among children with ADHD (see Barkley, 1989; Douglas & Parry, 1983; Haenlein & Caul, 1987). This state of affairs has led researchers such as Barkley (1989) to posit a motivational deficit among these children, which is optimally addressed through a combination of reinforcing and punishing contingencies.

A final factor that must be considered in recommending punishment strategies is their acceptability relative to other behavioral procedures by the general population. Not surprisingly, surveys presenting analogue case descriptions to parents, teachers, and undergraduate students consistently demonstrate a general preference for positive reinforcement over punishment procedures (e.g., Calvert & McMahon, 1987; Heffer & Kelley, 1987; Kazdin, 1980; Witt, Elliott, & Martens, 1984). Alternatively, milder punishment procedures such as response cost and nonexclusionary time out are rated more acceptable than more intrusive procedures (e.g., exclusion, spanking) and in some cases are rated similarly to positive reinforcement procedures (Frentz & Kelley, 1986; Heffer & Kelley, 1987; Von Brock & Elliott, in press). Acceptability of punishment procedures appears to depend not only on their effectiveness but also on the presence of adverse side effects (Kazdin, 1981), the concomitant use of a reward system (Kazdin, 1980), and practicality (Heffer & Kelley, 1987). Thus, the empirical evidence would seem to support the acceptability of using mild punishment procedures in combination with positive reinforcement in treating ADHD.

Home-Based Contingencies

A home-based reinforcement program involves evaluating the child's behavior at school over a specified time interval (e.g., one school day). At the end of each interval a report is sent home, and its contents determine the resultant consequences. This procedure has been found to serve as an effective supplement to or substitute for classroom-based behavior modification systems (see Atkinson & Forehand, 1979, for a review). The evaluation forms that have been developed vary with respect to target behaviors, frequency of evaluations, and complexity or detail of evaluation.

The system we have found to be most successful employs a card similar to that displayed in Figure 5.1. It permits up to six teachers (or one teacher across six subject areas) to rate the child's behavior in four different areas of classroom performance: participation, classwork completion, following rules or returning homework, and interaction with classmates. The teacher initials the card and enters his or her ratings in ink to circumvent possible forgery by the child. The student is responsible for getting the card to each teacher and returning it to his or her parents; a new card is used each day.

When the card is brought home, the parent briefly discusses the positive and negative ratings with the child. Then, points are assigned to

DAILY REPORT CARD

Name _____ Date _____

Please rate this child in each of the behavioral areas listed below as to how (s)he performed in school today using ratings of "1" to "5". "1" = excellent, "2" = good, "3" = fair, "4" = poor, "5" = terrible or did not work.

BEHAVIOR	CLASS PERIODS/SUBJECTS							
	1	2	3	4	5	6	7	8
Paying Attention								
Completing Classwork								
Work Accuracy								
Followed Rules								
Teacher's Initials								

COMMENTS:

Figure 5.1. Daily report card for use in a home-based reinforcement program.

the numbers on the card (e.g., each "1" earns +25 points, a "2" earns +15 points, a "3" earns +5 points, a "4" earns −15 points, and a "5" earns −25 points). These points are summed to yield the net total for the day. They can then be incorporated into the home token economy (e.g., poker-chip system) described in the section on parent training. Thus, points would be used to purchase various daily and/or weekly household privileges (e.g., television time, spending a night at a friend's house). The child's motivation to participate in such a program will obviously be greater the larger the number of daily privileges that are available.

The system can achieve several purposes. First, the child receives direct feedback from his or her teachers at the end of each class as to performance that day. Second, the parents receive daily feedback on the child's performance, thereby providing an excellent vehicle for teacher–parent communication (instead of relying solely on the child's daily report or waiting for an end-of-term report card). Finally, the card permits incentives offered at home to be contingent upon performance at school, which is especially helpful in situations where the classroom environment offers only a restricted number of privileges.

Like other token reinforcement programs, children under 6 years of age do not respond as well as older children, since delayed consequences are utilized. Thus, younger children will require an in-class behavior modification program to achieve changes in classroom performance. We have employed this system successfully with older children through high school, though clearly the reinforcers or privileges employed vary with this older age group.

Treatment Generalization

As is the case with home-based behavioral interventions, if generalization of treatment effects across time, classroom settings, and school personnel is to occur, it must be specifically included in the program design. Thus, specific contingencies must be applied across subject areas and classrooms for children who have more than one teacher or are having difficulties maintaining appropriate behavior throughout the school day. All the classroom interventions described above have included components to promote generalization across the school day. Although behaviorally based therapeutic programs have demonstrated short-term efficacy in the enhancement of ADHD children's school performance, information is lacking regarding their effects on academic and social performance over the long term. In fact, most research studies investigating these interventions have neglected to collect follow-up data even over a short time span. The evidence that is available would suggest that maintenance of treatment effects is optimized by a gradual fading of contingencies through the use of leaner schedules of reinforcement and longer delays between successful performance and receipt of reinforcement. For example, the use of a daily report card may be gradually replaced with a weekly report card wherein performance over the entire week is evaluated and reinforcement is delivered on the weekend. Given that one of the cardinal characteristics of an ADHD child is the inability to delay reinforcement (i.e., impulsivity), caution must be used when contingencies are being faded and school personnel should realize that these interventions must take place over the long term.

The specific variables targeted for intervention partly determine the extent to which treatment effects generalize to other classroom behaviors. While many empirical investigations have demonstrated the efficacy of behavior modification procedures in increasing the frequency of on-task behavior or reducing disruptiveness (e.g., Ayllon & Rosenbaum, 1977), these effects do not necessarily generalize to enhancement of academic productivity or accuracy. Alternatively, when academic variables (e.g., work completion and accuracy) are directly targeted for intervention, the behavioral chains (e.g., attention to task) that precede their production are indirectly positively effected (see for example Ayllon, Layman, & Kandel, 1975). Thus, behavioral products are the preferred targets of intervention for reasons of both practicality and generalizability.

Limitations to Classroom Interventions

Despite the generally positive outcome data obtained with the behavioral programs described above, several factors may limit their usefulness for individual children with ADHD. The primary limitation to a classroom program's successful implementation is teacher time and interest. For example, some teachers may hold philosophies of education that conflict with behavioral principles and methods—and in some cases this may require the parents to ask for a change to a new teacher. More often, the teacher finds it difficult to integrate these new program responsibilities into the classroom routine, particularly when he or she is charged with teaching a large group of heterogeneous students. In both cases, therapist sensitivity, skill, and diplomacy can go a long way toward persuading a recalcitrant teacher to try these programs. A second limiting factor is the severity of the child's behavioral control difficulties. The misbehaviors of some children will simply prove too disruptive to be treated within a regular classroom, thus necessitating placement in a more restrictive setting (e.g., special education class, residential program). Finally, the lack of parental interest or cooperation can limit program efficacy, particularly when home-based contingencies are involved. Obviously, a greater reliance on in-school consequences would be required in such cases.

OTHER TREATMENTS

This chapter has reviewed numerous treatment modalities for ADHD children which, through years of research, have proved efficacious. It is not within the purview of the present discussion to detail all the interventions that have been proposed and/or studied with this population. The described interventions are frequently augmented by individualized academic instruction, social-skills training (Pelham & Bender, 1982), or cognitive-behavioral strategies (Hinshaw,

Henker, & Whalen, 1984; Kendall & Braswell, 1985). More empirical data must be collected regarding the efficacy of these supplementary strategies before their value in treating ADHD can be determined (Whalen, Henker, & Hinshaw, 1985).

The techniques of traditional psychotherapy applied at either an individual or family level have minimal effectiveness in treating children with ADHD. These strategies typically assume that behavioral difficulties are caused by emotional or family-system disturbances. Since these latter variables have not been shown to play a role in the etiology of ADHD, it stands to reason that treatments based upon these assumptions would have limited success. More recently, certain "fad" therapies, such as megavitamin or amino acid supplementation, have been proposed. Like traditional therapies, these are based upon faulty etiological assumptions and are ineffective.

Many people seem to have accepted the notion that food additives and sugars are a major cause of behavior problems in young children (e.g., Feingold, 1975); thus, the removal of these substances from children's diets is presumed to be therapeutic. As discussed in the section on etiological factors, a plethora of research studies have been conducted that refute a causative role for food additives (see Conners, 1980; Mattes & Gittelman, 1981). In similar fashion, most of the well-controlled studies investigating the influence of sugar (sucrose) on normal and ADHD children's behavior have found only minor behavioral improvements associated with its removal from the diet (Milich & Pelham, 1986; Rosen et al., 1988).

CONCLUSION

The comprehensive treatment of children with ADHD is a long-term process that should not be undertaken by the uninitiated. These children typically present with a variety of problems (e.g., learning disabilities, social-skills deficits, conduct disorders) in addition to ADHD, which necessitate a working knowledge of the assessment and treatment of the most common psychological disorders of childhood. Therefore, a multimodal intervention approach must be adopted, wherein each component is designed to promote the common goal of coping with ADHD and associated difficulties.

The two treatment modalities that have proven

efficacy in ameliorating the symptoms of ADHD are psychostimulant medications and behavior modification techniques applied at home and/or in the classroom. A number of investigations have demonstrated that their combination is superior to either one alone in producing short-term academic and behavioral improvement (see Pelham & Murphy, 1986, for a review). Alternatively, traditional individual or family psychotherapy, dietary management, and removal of allergens have not proved useful in the management of ADHD. Frequently, the combination of stimulant medication and behavior modification is supplemented with special education instruction, social-skills and self-control training programs, and, to a lesser extent, residential placement to deal with associated behavioral or emotional difficulties. Surprisingly few (e.g., Satterfield et al., 1987) well-controlled studies have examined the long-term results of treatment with a multimodal intervention approach. Obviously, such studies are sorely needed to evaluate the efficacy of this approach.

It is apparent from the preceding discussion that ADHD is a common developmental disorder having an early onset, chronic course, and pervasive influence across many domains of adaptive functioning. No current treatment method can "cure" ADHD; however, significant improvements in child behavior can be attained when parents, teachers, and professionals consistently apply a combination of therapeutic techniques throughout the child's development. In sum, the optimal approach to coping with ADHD is to engineer and maintain a "best fit" between the characteristics of the ADHD child and the demands of the social environment.

REFERENCES

Ackerman, P. T., Dykman, R. A., & Peters, J. E. (1977). Teenage status of hyperactive and nonhyperactive learning disabled boys. *American Journal of Orthopsychiatry, 47,* 577–596.

American Academy of Pediatrics. (1987). Medications for children with an attention deficit disorder. *Pediatrics, 80,* 758–760.

American Psychiatric Association. (1980). *Diagnostic and statistical manual of mental disorders* (3rd ed.). Washington, DC: Author.

American Psychiatric Association. (1987). *Diagnostic and statistical manual of mental disorders* (3rd ed. rev.). Washington, DC: Author.

Anastopoulos, A. D., & Barkley, R. A. (1988). Biological factors in attention-deficit hyperactivity disorder. *The Behavior Therapist, 11,* 47–53.

Anastopoulos, A. D., & Barkley, R. A. (1989). A training program for parents of children with attention deficit-hyperactivity disorder. In C. E. Shaefer & J. Briesmeister (Eds.), *Handbook of parent training: Parents as cotherapists for children's behavior problems* (pp. 83–104). New York: John Wiley & Sons.

Atkinson, B. M., & Forehand, R. (1979). Home-based reinforcement programs designed to modify classroom behavior: A review and methodological evaluation. *Psychological Bulletin, 86,* 1298–1308.

Ayllon, T., Layman, D. & Kandel, H. (1975). A behavioral-educational alternative to drug control of hyperactive children. *Journal of Applied Behavior Analysis, 8,* 137–146.

Ayllon, T., & Rosenbaum, M. (1977). The behavioral treatment of disruption and hyperactivity in school settings. In B. Lahey & A. Kazdin (Eds.), *Advances in clinical child psychology* (Vol. 1, pp. 83–118). New York: Plenum Press.

Bacon, J. (1988). What's the best medicine for hyperactive kids? *USA Today,* February 17, p. 4D.

Barkley, R. A. (1977). A review of stimulant drug research with hyperactive children. *Journal of Child Psychology and Psychiatry, 18,* 137–165.

Barkley, R. A. (1981). *Hyperactive children: A handbook for diagnosis and treatment.* New York: Guilford Press.

Barkley, R. A. (1987). *Defiant children: A clinician's manual for parent training.* New York: Guilford Press.

Barkley, R. A. (1988). Attention-deficit hyperactivity disorder. In E. Mash & L. Terdal (Eds.), *Behavioral assessment of childhood disorders* (2nd ed., pp. 69–104). New York: Guilford Press.

Barkley, R. A. (1989). The problem of stimulus control and rule-governed behavior in children with attention deficit disorder with hyperactivity. In L. Bloomingdale & J. Swanson (Eds.), *Attention deficit disorders* (Vol IV). Elmsford, NY: Pergamon Press.

Barkley, R. A., & Cunningham, C. E. (1979).

The effects of Ritalin on the mother-child interactions of hyperactive children. *Archives of General Psychiatry, 36,* 201–208.

Barkley, R. A., & Cunningham, C. E. (1980). The parent–child interactions of hyperactive children and their modification by stimulant drugs. In R. Knights & D. Bakker (Eds.), *Treatment of hyperactive and learning disordered children* (pp. 219–236). Baltimore: University Park Press.

Barkley, R. A., Fischer, M., Newby, R., & Breen, M. (1988). Development of a multi-method clinical protocol for assessing stimulant drug responses in ADHD children. *Journal of Clinical Child Psychology, 17,* 14–24.

Barkley, R. A., Karlsson, J. & Pollard, S. (1985). Effects of age on the mother–child interactions of hyperactive children. *Journal of Abnormal Child Psychology, 13,* 631–38.

Barkley, R. A., Karlsson, J., Strzelecki, E., & Murphy, J. (1984). Effects of age and Ritalin dosage on the mother–child interactions of hyperactive children. *Journal of Consulting and Clinical Psychology, 52,* 750–758.

Baum, C. G., & Forehand, R. (1981). Long term follow-up of parent training by use of multiple outcome measures. *Behavior Therapy, 12,* 643–652.

Befera, M., & Barkley, R. A. (1985). Hyperactive and normal girls and boys: Mother–child interactions, parent psychiatric status, and child psychopathology. *Journal of Child Psychology and Psychiatry, 26,* 439–452.

Bell, R. Q. (1968). A reinterpretation of the direction of effects in studies on socialization. *Psychological Review, 75,* 81–95.

Bell, R. Q., & Harper, L. V. (1977). *Child effects on adults.* Hillsdale, NJ: Lawrence Erlbaum Associates.

Biederman, J., Munir, K., Knee, D., Armentano, M., Autor, S., Waternaux, C., & Tswang, M. (1987). High rate of affective disorders in probands with attention deficit disorders and in their relatives: A controlled family study. *American Journal of Psychiatry, 144,* 330–333.

Breen, M. (1985). *ADD-H in girls: An analysis of attentional, emotional, cognitive, and academic behaviors and parental psychiatric status.* Manuscript submitted for publication.

Breiner, J. L., & Forehand, R. (1981). An assessment of the effects of parent training on clinic-referred children's school behavior. *Behavioral Assessment, 3,* 31–42.

Brown, R. T., Borden, K. A., Wynne, M. E., Spunt, A. L., & Clingerman, S. R. (1987). Compliance with pharmacological and cognitive treatments for Attention Deficit Disorder. *Journal of the American Academy of Child and Adolescent Psychiatry, 26,* 521–526.

Brown, R. T., & Sleator, E. K. (1979). Methylphenidate in hyperkinetic children: Differences in dose effects on impulsive behavior. *Pediatrics, 64,* 408–411.

Calvert, S. C., & McMahon, R. J. (1987). The treatment acceptability of a behavioral parent training program and its components. *Behavior Therapy, 18,* 165–180.

Campbell, S. B., Schleifer, M., & Weiss, G. (1978). Continuities in maternal reports and child behaviors over time in hyperactive and comparison groups. *Journal of Abnormal Child Psychology, 6,* 33–45.

Cantwell, D. (1975). *The hyperactive child.* New York: Spectrum.

Chess, S. (1960). Diagnosis and treatment of the hyperactive child. *New York State Journal of Medicine, 60,* 2379–2385.

Clements, S. D. (1966). *Task force one: Minimal brain dysfunction in children* (National Institute of Neurological Diseases and Blindness, Monograph No. 3). Washington, DC: U.S. Department of Health, Education, and Welfare.

Conners, C. K. (1980). *Food additives and hyperactive children.* New York: Plenum Press.

Cunningham, C. E., Siegel, L. S., & Offord, D. R. (1985). A developmental dose response analysis of the effects of methylphenidate on the peer interactions of attention deficit disordered boys. *Journal of Child Psychology and Psychiatry, 26,* 955–971.

Deutsch, C. (1984, October). *Genetic studies of attention deficit disorder.* Paper presented at the High Point Hospital Conference on Attention and Conduct Disorder, Toronto.

Douglas, V. I. (1972). Stop, look, and listen: The problem of sustained attention and impulse control in hyperactive and normal children. *Canadian Journal of Behavioural Science, 4,* 259–282.

Douglas, V. I. (1983). Attention of cognitive problems. In M. Rutter (Ed.), *Developmental*

neuropsychiatry (pp. 280–329). New York: Guilford Press.

Douglas, V. I., Barr, R. G., O'Neill, M. E., & Britton, B. G. (1986). Short term effects of methylphenidate on the cognitive, learning, and academic performance of children with attention deficit disorder in the laboratory and the classroom. *Journal of Child Psychology and Psychiatry, 27,* 197–211.

Douglas, V. I., & Parry, P. A. (1983). Effects of reward on delayed reaction time task performance of hyperactive children. *Journal of Abnormal Child Psychology, 11,* 313–326.

Epstein, R. (1985). The positive side-effects of reinforcement: A commentary on Balsam and Bondy (1983). *Journal of Applied Behavior Analysis, 18,* 73–78.

Eyberg, S. M., & Robinson, E. A. (1982). Parent–child interaction training: Effects on family functioning. *Journal of Clinical Child Psychology, 11,* 130–137.

Feingold, B. (1975). *Why your child is hyperactive.* New York: Random House.

Feldman, S., Denhoff, E., & Denhoff, J. (1979). The attention disorders and related syndromes: Outcome in adolescence and young adult life. In E. Denhoff & L. Stern (Eds.), *Minimal brain dysfunction: A developmental approach.* New York: Masson Publishing.

Firestone, P. (1982). Factors associated with children's adherence to stimulant medication. *American Journal of Orthopsychiatry, 52,* 447–457.

Forehand, R., & McMahon, R. (1981). *Helping the noncompliant child: A clinician's guide to parent training.* New York: Guilford Press.

Forehand, R., Rogers, T., McMahon, R., Wells, K., & Griest, D. (1981). Teaching parents to modify child behavior problems: An examination of some follow-up data. *Journal of Pediatric Psychology, 6,* 313–322.

Forehand, R., Sturgis, E. T., McMahon, R. J., Aguar, D., Green, K., Wells, K., & Breiner, J. (1979). Parent behavioral training to modify child noncompliance: Treatment generalization across time and from home to school. *Behavior Modification, 3,* 3–25.

Forehand, R., Wells, K., & Griest, D. L. (1980). An examination of the social validity of a parent training program. *Behavior Therapy, 11,* 488–502.

Foster, S., Prinz, R., & O'Leary, K. D. (1983). Impact of problem-solving communication training and generalization programming procedures on family conflict. *Child and Family Behavior Therapy, 5,* 1–23.

Foster, S. L., & Robin, A. L. (1988). Family conflict and communication in adolescence. In E. Mash & L. Terdal (Eds.), *Behavioral assessment of childhood disorders.* (Vol. 2, pp. 717–775). New York: Guilford Press.

Fox, P. T., & Raichle, M. E. (1985). Stimulus rate determines regional brain blood flow in striate cortex. *Annals of Neurology, 17,* 303–305.

Frentz, C., & Kelley, M. L. (1986). Parents' acceptance of reductive treatment methods: The influence of problem severity and perception of child behavior. *Behavior Therapy, 17,* 75–81.

Gittelman, R. & Eskenazi, B. (1983). Lead and hyperactivity revisited. *Archives of General Psychiatry, 40,* 827–833.

Gittelman, R., Mannuzza, S., Shenker, R., & Bonagura, N. (1985). Hyperactive boys almost grown up. *Archives of General Psychiatry, 42,* 937–947.

Gordon, M. (1983). *The Gordon Diagnostic System.* Boulder, CO: Clinical Diagnostic Systems.

Gross, M. D. (1984). Effects of sucrose on hyperkinetic children. *Pediatrics, 74,* 876–878.

Haenlein, M., & Caul, W. F. (1987). Attention deficit disorder with hyperactivity: A specific hypothesis of reward dysfunction. *Journal of the American Academy of Child and Adolescent Psychiatry, 26,* 356–362.

Hanf, C. (1969). *A two stage program for modifying maternal controlling during mother–child interaction.* Paper presented at the Western Psychological Association Meeting. Vancouver, British Columbia.

Hartsough, C. S., & Lambert, N. M. (1985). Medical factors in hyperactive and normal children: Prenatal, developmental, and health history findings. *American Journal of Orthopsychiatry, 55,* 190–201.

Hechtman, L., Weiss, G., & Perlman, T. (1984). Young adult outcome of hyperactive children who received long-term stimulant treatment. *Journal of the American Academy of Child Psychiatry, 23,* 261–269.

Hechtman, L., Weiss, G., Perlman, R., & Amsel, R. (1984). Hyperactives as young adults: initial predictors of outcome. *Journal of the American Academy of Child Psychiatry, 23,* 250–260.

Heffer, R. W., & Kelley, M. L. (1987). Mothers' acceptance of behavioral interventions for children: The influence of parent race and income. *Behavior Therapy, 18,* 153–164.

Hinshaw, S. P., Henker, B., & Whalen, C. K. (1984). Cognitive-behavioral and pharmacologic interventions for hyperactive boys: Comparative and combined effects. *Journal of Consulting and Clinical Psychology, 52,* 739–749.

Hoy, E., Weiss, G., Minde, K., & Cohen, N. (1978). The hyperactive child at adolescence: Cognitive, emotional, and social functioning. *Journal of Abnormal Child Psychology, 6,* 311–324.

Humphreys, L., Forehand, R., McMahon, R., & Roberts, M. (1978). Parent behavioral training to modify noncompliance: Effects on untreated siblings. *Journal of Behavior Therapy and Experimental Psychiatry, 9,* 235–238.

Humphries, T., Kinsbourne, M., & Swanson, J. (1978). Stimulant effects on cooperation and social interaction between hyperactive children and their mothers. *Journal of Child Psychology and Psychiatry, 19,* 12–22.

Ingersoll, B. (1988). *Your hyperactive child: A parent's guide to coping with attention deficit disorder.* New York: Doubleday.

Kazdin, A. E. (1980). Acceptability of time out from positive reinforcement procedures for disruptive child behavior. *Behavior Therapy, 11,* 329–344.

Kazdin, A. E. (1981). Acceptability of child treatment techniques: The influence of treatment efficacy and adverse side-effects. *Behavior Therapy, 12,* 493–506.

Kendall, P. C., & Braswell, L. (1985). *Cognitive-behavioral therapy for impulsive children.* New York: Guilford Press.

Kinsbourne, M. (1977). The mechanism of hyperactivity. In M. Blaw, I. Rapin, & M. Kinsbourne (Eds.), *Topics in child neurology* (pp. 289–306). New York: Spectrum.

Klorman, R., Coons, H. W., & Borgstedt, A. D. (1987). Effects of methylphenidate on adolescents with a childhood history of attention deficit disorder: I. Clinical findings. *Journal of the American Academy of Child and Adolescent Psychiatry, 26,* 363–367.

Lambert, N. M., Hartsough, C. S., Sassone, D., & Sandoval, J. (1987). Persistence of hyperactivity symptoms from childhood to adolescence and associated outcomes.

American Journal of Orthopsychiatry, 57, 22–32.

Loney, J., Whaley-Klahn, M. A., Kosier, T., & Conboy, J. (1981, November). *Hyperactive boys and their brothers at 21: Predictors of aggressive and antisocial outcomes.* Paper presented at the Society of Life History Research, Monterey, CA.

Lopez, R. C. (1965). Hyperactivity in twins. *Canadian Psychiatric Association Journal, 10,* 421–426.

Lou, H. C., Henriksen, L., & Bruhn P. (1984). Focal cerebral hypoperfusion in children with dysphasia and/or attention deficit disorder. *Archives of Neurology, 41,* 825–829.

Mash, E. J., & Johnston, C. (1983). Parental perceptions of child behavior problems, parenting self-esteem, and mothers' reported stress in younger and older hyperactive and normal children. *Journal of Consulting and Clinical Psychology, 51,* 68–99.

Mattes, J. A., & Gittelman, R. (1981). Effects of artificial food colorings in children with hyperactive symptoms. *Archives of General Psychiatry, 38,* 714–718.

Milich, R., & Pelham, W. E. (1986). Effects of sugar ingestion on the classroom and playgroup behavior of attention deficit disordered boys. *Journal of Consulting and Clinical Psychology, 54,* 714–718.

Milich, R., Wolraich, M., & Lindgren, S. (1986). Sugar and hyperactivity: A critical review of empirical findings. *Clinical Psychology Review, 6,* 493–513.

O'Leary, K. D., & Wilson, G. T. (1987). *Behavior therapy: Application and outcome* (2nd ed.). Englewood Cliffs, NJ: Prentice-Hall.

Paternite, C., & Loney, J. (1980). Childhood hyperkinesis: Relationships between symptomatology and home environment. In C. K. Whalen & B. Henker (Eds.) *Hyperactive children: The social ecology of identification and treatment* (pp. 105–141). New York: Academic Press.

Patterson, G. (1976). The aggressive child: Victim and architect of a coercive system. In E. Mash, L. Hamerlynk, & L. Handy (Eds.), *Behavior modification and families* (pp. 267–316). New York: Brunner/Mazel.

Peed, S., Roberts, M., & Forehand, R. (1977). Evaluation of the effectiveness of a standardized parent training program in altering the interaction of mothers and their noncompliant children. *Behavior Modification, 1,* 323–350.

Pelham, W. E., & Bender, M. E. (1982). Peer relationships in hyperactive children: Description and treatment. In K. Gadow & E. Bialer (Eds.), *Advances in learning and behavioral disabilities* (Vol. 1, pp. 365–436). Greenwich, CT: JAI Press.

Pelham, W. E., Bender, M. E., Caddell, J., Booth, S., & Moorer, S. H. (1985). Methylphenidate and children with attention deficit disorder. *Archives of General Psychiatry, 42,* 948–952.

Pelham. W. E., & Murphy, H. A. (1986). Attention deficit and conduct disorders. In M. Hersen (Ed.), *Pharmacological and behavioral treatment* (pp. 108–148). New York: John Wiley & Sons.

Pfiffner, L. J., & O'Leary, S. G. (1987). The efficacy of all-positive management as a function of the prior use of negative consequences. *Journal of Applied Behavior Analysis, 20,* 265–271.

Pfiffner, L. J., Rosen, L. A., & O'Leary, S. G. (1985). The efficacy of an all-positive approach to classroom management. *Journal of Applied Behavior Analysis, 18,* 257–261.

Pliszka, S. R. (1987). Tricyclic antidepressants in the treatment of children with attention deficit disorder. *Journal of the American Academy of Child and Adolescent Psychiatry, 26,* 127–132.

Pollard, S., Ward, E. M., & Barkley, R. A. (1983). The effects of parent training and Ritalin on the parent-child interactions of hyperactive boys. *Child & Family Behavior Therapy, 5,* 51–69.

Pomeroy, J. C., Sprafkin, J., & Gadow, K. D. (1988). Minor physical anomalies as a biological marker for behavior disorders. *Journal of the American Academy of Child and Adolescent Psychiatry, 27,* 466–473.

Premack, D. (1965). Reinforcement theory. In D. Levine (Ed.), *Nebraska symposium on motivation.* Lincoln: University of Nebraska Press.

Quinn, P. O., & Rapoport, J. L. (1974). Minor physical anomalies and neurologic status in hyperactive boys. *Pediatrics, 53,* 742–747.

Rapoport, J., Quinn, P., Bradbard, G., Riddle, D., & Brooks, E. (1974). Imipramine and methylphenidate treatments of hyperactive boys. *Archives of General Psychiatry, 30,* 789–793.

Rapport, M. D. (1987). Attention deficit disorder with hyperactivity. In M. Hersen & V. B. Van Hasselt (Eds.). *Behavior therapy with children and adolescents: A clinical approach* (pp. 325–361). New York: John Wiley & Sons.

Rapport, M. D., DuPaul, G. J., & Kelly, K. L. (1989). Attention-deficit hyperactivity disorder and methylphenidate: The relationship between gross body weight and drug response in children. *Psychopharmacology Bulletin, 25,* 285–290.

Rapport, M. D., Jones, J. T., DuPaul, G. J., Kelly, K. L., Gardner, M. J., Tucker, S. B., & Shea, M. S. (1987). Attention deficit disorder and methylphenidate: Group and single-subject analyses of dose effects on attention in clinic and classroom settings. *Journal of Clinical Child Psychology, 16,* 329–338.

Rapport, M. D., Murphy, A., & Bailey, J. S. (1980). The effects of a response-cost treatment tactic on hyperactive children. *Journal of School Psychology, 18,* 98–111.

Rapport, M. D., Murphy, A., & Bailey, J. S. (1982). Ritalin versus response cost in the control of hyperactive children: a within-subject comparison. *Journal of Applied Behavior Analysis, 15,* 205–216.

Rapport, M. D., Stoner, G., DuPaul, G. J., Birmingham, B. K., & Tucker, S. B. (1985). Methylphenidate in hyperactive children: Differential effects of dose on academic, learning, and social behavior. *Journal of Abnormal Child Psychology, 13,* 227–244.

Rapport, M. D., Stoner, G., DuPaul, G. J., Kelly, K. L., Tucker, S. B., & Schoeler, T. (1988). Attention deficit disorder and methylphenidate: A multi-level analysis of dose-response effects on children's impulsivity across settings. *Journal of the American Academy of Child and Adolescent Psychiatry, 27,* 60–69.

Robin, A. L. (1981). A controlled evaluation of problem-solving communication training with parent-adolescent conflict. *Behavior Therapy, 12,* 593–609.

Robin, A. L., Kent, R., O'Leary, K. D., Foster, S. L., & Prinz, R. J. (1977). An approach to teaching parents and adolescents problem-solving communication skills: A preliminary report. *Behavior Therapy, 8,* 639–643.

Rosen, L. A., Booth, S. R., Bender, M. E., McGrath, M. L., Sorrell, S., & Drabman, R. S. (1988). Effects of sugar (sucrose) on children's behavior. *Journal of Consulting and Clinical Clinical Psychology, 56,* 583–589.

Rosen, L. A., O'Leary, S. G., Joyce, S. A., Conway, G., & Pfiffner, L. J. (1984). The importance of prudent negative consequences for maintaining the appropriate behavior of hyperactive students. *Journal of Abnormal Child Psychology, 12,* 581–604.

Ross, D. M., & Ross, S. A. (1982). *Hyperactivity: Current issues, research, and theory* (2nd ed.). New York: John Wiley & Sons.

Russo, D. C., Cataldo, M. F., & Cushing, P. J. (1981). Compliance training and behavioral covariation in the treatment of multiple behavior problems. *Journal of Applied Behavior Analysis, 14,* 209–222.

Rutter, M. (1977). Brain damage syndromes in childhood: Concepts and findings. *Journal of Child Psychology and Psychiatry, 18,* 1–21.

Rutter, M., Chadwick, O., & Schaffer, D. (1983). Head injury. In M. Rutter (Ed.), *Developmental neuropsychiatry* (pp. 83–111). New York: Guilford Press.

Satterfield, J. H., Hoppe, C. M., & Schell, A. M. (1982). A prospective study of delinquency in 110 adolescent boys with attention deficit disorder and 88 normal adolescent boys. *American Journal of Psychiatry, 139,* 795–798.

Satterfield, J. H., Satterfield, B. T., & Schell, A. M. (1987). Therapeutic interventions to prevent delinquency in hyperactive boys. *Journal of the American Academy of Child and Adolescent Psychiatry, 26,* 56–64.

Shaywitz, S. E., Cohen, D. J., & Shaywitz, B. A. (1978). The biochemical basis of minimal brain dysfunction. *Journal of Pediatrics, 92,* 179–187.

Shaywitz, S. E., Shaywitz, B. A., Cohen, D. J., & Young, J. G. (1983). Monoaminergic mechanisms in hyperactivity. In M. Rutter (Ed.), *Developmental neuropsychiatry* (pp. 330–347). New York: Guilford.

Skinner, B. F. (1938). *The behavior of organisms: An experimental analysis.* New York: Appleton-Century.

Skinner, B. F. (1953). *Science and Human Behavior.* New York: Macmillan.

Smith, L. (1976). *Your child's behavior chemistry.* New York: Random House.

Still, G. F. (1902). Some abnormal psychical conditions in children. *Lancet, 1,* 1008–1012, 1077–1082, 1163–1168.

Strauss, A. A., & Lehtinen, L. E. (1947). *Psychopathology and education of the brain-injured child.* New York: Grune & Stratton.

Tallmadge, J., & Barkley, R. A. (1983). The interactions of hyperactive and normal boys with their mothers and fathers. *Journal of Abnormal Child Psychology, 11,* 565–579.

Thorley, G. (1984). Review of follow-up and follow-back studies of childhood hyperactivity. *Psychological Bulletin, 96,* 116–132.

Varley, C. K. (1985). A review of studies of drug treatment efficacy for attention deficit disorder with hyperactivity in adolescents. *Psychopharmacology Bulletin, 21,* 216–221.

Von Brock, M. B., & Elliott, S. N. (in press). The influence of treatment effectiveness information on the acceptability of classroom interventions. *Journal of School Psychology.*

Vyse, S. A., & Rapport, M. D. (1987). *The effects of methylphenidate on learning in children with attention deficit disorder with hyperactivity.* Paper presented at the meeting of the American Psychological Association, New York, New York.

Wahler, R. (1980). The insular mother: Her problems in parent–child treatment. *Journal of Applied Behavior Analysis, 13,* 207–220.

Webster-Stratton, C. (1984). Randomized trial of two parent-training programs for families with conduct-disordered children. *Journal of Consulting and Clinical Psychology, 52,* 666–678.

Weiss, G., & Hechtman, L. (1986). *Hyperactive children grown up.* New York: Guilford Press.

Weiss, G., Hechtman, L., Milroy, T., & Perlman, T. (1985). Psychiatric status of hyperactives as adults: A controlled prospective 15-year follow-up of 63 hyperactive children. *Journal of the American Academy of Child Psychiatry, 24,* 211–220.

Weiss, G., Hechtman, L., & Perlman, T. (1978). Hyperactives as young adults: School, employer, and self-rating scales obtained during ten-year follow-up evaluation. *American Journal of Orthopsychiatry, 48,* 438–445.

Weiss, G., Hechtman, L., Perlman, T., Hopkins, J., & Wener, A. (1979). Hyperactives as young adults: A controlled prospective ten-year follow-up of 75 children. *Archives of General Psychiatry, 36,* 675–681.

Wells, K., & Forehand, R. (1985). Conduct and oppositional disorders. In P. H. Bornstein & A. E. Kazdin (Eds.), *Handbook of clinical behavior therapy with children* (pp. 218–265). Homewood IL: Dorsey Press.

Wender, P. H. (1971). *Minimal brain dysfunction in children.* New York: John Wiley & Sons.

Wender, P. H. (1987). *The hyperactive child, adolescent, and adult.* New York: Oxford University Press.

Wender, P. H., Reimherr, F. W., & Wood, D. R. (1981). Attention deficit disorder ("minimal brain dysfunction") in adults. *Archives of General Psychiatry, 38,* 449–456.

Werry, J. (1968). Developmental hyperactivity. *Pediatric clinics of North America, 19,* 9–16.

Werry, J., & Conners, C. K. (1979). Pharmacotherapy. In H. Quay & J. Werry (Eds.), *Psychopathological disorders of childhood* (2nd ed., pp. 336–386). New York: John Wiley & Sons.

Werry, J. S., & Sprague, R. L. (1970). Hyperactivity. In C. G. Costello (Ed.), *Symptoms of psychopathology* (pp. 397–417). New York: John Wiley & Sons.

Whalen, C., Collins, D., Henker, B., Alkus, S., Adams, D., & Stapp, J. (1978). Behavior observations of hyperactive children and methylphenidate (Ritalin) effects in systematically structured classroom environments. Now you see them, now you don't. *Journal of Pediatric Psychology, 3,* 177–187.

Whalen, C. K. & Henker, B. (Eds.). (1980). *Hyperactive children: The social ecology of identification and treatment.* New York: Academic Press.

Whalen, C. K., Henker, B., & Hinshaw, S. P. (1985). Cognitive-behavioral therapies for hyperactive children: Premises, problems, and prospects. *Journal of Abnormal Child Psychology, 13,* 391–410.

Willerman, L. (1973). Activity level and hyperactivity in twins. *Child Development, 44,* 288–293.

Willis, T. J., & Lovaas, I. (1977). A behavioral approach to treating hyperactive children: The parent's role. In J. B. Millichap (Ed.) *Learning disabilities and related disorders* (pp. 119–140). Chicago, IL: Yearbook Medical Publications.

Witt, J. C., Elliott, S. N., & Martens, B. K.

(1984). Acceptability of behavioral interventions used in classrooms: The influences of amount of teacher time, severity of behavior problem, and type of intervention. *Behavior Disorders, 9,* 95–104.

Wood, D. R., Reimherr, F. W., Wender, P. H., & Johnson, G. E. (1976). Diagnosis and treatment of minimal brain dysfunction in adults. *Archives of General Psychiatry, 33,* 1453–1460.

CHAPTER 6

ACADEMIC PROBLEMS

John Wills Lloyd
Daniel P. Hallahan
James M. Kauffman
Clayton E. Keller

When students are referred for special education, it is often or usually because they have academic problems (Anderson, Cronin, & Miller, 1986; Hutton, 1985; Lloyd, Kauffman, Landrum, & Roe, 1989). The size of the learning-disabilities category is testimony to the high prevalence of academic achievement difficulties in our nation's schools. The learning-disabilities classification, primarily comprising difficulties in academics, accounts for almost half of all handicapped children (U.S. Department of Education, 1987). There is also ample evidence that academic problems characterize two other relatively large groups receiving special education: students identified as behavior disordered and those identified as mentally retarded (Cullinan, Epstein, & Lloyd, 1983; Kauffman, 1989; MacMillan, 1982). When one includes pupils receiving special services under Chapter 1 funding—as well as the many "slow learners" who fall between the officially sanctioned categories of learning disabilities and mental retardation—then the number of students with academic problems is indeed staggering.

Because of the enormous number of pupils with academic problems and the wide range of difficulties these youngsters exhibit, considerable research attention has been directed toward determining effective interventions. In this chapter, we examine interventions based on the following major models: cognitive theory, behavioral theory, cognitive-behavioral theory, and Direct Instruction theory. (We have used capitals for Direct Instruction to discriminate it from the more common use of the term. In this regard, we have followed the lead of Becker and Carnine [1981]. The common use of the term [and variants such as "directive teaching"] refers to a set of specific teaching behaviors, while the capitalized version refers to the detailed set of teaching and instructional programming procedures associated with the work of Engelmann, Carnine, Becker, and Gersten [1988; to be discussed below]). In the immediately following section, we describe these models. In the next major section, we address five areas in which pupils commonly experience difficulties in the academic learning situation—attention to task, reading, handwriting, written expression, and arithmetic—and describe interventions for each based on the models. In the third and last major section, we discuss the integration of these models and their evidentiary bases into a comprehensive approach to the treatment and prevention of learning problems.

MODELS

Earlier examinations of the literature related to learning problems have included descriptions of medical, process, and behavioral conceptual models as the basis for intervention (e.g., Bateman, 1967; Ysseldyke & Salvia, 1974). However, for several reasons, these categories of models are not appropriate for the present review. First, the focus of the present review on school-based interventions makes discussion of medical interventions superfluous. For further discussion of medical aspects of disabilities, see Van Hasselt, Strain, and Hersen (1988; also see Kavale, 1982, and Reeve & Kauffman, 1988, for discussion of learning disabilities). Second, process training has been largely discredited as an approach to intervention in academic learning problems (e.g., Gersten & Carnine, 1984a; Hammill & Larsen, 1974; but see Kavale, 1981). Third, since the preparation of the earlier reviews, new findings have changed the conceptualization of learning problems. Finally, more recent interventions, such as those described by Pflaum and Pascarella (e.g., 1980) or Bryant and his colleagues (e.g., Bryant, Drabin, & Gettinger, 1981), clearly do not fit into medical, process, or behavioral categories.

We have organized our discussion of conceptual models around cognitive, behavioral, cognitive-behavioral, and Direct Instruction theories because these categories seem to us to be a reasonable framework for brief exposition of the current state of affairs—not because the models themselves have clearly different origins or because distinctions among educational interventions based on these models are always clear. Any description of conceptual models requires arbitrary decisions about how various theories and the interventions derived from them should be separated and grouped. That is, the theoretical roots and emphases of various models are often overlapping, so that the models are distinguished only by their *relative degree* of emphasis on such factors as how the student thinks about problems, the effects of setting events and consequences on academic performance, the student's sense of self-efficacy, or

the nature of the task presented to the student. For each of the four models we discuss, we shall briefly describe the theoretical roots of the basic concepts and the relative emphases in intervention strategies.

Cognitive Model

Cognitive approaches share an emphasis on the processes involved in human thinking, according these processes a role of greater importance than any of the other models. Advocates of cognitive approaches disagree as to what processes are considered important. Some emphasize the importance of metacognition (thinking about thinking), while others emphasize information processing factors (such as memory or rehearsal).

The distinctions between this model, the cognitive-behavioral model, and the Direct Instruction model illustrate the arbitrary nature of such divisions. Both of the latter models share the cognitive model's consideration of thinking. Although the cognitive model emphasizes thinking as the impetus for behavior, the cognitive-behavioral model reflects a greater interaction between overt behavior and covert thought processes. Similarly, although the cognitive model stresses traditional processes of thinking (e.g., memory), the Direct Instruction model stresses the formation of cognitive rules based on similarities and differences in the environment that are demonstrated during instruction. The most distinctive feature of the cognitive model is its focus on mental operations and their primacy in determining overt behavior. Proponents of the cognitive model tend to downplay the importance of the acquisition of specific academic skills, preferring to focus on mentation leading to generalized competence in problem solving.

Theoretical Roots

Proponents of cognitive approaches derive their ideas primarily from cognitive psychologists, most notably Piaget and his interpreters (e.g., Inhelder, Sinclair, & Bovet, 1974; Piaget & Inhelder, 1969a, b). Many other cognitive psychologists, particularly Flavell (e.g., Flavell, 1977) and Bruner (e.g., Bruner, Goodnow, & Austin, 1956), made significant contributions to the theoretical underpinnings of cognitive interventions.

The most important basic premise underlying cognitive approaches is that successful learners *actively* construct meaning from their prior experience *and* their thought processes about new information. They use "executive" or "meta-cognitive" processes—reflective consideration of their own approaches to solving problems—to determine how new information is sought, perceived, related to stored information, stored, selected, and recalled. What distinguishes a skilled learner from an unskilled one is the inability of the unskilled learner to use executive processes effectively and efficiently. Unlike the skilled learner, the unskilled one does not actively think about learning; metacognitive processes are not brought into play to guide perception, memory, and problem solving. Thus, basic research on the cognitive development of children and on the thought processes of successful and unsuccessful problem solvers provides the theoretical backdrop for cognitive interventions.

Emphases in Intervention

Cognitive interventions emphasize engaging students in activities that are meaningful and appropriately related to the their prior learning. "Effective instruction provides activities (in the broadest sense) to facilitate the *learner's ability to construct meaning* from experience" (Reid & Hresko, 1981, p. 49). In fact, some cognitive interventions involve "reciprocal teaching," in which teacher and student engage in dialogue intended to result in their joint construction of the meaning of text or algorithms (e.g., Palinscar, 1986; Palinscar & Brown, 1984). The hallmarks of cognitive interventions are an emphasis on (1) the meaning of learning for the student, (2) relating instructional activities to prior experiences of the student, (3) active involvement of the student in learning and planning for learning, and (4) long-term as opposed to short-term memory.

Cognitive interventions tend to emphasize "holistic" presentation of material to be learned under the assumption that material analyzed into its constituent parts is meaningless (cf., McNutt, 1984; Neal, 1984; Poplin, 1984, 1988a, b; Reid, 1988). "A cognitive approach assumes that children possess an 'umbrella' concept so that when details are presented, the children have a way of organizing them into that overall concept" (Reid & Hresko, 1981, p. 50). Thus some advocates of a cognitive approach to reading are likely to begin reading instruction by focusing on the meaning of reading—its function in a

child's life—and eschew instruction in details, such as accurate decoding of print into oral equivalents, until after the child has begun to read.

Cognitive interventions share the emphasis of cognitive-behavioral approaches on metacognitive processes and the active engagement of the learner. Unlike cognitive-behavioral approaches, however, cognitive interventions tend not to include direct measurement of student progress in acquiring the component skills of competent performance. For example, one would be less concerned with the rate at which students read stories or whether they could answer questions about the material and more concerned about whether the pupils' retelling of the story reflected an overall understanding of it.

Behavioral Model

Behavior modification has had a major effect on interventions for academic problems. Early studies (e.g., Zimmerman & Zimmerman, 1962; Haring & Hauck, 1969) revealed that behavioral principles could be applied to learning problems outside the laboratory setting. More recently, researchers influenced by behavioral principles have conducted studies in each of the academic areas. Reviews by Lahey (1976); Rose, Koorland, and Epstein (1982); and Witt, Elliott, and Gresham (1988) are available. Components of the behavioral model, particularly direct observation and measurement and an analytical view of component skills, are integrated into cognitive-behavioral and Direct Instruction approaches. Nevertheless, a strictly behavioral model does not include attribution of a causal role to internal thought processes (as does the cognitive-behavioral model), nor does it fully encompass the Direct Instruction model's logical analysis of instructional procedures. Its focus, rather, is on the analysis of the roles of environmental events in shaping and maintaining overt behavior.

Theoretical Roots

Behavioral theory holds as its most basic premise that behavior is a function of its consequences. Applications of the behavioral model to education are based on the laboratory and applied work of behavioral psychologists, most notably Skinner (e.g., Skinner, 1953; 1968). Applications of behavioral theory to academic learning grew rapidly with the contributions of other psychologists and educators such as Bijou (e.g., Bijou, 1970) and Haring (e.g., Haring, 1968; Haring, Lovitt, Eaton, & Hansen, 1978). A behavioral model maintains a focus on observable behavior. In its radical form, the behavioral model denies the causal role of internal events such as thought processes; it rejects all appeals to "mentalism" as explanations for behavior, proffering instead explanations based on analysis of directly observable events. Perhaps its most important features for application to education, however, are its insistence on direct measurement of behavior and its reliance on the experimental analysis of the causal roles of observable events following overt behavior.

Direct measurement of behavior involves frequent, usually daily, observation and recording of the target skills for which instruction is offered. Words read correctly, words written correctly, or problems solved correctly per minute, for example, might be target academic behaviors. The analysis of behavior and its controlling variables requires that the behavior be observed and recorded under conditions that are systematically altered, so that changes in the rate of behavior can be unambiguously attributed to specified, observable environmental events. Thus, for example, one would be expressly concerned with whether a reinforcement program caused improvement in the rate at which students complete arithmetic problems.

Behavioral theory underscores the importance of consequences in shaping and maintaining behavior, including the acquisition of discriminations and the competent performance of acquired skills. A behavioral analysis of learning difficulties looks first at the events that follow academic performance or approximations of academic responses. For example, a behavioral analysis of reading might examine the teacher's behavior after pupils have correctly answered a question. Because consequences are assumed to control both acquisition and performance of acquired skills, a behavioral analysis typically begins with programming a systematic change in events following desired performance (e.g., increase the frequency with which the teacher praises correct answers). Thus failure of a student to acquire or perform an academic task may prompt an analysis of the reinforcers the student acquires for performance or approximations of performance of a target skill.

Emphases in Intervention

Central elements in the behavioral model are consequences and discriminative stimuli. Consequences include both reinforcers and punishers, those events that follow the occurrence of a behavior and serve to increase or decrease the probability that it will recur. The range of interventions that have been studied by behaviorally oriented researchers is not, however, restricted to simplistic reinforcement and punishment procedures such as rewarding correct responses with small candies and punishing erroneous responses by loudly saying no. Complex social consequences, including those that are self-managed, have been employed as well. The behavioral model places tremendous emphasis on empirical verification of outcomes. Usually, this is accomplished by measuring specific behaviors (e.g., words read, problems solved, action verbs written in a story) and controlling the introduction of a teaching procedure so that comparisons can be made between students' performance under different conditions (usually baseline and treatment; see Tawney & Gast, 1984). In general, a behaviorally oriented educator requires or strongly encourages the collection of objective data about pupil performance and stresses the importance of basing teaching decisions on the outcomes of specific teaching tactics (cf., Lovitt, 1981; Haring et al., 1978).

Cognitive-Behavioral Model

The cognitive-behavioral model in education is an outgrowth of a larger movement in psychology which retained the empirical base of the behavioral approach but accepted as useful or essential certain features of radical behaviorism's nemesis, mentalism (thoughts and affective states as causal variables). Advocates of an integrated cognitive and behavioral approach, often called cognitive-behavior modification (CBM), often stress the role of metacogition (see previous discussion). Not only do cognitive-behaviorists contend that people's thoughts influence how they behave but they also place additional emphasis on specific kinds of thoughts such as a sense of personal effectiveness, student involvement in instruction, and so forth.

For the most part, CBM interventions are designed to increase self-awareness and self-control and, therefore, to improve academic behavior. Gerber (1987), Kendall and Cummings

(1988), Kneedler and Meese (1988), Loper and Murphy (1985), and Wong (1985a) have provided reviews of the literature in this area.

Theoretical Roots

The theory underlying cognitive-behavioral approaches is derived from principles of social learning, which melds cognitive and behavioral concepts. Principal among those whose ideas gave rise to cognitive-behavioral strategies are Bandura (e.g., Bandura, 1977, 1986), Mahoney (e.g., Mahoney, 1974), Meichenbaum (e.g., Meichenbaum, 1977), and Mischel (e.g., Mischel, 1973). In contrast to a strictly cognitive approach, cognitive-behavioral theory recognizes the considerable influence of contingencies of reinforcement on learning; in contrast to radical behaviorism, it views the self—including one's mental activities and affective states—as actively involved in determining behavior. A key concept in cognitive-behavioral theory is reciprocal determinism: the notion that behavior, environmental events, and internal variables (i.e., "self" or "person" variables such as thoughts and feelings) mutually affect one another. Thus management of external events, such as the consequences of behavior, is a legitimate intervention strategy. Likewise, a strategy designed to alter cognitive processing of information is legitimate. Indeed, cognitive-behavioral theory posits that the most effective strategies will combine behavioral and cognitive methods for overcoming learning and behavioral problems.

Emphases in Intervention

Like the cognitive approach, cognitive-behavioral interventions emphasize actively involving the student in learning, particularly in learning to monitor and direct his or her own thought processes. This emphasis is combined, however, with concern for measuring directly the behavioral outcomes of intervention and for teaching the component skills involved in academic performance. Thus a student might be taught word-attack skills in beginning reading, but these skills would likely be taught along with cognitive strategies for applying them. These and similar topics are discussed in greater detail by Braswell and Kendall (1988), Keogh and Hall (1984), and Whitman, Burgio, and Johnston (1984).

In cognitive-behavioral interventions, considerable emphasis is placed on self-control. Self-monitoring, self-assessment, self-recording, self-

management of reinforcement, and so on are commonly used strategies. These are often effective, however, only if students are helped to become aware of their own thinking about their behavior and the strategies they are using (or not using) to approach problems. Thus metacognitive strategy training is often a critical part of these interventions. Self-control interventions are also dependent on prior learning of skills by a particular self-procedure. For example, in order for pupils to use a self-instructional strategy to guide their completion of a long-division task, they must learn not only the steps in the self-guiding strategy but also the steps in completing long division problems.

Direct Instruction Model

The Direct Instruction model has generated much research in academic learning. Although the generic term "direct instruction" (e.g., Rosenshine & Stevens, 1986) gained great currency in the late 1970s and early 1980s, Direct Instruction (DI) as used here differs from it in some specific ways. In both the Direct Instruction and the generic direct instruction approach, there is emphasis on specific control of teacher behavior (particularly in the form of correction, reinforcement, and provision of practice opportunities); but in the Direct Instruction model, relatively greater emphasis is placed on the logical analysis of instructional communications (Engelmann & Carnine, 1982). Indeed, Direct Instruction researchers have conducted many studies of these instructional programming principles, both with normally achieving students (e.g., Carnine, 1980) and handicapped learners (e.g., Gersten, White, Falco, & Carnine, 1982). A meta-analytic review of research in DI revealed an average effect size of 0.81 for academic measures (White, 1988).

Theoretical Roots

Direct Instruction is most closely associated with the work of Engelmann, Carnine, Becker, and Bereiter (e.g., Becker, Engelmann, & Thomas, 1975; Bereiter & Engelmann, 1966; Carnine & Silbert, 1979; Engelmann, 1969; Engelmann, Becker, Carnine, & Gersten, 1988; Engelmann & Carnine, 1982). Observation of DI lessons would immediately reveal that the model owes a great deal to behavioral principles. Lessons are highly structured and rich with praise and, particularly for low-achieving students, rewards (e.g., points). Nevertheless, a closer examination of the content and structure of lessons reveals a debt to other literatures that are not directly in the behavioral tradition. For instance, one of the central features of the commercially available instructional programs authored by Engelmann and his colleagues is the extensive use of examples and not-examples and their sequencing, as developed in the concept learning literature.

Emphases in Intervention

Direct Instruction emphasizes control of the details of the instructional interaction between teachers and students. Academic lessons are presented by teachers according to carefully field-tested scripts. In a typical lesson, the teacher frequently asks small groups of students questions having specific answers. The students answer chorally and, depending on the accuracy of the answer, the teacher provides praise or corrective feedback. Figure 6.1 shows one of a series of scripts for teaching students the structure and use of analogies.

The logical analysis of instruction proposed by Engelmann and Carnine (1982) is designed to admit to one and only one interpretation of a task. A central tenet of this approach is that if the instructional presentation admits to more than one interpretation, some students will learn the wrong interpretation and, thus, will fail to learn the skill or concept being taught. Pupils with atypical learning characteristics may be more likely than normals to adopt the "misrules" that faulty instruction provides. Engelmann and Carnine call instruction that prevents mislearning "faultless instruction."

PROBLEM AREAS

Students who encounter problems with learning in school tasks may experience difficulties in any of one or more areas. According to some views of these difficulties, the problems are reflections of more fundamental problems in other areas, such as memory or the processing of stimuli, but the nature and extent of the relationship between such underlying capabilities and achievement problems is regularly a source of disagreement. (For a more extensive treatment of these issues see Hallahan, Kauffman, & Lloyd, 1985.) At the very least, however, these difficulties are clearly manifested in performance deficits in the basic academic areas (reading, writing, and arithmetic) and related

school areas (attention). We focus the remainder of this chapter on these problem areas. Thus, the following material is arranged according to problem area (attention to task, reading, handwriting, written expression, and arithmetic), with a separate discussion of how each of the previously discussed models approaches each problem.

Attention to Task

One need spend only a few minutes in a teachers' lounge before hearing about problems in attention to task. Difficulties in securing pupils' attention to teacher presentations or individual assignments are regularly described in the educational literature (e.g., Hallahan et al., 1985). Behaviorally, the problem is primarily one of what the pupil looks at during instruction. Looking at assigned work or at the teacher is considered attending to task, while staring out the window, playing with objects during a lecture, and so forth are considered nonattending. Many are also concerned with whether the pupil is actually thinking about the assigned work or the teacher's presentation; but the extent of this problem has not yet been successfully measured. Table 6.1 shows some interventions that have been used with attention problems. In the following subsections, we discuss the evidence about interventions associated with the behavioral, cognitive-behavioral, and Direct Instruction models.

Behavioral Model

There have been many demonstrations of reinforcement-based interventions for deficits in study behavior or attention to task. Indeed, the first article in the *Journal of Applied Behavior Analysis* described the beneficial effects of contingent praise on study behavior (Hall, Lund, & Jackson, 1968). Since that time there have been myriad similar studies demonstrating similar effects. However, one of the difficulties with the behavioral approach has been that manipulation of attending behavior has not uniformly led to concomitant improvements in pupils' academic performance. Ferritor, Buckholdt, Hamblin, and Smith (1972) reported that contingent reinforcement of attending behavior did not consistently affect the amount of work pupils accomplished; but contingent reinforcement of completing work affected levels of attending behavior.

Lesson 21   Lesson 42

THINKING OPERATIONS

● **EXERCISE 1**   Analogies
Task A
The first Thinking Operation today is Analogies.
1. **We're going to make up an analogy that tells how animals move. What is the analogy going to tell?** Signal. *How animals move.* Repeat until firm.
2. **The animals we're going to use in the analogy are a hawk and a whale. Which animals?** Signal. *A hawk and a whale.*
3. **Name the first animal.** Signal. *A hawk.* **Yes, a hawk. How does that animal move?** Signal. *It flies.* **Yes, it flies.**
4. **So, here's the first part of the analogy. A hawk is to flying. What's the first part of the analogy?** Signal. *A hawk is to flying.* **Yes, a hawk is to flying.** Repeat until firm.
5. **The first part of the analogy told how an animal moves. So, the next part of the analogy must tell how another animal moves.**
6. **You told how a hawk moves. Now you're going to tell about a whale. What animal?** Signal. *A whale.* **How does that animal move?** Signal. *It swims.* **Yes, it swims.**
7. **So, here's the second part of the analogy. A whale is to swimming. What's the second part of the analogy?** Signal. *A whale is to swimming.* **Yes, a whale is to swimming.**
8. Repeat steps 2–7 until firm.
9. **Now we're going to say the whole analogy. First, we're going to tell how a hawk moves and then we're going to tell how a whale moves. Say the analogy with me.** Signal. Respond with the students. **A hawk is to flying as a whale is to swimming.** Repeat until the students are responding with you.
10. **All by yourselves. Say that analogy.** Signal. *A hawk is to flying as a whale is to swimming.* Repeat until firm.
11. **That analogy tells how those animals move. What does that analogy tell?** Signal. *How those animals move.*
12. Repeat steps 10 and 11 until firm.
Individual test
Call on individual students to do step 10 or 11.

● **EXERCISE 12**   Analogies: opposites
Now we're going to do some more Analogies.
1. **Here's an analogy about words. Old is to young as asleep is to . . .** Pause 2 seconds. **Get ready.** Signal. *Awake.* **Everybody, say the analogy.** Signal. *Old is to young as asleep is to awake.* Repeat until firm.
2. **What are old and asleep?** Signal. *Words.* **To correct students who say** *Opposites:*
   a. **Old and asleep are words.**
   b. Repeat step 2.
   Old is to young as asleep is to awake. That analogy tells something about those words. Pause. **What does that analogy tell about those words?** Signal. *What opposites those words have.* Repeat until firm.
3. **Say the analogy.** Signal. *Old is to young as asleep is to awake.* Repeat until firm.
4. **And what does that analogy tell about those words?** Signal. *What opposites those words have.*
5. Repeat steps 3 and 4 until firm.

EXERCISE 13   Analogies
Note: Praise all reasonable responses in this exercise, but have the group repeat the responses specified in the exercise.
1. **Everybody, what class are a towel and a plate in?** Signal. *Objects.*
2. **Finish this analogy. A towel is to rectangular as a plate is to . . .** Pause 2 seconds. **Get ready.** Signal. *Round.*
3. **Everybody, say that analogy.** Signal. *A towel is to rectangular as a plate is to round.* Repeat until firm.
4. **The analogy tells something about those objects.** Pause. **What does that analogy tell about those objects?** Signal. *What shape those objects are.*
5. Repeat steps 3 and 4 until firm.
6. **A towel is to cloth as a plate is to . . .** Pause 2 seconds. **Get ready.** Signal. *Plastic.*
7. **Everybody, say that analogy.** Signal. *A towel is to cloth as a plate is to plastic.* Repeat until firm.
8. **The analogy tells something about those objects.** Pause. **What does that analogy tell about those objects?** Signal. *What material those objects are made of.*
9. Repeat steps 7 and 8 until firm.

Figure 6.1. Sample teaching scripts from a Direct Instruction program. Note that the scripts come from two different lessons, the second of which would normally be taught about a month after the first. From the careful selection of multiple examples and systematic reduction of teacher assistance, pupils learn great facility with language skills such as understanding and using analogies. From *Thinking basics: Corrective reading comprehension A.* (pp. 121, 251) by S. Engelmann, P. Haddox, S. Hanner, and J. Osborn, 1978, Chicago: Science Research Associates. Copyright 1978 by Science Research Associates. Reprinted by permission of publisher.

Table 6.1. Selected Studies Illustrating Techniques for Treating Attention Problems

CITATION	INDEPENDENT VARIABLE
Bailey, Wolf, & Phillips, 1970	Home-based reinforcement
Carnine, 1976	Pacing of teacher questioning
Ferritor, Buckholt, Hamblin, & Smith, 1972	Token reinforcement of attending versus completing work
Hall, Lund, & Jackson, 1968	Teacher praise
Hallahan, Lloyd, Kosiewicz, Kauffman, & Graves, 1979	Self-recording
Hallahan, Lloyd, Kneedler, & Marshall, 1982	Self- versus teacher-assessed self-recording
Harris, 1986	Self-recording of attention versus productivity
Lloyd, Bateman, Landrum, & Hallahan, 1989	Self-recording of attention versus productivity
McLaughlin, 1984	Self-recording with and without consequences
Packard, 1970	Group contingency
Walker & Buckley, 1968	Token reinforcement

Cognitive-Behavioral Model

Self-recording is an example of a cognitive-behavioral intervention for deficits in attention to task. Self-recording of attending behavior has been extensively studied with atypical learners. Because theoretical opinions (see Nelson & Hayes, 1981) differ about whether self-recording's beneficial effects are the result of its behavioral components (i.e., it makes environmental cues more salient) or its cognitive components (i.e., it makes the individual more aware of his or her behavior), it is difficult to achieve consensus about whether it is a behavioral or a cognitive intervention. We treat it here as a cognitive-behavioral technique because it seems to straddle the two camps and because previous work has treated it in that way (e.g., Hallahan, Kneedler, & Lloyd, 1983).

In studies of self-recording of attention to task, teachers have provided their pupils with intermittent cues (via a preprogrammed audiotape recording) which prompted the students to ask themselves whether they were paying attention to their assigned tasks. Students were taught to record their answers to the question (either yes or no) and then return to work. Box 6.1 illustrates (1) how a teacher might introduce self-recording of attention to a pupil and (2) how the pupil might implement it on subsequent days. (For a detailed description of the research on self-recording of attention, see Lloyd & Landrum, in press.)

Overall, the results of these studies have indicated that the introduction of self-recording causes substantial and consistent improvements in attention to task as recorded by independent observers. Moreover, the studies have revealed (1) that the children benefit from having the cues and being required to perform the recording act during the period when they are learning to record their attention-to-task behavior, (2) that children can be weaned from reliance on the tape-recorded cues and the recording, (3) that these improvements are often accompanied by improvements in the rate of correct answering on assigned tasks, and (4) that self-recording has greater effects than a similar procedure in which the teacher makes the assessment and directs the pupil to record. Research comparing self-recording of attention to task and self-recording of academic productivity has shown that both procedures have substantial effects on measures of both behaviors, that for most students neither procedure is consistently more effective than the other, and that pupils' preference for one or the other procedure is probably influenced by the ease with which either may be used (e.g., Lloyd, Bateman, Landrum, & Hallahan, 1989).

Direct Instruction Model

According to the Direct Instruction view, one of the requirements of teaching is to make the instruction so engaging that pupils attend at a very high rate. To accomplish this, teachers should keep lessons moving at a lively pace. Carnine (1976) illustrated the effectiveness of this approach by manipulating the rate of teacher questions and recording the percentage of time pupils were attending to the teacher and the probability of correct answering. He found that

---

BOX 6.1. CASE STUDY: TRAINING AND IMPLEMENTATION OF A SELF-MONITORING PROGRAM

SCRIPT FOR TEACHER INTRODUCTION
OF SELF-MONITORING

"Edwin, you know how paying attention to your work has been a problem for you. You've heard teachers tell you, 'Pay attention,' 'Get to work,' 'What are you supposed to be doing?' and things like that. Well, today we're going to start something that will help you help yourself pay attention better. First we need to make sure that you know what paying attention means. This is what I mean by paying attention." (Teacher models immediate and sustained attention to task.) "And this is what I mean by not paying attention." (Teacher models inattentive behaviors such as glancing around and playing with objects). "Now you tell me if I was paying attention." (Teacher models attentive and inattentive behaviors and requires the student to categorize them.) "Okay, now let me show you what we're going to do. While you're working, this tape recorder will be turned on. Every once in awhile, you'll hear a little sound like this": (Teacher plays tone on tape). "And when you hear that sound, quietly ask yourself, 'Was I paying attention?' If you answer yes, put a check in this box. If you answer no, put a check in this box. Then go right back to work. When you hear the sound again, ask the question, answer it, mark your answer, and go back to work. Now, let me show you how it works." (Teacher models entire procedure.) "Now, Edwin, I bet you can do this. Tell me what you're going to do every time you hear a tone. Let's try it. I'll start the tape and you work on these papers." (Teacher observes student's implementation of the entire procedure, praises its correct use, and gradually withdraws her presence.)

THE NEXT DAY

SCENE: A classroom of students engaged in various activities. One teacher is walking about the room, preparing for her next activity. Some students are sitting in a semicircle facing another teacher and answering questions he poses. Other students are sitting at their desks and writing on papers or in workbooks. Edwin is working at his own desk. The teacher picks up some work pages that have green strips of paper attached to their tops.

TEACHER: (Walking up to Edwin's desk.) "Edwin, here are your seat-work pages for today. I'm going to start the tape and I want you to self-record like you have been doing. What are you going to ask yourself when you hear the beep?"

EDWIN: (Taking papers.) "Was I paying attention?"

TEACHER: "Okay, that's it." (Turning away.) "Bobby, Jackie, and Anne; it's time for spelling group." (Starts a tape recorder and walks toward front of room where three students are gathering.)

EDWIN: (Begins working on his assignments; he is continuing to work when a tone comes from the tape recorder. Edwin's lips barely move as he almost inaudibly whispers.) "Was I paying attention? Yes." (He marks the green strip of paper and returns to work. Later, another tone comes from the tape recorder. Edwin whispers.) "Was I paying attention? Yes." (He marks the green strip of paper and returns to work. Later, as the students in one group laugh, Edwin looks up and watches them. While he is looking up, a tone occurs.) "Was I paying attention? No." (He marks the strip of paper and begins working again. He continues working, questioning himself when the tone occurs and recording his answers.)

---

at higher rates of teacher questions directed toward the entire group of pupils (approximately 12 questions per minute), students both attended better and were more likely to answer correctly than at lower rates of teacher questioning (approximately 6 questions per minute). Of course, the latter rate of questioning is still far more rapid than the rate of questioning in many classrooms, where pupils may only be called on to answer one or two questions in an entire lesson.

Outside of the pacing of teacher-directed lessons, DI recommendations for maintaining high levels of attending to task resemble those discussed in previous sections. Teachers may set time limits, praise appropriate attending behavior, and so forth.

Reading

Of the academic performance areas, reading is regularly judged to be of primary importance. In fact, reading difficulties constitute the most common problem of learning-disabled students

(Norman & Zigmond, 1980) and are the focus of teachers' greatest efforts (Kirk & Elkins, 1975). Problems in reading range from difficulties with converting print into spoken equivalents to failing to group the content of material being read. In this section, we describe contributions from each of the models to the improvement of reading performance (see Table 6.2).

Cognitive Model
In the area of reading, there is a great deal of overlap among the various models' approaches. For example, Brown, Campione, and Day (1980) call parts of their procedures "self-control" training, a term that evokes the cognitive-behavior modification model even though their work shares many characteristics with the cognitive model. For this reason it is hard to designate an intervention as representative of only one model. However, there are some studies of interventions that seem to fit better here than under the other categories.

A report by Williams (1980) provides an excellent illustration of the application of cognitive psychology to reading. Williams developed a program for teaching beginning reading that is based on extensive research about the component skills of prereading and reading. The program is very similar to other programs (e.g., those developed by Engelmann, 1969 and Wallach & Wallach, 1976), but was designed ex-

pressly for use with pupils identified or likely to be identified as learning-disabled. The program taught the skills of phonemic analysis, sound blending, and basic decoding during the primary grades. Williams's carefully conducted field test indicated that it was effective, in that pupils who were taught according to these principles were less likely to fail to acquire rudimentary reading skills.

Borkowski and his colleagues have studied the contribution of metacognitive processes and affective beliefs to reading performance (e.g., Borkowski, Weyhing, & Carr, 1988). Borkowski et al. tested an intervention for deficits in reading comprehension; it incorporated components focused on specific strategy knowledge, metacognitive routines, and attributions about effectiveness. Students in one group received the intervention described in Box 6.2, while other groups participated in various control conditions. Some of the pupils were not only taught how to perform reading comprehension tasks but also encouraged to attribute their successes to their own efforts. These pupils performed significantly better than those who received only training in reading strategies or attributions.

Palincsar and Brown's work on reciprocal teaching (Brown & Campione, 1984; Brown & Palincsar, 1982; Palincsar, 1986; Palincsar & Brown, 1984) is another example of programmatic research in reading developed from cog-

Table 6.2. Selected Studies Illustrating Techniques for Treating Reading Problems

CITATION	INDEPENDENT VARIABLE
Brown, Campione, & Day, 1980	Self-control training
Carnine, Kameenui, & Coyle, 1984	Training pupils to use context with vocabulary words
Freeman & McLaughlin, 1984	Audiotaped modeling of reading words
Hendrickson, Roberts, & Shores, 1978	Modeling versus correction
Jenkins & Larson, 1979	Error-correction techniques
Knapcyzk & Livingston, 1974	Encouraging students to ask questions
Levin, 1973	Imagery training
Lloyd, Epstein, & Cullinan, 1981	Direct Instruction programs
Lovitt & Hansen, 1976	Skipping and drilling contingent on fluency and accuracy
Pascarella & Pflaum, 1981	Self-correction
Rose, 1985	Previewing of material to be studied
Schumaker, Deshler, Alley, Warner, & Denton, 1982	Study strategy instruction
Scruggs, Mastropieri, McLoone, Levin, & Morrison, 1987	Mnemonic strategy training
Swanson, 1981a	Self-recording and reinforcement contingencies

---

**BOX 6.2. AN EXAMPLE OF A READING INTERVENTION THAT INCORPORATES
ATTRIBUTION TRAINING**

In a study by Borkowski and his colleagues (Borkowski et al., 1988), a group of pupils identified as having learning disabilities received an intensive training program. This was designed to remediate the pupils' reading comprehension deficits not only by teaching reading comprehension skills but also by encouraging the use of metacognitive routines and re-forming attributions about the value of using strategies in learning.

Pupils in the experimental group were taught memory strategies during the first sessions. For example, to help a student remember paired associates, the experimenter showed the pupil how to use an imagery strategy (i.e., the item pair *turtle-bus* might be imagined as a school bus with a turtle shell on it). To help them remember items in a free-recall task, pupils were taught a categorization strategy (sort items into categories of, for instance, clothes, vehicles, or animals). Also during these sessions the trainers repeatedly told the pupils about the importance of exerting effort in making the strategies work effectively and of attributing failure and success to the appropriate use of strategies. For example, after making a mistake while modeling the procedure, the trainer might say, "I need to try and use the strategy" (Borkowski et al., 1988, p. 49).

In later sessions, the pupils were taught strategies for summarizing the content of written materials. For example, in summarizing what they had read, students were taught to (1) create titles for paragraphs, (2) locate the main idea (topic sentence), and (3) find a rationale for the main idea. Again, the trainer emphasized the importance of attributing success and failure to the use of the strategies.

Thus, the experimenters gave pupils prior teaching in how to use strategies and how to link their success in completing tasks to the employment of strategies. They then taught the students how to use strategies and appropriate attributions when attacking reading tasks. The result was that pupils who received this sort of training had higher scores on certain follow-up tests.

---

nitive psychology. Based on Vygotsky's theory of the importance of a social context for learning, reciprocal teaching involves dialogues between teachers and students as they consider portions of text. Four strategies are used in the dialogues: summarizing, question generating, clarifying, and predicting. Teachers and students (or, in some cases, just students) take turns leading discussions of the texts. At first, the teachers provide more structure for the students as the students lead the dialogues; gradually, the students take over more responsibility for leading the dialogues themselves. The reciprocal teaching technique has (1) been successful in both one-to-one situations and small groups, (2) led to improvements not only in reading comprehension but in other subjects that require reading skills, and (3) shown durable effects (Palincsar & Brown, 1984).

Behavioral Model

One of the most ubiquitous findings in the behavior modification literature is that behavior can be influenced by its consequences. When one conceives of reading—particularly oral reading or the answering of questions about what was read—as behavior, it is easy to understand why there are so many studies demonstrating the influence of reinforcement in reading.

Haring and Hauck (1969) examined changes in 4 elementary school-aged boys' reading performance. They compared the boys' skills under baseline conditions to their performance when programmed reading materials and token reinforcement were provided. Although their design was not frankly experimental, their results were consistent with much of the more recent research: when programmed learning materials, a more structured environment, and reinforcement were provided, the frequency of correct responding increased. Studies such as those by Lahey, McNees, and Brown (1973) and Jenkins, Barksdale, and Clinton (1978) have extended these findings in a systematic way. Similarly, clever arrangements of contingencies show that the consequences controlling reading need not be tangible (e.g., tokens) or even social (praise). Lovitt and Hansen (1976) found that when rapid progress was made contingent on performance, there were substantial improvements in the pupils' reading performance.

Of course, not all behaviorally based interventions require manipulation of consequences. For example, working with a boy and a girl from the primary grades who were identified as learning-disabled, Smith (1979) found that the rate of oral reading could be positively affected simply by having the teacher model fluent reading before the students were required to read. In a second study, she also observed that modeling influenced the oral reading rate and accuracy of an elementary-aged boy identified as learning-disabled, but that additional interventions (e.g., corrections) enhanced these effects. Hendrickson, Roberts, and Shores (1978) reported the results of their work with 2 primary-aged boys with reading disabilities. Having examined the effects of modeling and correction on the frequency with which the boys read words correctly, they reported that modeling led to more rapid acquisition of word-reading responses than did correction; however, although both procedures led to acquisition of the training words, neither procedure produced generalized word-reading skills. Because these procedures are not instructional in the sense that they teach students how to read words, the absence of transfer to new words is understandable.

Cognitive-Behavioral Model

Swanson (1981a, b) examined the effects of self-recording and reinforcement techniques on reading performance. In a series of studies (1981a), he found that these variables positively influenced oral reading accuracy, silent reading rate, and accuracy in answering comprehension questions. Malamuth (1979) evaluated a broad-based self-management program. Using assorted materials, the students were taught to scan them during reading. Although conventional significance levels were not obtained, Malamuth interpreted the results as indicating that the experimental program aided performance on reading tasks. However, Lloyd, Kneedler, and Cameron (1982) reported that requiring learning-disabled pupils to use a self-verbalized strategy for reading words did not facilitate word-reading accuracy.

Research by Wong and others (see Wong, 1985a, b, for reviews) has examined the efficacy of training in another metacognitive process—self-questioning—to improve the reading comprehension of learning-disabled students. In self-questioning interventions, pupils are trained to ask themselves the types of questions that monitor their understanding of what they are reading. For example, Wong and Jones (1982) trained learning-disabled and nonhandicapped students to use a five-step self-questioning procedure that focused on (1) determining the purpose of reading the passage, (2) finding the main ideas, (3) learning the answers to the question, and (4) looking back at the sequence of previous questions and answers. The intervention facilitated the learning-disabled students' reading comprehension and improved both their awareness of which parts of the passages were important and the quality of the questions they generated. However, the training did not produce similar results in the nonhandicapped pupils.

Direct Instruction Model

Direct Instruction reading programs have one of the best-documented records for effects on reading performance (Abt Associates, 1976, 1977; Becker & Carnine, 1981; Engelmann, Becker, Carnine, & Gersten, 1988). Although this record reflects primarily work with children identified as disadvantaged, the programs have also been evaluated with atypical learners. In one study, Serwer, Shapiro, and Shapiro (1973) reported that pupils identified as at risk who received DI reading instruction performed the same on most criterion measures as pupils receiving perceptual-motor remedial training or both conditions. Although the DI group did less well on two measures of motor skills and on measures of handwriting and arithmetic, it obtained a better score on the measure of wrong endings on words, the only significant difference on a measure of reading. Other studies are more supportive.

At the beginning reading level, a study by Stein and Goldman (1980) compared DI and another beginning reading program with a sample identified as having "minimum brain dysfunction." The pupils given DI reading instruction did significantly better according to scores on an achievement test. At the remedial level, Lloyd, Epstein, and Cullinan (1981; Lloyd, Cullinan, Heins, & Epstein, 1980) reported the results of an intervention program based in part on the DI model and implemented with learning-disabled pupils. After six months of instruction, their reading scores were compared to the reading scores of a randomly assigned comparison group. The pupils in the DI groups had significantly higher scores on (1) word reading, (2) passage reading, (3) passage comprehension. The authors reported that the effect sizes for these measures were 0.71 or greater.

Other studies have investigated programmatic effects (e.g., Gregory, Hackney, & Gregory, 1982) and more specific aspects of DI programming in reading (e.g., Carnine, Prill, & Armstrong, 1978; Darch & Gersten, 1986; Doomes, Gersten, & Carnine, 1984; Kameenui, Carnine, & Maggs, 1980), often using low-performing pupils as subjects.

Handwriting

Handwriting has received considerably less study than some other areas of academic performance. Most of the studies that have been done in this area are based on either the behavioral or the cognitive-behavioral model.

Behavioral Model

Handwriting problems have been repeatedly studied by behaviorally oriented special educators. Despite having ignored psychological and physiological explanations of these problems, these specialists have developed what is nearly a "cure" for problems such as reversals. The procedure they have used is based on differential reinforcement contingencies: When the student writes a target letter, numeral, or word correctly, reinforcement (praise, for example) is provided; when the student writes an item incorrectly, he or she is required to correct it. Studies of this type of procedure or one very similar to it have repeatedly shown its effectiveness (Faukc, Burnett, Powers, & Sulzer-Aza-

roff, 1973; Hasazi & Hasazi, 1972; Lahey, Busemeyer, O'Hara, & Beggs, 1977; Smith & Lovitt, 1973; Stromer, 1975, 1977). The procedure is illustrated in Box 6.3.

Cognitive-Behavioral Model

Advocates of the cognitive-behavioral model have encouraged teaching students to use self-verbalization to guide their behavior. In the area of handwriting, it has been recommended that students guide themselves verbally while forming letters. For example, while writing the letter "b," the pupil might say, "First I make a tall stick: I start here and go all the way down. Then I make a ball: I start at the middle and go all the way around so it just touches the stick." Studies of such procedures (Hayes, 1982; Robin, Armel, & O'Leary, 1975) have shown that they produce small beneficial effects on handwriting. However, Graham (1983) did not find these effects with learning-disabled pupils.

More extensive self-instruction procedures have been developed in order to improve handwriting performance. Kosiewicz, Hallahan, Lloyd, and Graves (1982) evaluated the effects of having a pupil use detailed self-guiding statements to help him copy handwriting materials more accurately and neatly. They found that these self-instructions—they had the boy repeat the word aloud, repeat it in syllables, repeat each letter in the syllable, and then repeat each letter as he wrote it—resulted in substantial improvements in the boy's handwriting. Similarly, Blandford and Lloyd (1987) found that having pupils consult a card that prompted self-

---

BOX 6.3. A CASE ILLUSTRATION OF THE REMEDIATION OF HANDWRITING PROBLEMS

Benjamin B. Lahey and his colleagues (Lahey, Busmeyer, O'Hara, & Beggs, 1977) reported the results of two studies demonstrating the effects of a behavior modification program on handwriting problems. In the second of these studies, they described a boy who was nearly 10 years old and had been identified as learning-disabled. They noted that the boy was considered untestable and that he usually looked at academic materials out of the side of his eye. In addition to his many other problems, the boy had very poor handwriting skills.

After obtaining baseline assessments of the boy's handwriting, Lahey and colleagues instituted a program of reinforcement and correction. When the boy wrote a word correctly, he was told that he had written it correctly and was given a token, which he could later exchange for raisins. When he wrote a word incorrectly, he was told that he erred and was given directions about how to write the word correctly; for example, the trainer said, " 'These letters are backwards. Watch me; they should go like this' " (p. 128). Later, the correction-and-reinforcement program was withdrawn and then reinstated; thus the program was evaluated across four phases: baseline, first treatment, second baseline, and second treatment.

Figures 6.2 and 6.3 illustrate the effects of this treatment on the boy's handwriting. Clearly, this program helped this pupil.

Figure 6.2. An example of one pupil's handwriting from the study by Lahey et al. (1977). The first panel shows the pupil's responses during the first baseline phase; the second, third, and fourth panels show the pupil's responses during the first treatment, second baseline, and second treatment phases. From B. B. Lahey, M. K. Busemeyer, C. O'Hara, and V. E. Beggs, "Treatment of severe perceptual-motor disorders in children diagnosed as Learning Disabled." *Behavior Modification 1(1)*, pp. 135–136, copyright 1977 by Sage Publications. Reprinted by permission of Sage Publications, Inc.

questioning about handwriting performance (e.g., "Are all my letters sitting on the line?") produced improvement in handwriting quality. They were able to withdraw the task card while the effects were maintained.

Written Expression

In written expression, we have included both spelling and composition. These are substantial areas of deficit in atypical learners and have received considerable interest (see, e.g., Graham & Harris, 1988; Harris, Graham, & Pressley, in press). A selection of interventions is shown in Table 6.3. Some reports about interventions in this area do not fit into the organization of models presented here. For example, Bryant et al. (1981) and Gettinger, Bryant, and Fayne (1982) developed means of modifying usual spelling instructional programs to increase their effectiveness with learning-disabled children. Among the modifications they studied were (1) reductions in the number of words taught in any one lesson, (2) distribution of practice opportunities to increase retention, and (3) organization of spelling words to facilitate transfer from word to word. Their studies indicate that incorporation of these variables in spelling lessons improves the spelling performance of elementary school pupils with learning disabilities. These modifications illustrate the application of effective teaching precepts to the instruction of the learning-disabled. In this regard, they are important for all of the models.

Behavioral Model
Behavioral researchers have also studied the modification of written expression. The reinforcement of changes in particular parts of compositions has been examined repeatedly (Brigham, Graubard, & Stans, 1972; Maloney & Hopkins, 1973; Maloney, Jacobsen, & Hopkins, 1975) and has led to these conclusions: Reinforcement contingent on (1) writing more words increases the number of words written, (2) writing more action verbs (e.g., "hit" and "fly" but not "is" and "do") increases the number of action verbs in composition, and (3) using different words leads to a wider vocabulary. However, reinforcing one aspect of writing usually does not influence other parts.

To obtain broader effects using reinforcement, it will probably be necessary to design a system that reinforces multiple different aspects of composing at the same time. Also, it is unlikely that reinforcement will induce new sentence structures (unless it is contingent on their use). This reemphasizes the theme that students must be shown how to write communicatively (Lloyd, 1988).

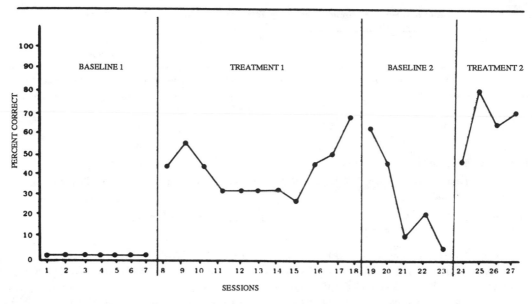

Figure 6.3. A graph showing the handwriting performance for the student in the Lahey et al. (1977) study. The graph reveals that the percent of correct responses in handwriting varied as a function of the reinforcement-and-correction treatment the authors implemented. From B. B. Lahey, M. K. Busemeyer, C. O'Hara, and V. E. Beggs, "Treatment of severe perceptual-motor disorders in children diagnosed as Learning Disabled." *Behavior Modification 1(1)*, pp. 135–136, copyright 1977 by Sage Publications. Reprinted by permission of Sage Publications, Inc.

Cognitive-Behavioral Model

Studies from the cognitive-behavioral perspective have revealed that the type of instruction provided to pupils may interact with those pupils' characteristics. Bendall, Tollesfson, and Fine (1980) identified an aptitude-by-treatment interaction. Students with relatively internal attributions learned more spelling words when they studied them in any way they wished than they did when their study methods were prescribed for them. However, students with relatively external attributions for success learned more words during the high-structure than the low-structure condition.

Peer editing and self-evaluation are other techniques that have been found to be effective in teaching composition. Karegianes, Pascarella, and Pflaum (1980) taught students to use an editing and rating system for evaluating their peers' essays. They found that students in the peer-editing condition scored higher on a posttest than did others in a comparable condition in which teachers edited the essays. Also, third-graders have been taught to check their own writing assignments according to guidelines (Ballard & Glynn, 1975). The self-evaluation procedure required that they count the number of sentences, words, and various types of words used; also, they took other simple measures of writing. On the basis of their counts, students assigned themselves points in a reward system depending on how they had done in their essays. This combination of self-evaluation and self-reward had positive effects on the students' writing. Self-evaluation has been incorporated into writing programs as well (Harris & Graham, 1985; Moran, Schumaker, & Vetter, 1981).

Arithmetic

Arithmetic deficits have been extensively addressed and a wide range of interventions studied (see Table 6.4). Arithmetic difficulties range from deficits in simple computation to deficits in solving multistep problems. The following paragraphs describe some interventions.

Cognitive Model

Recent work by cognitive psychologists and mathematics educators in the domain of mathematics has shown the importance of cognitive and metacognitive processes for understanding the nature, acquisition, and use of mathematical knowledge and skills. (For summaries of the work in this area, see Baroody, 1984; Carpenter, Moser, & Romberg, 1982; Ginsburg, 1983; Hiebert, 1986; Lesh & Landau, 1983; Pellegrino &

Table 6.3. Selected Studies Illustrating Techniques for Treating Writing Problems

CITATION	INDEPENDENT VARIABLE AND AREA OF INSTRUCTION
Bendall, Tollefson, & Fine, 1980	Self- versus teacher-directed study conditions in spelling
Brigham, Graubard, & Stans, 1972	Reinforcement contingent on using certain types of words in compositions
Gettinger, Bryant, & Fayne, 1982	Lesson structure in spelling
Harris & Graham, 1985	Self control training in composition
Karegianes, Pascarella, & Pflaum, 1980	Peer editing effects on compositions
Kauffman, Hallahan, Haas, Brame, & Boren, 1978	Contingent imitation of errors in spelling
MacArthur & Graham, 1987	Mechanisms for producing compositions
Stephens & Hudson, 1984	Direct Instruction effects on spelling

Goldman, 1987; Resnick & Ford, 1981; Romberg & Carpenter, 1986; Schoenfeld, 1987). By examining the cognitive demands of mathematical tasks, researchers in this area have determined (1) the procedural knowledge individuals need in order to accomplish different mathematical tasks, (2) the conceptual and factual knowledge they need for the tasks, and (3) how these types of knowledge interact as the tasks are done.

There are few interventions for arithmetic difficulties that reflect a strictly cognitive model, despite the model's close connection to this developed body of research. It may be that the cognitive model's emphases—as on a holistic presentation of content within a given domain and the active involvement of the learner in constructing knowledge—may, in the case of mathematics, make interventions more amenable to presentation in the form of a curriculum than in a discrete series of procedural steps

targeting a specific task (for instance, subtraction computation or two-step word problems).

As an example of this last point, Reid and Hresko (1981) suggest that the Project MATH program developed by Cawley and his associates (Cawley et al., 1976) represents a more cognitively oriented approach to mathematics instruction for learning-disabled students. Project MATH emphasizes not only the acquisition of mathematics principles but also their integration into everyday living situations. Preliminary tests have supported the efficacy of Project MATH (Cawley, Fitzmaurice, Shaw, Kahn, & Bates, 1978), although additional evaluations of the program should be conducted and reported.

Behavioral Model

Behavioral work in the area of arithmetic is equally diverse and extensive. The independent variables of some behavioral studies of arith-

Table 6.4. Selected Studies Illustrating Techniques for Treating Arithmetic Problems

CITATION	INDEPENDENT VARIABLE
Albion & Salzberg, 1982	General and specific self-instruction
Greenwood et al., 1984	Peer tutoring
Holman & Baer, 1979	Self-recording
Johnston & Whitman, 1987	Self-instruction
Kelly, Carnine, Gersten, & Grossen, 1986	Direct Instruction using videodisc
Leon & Pepe, 1983	Self-instruction
Lloyd, Saltzman, & Kauffman, 1981	Strategy training
Schunk & Cox, 1986	Strategy training and attributional feedback
Smith & Lovitt, 1975	Modeling and demonstrations
Smith & Lovitt, 1976	Reinforcement contingencies
Thackwray, Meyers, Schlesser, & Cohen, 1985	Specificity of self-instructional strategies

metic were shown in Table 6.1, and examples of these studies are discussed in the following paragraphs.

Smith and Lovitt (1976) demonstrated an important relationship between reinforcement and academic performance. In two studies, they assessed the arithmetic computational performance of 10 elementary-aged boys (3 in one study and 7 in the other) identified as learning-disabled. Their results indicated that reinforcement contingencies have little effect on rate or accuracy unless the pupils know how to perform the required operations. A comparable finding is apparent in other studies (e.g., Grimm, Bijou, & Parsons, 1973). In a similar vein, Smith and Lovitt (1975) studied the effects of providing pupils with a demonstration of the steps in a solution algorithm and then leaving them a model showing how to follow those steps. They found that the pupils' performance increased dramatically when they were taught by this procedure.

Cognitive-Behavioral Model

Cognitive-behavioral interventions for students having difficulty in mathematics make use of the types of cognitive and metacognitive processes that are studied by cognitive psychologists and mathematics educators. These cognitive and metacognitive processes are used in cognitive-behavioral interventions in two general ways (Keller & Lloyd, 1989; Lloyd & Keller, 1989).

Some interventions have used procedures that facilitate access to the appropriate content knowledge for a task. For example, Parsons (1972) studied the effects on arithmetic accuracy of having pupils both circle and name the operation symbol before performing addition and subtraction computations. Similarly, Lovitt and Curtiss (1968) required a student to read each problem aloud before beginning to solve it. This procedure improved arithmetic performance. The positive effects of these tactics have been interpreted as support for the idea that antecedent self-verbalization is a desirable component of CBM programs.

Other cognitive-behavioral approaches have trained students to use combinations of both metacognitive processes and content knowledge, usually in the form of an algorithm's procedures. The distinction between these two intervention components blurs at times, however, for two reasons (Keller & Lloyd, 1989). Some steps in solving mathematical tasks—such as (1) identifying the pertinent information in a word problem, (2) identifying the question, and (3)

planning how to answer the question—are identical to metacognitive processes in other situations. Also, it is not always clear from the descriptions of cognitive-behavioral interventions how the metacognitive components of the interventions are being used. Are the students trained to use the metacognitive processes to guide the other, more task-specific components of the intervention—more in line with the nature of metacognition—or are the metacognitive processes and content procedures taught as separate components?

As examples of interventions using metacognitive components, Johnston, Whitman, and Johnson (1981), Johnston and Whitman (1987), and Whitman and Johnston (1983) evaluated the effects of a self-instructional intervention for teaching arithmetic computation skills. In both studies, pupils were taught algorithms for solving specific types of arithmetic problems. The results indicated that this intervention had clear and substantial effects on the students' performance. Several other studies (Albion & Salzberg, 1982; Cameron & Robinson, 1980; Leon & Pepe, 1983; Thackwray, Meyers, Schleser, & Cohen, 1985) have also examined self-instructional interventions for students with difficulties in arithmetic. Johnston and Whitman (1987), though, found that a set of self-instructions focusing on both general and specific strategies, when taught through a self-instructional format, was more effective than (1) the same instructions taught through a didactic format and (2) a set of only specific self-instructions taught through either format. Follow-up analyses showed that these results held for those students who had less ability in math, too.

Direct Instruction Model

Direct Instruction studies of arithmetic have revealed that pupils who are likely to have problems acquiring arithmetic skills and knowledge can learn at a rate consistent with that of their nonhandicapped peers. Becker and Carnine (1981) and Gersten and Carnine (1984b) reported that among the nine major model sponsors in Project Follow Through, the Direct Instruction model was one of only two to have positive effects on pupils' mathematics achievement. Furthermore, although the pupils participating in Follow Through were expected to perform at about the 20th percentile, the average Metropolitan Achievement Test (MAT) total math score for students receiving mathematics instruction under the Direct Instruction model was at the 48th percentile; furthermore, the average score for the other eight models was at the 17th percentile (see Abt Associates, 1976, 1977). Although results on other measures on which more limited skills are required (e.g., the Wide Range Achievement Test) are consistent with these data, it is important to note that the MAT scores are based on a combination of computation skill, problem solving, and conceptual knowledge. In addition, analyses of data for subjects who entered school with IQs of 80 or lower (Gersten, Becker, Heiry, & White, 1984) are also instructive: "Those entering with low IQ scores tended to begin and end with lower MAT scores than their peers, *but they still maintained the same average growth rate of 1.0 grade-equivalent units a year*" (Gersten & Carnine, 1984b, italics in original).

Although research on Direct Instruction has focused almost exclusively on nonhandicapped pupils, some studies have been conducted with handicapped students. Lloyd, Saltzman, and Kauffman (1981) examined the effects of "strategy training," an instructional procedure based on the Direct Instruction model's principle of teaching cognitive operations by isolating and teaching a series of steps that lead to solution of a type of problem (cf., Lloyd, 1980). The authors found that transfer of training was predictable on the basis of the instruction given to learning-disabled pupils. The results are consistent with the findings of Carnine (1980), who reported that young nonhandicapped pupils who were instructed in the component skills of a multiplication strategy showed more rapid acquisition of the strategy and greater transfer of it to untrained items than did young nonhandicapped pupils who were taught the component skills and the strategy at the same time.

INTEGRATION

Based on the evidence reviewed in this chapter, one generalization we can make is that research has established the effectiveness of interventions falling under each of the four models. Considering the variety of academic behaviors that have been improved by such interventions, we can also conclude that their effectiveness is very wide-ranging. Because research has documented the efficacy of each model, it is tempting to suggest that clinicians—teachers or psychologists—need only use any one of these approaches to be successful in ameliorating the

academic achievement difficulties of handicapped students. And indeed, there is little doubt that a professional well-versed in any one of these models would be preferable to one who is unfamiliar with all of them. A research question worth pursuing, however, is whether a clinician equipped with techniques falling under more than one model (perhaps as many as all four) would be effective with more students and more kinds of academic disabilities than a clinician who followed just one approach.

As a first step in pursuing the question of a single- versus a combined-model approach, it is, perhaps, useful to consider how each of these models interacts with three variables: teacher, learner, and task. It may be that some of these models are more or less effective when used by certain types of teachers with certain types of students for specific kinds of academic tasks. We shall tentatively hypothesize some ways in which these models may interact with teachers, learners, and tasks.

Teacher Characteristics

No matter how powerful and appropriate the intervention procedure itself, its value is undoubtedly diminished if the teacher does not use it thoroughly or appropriately. For years many educational researchers and practitioners have naively assumed that teachers execute interventions fully and equally. That is, they have presumed that all teachers, when asked to use a set of educational procedures, will use them thoroughly. And when researchers have recognized that teachers differ in the degree to which they implement given interventions, they have usually chosen to treat this as a random variation to be controlled for by standard research designs.

In the past few years, however, intervention researchers have begun to consider the importance of the implementation dimension (cf. Abt Associates, 1976; Wang, Nojan, Strom, & Walberg, 1984). Some have warned that in order to assess the effectiveness of interventions, it is first necessary to undertake some measure of the degree to which the interventions under study have, in fact, been implemented. They have documented wide variation in how thoroughly teachers use given treatments, and they have found relationships between degree of implementation and student performance outcomes.

We believe that this line of reasoning, which recognizes the importance of intervention execution, can be taken a step further. Researchers also need to investigate why teachers differ in their degree of implementation. One obvious factor is a teacher's ability to carry out the desired intervention procedures. Another factor—which should be obvious but has not received the attention it has deserved until recently—is how well particular techniques fit in with the individual teacher's teaching styles and philosophy of the teaching–learning process (see Clark & Peterson, 1986, for a discussion of teacher thought processes). With regard to the models discussed in this chapter, for example, it might be important to consider the degree to which each stresses teacher-directed versus child-directed learning. We suggest that on a continuum ranging from dependence on to independence from the teacher, the models can be roughly ordered as follows: behavioral, DI, CBM, cognitive. A fruitful area of research would be the investigation of the relationship between teachers' beliefs regarding the use of teacher- versus child-directed approaches and their success at using behavioral, DI, CBM, and cognitive methods. Subsumed under this area of research would be the question of teachers' flexibility in adapting their teaching styles to the different models. Would those teachers who can and are willing to assume varying amounts of directiveness be able to use more models and hence be more effective with a greater number of students?

Learner Characteristics

It is also worth pursuing the notion that different types of students will respond differently to the four models of instruction. Although we are not sanguine about interactions between learner characteristics and instructional programs (Lloyd, 1984), one of the challenges in this regard is to determine those student characteristics that might interact with models of instruction. Again, given the concept that these models differ along a continuum of teacher direction, one potential characteristic would appear to be the child's ability to work independently. There is a sizable body of literature supporting the idea that many mildly handicapped children have problems in working without teacher direction (see Hallahan et al., 1985, for a review of some of this literature). It is tempting to conclude that such students should be taught using procedures contained in the highly teacher-controlled models. On the other hand, a convincing case can be made for attempting to increase their independence from the teacher (Lloyd, Hallahan, & Kauffman, 1980). And as we have already noted, investigators have successfully used the CBM technique of self-monitoring with these kinds of students. It may be that the optimum way to approach children needing a high degree of teacher structure is sequentially, starting with methods involving high teacher direction and moving toward methods requiring greater amounts of independence.

Task Characteristics

Some academic tasks—such as counting, letter-sound associations, and vocabulary—involve learning relatively arbitrary content (i.e., there is only one correct answer). However, other tasks—such as comparing concepts or composing essays—are more meaningful and divergent (i.e., there are several correct answers). Many tasks of the latter type can be approached by performing a series of steps in order to reach a correct solution consistently. Teaching pupils strategies or algorithms for attacking such tasks is probably essential to successful interventions for atypical learners (e.g., Lloyd, 1988). Direct Instruction, cognitive-behavioral, and cognitive models emphasize teaching pupils systematic ways of approaching problems, and many interventions implemented under the rubric of behavior modification have done so as well. For this reason, it is important to illustrate how strategies work; a strategy for an arithmetic task is illustrated in Box 6.4. Illustrations of other complex strategies are available in the areas of composition (Englert & Raphael, 1988) and reading comprehension (Palincsar & Brown, 1984) as well as other areas.

However, it is also reasonable to assume that some models will be more effective and efficient when used with certain types of tasks than with others. It might be, for example, that the more the task involves higher-level cognitive operations, the more it calls for the use of the more cognitively oriented models, such as CBM. On the other hand, problems that require less inference may be better handled through the use of the behavioral or DI models. There are, admittedly, several examples of the successful use of behavioral and DI approaches with high-inference tasks (e.g., Bijou, Birnbrauer, Kidder, &

BOX 6.4. ILLUSTRATION OF A STRATEGY THAT PUPILS CAN USE TO ATTACK AN ARITHMETIC TASK

Arithmetic tasks can easily be approached by systematically completing a series of steps. For example, young children often count out objects for each addend in an additional problem and then count the combined sets in order to derive the sum. The following example illustrates how a more complicated task—finding an equivalent fraction—can be approached strategically. An important advantage of such strategies is that they make it possible to teach explicitly what are usually covert steps performed in reaching solutions. (See Figure 6.4.) Initially, students may need a great deal of prompting and assistance in using a strategy. As students become proficient in applying a given strategy, however, they often streamline it and may no longer even appear to be using it.

Example of a Solution Algorithm for Finding Equivalent Fractions

Step	Description	Action	
1: Read	Pupil reads problem to him- or herself.	"Let's see . . . um, 9/17ths is equal to how many 102nds?"	$\frac{9}{17} = \frac{?}{102}$
2: Plan	Pupil describes general process to him- or herself.	"Okay, I've got to multiply 9/17ths by some fraction that's the same as 1, and then I can get the number of 102nds that it equals."	$\frac{9}{17} = \frac{?}{102}$
3: Rewrite	Pupil rewrites problem, providing space for work. Note: This step can be completed while performing step 2.	"Here's my workspace. . . ."	$\frac{9}{17}(-) = \frac{?}{102}$
4: Identify known part	Pupil identifies part of equivalence for which numbers are known.	"Okay. I've got two out of three numbers here (pointing to denominators), so I can start on that part."	$\frac{9}{17}(-) = \frac{?}{102}$
5: Solve known part	Pupil uses prior knowledge to solve for missing multiplier.	"So, 17 times something equals 102 . . . um . . . I'll just figure that out . . . 17 is almost 20 and 20 goes into 100 five times, so I'll try that . . . nope, 17 leftover, so it's 6 times . . . great! It's even."	$\frac{9}{17}(-) = \frac{?}{102}$ $17\overline{)102}$
6: Substitute	Pupil uses information derived in Step 5 to complete fraction in equation.	"And that means this (writing) is 6 over 6 . . . which is the same as 1, so . . ."	$\frac{9}{17}\left(\frac{6}{6}\right) = \frac{?}{102}$
7: Derive missing numerator	Pupil solves for missing numerator using information from Step 6.	"Now, I can just multiply these 'cause I've got two out of three and . . . 6 times 9 is 54, sooo. . ."	$\frac{9}{17}\left(\frac{6}{6}\right) = \frac{?}{102}$
8: Read	Pupil reads completed problem.	"9/17th is equal to 54/102nds."	$\frac{9}{17}\left(\frac{6}{6}\right) = \frac{54}{102}$

Figure 6.4. An example of a solution algorithm for finding equivalent fractions. This example shows the steps in the algorithm, a description of what the student does as she or he solves the problem, some possible covert verbalizations that might accompany the pupil's performance, and the written product of the actions. From "Effective mathematics instruction" by J. W. Lloyd and C. E. Keller, 1989, *Focus on Exceptional Children, 21*(7), p. 8. Copyright 1989 by Love Publishing. Reprinted by permission.

Tague, 1966; Brigham, Graubard, & Stans, 1972; Lovitt, 1973; Maloney & Hopkins, 1973). But given that there are no thorough direct comparisons of behavioral versus cognitive techniques, we believe it would be worth investigating their effectiveness and especially their efficiency.

Research Methodology Considerations

A research methodology that might prove particularly useful in teasing out matches between student characteristics and educational treatments and between teacher characteristics and educational treatments is cluster analysis. McKinney and his colleagues, for example, have been able to identify several different subtypes of learning-disabled children based on behavioral, language, and perceptual characteristics (McKinney, 1988). And there is work under way on the subtyping of teachers based on observations of their use of behaviors associated with the effective teaching literature (Hallahan, McNergney, & McKinney, 1986).

Although earlier investigations of instruction based on an aptitude-by-treatment interaction model have been unsuccessful for the most part (Cronbach & Snow, 1977; Lloyd, 1984), some researchers have begun to use subtyping to explore matches between child characteristics and educational techniques. In general, the hope for these studies is greater than it has been previously because the research is far more systematic. For example, Osborne and McKinney are currently investigating whether self-recording of attention is the treatment of choice for students who fall into the attention-deficit subtype, a subgroup at substantial risk for continued academic failure. Lyon, too, has begun to use cluster analysis to investigate the match between educational treatments and student characteristics. His results tentatively suggest that learning-disabled students with phonological decoding and auditory memory deficits profit from instruction based on whole-word and analytic phonics principles (Lyon, 1985a, b). In the area of mathematics, Rourke and Strang (1983; Strang & Rourke, 1985) validated conceptually derived subtypes of learning-disabled students by qualitatively analyzing errors from the students' arithmetic scores. Students in the subtype with reading and spelling achievement even lower than their already low achievement in arithmetic made (1) fewer errors, (2) fewer different types of errors, and (3) fewer errors related to judgment and reasoning than did students in the subtype with higher levels of reading and spelling achievement relative to their low achievement in arithmetic (Strang & Rourke, 1985).

SUMMARY

Evidence about interventions for academic problems indicates that clinicians can select effective procedures from each of the various models discussed here. However, we do not believe that the breadth of possibilities implies that a person charged with designing or delivering interventions may chose among them eclectically. Rather than making decisions on the basis of consistency with the model they prefer, we recommend that practitioners use interventions based on a complex of ecological variables—including learner, teacher, and task characteristics—as well as a systematic evaluation of program effects (e.g., Fuchs, 1986; Howell & Morehead, 1987). This will permit the practitioner to make ongoing program decisions based on performance data. We believe that the judicious and data-reactive application of interventions such as those described in this chapter will help relieve the academic problems experienced by many students for whom professionals must provide or design therapeutic programs.

REFERENCES

Abt Associates. (1976). *Education as experimentation: A planned variation model* (Vol. 3A). Cambridge, MA: Author.

Abt Associates. (1977). *Education as experimentation: A planned variation model* (Vol. 4). Cambridge, MA: Author.

Albion, F. M., & Salzberg, C. (1982). The effect of self-instructions on the rate of correct addition problems with mentally retarded children. *Education and Treatment of Children, 5,* 121–131.

Anderson, P. L., Cronin, M. E., & Miller, J. H. (1986). Referral reasons for learning disabled students. *Psychology in the Schools, 23,* 388–395.

Bailey, J. W., Wolf, M. M., & Phillips, E. L. (1970). Home-based reinforcement and the modification of predelinquents' classroom behavior. *Journal of Applied Behavior Analysis, 3,* 223–233.

Ballard, K. D., & Glynn, T. L. (1975). Behavioral self-management in story writing with elementary school children. *Journal of Applied Behavior Analysis, 8,* 387–398.

Bandura, A. (1986). *Social foundations of thought and action.* Englewood Cliffs, NJ: Prentice-Hall.

Bandura, A. (1977). *Social learning theory.* Englewood Cliffs, NJ: Prentice-Hall.

Baroody, A. J. (1984). The case of Felicia: A young child's strategies for reducing memory demands during mental addition. *Cognition and Instruction, 1,* 109–116.

Bateman, B. (1967). Three approaches to diagnosis and educational planning for children with learning disabilities. *Academic Therapy, 3,* 215–222.

Becker, W. C., & Carnine, D. (1981). Direct instruction: A behavior theory model for comprehensive educational intervention with the disadvantaged. In R. Ruiz & S. W. Bijou (Eds.), *Behavior modification: Contributions to education* (pp. 145–210). Hillsdale, NJ: Lawrence Erlbaum Associates.

Becker, W. C., Engelmann, S., & Thomas, D. R. (1975). *Teaching 2: Cognitive learning and instruction.* Chicago: Science Research Associates.

Bendall, D., Tollefson, N., & Fine, M. (1980). Interaction of locus-of-control orientation and the performance of learning disabled adolescents. *Journal of Learning Disabilities, 13,* 83–86.

Bereiter, C., & Engelmann, S. (1966). *Teaching disadvantaged children in the preschool.* Englewood Cliffs, NJ: Prentice-Hall.

Bijou, S. W. (1970). What psychology has to offer education—now. *Journal of Applied Behavior Analysis, 3,* 65–71.

Bijou, S. W., Birnbrauer, J. S., Kidder, J. D., & Tague, C. (1966). Programmed instruction as an approach to teaching of reading, writing, and arithmetic to retarded children. *Psychological Record, 16,* 505–522.

Blandford, B. J., & Lloyd, J. W. (1987). Effects of a self-instructional procedure on handwriting. *Journal of Learning Disabilities, 20,* 342–346.

Borkowski, J. G., Weyhing, R. S., & Carr, M. (1988). Effects of attributional retraining on strategy-based reading comprehension in learning-disabled students. *Journal of Educational Psychology, 80,* 46–53.

Braswell, L., & Kendall, P. C. (1988). Cognitive-behavioral methods with children. In K. S. Dobson (Ed.), *Handbook of cognitive-behavioral therapies* (pp. 167–213). New York: Guilford Press.

Brigham, T. A., Graubard, P. S., Stans, & A. (1972). Analysis of the effects of sequential reinforcement contingencies on aspects of composition. *Journal of Applied Behavior Analysis, 5,* 421–429.

Brown, A. L., & Campione, J. C. (1984). Three faces of transfer: Implications for early competence, individual differences, and instruction. In M. E. Lamb, A. L. Brown, & B. Rogoff (Eds.), *Advances in developmental psychology* (Vol. 3, pp, 143–192). Hillsdale, NJ: Lawrence Erlbaum Associates.

Brown, A. L., Campione, J. C., & Day, J. D. (1980, April). *Learning to learn: On training students to learn from texts.* Paper presented at the annual meeting of the American Educational Research Association meeting, Boston.

Brown, A. L., & Palincsar, A. S. (1982). Inducing strategic learning from text by means of informed, self-control training. *Topics in Learning and Learning Disabilities, 2,* 1–17.

Bruner, J. S., Goodnow, J. J., & Austin, G. A. (1956). *A study of thinking.* New York: John Wiley & Sons.

Bryant, N. D., Drabin, I. R., & Gettinger, M. (1981). Effects of varying units size on spelling achievement in learning disabled children. *Journal of Learning Disabilities, 14,* 200–203.

Cameron, M. I., & Robinson, J. J. (1980). Effects of cognitive training on academic and on-task behavior of hyperactive children. *Journal of Abnormal Child Psychology, 8,* 405–419.

Carnine, D. W. (1976). Effects of two teacher-presentation rates on off-task behavior, answering correctly, and participation. *Journal of Applied Behavior Analysis, 9,* 199–206.

Carnine, D. W. (1980). Preteaching versus concurrent teaching on the component skills of a multiplication problem-solving strategy. *Journal for Research in Mathematic Education, 11,* 375–379.

Carnine, D. W., Kameenui, E., & Coyle, G. (1984). Utilization of contextual information in determining the meanings of unfamiliar words in context. *Reading Research Quarterly, 19,* 343–356.

Carnine, D. W., Prill, N., & Armstrong, J. (1978). *Teaching slower performing students general case strategies for solving comprehension items*. Eugene, OR: University of Oregon Follow Through Project.

Carnine, D., & Silbert, J. (1979). *Direct instruction reading*. Columbus, OH: Charles E. Merrill.

Carpenter, T. R., Moser, J. M., & Romberg, T. A. (Eds.). (1982). *Addition and subtraction: A cognitive approach*. Hillsdale, NJ: Lawrence Erlbaum Associates.

Cawley, J. F., Fitzmaurice, A. M., Goodstein, H. A., Lepore, A. V., Sedlak, R., & Althaus, V. (1976). *Project MATH*. Tulsa, OK: Educational Development Corporation.

Cawley, J. F., Fitzmaurice, A. M., Shaw, R., Kahn, H., & Bates, H., III. (1978). Mathematics and learning disabled youth: The upper grade levels. *Learning Disability Quarterly, 1*(4), 37–52.

Clark, C. M., & Peterson, P. L. (1986). Teachers' thought processes. In M. C. Wittrock (Ed.), *Handbook of research on teaching* (3rd ed., pp. 255–296). New York: Macmillan.

Cronbach, L. J., & Snow, R. E. (1977). *Aptitudes and instructional methods*. New York: Irvington.

Cullinan, D., Epstein, M. H., & Lloyd, J. W. (1983). *Behavior disorders of children and adolescents*. Englewood Cliffs, NJ: Prentice-Hall.

Darch, C., & Gersten, R. (1986). Direction setting activities in reading comprehension: A comparison of two approaches. *Learning Disability Quarterly, 9*, 235–243.

Dommes, P., Gersten, R., & Carnine, D. (1984). Instructional procedures for increasing skill-deficient fourth graders' comprehension of syntactic structures. *Educational Psychology, 4*, 155–165.

Engelmann, S. (1969). *Preventing failure in the primary grades*. Chicago: Science Research Associates.

Engelmann, S., Becker, W. C., Carnine, D., & Gersten, R. (1988). The Direct Instruction Follow Through Model: Design and outcomes. *Education and Treatment of Children, 11*, 303–317.

Engelmann, S., & Carnine, D. (1982). *Theory of instruction*. New York: Irvington.

Englert, C. S., & Raphael, T. E. (1988). Constructing well-formed prose: Process, structure, and metacognitive knowledge. *Exceptional Children, 54*, 513–520.

Fauke, J., Burnett, J., Powers, M. A., & Sulzer-Azaroff, B. (1973). Improvement of handwriting and letter recognition skills: A behavior modification procedure. *Journal of Learning Disabilities, 6*, 296–300.

Ferritor, D. C., Buckholdt, D., Hamblin, R. L., & Smith, L. (1972). The noneffects of contingent reinforcement for attending behavior on work accomplished. *Journal of Applied Behavior Analysis, 5*, 7–17.

Flavell, J. H. (1977). *Cognitive development*. Englewood Cliffs, NJ: Prentice-Hall.

Freeman, T. J., & McLaughlin, T. F. (1984). Effects of taped-words treatment procedure on learning disabled students' sight-word oral reading. *Learning Disability Quarterly, 7*, 49–54.

Fuchs, L. S. (1986). Monitoring the performance of mildly handicapped students: Review of current practice and research. *Remedial and Special Education, 7*, 5–12.

Gerber, M. M. (1987). Application of cognitive-behavioral training methods to teaching basic skills to mildly handicapped elementary school students. In M. C. Wang, M. C. Reynolds, & H. J. Walberg (Eds.), *Handbook of special education: Research and practice. Vol. 1, Learner characteristics and adaptive education* (pp. 167–186). Elmsford, NY: Pergamon Press.

Gersten, R. M., Becker, W. C., Heiry, T. J., & White, W. A. T. (1984). Entry IQ and yearly academic growth of children in Direct Instruction programs: A longitudinal study of low SES children. *Educational Evaluation and Policy Analysis, 6*, 109–121.

Gersten, R., & Carnine, D. (1984a). Auditory-perceptual skills and reading: A response to Kavale's meta-analysis. *Remedial and Special Education, 5*(1), 16–19.

Gersten, R., & Carnine, D. (1984b). Direct instruction mathematics: A longitudinal evaluation of low-income elementary school students. *The Elementary School Journal, 84*(4), 395–407.

Gersten, R. M., White, W. A. T., Falco, R., & Carnine, D. (1982). Teaching basic discriminations to handicapped and non-handicapped individuals through a dynamic presentation of instructional stimuli. *Analysis and Intervention in Developmental Disabilities, 2*, 305–317.

Gettinger, M., Bryant, N. D., & Fayne, H. R. (1982). Designing spelling instruction for learning-disabled children: An emphasis on unit size, distributed practice, and training for transfer. *Journal of Special Education, 16,* 439–448.

Ginsburg, H. P. (Ed.). (1983). *The development of mathematical thinking.* New York: Academic Press.

Graham, S. (1983). The effect of self-instructional procedures on LD students' handwriting performance. *Learning Disability Quarterly, 6,* 231–234.

Graham, S., & Harris, K. R. (Eds.). (1988). Research and instruction in written language [Special issue]. *Exceptional Children, 54*(6).

Greenwood, C. R., Dinwiddie, G., Terry, B., Wade, L., Stanley, S. O., Thibadeau, S., & Delquadri, J. C. (1984). Teacher- versus peer-mediated instruction: An ecobehavioral analysis of achievement outcomes. *Journal of Applied Behavior Analysis, 17,* 521–538.

Gregory, R. P., Hackney, C., & Gregory, N. M. (1982). Corrective reading programme: An evaluation. *British Journal of Education Psychology, 52,* 33–50.

Grimm, J. A., Bijou, S. W., & Parson, J. A. (1973). A problem-solving model for teaching remedial arithmetic to handicapped young children. *Journal of Abnormal Child Psychology, 1,* 26–39.

Hall, R. V., Lund, D., & Jackson, D. (1968). Effects of teacher attention on study behavior. *Journal of Applied Behavior Analysis, 1,* 1–12.

Hallahan, D. P., Kauffman, J. M., & Lloyd, J. W. (1985). *Introduction to learning disabilities.* (2nd ed.). Englewood Cliffs, NJ: Prentice-Hall.

Hallahan, D. P., Kneedler, R. D., & Lloyd, J. W. (1983). The theory and application of cognitive behavior modification. In J. D. McKinney & L. Feagans (Eds.), *Current topics in learning disabilities* (Vol. 1, pp. 207–244). New York: Ablex.

Hallahan, D. P., Lloyd, J. W., Kneedler, R. D., & Marshall, K. J. (1982). A comparison of the effects of self- versus teacher-assessment of on-task behavior. *Behavior Therapy, 13,* 715–723.

Hallahan, D. P., Lloyd, J. W., Kosiewicz, M. M., Kauffman, J. M., & Graves, A. W. (1979). Self-monitoring of attention as a treatment for a learning disabled boy's off-task behavior. *Learning Disability Quarterly, 2*(3), 24–32.

Hallahan, D. P., McNergney, R. M., & McKinney, J. D. (1986). *Improving teacher effectiveness with learning-disabled mainstreamed students.* Proposal funded by Office of Special Education Programs, U.S. Department of Education.

Hammill, D. D., & Larsen, S. C. (1974). The effectiveness of psycholinguistic training. *Exceptional Children, 41,* 5–14.

Haring, N. G. (1968). *Attending and responding.* San Rafael, CA: Dimensions.

Haring, N. G., & Hauck, M. (1969). Improved learning conditions in the establishment of reading skills with disabled readers. *Exceptional Children, 35,* 341–351.

Haring, N. G., Lovitt, T. C., Eaton, M. D., & Hansen, C. L. (1978). *The fourth R: Research in the classroom.* Columbus, OH: Charles E Merrill.

Harris, K. (1986). Self-monitoring of attentional behavior versus self-monitoring of productivity: Effects on on-task behavior and academic response rate among learning disabled children. *Journal of Applied Behavior Analysis, 19,* 417–423.

Harris, K. R., & Graham, S. (1985). Improving learning disabled students' composition skills: A self-control strategy training approach. *Learning Disability Quarterly, 8,* 27–36.

Harris, K. R., Graham, S., & Pressley, M. (in press). Cognitive-behavioral approaches in reading and written language: Developing self-regulated learners. In N. N. Singh & I. L. Beale (Eds.), *Current perspectives in learning disabilities; Nature, theory, and treatment.* New York: Springer-Verlag.

Hasazi, J. E., & Hasazi, S. E. (1972). Effects of teacher attention on digit-reversal behavior in an elementary school child. *Journal of Applied Behavior Analysis, 5,* 157–162.

Hayes, D. (1982). Handwriting practice: The effects of perceptual prompts. *The Journal of Educational Research, 75,* 169–172.

Hendrickson, J., Roberts, M., & Shores, R. E. (1978). Antecedent and contingent modeling to teach basic sight vocabulary. *Journal of Learning Disabilities, 11,* 524–528.

Hiebert, J. (Ed.). (1986). *Conceptual and procedural knowledge: The case of mathematics.* Hillsdale, NJ: Lawrence Erlbaum Associates.

Holman, J., & Baer, D. M. (1979). Facilitating generalization of on-task behavior through self-monitoring of academic tasks. *Journal of Autism and Developmental Disabilities, 9,* 429–446.

Howell, K. W., & Morehead, M. K. (1987). *Curriculum-based evaluation for special and remedial education: A handbook for deciding what to teach.* Columbus, OH: Charles E Merrill.

Hutton, J. B. (1985). What reasons are given by teachers who refer problem behavior students? *Psychology in the Schools, 22,* 79–82.

Inhelder, B., Sinclair, H., & Bovet, M. (1974). *Learning and the development of cognition.* Cambridge, MA: Harvard University Press.

Jenkins, J. R., Barksdale, A., & Clinton, L. (1978). Improving reading comprehension and oral reading: Generalization across behaviors, settings, and time. *Journal of Learning Disabilities, 11,* 607–617.

Jenkins, J. R., Larson, K. (1979). Evaluating error-correction procedures for oral reading. *Journal of Special Education, 13,* 145–156.

Johnston, M. B., & Whitman, T. (1987). Enhancing math computation through variations in training format and instructional content. *Cognitive Therapy and Research, 11,* 381–397.

Johnston, M. B., Whitman, T. L., & Johnson, M. (1981). Teaching addition and subtraction to mentally retarded children: A self-instructional program. *Applied Research in Mental Retardation, 1,* 141–160.

Kameenui, E., Carnine, D. W., & Maggs, A. (1980). Instructional procedures for teaching reversible passive voice and clause constructions to three mildly handicapped children. *The Exceptional Child, 27*(1), 29–41.

Karegianes, M. L., Pascarella, E. T., & Pflaum, S. W. (1980). The effects of peer editing on the writing proficiency of low-achieving tenth grade students. *Journal of Educational Research, 73,* 203–207.

Kauffman, J. M. (1989). *Characteristics of children's behavior disorders.* (4th ed.). Columbus, OH: Charles E Merrill.

Kauffman, J. M., Hallahan, D. P., Haas, K., Brame, T., & Boren, R. (1978). Imitating children's errors to improve their spelling performance. *Journal of Learning Disabilities, 11,* 217–222.

Kavale, K. (1981). Functions of the Illinois Test of Psycholinguistic Abilities (ITPA): Are they trainable? *Exceptional Children, 47,* 495–510.

Kavale, K. (1982). The efficacy of stimulant drug treatment for hyperactivity: A meta-analysis. *Journal of Learning Disabilities, 15,* 280–289.

Keller, C. E., & Lloyd, J. W. (1989). Cognitive training: Implications for arithmetic instruction. In J. N. Hughes & R. J. Hall (Eds.), *Cognitive behavioral approaches in educational settings* (pp. 280–304). New York: Guilford Press.

Kelly, B., Carnine, D., Gersten, R., & Grossen, B. (1986). The effectiveness of videodisc instruction in teaching fractions to learning-disabled and remedial high school students. *Journal of Special Education Technology, 8*(2), 5–17.

Kendall, P. C., & Cummings, L. (1988). Thought and action in educational interventions: Cognitive-behavioral approaches. In J. C. Witt, S. N. Elliott, & F. M. Gresham (Eds.), *Handbook of behavior therapy in education* (pp. 403–418). New York: Plenum Press.

Keogh, B. K., & Hall, R. J. (1984). Cognitive training with learning-disabled pupils. In A. W. Meyers & W. E. Craighead (Eds.), *Cognitive behavior therapy with children* (pp. 163–191). New York: Plenum Press.

Kirk, S. A., & Elkins, J. (1975). Characteristics of children enrolled in the child service demonstration centers. *Journal of Learning Disabilities, 8,* 630–637.

Knapczyk, D. R., & Livingston, G. (1974). The effects of prompting question-asking upon on-task and reading comprehension. *Journal of Applied Behavior Analysis, 7,* 115–121.

Kneedler, R. D., & Meese, R. L. (1988). Learning-disabled children. In J. C. Witt, S. N. Elliott, & F. M. Gresham (Eds.), *Handbook of behavior therapy in education* (pp. 601–629). New York: Plenum Press.

Kosiewicz, M. M., Hallahan, D. P., Lloyd, J., & Graves, A. W. (1982). Effects of self-instruction and self-correction procedures on handwriting performance. *Learning Disability Quarterly, 5,* 71–78.

Lahey, B. B. (1976). Behavior modification with learning disabilities and related problems. In M. Hersen, R. M. Eisler, & P. M. Miller, (Eds.), *Progress in behavior modification* (Vol. 3, pp. 173–205). New York: Academic Press.

Lahey, B. B., Busemeyer, M. K., O'Hara, C., & Beggs, V. E. (1977). Treatment of severe perceptual-motor disorders in children diagnosed as learning disabled. *Behavior Modification, 1,* 123–140.

Lahey, B. B., McNees, M. P., & Brown, C. C. (1973). Modification of deficits in reading for comprehension. *Journal of Applied Behavior Analysis, 6,* 475–480.

Leon, J. A., & Pepe, H. J. (1983). Self-instructional training: Cognitive-behavior modification for remediating arithmetic deficits. *Exceptional Children, 50,* 54–60.

Lesh, R., & Landau, M. (Eds.). (1983). *Acquisition of mathematics concepts and processes.* New York: Academic Press.

Levin, J. R. (1973). Inducing comprehension in poor readers: A test of a recent model. *Journal of Educational Psychology, 65,* 19–24.

Lloyd, J. (1980). Academic instruction and cognitive-behavior modification: The need for attack strategy training. *Exceptional Education Quarterly, 1*(1), 53–63.

Lloyd, J. W. (1984). How shall we individualize instruction—or should we? *Remedial and Special Education, 5,* 7–15.

Lloyd, J. W. (1988). Direct academic interventions in learning disabilities. In M. C. Wang, M. C. Reynolds, & H. J. Walberg (Eds.), *The handbook of special education: Research and practice* (Vol. 2, pp. 345–366). Oxford, England: Pergamon Press.

Lloyd, J. W., Bateman, D. F., Landrum, T. J., & Hallahan, D. P. (1989). Self-recording of attention versus productivity. *Journal of Applied Behavior Analysis, 22,* 315–323.

Lloyd, J. W., Cullinan, D., Heins, E. D., & Epstein, M. H. (1980). Direct instruction: Effects on oral and written language comprehension. *Learning Disability Quarterly, 3*(4), 70–77.

Lloyd, J., Epstein, M. H., & Cullinan, D. (1981). Direct teaching for learning disabilities. In J. Gottlieb & S. S. Strichart (Eds.), *Developmental theory and research in learning disabilities* (pp. 278–309). Baltimore, MD: University Park Press.

Lloyd, J. W., Hallahan, D. P., & Kauffman, J. M. (1980). Learning disabilities: Selected topics. In L. Mann & D. Sabatino (Eds.), *The fourth review of special education* (pp. 35–60). New York: Grune & Stratton.

Lloyd, J. W. Kauffman, J. M., Landrum, T. J., & Roe, D. L. (1989). *Why do teachers refer pupils? An analysis of referrals records.* Unpublished manuscript, University of Virginia, Charlottesville.

Lloyd, J. W., Keller, C. E. (1989). Effective mathematics instruction. *Focus on Exceptional Children, 21*(7), 1–10.

Lloyd, J. W., Kneedler, R. D., & Cameron, N. A. (1982). Effects of verbal self-guidance on word reading accuracy. *Reading Improvement, 19,* 84–89.

Lloyd, J. W., & Landrum, T. J. (in press). Self-recording of attending to task: Treatment components and generalization of effects. In T. Scruggs & B. Y. L. Wong (Eds.), *Intervention research in learning disabilities.* New York: Springer-Verlag.

Lloyd, J., Saltzman, N. J., & Kauffman, J. M. (1981). Predictable generalization in academic learning as a result of pre-skills and strategy training. *Learning Disability Quarterly, 4,* 203–216.

Loper, A. B., & Murphy, D. M. (1985). Cognitive self-regulatory training for underachieving children. In D. Forrest-Pressley, G. E. MacKinnon, & T. G. Waller (Eds.), *Metacognition, cognition, and human performance* (Vol. 2, pp. 223–265). New York: Plenum Press.

Lovitt, T. C. (1973). *Applied behavior analysis techniques and curriculum research.* Report submitted to the National Institute of Education.

Lovitt, T. C. (1981). Charting academic performances of mildly handicapped youngsters. In J. M. Kauffman & D. P. Hallahan (Eds.), *Handbook of special education* (pp. 393–417). Englewood Cliffs, NJ: Prentice-Hall.

Lovitt, T. C., & Curtiss, K. A. (1968). Effects of manipulating an antecedent event on mathematics response rate. *Journal of Applied Behavior Analysis, 1,* 329–333.

Lovitt, T. C., & Hansen, C. L. (1976). The use of contingent skipping and drilling to improve oral reading and comprehension. *Journal of Learning Disabilities, 9,* 481–487.

Lyon, G. R. (1985a). Educational validation studies of learning disability subtypes. In B. P. Rourke (Ed.), *Neuropsychology of learning disabilities: Essentials of subtype analysis* (pp. 228–253). New York: Guilford Press.

Lyon, G. R. (1985b). Identification and remediation of learning disability subtypes: Preliminary findings. *Learning Disabilities Focus, 1*(1), 21–35.

MacArthur, C. A., & Graham, S. (1987). Learning disabled students' composing under three methods of text production: Handwriting, word processing, and dictation. *Journal of Special Education, 21,* 22–42.

MacMillan, D. L. (1982). *Mental retardation in school and society.* (2nd ed.). Boston: Little, Brown.

Mahoney, M. J. (1974). *Cognition and behavior modification.* Cambridge, MA: Ballinger.

Malamuth, Z. N. (1979). Self-management training for children with reading problems: Effects on reading performance and sustained attention. *Cognitive Therapy and Research, 3,* 279–289.

Maloney, K. B., & Hopkins, B. L. (1973). The modification of sentence structure and its relationship to subjective judgments of creativity in writing. *Journal of Applied Behavior Analysis, 6,* 425–433.

Maloney, K. B., Jacobson, C. R., & Hopkins, B. L. (1975). An analysis of the effects of lecture, requests, teacher praise, and free time on the creative writing behaviors of third-grade children. In E. Ramp & G. Semb (Eds.), *Behavior analysis: Areas of research and application* (pp. 244–260). Englewood Cliffs, NJ: Prentice-Hall.

McKinney, J. D. (1988). Research on conceptually and empirically derived subtypes of specific learning disabilities. In M. C. Wang, M. C. Reynolds, & H. J. Walberg (Eds.), *Handbook of special education research and practice. Vol. 2. Mildly handicapping conditions* (pp. 253–281). Oxford, London: Pergamon Press.

McLaughlin, T. F. (1984). A comparison of self-recording plus consequences for on-task and assignment completion. *Contemporary Educational Psychology, 9,* 185–192.

McNutt, G. (1984). A holistic approach to language arts instruction in the resource room. *Learning Disability Quarterly, 7,* 315–320.

Meichenbaum, D. (1977). *Cognitive-behavior modification: An integrative approach.* New York: Plenum Press.

Mischel, W. (1973). Toward a cognitive social learning reconceptualization of personality. *Psychological Review, 80,* 252–283.

Moran, M. R., Schumaker, J. B., & Vetter, A. F. (1981). *Teaching a paragraph organization strategy to learning disabled adolescents* (Research Report No. 54). Lawrence, KS: University of Kansas Institute for Research in Learning Disabilities.

Neal, C. (1984). The holistic teacher. *Learning Disability Quarterly, 7,* 309–313.

Nelson, R. O., & Hayes, S. N. (1981). Theoretical explanations for reactivity in self-monitoring. *Behavior Modification, 5,* 3–14.

Norman, C., & Zigmond, N. (1980). Characteristics of children labeled and served as learning disabled in school systems affiliated with child service and demonstration centers. *Journal of Learning Disabilities, 13,* 542–547.

Packard, R. G. (1970). The control of "classroom attention": A group contingency for complex behavior. *Journal of Applied Behavior Analysis, 3,* 13–28.

Palinscar, A. S. (1986). Metacognitive strategy instruction. *Exceptional Children, 53,* 118–124.

Palinscar, A. S., & Brown, A. L. (1984). The reciprocal teaching of comprehension fostering and comprehension monitoring activities. *Cognition and Instruction, 1,* 117–175.

Parsons, J. A. (1972). The reciprocal modification of arithmetic behavior and program development. In G. Semb (Ed.), *Behavior analysis and education—1972* (pp. 185–199). Lawrence, KS: Kansas University Department of Human Development.

Pascarella, E. T., & Pflaum, S. W. (1981). The interaction of children's attribution and level of control over error correction in reading instruction. *Journal of Educational Psychology, 73,* 533–540.

Pellegrino, J. W., & Goldman, S. R. (1987). Information processing elementary mathematics. *Journal of Learning Disabilities, 20,* 23–32, 57.

Pflaum, S. W., & Pascarella, E. T. (1980). Interactive effects of prior reading achievement and training in context on the reading of learning disabled children. *Reading Research Quarterly, 16,* 138–158.

Piaget, J., & Inhelder, B. (1969a). *Memory and intelligence.* New York: Basic Books.

Piaget, J., & Inhelder, B. (1969b). *The psychology of the child.* New York: Basic Books.

Poplin, M. S. (1984). Toward an holistic view of persons with learning disabilities. *Learning Disability Quarterly, 7,* 290–294.

Poplin, M. S. (1988a). Holistic/constructivist principles of the teaching/learning process: Implications for the field of learning disabilities. *Journal of Learning Disabilities, 21*(7), 401–416.

Poplin, M. S. (1988b). The reductionist fallacy in learning disabilities: Replicating the past by reducing the present. *Journal of Learning Disabilities, 21*(7), 389–400.

Reeve, R. E., & Kauffman, J. M. (1988). Learning disabilities. In V. B. Van Hasselt, P. S. Strain, & M. Hersen (Eds.), *Handbook of developmental and physical disabilities* (pp. 316–335). Elmsford, NY: Pergamon Press.

Reid, P. K. (1988). Reflections on the pragmatics of a paradigm shift. *Journal of Learning Disabilities, 21*, 417–420.

Reid, D. K., & Hresko, W. P. (1981). *A cognitive approach to learning disabilities*. New York: McGraw-Hill.

Resnick, L. B., & Ford, W. W. (1981). *The psychology of mathematics for instruction*. Hillsdale, NJ: Lawrence Erlbaum Associates.

Robin, R. L., Armel, S., & O'Leary, K. D. (1975). The effects of self-instruction on writing deficiencies. *Behavior Therapy, 6*, 73–77.

Romberg, T. A., & Carpenter, T. P. (1986). Research on teaching and learning mathematics: Two disciplines of scientific inquiry. In M. C. Wittrock (Ed.), *Handbook of research on teaching* (3rd ed., pp. 850–873). New York: Macmillan.

Rose, T. L. (1985). The effects of two prepractice procedures on oral reading. *Journal of Learning Disabilities, 16*, 544–548.

Rose, T. L., Koorland, M. A., & Epstein, M. H. (1982). A review of applied behavior analysis with learning disabled children. *Education and Treatment of Children, 5*, 41–58.

Rosenshine, B., & Stevens, R. (1986). Teaching functions. In M. C. Wittrock (Ed.), *Handbook of research on teaching* (3rd ed., pp. 376–391). New York: Macmillan.

Rourke, B. P., & Strang, J. D. (1983). Subtypes of reading arithmetical disabilities: A neuropsychological analysis. In M. Rutter (Ed.), *Developmental neuropsychiatry* (pp. 473–488). New York: Guilford Press.

Schoenfeld, A. H. (1987). *Mathematical problem solving*. Orlando, FL: Academic Press.

Schumaker, J. B., Deshler, D. D., Alley, G. R., Warner, M. M., & Denton, P. H. (1982). Multipass: A learning strategy for improving reading comprehension. *Learning Disability Quarterly, 5*, 295–304.

Schunk, D. H., & Cox, P. D. (1986). Strategy training and attributional feedback with learning disabled students. *Journal of Educational Psychology, 78*, 201–209.

Scruggs, T. E., Mastropieri, M. A., McLoone, B. B., Levin, J. R., & Morrison, C. (1987). Mnemonic facilitation of text-embedded science facts with LD students. *Journal of Educational Psychology, 78*, 27–34.

Serwer, B. L., Shapiro, B. J., & Shapiro, P. P. (1973). The comparative effectiveness of four methods of instruction of the achievement of children with specific learning disabilities. *Journal of Special Education, 7*, 241–249.

Skinner, B. F. (1953). *Science and human behavior*. New York: Macmillan.

Skinner, B. F. (1968). *The technology of teaching*. New York: Appleton-Century-Crofts.

Smith, D. D. (1979). The improvement of children's oral reading rate through the use of teacher modeling. *Journal of Learning Disabilities, 12*, 172–175.

Smith, D. D., & Lovitt, T. C. (1973). The educational diagnosis and remediation of written b and d reversal problems: A case study. *Journal of Learning Disabilities, 6*, 356–363.

Smith, D. D., & Lovitt, T. C. (1975). The use of modeling techniques to influence the acquisition of computational arithmetic skills in learning-disabled children. In E. Ramp & G. Semb (Eds.), *Behavior analysis: Areas of research and application* (pp. 282–308). Englewood Cliffs, NJ: Prentice-Hall.

Smith D. D., & Lovitt, T. C. (1976). The differential effects of reinforcement contingencies on arithmetic performance. *Journal of Learning Disabilities, 9*, 21–29.

Stein, C. L'E., & Goldman, J. (1980). Beginning reading instruction for children with minimal brain dysfunction. *Journal of Learning Disabilities, 13*, 219–222.

Stephens & Hudson. (1984). A comparison of the effects of direct instruction and remedial English classes on the spelling skills of secondary students. *Educational Psychology, 4*, 261–267.

Strang, J. D., & Rourke, B. P. (1985). Arithmetic disability subtypes: The neuropsychological significance of specific arithmetical impairment in childhood. In B. P. Rourke (Ed.), *Neuropsychology of learning disabilities: Essentials of subtype analysis* (pp. 167–183). New York: Guilford Press.

Stromer, R. (1975). Modifying letter and number

reversals in elementary school children. *Journal of Applied Behavior Analysis, 8,* 211.

Stromer, R. (1977). Remediating academic deficiencies in learning disabled children. *Exceptional Children, 43,* 432-440.

Swanson, L. (1981a). Modification of comprehension deficits in learning disabled children. *Learning Disability Quarterly, 4,* 189-202.

Swanson, L. (1981b). Self-monitoring effects on concurrently reinforced reading behavior of a learning disabled child. *Child Study Journal, 10,* 225-232.

Tawney, J. W., & Gast, D. L. (1984). *Research in special education.* Columbus, OH: Charles E. Merrill.

Thackwray, D., Meyers, A., Schlesser, R., & Cohen, R. (1985). Achieving generalization with general versus specific self-instructions: Effects of academically deficient children. *Cognitive Therapy and Research, 9,* 291-308.

U.S. Department of Education. (1987). *Ninth annual report to congress on the implementation of the Education of the Handicapped Act.* Washington, DC: U.S. Government Printing Office.

Van Hasselt, V. B., Strain, P. S., & Hersen, M. (Eds.) (1988). *Handbook of developmental and physical disabilities.* Elmsford, NY: Pergamon Press.

Walker, H. M, & Buckley, N. K. (1968). The use of positive reinforcement in conditioning attending behavior. *Journal of Applied Behavior Analysis, 1,* 245-250.

Wallach, M. A., & Wallach, L. (1976). *Teaching all children to read.* Chicago: University of Chicago Press.

Wang, M. C., Nojan, M., Strom, C. D., & Walberg, H. J. (1984). The utility of degree of implementation measures in program evaluation and implementation research. *Curriculum Inquiry, 14,* 249-286.

White, W. A. T. (1988). A meta-analysis of the effects of direct instruction in special education. *Education and Treatment of Children, 11,* 364-374.

Whitman, T., Burgio, L., & Johnston, M. B. (1984). Cognitive behavioral interventions with mentally retarded children. In A. W. Meyers & W. E. Craighead (Eds.), *Cognitive behavior therapy with children* (pp. 193-227). New York: Plenum Press.

Whitman, T., & Johnston, M. B. (1983). Teaching addition and subtraction with regrouping to educate mentally retarded children: A group self-instructional training program. *Behavior Therapy, 14,* 127-143.

Williams, J. P. (1980). Teaching decoding with an emphasis on phoneme analysis and phoneme blending. *Journal of Educational Psychology, 72,* 1-15.

Witt, J. C., Elliott, S. N., & Gresham, F. M. (Eds.) (1988). *Handbook of behavior therapy in education.* New York: Plenum Press.

Wong, B. Y. L. (1985a). Metacognition and learning disabilities. In D. L. Forrest-Pressley, G. E. MacKinnon, & T. G. Waller (Eds.), *Metacognition, cognition, and human performance* (Vol. 2, pp. 137-180). New York: Academic Press.

Wong, B. Y. L. (1985b). Issues in cognitive-behavioral interventions in academic skill areas. *Journal of Abnormal Child Psychology, 13,* 425-441.

Wong, B. Y. L., & Jones, W. (1982). Increasing metacomprehension in learning disabled and normally achieving students through self-question training. *Learning Disability Quarterly, 5,* 228-240.

Ysseldyke, J. E., & Salvia, J. (1974). Diagnostic-prescriptive teaching: Two models. *Exceptional Children, 41,* 181-186.

Zimmerman, E. H., & Zimmerman, J. (1962). The alteration of behavior in a special classroom situation. *Journal of Experimental Analysis of Behavior, 5,* 59-60.

CHAPTER 7

AGGRESSIVE BEHAVIOR AND CONDUCT DISORDER

Alan E. Kazdin

INTRODUCTION

Definition

Conduct disorder encompasses a broad range of antisocial behaviors such as aggressive acts, theft, vandalism, fire setting, lying, truancy, and running away. Although these behaviors are diverse, their common characteristic is that they tend to violate major social rules and expectations. Many of the behaviors often reflect actions against the environment, including both persons and property. Antisocial behaviors emerge in some form over the course of normal development. Fighting, lying, stealing, destruction of property, and noncompliance are relatively common at different points in childhood (Achenbach & Edelbrock, 1981; MacFarlane, Allen, & Honzik, 1954). For the most part, these behaviors diminish over time, do not interfere with everyday functioning, and do not predict untoward consequences in adulthood.

The term "conduct disorder" is usually reserved for a pattern of antisocial behavior that is associated with significant impairment in everyday functioning at home or school, and with concerns of significant others that the child or adolescent is unmanageable. Clinically severe antisocial behavior is likely to bring the youth into contact with various social agencies. Mental health services (clinics, hospitals) and the criminal justice system (police, courts) are the major sources of contact for youths whose behaviors are identified as severe. Within the educational system, special services, teachers, and classes are often provided to manage such children.

Conduct disorder raises special challenges in relation to treatment. The present chapter ex-

Completion of this chapter facilitated by a Research Scientist Development Award (MH00353) and a grant (MH35408) from the National Institute of Mental Health.

amines and illustrates the application of several treatments of conduct disorder. The focus, effectiveness, and limitations of alternative techniques are reviewed. Evaluation of alternative treatments depends on clarifying the full range of characteristics of conduct disorder to determine the areas that treatment may need to address to be effective.

Historical Background

Conduct disorder has long been recognized, in part because of the social impact of the constituent behaviors. Antisocial behaviors that comprise conduct disorder include aggressive behavior, theft, and vandalism and have been of interest as part of legal codes for children and adults. Within clinical work, the dysfunction has been identified readily as well. Conduct disorder reflects externalizing behaviors that act against the environment and are more easily recognized diagnostically than many internalizing disorders that reflect reactions directed inward (e.g., social withdrawal, depression).

Early studies of clinical disorders among children identified antisocial behaviors quite clearly. For example, one of the earliest studies that utilized statistical techniques to examine childhood disorders was completed by Hewett and Jenkins (1946). These investigators analyzed the case records of children ($N = 500$) referred to a child guidance clinic. They measured several different symptoms from the records to identify the joint occurrence of specific problems. On the basis of the pattern of intercorrelations, they identified three major behavioral syndromes: unsocialized aggressive, socialized delinquent, and overinhibited. The first two of these reflect antisocial behavior and have clear parallels in contemporary views of conduct (see Kazdin, 1987a; Quay, 1986a).

The significance of antisocial behavior has been made salient by longitudinal studies. In the 1950s, Glueck and Glueck (1950, 1959) examined characteristics of delinquent youths and attempted to identify child, parent, and family predictors of delinquency and recidivism. In 1966, Robins completed the now classic study that followed clinically referred youths 30 years later. The study demonstrated the long-term consequences of antisocial behavior, as reflected in psychiatric symptoms, criminal behaviors, and physical and social adjustment prob-

lems. These findings were replicated with separate samples and with follow-up evaluations of different durations (see Robins, 1978, 1981). These studies made salient the severity and stability of antisocial behavior over the developmental spectrum.

Characteristics of Conduct Disorder

Central Features
There are several features of conduct disorder that make the behaviors discrepant from what is seen as part of "normal development." First, many of the behaviors such as fighting, temper tantrums, stealing, and others are relatively frequent. In some cases, the behaviors may be of a low frequency (e.g., fire setting), in which case intensity or severity is the central characteristic. Second, repetitiveness and chronicity of the behaviors are critical features. The behaviors are not likely to be isolated events or to occur within a brief period where some other influences or stressors (e.g., change in residence, divorce) is operative. Third, the breadth of the behaviors is central as well. Rather than an individual symptom or target behavior, there are usually several behaviors that occur together and form a syndrome or constellation of symptoms.

Conduct disorder, as a syndrome, includes several core features such as fighting, engaging in temper tantrums, theft, truancy, destroying property, defying or threatening others, and running away. The syndrome is recognized in clinically derived diagnostic systems such as the *Diagnostic and Statistical Manual of Mental Disorders* (American Psychiatric Association, 1987). In addition, multivariate analyses have consistently identified conduct disorder as a distinct syndrome (see Quay, 1986b).

Associated Features
The central features of conduct disorder comprise antisocial, aggressive, and defiant behaviors. There are several correlates or associated features as well. Among alternative symptoms that have been found among antisocial children, those related to hyperactivity have been the most frequently identified. These symptoms include excessive motor activity, restlessness, impulsiveness, and inattentiveness. In fact, the cooccurrence of hyperactivity and conduct disorder has made their diagnostic delineation and

assessment a topic of considerable research (e.g., Hinshaw, 1987). Several other behaviors—such as boisterousness, showing off, and blaming others—have been identified as problematic among antisocial youths. Many of these, in comparison to various acts that invoke damage to persons or property, appear to be relatively mild forms of obstreperous behavior.

Children with conduct disorder are also likely to suffer from academic deficiencies, as reflected in achievement level, grades, and specific skill areas, especially reading (e.g., Ledingham & Schwartzman, 1984; Sturge, 1982). Such children are often viewed by their teachers as uninterested in school, unenthusiastic about academic pursuits, and careless in their work (Glueck & Glueck, 1950). They are more likely to be left behind in grades, to show lower achievement levels, and to end their schooling sooner than their peers matched in age, socioeconomic status, and other demographic variables (Bachman, Johnston, & O'Malley, 1978; Glueck & Glueck, 1968).

Poor interpersonal relations correlate with antisocial behavior. Children high in aggressiveness or other antisocial behaviors are rejected by their peers and show poor social skills (e.g., Behar & Stewart, 1982; Carlson, Lahey, & Neeper, 1984). Such youths are socially ineffective in their interactions with an array of adults (e.g., parents, teachers, community members). Specifically, antisocial youths are less likely to defer to adult authority, to act politely, and to respond in ways that promote further positive interactions (Freedman, Rosenthal, Donahoe, Schlundt, & McFall, 1978; Gaffney & McFall, 1981).

The correlates of antisocial behavior involve not only overt behaviors but also a variety of cognitive and attributional processes. Antisocial youths are deficient in cognitive problem-solving skills that underlie social interaction (Dodge, 1985; Kendall & Braswell, 1985). For example, such youths are more likely than their peers to interpret gestures of others as hostile and hence to react aggressively. They are less able to identify solutions to interpersonal problem situations and to take the perspective of others. In addition, conduct-disordered youths are higher than non-conduct-disordered peers on measures of cognitive-perceptual characteristics such as resentment, suspiciousness, and irritability (becoming upset) in response to others (Kazdin, Rodgers, Colbus, & Siegel, 1987).

Course and Prognosis

For the children with conduct disorder who are seen clinically, the course and prognosis are relatively clear. Longitudinal studies have consistently shown that antisocial behavior identified in childhood or adolescence predicts a continued course of social dysfunction, problematic behavior, and poor school adjustment (see Kazdin, 1987a). One of the most dramatic illustrations of the long-term prognosis of clinically referred children was the previously mentioned study by Robins (1966). The results demonstrated that antisocial behavior in childhood predicted psychiatric symptoms, criminal behavior, physical dysfunction, and social maladjustment in adulthood. Even though conduct disorder in childhood portends a number of other significant problems in adulthood, not all antisocial children suffer impairment as adults. Robins (1978) noted that less than 50% of the most severely antisocial children become antisocial adults; but this percentage is still quite high. In addition, among those who do not continue antisocial behavior, social maladjustment (e.g., frequent unemployment, divorce, contact with the law) and clinical dysfunction reflecting impairment other than antisocial behavior are evident.

Major factors that influence whether antisocial youths are likely to continue their behavior into adulthood include parent antisocial behavior, alcoholism, poor parental supervision of the child, harsh or inconsistent disciplinary practices, marital discord in the family, large family size, older siblings who are antisocial, and so on. The most significant predictors of long-term outcome are characteristics of the child's antisocial behavior, including early onset of these behaviors, antisocial acts across multiple settings (e.g., home and school), and many and diverse antisocial behaviors (e.g., several versus few, covert versus overt acts) (Loeber & Dishion, 1983; Rutter & Giller, 1983).

Prevalence

The prevalence of conduct disorder is difficult to estimate, given the very different definitions that have been used and variations in rates for children of different ages, sex, socioeconomic class, and geographical locale. Estimates of the rate of conduct disorder among children have ranged from approximately 4% to 10% (Rutter,

Cox, Tupling, Berger, & Yule, 1975; Rutter, Tizard, & Whitmore, 1970). When rates are evaluated for specific behaviors that comprise conduct disorder and youths themselves report on their activities, the prevalence rates are extraordinarily high. For example, among youths (ages 13 to 18), more than 50% admit to theft, 35% admit to assault, 45% admit to property destruction, and 60% admit to engaging in more than one type of antisocial behavior (such as aggressiveness, drug abuse, arson, vandalism) (see Feldman, Caplinger, & Wodarski, 1983; Williams & Gold, 1972). The extent of the problem is attested further by the rates of referrals of conduct disorder to clinical services. Estimates have indicated that referrals to outpatient clinics for aggressiveness, conduct problems, and antisocial behaviors encompass from one third to one half of all child and adolescent cases (Gilbert, 1957; Robins, 1981).

Conduct disorder in children and adolescents varies as a function of sex (Gilbert, 1957; Robins, 1966). The precise sex ratio is difficult to specify because of varying criteria and measures of conduct disorder among the available studies. Nevertheless, antisocial behavior appears to be at least three times more common among boys (Graham, 1979). Sex differences also are apparent in the age of onset of dysfunction. Robins (1966) found that the median age of onset of dysfunction for children referred for antisocial behavior was in the 8- to 10-year age range. Most (57%) boys had an onset before age 10 (median = age 7). For girls, onset of antisocial behavior was concentrated in the 14- to 16-year age range (median = age 13). Characteristic symptom patterns were different as well. Theft was more frequent as a basis of referral among antisocial boys than among antisocial girls. For boys, aggression was also likely to be a presenting problem. For girls, antisocial behavior was much more likely to include sexual misbehavior.

Underlying Bases and Correlates

The development of conduct disorders has been well studied. Rather than clear causal paths, several factors have been identified that place individuals at risk for conduct disorder. To be "at risk" refers to the increased likelihood, above base rates in the population, that persons will show the behavior of interest. Table 7.1 lists several factors that predispose children and adolescents to antisocial behavior (see Kazdin, 1987a). Among the factors listed, those that reflect early signs of antisocial behavior are the most robust predictors of subsequent conduct disorder. The degree to which individuals evince particular risk factors or the range of factors can vary widely. Moreover, the list of risk factors in Table 7.1 is incomplete. Additional risk factors can be identified, such as mental retardation of the parent, early marriage of the parents, lack of parental interest in the child's school performance, lack of participation of the family in religious or recreational activities, and many other parental and family factors (Glueck & Glueck, 1968; Wadsworth, 1979).

The risk factors do not, of course, convey the causes of antisocial behavior or the specific mechanisms through which they operate. Several lines of evidence have emerged in support of the role of the genetic factors. Twin studies have shown greater concordance of criminality and antisocial behavior among monozygotic ("identical") rather than dizygotic ("fraternal") twins (e.g., Christiansen, 1974; Cloninger, Christiansen, Reich, & Gottesman, 1978). Attribution of the differences in concordance between monozygotic and dizygotic twins to genetic factors assumes that the environments for different types of twins are equated. Yet environmental factors may be more similar for monozygotic than for dizygotic twins (Christiansen, 1974). Adoption studies separate genetic and environmental influences better because the child often is separated from the biological parent at birth. Adoption studies have shown that antisocial behavior and criminality in the offspring are more likely when the biological relative has shown such behavior than when the relative has not (e.g., Cadoret, 1978; Crowe, 1974).

The relatively frequent replication of the increased risk due to antisocial behavior in the biological parent of adoptees establishes the role of genetics in accounting for some portion of variance in the emergence of conduct disorder. Yet, genetic factors alone cannot account for current findings. For example, criminality aggregates among siblings in the home more often than can be currently explained by genetic factors (Cloninger, Reich, & Guze, 1975). Adoption studies have also affirmed the influence of such environmental factors as adverse conditions in

Table 7.1. Risk Factor Associated With the Onset of Conduct Disorder

RISK FACTOR	RELATION TO CONDUCT DISORDER
Child Temperament	Children who have "difficult" temperaments as characterized by negative mood, reluctance to approach new stimuli, low adaptability to change, and more intense reactions to new stimuli are at greater risk than nondelinquent children (Shanok & Lewis, 1981); early neurological signs, when evident, may well be the result of risk-taking behavior and adverse family conditions (e.g., abuse of the child).
Subclinical Levels of Antisocial Behavior	Early signs of aggressiveness and unmanageability place youth at risk for conduct disorder. Early onset, increased number of these early signs, and behaviors across multiple situations increase risk.
Academic and Intellectual Performance	Academic deficiencies and lower levels of intellectual functioning are associated with increased risk of conduct disorder.
Parental Psychopathology and Criminal Behavior	Psychopathology in the parents places the child at risk for psychological disturbance in general. Criminal behavior and alcoholism, particularly of the father, are two of the stronger and more consistently demonstrated parental factors that increase the child's risk for conduct disorder.
Parent Discipline Practices	Harsh, lax, and inconsistent discipline practices increase risk for conduct disorder.
Poor Parental Supervision	Low levels of monitoring child whereabouts or arranging for care when parents are temporarily away from the home, not setting rules for where child can go and when to return increase risk.
Marital Discord	Unhappy marital relations, interpersonal conflict, and aggression between the parents increase risk of the child.
Birth Order	Risk is greater among middle children in comparison to only, firstborn, or youngest children.
Family Size	Risk is associated with increased family size. This risk for a given child is augmented if older male siblings in the home display antisocial behaviors.
School-Related Characteristics	Low standing of a school on such factors as an emphasis on academics, teacher time on lessons, teacher use of praise and appreciation for schoolwork, emphasis on individual responsibility of the students, good working conditions for pupils (e.g., clean classroom, furniture in good repair), availability of the teacher to deal with children's problems, and consistent teacher expectancies, among others, increase child risk for antisocial behavior. The combination of several factors, rather than any single variable, contributes to child outcomes.

NOTE: These factors and the research on which they are based have been reviewed elsewhere in greater detail (Kazdin, 1987a).

the home (e.g., marital discord, psychiatric dysfunction), exposure to discontinuous mothering before being placed in the final adoptive setting, and the age at which the child has been adopted (Cadoret & Cain, 1981; Crowe, 1974; Hutchings & Mednick, 1975). This work suggests the combined role of genetic and environmental factors.

The dual contribution of genetic and environ-mental influences can be seen in studies which show that antisocial behavior in both the biological and adoptive parent increases the risk of antisocial behavior in the child (Mednick & Hutchings, 1978), although the impact of the biological parent is much greater. Other studies examining a number of variables have shown that the risk is greatly increased when both genetic and environmental influences are present (e.g., Cadoret, Cain, & Crowe, 1983; Cloninger, Sigvardsson, Bohman, & von Knorring, 1982). Yet, there are important nuances showing the interaction of genetic and environmental factors with other variables.

For example, sex of the child interacts with the influence of genetic and environmental factors. In studies of adoptees, Cadoret and Cain (1980, 1981) found that having an alcoholic biological relative, adverse home conditions in the adoptive home, and discontinuous mothering predicted antisocial behavior in adolescent males. However, for female adolescents, only having an antisocial or mentally retarded biological parent predicted antisocial behavior. Thus, environmental factors (home conditions and mothering practices) only emerged as predictors for males, suggesting their greater susceptibility to environmental influences. Other studies have suggested differences in vulnerability of males and females to environmental factors (e.g., divorce or institutional care) that may place the child at risk for antisocial behavior, although many of the influences appear to be a matter of degree rather than an all-or-none phenomenon (Cloninger, Reich, & Guze, 1978; Rutter, 1972; Wolkind & Rutter, 1973).

CURRENT TREATMENTS

The Challenges of Treatment

The purpose in describing conduct disorder and its many characteristics is not to paint a bleak picture but rather to highlight what is known about the dysfunction. Many aspects of conduct disorder have major implications for the implementation and evaluation of alternative treatments. Key characteristics to bear in mind for effective intervention are the pervasiveness and stability of conduct disorder. Youths with conduct disorder are likely to show dysfunction in diverse areas of their lives. They are likely to function poorly at home and at school, and multiple problems are likely to be evident within a given setting. For example, at school, antisocial youths often perform poorly on academic tasks and have few prosocial relations with their peers. The core symptoms of the conduct disorder appear to begin a sequence of events that support continued dysfunction. Thus, failure to complete homework and possible truancy or lying are likely to portend further deterioration

(expulsion, school transfer). In general, the associated features of conduct disorder convey the breadth of dysfunction in academic, cognitive, and interpersonal domains.

Apart from pervasive dysfunction, parental and family correlates raise critical issues as well. Parents and the family may suffer significant dysfunction that is related to the child's problems. Parental psychopathology and harsh child-rearing practices, already mentioned, may contribute directly to the development of antisocial behavior in the child (Patterson, 1986). In general, the challenge of antisocial behavior derives in part from the range of characteristics with which it is associated and the implications regarding where to intervene.

Overview of Current Treatments

Several treatments have been implemented for antisocial behavior, including diverse forms of individual and group therapy, behavior therapy, residential treatment, pharmacotherapy, psychosurgery, and a variety of innovative community-based treatments (Kazdin, 1985; McCord, 1982; O'Donnell, 1985). At present no treatment has been shown to ameliorate conduct disorder and to controvert its poor prognosis. The absence of effective treatments has not resulted from a paucity of creative efforts or available techniques. Indeed, many different classes of treatment can be identified. Table 7.2 highlights major classes of treatment and their therapeutic focus.

Most treatments focus on the individual by altering a particular facet of functioning or processes within the child. Diverse approaches that focus on changing the individual child include individual and group therapy, behavioral and cognitive therapies, and pharmacotherapies. A number of other treatments focus on the family. Treatment is aimed at altering interaction patterns or other family processes in the home; techniques such as family therapy and parent management training are examples. Other treatments are worth delineating on the basis of their use or incorporation of therapeutic influences in the context of the community. The influence of direct contact and involvement of the youth with prosocial peers and community services is accorded major weight. Community-based techniques often rely on other treatments, such as psychotherapy and behavior therapy. Yet these are integrated within a larger social, organiza-

Table 7.2. Therapeutic Focus and Processes of Major Classes of Treatment for Antisocial Behavior

TYPES OF TREATMENT	FOCUS	KEY PROCESSES
Child-Focused Treatments		
Individual Psychotherapy	Focus on intrapsychic bases of antisocial behavior, especially conflicts and psychological processes that were adversely affected over the course of development.	Relationship with the therapist is the primary medium through which change is achieved. Treatment provides a corrective emotional experience by providing insight and exploring new ways of behaving.
Group Psychotherapy	Processes of individual therapy, as noted above. Additional processes are reassurance, feedback, and vicarious gains by peers. Group processes such as cohesion and leadership also serve as the focus.	Relationship with the therapist and peers as part of the group. Group processes emerge to provide children with experiences and feelings of others and opportunities to test their own views and behaviors.
Behavior Therapy	Problematic behaviors are presented as target symptoms. Prosocial behaviors are trained directly.	Learning of new behaviors through direct training, via modeling, reinforcement, practice and role playing. Training in the situations (e.g., at home, in the community) where the problematic behaviors occur.
Problem-Solving Skills Training	Cognitive processes and interpersonal cognitive problem-solving skills that underlie social behavior.	Teach problem-solving skills to children by engaging in a step-by-step approach to interpersonal situations. Use of modeling, practice, rehearsal, and role play to develop problem-solving skills. Development of an internal dialogue or private speech that utilizes the processes of identifying prosocial solutions to problems.
Pharmacotherapy	Designed to affect the biological substrates of behavior, especially in light of laboratory-based findings on neurohumors, biological cycles, and other physiological correlates of aggressive and emotional behavior.	Administration of psychotropic agents to control antisocial behavior. Lithium carbonate and haloperidol have been used because of their antiaggressive effects.
Residential Treatments	Means of administering other techniques in day treatment or residential setting. Foci of other techniques apply.	Processes of other techniques apply. Also, separation of the child from parents or removal from the home situation may help reduce untoward processes or crises that contribute to the clinical problem.
Family-Focused Treatments		
Family Therapy	Family as a functioning system serves as focus rather than the identified patient. Interpersonal relationships, organization, roles, and dynamics of the family.	Communication, relationships, and structure within the family and such processes as developing autonomy, problem solving skills, and the ability to negotiate.
Parent Management Training	Interactions in the home, especially those involving coercive exchanges.	Direct training of parents to develop prosocial behavior in their children. Explicit use of social-learning techniques to influence the child.
Community-Based Treatments		
Community-Wide Interventions	Focus on activities and community programs to foster competence and prosocial peer relations.	Develop prosocial behavior and connections with peers. Activities are seen to promote prosocial behavior and to be incompatible with antisocial behavior.

tional, and peer-group context. Within a given class of treatment, several variations can be identified. For example, individual psychotherapy consists of psychodynamic, nondirective, and play therapies as well as others. Similarly, behavioral therapy can include a range of techniques such as social-skills training, contingency management, and token economies. At the level of specific techniques rather than the more generic classes of treatment, the number of available procedures is great.

The plethora of available treatments might be viewed as a healthy sign that the field has not become rigidly set on one or two techniques. On the other hand, the diversity of procedures suggests that no particular approach has ameliorated clinically severe antisocial behavior. Four classes of treatment that have been utilized and evaluated are detailed here. These include operant conditioning based interventions, social-skills training, parent- and family-based treatments, and cognitively based treatments.

OPERANT CONDITIONING TECHNIQUES

The principles of operant conditioning have generated a large number of intervention techniques applied to antisocial behavior. The techniques can be distinguished on the basis of whether they attempt to increase the frequency of appropriate (e.g., nonaggressive) behavior or to decrease the frequency of inappropriate behavior. In fact, the procedures are often combined. However, the specific techniques can be better illustrated separately.

Reinforcement Techniques

Characteristics
Many applications of operant conditioning are based on the administration of positive reinforcement to increase appropriate (prosocial) behavior. Positive reinforcers usually include the delivery of praise, attention from others, privileges, and tangible rewards such as prizes. Many programs incorporate a large number of rewards in the form of a token economy (Kazdin, 1977) in which the child earns tokens (e.g., stars, tickets, points, money) for specific behaviors. The tokens are exchangeable for a variety of rewards, privileges, and activities (backup reinforcers). Token economies may be individ-

ually designed for only one child or may be applied to an entire classroom, hospital ward, family, or group of children.

Illustrations
As an example of token reinforcement applied to an individual child, Bristol (1976) reports a program for an 8-year-old boy in a second-grade classroom who constantly engaged in fighting. The program involved the cooperation of parents, the teacher, and the child, who agreed to the contingencies and signed a "contract" to that effect. Each morning the child received a card with a smiling face on it. In the morning, at lunch, and at the end of the day, the teacher signed the card if the boy had not engaged in fighting. The teacher's signatures served as points that could be accumulated toward backup rewards such as being a student helper in class, going to the library for free reading, or staying up 15 minutes later at bedtime. Experimental evaluation demonstrated that fighting decreased whenever the program was in effect. By the end of the project, fighting was eliminated over a 3-week period. A report obtained 7 months after the program was terminated indicated that the boy was doing well without any special program.

A novel application of token reinforcement was reported by Blue, Madsen, and Heimberg (1981), who increased the coping behaviors of elementary school children identified as aggressive by teachers and peers. Children received token reinforcement exchangeable for backup reinforcers in 10 treatment sessions in which they participated in a "taunting game." The game was designed to provoke aggressive behavior. Peer assistants (not in need of treatment) were trained to provoke anger in the target children by teasing or yelling as part of the game. The children earned rewards for coping (i.e., not engaging in verbal or physical aggression) and providing verbal statements (e.g., "leave me alone") that did not respond to the provocation. Token reinforcement led to significantly greater changes in coping behavior during the game in these children relative to waiting-list and attention-placebo (discussion of aggressive behavior) control groups. However, groups did not differ in coping responses assessed on the playground.

In most applications of reinforcement, specific inappropriate behaviors are identified and rewarded. Yet there are many other effective ways of administering reinforcement. One procedure, referred to as differential reinforcement of other behavior (DRO), consists of providing reinforcement for nonoccurrences of the undesired behaviors. As an example, Frankel, Moss, Schofield, and Simmons (1976) used DRO to modify the aggressive behaviors of a 6-year-old mentally retarded girl. The child engaged in a high level of pinching, biting, and hair pulling directed toward others, as well as head banging. The child was praised and given candy every 5 seconds for quiet, appropriate behavior in class and every 60 seconds during free time. Intervals were timed with a stopwatch by an observer behind a one-way mirror and were communicated to the teacher through a "bug in the ear." The teacher administered the reinforcers. After 4 days, the rates of aggression began to decrease. The intervals between reinforcer delivery were gradually lengthened until the entire procedure was eliminated 16 days later, without reappearance of the aggression.

The application of operant techniques may involve more than the administration of consequences. Often the stimulus conditions are altered as well, in order to help promote the desired behaviors so they can be reinforced. For example, Murphy, Hutchinson, and Bailey (1983) reorganized play activities and also altered consequences to decrease the aggressive behavior of elementary school children. The children included 344 first- and second-graders who played outside before the beginning of class. During this time, high rates of aggressive behavior (e.g., striking, slapping, tripping, kicking, pushing, or punching others) were observed. After collecting baseline information, the investigators initiated an intervention that included several components. The major component was structured (organized) game activities including rope jumping and foot races supervised by playground aides. During the activities, aides praised appropriate behavior (reinforcement) and invoked time out (punishment) by placing disruptive children on a bench for 2 minutes for particularly unruly behavior. The program was alternately implemented and withdrawn over time to evaluate its effects. The results, presented in Figure 7.1, illustrate that aggressive behavior decreased when the intervention was in effect.

Recommendations

Several basic steps are involved in instituting a positive reinforcement program. The target behaviors must be carefully defined and measured prior to the intervention. There will be at least two target behaviors to assess: the aggressive behavior (to be eliminated) and a more socially appropriate behavior (to be increased). Following the assessment of baseline (pretreatment) rates of these behaviors, positive reinforcement can begin. The choice of an effective positive reinforcer is often an empirical question with each child. Possibilities may be explored by asking the child about things he or she would like to earn or by observing the types of free-time activities in which the child engages. If observable changes in target behaviors are not obtained within several days of reinforcement, substitution of another reinforcer should be considered. With some children, social reinforcement (verbal praise) alone may be effective for changing behavior. If praise is used, designating the specific act for which the child is being commended results in greater behavioral change than making general comments such as "Good, Susie" (Drabman & Tucker, 1974; Forehand & Peed, 1979). Because social reinforcers may have little value with aggressive children (Agee, 1979), it is desirable to pair praise with material reinforcers. Praise may eventually acquire reinforcing properties through association.

To maximize the effects of positive reinforcement, the desired response should be reinforced frequently. After the response is strengthened, the schedule of reinforcement should be "thinned" gradually (partial reinforcement) to maintain behavior. The type of reinforcer should also be adjusted gradually until it resembles those more typically available to the child in the natural environment (Kazdin, 1989).

In addition to these basic points, there are other considerations specific to the individual techniques. The token economy involves the choice of token to be used. Although physical tokens (e.g., tickets, cards, coins) are useful because individuals may enjoy their accumulation, they may also be lost, destroyed, stolen, or traded. As a result, point systems involving check marks or records of earnings are usually preferred. Also, before beginning a token economy, it is necessary to specify the desired and undesired behaviors and the rules for obtaining rewards. Children are frequently offered a choice of backup reinforcers, which are described with their costs on a "reward menu." Several program options are available that vary the specific way in which the contingencies can be implemented (see Kazdin, 1989).

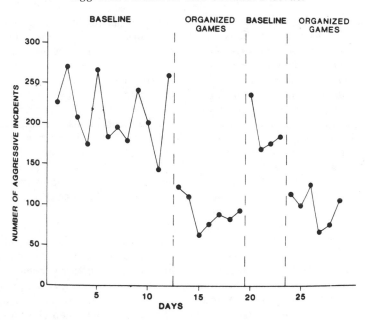

Figure 7.1. Number of incidents of aggressive behavior recorded on the playground before school started. Baseline—no intervention. Intervention—organized activities, praise, and time out. Reversal—return to baseline conditions. Intervention—return to the activities, praise, and time-out procedures. From "Behavioral school psychology goes outdoors: The effects of organized games on playground aggression" by H. A. Murphy, J. M. Hutchinson, and J. S. Bailey, 1983, *Journal of Applied Behavior Analysis, 16,* 29–35. Copyright 1983 by the Society for the Experimental Analysis of Behavior, Inc. Reprinted by permission.

Punishment Techniques

Characteristics

Punishment techniques also have been used to suppress or eliminate antisocial behaviors. The punishment procedures differ from the usual consequences applied to behavior in everyday life, and they are implemented somewhat differently. Punishment procedures in the context of treatment typically consist of the withdrawal of reinforcers.

Illustrations

One procedure is referred to as "time out from reinforcement" and consists of the removal of positive reinforcers for a brief period of time. During time out, the child does not have access to positive reinforcers that are normally available in the setting. The crucial feature of time out is delineating a time period in which reinforcers are unavailable. Typically, time out consists of social isolation, where the child is removed from the situation for a brief period (e.g., 5 minutes). Extended periods are not necessary for time out to be effective.

As an example, Drabman and Spitalnik (1973) applied a social isolation program to a class of 9- to 11-year-old aggressive boys in a residential psychiatric setting. When a target behavior such as hitting another child occurred, a classroom observer unobtrusively signaled the teacher. The teacher immediately identified the child and said, "You have misbehaved. You must leave the class." The child was then escorted without further comment to a small, dimly lit isolation room (a music practice room). A teaching assistant stayed nearby to ensure the child's safety. After 10 minutes, the child was returned to the class, where observations began again. There was no limit to the number of times a child could be sent out of the room. After 16 days of the program, this procedure resulted in a marked decrease in aggressive acts. Similarly, in other studies, social isolation has been effective in reducing such problem behaviors as aggressiveness and noncompliance (e.g., Patterson, Cobb, & Ray, 1973; Roberts, Hatzenbuehler, & Bean, 1981; Wahler, 1972). Other variations of time out include withdrawal of attention and suspension of the opportunity to earn reinforcers (see Kazdin, 1989). In each case, relatively brief time outs have effectively suppressed behaviors.

"Response cost" is another type of punishment used to decrease inappropriate behavior. It usually involves the loss of a positive reinforcer. Unlike time out, there is no necessary time period involved in the punishment. The most common use of response cost involves taking away tokens or points for inappropriate behavior as a part of a token economy. A child may earn tokens for appropriate behavior but lose them for inappropriate behavior. For example, Burchard and Barrera (1972) used a response-cost token program with 11 mildly retarded adolescents who had a history of antisocial behavior. Swearing, disobedience, and aggression were identified as behaviors to be eliminated. When a child engaged in one of the target behaviors, he was required to give up either 5 or 30 of his tokens or to take 5 or 30 minutes of time out. Each child experienced each type of penalty over the course of the program. Both response cost and time out were effective in reducing aggressive behaviors, with the more severe penalties resulting in greater behavior change.

"Overcorrection" is also designed to reduce inappropriate behavior. The technique includes two components. The first, restitution, consists of having the child correct the environmental effects of the inappropriate behavior. The second component, positive practice, consists of repeatedly practicing the appropriate behaviors in the situation. Both components are combined to suppress deviant behavior.

For example, Foxx and Azrin (1972) used overcorrection with a hospitalized 50-year-old profoundly retarded woman who had engaged in severely disruptive and aggressive behavior, especially throwing things. After baseline observations were made, overcorrection was implemented. When the patient performed a disruptive behavior (e.g., overturning a bed), she was required to "correct" (make restitution for) the physical effects of her behavior on the environment (i.e., turn the bed to its correct position and straighten the spread and pillows). In addition, she was required to rehearse the correct behavior by straightening all the other beds on the ward (positive practice). After 11 weeks of training, the patient no longer threw things.

For many behaviors, it is not possible to have people "correct" the environmental consequences because their behaviors have not altered the environment in a tangible fashion. In such cases, positive practice is often used alone, with the person being required to perform the appropriate behavior. For example, Azrin and Powers (1975) used positive practice to control the classroom behavior of 6 disruptive boys. Talking out and leaving one's seat were decreased after the children practiced appropriate classroom behavior by sitting in their seats, raising their hands, being recognized by the teacher, and asking permission to get up. Overcorrection and positive practice include a number of variations that have been applied effectively to a wide range of disruptive behaviors (see Kazdin, 1989).

Recommendations

As with positive reinforcement methods, punishment procedures require clear definition and measurement of target behaviors before treatment is implemented. In addition, it is important that punishment programs be written in an explicit manner and then closely followed. Those involved in administering such a program should be carefully monitored for adherence to the written conditions. Perhaps the most important single practice when punishment is used is to ensure that alternative (prosocial) behaviors are reinforced directly. When punishment for undesired behaviors is embedded in a larger behavioral program that includes positive reinforcement, behavior change is likely to be more rapid and not to result in many of the untoward side effects that may appear when punishment is used alone.

Research with time out has revealed several important parameters. To begin with, longer time outs are not necessarily more effective than shorter ones. Intervals of social isolation as brief as one or a few minutes have been shown to be effective (Hobbs, Forehand, & Murray, 1978; White, Nielsen, & Johnson, 1972). Periods exceeding 30 minutes do not appear to possess much additional punishment value. Time out should be administered at each occurrence of the undesirable behavior until the behavior has been reduced, at which time an intermittent schedule can maintain suppression (Calhoun & Lima, 1977; Jackson & Calhoun, 1977). Release from time out may be contingent on a 15-second period of appropriate behavior at the end of the interval. This method has been found to decrease noncompliance in preschoolers. In general, time out is effective when the situation from which the child has been removed is reinforcing (Solnick, Rincover, & Peterson, 1977).

Thus, if a child detests being in the classroom, removal from the class for aggressive acts could conceivably *increase* the unwanted behaviors.

If response cost is used, the program must provide the child with the opportunity to receive positive reinforcement for appropriate behavior. Once earned, the tokens or points can be withdrawn for inappropriate behaviors. Often small costs are very effective. Here too the effectiveness can be augmented by a program that provides continuous reinforcement for prosocial behaviors that compete with the undesired target behavior.

As for overcorrection, brief periods of restitution and practice (only a few minutes) have been effective in suppressing behavior (see Foxx & Bechtel, 1983). Other research suggests that requiring positive practice of behaviors that are topographically similar to the target behavior results in larger initial behavior change and longer maintenance (Ollendick, Matson, & Martin, 1978). Persons employing overcorrection should carefully observe for side effects, such as the development of other undesirable behaviors, and terminate treatment if necessary. Because physical guidance is often necessary, overcorrection should be attempted only with those children who are not physically more powerful than the supervising adults.

In general, aversive consequences can often suppress antisocial behavior. However, such consequences should be embedded in a larger program that emphasizes positive reinforcement for prosocial behavior. It is not likely that programs emphasizing aversive consequences would be effective in the long run in altering conduct-disorder behaviors. Indeed, many of the side effects of punishment (e.g., emotional reactions, escape from adults, aggression) are already well established in the repertoires of such youths and could be exacerbated by a punishment program.

Multifaceted Operant Conditioning Programs

The previous discussion conveys relatively circumscribed interventions in the sense that one or two contingencies were invoked to alter one or two behaviors. Many programs are multifaceted and combine several reinforcement and punishment contingencies to change multiple behaviors. Most programs have dealt with delinquent youths and the literature is quite extensive (e.g., see Stumphauzer, 1979). Selected programs are illustrated here to convey the application of more complex interventions than isolated reinforcement or punishment contingencies.

Illustrations

Multifaceted behavioral programs have been conducted in several different settings, including special home-style facilities, psychiatric hospitals, prisons, schools, and the community at large. Perhaps the best known of behavioral interventions is the program at Achievement Place (in Kansas) which is conducted for youths (ages 10 to 16) who have been adjudicated for a variety of offenses, primarily felonies. Diverse diagnoses have been applied to the population, including personality disorder, adjustment reaction, and conduct disorder. Because the program is community-based and youths are not confined to the facility, children who commit violent offenses (murder, rape, armed robbery) and who might require restriction are excluded (Kirigin, Wolf, Braukmann, Fixsen, & Phillips, 1979).

The program is conducted in a home-style situation in which a small number of boys or girls (usually 6 to 8) live with a specially trained married couple referred to as teaching parents. In the setting, the children participate in a token economy in which a variety of self-care (e.g., room cleaning), social (e.g., communicating with peers, participating in group activity), and academic (e.g., reading, completing homework) behaviors are reinforced. The reinforcers are provided in a point system, with several rewards and privileges that can be earned. The latter include an allowance; access to TV, games, and tools; and permission to go downtown or stay up late. Points can be lost for failure to meet particular responsibilities (e.g., to maintain passing\grades in school) or violation of rules (e.g., being late in returning home, lying, stealing). The program is managed by the teaching parents, who complete special training in the general principles and practical skills needed to administer the program effectively. In addition to reinforcement and punishment techniques, several other procedures are included, such as training children in specific skill areas (e.g., vocational training); offering them experience in self-government, whereby they decide many of the consequences for their behavior; and providing a close interpersonal relationship with the teaching parents as well as a structured family situation (e.g., Wolf et al., 1976).

Several studies have demonstrated the effects of reinforcement and punishment contingencies on such behaviors as aggressive statements, completion of homework and chores, keeping up on current events, and communication skills (e.g., Phillips, Phillips, Wolf & Fixsen, 1973; Werner et al., 1975). In addition, while the youths were in the program, the gains were reflected in a reduction in criminal offenses in the community. The youths engaged in fewer criminal offenses than did others in community-based or more traditional institutional programs (Kirigin, Braukmann, Atwater, & Wolf, 1982).

The teaching-family model has been extended to over 150 group homes throughout the United States and in a few foreign countries (Jones, Weinrott, & Howard, 1981). Evaluations of these extensions across multiple settings have not supported the efficacy of the procedures on community measures. Measures of offenses and reinstitutionalization—for from 1 to 3 years after participation in the program—are no different for youths who complete the program than for those who participate in more traditional programs (Jones et al., 1981; Kirigin et al., 1979, 1982). Thus, the evidence has been relatively consistent in showing gains during treatment but not thereafter.

Multifaceted behavioral programs for delinquent youths have been conducted in institutional settings where youths are confined. For example, Hobbs and Holt (1976) utilized a token economy for 125 adjudicated boys (ages 12 to 15) in a correctional institution. The majority had six or more charges ranging from truancy and unmanageability to arson and homicide. The program was implemented in separate cottages in the facility. Target behaviors included engaging in appropriate peer interaction, following the rules of the cottage, following instructions from staff, and not engaging in verbal and physical aggression. Tokens delivered for these appropriate behaviors were backed by candy, toys, games, the opportunity to go home on a pass or attend athletic events, and other rewards. The effects of the program were evaluated in a multiple-baseline design across separate cottages over a 14-month period. As evident in Figure 7.2, when treatment was introduced to each cottage, appropriate behavior increased. The program was not introduced and at one of the cottages (D), which served as a control, no changes were evident there. The pattern of results across the cottages reflects the impact of the program. However, no data were provided on the impact of treatment after the youths left the cottage setting.

Walker, Hops, and Greenwood (1981) have reported a multifaceted program for remediation of aggressive behavior among elementary school children (kindergarten through third grade). The target behaviors were identified through initial work on characteristics that distinguish aggressive children from their normal peers. A number of behaviors were selected (e.g., teasing, provoking fights, arguing, making threats, speaking in an irritable fashion). The program was conducted both on the playground and in the classroom; it included several procedures to alter negative and aggressive behavior. Social-skills training was provided by a trainer who taught children to discriminate appropriate and inappropriate behaviors. Reinforcement and punishment contingencies on the playground consisted of praise for appropriate interactions and response cost (loss of points given at the beginning of recess) for aggressive social interactions or violation of rules of the playground. Time out was also used (sitting out the recess period) if all points were lost. A similar program was use in the classroom if the child's behavior was a problem there. Group and individual contingencies were often combined to obtain peer support and reinforcement of the child's appropriate behavior.

The program involved several persons, including a special consultant to help design and implement the procedures, the teacher, parents, and peers. All were involved in some way to promote change across different settings and to maximize generalization. Evaluation of the special program showed that reinforcement and punishment contingencies were effective in reducing negative and aggressive behavior to within the range of normal peers. Although some of the gains were lost when the program was discontinued and children returned to regular classes, improvements were still evident. Moreover, the gains generalized to classroom and playground periods where the intervention was not in effect.

A final illustration conveys the use of reinforcement procedures on an outpatient basis. Fo and O'Donnell (1974, 1975) developed a large-scale program for youths (ages 11 to 17) with various behavioral and academic problems. The youths were referred from public schools, the police, courts, and social welfare agencies. Adults were recruited from the community to work as therapists and to conduct behavior modification programs individually with the youths. They met

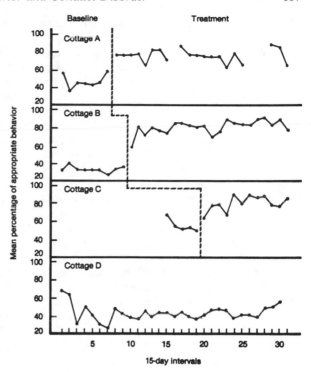

Figure 7.2. Mean percentage of appropriate behavior as treatment was introduced across each cottage in a multiple-baseline design. The final cottage served as a no-treatment control condition. From "The effects of token reinforcement on the behavior of delinquents in cottage settings," by T. R. Hobbs and M. M. Holt, 1976, *Journal of Applied Behavior Analysis, 9,* 189–198. Copyright 1976 by the Society for the Experimental Analysis of Behavior, Inc. Reprinted by permission.

with the youths, engaged in a variety of activities (e.g., arts and crafts, fishing, camping), and implemented and evaluated behavior modification programs. Individualized reward programs focused on such behaviors as truancy, fighting, completing chores at home, and homework. Social and token reinforcement (money) were used to alter these behaviors. The results indicated changes in truancy, fighting, staying out late, and other problem behaviors in relation to the behavior of control youths who did not receive treatment (Fo & O'Donnell, 1975). Also, over a 2-year follow-up period, arrest records reflected treatment gains relative to no-treatment controls (O'Donnell, Lydgate, & Fo, 1979). However, the effects of the program varied as a function of whether the children had a prior record of offenses. Youths who completed the program and who had no prior arrest record became worse with treatment, as reflected by an increase in their rates of major offenses. This finding was possibly due to the contact that these children had, over the course of the project, with others who had committed more serious offenses. In any case, the results were mixed, showing clearly beneficial and deleterious effects as a function of different histories of deviant behavior among the youths.

The multifaceted behavioral programs highlight the use of relatively complex procedures beyond isolated reinforcement or punishment contingencies. Gains during or after treatment cannot be attributed to any particular component of the program. Indeed, factors regarded as particularly significant in traditional treatment procedures, such as the therapeutic relationship, may play a major role in outcome. For example, in the Achievement Place program, the number of delinquent and behavioral-problem acts the youths performed during their stay at the home was inversely correlated with variables that reflect the relationships youths had with the teaching parents. In separate reports encompassing over 10 homes, self-reported or recorded acts of delinquency were inversely correlated with the amount of time the youths spent talking with or in close proximity to their teaching parents and to the youths' ratings of the fairness, concern, pleasantness, and similar characteristics of these parents (Kirigin et al., 1982; Solnick, Braukmann, Bedington, Kirigin & Wolf, 1981).

Recommendations

Multifaceted programs are based on combinations of the reinforcement and punishment contingencies noted previously. Consequently, specific recommendations for their constituent techniques readily apply. Multifaceted programs often include additional complexities such as special settings and contingencies that are implemented to alter behavior in less structured situations. For example, a program implemented in family-style setting that addresses chores, interpersonal interaction, mealtime behavior, and self-care is more than a minor extension of a circumscribed reinforcement program such as one implemented in a classroom to control on-task behavior. As a result of this difference, often more staff and more highly trained staff are required in multifaceted intervention programs. Implementation of the desired contingencies and—perhaps as important—administration of consequences for the many desired behaviors that might fall outside of these contingencies are critical. Thus, in everyday interaction in an institutional setting or on the playground at a school, praise for appropriate behavior is critical and extends beyond the contingencies that might be administered in a highly circumscribed program. Training of staff and ensuring that the contingencies are implemented are always critical. However, as the program becomes more complex, there are increased opportunities for decay.

Overall Evaluation

Reinforcement, punishment, and combined programs discussed previously only sample the vast literature on various disruptive behaviors and conduct problems with children and adolescents. The examples fail to represent the range of effective consequences and the settings in which they have been applied. For example, many programs are based upon the use of reinforcing activities, privileges, and various consumable and social reinforcers to alter aggressive behavior in children (e.g., Doke, Wolery, & Sumberg, 1983). Also, in some programs, contingencies are implemented in quite novel settings such as at summer camps (e.g., Hughes, 1979). In addition, a variety of different types of reinforcement schedules are available to decrease or eliminate undesirable behaviors (Kazdin, 1989). The examples also fail to convey the obvious, namely, that incentive systems do not always alter antisocial behavior (Weathers & Liberman, 1975; Wodarski & Pedi, 1978).

In most applications, reinforcement and punishment techniques are combined, so that consequences for appropriate and inappropriate behavior are provided. Punishment alone may decrease specific behaviors, but it does not develop acceptable behaviors. Consequently, re-

inforcement techniques are usually emphasized. In some applications with children with conduct problems, reinforcement alone, such as social approval for appropriate behavior, shows little or no effect without the simultaneous use of mild punishment, such as time out (Herbert et al., 1973; Wahler & Fox, 1980a). In general, the combined use of reinforcement and punishment appears to maximize the behavior change in operant conditioning programs and is more effective than either procedure alone (e.g., Pfiffner & O'Leary, 1987; Walker et al., 1981).

In light of the above, there is little question that operant conditioning-based interventions can reduce aggressive behavior and conduct disorder and increase prosocial behavior. An advantage of the techniques is that they provide relatively clear guidelines for intervention strategies. There are limitations in what the studies have shown in relation to aggressive behavior and conduct disorder. These include the tendency to focus on one or a few target behaviors rather than on the larger constellation of antisocial behaviors in which that behavior may be embedded. Thus, the often dramatic effects achieved with a particular behavior is tempered by the absence of information on related behaviors that may not have been addressed.

The infrequent evaluation of long-term effects raises another issue. Because of the recalcitrance of antisocial behaviors to change, there is a strong likelihood that conduct problems will return and continue. Consequently, demonstrations of long-term impact on the constellation of antisocial behavior are also greatly needed. At this point, the literature is impressive in demonstrating the range of techniques that can be used to alter aggressive behavior in diverse settings. Further demonstrations are needed that apply the approach more broadly—that is, to address multiple behaviors and domains of functioning.

SOCIAL-SKILLS TRAINING

Characteristics
Social skills training (SST) refers to a behavioral treatment approach that has been widely applied to children, adolescents, and adults. Training focuses on the verbal and nonverbal behaviors that affect social interactions. Specific behaviors are developed to enhance the child's ability to influence his or her environment, to obtain ap-

propriate outcomes, and to respond appropriately to the demands of others.

The underlying rationale for SST is drawn from the notion that conduct problems in children are basically interpersonal problems. Children are often identified as in need of treatment because their behaviors have deleterious effects on others, as evidenced by aggressive acts, destruction of property, noncompliant behavior, negativism, and tantrums. Several maladaptive patterns of social interaction among children have been implicated in clinical dysfunction. For example, asocial behavior, social isolation, and unpopularity in childhood are risk factors for childhood psychopathology, delinquency and conduct problems, dropping out of school, and antisocial behavior in adulthood (e.g., Cowen et al., 1973; Hartup, 1970; Roff, Sells, & Golden, 1972).

SST has been applied to withdrawn, isolated, and aggressive children (see Michelson, Sugai, Wood, & Kazdin, 1983). In each case, the assumption is made that children suffer from social skills deficits (i.e., a lack of responses in their repertoires that will enable them to act appropriately in their environment). Different lines of evidence suggest that children with conduct problems suffer deficiencies in their responses in social situations. For example, children who are disruptive at school and are delinquent are less likely than their normal peers to identify appropriate solutions to interpersonal problems (e.g., Deluty, 1981; Freedman et al., 1978; Richard & Dodge, 1982; Spivack, Platt, & Shure, 1976). Moreover, the solutions to interpersonal problems that are suggested often rely on physical force, such as aggressive responses to others.

SST develops a variety of interpersonal skills, usually in the context of individual treatment sessions. Typically, training includes several procedures to develop the skills, including instructions, modeling by the therapist, practice by the child, corrective feedback, and social reinforcement (praise) for appropriate performance. The sequence of these procedures is enacted with several interpersonal situations, as in interactions with parents, siblings, and peers. In each situation, the child and therapist role-play the appropriate behaviors. Instructions convey what the child is to do, what the overall purpose is (e.g., "It is important to be positive when interacting with others. Look at the other person when talking."), and what features of

the behavior actually are to be emphasized. Modeling by the therapist shows exactly how the behavior should be performed. Feedback from the therapist conveys how the child's responses might be improved. The therapist may model what the child has done and show the child how the action may be done differently. The child again enacts the desired behaviors. If they are appropriate, the therapist provides social reinforcement. The general sequence is continued until the child's responses are appropriate in particular situations and across a large number of different situations.

Illustrations

As an example, Elder, Edelstein, and Narick (1979) used SST with four adolescents who had been hospitalized (from 2 months to 5 years). Each had a history of verbal and physical aggressiveness. Based on the behavior checklist ratings and interviews with the youths, the following behaviors were selected for treatment: interrupting others, responding to negative provocation, and making requests of others. Role-play situations were devised in which training was conducted. Training was carried out in a group in which each person had an opportunity to role-play and to observe others enact the situation. Treatment was evaluated in a multiple-baseline design in which the behaviors were trained in sequence using instructions, modeling, practice, and feedback, as highlighted earlier. The effects of training on those situations in which behaviors were developed (training scenes) and in novel situations in which there was no specific skills training (generalization scenes) can be seen in Figure 7.3. The results indicated improvements when the training regimen was introduced for each particular behavior. The improvements were associated with increases in social behaviors on the ward and with decreases in the frequency of seclusion for inappropriate behavior. Three of the four subjects were discharged and were reported to have maintained their gains up to 9 months later.

As another example, Spence and Marzillier (1981) applied SST to male offenders (ages 10 to 16) who resided in a special school. SST consisted of 12 one-hour sessions that utilized instructions, modeling, role play, feedback, reinforcement, and other components. Attention-placebo subjects met for an equal amount of time, viewed films, and enacted and taped their

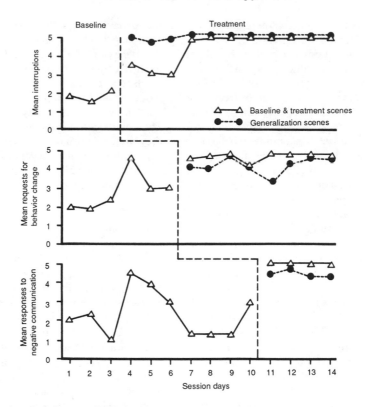

Figure 7.3. Ratings of target behaviors during baseline (pretreatment) and treatment phases for scenes used in treatment and novel scenes used to measure generalization. Higher ratings reflect more socially appropriate behaviors. From J. P. Elder, B. A. Edelstein, and M. M. Narick, "Adolescent psychiatric patients: Modifying aggressive behavior with social skills training." *Behavior Modification, 3,* pp. 161–178, copyright by Sage Publications. Reprinted by permission of Sage Publications, Inc.

own social play situations. No-treatment control subjects had no contact with therapists but were in the same residential program as the other youths. The results indicated that SST improved behaviors on role-play measures (e.g., eye contact) in comparison to the other groups. On broader measures of social skills, including staff ratings of social behavior; social workers' ratings of work, school, and family relationships; and self-report and police records of offenses (up to 6 months after treatment), there were no consistent differences favoring SST. Thus, training had an impact on highly specific measures of social skills included in training, but the effects were not evident on broader measures of social behavior.

Evaluation

Several studies have demonstrated that social skills can be developed in aggressive and conduct-problem children and adolescents (Born-

stein, Bellack, & Hersen, 1980; Matson, Kazdin, & Esveldt-Dawson, 1980). In such investigations, the focus is usually on specific behaviors in simulated social situations. These behaviors include hostile tone of voice, eye contact, content of verbal statements, making appropriate requests of others, and responding appropriately to unreasonable requests. The evidence on the effectiveness of training for aggressive children comes mainly from studies with small samples of only one or a few children. Group studies on the effectiveness of SST have been conducted primarily with socially withdrawn children (Michelson et al., 1983). The effects of SST on adjustment in the community and over the course of follow-up have been evaluated infrequently (e.g., Gross, Brigham, Hopper, & Bologna, 1980). Thus, the therapeutic impact, apart from changes in highly specific behaviors within the treatment setting, is difficult to evaluate.

Recommendations

The techniques designed to develop social skills are relatively straightforward in the sense that they reflect application of instructions, modeling, practice, feedback, and reinforcement. These are used repeatedly until the individual acquires the target behaviors and performance reaches a criterion level. A number of manuals are available that describe and illustrate the manner in which training is conducted (Kelly, 1982; Michelson et al., 1983). Critical issues must be addressed before training begins. An initial issue is to identify the specific behaviors that are to be developed. In many social-skills studies, behaviors such as initiating conversation, making requests assertively rather than aggressively, refusing unreasonable requests from others, making eye contact with the other person, and responding to the friendly overtures of others have served as the focus. It is likely that antisocial youths have deficits in these areas. However, that alone does not serve as a strong warrant for their focus in treatment. Selecting behaviors for training requires a stronger conceptual or empirical connection that establishes how the development of these social skills will alter the constellation of conduct disorder. It is not clear that the teaching of social skills will address the antisocial behaviors that serve as the primary basis of concern. In any case, for the application of treatment, selection of the target behaviors should be as closely related as possible to the areas that relate to antisocial behavior.

A related issue is selection of the stimulus conditions in which the behaviors are developed. Typically, a number of situations in which the social skills are practiced are selected. These often address generic social situations. It might be advisable to sample a wide range of situations emphasizing those related to the performance of antisocial behavior. Training and generalization situations are often included in studies of social-skills training. Generalization in this context usually involves novel situations that were not included in training. In using this approach, it is important to consider another use of generalization in the sense of training social behaviors broadly across a variety of situations involving interactions with parents, teachers, peers, and siblings, and under a variety of circumstances (e.g., shopping with parents, being tempted by peers).

Finally, treatment may be enhanced if practice and reinforcement of the skills extends to situations other than specific training sessions. Others such as parents, teachers, and peers might be incorporated into training to help the child develop skills in everyday interactions. Practice assignments for the child and reinforcement contingencies administered by parents and teachers are examples of procedures that might be useful to incorporate into training. As part of treatment, it is essential to show that the changes have impact on measures of conduct. The assumption that overcoming deficits in social skills will reduce antisocial behaviors and increase prosocial behaviors has rarely been tested.

PARENT- AND FAMILY-BASED TREATMENT

Parent Management Training

Characteristics

Parent management training (PMT) refers to procedures in which a parent or parents are trained to interact differently with their child. Training is based on the general view that problem behavior is inadvertently developed and sustained in the home by maladaptive parent–child interactions. In fact, research has shown that parents of antisocial youths engage in several practices that promote aggressive behavior and suppress prosocial behavior (Patterson, 1982). These practices include the inadvertent and direct reinforcement of aggressive behavior, frequent use of commands, nonreinforcement of prosocial behaviors, and others. PMT alters the pattern of interchanges between parent and child so that prosocial, rather than aggressive, behavior is directly fostered within the family.

Although many variations of PMT exist, several common characteristics can be identified. First, treatment is conducted primarily with the parents, who directly implement several procedures in the home. There usually is no direct intervention by the therapist with the child. Second, parents are trained to identify, define, and observe problem behavior in new ways. The careful specification of the problem is essential for the delivery of reinforcing or punishing consequences and for evaluating the program's effectiveness.

Third, the treatment sessions cover social-learning principles and the procedures that follow from them, including positive reinforcement (e.g., the use of social praise and tokens or points for prosocial behavior), mild punishment (e.g., use of time out from reinforcement, loss of privileges), negotiation, and contingency contracting. Fourth, the sessions provide opportunities for parents to see how the techniques are implemented, to practice using the techniques, and to review the behavior change programs in the home.

The immediate goal of the program is to develop specific skills in the parents. This is usually achieved by having parents apply their skills to relatively simple behaviors that can be observed easily and are not enmeshed with more provoking interactions (e.g., punishment, battles of will, coercive interchanges). As the parents become more proficient, the program can address the child's most severely problematic behaviors and encompass other problem areas (e.g., school behavior).

Case Study

The application of PMT can be illustrated by the case of Shawn, a 7-year-old boy referred for treatment because of his aggressive outbursts toward his two younger sisters at home as well as his peers at school. He argued and had severe tantrums at home, stayed out late at night, and occasionally stole from his stepfather, who lived in the home. At school, his behavior in class was difficult to control. He fought with peers, argued with the teacher, and disrupted the class. PMT was provided to the mother. The stepfather could not attend the meetings on a regular basis because of his work as a trucker and his extended periods away from home. Training began by discussing Shawn's behavior and childrearing practices that might be useful in making him more sociable as well as in reducing or eliminating the problems for which he was referred.

A master's degree-level clinician trained in PMT for over 2 years administered treatment. She agreed to meet with the parents once each week for approximately 16 sessions. The overall goal of treatment was to train the parents to behave differently in relation to Shawn and their other children. Specifically, the mother, who attended all the sessions, was trained to identify concrete behaviors to address her and her husband's concerns, to observe these behaviors systematically, to implement positive reinforcement programs, to provide mild punishment as

needed, and to negotiate such programs directly with the child.

The contents of the 16 sessions provided to the mother are highlighted in Table 7.3. In each session, the trainer reviewed the previous week's data collection and implementation of the program. The purpose was to see how both of the parents behaved in relation to their children. Queries were made to review precisely what the parents did (e.g., praise, administer points or tokens, send the child to time out) in response to the child's behavior. In the sessions, the mother would invariably focus on the behavior of the child and how well or poorly the child was doing. However, the trainer directed the conversation toward the behaviors that the parents performed in relation to the child. The trainer and the mother role-played situations to show how the parents might have responded more effectively. The mother practiced delivering the consequences and received feedback and reinforcement for this behavior from the trainer. Any problems in the programs, ambiguity of the observation procedures, or other facets were discussed. Thus, the initial portion of the session was used to review practical issues and applications for the previous week. After the program was reviewed, new material was taught, as outlined in Table 7.3.

Each session with Shawn's mother lasted about 2 hours. Between the weekly sessions, the trainer called the parent on two occasions to find out how the programs were working and to handle problems that had arisen. The calls between sessions were designed to correct problems immediately instead of waiting until the end of the week. Shawn's mother and the therapist developed a program to increase Shawn's compliance with requests. Simple chores were requested (e.g., cleaning his room, setting the table) in the first few weeks of the program to help both parents apply what the mother had learned. Time out from reinforcement was introduced to provide mild punishment for fighting. Any fights in the home led to Shawn's being isolated in the hall near the kitchen of his home for a period of 5 minutes. If he went to time out immediately upon instructions from his mother or stepfather, the duration of time out was automatically reduced to 2 minutes.

Over time, several behaviors were incorporated into a program where Shawn earned points that could be exchanged for special privileges (e.g., staying up 15 minutes beyond bedtime,

Table 7.3. Parent Management Training Sessions for the Case of Shawn

SESSION	TOPIC	BRIEF DESCRIPTION
1.	Introduction and Overview	This session provided the mother with an overview of the program and outlined the demands placed upon them and the focus of the intervention.
2.	Defining and Observing	This session trained the mother to pinpoint, define, and observe behavior. The mother and trainer defined specific problems that could be observed and developed a specific plan to begin observations.
3.	Positive Reinforcement	This session focused on learning the concept of positive reinforcement, factors that contribute to the effective application, and rehearsal of applications in relation to the target child. Specific programs were outlined where praise and points were to be provided for the behaviors observed during the week.
4.	Review of the Program and Data	Observations of the previous week as well as application of the reinforcement program were reviewed. Details about the administration of praise, points, and backup reinforcers were discussed and enacted as needed so the trainer could identify how to improve parent performance. Changes were made in the program as needed.
5.	Time Out From Reinforcement	The mother learned about time out and the factors related to its effective application. The use of time out was planned for the next week for specific behaviors.
6.	Shaping	The mother was trained to develop behaviors by reinforcement of successive approximations and to use prompts and fading of prompts to develop terminal behaviors.
7.	Review and Problem Solving	In this session, the concepts discussed in all prior sessions were thoroughly reviewed. The mother was asked to apply these concepts to hypothetical situations presented within the session. Areas of weakness in understanding the concepts or their execution in practice served as the focus.
8.	Attending and Ignoring	In this session, the mother learned about attending and ignoring and chose undesirable behavior that she would ignore and a positive opposite behavior to which she would attend. These procedures were practiced within the session.
9.	School Intervention	In this session, plans were made to implement a home-based reinforcement program to develop school-related behaviors. Prior to this session, discussions with the teachers and parents had identified specific behaviors to focus on in class (e.g., deportment) and at home (e.g., homework completion). These behaviors were incorporated into the reinforcement system.
10.	Reprimands	The mother was trained in effective use of reprimands.
11.	Family Meeting	At this meeting, the child and both parents were brought into the session. The programs were discussed along with any problems. Revisions were made as needed to correct misunderstandings or to alter facets that may not have been implemented in a way that was likely to be effective.
12.	Review of Skills	Here the programs were reviewed along with all concepts about the principles. The mother was asked to develop programs for a variety of hypothetical everyday problems at home and at school. Feedback was provided regarding program options and applications.
13.	Negotiating and Contracting	The child and mother met together to negotiate new be-

Table 7.3. Parent Management Training Sessions for the Case of Shawn (*continued*)

SESSION	TOPIC	BRIEF DESCRIPTION
		havioral programs and to place them in contractual form.
14.	Low-Rate Behavior	The mother was trained to deal with low-rate behaviors such as fire setting, stealing, or truancy. Specific punishment programs were planned and presented to the child as needed for behaviors characteristic of the case.
15, 16, & 17.	Review, Problem Solving, and Practice	Material from other sessions was reviewed in theory and practice. Special emphasis was given to role-playing application of individual principles as they were enacted with the trainer. The mother practiced designing new programs, revising ailing programs, and responding to a complex array of situations in which principles and practices discussed in prior sessions were reviewed.

having a friend sleep over, small prizes, time to play his video game). About halfway through treatment, a home-based reinforcement program was developed to alter Shawn's behaviors at school. Two teachers at the school were contacted and asked to identify target behaviors. For their part in the program, they were asked to initial cards carried by Shawn to indicate how well he behaved in class and whether he completed his homework. On the basis of these daily teacher evaluations, Shawn earned additional points at home.

After approximately 5 months, Shawn had improved greatly in his behavior at home. He argued very little with his mother and sisters. His parents felt they were able to manage him much better. At school, Shawn's teacher reported that he could remain in class like other children. Occasionally, he would not listen to the teacher or get into heated arguments with peers on the playground. However, he was less physically aggressive than he had been prior to treatment.

Evaluation

The effectiveness of PMT has been evaluated in scores of outcome studies with behavior-problem children varying in age and degree of severity of dysfunction (see Kazdin, 1985). The work of Patterson and his colleagues, spanning more than two decades, exemplifies the ongoing development of a conceptual model and outcome research on parent training with antisocial youths (see Patterson, 1986). Over 200 families have been seen that include primarily aggressive children (ages 3 to 12 years) referred for outpatient treatment (see Patterson, 1982). Several controlled studies have demonstrated marked

improvements at home and at school in child behavior over the course of treatment. Moreover, these changes surpass those achieved with variations of family-based psychotherapy, attention-placebo (discussion), and no-treatment conditions (Patterson, Chamberlain, & Reid, 1982; Walter & Gilmore, 1973; Wiltz & Patterson, 1974). PMT has brought the problematic behaviors of treated children within normative levels of their peers who are functioning adequately (Eyberg & Johnson, 1974; Patterson, 1974; Wells, Forehand, & Griest, 1980). Improvements often remain evident 1 year after treatment (e.g., Fleischman & Szykula, 1981); the continued benefits of treatment have been evident with noncompliant children to 4.5 years later (Baum & Forehand, 1981). The impact of PMT is relatively broad. The effects of treatment are evident for child behaviors not focused on directly as part of training. Also, siblings improve, even though they are not directly focused on during treatment. In addition, maternal psychopathology, particularly depression, decreases systematically following PMT. These changes suggest that PMT alters multiple aspects of dysfunctional families (see Kazdin, 1985).

Several characteristics of the treatment and the families who participate contribute to treatment outcome. Duration of treatment appears to influence outcome. Brief and time-limited treatments (e.g., less than 10 hours) are less likely to show benefits with clinical populations. More dramatic and durable effects are evident with protracted or time-unlimited programs extending up to 50 or 60 hours of treatment (see Kazdin, 1985). Specific training components such as providing parents with in-depth knowledge of social-learning principles and utilizing time out from reinforcement in the home enhance treatment effects (e.g., McMahon, Forehand, & Griest, 1981; Wahler & Fox, 1980a). Third, therapist training and skill appear to be associated with the magnitude and durability of therapeutic changes (Fleischman, 1982; Patterson, 1974), although these have yet to be carefully tested.

Parent and family characteristics also relate to treatment outcome. As might be expected, families characterized by many risk factors associated with childhood dysfunction (e.g., marital discord and parent psychopathology) tend to show fewer gains in treatment than families without these characteristics (e.g., Strain, Young, & Horowitz, 1981). Moreover, when gains are achieved in treatment, they are unlikely to be maintained in families with socioeconomic disadvantages. The social support system of the mother outside of the home also contributes to the efficacy of PMT (Dumas & Wahler, 1983). Mothers who are insulated from social supports outside the home (i.e., have few positive social contacts with relatives and friends) are less likely to profit from treatment. Thus, variables beyond the specific parent–child interactions need to be considered in treatment.

Many issues regarding the effects of PMT remain. Perhaps most significant is the need for long-term follow-up with clinically dysfunctional samples. With antisocial youths referred for aggressive behavior, follow-up typically has been completed up to 1 year. Given the recalcitrance of severe antisocial behavior, evidence is needed to assess the long-term impact.

Recommendations
PMT is one of the best-researched techniques to alter antisocial behavior among children (Kazdin, 1987b). There are many critical steps upon which effective application is likely to depend. The first has to do with the training of the persons who administer the interventions. Such persons require clear mastery of the reinforcement and punishment procedures discussed previously. It is critical for trainers to understand the principles and to be able to translate these into a wide array of feasible practices that can be implemented in the home.

The actual lesson content can vary across a variety of programs. Central to virtually all programs are sessions on the administration of reinforcement techniques and mild forms of punishment. A number of different treatment manuals are available to guide trainers regarding specific content (see Ollendick & Cerny, 1981, for a list). In addition, a number of books have been made available that are designed for parents to read as a supplement to training sessions (e.g., Clark, 1985; Patterson, 1975).

Although therapist training and treatment content are obviously important, selection of the family may be critical as well. PMT is a demanding form of treatment. Parents are required to master educational materials that convey major principles underlying the program, to observe deviant child behavior, to implement multiple procedures at home, and to respond to frequent telephone contacts made by the therapist. Many parents firmly believe that the child has the problem and has to be treated by a therapist. Requests to see the parents in treatment sessions, even when couched in a detailed rationale, are occasionally met with reluctance. In addition, families of conduct-disordered youths are often characterized by a variety of stressors, as identified in the discussion of risk factors. These factors often discourage parents from coming to sessions. In general, parents under severe stress or social disadvantage, not at all rare in clinical samples, may profit little from PMT.

Notwithstanding the potential limitations, PMT is one of the better-developed and researched techniques for conduct disorder. Among the strengths of the approach is the fact that it permits integration of several domains of the child's maladaptive functioning. Specifically, the child's interactions and behavior at home are central to the development of antisocial behavior. In addition, school behavior can be integrated into treatment. This is usually accomplished by the use of contingencies to address school-related behaviors at home (e.g., completion of homework) or to develop home-based reinforcement in which teachers evaluate the child's deportment (e.g., in-class behavior) and parents provide backup reinforcers at home on the basis of the teachers' evaluations.

Functional Family Therapy

Characteristics
Functional family therapy (FFT) reflects an integrative approach to treatment that has relied on two perspectives of human behavior and therapeutic change. The first perspective is a systems approach in which clinical problems are conceptualized from the standpoint of the func-

tions they serve in the family as a system as well as for individual family members. The assumption is that problem behavior evident in the child is the only way some interpersonal functions (e.g., intimacy, distancing, support) can be met among family members. Maladaptive processes within the family are considered to preclude a more direct means of fulfilling these functions. The goal of treatment is to alter interaction and communication patterns in such a way as to foster more adaptive functioning. The second perspective is an operational behavioral perspective. This is based on learning theory and focuses on specific stimuli and responses that can be used to produce change. Behavioral concepts and procedures identifying specific behaviors for change and reinforcing new, appropriate, adaptive ways of responding and empirically evaluating and monitoring change are included in this perspective.

More recent formulations of FFT have included a third perspective, which emphasizes cognitive processes (Morris, Alexander, & Waldron, in press). This perspective focuses on the attributions, attitudes, assumptions, expectations, and emotions of the family. Family members may begin treatment with attributions that focus on blaming others or themselves. New perspectives may be needed to help serve as the basis for developing new ways of behaving.

FFT requires that the family see the clinical problem from the relational functions it serves within the family. The therapist points out interdependencies and contingencies between family members in their day-to-day functioning and with specific reference to the problem that has served as the basis for seeking treatment. Once the family sees alternative ways of viewing the problem, the incentive for interacting more constructively is increased.

The main goals of treatment are to increase reciprocity and positive reinforcement among family members, to establish clear communication, to help specify behaviors that family members desire from each other, to negotiate constructively, and to help identify solutions to interpersonal problems. In order to develop familiarity with the concepts used in treatment, the family members read a manual that describes social-learning principles. In therapy, family members identify behaviors they would like others to perform. Responses are incorporated into a reinforcement system in the home to promote

adaptive behavior in exchange for privileges. However, the primary focus is on the treatment sessions, where family communication patterns are altered directly. During the sessions, the therapist provides social reinforcement (verbal and nonverbal praise) for communications that suggest solutions to problems, clarify problems, or offer feedback to other family members.

Illustration

An illustration of the entire process of FFT is difficult to convey because of the complex set of techniques, their relation to the nature of family functioning, and their dependence on individual features of the family. The technique is well illustrated elsewhere, where guidelines are provided for therapists (Alexander & Parsons, 1982). Selected features of the techniques can be described and illustrated to show how the technique works.

The technique requires understanding of several types of functions that behaviors can serve within the family. These functions include behaviors that family members perform to sustain contact and closeness (merging), to decrease psychological intensity and dependence (separating), and to provide a mixture of merging and separating (midpointing). These processes are intricate because they usually involve the relations of all family members with each other. Also, the behaviors of a given family member may serve multiple and opposing functions in relation to different individuals within the family. Thus, a behavior that may draw one family member close may distance another. Finally, several different behaviors (e.g., the fighting of a child with a sibling, getting into trouble at school, running away from home overnight) may serve quite similar functions (e.g., to bring the mother and father together).

During the course of treatment, all family members meet. The focus of treatment is to identify consistent patterns of behavior, the range of functions they serve, and messages they send. A number of specific techniques that can be used to focus on relations in therapy are used. The specific techniques, goals, and illustrations are presented in Table 7.4.

A number of other strategies are employed during the course of treatment. These include not blaming individuals; relabeling thoughts, feelings, and behaviors to take into account relational components; discussing the implications of symptom removal; changing the context

Table 7.4. Selected Therapy Techniques in Functional Family Therapy

TECHNIQUE	GOAL
Asking Questions	To help focus on the relationships raised by the issue or problem. Example: After a description of an event involving the child (named Ginger) and the mother, the therapist may ask the father, "How do you fit into all of this?"
Making Comments	To help identify and clarify relationships. Example: The therapist may say to the father, "So you are drawn into this argument when your wife gets upset."
Offering Interpretations	To go beyond the obvious observations by inferring possible motivational states, effects on others, and antecedents. Example: The therapist may say, "So when you have an argument, you believe that this is a message that you are needed. But at the same time you feel pushed away."
Identifying Sequences	To point to the relations among sequences or patterns of behavior to see more complex effects of interactions, i.e., several functional relations over time. Example: The therapist says (to mother), "It seems to me that the argument between Ginger and you make both you and your husband upset. This leads to everyone arguing for a while about who did what and what has to be done and no one agrees. But after the dust settles, you both (to mother and father) have something to talk about and to work on. This brings you both together at least for a little while. And this may help you a lot too, Ginger, because you don't get to see your mother and father talking together like this very often."
Using the Therapist as a Direct Tool	To have the therapist refer to his or her relation to the family within the session and what functions this could serve. Example: The therapist says, "I feel as if I am still being asked to choose sides here because it may serve a function similar to the one that Ginger serves. That is, to help bring you two together. That's not good or bad. But we need to see how we can get you two together when there is no argument or battle with a third party."
Stopping and Starting Interaction	To intervene to alter interactions between or among family members. The purpose may be to induce new lines of communication, to develop relations between members not initiating contact, or to point out functions evident at the moment. Example: The therapist says to Ginger and father, "What do you two have to say about the effect that this has on each of you?" (Without asking the mother to comment here.)

of the symptom to help alter the functions it may have served; and shifting the focus from one problem or person to another. FFT is designed not merely to identify functional relations but also to build new and more adaptive ways of functioning. Communication patterns are altered and efforts are made to provide families with concrete ways of behaving differently, both in the sessions and at home (see Alexander & Parsons, 1982).

Evaluation
The few available outcome studies of FFT have shown relatively clear effects. The initial study included male and female delinquent adolescents referred to juvenile court for such behav-iors as running away, truancy, theft, and unmanageability (Parsons & Alexander, 1973). Cases were assigned to FFT, an attention-placebo condition (group discussion and expression of feeling), or a no-treatment control group. Posttreatment evaluation after 8 treatment sessions revealed that FFT led to greater discussion among family members, more equitable speaking, and more spontaneous speech than did the attention-placebo and no-treatment conditions.

In an extension of the above program, Alexander and Parsons (1973) compared FFT, client-centered family groups, psychodynamically oriented family therapy, and no treatment. The FFT group showed greater improvement on family interaction measures and lower recidivism rates from juvenile court records up to 18 months after treatment. Follow-up data obtained 2½ years later indicated that the siblings of those who received FFT showed significantly lower rates of referral to juvenile courts (Klein, Alexander, & Parsons, 1977). Thus, the results suggest significant changes on index children as well as their siblings.

FFT shows obvious promise, notwithstanding the paucity of studies and independent replication attempts. From the few available studies, several statements can be supported. First, the effectiveness of treatment is influenced by the relationship (e.g., warmth, integration of affect and behavior) and structuring (e.g., directiveness) skills of the therapist (Alexander, Barton, Schiavo, & Parsons, 1976). Second, process measures of family interactions at posttreatment are related to subsequent recidivism (Alexander & Parsons, 1973). This finding lends credence to the model from which treatment was derived. Finally, in the outcome studies, client-centered and psychodynamically oriented forms of family-based therapies have not achieved the positive effects of FFT. Thus treatment of the clinical problem at the level of the family per se does not appear to be sufficient to alter antisocial behavior.

Recommendations

FFT represents a promising treatment for families with antisocial children. As with parent training, there are some obvious minimal conditions that need to be invoked to carry out therapy. To begin, the family obviously needs to agree to come to treatment. In clinically referred families this requirement excludes a large percentage of cases. It is often difficult to obtain one parent because some of the conditions surrounding antisocial behavior (e.g., parent psychopathology, social disadvantage, large family size) affect the priority of treatment for the parents or the feasibility of attending sessions.

Second and related, for many families a functional approach is likely to be problematic. Many parents clearly believe the problem is "in the child" and that a no-nonsense approach (e.g., teach the child to act differently, punish the child) is needed. In such cases, the prospect of entering into the dynamics of family life is often not welcome or understood. The therapist's task, of course, is to reframe the "child's problem" into a larger family and interactional context.

For many clinically dysfunctional families, this may be an insurmountable task.

The extent to which the reservations noted here restrict the application of FFT is not known. Hence, in advance, they should not be used to preclude the application of the intervention. Currently available materials (e.g., Alexander & Parsons, 1982) suggest that the approach does not engage in a high level of inference away from the direct observations of family interaction and discussion. It is relatively straightforward in addressing interactions concretely and providing directives regarding new ways to change such interactions. These advantages may counteract the points noted previously.

COGNITIVELY BASED TREATMENT

Alternative interventions have focused on those cognitive processes (perceptions, self-statements, attributions, and problem-solving skills) that are presumed to underlie the child's maladaptive behavior. Cognitive processes are frequently accorded a major role in aggressive behavior (Berkowitz, 1977; Novaco, 1978). Aggression is not triggered by environmental events alone but also by the way in which these events are perceived and processed. This processing involves the child's appraisals of the situation, anticipated reactions of others, and self-statements in response to particular events. Clinic and nonreferred children identified as aggressive have shown a predisposition to attribute hostile intent to others, especially in social situations where the cues of actual intent are ambiguous (Dodge, 1985). Understandably, when situations are initially perceived as hostile, children are more likely to react aggressively. The ability to take the perspective of or empathize with other persons is also related to aggressive behavior. For example, among delinquents, those who are aggressive (i.e., who have committed acts against other persons or property) are less empathic than nonaggressive delinquents (see Ellis, 1982). Perspective taking appears to increase with age among normal children and adolescents and to be inversely related to the expression of aggression (Feshbach, 1975).

Problem-Solving Skills Training

The relationship between cognitive processes and behavioral adjustment has been evaluated extensively by Spivack and Shure (1982; Shure

& Spivack, 1978; Spivack et al, 1976). These investigators have identified different cognitive processes or interpersonal cognitive problem-solving skills that underlie social behavior (see Table 7.5). The ability to engage in these processes is related to behavioral adjustment, as measured in teacher ratings of disruptive behavior and social withdrawal. Disturbed children tend to generate fewer alternative solutions to interpersonal problems, to focus on ends or goals rather than the intermediate steps to obtain them, to see fewer consequences associated with their behavior, to fail to recognize the causes of other people's behavior, and to be less sensitive to interpersonal conflict.

Characteristics

Problem-solving skills training (PSST) consists of developing those interpersonal problem-solving skills in which children with conduct problems are considered to be deficient. Many variations of PSST have emerged (Camp & Bash, 1985; Kendall & Braswell, 1985; Spivack et al., 1976), and these variations share many characteristics. First, the emphasis is on how children approach situations. Although it is obviously important that children ultimately select appropriate means of behaving in everyday life, the primary focus is more on the thought process rather than on the outcomes or specific behavioral acts that result. Second, children are taught to engage in a step-by-step approach to solving interpersonal problems. They make statements to themselves that direct attention to certain aspects of the problem and to the steps that will lead to effective solutions. Third, treatment utilizes structured academic activities, and stories. Over the course of treatment, the cognitive problem-solving skills are increasingly applied

to real-life situations. Fourth, the therapist usually plays an active role in treatment. He or she models the cognitive processes by making verbal self-statements, applies the sequence of statements to particular problems, provides cues to prompt use of the skills, and delivers feedback and praise to develop correct use of the skills. Finally, treatment usually combines several different procedures, including modeling and practice, role playing, and reinforcement and mild punishment (loss of points or tokens).

Case Study

The application of PSST can be illustrated more concretely in a case application. Cory, a 10-year-old boy, was hospitalized in a short-term children's inpatient unit. He was to begin a treatment regimen designed to control his aggressive and disruptive behavior at home and at school. At home, Cory constantly fought with his siblings, stole personal possessions from all family members, swore, disobeyed family rules, and refused to participate in family activities. He had been caught on three occasions playing with matches and setting fires in his room. At school, Cory had been in fights with several of his peers in class. He threatened peers, ran around the classroom throwing crayons and pencils as if they were darts, and hit the teacher with various toys and supplies. Before coming for treatment, he was suspended from school for assaulting a classmate and choking him to the point that the child almost lost consciousness.

PSST was begun and completed while Cory was in the hospital because his parents said they could not bring him back for treatment on an outpatient basis once hospitalization had ended. Cory received 20 individual sessions of PSST,

Table 7.5. Interpersonal Cognitive Problem-Solving Skills

SKILL	DESCRIPTION
Alternative Solution Thinking	The ability to generate different options (solutions) that can solve problems in interpersonal situations.
Means-End Thinking	Awareness of the intermediate steps required to achieve a particular goal.
Consequential Thinking	The ability to identify what might happen as a direct result of acting in a particular way or choosing a particular solution.
Causal Thinking	The ability to relate one event to another over time and to understand why one event led to a particular action of other persons.
Sensitivity to Interpersonal Problems	The ability to perceive a problem when it exists and to identify the interpersonal aspects of the confrontation that may emerge.

Adapted from Spivack et al. (1976).

with two to three sessions being held each week. The treatment was administered by a master's degree-level social worker with special training in PSST. During the first treatment sessions, Cory was taught the problem-solving steps. These consist of specific self-statements, each representing a step for solving a problem. They are as follows:

1. What am I supposed to do?
2. I have to look at all my possibilities.
3. I have to concentrate and focus in.
4. I need to make a choice and select a solution.
5. I need to find out how I did.

In the first session, Cory was taught the steps so he could recall them without special reminders or cues from the therapist. In the next several sessions, he learned to apply the steps to simple problems involving various academic tasks (e.g., arithmetic problems) and board games (e.g., checkers). In each of these sessions, Cory's task was to find out what the goal was (e.g., to move his checkers without being jumped), what the choices were and the consequences of each, what the best choice was, and so on. In the sessions, Cory and the therapist took turns using the steps to work on the task. In these early sessions, the focus was on teaching the steps and training Cory to become facile in applying them to diverse but relatively simple situations. After session 8, the games were withdrawn and the focus shifted to applying the steps to problems that were related to interactions with parents, teachers, siblings, peers, and others.

Cory was also given assignments outside of treatment. These initially involved identifying "real" problems (e.g., with another child on the inpatient service) where he could use the steps. When he brought one of these situations to the session, he described how the steps could have been used. He earned points for bringing in such a situation, and these points could be exchanged for small prizes. As the sessions progressed, he received points not only for thinking of situations outside of treatment but also for using the steps in the actual situations. His use of the steps was checked by asking him exactly what he did, role-playing the situation within the session, and asking other staff on the ward if the events were accurate.

Most of the treatment consisted of applying the steps in the session to situations where Cory's aggressive and antisocial behaviors had emerged. To illustrate this, portions of session 17 follow:

Therapist: Well, Cory today we are going to act out some more problem situations using the steps. You have been doing so well with this that I think we can use the steps today in a way that will make it even easier to use them in everyday life. When you use the steps today, I want you to think in your mind what the first steps are. When you get to step 4, say that one out loud before you do it. This will let us see what the solution is that you have chosen. Then, step 5, when you evaluate how you did, can also be thought in your mind. We are going to do the steps in our heads today like this so that it will be easier to use them in everyday life without drawing attention to what we are doing. The same rules apply as in our other sessions. We still want to go slowly in using the steps and we want to select good solutions.

O.K., today I brought in a lot of difficult situations. I think it is going to be hard to use the steps. Let's see how each of us does. I have six stacks of cards here. You can see the stacks are numbered from 1 to 6. We will take turns rolling the die and take a card from the stack with the same number. As we did in the last session, we are going to solve the problem as we sit here, then we will get up and act it out as if it is really happening. O.K., why don't you go first and roll the die?

Cory: (rolls the die) I got a 4.

Therapist: O.K., read the top card in that stack (therapist points).

Cory: (reads the card) "The principal of your school is walking past you in the hall between classes when he notices some candy wrappers that someone has dropped on the floor. The principal turns to you and says in a pretty tough voice, 'Cory, we don't litter in the halls at this school! Now pick up the trash!' "

Therapist: This is a tough one—how are you going to handle this?

Cory: Well, here goes with the steps. (Cory holds his first finger up and appears to be saying step 1 to himself; he does this with steps 2 and 3 as well. When he gets to step 4 he says out loud) I would say to him that I did not throw the wrappers down and I would keep walking.

Therapist: Well, it was *great* that you did not get mad and talk back to him. He was sort of accusing you and you hadn't really thrown the papers down. But if you just say, "I didn't do it," and walk away, what might happen?

Cory: Nothing. Because I didn't do it.

Therapist: Yeah, but he may not believe you—maybe especially because you got into trouble before with him. Also, he asked you for a favor and you could help a lot by doing what he asked. Try going through the steps again and see if you can turn your pretty good solution into a great one.

Cory: (goes through steps 1, 2, and 3 again; at step 4 he says) I would say to him that I did not throw the wrappers down but that I would gladly pick 'em up and toss them in the trash.

Therapist: (with great enthusiasm) That's great—that's a wonderful solution! O.K. Go to step 5, how do you think you did?

Cory: I did good because I used the steps.

Therapist: That's right, but you did more than that. You nicely told the principal that you did not do it *and* you did the favor he asked: What do you think he will think of you in the future? Very nicely done. O.K. Now let's both get up and act this out. I am the principal. Why don't you stand over there (pointing to the opposite corner of the treatment room). O.K., let's start. "Hey, Cory, pick up those wrappers on the floor, you are not supposed to litter in the halls, you know better than that."

Cory: (carries out steps 1, 2, and 3 in his head. At step 4 he acts out the step directly in face-to-face interaction with the principal [i.e., therapist] and says) "Mr. Putnam, I didn't

throw these on the floor, but if you want I will pick them up and toss them in the trash."

Therapist: (acting as principal) Yeah, that would be great. Thanks for helping out; these kids make a mess of this place.

Therapist: (as herself) Well, Cory how do you think you did?

Cory: Pretty good because I used the steps and got a good solution.

Therapist: (as herself) I think you did great!

The treatment session continues like this with a variety of situations. When the child does especially well, the situation may be made a little more difficult or provocative to help him apply the steps under more challenging circumstances.

Additional Illustration

Another illustration of PSST was provided in a recent report of eight adolescents (ages 13 to 19) who resided in a state hospital (Tisdelle & St. Lawrence, 1988). Problem-solving skills were taught across different components of the problem-solving skill. Training consisted in a group format, with 45-minute sessions twice per week for a total of 13 sessions. In each session, training consisted of providing the rationale and instructions for the skill component, modeling of the component by the trainer, practice by the youths, and feedback and verbal reinforcement for use of the skill. Assessment consisted of presenting the situations used in training and evaluating how well individual skill components had been assimilated. Additional novel situations were presented in this fashion to evaluate transfer of the skills to new areas. In addition, in vivo situations in the hospital were devised to present the youths with situations that would test their new problem-solving skills.

The effects of training can be seen in Figure 7.4, which shows that each problem-solving component changed as it was addressed in training in a multiple-baseline design. The figure also shows that the skills generalized to nontraining scenes as well. Not included in the figure are the data on performance on the hospital ward itself, where in vivo assessment of skill use was conducted. The results indicated that the youths had not improved in their effectiveness in problem solving and had not applied the skills they learned. One month after treatment was completed, improvements in the in vivo situations were evident for 3 of the original 8 who were still inpatients. Staff ratings of adjustment of the patients from pre- to posttreatment had indicated no significant improvements in adjustment. Thus, the results are somewhat mixed, showing clear and robust changes on measures on the hypothetical problems during assessment but little or no change on measures of adjustment or functioning in everyday situations.

Evaluation

A number of researchers have conducted programmatic series of studies showing the efficacy of PSST (see Kendall & Braswell, 1985; Spivack & Shure, 1982). Research has established the efficacy of alternative variations on treatment. The majority of studies, however, have evaluated the impact of training on cognitive processes and laboratory-task performance rather than deviant child behavior at home or at school (see Gresham, 1985; Kazdin, 1987b). In some studies with impulsive or aggressive children and adolescents, cognitively based treatment has led to significant changes in behavior at home, at school, and in the community, and these gains were evident up to a year later (Arbuthnot & Gordon, 1986; Kazdin, Esveldt-Dawson, French, & Unis, 1987; Kendall & Braswell, 1982; Lochman, Burch, Curry, & Lampron, 1984). However, the magnitude of the changes must be greater than those currently achieved to return children to normative or adaptive levels of functioning at home and at school.

PSST at this point in time has not been shown to be an effective treatment for antisocial behavior. It can often help children with mild adjustment problems. That change is achieved at all, and that these changes cannot be attributed to such influences as exposure to specific tasks or stimulus materials and discussion of interpersonal situations, should not be treated lightly. Few studies have evaluated factors that contribute to treatment outcome. Some evidence has suggested that the greater the level of child aggression, the less effective the treatment (Kendall & Braswell, 1985). Duration of treatment influenced outcome in one study with longer treatment (more than 18 sessions), leading to greater change than shorter treatment (Lochman, 1985). However, further tests of the effects of duration among different treatments are needed.

Age and cognitive development may influence outcome as well, although these have yet to be explored in the context of clinical treatment

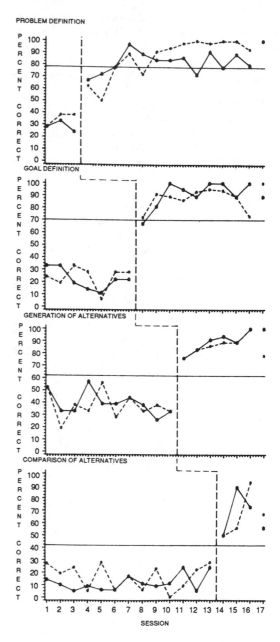

Figure 7.4. Mean percentage of occurrence for each problem-solving component by session. The solid horizontal line represents the mean for normal (nonreferred) adolescents. The solid and dashed lines represent trained and generalization problem situations which show the same pattern of improvements. From "Adolescent interpersonal problem-solving skills training: Social validation and generalization" by D. A. Tisdell, and J. S. St. Lawrence, 1988, *Behavior Therapy, 19,* 171–182. Copyright 1988 by the Association for Advancement of Behavior Therapy. Reprinted by permission of the publisher and author.

trials (Cole & Kazdin, 1980). Cognitive processes highly significant at one age (e.g., means–ends thinking in adolescents) may be less critical at other ages, such as early childhood (Spivack et al., 1976). Consequently, further work is needed to evaluate whether treatment efficacy is influenced by the type of child being treated and other factors.

Research to date has generally adopted the view that children with problems of adjustment, broadly conceived, have cognitive deficits. For example, Spivack et al. (1976) have found similar cognitive deficits of children who are socially withdrawn or who act out. Their work with adolescents and adults has also shown that drug addicts, delinquents, and schizophrenic patients evince cognitive deficits compared to nonreferred samples matched on various demographic variables. Finer distinctions must be explored to delineate the cognitive correlates or underpinnings of specific clinical problems (cf. Dodge, 1985). In turn, these distinctions may lead to more highly focused interventions that have greater impact on antisocial behavior.

Other Variations of Treatment

Most outcome studies have evaluated variations of problem-solving strategies described earlier. Other variations are worth noting in passing to convey the range of interventions included in cognitively based training, even though outcome evidence for their efficacy is sparse.

A major variation has focused on training children to take the perspective of other persons. Training in perspective- or role-taking ability is often part of a comprehensive approach to develop problem-solving skills. Applications have focused on this skill by itself with some success. The most promising work was completed by Chandler (1973), who developed role-taking skills in delinquent boys aged 11 to 13. The boys had multiple contacts with the police and had committed felonies. The treatment programs, conducted one-half day per week for 10 weeks, utilized drama and films as a means of helping the subjects to see themselves from the perspective of others and to take the roles of other people. During the sessions, the children were encouraged to develop, portray, and actually film brief skits dealing with other people their own age. Skits were repeated and filmed until each person (working in a small group) had the opportunity to participate in each role in the

plot. The films of these skits were reviewed and discussed to identify ways behavior could be improved. Trained youths improved in their role-taking skills on a standard laboratory-based measure (involving characters in cartoon sequences) relative to a no-treatment group and a placebo-control group that met to make films but did not focus on role taking. More importantly, at a follow-up assessment 1½ years later, police and court records revealed that treated subjects had fewer documented delinquent acts than control subjects.

In a subsequent study, Chandler, Greenspan, and Barenboim (1974) developed role-taking skills in institutionalized psychiatric patients (ages 9 to 14) whose diagnoses included primarily antisocial behavior. Two treatments, role taking and communication training, were compared to no treatment. Communication training consisted of encouraging the children to identify and correct miscommunications, using a gamelike format, and focused on improving peer communication. Both treatments led to improvements on a test of role-taking skills. A 1-year follow-up showed that improvement in either role-taking or communication skills was moderately correlated with ratings of behavioral improvement in the institution. Although ratings of behavioral improvement favored role-taking and communication-training groups, they were not statistically different from those of no-treatment controls. In several other studies, children were trained in role-taking skills by enacting the roles of others; discussing thoughts, feelings, or motives of others; and switching roles (e.g., Iannotti, 1978; Little & Kendall, 1979). Yet, these studies have not provided firm evidence that behavior changes occur outside of the context of the treatment setting after training.

In some variations of cognitive therapy, parents are occasionally involved in training. Utilization of parents is a reasonable extension, given that many behavior problems of children emerge and are evident in the home and in relation to the parents (e.g., noncompliance). Moreover, the problem-solving skills that parents use to resolve problems with their children and their manner of interacting with their children more generally are related to the child's problem-solving skills and classroom behavior (Shure & Spivack, 1978). Thus, training the parent to interact in ways that promote problem-solving skills may have broad effects both on the parent and on the child.

As part of the Shure and Spivack (1978) program for preschool children, mothers have been trained to develop problem-solving skills in their children. Treatment led to improvements in the children's problem-solving skills and in teacher ratings of classroom behavior as well as to changes in the mothers' problem-solving skills and approach toward child rearing. This study suggests that training mothers may not only have direct impact on the child but also change several aspects of the child's interpersonal environment that may contribute to deviant or prosocial behavior.

In other studies, youths who have engaged in aggressive behavior or who represent serious behavioral problems at school, as well as institutionalized delinquents, have been exposed to variations of cognitively based interventions. The treatments have combined self-instruction and training in problem-solving skills, relaxation, and the use of imagery to cope with anger (e.g., Feindler, Marriott, & Iwata, 1984; Garrison & Stolberg, 1983; Schlichter & Horan, 1981). These studies have shown treatment effects on measures of problem-solving and coping skills and on role-play measures, with mixed effects on measures of problem behavior outside of treatment.

A final variation of cognitively based therapy mentioned only in passing pertains to programs conducted in the schools. Much of the work of Spivack and Shure, already discussed, has been conducted by training teachers to introduce specific lessons in class to develop problem-solving skills (Spivack et al., 1976). Several programs have emerged from this work and are intended to develop large-scale classroom applications of problem-solving training for children at risk for social maladjustment. For example, Weissberg and Gesten (1982) devised and evaluated a problem-solving curriculum for elementary school children (grades 2 through 4). In one variation of the program, children receive 34 lessons of 20 to 30 minutes each in addition to opportunities to review skills and practice resolving interpersonal conflicts. The major units of the curriculum include recognizing feelings in oneself and others, identifying problems, generating alternative solutions, considering consequences, and integrating diverse problem-solving behaviors. Use of the skills covered in the lessons is integrated with classroom activities (e.g., solving minor problems between children). The results of several evaluations of the program have shown that cognitive skills improve significantly relative to those of untreated children. However, the impact of training on teacher ratings of classroom adjustment has been equivocal; some studies have shown gains but other studies have not (Gesten et al., 1982; Weissberg et al., 1981).

The school applications of problem-solving training are important to mention, even though they are not necessarily applied for purposes of "treatment" of children whose behaviors have been identified as problems. Problem-solving skills can be taught as part of ordinary classroom curriculums and perhaps improve the behaviors of many children. Integrating problem-solving training in the early elementary grades as part of the routine curriculums also raises intriguing possibilities for the prevention of deviant behaviors.

Recommendations

In conveying the techniques, it is important to note that many distinctions might be made among alternative approaches. These differences can be seen in the available treatment manuals (e.g., Camp & Bash, 1985; Kendall & Braswell, 1985). The techniques were included under a single rubric because of their common focus on cognitive processes considered to underlie disruptive behavior and because of distinctions among alternative techniques in practice are often difficult to invoke.

The techniques usually focus on developing a problem-solving approach to a variety of different situations. As such, many of the recommendations discussed in relation to social-skills training may be relevant here as well. Special importance may be placed on identifying the specific situations in which the problem-solving approach is to be applied and sampling these broadly to incorporate many different types of interactions (home, school, community) with many different participants (parents, teacher, peers, siblings, and others). In addition, it would probably be useful to extend the approach outside of the sessions and to involve others to support, foster, or reinforce such applications directly. Because generality of treatment effects beyond laboratory tasks and treatment sessions has been somewhat problematic in the outcome studies with approaches based on problem solving, these latter points may be especially important.

APPROACHES TO TREATMENT: EXEMPLARY STUDIES

The previous discussion illustrates alternative treatment techniques. Although it is critical to convey specific techniques, it is also important to go beyond the focus on techniques alone. Techniques are likely to vary in their efficacy as a function of many factors related to the nature of the dysfunction, children, families, therapists, and others. In the area of child psychotherapy in general, relatively few studies examine alternative techniques and conditions that influence their effectiveness (see Kazdin, 1988). Two exemplary studies are detailed below to convey alternative approaches to conduct disorder and as well the more complex questions that must be considered in selecting intervention techniques.

School-Based Treatments of Neurotic and Antisocial Behavior

Kolvin et al. (1981) conducted an ambitious outcome study in England between 1972 and 1979 to examine the impact of different treatments on different types of clinical problems with children at different stages of development and dysfunction. Two different types of child dysfunction were investigated, namely neurotic and conduct disorder. Neurotic disorder was defined broadly to include internalizing types of dysfunction (e.g., neuroses, depression, anxiety); conduct disorder was defined to include externalizing types of dysfunction (e.g., disruptive behavior, bullying, delinquency). Because of the potential significance of developmental stage on the nature of child dysfunction and response to treatment, two different age levels were selected. Children aged 7 to 8 and 11 to 12 years old were included and referred to, respectively, as juniors and seniors. Screening of 4,300 children was undertaken to identify the final group (slightly less than 600) of children included in the study. Screening criteria were invoked to identify children who showed maladjustment problems at school and were at risk for psychiatric impairment (juniors) or who already evinced psychiatric disturbance (seniors). Multiple measures involving parent, teacher, peer, and clinician evaluations were used to conduct screening and to evaluate treatment outcome. Major characteristics of the study are highlighted in Table 7.6.

Once identified, children were assigned randomly to one of four conditions. The conditions varied slightly for younger and older children (see Table 7.6), but for each group there was a no-treatment control group that provided the basis for comparison over the course of treatment and follow-up. Parent-counseling plus teacher-consultation consisted of social work consultation with parents and teachers in an effort to coordinate school and home activities, casework with the family, and support for the teacher. Nurture work consisted of providing enrichment activities for the children, close interaction with each child, and behavioral shaping for individual child goals. Group therapy was based on client-centered principles and practices and consisted of play group therapy (for younger children) or discussion (more traditional) group therapy for older children. In each case, the focus was on the expression of feelings, acceptance of the child, warmth, and the therapeutic relationship. The behavior modification program (for seniors only) consisted of classroom reinforcement systems relying on social and token reinforcement to improve deportment and classroom performance.

The treatments involved different models of care delivery and different personnel (e.g., social workers, teachers, teacher aides). The treatments were carefully developed, structured, and implemented. Training of staff provided formal and informal supervision and discussion as well as reading and background information on the principles and practices underlying treatment.

The effects of treatments are not easily summarized, given the large number of outcome measures and different sources of information. In general, for the younger children, play-group therapy and nurture work led to significantly greater changes than the no-treatment or parent–teacher conditions. These effects were evident primarily for neurotic rather than conduct-problem behavior. For the older children, group therapy and behavior modification led to greater changes than controls and the parent–teacher condition.

Among the different treatments, children with neurotic disorders, as defined earlier, responded better than children with conduct disorders. Also, girls responded better than did boys. There were no consistent interactions between the type of treatment and type of child disorder between treatment and child sex. However, neurotic behavior appeared to be more amenable to change

Table 7.6. Selected Characteristics of the Outcome Study Conducted by Kolvin et al. (1981)

DOMAIN	MAJOR CHARACTERISTICS
Sample	Ages 7 to 8 (juniors) or 11 to 12 (seniors)
Sample Size	60 to 90 youths per group ($N = 574$)
Screening	Multistage screening to identify dysfunctional youths
Setting	Regular public schools
Treatments (Juniors)	Parent-counseling/teacher consultation Nurture work Group (play) therapy No treatment
Treatments (Seniors)	Parent-counseling/teacher consultation Group (nondirective, discussion) therapy Behavior modification No treatment
Treatment Sessions	Number and duration varied for each treatment
Sources of Data	Parent, teacher, peer, self, and clinician ratings
Assessment Domain	Adjustment, psychopathology, cognitive, and social functioning
Major Outcome Measures	Rutter Teacher and Parent Scales—parent interview to assess neurotic, antisocial, and psychosomatic behavior, Junior Eysenck Personality Inventory, Devereax Elementary School Behavior Rating Scale—measures of vocabulary, intelligence, and reading ability, sociometric data
Assessment Periods	Pretreatment, posttreatment, follow-up (18 months after treatment ended)
Training of Therapists	Special programs for trainers involving formal and informal instruction and supervision, varying as needed by condition

in boys than in girls, whereas conduct problems appeared to be more amenable to change in girls than in boys.

The treatments sampled different dimensions of interest in contemporary work. One dimension is the extent to which treatment is direct versus indirect. Direct treatment consists of face-to-face interaction with the child (e.g., group therapy), whereas indirect treatment consists of working with significant others (e.g., parents and teachers) who treat the child (e.g., parent–teacher consultation). Another dimension is whether treatment focuses on intrapsychic process versus overt behavior (e.g., group therapy versus behavior modification, respectively). Finally, treatments varied markedly in duration and intensity with a brief versus more extended treatment (e.g., 10 sessions of group therapy versus 20 weeks of daily behavioral treatment).

In the present project, each of these dimensions was not fully represented or extensively sampled. Nevertheless, at the end of the project tentative conclusions could be drawn. Indirect treatment (parent–teacher consultation) did not appear to produce major changes; more direct treatments—including group therapy and behavioral approaches—produced the most significant changes. Treatment focus, whether intrapsychic or behavioral, did not seem to be the crucial determinant, given the impact of both group therapy and behavioral approaches. Dura-

tion of treatment did not seem to be an issue, because relatively shorter and longer treatments (e.g., group therapy and behavior modification) led to greater change. Again, each of the dimensions of possible interest was not carefully sampled, so the conclusions of the study can be applied only to the specific condition.

There are a number of excellent features of this study. The use of multiple measures for screening, a comparison of separate treatments with a randomly comprised no-treatment control group, assessment of multiple domains of functioning (maladjustment, cognitive functioning, social relations with peers), and the evaluation of follow-up make this study truly outstanding. Kolvin et al. (1981) addressed treatment at the level of complexity that avoids highly diluted and diffuse conclusions. The focus on different treatments and clinical problems and on children of different ages within a single study serves as an excellent basis for drawing conclusions about treatment.

Community-Based Treatment for Antisocial Youths

Feldman et al. (1983) conducted a community-based treatment project for antisocial youths. Community-based treatment attempts to take advantage of the resources in the everyday environment that can support prosocial behavior.

Integration of treatment in existing community programs reduces the problem of ensuring carryover of prosocial behavior from treatment to the community settings. This problem is likely to arise if the youths are removed from the community (e.g., psychiatric hospital, juvenile correctional facility) for their treatment.

Another characteristic of community-based treatment is an effort to include problem youths as well as their prosocial peers. If positive peer-group influences are to be fostered in treatment, it is critical that the peers not be restricted to other deviant youths. Segregation of deviant youths in residential settings in particular provides them with models for further deviant behavior.

Feldman et al. (1983) conducted a large-scale community-based program that was integrated with activities of the Jewish Community Centers Association in St. Louis, Missouri. The St. Louis Experiment, as it was called, included youths (ages 8 to 17) who were referred for antisocial behavior (referred youths) or who normally attended the regular activities programs and were not identified as showing problem behavior (nonreferred youths). The project began with approximately 700 youths; this number declined to approximately 450 by the end of treatment.

The design of the study was complex because of the interest in evaluating the separate and combined effects of different influences on outcome (see Table 7.7). The study evaluated the effects of three types of treatment, two levels of therapist experience, and three different ways to compose the groups. The three treatments were traditional group social work (focus on group processes, social organization and norms within the group), behavior modification (use of reinforcement contingencies, focus on prosocial behavior), and minimal treatment (no explicit application of a structured treatment plan; spontaneous interactions of group members). Activity groups within the center were formed and assigned to one of these three interventions. The groups were led by trainers, some of whom were experienced (graduate students of social work with previous experience) and others who were inexperienced (undergraduate students). Finally, the groups were composed in three ways: all members were youths referred for antisocial behavior, all members were nonreferred ("normal") youths, and a mixture of referred and nonreferred.

The main objective was to evaluate changes in antisocial behavior of referred youths over the course of the intervention. Measures were obtained from parents, referral agents, the youths, and group leaders as well as direct observations of the groups. The intervention was conducted over a period of a year, in which the youths attended sessions and engaged in a broad range of activities (e.g., sports, arts and crafts, fund raising, discussions). The specific treatments were superimposed on the usual activity of the com-

Table 7.7. Selected Characteristics of the Outcome Study Conducted by Feldman et al. (1983)

DOMAIN	MAJOR CHARACTERISTICS
Sample	Referred for antisocial behavior (ages 8–17, $m = 11.2$).
Sample Size	$N = 452$ participants, $N = 54$ at follow-up.
Screening	Severity of antisocial behavior on checklists completed by referral agent and parent.
Setting	Jewish Community Center
Treatments	Traditional group social work Behavior modification Minimal treatment (no explicit or structured plan)
Treatment Sessions	Range from 8 to 29 sessions ($m = 22.2$ sessions) of 2 to 3 hours each.
Sources of Data	Referral agency, parents, children, therapists.
Assessment Domain	Antisocial, prosocial, nonsocial behavior.
Major Outcome Measures	Checklist questions designed to measure prosocial, antisocial, and nonsocial behavior completed by professionals at referral agencies, parents, therapists, and youths; direct observations of youths in the groups designed to measure prosocial, antisocial, and nonsocial behavior; therapist and observer completed measures of group norms, child and peer relations; aggression scale completed by youths.
Therapists	Experienced (social work graduate students) versus inexperienced (undergraduates).
Training of Therapists	In-service training; prior course work and practical training for "experienced" therapists.

munity facility. Treatment sessions ranged from 8 to 29 sessions (mean = 22.2 sessions), each lasting about 2 to 3 hours.

The results indicated that treatment, trainer experience, and group composition exerted impact on at least some of the measures. Youths showed greater reductions in antisocial behavior with experienced rather than inexperienced leaders. Referred (antisocial) youths in mixed groups (that included nonreferred children) showed greater improvements than similar youths in groups comprising only antisocial youths. Treatments also differed; behavior modification led to greater reductions in antisocial behavior than did traditional group treatment. Traditional treatment led to some decrements in antisocial behavior relative to the minimal-contact group. However, treatment accounted for only a small amount of variance in predicting outcome.

Overall, antisocial youths benefited from the program, especially those who received the most favorable intervention condition (i.e., behavior modification with an experienced leader and in a mixed group of referred and nonreferred peers). For a small subsample ($N = 54$), follow-up data were available a year later. The follow-up data revealed slight (nonsignificant) increases in antisocial behavior based on data from parent and referral-agent reports. Yet, the size of the follow-up sample precluded evaluation of the effects of treatment, trainer experience, and group composition.

Overall Evaluation
There remain some ambiguities regarding the impact of alternative treatments. Checks on how treatment was carried out revealed a breakdown in treatment integrity. For example, observations of treatment sessions revealed that approximately 35% of the leaders did not implement the behavior-modification procedures appropriately for two of the three sessions observed; approximately 44% of the minimal-treatment leaders carried out systematic interventions even though none was supposed to; finally, only 25% of the leaders in the traditional group treatment condition carried out the intervention appropriately. It is difficult to draw conclusions about the relative impact of alternative treatments. Yet it is rare for child-treatment studies even to assess treatment integrity. Consequently, attention should be directed to this superb methodological feature instead of faulting the study for departures from the intended

interventions. Nevertheless, it is still possible that there would have been greater differences in outcome if the treatments had been conducted as intended and even substantially different conclusions about individual treatment conditions.

The absence of stronger follow-up data raises other problems. Follow-up was restricted to ratings on nonstandardized measures of antisocial behavior and was available for only 12% (54/450) of the sample. From these data, it is not possible to tell how the vast majority of youths fared. Follow-up data are critical, given the possibility that the results might differ from, and even be diametrically opposed to, the pattern evident immediately after treatment. Nevertheless, the St. Louis Experiment represents a major contribution to the treatment literature. The project shows that interventions can be delivered on a relatively large scale and can provide benefits for referred (and nonreferred) youths.

General Comments

The two previously noted studies illustrate very special efforts to evaluate alternative treatments for conduct disorder. The studies share several characteristics, such as the evaluation of multiple treatments, the reliance upon multiple measures and perspectives to examine outcome, and the sampling of different types of youths to examine the differential responsiveness of clients to treatment. More than the specific commonalities, both studies focus on questions involving the interaction of treatment outcome with other variables (e.g., clinical problem, child age, referral status). This level of specificity is needed in outcome research, a fact widely recognized but rarely translated into action in the child-therapy literature.

GENERALITY OF TREATMENT EFFECTS

Generality of treatment can refer to different phenomena, including the generality of behavior over time, across settings, across behaviors, and other forms as well (Kazdin, 1989). Only very preliminary statements about different types of generalization can be made, given the paucity of controlled outcome studies demonstrating effective treatments with aggressive children. Indeed, most of the research has neglected issues of generality. Research on parent management training is a partial exception and will be emphasized here.

Maintenance of Behavior

Maintenance of behavior or durability of therapeutic change can be conceived of as generality of treatment effects over time. Maintenance of behavior is obviously important because it represents the ultimate success of treatment. Also, treatments that are more (or less) effective than alternatives at posttreatment may be very different in their effects at follow-up. Thus, conclusions reached about outcome immediately after treatment may vary from those reached at follow-up.

Follow-up data have been obtained in a number of parent management training programs. For example, in separate reports children still continued to show significant reductions in deviant behavior up to a year after treatment relative to initial baseline (see Fleischman, 1981; Fleischman & Szykula, 1981; Patterson & Fleischman, 1979). Moreover, in Patterson's program, deviant behavior in the homes of over 80% of the children whose parents received training fell within the range of their nondeviant peers who were functioning adequately.

Longer-term follow-up assessment has led to mixed results. In some cases, the superiority of parent training relative to other conditions such as client-centered therapy at posttreatment have not been maintained 2 to 5 years later (Bernal, Klinnert, & Schultz, 1980; Christophersen, Barnard, Barnard, Gleeson, & Sykes, 1980). Overall, maintenance of treatment has been evident in a few studies, but the data are difficult to evaluate because of different child populations, versions of treatment, and family characteristics. Also, in some studies, booster sessions are provided to families during the follow-up interval (Patterson, 1974; Wahler, 1975). Long-term effects (e.g., beyond 2 years) have been rarely evaluated. Evaluations up to a year rarely include groups assigned to different treatments or no-treatment to permit evaluation of durability of treatment effects associated with a particular intervention (see Fleischman & Szykula, 1981). For most treatments discussed in the present chapter, follow-up has rarely been assessed at all.

The factors that influence durability of treatment effects have only begun to be explored.

For example, with parent management training, Wahler, Leske, and Rogers (1979) demonstrated that treatment effects and maintenance of change are less likely, if apparent at all, among high-risk families as defined by marked poverty, low rate of parental social contact with others, poor education, single parents, crowded living conditions, and residence in high-crime areas.

The durability of treatment effects is very likely to depend on characteristics of the family to which the child returns. For example, Stewart, Cummings, and Meardon (1978) followed up hospitalized aggressive boys after discharge from an inpatient treatment program. The follow-up status of the children between 1½ and 2 years after hospitalization depended on departure from the child's home of a deviant parent or the child's separation from such a parent through placement in a foster home. Greater antisocial behavior was evident in boys who had returned to families where an antisocial or alcoholic father was present.

Griest et al. (1982) compared variations of parent training that differed in their consideration of family variables. Parent training alone was compared with parent training plus a focus on parental personal adjustment, marital adjustment, parent perceptions of child behavior, and extrafamilial relations. Although both treatments, compared to a no-treatment control condition, led to significant improvements in the child, improvements in children and their families at a 2-month follow-up assessment were maintained significantly better for the group in which treatment had considered family variables.

These studies have begun to explore the factors that may contribute to maintenance of therapeutic change. Maintenance of treatment effects may vary across studies as a function of extratreatment variables. If children are returned to conditions that promote continued deviance, the impact of treatment may be minor. The difficulty at present is understanding the conditions to which children are returned and how these interact with treatment effects (that is, where such interactions exist).

Generality Across Settings

A major reason for implementing treatment at all is to induce change beyond the clinic setting. In parental management training, generalization from clinic to home is not exactly a test of generality. The focus of treatment is on parent–child interaction in the home. Typically, treatment requires parents to assess their behavior or that of their child and to complete homework assignments where they apply behavior-change procedures directly. Change at home constitutes the primary therapeutic focus. Generality across settings is still of interest, because many children whose parents receive training have problems at school as well. Programs that produce behavior change at home have not demonstrated improvements in the child's behavior at school (e.g., Wahler, 1969). Indeed, in one investigation, increases in deviant behavior at school were evident during treatment of behavior at home (Wahler, 1975). Yet, when treatment is extended to the school, direct effects are evident there as well. An obvious limitation of existing studies is the lack of data on generality of treatment effects across settings.

Generality Across Behaviors

The extent to which treatment effects spread to areas of behavior that are not focused on directly raises interesting questions. If nontargeted behaviors change, the basis for these changes is not always clear. For example, with parent management training, it is possible that behaviors not focused on directly change because parents extend their newly learned skills to behaviors not identified for treatment. Alternatively, the improvements in specific child behaviors may trigger additional changes, even though these latter changes were not the direct effects of treatment. Similarly, with cognitively based therapy, the focus is not on a single set of behaviors but rather on the strategy the child uses to identify effective responses. Changes across a large range of behaviors might not necessarily reflect generalization if the trained response is conceived as a general approach.

Major issues about the generality across behaviors have been illuminated by Wahler and his colleagues, who have examined the organization of behavior and the nature of multiple response changes in conduct problem children (see Wahler, Berland, & Coe, 1979). Several studies completed by Wahler have shown that responses in children tend to covary, so that changes in one response are likely to be reflected in changes in other responses with which it is correlated. The breadth of changes likely to result from treatment is delineated by identifying what behaviors are positively and negatively correlated with a particular response.

Information about response covariation has been utilized to treat aggressive behavior in children. Wahler and Fox (1980a) treated four children who were oppositional and aggressive. Previous research (Wahler & Fox, 1980b) had suggested that oppositional behavior was negatively correlated with engaging in solitary play. Wahler and Fox (1980a) trained parents to reward solitary play, which led to systematic reductions in oppositional behavior. The reduction could not be accounted for by merely isolating children from others (e.g., parents, siblings) with whom oppositional behavior might be manifest or observing behavior at times when solitary play was reinforced.

Response covariation has important implications for the study of generality of responses and treatment evaluation (Kazdin, 1982; Voeltz & Evans, 1982). Interventions designed to alter a particular behavior are likely to have broad effects. Research has already shown that not all of the effects might be considered to be positive or negative. For example, some of the changes may be regarded as desirable (e.g., increased social interaction, reduced self-stimulation) or undesirable (e.g., increased classroom disruption, provocation of peers) side effects of treatment. Few outcome studies have assessed a wide range of behaviors that might covary with treatment.

Recommendations

More evidence has been obtained for the durability of therapeutic change than for other types of generality. Even so, few studies exist with untreated subjects or alternative treatments to examine whether sustained improvements can be attributed to a particular treatment. Other forms of generality raise critical assessment issues that have yet to be adequately addressed. The resources to assess generality across settings, behaviors, or siblings raise practical obstacles for research. Also, generality data, once obtained, are difficult to interpret unless an additional assessment effort is made to determine the basis for the spread of treatment effects. At present, demonstration of effective treatments with replicable effects continues as the highest priority in research and supersedes examination of the more subtle, albeit important, questions about generality.

Despite general paucity of investigations specifically evaluating generality of treatment effects with aggressive children, tentative recommendations for promoting generality can be made by drawing upon a larger literature on the topic (see Albin, Horner, Koegel, & Dunlap, 1987; Kazdin, 1989; Stokes & Osnes, 1986). First, the areas for which generality is desired must be incorporated directly into treatment. For example, if changes resulting from parent management training are desired in the home and at school, both settings must be incorporated into the contingencies. Because more parent training programs alter behavior in the home, supplementary techniques might be used to develop classroom performance. The child may carry a card that the teacher completes to evaluate performance. Parents can then provide consequences (home-based reinforcement) when the child returns home. Alternatively, if it is possible to solicit greater school participation, teachers can be trained directly to implement the program to obtain classroom changes. Similarly, for other forms of generality, direct intervention is probably superior to passive expectation of the spread of beneficial treatment effects. Thus, if specific behaviors eventually need to be changed, they should be incorporated directly at some point in treatment.

Second, training should explicitly incorporate the application of treatment to new situations, settings, and persons. Not all of the problem areas to which skills need to be applied can be anticipated in advance in the course of treatment and specifically trained. Thus, training should include a broad range of circumstances to provide opportunities for practice so that the skills learned in treatment are more likely to be applied in the face of new situations. For example, in parent training, parents should have opportunities to generate and develop reinforcement and punishment contingencies beyond those of direct interest to them for the immediate child problems that provided the impetus for treatment. In simulated situations, parents can be asked to generate programs to alter behaviors that might arise, to identify several different program options, and to rectify hypothetical programs that have failed to produce the desired change. Training parents to apply skills broadly is more likely to lead to generality of training effects. Stated simply, if broad effects are desired, broad parent management skills may need to be trained. Similarly, in cognitively based

therapy, children probably need to be trained to use problem-solving steps in a broad variety of situations. If the child is to apply the skills to situations that cannot be completely anticipated in treatment, the next best alternative is to train broad applications of the skills to interactions with peers, siblings, parents, teachers, strangers, police, and other community members. Practice in broad application of the cognitive skills is likely to lead to broad treatment effects. Finally, the extension of training effects to new situations should be measured occasionally to evaluate if training has achieved its goal or if additional training is needed. The first and most important feature of generality is knowing to what degree treatment effects have spread. Hence, some effort should be made to assess the breadth of the impact of treatment.

CURRENT ISSUES

Severity of Dysfunction

There remain several issues that cloud the evaluation of current treatments (see Kazdin, 1988). Perhaps the most critical is the need to specify the clinical dysfunction in a way that permits comparisons among studies. Children who have been referred to as conduct-disordered or conduct problems within the treatment literature vary widely in terms of the severity and breadth of their dysfunction. Noncompliance and oppositional behavior, as well as repeated fighting and stealing, have been grouped under a single rubric. The point here is not to say that some of these cases are conduct-disordered and others not. Presumably the continuum of dysfunctions is worth treating. However, it is quite likely that the effectiveness of treatment will vary as a function of the severity and breadth of the antisocial behaviors of the children. Youths who engage in more severe and diverse forms of antisocial behavior, who exhibit these across more situations, and who do so for a longer period of time are more likely to continue these behaviors over time. In evaluating any intervention, it is important to know how the children fare on these dimensions.

It would be useful if researchers would adopt a standardized descriptive system in reference to conduct-disordered youths so that the results of different studies could be compared. There are standard ways of classifying dysfunction, including the use of a diagnostic system such as

DSM-III-R (APA, 1987). The advantage of such a system is that it provides a widely used, even if not maximally explicit, means of delineating severity, breadth, and chronicity of dysfunction. The knowledge that children in an investigation met the criteria for conduct disorder would not resolve all the ambiguities. However, the information conveys that at least a minimum level of dysfunction existed. Use of other facets of current diagnosis (severity ratings, subtype of conduct disorder, multiple axes) can help to further elaborate potentially important descriptive characteristics of the sample.

Psychiatric diagnosis is only one means to better convey the level, type, and severity of clinical dysfunction. Diagnosis does not resolve many issues in the search for consistencies in delineating dysfunction, because the diagnostic criteria have undergone periodic revisions. In addition, individuals with a diagnosis of conduct disorder can be extremely heterogenous in the specific symptoms they evince and the severity and chronicity of each. Thus, diagnosis can help to describe some features, but it also obscures others.

An alternative is to use standardized measures, such as parent and teacher checklists. For example, the Child Behavior Checklist (Achenbach & Edelbrock, 1983) assesses multiple symptom domains, broad scales (internalizing, externalizing), and prosocial behavior (participation in activities, social interaction, progress at school). The measure permits evaluation of these characteristics in relation to same-age peers functioning adequately in everyday life. The normative basis of this and other measures would also be helpful for better specifying the population that has been treated.

Subscales especially relevant to conduct disorder (e.g., aggression, delinquency, hyperactivity) can be compared across investigations to evaluate severity of dysfunction in relation to normative and clinic samples. Other measures more specific to antisocial behavior are available (see Kazdin, 1987a). For example, the Eyberg Child Behavior Inventory (Eyberg & Robinson, 1983) is specifically designed to examine frequency and severity of conduct problems. Use of this or other measures in a more consistent fashion across studies would greatly improve the evaluation of the effectiveness of alternative treatments.

The point made here regarding the need to specify the severity, breadth, and chronicity of dysfunction might be extended to evaluation of the family. Clearly the effectiveness of treatment varies as a function of family characteristics (e.g., social disadvantage, mother isolation from positive social contacts) (Dumas & Wahler, 1983; Wahler, Leske, & Rogers, 1979). Thus it would be useful to convey further details about the parents and families of children included in a treatment trial. Although such assessment is a laudable goal, there are obstacles—such as the absence of widely agreed upon assessment tools or diagnostic systems that are designed to focus on characteristics of families of antisocial youth. At this point, a basic priority is the need to specify operationally and in more detail the nature of the child's dysfunction. Better specification will help identify the children for whom some treatments may be effective.

Focusing on the Constellation of Behaviors

An important issue for many interventions is the focus of treatment. Often one or two salient behaviors serve as the target focus. For example, reinforcement and punishment techniques frequently focus on individual target behaviors. A demonstration that misbehavior—such as fighting in the classroom or obeying parents at home—is altered dramatically is noteworthy. Yet, the short- and long-term impact of a restricted focus is of unclear or limited clinical value. It is very likely that a pattern of dysfunction and a package of symptoms will have to be altered.

It is not clear that all domains of a child's dysfunction must be treated for the child to function well in everyday life. However, it is critical to evaluate child functioning across a wide range of problematic domains. Thus, decreases in classroom fighting are important. Additional assessment is needed to evaluate functioning in class (e.g., deportment or other measures, academic functioning), at home (e.g., compliance with parents, interactions with others), and in the community (e.g., staying out overnight, stealing with peers). The importance of assessment across many domains of functioning is usually argued as a generally advisable strategy. In the case of conduct disorder, the strategy would appear to be essential because of the pervasive nature of the dysfunction. Also, the effective alteration of one or a few behaviors, while impressive, may have no clear impact on the child's overall functioning across other relevant behaviors and situations.

Developing Prosocial Behaviors

Treatments for conduct-disordered youths probably need to include specific efforts to develop prosocial behavior as well as to decrease deviant behavior. "Prosocial functioning" refers to the presence of positive adaptive behaviors and experiences such as participation in social activities, social interaction, and making friends. There are separate reasons to advocate the dual approach of decreasing symptoms and increasing prosocial behaviors. To begin with, reducing deviant behavior does not by itself ensure an increase in positive prosocial behaviors. For example, decreasing fighting with teachers and peers is very unlikely to develop positive interactions with either. Evidence in the study of childhood dysfunction more generally has suggested that the overlap of symptom reduction and positive prosocial functioning may not be great. Indeed, correlations between measures of symptoms and prosocial behavior, whether completed by parents or children, are in the low to moderate range (e.g., -0.3 to -0.5) (Kazdin, 1986). The small amount of shared variance between the scales indicates that a low level of deviant behavior does not mean the presence of prosocial behavior, and vice versa.

Another reason for focusing on prosocial behaviors is their possible relevance to long-term adjustment. For example, it is likely that the development of academic competence would be an important prosocial focus, apart from reduction of antisocial behaviors. Poor academic functioning is frequently associated with conduct disorder and suggests a poor long-term prognosis. Neglecting the development of positive competencies in this area may detract from effective interventions designed to reduce maladaptive behaviors.

Many treatments emphasize reduction of symptoms or development of prosocial behavior. The implicit assumption has been that a focus on one of these will invariably help the other. However, it is quite likely that the reduction of symptoms and increase of prosocial behavior require separate attention. This does not necessarily mean that entirely separate interventions are needed. Rather, the program focus should probably include and assess impact on behaviors within these two broad domains.

CONCLUSIONS

The treatment of conduct disorder represents a significant priority because of the prevalence of the problem and the poor prognosis. Because of the impact of the problem on others (e.g., victims) and society at large and the transmission across generations, the problem is clinically and socially significant. Current treatments have shown that antisocial behaviors can be altered. The challenges are primarily in the areas of establishing impact on multiple behaviors of the constellation, obtaining effects that are sustained, and effecting large enough changes to be clinically significant.

The difficulties in effecting change in these areas might suggest a variety of different directions. In clinical work, the direction is likely to be to combine multiple approaches to achieve change. The goal would be to address all the many domains of dysfunction (family life, school, peer interactions) that are involved. Even with broad foci of clinical work, it is often difficult to consider critical domains. For example, academic dysfunction is problematic for many antisocial youths. Academic dysfunction predicts long-term antisocial behavior and may be hazardous to neglect. Yet persons who are most likely to be responsible for clinical intervention in treatment settings (i.e., mental-health professionals) may not be familiar with or trained in procedures to develop academic competencies in children. In short, even broad-based approaches may omit critical domains.

Because of the demonstrated but often insufficiently strong changes with many current treatments, alternative models of intervention have been suggested. One approach includes the use of more protracted treatments, perhaps spanning years and/or continued on an as-needed basis for severely antisocial youth (e.g., Kazdin, 1987a; Wolf, Braukmann, & Ramp, 1987). It is reasonable to assume at this time that a core group of conduct-disorder youths are likely to continue their dysfunction after the most potent available treatment approaches have been applied. At the same time, it is clear that studies referring to conduct-disordered youths include many persons who are oppositional, noncompliant, and mildly aggressive but not of the ilk that might require such treatment. Improved efforts are needed to help identify different levels or types of conduct disorder and to monitor those who have been treated to see if further help is needed.

REFERENCES

Achenbach, T. M., & Edelbrock, C. S. (1981). Behavioral problems and competencies reported by parents of normal and disturbed children aged four through sixteen. *Monographs of the Society for Research in Child Development, 46,* 188.

Achenbach, T. M., & Edelbrock, C. S. (1983). *Manual for the child behavior checklist and revised child behavior profile.* Burlington, VT: University Associates in Psychiatry.

Agee, V. L. (1979). *Treatment of the violent incorrigible adolescent.* Lexington, MA: Lexington Books.

Albin, R. W., Horner, R. H., Koegel, R. L., & Dunlap, G. (Eds.). (1987). *Extending competent performance: Applied research on generalization and maintenance.* Eugene, OR: University of Oregon.

Alexander, J. F., Barton, C., Schiavo, R. S., & Parsons, B. V. (1976). Systems-behavioral intervention with families of delinquents: Therapist characteristics, family behavior, and outcome. *Journal of Consulting and Clinical Psychology, 44,* 656–664.

Alexander, J. F., & Parsons, B. V. (1973). Short-term behavioral intervention with delinquent families: Impact on family process and recidivism. *Journal of Abnormal Psychology, 81,* 219–225.

Alexander, J. F., & Parsons, B. V. (1982). *Functional family therapy.* Monterey, CA: Brooks/Cole.

American Psychiatric Association. (1987). *Diagnostic and statistical manual of mental disorders* (3rd ed. rev.). Washington, DC: Author.

Arbuthnot, J., & Gordon, D. A. (1986). Behavioral and cognitive effects of a moral reasoning development intervention for high-risk behavior-disordered adolescents. *Journal of Consulting and Clinical Psychology, 54,* 208–216.

Azrin, N. H., & Powers, M. A. (1975). Eliminating classroom disturbances of emotionally disturbed children by positive practice procedures. *Behavior Therapy, 6,* 525–534.

Bachman, J. G., Johnston, L. D., & O'Malley, P. M. (1978). Delinquent behavior linked to educational attainment and post-high school experiences. In L. Otten (Ed.), *Colloquium on the correlates of crime and the determinants of criminal behavior* (pp. 1–43). Arlington, VA: The MITRE Corp.

Baum, C. G., & Forehand, R. (1981). Long-term follow-up assessment of parent training by use of multiple outcome measures. *Behavior Therapy, 12,* 643–652.

Behar, D., & Stewart, M. A. (1982). Aggressive conduct disorder of children. *Acta Psychiatrica Scandinavica, 65,* 210–220.

Berkowitz, L. (1977). Situational and personal conditions governing reactions to aggressive cues. In D. Magnusson & N. S. Endler (Eds.), *Personality at the crossroads: Current issues in interactional psychology* (pp. 165–171). Hillsdale, NJ: Lawrence Erlbaum Associates.

Bernal, M. E., Klinnert, M. D., & Schultz, L. A. (1980). Outcome evaluation of behavioral parent training and client-centered parent counseling for children with conduct problems. *Journal of Applied Behavior Analysis, 13,* 677–691.

Blue, S. W., Madsen, C. H., Jr., & Heimberg, R. G. (1981). Increasing coping behavior in children with aggressive behavior: Evaluation of the relative efficacy of the components of a treatment package. *Child Behavior Therapy, 3,* 51–60.

Bornstein, M., Bellack, S., & Hersen, M. (1980). Social skills training for highly aggressive children: Treatment in an inpatient setting. *Behavior Modification, 4,* 173–186.

Bristol, M. M. (1976). Control of physical aggression through school- and home-based reinforcement. In J. D. Krumboltz & C. E. Thoresen (Eds.), *Counseling methods* (pp. 180–186). New York: Holt, Rinehart & Winston.

Burchard, J. D., & Barrera, F. (1972). An analysis of time out and response cost in a programmed environment. *Journal of Applied Behavior Analysis, 5,* 271–282.

Cadoret, R. J. (1978). Psychopathology in adopted-away offspring of biological parents with antisocial behavior. *Archives of General Psychiatry, 35,* 176–184.

Cadoret, R. J., & Cain, C. (1980). Sex differences in predictors of antisocial behavior in adoptees. *Archives of General Psychiatry, 37,* 1171–1175.

Cadoret, R. J., & Cain, C. (1981). Environmental and genetic factors in predicting adolescent antisocial behavior. *The Psychiatric Journal of the University of Ottawa, 6,* 220–225.

Cadoret, R. J., Cain, C. A., & Crowe, R. R. (1983). Evidence for gene-environment interaction in the development of adolescent antisocial behavior. *Behavior Genetics, 13,* 301–310.

Calhoun, K. S., & Lima, P. P. (1977). Effects of varying schedules of time out on high- and low-rate behaviors. *Journal of Behavior Therapy and Experimental Psychiatry, 8,* 189–194.

Camp, B. W., & Bash, M. A. S. (1985). *Think aloud: Increasing social and cognitive skills— a problem solving program for children.* Champaign, IL: Research Press.

Carlson, C. L., Lahey, B. B., & Neeper, R. (1984). Peer assessment of the social behavior of accepted, rejected, and neglected children. *Journal of Abnormal Child Psychology, 12,* 189–198.

Chandler, M. J. (1973). Egocentrism and antisocial behavior: The assessment and training of social perspective-taking skills. *Developmental Psychology, 9,* 326–332.

Chandler, M. H., Greenspan, S., & Barenboim, C. (1974). Assessment and training of role-taking and referential communication skills in institutionalized emotionally disturbed children. *Developmental Psychology, 10,* 546–553.

Christiansen, K. O. (1974). Seriousness of criminality and concordance among Danish twins. In R. Hood (Ed.), *Crime, criminology and public policy* (pp. 63–67). London: Heinemann.

Christophersen, E. R., Barnard, S. R., Barnard, J. D., Gleeson, S., & Sykes, B. W. (1980). Home-based treatment of behavior disordered and developmentally delayed children. In M. J. Begab, H. C. Haywood, & H. T. Garber (Eds.), *Prevention of retarded development and psychosocially disadvantaged children.* Baltimore: University Park Press.

Clark, L. (1985). *SOS! Help for parents.* Bowling Green, KY: Parents Press.

Cloninger, C. R., Christiansen, K. O., Reich, T., & Gottesman, I. I. (1978). Implications of sex differences in the prevalences of antisocial personality, alcoholism, and criminality for familiar transmission. *Archives of General Psychiatry, 35,* 941–951.

Cloninger, C. R., Reich, T., & Guze, S. B. (1975). The multifactorial model of disease transmission: II. Sex differences in the familial transmission of sociopathy (antisocial personality). *British Journal of Psychiatry, 127,* 11–22.

Cloninger, C. R., Reich, T., & Guze, S. B. (1978). Genetic-environmental interactions and antisocial behaviour. In R. D. Hare & D. Schalling (Eds.), *Psychopathic behaviour: Approaches to research* (pp. 225–237). Chichester, England: John Wiley & Sons.

Cloninger, C. R., Sigvardsson, S., Bohman, M., & von Knorring, A. (1982). Predisposition to petting criminality in Swedish adoptees: II. Cross-fostering analysis of gene-environment interaction. *Archives of General Psychiatry, 39,* 1242–1247.

Cole, P. M., & Kazdin, A. E. (1980). Critical issues in self-instruction training with children. *Child Behavior Therapy, 2,* 1–23.

Cowen, E. L., Pederson, A., Babigan, U., Izzo, L. D., & Trost, N. (1973). Long-term follow-up of early detected vulnerable children. *Journal of Consulting and Clinical Psychology, 41,* 438–446.

Crowe, R. (1974). An adoption study of antisocial personality. *Archives of General Psychiatry, 31,* 786–791.

Deluty, R. H. (1981). Alternative-thinking ability of aggressive, assertive, and submissive children. *Cognitive Therapy and Research, 5,* 309–312.

Dodge, K. A. (1985). Attributional bias in aggressive children. In P. C. Kendall (Ed.), *Advances in cognitive-behavioral research and therapy* (Vol. 4, pp. 73–110). Orlando, FL: Academic Press.

Doke, L., Wolery, M., & Sumberg, C. (1983). Treating chronic aggression: Effects and side effects of response-contingent ammonia spirits. *Behavior Modification, 7,* 531–556.

Drabman, R., & Spitalnik, R. (1973). Social isolation as a punishment procedure: A controlled study. *Journal of Experimental Psychology, 16,* 236–249.

Drabman, R. S., & Tucker, R. (1974). Why classroom economies fail. *Journal of School Psychology, 12,* 178–188.

Dumas, J. E., & Wahler, R. G. (1983). Predictors of treatment outcome in parent training: Mother insularity and socioeconomic disadvantage. *Behavioral Assessment, 5,* 301–313.

Elder, J. P., Edelstein, B. A., & Narick, M. M. (1979). Adolescent psychiatric patients: Modifying aggressive behavior with social skills training. *Behavior Modification, 3,* 161–178.

Ellis, P. L. (1982). Empathy: A factor in antisocial behavior. *Journal of Abnormal Child Psychology, 10,* 123–134.

Eyberg, S. M., & Johnson, S. M. (1974). Multiple assessment of behavior modification with families: Effects on contingency contracting and order of treated problems. *Journal of Consulting and Clinical Psychology, 42,* 594–606.

Eyberg, S. M., & Robinson, E. A. (1983). Conduct problem behavior: Standardization of a behavioral rating scale with adolescents. *Journal of Clinical Child Psychology, 12,* 347–354.

Feindler, E. L., Marriott, S. A., & Iwata, M. (1984). Group anger control training for junior high school delinquents. *Cognitive Therapy and Research, 8,* 299–311.

Feldman, R. A., Caplinger, T. E., & Wodarski, J. S. (1983). *The St. Louis conundrum: The effective treatment of antisocial youths.* Englewood Cliffs, NJ: Prentice-Hall.

Feshbach, N. (1975). Empathy in children: Some theoretical and empirical considerations. *Counseling Psychologist, 5,* 25–30.

Fleischman, M. J. (1981). A replication of Patterson's "Intervention for boys with conduct problems." *Journal of Consulting and Clinical Psychology, 49,* 343–351.

Fleischman, M. J. (1982). Social learning interventions for aggressive children: From the laboratory to the real world. *The Behavior Therapist, 5,* 55–58.

Fleischman, M. J., & Szykula, S. A. (1981). A community setting replication of a social learning treatment for aggressive children. *Behavior Therapy, 12,* 115–122.

Fo, W. S. O., & O'Donnell, C. R. (1974). The buddy system: Relationship and contingency conditions in a community intervention program for youth with nonprofessionals as behavior change agents. *Journal of Consulting and Clinical Psychology, 42,* 163–169.

Fo, W. S. O., & O'Donnell, C. R. (1975). The buddy system: Effect of community intervention on delinquent offenses. *Behavior Therapy, 6,* 522–524.

Forehand, R., & Peed, S. (1979). Training parents to modify the noncompliant behavior of their children. In A. J. Finch & P. C. Kendall (Eds.), *Clinical treatment and research in child psychopathology* (pp. 159–184). New York: Spectrum Publications.

Foxx, R. M., & Azrin, N. H. (1972). Restitution: A method of eliminating aggressive-disruptive behavior of retarded and brain damaged patients. *Behaviour Research and Therapy, 10,* 15–27.

Foxx, R. M., & Bechtel, D. R. (1983). Overcorrection: A review and analysis. In S. Axelrod & J. Apsche (Eds.), *The effects of punishment on human behavior* (pp. 133–220). New York: Academic Press.

Frankel, F., Moss, D., Schofield, S., & Simmons, J. Q. (1976). Case study: Use of differential reinforcement to suppress self-injurious and aggressive behavior. *Psychological Reports, 39,* 843–849.

Freedman, B. J., Rosenthal, L., Donahoe, C. P., Schlundt, D. G., & McFall, R. (1978). A social-behavioral analysis of skills deficits in delinquent and nondelinquent boys. *Journal of Consulting and Clinical Psychology, 46,* 1448–1462.

Gaffney, L. R., & McFall, R. M. (1981). A comparison of social skills in delinquent and nondelinquent adolescent girls using a behavioral role-playing inventory. *Journal of Consulting and Clinical Psychology, 49,* 959–967.

Garrison, S. R., & Stolberg, A. L. (1983). Modification of anger in children by affective imagery training. *Journal of Abnormal Child Psychology, 11,* 115–130.

Gesten, E. L., Rains, M., Rapkin, B. D., Weissberg, R. G., Flores de Apodaca, R., Cowen, E. L., & Bowen, G. (1982). Training children in social problem-solving competencies: A first and second look. *American Journal of Community Psychology, 10,* 95–115.

Gilbert, G. M. (1957). A survey of "referral problems" in metropolitan child guidance centers. *Journal of Clinical Psychology, 13,* 37–42.

Glueck, S., & Glueck, E. (1950). *Unravelling juvenile delinquency.* Cambridge, MA: Harvard University Press.

Glueck, S., & Glueck, E. (1959). *Predicting delinquency and crime.* Cambridge, MA: Harvard University Press.

Glueck, S., & Glueck, E. (1968). *Delinquents and nondelinquents in perspective.* Cambridge, MA: Harvard University Press.

Graham, P. (1979). Epidemiological studies. In H. C. Quay & J. S. Werry (Eds.), *Psychopathological disorders of childhood* (2nd ed., pp. 185–209). New York: John Wiley & Sons.

Gresham, F. M. (1985). Utility of cognitive-behavioral procedures for social skills training with children: A critical review. *Journal of Abnormal Child Psychology, 13,* 411–423.

Griest, D. L., Forehand, R., Rogers, T., Breiner, J., Furey, W., & Williams, C. A. (1982). Effects of parent enhancement therapy on the treatment outcome and generalization of a parent training program. *Behaviour Research and Therapy, 20,* 429–436.

Gross, A. M., Brigham, T. A., Hopper, C., & Bologna, N. C. (1980). Self-management and social skills training: A study with predelinquent and delinquent youths. *Criminal Justice and Behavior, 7,* 161–184.

Hartup, W. W. (1970). Peer interaction and social organization. In P. Mussen (Ed.), *Carmichael's manual of child psychology* (Vol. 2). New York: John Wiley & Sons.

Herbert, E. W., Pinkston, E. M., Hayden, M., Sajwaj, T. E., Pinkston, S., Cordua, G., & Jackson, C. (1973). Adverse effects of differential parental attention. *Journal of Applied Behavior Analysis, 6,* 15–30.

Hewett, L. E., & Jenkins, R. L. (1946). *Fundamental patterns of maladjustment: The dynamics of their origin.* Springfield, IL: State of Illinois.

Hinshaw, S. P. (1987). On the distinction between attentional deficits/hyperactivity and conduct problems/aggression in child psychopathology. *Psychological Bulletin, 101,* 443–463.

Hobbs, S. A., Forehand, R., & Murray, R. G. (1978). Effects of various durations of time out on the noncompliant behavior of children. *Behavior Therapy, 9,* 652–656.

Hobbs, T. R. & Holt, M. M. (1976). The effects of token reinforcement on the behavior of delinquents in cottage settings. *Journal of Applied Behavior Analysis, 9,* 189–198.

Hughes, H. M. (1979). Behavior change in children at a therapeutic summer camp as a function of feedback and individual versus group contingencies. *Journal of Abnormal Child Psychology, 7,* 211–219.

Hutchings, B., & Mednick, S. A. (1975). Registered criminality in the adoptive and biological parent of registered male criminal adoptees. In R. R. Fieve, D. Rosenthal, & H. Brill (Eds.), *Genetic research in psychia-* try. Baltimore: Johns Hopkins University Press.

Iannotti, R. (1978). Effect of role-taking experiences on role-taking, empathy, altruism, and aggression. *Developmental Psychology, 14,* 119–124.

Jackson, J. L., & Calhoun, K. S. (1977). Effects of two variable-ratio schedules of time out: Changes in target and nontarget behaviors. *Journal of Behavior Therapy and Experimental Psychiatry, 8,* 195–199.

Jones, R. R., Weinrott, M. R., & Howard, J. R. (1981, June). *The national evaluation of the teaching family model.* Final report to the National Institute of Mental Health, Center for Studies in Crime and Delinquency.

Kazdin, A. E. (1977). *The token economy.* New York: Plenum Press.

Kazdin, A. E. (1982). Symptom substitution, generalization, and response covariation: Implications for psychotherapy outcome. *Psychological Bulletin, 91,* 349–365.

Kazdin, A. E. (1985). *Treatment of antisocial behavior in children and adolescents.* Homewood, IL: Dorsey Press.

Kazdin, A. E. (1986, December). *Hospitalization of antisocial children: Clinical course, follow-up status, and predictors of outcome.* Presented at the Rivendell Conference for Clinical Practitioners, Memphis, Tennessee.

Kazdin, A. E. (1987a). *Conduct disorder in childhood and adolescence.* Newbury Park, CA: Sage Publications.

Kazdin, A. E. (1987b). Treatment of antisocial behavior in children: Current status and future directions. *Psychological Bulletin, 102,* 187–203.

Kazdin, A. E. (1988). *Child psychotherapy: Developing and identifying effect treatments.* Elmsford, NY: Pergamon Press.

Kazdin, A. E. (1989). *Behavior modification in applied settings* (4th ed.). Pacific Grove, CA: Brooks/Cole.

Kazdin, A. E., Esveldt-Dawson, K., French, N. H., & Unis, A. S. (1987). Problem-solving skills training and relationship therapy in the treatment of antisocial child behavior. *Journal of Consulting and Clinical Psychology, 55,* 76–85.

Kazdin, A. E., Rodgers, A., Colbus, D., & Siegel, T. (1987). Children's Hostility Inventory: Measurement of aggression and hostility in psychiatric inpatient children. *Journal of Clinical Child Psychology, 16,* 320–328.

Kelly, J. A. (1982). *Social skills training: A*

practical guide for interventions. New York: Springer.

Kendall, P. C. & Braswell, L. (1982). Cognitive-behavioral self-control therapy for children: A components analysis. *Journal of Consulting and Clinical Psychology, 50,* 672–689.

Kendall, P. C., & Braswell, L. (1985). *Cognitive-behavioral therapy for impulsive children.* New York: Guilford Press.

Kirigin, K. A., Braukmann, C. J., Atwater, J. D., & Wolf, M. M. (1982). An evaluation of teaching-family (Achievement Place) group homes for juvenile offenders. *Journal of Applied Behavior Analysis, 15,* 1–16.

Kirigin, K. A., Wolf, M. M., Braukmann, C. J., Fixsen, D. L., & Phillips, E. L. (1979). Achievement Place: A preliminary outcome evaluation. In J. S. Stumphauzer (Ed.), *Progress in behavior therapy with delinquents* (pp. 118–145). Springfield, IL: Charles C Thomas.

Klein, N. C., Alexander, J. F., & Parsons, B. V. (1977). Impact of family systems intervention on recidivism and sibling delinquency: A model of primary prevention and program evaluation. *Journal of Consulting and Clinical Psychology, 45,* 469–474.

Kolvin, I., Garside, R. F., Nicol, A. E., MacMillan, A., Wolstenholme, F., & Leitch, I. M. (1981). *Help starts here: The maladjusted child in the ordinary school.* London: Tavistock.

Ledingham, J. E. & Schwartzman, A. E. (1984). A 3-year follow-up of aggressive and withdrawn behavior in childhood: Preliminary findings. *Journal of Abnormal Child Psychology, 12,* 157–168.

Little, V. L., & Kendall, P. C. (1979). Cognitive-behavioral interventions with delinquents: Problem solving, role-taking, and self-control. In P. C. Kendall & S. D. Hollon (Eds.), *Cognitive behavioral interventions: Theory, research, and procedures* (pp. 81–115). New York: Academic Press.

Loeber, R., & Dishion, T. J. (1983). Early predictors of male delinquency: A review. *Psychological Bulletin, 94,* 68–99.

Lochman, J. E. (1985). Effects of different treatment lengths in cognitive behavioral interventions with aggressive boys. *Child Psychiatry and Human Development, 16,* 45–56.

Lochman, J. E., Burch, P. R., Curry, J. F., & Lampron, L. B. (1984). Treatment and generalization effects of cognitive-behavioral and goal-setting interventions with aggressive boys. *Journal of Consulting and Clinical Psychology, 52,* 915–916.

MacFarlane, J. W., Allen, L., & Honzik, M. P. (1954). *A developmental study of the behavior problems of normal children between 21 months and 14 years.* Berkeley, CA: University of California Press.

Matson, J. L., Kazdin, A. E., & Esveldt-Dawson, K. (1980). Training interpersonal skills among mentally retarded and socially dysfunctional children. *Behaviour Research and Therapy, 18,* 419–427.

McCord, W. (1982). *The psychopath and milieu therapy: A longitudinal study.* New York: Academic Press.

McMahon, R. J., Forehand, R., & Griest, D. L. (1981). Effects of knowledge of social learning principles on enhancing treatment outcome and generalization in a parent training program. *Journal of Consulting and Clinical Psychology, 49,* 526–532.

Mednick, S. A., & Hutchings, B. (1978). Genetic and psychophysiological factors in asocial behaviour. In R. D. Hare & D. Schalling (Eds.), *Psychopathic behaviour: Approaches to research* (pp. 239–253). Chichester, England: John Wiley & Sons.

Michelson, L., Sugai, D. P., Wood, R P., & Kazdin, A. E. (1983). *Social skills assessment and training with children.* New York: Plenum Press.

Morris, S. B., Alexander, J. F., & Waldron, H. (in press). Functional family therapy: Issues in clinical practice. In I. R. H. Falloon (Ed.), *Handbook of behavior therapy.* New York: Guilford Press.

Murphy, H. A., Hutchinson, J. M., & Bailey, J. S. (1983). Behavioral school psychology goes outdoors: The effect of organized games on playground aggression. *Journal of Applied Behavior Analysis, 16,* 29–36.

Novaco, R. W. (1978). Anger and coping with stress: Cognitive behavioral intervention. In J. P. Foreyt & D. P. Rathjen (Eds.), *Cognitive behavioral therapy: Research and application* (pp. 135–173). New York: Plenum Press.

O'Donnell, C. R., Lydgate, T., & Fo., W. S. O. (1979). The buddy system: Review and follow-up. *Child Behavior Therapy, 1,* 161–169.

O'Donnell, D. J. (1985). Conduct disorders. In J. M. Weiner (Ed.), *Diagnosis and psychopharmacology of childhood and adolescent disorders.* New York: John Wiley & Sons.

Ollendick, T. H., & Cerny, J. A. (1981). *Clinical behavior therapy with children.* New York: Plenum Press.

Ollendick, T. H., Matson, J. L., & Martin, J. E. (1978). Effectiveness of hand overcorrection for topographically similar and dissimilar self-stimulatory behavior. *Journal of Experimental Child Psychology, 25,* 396–403.

Parsons, B. V., & Alexander, J. F. (1973). Short-term family intervention: A therapy outcome study. *Journal of Consulting and Clinical Psychology, 42,* 471–481.

Patterson, G. R. (1974). Interventions for boys with conduct problems: Multiple settings, treatments, and criteria. *Journal of Consulting and Clinical Psychology, 42,* 471–481.

Patterson, G. R. (1975). *Families.* Champaign, IL: Research Press.

Patterson, G. R. (1982). *Coercive family process.* Eugene, OR: Castalia.

Patterson, G. R. (1986). Performance models for antisocial boys. *American Psychologist, 41,* 432–444.

Patterson, G. R., Chamberlain, P., & Reid, J. B. (1982). A comparative evaluation of a parent-training program. *Behavior Therapy, 13,* 638–650.

Patterson, G. R., Cobb, J. A., & Ray, R. S. (1973). A social engineering technology for retraining the families of aggressive boys. In H. E. Adams & I. P. Unikel (Eds.), *Issues and trends in behavior therapy* (pp. 139–210). Springfield, IL: Charles C Thomas.

Patterson, G. R., & Fleischman, M. J. (1979). Maintenance of treatment effects: Some considerations concerning family systems and follow-up data. *Behavior Therapy, 10,* 168–185.

Pfiffner, L. J., & O'Leary, S. G. (1987). The efficacy of all-positive management as a function of the prior use of negative consequences. *Journal of Applied Behavior Analysis, 20,* 265–271.

Phillips, E. L., Phillips, E. A., Wolf, M. M., & Fixsen, D. L. (1973). Achievement Place: Development of the elected manager system. *Journal of Applied Behavior Analysis, 6,* 541–561.

Quay, H. C. (1986a). Classification. In H. C. Quay & J. S. Werry (Eds.), *Psychopathological disorders of childhood* (3rd ed., pp. 1–34). New York: John Wiley & Sons.

Quay, H. C. (1986b). A critical analysis of DSM-III as a taxonomy of psychopathology in childhood and adolescence. In T. Millon &

G. Klerman (Eds.), *Contemporary issues in psychopathology* (pp. 151–165). New York: Guilford Press.

Richard, B. A., & Dodge, K. A. (1982). Social maladjustment and problem solving in school-aged children. *Journal of Consulting and Clinical Psychology, 50,* 226–233.

Roberts, M. W., Hatzenbuehler, L. C., & Bean, A. W. (1981). The effects of differential attention and time out on child noncompliance. *Behavior Therapy, 12,* 93–99.

Robins, L. N. (1966). *Deviant children grown up.* Baltimore: Williams & Wilkins.

Robins, L. N. (1978). Sturdy childhood predictors of adult antisocial behavior: Replications from longitudinal studies. *Psychological Medicine, 8,* 611–622.

Robins, L. N. (1981). Epidemiological approaches to natural history research: Antisocial disorders in children. *Journal of the American Academy of Child Psychiatry, 20,* 566–680.

Roff, M., Sells, S. B., & Golden, M. M. (1972). *Social adjustment and personality development in children.* Minneapolis, MN: University of Minnesota Press.

Rutter, M. (1972). *Maternal deprivation reassessed.* Harmondsworth, Middlesex: Penguin Books.

Rutter, M., Cox, A., Tupling, C., Berger, M., & Yule, W. (1975). Attainment and adjustment in two geographical areas. I. The prevalence of psychiatric disorder. *British Journal of Psychiatry, 126,* 493–509.

Rutter, M., & Giller, H. (1983). *Juvenile delinquency: Trends and perspectives.* New York: Penguin Books.

Rutter, M., Tizard, J., & Whitmore, K. (Eds.). (1970). *Education, health and behaviour.* London: Longmans.

Schlichter, K. J., & Horan, J. J. (1981). Effects of stress innoculation on the anger and aggression management skills of institutional juvenile delinquents. *Cognitive Therapy and Research, 5,* 359–365.

Shanok, S. S., & Lewis, D. O. (1981). Medical histories of female delinquents: Clinical and epidemiological findings. *Archives of General Psychiatry, 38,* 211–213.

Shure, M. B., & Spivack, G. (1978). *Problem-solving techniques in child-rearing.* San Francisco: Jossey-Bass.

Solnick, J. V., Braukmann, C. J., Bedington, M. M., Kirigin, K. A., & Wolf, M. M. (1981). The relationship between parent–youth interaction and delinquency in group homes. *Journal of Abnormal Child Psychology, 9,* 107–119.

Solnick, J. V., Rincover, A., & Peterson, C. R. (1977). Some determinants of the reinforcing and punishing effects of time out. *Journal of Applied Behavior Analysis, 10,* 415–424.

Spence, S. H., & Marzillier, J. S. (1981). Social skills training with adolescent male offenders. II. Short-term, long-term, and generalized effects. *Behavior Research and Therapy, 19,* 349–368.

Spivack, G., & Shure, M. B. (1982). The cognition of social adjustment: Interpersonal cognitive problem solving thinking. In B. B. Lahey, & A. E. Kazdin (Eds.), *Advances in clinical child psychology* (Vol. 5, pp. 323–372). New York: Plenum Press.

Spivack, G., Platt, J. J., & Shure, M. B. (1976). *The problem-solving approach to adjustment.* San Francisco: Jossey-Bass.

Stewart, M. A., Cummings, C., & Meardon, J. K. (1978). Unsocialized aggressive boys: A follow-up study. *Journal of Clinical Psychiatry, 39,* 797–799.

Stokes, T. F., & Osnes, P. G. (1986). Programming the generalization of children's social behavior. In P. S. Strain, M. J. Guralnick, & H. M. Walker (Eds.), *Children's social behavior: Development, assessment, and modification* (pp. 407–443). New York: Academic Press.

Strain, P. S., Young, C. C., & Horowitz, J. (1981). Generalized behavior change during oppositional child training: An examination of child and family demographic variables. *Behavior Modification, 5,* 15–26.

Stumphauzer, J. S. (Ed.). (1979). *Progress in behavior therapy with delinquents.* Springfield, IL: Charles C Thomas.

Sturge, C. (1982). Reading retardation and antisocial behaviour. *Journal of Child Psychology and Psychiatry, 23,* 21–31.

Tisdell, D. A., & St. Lawrence, J. S. (1988). Adolescent interpersonal problem-solving skills training: Social validation and generalization. *Behavior Therapy, 19,* 171–182.

Voeltz, L. M., & Evans, I. M. (1982). The assessment of behavioral interrelationships in child behavior therapy. *Behavioral Assessment, 4,* 131–165.

Wadsworth, M. (1979). *Roots of delinquency: Infancy, adolescence and crime.* New York: Barnes & Noble.

Wahler, R. G. (1969). Setting generality: Some specific and general effects of child behavior therapy. *Journal of Applied Behavior Analysis, 2,* 239–246.

Wahler, R. G. (1972). Some ecological problems in child behavior modification. In S. W. Bijou & E. Ribes-Inesta (Eds.), *Behavior modification: Issues and extensions.* New York: Academic Press.

Wahler, R. G. (1975). Some structural aspects of deviant child behavior. *Journal of Applied Behavior Analysis, 8,* 27–42.

Wahler, R. G., Berland, R. M., & Coe, T. D. (1979). Generalization processes in child behavior change. In B. B. Lahey & A. E. Kazdin (Eds.), *Advances in clinical child psychology* (Vol. 2, pp. 36–69). New York: Plenum Press.

Wahler, R. G., & Fox, J. J. (1980a). Solitary toy play and time out: A family treatment package for children with aggressive and oppositional behavior. *Journal of Applied Behavior Analysis, 13,* 23–29.

Wahler, R. G., & Fox, J. J. (1980b, October). *Response structure in deviant child-parent relationships: Implications for family therapy.* Paper presented to the Nebraska Symposium on Motivation, University of Nebraska, Lincoln, Nebraska.

Wahler, R. G., Leske, G., & Rogers, E. S. (1979). The insular family: A deviance support system for oppositional children. In L. A. Hamerlynck (Ed.), *Behavioral systems for the developmentally disabled: I. School and family environments.* New York: Brunner/Mazel.

Walker, H. M., Hops, H., & Greenwood, C. R. (1981). RECESS: Research and development of a behavior management package for remediating social aggression in the school setting. In P. S. Strain (Ed.), *The utilization of classroom peers as behavior change agents.* New York: Plenum Press.

Walter, H. I., & Gilmore, S. K. (1973). Placebo versus social learning effects in parent training procedures designed to alter the behavior of aggressive boys. *Behavior Therapy, 4,* 361–377.

Weathers, L., & Liberman, R. P. (1975). Contingency contracting with families of delinquent adolescents. *Behavior Therapy, 6,* 356–366.

Weissberg, R. P., & Gesten, E. L. (1982). Considerations for developing effective school-based social problem-solving (SPS) training programs. *School Psychology Review, 11,* 56–63.

Weissberg, R. P., Gesten, E. L., Rapkin, B. D., Cowen, E. L., Davidson, E., Flores de Apodaca, R., & McKim, B. J. (1981). The evaluation of a social problem solving training program for suburban and inner-city third grade children. *Journal of Consulting and Clinical Psychology, 49,* 251–261.

Wells, K. C., Forehand, R., & Griest, D. L. (1980). Generality of treatment effects from treatment to untreated behaviors resulting from a parent training program. *Journal of Clinical Child Psychology, 9,* 217–219.

Werner, J. S., Minkin, N., Minkin, B. L., Fixsen, D. L., Phillips, E. L., & Wolf, M. M. (1975). "Intervention package:" An analysis to prepare juvenile delinquents for encounters with police officers. *Criminal Justice and Behavior, 2,* 55–83.

White, G. D., Nielsen, G., & Johnson, S. M. (1972). Timeout duration and the suppression of deviant behavior in children. *Journal of Applied Behavior Analysis, 5,* 111–120.

Williams, J. R., & Gold, M. (1972). From delinquent behavior to official delinquency. *Social Problems, 20,* 209–229.

Wiltz, N. A., & Patterson, G. R. (1974). An evaluation of parent training procedures designed to alter inappropriate aggressive behavior of boys. *Behavior Therapy, 5,* 215–221.

Wodarski, J. S., & Pedi, S. J. (1978). The empirical evaluation of the effects of different group treatment strategies against a controlled treatment strategy on behavior exhibited by antisocial children, behaviors of the therapist, and two self-rating scales that measure antisocial behavior. *Journal of Clinical Psychology, 34,* 471–481.

Wolf, M. M., Braukmann, C. J., & Ramp, K. A. (1987). Serious delinquent behavior as part of a significantly handicapping condition: Cures and supportive environments. *Journal of Applied Behavior Analysis, 20,* 347–359.

Wolf, M. M., Phillips, E. L., Fixsen, D. L., Braukmann, C. J., Kirigin, K. A., Willner, A. G., & Schumaker, J. B. (1976). Achievement Place: The teaching-family model. *Child Care Quarterly, 5,* 92–103.

Wolkind, S., & Rutter, M. (1973). Children who had been "in care" — An epidemiological study. *Journal of Child Psychology and Psychiatry, 14,* 97—105

CHAPTER 8

SOMATIC DISORDERS

Lawrence J. Siegel
Karen E. Smith

INTRODUCTION

Since antiquity, psychological factors have been regarded as important in the understanding of disease. The interrelationship between the mind and body has fascinated people for centuries and continues to be a topic of considerable interest to researchers and clinicians. Debates over a mind–body dichotomy led to a distinction between disorders caused by "physical" factors and disorders caused by "emotional" or "psychological" factors. This conceptual approach to disease gave rise in the early 1900s to the field generally referred to as psychosomatic medicine. In more recent times, the term "psychophysiological" was applied to disorders that have traditionally been called psychosomatic illnesses (American Psychiatric Association [APA], 1968). Psychosomatic or psychophysiological disorders have been defined as disorders in which:

> There is a significant interaction between somatic and psychological components, with varying degrees of weighting in each component. Psychophysiological disorders may be precipitated and perpetuated by psychological or social stimuli of a stressful nature. Such disorders ordinarily involve those organ systems that are innervated by the autonomic or involuntary portion of the central nervous system. . . .
>
> Structural change occurs . . . , continuing to a point that may be irreversible and that may threaten life in some cases. (Group for the Advancement of Psychiatry, 1966, p. 258)

In the most recent revision of the *Diagnostic and Statistical Manual of Mental Disorders* (APA, 1987), the diagnostic category of psychophysiological disorders is no longer included. Instead, DSM-III-R has several diagnostic categories that subsume the disorders previously referred to as psychophysiological. These new categories include: (1) "psychological factors affecting physical condition" pertaining to disorders in which psychological factors are presumed to cause or exacerbate a physical condition, and (2) "somatoform disorders" defined as physical symptoms with "no demonstrable organic findings or known physiological mechanisms and for which there is positive evidence, or a strong presumption, that the symptoms are linked to psychological factors or conflicts" (APA 1987, p. 255). Among the disorders included in this diagnostic category are conversion disorder, somatization disorder, psychogenic pain disorder, and hypochondriasis.

At the present time, it is the general consensus that the concepts "psychosomatic," "psychophysiological," or "somatopsychic" are of limited usefulness and lead to a simplistic notion about the relationship between psychological factors and a *distinct* group of physical or somatic disorders. The prevailing view is that an interaction of multiple, complex factors (i.e., biological, environmental, psychological, and social) contributes to the development and maintenance of most physical disorders (Kimball, 1970; Lipton, Sternschneider, & Richmond, 1966; Schwab, McGinnis, Morris, & Schwab, 1970). This view is expressed by Lipowski (1977):

> The concept of psychogenesis of organic disease . . . is no longer tenable and has given way to the multiplicity of all disease. . . . The relative contributions of these factors [social and psychological] varies from disease to disease, from person to person, and from one episode of the same disease in the same person to another episode. . . . If the foregoing arguments are accepted then it becomes clear that to distinguish a class of disorders as "psychosomatic disorders" and to propound generalizations about psychosomatic patients is misleading and redundant. Concepts of single causes and unilinear causal sequences for example from psyche to soma and vise versa are simplistic and obsolete. (p. 234)

Davidson and Neale (1974) similarly have noted that:

> Many diseases are viewed as being partially caused by emotional or psychological factors. The list, a long one, includes multiple sclerosis, pneumonia, cancer, tuberculosis, and the common cold. In fact, the emotional state of the patient is now recognized as playing an important role in the precipitation or exacerbation of many illnesses. (p. 152)

To avoid this arbitrary distinction between "psychosomatic disorders" and other health-related problems, Siegel and Richards (1978) have proposed that the term "somatic disorder" be used to refer to any bodily dysfunction irrespective of the presumed etiology. Therefore, this chapter will use the more generic term "somatic disorder" to refer to a diverse array of problems associated with dysfunctions of various organ systems of the body.

THEORETICAL MODELS OF SOMATIC DISORDERS

During the past several decades, numerous theories have been put forth to account for the etiology of somatic disorders in which psychological or emotional factors are presumed to play a significant role. There are four major theoretical models that dominate the field at the present time: the stress model, the family-systems model, the cognitive-perceptual model, and the behavioral model. Each of these models will be briefly reviewed.

Stress Model

Psychological stress has been implicated as an important factor in the development and maintenance of many somatic problems. A number of theories have been proposed to account for the relationship between stress and disease. One of the earliest theories to link stress to illness was the general adaptation syndrome proposed by Selye (1956). According to Selye, a noxious or stressful stimulus results in increased physiological activity which, if prolonged, can lead to lowered resistance of the body systems and eventually to disease.

A major research focus in recent years has been on the effects of stressful life events on health-related problems. It has been proposed that life changes, whether positive or negative, require some readjustment by the person affected. A consequence of frequent life-change events is an enhanced susceptibility to disease (Holms & Rahe, 1967). A large body of literature has demonstrated a significant relationship between measures of life change and the occurence of a wide range of somatic disorders (Johnson & Bradlyn, 1988), although the etiological link between stressful life events and physical problems remains open to debate. The complexity of this relationship is further illustrated by a number of factors that serve as moderator variables, such as the role of appraisal of life events as stressful or not stressful and the availability of personal resources (e.g., coping behaviors, social support) (Lazarus, 1966). Similar findings with health-related outcomes have also been reported with the occurrence of daily hassles, which represent common, daily events that are irritating, frustrating, and annoying (Kanner, Coyne, Schaefer, & Lazarus, 1980).

The field of psychoneuroimmunology, which has proliferated during the past decade, is concerned with the study of biological mechanisms that serve to link stress-related factors and the onset and exacerbation of disease processes. Research suggests that the body's immune system, in interaction with the neuroendocrine system, is responsive to a variety of psychological events. In particular, acute and chronic stress can suppress different aspects of the immune system (Rogers, Dubey, & Reich, 1979). While conclusive evidence remains to be empirically demonstrated, it has been suggested that the resulting immune suppression can result in disease onset and maintenance (Keicolt-Glaser & Glaser, 1988).

Family-Systems Model

Various theories have addressed the role that the family plays in the etiology and maintenance of physical symptoms among its members (Payne & Norfleet, 1986; Turk & Kerns, 1985). The literature in this area is represented by a preponderance of theorists who subscribe to a family-systems model. Family-systems theorists are particularly concerned with the nature of the family's interaction patterns and regard the somatic symptoms as having a functional significance in stabilizing and maintaining the status quo of the family system (Haggerty, 1983; Meisner, 1974).

Minuchin and his colleagues (Minuchin, Baker, Liebman, Milman, & Todd, 1975; Minuchin, Rosman, & Baker, 1978) have developed one of the most comprehensive and influential theories pertaining to family relationships and somatic symptoms. These researchers observed that families of children diagnosed as having severe "psychosomatic" symptoms—such as asthma, diabetes, and anorexia nervosa—demonstrated a number of consistent characteristics, particularly when threatened by stresses. These families were found to be rigid in their rules and expectations at times when flexibility and change were important; they lacked appropriate conflict-resolution skills, so that the somatic symptoms served to distract the family from solving significant family problems; and there was excessive and inappropriate overprotectiveness. Support for this theory is limited primarily to reports from Minuchin and his colleagues; these

indicate the successful treatment of somatic symptoms in children by means of intervention programs designed to change dysfunctional patterns of family organization and interaction.

Cognitive-Perceptual Model

A number of diverse theories examine the role that cognitive-perceptual processes play in the development of physical symptoms. A common theme of these theoretical approaches is that the preoccupation with or heightened sensitivity to bodily states contributes to symptom development.

Pennebaker and Skelton (1978) argue that attending to one's internal states serves to enhance the perceived intensity of physical symptoms. Using the concept of private body consciousness, investigators have shown that persons who tend to focus on normal bodily sensations also report more somatic symptoms (Ahles, Cassens, & Stallings, 1983). Similarly, Mechanic (1983) refers to the notion of introspectiveness, which he defines as a learned focus on inner thoughts and feelings that can lead to a greater sensitivity to bodily changes. He suggests that an increased reporting of somatic symptoms during adolescence can be attributed to a greater degree of introspectiveness and self-monitoring during this period of rapid bodily changes. Finally, Barsky and his colleagues (Barsky & Klerman, 1983; Barsky, Goodson, Lane, & Cleary, 1988) propose the concept of an "amplifying somatic style" to account for persons who report frequent somatic complaints. Such individuals exhibit a tendency to experience normal physiological sensations as disturbing and respond to such sensations with hypervigilance. As a result, these sensations are amplified and misinterpreted.

While the theories included under the cognitive-perceptual model are relatively new, cognitive-behavioral intervention techniques that focus on a person's cognitions and appraisals can easily incorporate this perspective. Hypervigilance and misinterpretation of bodily sensations, once identified as a part of the problem, can become targets for change using cognitive-behavioral approaches.

Behavioral Model

There is considerable research evidence that learning mechanisms can play a significant role in a variety of somatic disorders, regardless of the specific etiology involved. Research has shown that the body's physiological responses can be influenced and modified by specified learning experiences. Autonomic or visceral responses can be affected or altered by both respondent (classical) conditioning or operant (instrumental) conditioning (cf. Blanchard & Young, 1974; Miller, 1969; Schwartz, 1973; Shapiro & Surwit, 1976). It was presumed until very recently that autonomic responses were "involuntary" and as such could be modified only through the process of respondent conditioning. However, there is now substantial clinical and research evidence, accumulated over the last decade, indicating that many autonomic or visceral responses such as heart rate (Brener, 1974; Engle, 1972), blood pressure (Elder, Ruiz, Deabler, & Dillenkoffer, 1973; Shapiro, Tursky, & Schwartz, 1970), skin temperature (Roberts, Kewan, & Macdonald, 1973; Sargent, Green, & Walters, 1973), brain-wave activity (Beatty, 1977), and muscular activity (Basmajian, 1977) are in fact subject to voluntary control through operant conditioning mechanisms. These findings have led to significant developments in our basic understanding of the etiology and treatment of numerous somatic disorders. However, Davison and Neale (1974) have proposed that the primary role of operant and respondent conditioning mechanisms in physical disorders "is probably best viewed as a factor that can exacerbate an already existing illness rather than cause it" (p. 157).

In another, more detailed conceptualization of physical illnesses within a behavioral framework—described by Whitehead, Fedoravicius, Blackwell, and Wooley (1979)—somatic symptoms are regarded as the result of interactions between stress reactions and operant and respondent conditioning. This behavioral model of somatic disorders is illustrated in a case described by Siegel and Richards (1978). An 8-year-old child had experienced severe abdominal pains for several days as a result of gastrointestinal problems that developed during a viral infection. When the child drank milk during this illness, the stomach pains worsened, becoming more intense. As a result of this repeated, learned association between the stomachaches and the milk, the act of drinking milk alone was sufficient to elicit the stomach pains, despite the fact that the child no longer had the virus. Therefore, each time the child subsequently attempted to drink milk, stomach pains occurred for a short time. This learned association between the abdominal pains and the drinking of milk can be accounted for by the process of respondent conditioning, in which involuntary or reflexive behaviors (i.e., contractions of the gastrointestinal tract) can be made to occur in the presence of a previously neutral stimulus (e.g., the milk) which does not naturally elicit the physiological response. It is also possible for physical symptoms to be shaped and maintained by operant conditioning mechanisms. "Operant conditioning" refers to a learning process that involves the occurrence of a response (e.g., stomach pains) and the consequences that contingently and systematically follow it. The response is more or less likely to occur in the future depending on whether the consequences that follow it are reinforcing, punishing, or neutral. For example, in the case of the child with stomach pains, it is possible that upon exhibiting verbal and/or nonverbal pain behaviors, a number of positive events or benefits (sometimes referred to as secondary gains) may follow in a contiguous manner. The child, for instance, may receive considerable adult attention and comfort for the reported pain. In addition, as a result of the stomach pains, the parents may permit the child to remain home from school or to avoid unpleasant activity, such as completing household chores or doing homework assignments. These reinforcing consequences can then perpetuate the symptomatic behaviors even when the illness, which may have initially precipitated the abdominal pains, no longer exists. Other learning-based intervention procedures, such as modeling, have received little attention in the treatment of somatic disorders in children, although a more comprehensive behavioral model of treatment has recently been proposed (Wooley, Blackwell, & Winget, 1978). It is within this conceptual model that behavioral procedures have developed as an effective treatment approach for many somatic disorders in children.

INTERVENTION STRATEGIES WITH SOMATIC DISORDERS

An understanding of the etiology of a particular somatic disorder is important primarily to the extent that organic or physical factors, if present, need to be identified for appropriate medical intervention. Where any physical or somatic complaints are presented as a problem, a thorough medical examination is imperative to evaluate the need for medical treatment prior to any treatment by psychological methods. Furthermore, many somatic disorders, despite their etiology, can result in extensive tissue damage or physical changes in a particular organ system, so that a combination of medical and psychological interventions may be required. For example, while enuresis typically has a nonorganic etiology, in some instances it can be caused by such organic factors as a urinary-tract infection, a neurological disorder, or a defect in the urogenital tract. Therefore, while less than 10% of the cases of childhood enuresis can be attributed to organic causes (Pierce, 1967), the effectiveness of any psychological treatment might be impeded should any of these conditions exist. In addition, the disorder may even worsen if psychological treatment is pursued in the context of an inadequate medical evaluation.

It should be emphasized, however, that the need for medical treatment does not preclude the simultaneous use of empirically derived psychological interventions. Behavioral procedures have served a useful and highly effective adjunctive role in the direct treatment of somatic disorders and indirectly through patient management (Melamed & Siegel, 1980). The concurrent application of behavioral methods and medical procedures has been effective in preventing the exacerbation of symptomatic behaviors and in alleviating discomfort in a variety of somatic disorders. Because it is generally recognized that psychological, environmental and physiological factors contribute to the development of many health problems, treatment strategies beyond traditional medical approaches are clearly warranted in many cases. Our knowledge of the multiple determinants of problems of health and illness underscores the need for a multifaceted treatment approach that integrates behavioral as well as medical methods of treatment for somatic disorders. In this regard, Katz and Zlutnick (1975) have noted that:

> In conjunction with already established medical technology, behavioral techniques allow for a more comprehensive approach to patient care. In contrast, lack of attention to the environmental, behavioral, and social components of health problems may result in a less than satisfactory outcome. Clearly, the patient profits from the collaboration between medical practitioners and behavioral scientists. (p. xv)

The merits of this interdisciplinary approach to the treatment of health problems have been recognized in recent years. This new orientation to health and illness has given rise to several fields or disciplines variously referred to as behavioral medicine, psychomatic medicine, and health psychology.

The remainder of this chapter presents various behavioral intervention methods which have been demonstrated to be effective or show considerable promise in the treatment of several somatic disorders in children. This chapter presents an overview of some of the psychological treatment approaches that have been used either alone or in combination with medical procedures to alleviate or reduce the symptomatic behaviors associated with various somatic disorders in children. In some cases, these psychological approaches have been used successfully to treat somatic disorders when medical interventions have failed to affect any changes in the bodily dysfunction. Furthermore, various psychological interventions have shown considerable promise in the treatment of physical disorders that have potentially debilitating or life-threatening consequences for the child.

The past decade has witnessed a proliferation of the literature in this area (cf. Magrab, 1978; Melamed & Siegel, 1980; Schaefer, Millman, & Levine, 1979; Siegel & Richards, 1978). It is, therefore, not possible in a single chapter to present a comprehensive review of all somatic problems in children which have been treated by psychological approaches. This chapter will focus on the treatment of several bodily dysfunctions that occur with a sufficient frequency to be of particular interest to practitioners from various disciplines who work with children. Included in this review is a discussion of intervention methods for eating disorders, enuresis, and headaches. An emphasis is placed on treatment strategies which are consistent with learning-based behavioral approaches to modifying disordered behavior. Behavioral procedures have shown considerable promise in this area and many innovative treatment programs have been developed by behavioral practitioners. Most impressively, research has demonstrated that behavioral methods, in contrast to other medical and nonmedical approaches, have been the most effective therapeutic strategies with several somatic disorders in children. While other intervention strategies, such as family therapy approaches, may also be clinically useful, less empirical data are available to document their efficacy.

Eating Disorders

Diagnostic categories within the DSM-III-R eating disorders subclass include anorexia nervosa, bulimia nervosa, pica, and rumination disorder, (APA, 1987). Eating disorder not otherwise specified is also included and applicable when a person does not meet all the criteria for either anorexia or bulimia. Other eating-related problems that are not included in DSM-III-R but are of importance psychologically are obesity, food refusal, and restricted eating patterns. Obesity is a significant somatic problem in which treatment components often involve psychological techniques. Food refusal and restricted eating patterns may present during the early ages of childhood, when food preferences typically develop. Treatment issues related to obesity and anorexia will be reviewed in this section because, clinically, these disorders are found more often in childhood or adolescence than pica, rumination, or food refusal and have received more attention in the literature. While bulimia nervosa is seen during adolescence (Howat & Saxton, 1988), it is beyond the scope of this chapter to review all areas. The reader is referred to reviews of treatment approaches to bulimia by Johnson (1984) and Johnson, Conners, and Tobin (1987). Siegel (1983) has reviewed the treatment of food refusal, restricted eating patterns, rumination, and vomiting.

Obesity

Obesity is usually defined as a weight that is 20% above the ideal, which, for children, is based on height, age, and gender (Epstein & Wing, 1987). While the problem of obesity in adults has been extensively investigated (Brownell & Jeffrey, 1987), only in the past decade has greater emphasis been placed on this problem in children and adolescents. The increased interest may be due in part to the fact that weight reduction with obese adults has resulted in little long-term success (Brownell, 1982; Brownell & Jeffrey, 1987) and that being overweight as a child places a person at greater risk for obesity during adulthood. The risk factor increases from approximately 2 during infancy to 6.5 by the preadolescent years (e.g., Epstein, 1986). In addition, the prevalence of obesity in children appears to be increasing. While one recent study has estimated it at only about 9%, among adolescents this represents a substantial increase (39% for obesity; 64% for superobesity) from

the previous results of the National Health and Examination Survey, Cycle 1 (Gortmaker, Dietz, Sobol, & Wehler, 1987). A similar trend has been noted in younger children, with greater increases noted in boys 6 to 11 years of age and adolescent girls (Gortmaker et al., 1987).

As with adults, childhood obesity can have significant medical impact, including increased risk for hypertension, hypercholesterolemia, carbohydrate intolerance, increased insulin secretion, and decreased growth hormone release (Chiumello, del Guercio, Carnelutti, & Bidone, 1969; Gillum et al., 1983; Heald, 1971; Lauer, Conner, Leaverton, Reiter, & Clark, 1975; Laskarzewski et al., 1979; Londe, Bourgoignie, Robson, & Goldring, 1972). The psychological impact of being overweight, while intuitively appealing, has not been consistently documented. Some studies have found lower self-esteem in obese children relative to normal-weight peers (Sallade, 1973), while others have found no significant differences (Wadden, Foster, Brownell, & Finley, 1984). Given society's emphasis on thinness, being overweight can have social repurcussions (e.g., Millman, 1980). Studies have indicated that, given a choice of several visible physical disabilities, a child is least likely to select an overweight person as a friend (Staffieri, 1967). Further investigation in this area is warranted, as children seeking treatment for their obesity may do so as a result of teasing by peers or concerns about acceptance by peers. These children may look different on standardized measures of psychological adjustments (Wadden et al., 1984). It would be interesting to know if emotional discomfort results in greater motivation both to seek and to follow through with treatment.

Etiological Factors. Simply stated, obesity is the result of an energy imbalance; that is, a person consumes more calories than are expended in the output of energy (Garrow, 1986). While this etiology seems simple enough, the attempt to understand why some children have more difficulty maintaining an optimum energy balance than others becomes very complex because so many factors (e.g., metabolic rate, responsive of metabolism to food and exercise) are related to energy balance (Garrow, 1986; Keesey, 1986). Research on the etiology of obesity has been plagued with the problem inherent in trying to untangle genetic and environmental influences.

Only a cursory overview of this debate and biological theories of obesity will be presented.

On the side of genetics, children of obese parents are more likely to be fat than children of thin parents, and this risk increases when both parents are overweight (Epstein, 1986). In addition, researchers have suggested that it is easier for obese children of thin parents to lose and maintain their weight loss than it is for children with obese parents (Epstein, Wing, Koeske, & Valoski, 1987; Epstein, Wing, Valoski, & Gooding, 1987). Twin studies have revealed an increased concordance of obesity in monozygotic twins relative to other sibling pairs (Foch & McClearn, 1980). Yet the most convincing evidence for a genetic component has been provided by Stunkard and his colleagues (Stunkard et al., 1986) in an adoption study, which showed greater correlations between the weight of adopted children and their biological parents than the children and their adopted parents. Other studies have suggested that genetics differentially affects different types of body fat (i.e., internal versus subcutaneous) (Bouchard, Perusse, LeBlanc, Tremblay, & Theriault, 1988). These studies would certainly argue for some degree of genetic involvement in the development of obesity.

If genetics plays a role, then what is inherited? Current theories regarding obesity suggest that weight is physiologically regulated, so that attempts to reduce weight through restricted diet may lower the metabolic rate and thus the required number of calories to maintain the original weight (Keesey, 1986). That is, some obese individuals may have a higher set point for their body weight. The reader is referred to Keesey (1986) for a more detailed discussion of the set-point theory of obesity. Other researchers have focused on the number and size of fat cells (Sjostrom, 1980) as being at least in part genetically determined.

On the side of environmental influences, studies suggest that parents can influence their children's preferences for particular types of foods, as well as the amounts of food they consume through exposure, prompting, reinforcement, and modeling (e.g., Birch & Marlin, 1982; Duncker, 1938; Epstein, Masek, & Marshall, 1978; Harper & Sanders, 1975; Klesges et al., 1983). These behavioral principles have been noted to apply to the amount of physical activity in which children engage as well (Epstein, Woodall, Goreczny, Wing, & Robertson, 1984; Klesges, Malott, Boschee, & Weber, 1986). In addition,

parental expectations regarding food consumption and amount of physical activity may play a role, as it has been shown that parents feel their obese children need more to eat and will be less active relative to their thinner siblings (Waxman & Stunkard, 1980). These studies would suggest that behavioral factors such as exposure to and availability of foods (e.g., stimulus control), reinforcement principles, and cognitive variables such as expectations and modeling are also involved in the development of obesity in childhood.

While behavioral factors have been shown to influence food consumption and activity level, the data are less consistent as to whether obese children actually differ from thin children in these ways (O'Brien, Walley, Anderson-Smith, & Drabman, 1982; Woodall & Epstein, 1983). There is evidence that obese and thin children differ in their perception of different types of physical activities and foods, but it is unclear if these perceptions preceded the obesity (Worsley, Coonan, Leitch, & Crawford, 1984; Worsley, Peters, Worsley, Coonan, & Baghurst, 1984). Other studies have suggested that obese children differ in their eating styles (Geller, Keane, & Scheirer, 1981) and have more difficulty delaying gratification when food is involved (Bonato & Boland, 1983; Sobhany & Rogers, 1985).

Though not a comprehensive review, these studies suggest that genetic, behavioral, and environmental factors can all contribute to obesity in children. The degree to which each factor is involved will likely vary between children. For example, a genetic component which may predispose children to gain weight more easily may be a major factor in some children, while obesity in others may be due primarily to self-regulatory difficulties with regard to food and activity. Certainly further investigations are needed in order to individualize treatment programs for children with different reasons for being overweight. In particular, continued evaluation of differences between obese and nonobese children with regard to eating and activity behaviors is needed to clarify what behavioral treatment components are needed. In the future particular attention should be paid to whether behaviors are a cause or result of increased weight.

Overview of Treatment Approaches. Treatment approaches for childhood obesity have been patterned primarily after those used with adults, with behavioral techniques as the major treatment components. One important difference between adult and child weight reduction is that, since children are still growing both in height and in weight, any methods used, especially dietary, must consider the child's nutritional needs to promote optimal growth (Epstein & Wing, 1987). Therefore, it is important to ensure that children receive recommended daily allowances of nutrients and to monitor changes in height carefully during treatment. In addition, it is usually best to base treatment success on decreases in percent overweight rather than actual pounds lost. For example, a child may maintain baseline weight and still decrease percent overweight with an increase in height. Finally, developmental differences that can affect understanding of the rationale for treatment as well as adherence to various treatment components should be considered (Wolfe, Farrier, & Rogers, 1987).

In general, treatment should include two phases: the initial weight loss or decrease in percent overweight and the maintenance of gains made during the initial period (Epstein & Wing, 1987). Studies with adults have suggested that duration of initial treatment is correlated with amount of weight lost (Brownell & Jeffrey, 1987). While it is relatively easy to achieve some initial weight loss, the success of a program is best judged by long-term maintenance (e.g., 1 to 5 years) (Brownell & Jeffrey, 1987).

A typical program for children and adolescents usually includes behavioral techniques such as self-monitoring, stimulus control, and reinforcement of behavior change. Most programs include dietary modifications and exercise components as well. A typical program and factors related to successful initial "losers" and "maintainers" will be reviewed in greater depth. Other approaches used with adults—such as pharmacotherapy (e.g., appetite suppressants) and surgical techniques that have not been a primary clinical or research focus with children—are not reviewed. Readers are referred to other sources for information regarding these types of interventions (Cohen & Stunkard, 1983; Kral & Kissileff, 1987).

A typical program involves having the child and/or parent "self-monitor" or keep records of various treatment components, which may include type and amount of food consumed, type and duration of exercise, actual weight, and reinforcements earned. The child's age and the complexity of the record keeping are usually determinants of who maintains the records,

though even younger children can be involved in some way (e.g., "helping" the parent record data). Most programs include education on the role of stimulus control, diet, activity, and use of reinforcements. Stimulus control involves reducing the number of cues associated with eating. For example, rather than eating in front of the television or while studying, the child consumes all foods at the dinner table. High-calorie foods are either not kept at home or are stored in opaque containers or on shelves out of children's reach. Low-calorie foods, such as carrots or celery, are prepared and placed in a prominent location in the refrigerator for easy access. Specific eating behaviors—such as using smaller plates with smaller portions of food, putting the fork down between bites, and chewing food a specified number of times—may be taught as well.

As food intake is one major part of the energy-balance equation, most programs include detailed education about the nutritional and caloric value of various foods. Epstein and his colleagues (Epstein, Masek, & Marshall, 1978) have developed the "Traffic Light Diet," which is easily understood by younger children because foods are divided into green—eat all you want, low calorie foods; yellow—all right to eat but use caution in amount consumed; and red—high-calorie, low-nutritional-value foods that should be limited. Successful weight reduction using this diet has been correlated with limiting the number of foods rated red eaten each week (Epstein, Wing, Koeske, Andrasik, & Ossip, 1981).

One of the difficulties with most typical weight-loss programs is that despite decreases in percent overweight, most children do not achieve a nonobese status, especially if they are markedly obese. The use of very low calorie protein-sparing diets has gained considerable attention with adults as one means of achieving even greater initial weight loss, with behavioral components being used to facilitate maintenance (Blackburn, Lynch, & Wong, 1986; Kirschner, Schneider, Ertel, & Gorman, 1988). These diets require close medical supervision, but there is some evidence that this approach can be used with children and adolescents without adverse effects (Blackburn et al., 1986; Merrit, 1978). Further collaborative investigations with physician colleagues will be important to carefully explore the safe application of this type of diet with children.

Activity level, the other major component in

the equation, has gained more attention and is now included in most programs. Exercise not only increases energy expenditure but also decreases the loss of lean body mass during a diet, improves psychological functioning, and may act to suppress appetite and offset the decline in basal metabolic rate associated with dieting (Brownell & Stunkard, 1980). Low-intensity activity (e.g., walking) that is equivalent in energy expenditure to a high-intensity, programmed activity (e.g., aerobics) is more likely to result in adherence to the program and to be associated with greater maintenance of fitness and weight loss (Epstein, Wing, Koeske, & Valoski, 1985; Epstein, Wing, Koeske, Ossip, & Beck, 1982). Shaping of the desired exercise behavior may be needed for children who are moderately obese and/or sedentary; this can be accomplished by setting a short-term goal that is increased each week until the desired endpoint is attained.

The use of reinforcements by other family members, such as praise contingent on changes in eating or activity levels, is another component included in most programs (e.g., Epstein et al., 1981). For some children a point system, where achieving daily or weekly treatment goals or adhering to specific behaviors can earn points that can be used to "buy" backup reinforcers, can be an additional motivator. Like reinforcement, contingency contracting is often used where monetary deposits are made prior to treatment and a specified amount is returned contingent on either attendance or weight loss (Epstein et al., 1987; Kirschenbaum, Harris, & Tomarken, 1984). There is some suggestion that contracts contingent on weight loss as opposed to adherence results in greater weight loss (Epstein et al., 1987; Coates, Jeffrey, Slinkard, Killen, & Danaher, 1982). No investigations have compared the utility of contracting contingent on weight loss with no contracting in children, though it has resulted in greater weight loss in adults (Brownell & Jeffrey, 1987).

While many programs are provided through medical or psychological clinics, there is evidence that weight-reduction programs can be implemented within the school setting (Brownell & Kaye, 1982; Foster, Wadden, & Brownell, 1985; Lansky & Brownell, 1982). Generally, school-based programs have resulted in smaller weight losses than clinic-based programs; evidence of maintenance of losses or behavioral changes that may stabilize weight are needed (Foster et al., 1985).

Factors Related to Weight Loss and Maintenance. In assessing factors related to weight loss, the issue of how and when to include parents has been a focus of research. There is some evidence that adolescents are best treated in groups separate from the parents, though both receive the same information (Brownell, Kelman, & Stunkard, 1983). In treating children 9 to 13 years of age, no differences were found in weight lost between children treated with parents in the same group or children treated alone, with parents receiving detailed written information (Kirschenbaum, Harris, & Tomarken, 1984). Attrition was lower in the group that included the parents. As adolescence is a time for developing independence, separate treatment may be more important for adolescents than for younger children.

Epstein et al. (1987) have found that targeting both parent and child for weight loss results in greater maintenance for the child at 5-year follow-up, despite the fact that parents regained their weight. While parent modeling and support can account for changes during treatment, modeling is unlikely to be related to maintenance, though continued support may be of importance. Israel, Stolmaker, and Andrian (1985) have noted that adding a general behavioral-management training component to the weight-reduction program resulted in greater maintenance of weight loss at 1-year follow-up. These parents may have been able to generalize their additional training to other problem situations that may have occurred during the follow-up year; absence of such generalization may have contributed to relapse in the standard treatment group (Epstein & Wing, 1987).

In addition to parental involvement, greater weight loss at posttreatment has been predicted by children's perceptions of greater personal control over their weight, that weight loss would be difficult, and that their excess weight is not due to family problems. Parental perception that the child was less likely to be overweight in the future was also a significant predictor (Uzark, Becker, Dielman, Rocchini, & Katch, 1988). Similarly, Flanery and Kirschenbaum (1986) found that flexible problem solving and attributions of ability and lack of effort predicted greater maintenance of weight loss, though keeping a weight chart was predictive as well. Cohen, Gelfand, Dodd, Jensen, and Turner (1980) found that greater self-regulation and physical exercise distinguished "maintainers" from "regainers" and normal-weight peers. Regainers also reported greater parental regulation of weight management relative to normal-weight peers. Though few in number, these studies suggest that children's self-efficacy (Bandura, 1977), attributions about the ability to lose weight, thoughts regarding relapse events, and ability to continue to self-monitor are important variables during the maintenance phase of weight loss. Parental support and expectations regarding success are probably important factors during this phase as well.

Though investigations with adults have focused on factors related to maintenance, such as continued therapist contact and the inclusion of a relapse component in the program (Perri, Shapiro, Ludwig, Twentyman, & McAdoo, 1984), these factors have not been empirically assessed in younger samples. Given that obesity may well be a chronic condition requiring continuous application of behavioral techniques and self-restraint, continued therapist contact may be one means of solidifying important behavioral changes and providing external motivation during periods of relapse.

Anorexia Nervosa

The most serious form of food refusal is known as anorexia nervosa. This disorder is characterized by a refusal to eat and extreme weight loss without any organic causes (American Psychiatric Association, 1987). Current DSM-III-R criteria for weight loss are less stringent than DSM-III (American Psychiatric Association, 1980) with 15% versus 25% of original body weight being one criterion. For children and adolescents, weight gain attributable to growth should be included in the 15% figure as well. Anorexia can pose a grave danger to the patient, with estimates of mortality as high as 15% (Dally, 1969; Palla & Litt, 1988). This disorder typically begins during adolescence, with most cases occurring by young adulthood; however, cases have been diagnosed in 7- to 14-year-olds (Fosson, Knibbs, Bryant-Waugh, & Lask, 1987). Anorexia occurs most frequently in females (Halmi, 1974) and in middle and upper socioeconomic classes (Garfinkel & Garner, 1982). In addition to profound weight loss, anorexia nervosa is typically associated with cessation of menstruation, serious electrolyte imbalances, and other medical abnormalities (Palla & Litt, 1988). Other common features of this disorder include distorted perceptions of body image, preoccupation with food preparation, unrealistic fears of being overweight, and lack of sensitivity to internal cues of hunger. The anorexic may also engage in compulsive overeating, followed by self-induced vomiting, laxative use, or high activity levels to avoid the intense fear of weight gain (Crisp, Hsu, Harding, & Hartshorn, 1980). Estimates of the prevalence of anorexia have ranged from 0.5% to 2.1%, and epidemiological studies have suggested that the incidence of the disorder is increasing (Strober, 1986).

Etiological Factors. The etiology of anorexia nervosa is unknown, though many theories have been suggested to account for it (Bemis, 1978). Given the multiple physiological abnormalities found in these patients and the fact that in some amenorrhea precedes weight loss, some researchers have suggested a hypothalamic dysfunction (Garfinkel & Kaplan, 1986). Yet studies have found that the majority of physiological abnormalities are the result of weight loss and calorie restriction. Studies of semistarved samples have reported obsessive food-related thoughts and behaviors similar to those in anorexic patients (Keys, Brozek, Henschel, Mickelsen, & Taylor, 1950). A genetic component has been hypothesized, based on evidence that eating disorders are more prevalent in relatives of anorexic patients (Strober, Morrell, Burroughs, Salkin, & Jacobs, 1985), and twin studies have documented greater concordance in monozygotic than dizygotic twins for anorexia (Holland, Hall, Murray, Russell, & Crisp, 1984). In addition, an increased prevalence of affective disorders has been found in first-degree relatives of anorexics, although the reverse is not true (e.g., there is not a higher prevalence of anorexia in relatives of depressed patients) (Gershon, et al., 1983). Sociocultural values have been implicated in the onset of anorexia, as the high value society places on thinness may interact with personality variables (Garner, Garfinkel, & Olmstead, 1983).

Psychological studies have suggested that, as a group, anorexics tend to be perfectionistic, to feel more personally ineffective, to exhibit greater interpersonal distrust, and to lack awareness of or exhibit confusion over internal emotional and physiological states (Bruch, 1977; Crisp, 1980; Garner et al., 1983; Strober, 1980). Crisp (1980) has described anorexics as having a "weight phobia," which results from a fear of maturation and sexuality. This fits well with behavioral conceptualizations that anorexic behavior is an example of a conditioned avoidance response to real or perceived fears related to weight, development, and performance (Garner, 1986). In addition, in a context of feeling ineffective, the ability to master a specific part of one's life can be highly reinforcing and may account for the perpetuation of the behaviors despite an emaciated condition (Garner, 1986). Cognitive-behavioral theorists have pointed to misperceptions regarding self-concept, separation, perfectionism, and relationships (Garner, 1986)—issues which seem consistent with the views of psychodynamic theorists. Family interactional patterns have also been hypothesized as contributing to the onset and perpetuation of the disorder through patterns such as overprotection, enmeshment, inability to express and resolve conflict openly, detachment, and lack of empathy and affection (Minuchin, et al., 1975; Strober & Humphrey, 1987). In a review of family contributions to both anorexia and bulimia, Strober and Humphrey (1987) interpret the available literature as suggesting that a family environment characterized by the above interactional patterns may interfere with the development of a stable identity and feelings of independence and self-efficacy. These authors call for more sophisticated investigations of family interactional patterns to support this hypothesis.

Overview of Treatment Approaches. Given that anorexia is probably the result of a complex interaction of social, familial, biological, and personality factors, careful assessment is needed to develop an appropriate treatment plan. A team approach that includes close collaboration between physician and therapist is imperative in the treatment of these patients. Most clinicians would agree that anorexia is a very difficult disorder to treat. Many patients with anorexia are reluctant to seek treatment, as their symptoms are not perceived as a problem. Therefore, the initial phases of any treatment approach will be to engage the patient in the therapeutic relationship in a collaborative manner. Garner, Rocket, Olmstead, Johnson, and Coscina (1985) have suggested that educational material on anorexia, the effects of starvation, medical complications, nutrition, physiology of weight regulation, and consequences of dieting can be helpful in this context.

Attention to eating habits and physical con-

dition are an important part of the treatment and likely to be the initial focus. Depending upon the degree of weight loss and medical condition, treatment may be instituted in a hospital or in an outpatient setting (Anderson, 1986; Palla & Litt, 1988). Contracts regarding a minimal acceptable weight and contingencies related to hospitalization are a part of many outpatient treatments. Behavioral approaches to treatment have helped patients to increase their weight through control of factors associated with the maladaptive eating patterns. Typically, the focus of treatment is on weight gain rather than eating per se. This approach places greater responsibility for eating on the patient and avoids problems of the patient engaging in vomiting after eating. The most frequently used procedure has been the manipulation of environmental contingencies in order to maximize calorie intake, food consumption, and weight gain. This has been accomplished by making activities, privileges, and reinforcers contingent on eating behavior or weight gain (Bemis, 1987). These procedures have been effective in cases where other treatment approaches—such as tube feeding, insulin, tranquilizers, and traditional psychotherapy—have failed to modify the symptomatic behavior (Walen, Hauserman, & Lavin, 1977).

With some resolution of the patient's semi-starved state, the therapeutic focus can shift to other issues regarding the misperceptions and fears noted previously. Yet attention to weight should be given throughout treatment in order to deal quickly with relapses. Several treatment programs for anorexia have been reported in which behavioral techniques have been combined with drug therapy (Munford, 1980) or family therapy (Lagos, 1981). Other behavioral approaches have focused primarily on the fear component of the disorder, using systematic desensitization to reduce fears of weight gain, criticism, and rejection; concerns about appearance; and fears of specific foods. Cognitive-behavioral techniques have been useful in changing misperceptions and distortions in thinking, symptoms that persist even after weight is gained (Garner, 1986). Various approaches to the treatment of anorexia nervosa have been reviewed by Bemis (1987) and Murray (1986). As the majority of the empirical literature has focused on behavioral techniques, several of these approaches will be described. Unfortunately relatively few empirical studies are available regarding psychodynamic and family approaches to treatment.

Premack Principle. Based on their observation that many anorexic patients exhibit a high level of activity, Blinder, Freeman, and Stunkard (1970) used access to physical activity as a reinforcer for weight gain in several adolescent girls diagnosed as having anorexia nervosa. Previous research has demonstrated that access to high-frequency behaviors can be used to reinforce contingently low-frequency behaviors (Premack, 1965). Therefore, physical activity, a high-frequency behavior in these patients, was used as a positive reinforcer for weight gain. Previous treatment with medication and traditional psychotherapy had failed to result in any improvements in these girls' physical condition. In the behavioral treatment program, each patient was permitted 6 hours outside the hospital on days when her morning weight check indicated that she was at least ½ pound above the previous day's weight. This treatment approach provided a rapid weight gain for all the girls. There was an increase of approximately 4 pounds each week for all patients over a 6-week period. These weight gains were maintained or increased after discharge from the hospital, as revealed by an 8- to 10-month follow-up assessment. Similar results with adolescent anorexic patients using a variety of reinforcers for food consumption and weight gain are reported by Garfinkel, Kline, and Stancer (1973); Halami, Powers, and Cunningham (1975); Leitenberg, Agras, and Thompson (1968); and Werry and Bull (1975).

Systematic Desensitization. Hallsten (1965) treated a 12-year-old anorexic girl by systematic desensitization. Several years prior to treatment, the patient had been teased for being overweight; she then went on a diet and lost an excessive amount of weight. She expressed a fear of being fat and periodically induced vomiting. After training in deep-muscle relaxation, a hierarchy of items was constructed that related to her fears of becoming fat and of being teased by her peers for being overweight. Hierarchy items included visualizing herself being called to the table, eating at the table, eating fattening foods, standing in front of the mirror observing that she was gaining weight, and so on. Treatment was conducted over 12 sessions, during which she began to eat complete meals. There was a concomitant increase in her weight. These improvements in her eating pattern and weight were maintained at a 5-month follow-up.

Reinforcement, Feedback, and Meal Size. In a series of single case studies, Agras, Barlow, Chapin, Abel, and Leitenberg (1974) systematically investigated several variables to determine their relative importance in the behavioral treatment of anorexia nervosa. The first study investigated the effects on several children 10 and 17 years old of reinforcing weight gain. The patients recorded the number of mouthfuls eaten and calories consumed at each meal. They were also informed of their daily weight and asked to keep records of their progress through self-monitoring. Daily weight gain of a specified amount was reinforced with access to serious activities in the hospital. These procedures resulted in a rapid increase in weight. Using a reversal procedure in which contingent reinforcement was discontinued, the patients continued to show a weight gain. While only suggestive, these results indicated that reinforcement was instrumental in establishing weight gain, but that the maintenance and additional increase in weight were the result of other factors.

In a second experiment, reinforcement without self-monitoring was delivered contingent on weight gain. This produced an increase in daily caloric intake and weight. However, when reinforcement was provided noncontingently, there was a decline in the rate of weight gain and a marked decrease in caloric intake. When reinforcement was again made contingent on weight gain, there was a significant increase in both caloric intake and weight.

In the third series of experiments, Agras et al. (1974) systematically evaluated the effects of reinforcement and information feedback. The reinforcement contingencies, like those in early experiments, remained in effect during this investigation. Information feedback, in which the patient received information about the number of calories and mouthfuls eaten and about daily weight, was introduced for several days, discontinued, and reintroduced. The results of this experiment revealed that maximum increases in caloric intake and weight gain were obtained only when the information-feedback condition was in effect. The investigators suggested that information regarding caloric intake and weight may enhance the effectiveness of reinforcement because it provides a cue for the patient that reinforcement is forthcoming.

The final experiment reported by Agras et al. (1974) demonstrated that the size of the meal given to an anorexic patient may affect the quantity of food eaten. When a large meal was provided, the patient's caloric intake increased, even when not all of the meal was eaten. However, when the size of the meal was decreased, there was a concomitant decrease in the number of calories consumed.

Operant Reinforcement and Family Therapy. Minuchin and his colleagues (Liebman, Minuchin, & Baker, 1974; Minuchin, Rosman, & Baker, 1978) have described a comprehensive treatment program for anorexic patients in which behavioral procedures in the hospital and at home are combined with family therapy. They propose that weight gain alone should not be the primary goal of treatment but should also include a restructuring of dysfunctional patterns of family interaction; this is intended to prevent relapses and promote weight gain once the patient is discharged from the hospital. It is assumed that these maladaptive relationship patterns within the family serve to maintain the child's anorexic behaviors. If hospitalization is warranted for medical reasons, the child is admitted to the hospital to facilitate weight gain and to engage the family in treatment. In operant reinforcement programs, family lunch sessions in the hospital are used to initiate weight gain. Weight gain (as assessed each morning) of at least ½ pound enables the patient to remain out of bed, watch television, have visitors, and have 4 hours of unrestricted hospital activity. Family therapy sessions continue on an outpatient basis when the child is discharged from the hospital. In this program, the patient is typically hospitalized for several weeks and weekly family therapy sessions occur over a period of 5 to 12 months.

Minuchin et al. (1978) have reported on 53 anorexic patients (ages 9 to 21) who were treated with this intervention program. Based on their criteria for treatment effectiveness (i.e., no evidence of eating disturbances and good adjustment at home and at school), they report a success rate of approximately 86% after a follow-up period ranging from 4 months to 4 years.

Factors Related to Treatment Outcome. As noted, anorexia is a very difficult, often recalcitrant disorder to treat. While prognostic indicators have been difficult to determine, anorexic patients who also exhibit bulimic symptoms appear to have a more chronic course than patients who do not engage in vomiting or purging (Casper, Eckert, Halmi, Goldberg, & Davis, 1980; Garfinkel, Moldofsky, & Garner, 1977). Bulimic anorexics are more likely to have a history of childhood maladjustment and obesity; they are also more likely to experience depression and to have impulse-control problems such as alcoholism. Families of bulimic anorexics are characterized as more conflictual and negative in their interactions, and a family history of obesity is more likely (Casper, Eckert, Halmi, Goldberg, & Davis, 1980; Garfinkel, Moldofsky, & Garner, 1980; Strober, 1981). Other factors which have been associated with a poorer prognosis in anorexics as a group include older age of onset, longer duration of illness, lower body weight, poorer childhood adjustment, disturbed family relationships, and a history of previous psychiatric treatment (Szmuckler & Russell, 1986).

In a review of studies that provide long-term results, Szmukler and Russell (1986) conclude that outcome is quite variable even within the same treatment centers. Some patients make complete recoveries, others appear to have more chronic courses, and some die. There is evidence that the percentage of patients who recover continues to increase up to about 4 years after treatment (Szmuckler & Russell, 1986), although it was not clear whether patients continued to receive treatment during the follow-up period. Szmuckler and Russell (1986) thoughtfully reflect on what constitutes a cure in these patients: successful maintenance of a specific body weight and menses, change in eating habits, and/or change in psychological disturbance or misperceptions.

At present, though behavioral approaches appear to be effective in producing initial weight gain, there are few comparative studies suggesting that one approach is superior to another (Szmuckler & Russell, 1986). While Bruch (1974) has argued that behavior modification can result in further psychological damage to the anorexic patient (because the therapist takes control), empirical data supporting this hypothesis are lacking. One recent study that compared family therapy with individual therapy in treating anorexia and bulimia suggested that, after 1 year of treatment, family therapy was more effective than individual therapy for patients who had developed their condition before age 19 and who had their symptoms for a shorter period of time prior to treatment (Russell, Szmukler, Dare, & Eisler, 1987). In the description of both therapies, it was clear that a variety of techniques were used under the headings of "family therapy" and "individual therapy." This points out one of the research challenges to therapists: the need to define what specific therapies are being used and to determine what components of a multicomponent treatment approach are effective for different patients. Different types of interventions may impact the various characteristics of anorexia differentially or different interventions may work better with certain as yet unidentified subgroups of patients. Some treatment approaches have integrated a variety of behavioral, family, and psychodynamic components in an attempt to address the complexity involved in this disorder (e.g., Anderson, 1986; Geller, 1975; Liebman et al., 1974).

Discussion
While some eating disorders—such as pica, vomiting, and rumination—continue to have relatively low base rates, other eating-related problems—such as obesity and anorexia—appear to be increasing. Factors related to these increases are not well understood, though television has been suggested as one culprit in the increase in obesity (Dietz & Gortmaker, 1985). Certainly, society continues to value thinness highly, particularly in women, often equating a slim physique with power and attractiveness. At present, dieting appears to be a normative behavior (Polivy & Herman, 1987; Rosen & Gross, 1987) which has prompted investigators to consider the relationship between normal eating behavior (e.g., dieters) and disordered eating. Polivy and Herman (1987) offer a conceptualization of "reordered" eating behaviors where obese, anorexic, and bulimic patients use other than physiological boundaries (e.g., hunger and satiety) to govern their eating behavior—boundaries that are similar to those used by dieters, though more extreme. Differences between dieters and eating-disordered patients become more apparent when in comparisons of personality traits such as self-esteem, interpersonal trust and relationships, ability to recognize feeling states accurately, and family relationships (Polivy & Herman, 1987; Humphrey, 1988). As previously

noted, there appears to be some overlap between anorexic and bulimic behaviors. Other studies have provided evidence that a significant proportion of obese patients engage in binging behavior, which may be related to higher levels of dietary restraint and ability to control urges to eat (Marcus & Wing, 1987). This suggests a possible overlap between these two eating-related disorders. Further investigations regarding the similarities and differences between these disorders will be important, particularly if a preventive approach is to be utilized in the future.

Numerous intervention approaches have been applied to the treatment of inappropriate food preferences—including anorexia nervosa, the most serious condition—with varying degrees of success. Many children who exhibit these disorders are in imminent physical danger because of extreme weight loss and biochemical imbalances in bodily functioning; therefore an immediate goal of treatment is to bring their weight up to safe levels as quickly as possible. Taken together, the available evidence suggests that, in the most extreme cases of food refusal, behavioral techniques can provide a useful strategy for *rapidly* restoring children's eating behavior and weight. The most frequently used technique in the behavioral treatment of food refusal has been the contingent reinforcement of food consumption, caloric intake, and weight gain. A critical factor in the success of these treatment programs has been the selection of potent reinforcers that can supersede the strong avoidance-of-eating behaviors exhibited by children with eating disorders. The observation that high-frequency behaviors can be used as reinforcers for low-frequency behaviors (Premack, 1965) provides an effective and efficient means for selecting appropriate reinforcers to reinstate normal eating and accelerate weight gain in a relatively short time.

With older adolescents, the reinforcement of weight gain per se, rather than food consumption, seems to be an effective strategy. This approach appears to avoid many manipulative and undesirable behaviors, such as self-induced vomiting, that sometimes occur when the target response is amount of food eaten. However, with younger children, reinforcing responses that are temporally and topographically as close as possible to the target response may be more effective than a strategy involving a longer delay between the response and reinforcement, as is the case with reinforcing weight gain. Thus, food consumption with younger children would be a much closer target response than is weight gain. Some research efforts—such as those reported by Agras et al. (1974)—have attempted to isolate the essential treatment variables in the behavioral treatment of anorexia nervosa through controlled investigations. They appear to be the most fruitful in providing empirical documentation of treatment efficacy, but such a detailed analysis of eating behavior may inadvertently foster the development of other abnormal eating habits (Bemis, 1987). Certainly future investigations of treatment approaches will have to consider the impact of treatment on eating behavior over the long term.

It appears that for the disorders reviewed here, the treatment approaches must include several phases. Van Buskirk (1977) has noted that the efficacy of treatment techniques for anorexia nervosa must be evaluated from two perspectives: their effects on facilitating rapid weight gain to restore the patient to a safe level of physical functioning and their effects on long-term maintenance of appropriate weight and adequate psychological adjustment. While behavioral techniques have shown particular effectiveness in the initiation of rapid weight gain in children in critical physical condition who require immediate intervention in the acute phase of the disorder, their *long-term* results have been disappointing (Bemis, 1978). Similar comments can be made regarding obesity, as treatment for this involves initial weight reduction and then long-term maintenance of weight loss or return to age-appropriate weight gain for height (Epstein, 1986). While behavioral techniques have proven effective, other techniques to facilitate initial weight loss in extremely obese children— such as the very low calorie diet—warrant further investigation. With regard to maintenance of weight loss, more emphasis on including relapse techniques and/or continued therapist contact in some manner would appear to be useful (Perri et al., 1984). These strategies in children, however, await further empirical evidence.

Enuresis

A common problem of childhood, which may continue into adolescence, is enuresis. Specifically, functional enuresis is defined by DSM-III-R (APA, 1987) as: (1) repeated voiding of urine during the day or night into bed or clothes,

whether involuntary or intentional; (2) at least two such events per month for children between the ages of 5 and 6 and at least one event per month for older children; (3) chronological age of at least 5 and mental age of at least 4; and (4) absence of a causative physical condition such as diabetes, urinary tract infection, or seizure disorder (p. 85). Childhood enuresis may take the form of wetting during the day (diurnal) or at night (nocturnal), the latter being more frequent. Enuresis has also been classified as primary or secondary. In primary enuresis, the child has never attained daytime or nighttime bladder control. Secondary enuresis, on the other hand, refers to the loss of previously acquired bladder control after at least a year of continence (APA, 1987; Forsythe, Merrett, & Redmond, 1972).

Estimates of incidence vary; however, enuresis appears to be a common problem, with more than 3 million children in this country exhibiting some form of it (Baller, 1975). Approximately 20% of 5-year-olds continue to wet their beds. Half of these children remain enuretic at 10 years of age. Nocturnal enuresis also occurs twice as often in boys as in girls, and it diminishes with age (Lovibond & Coote, 1970; Oppel, Harper, & Rowland, 1968). Approximately 30% of children who are nocturnally enuretic also exhibit diurnal enuresis (Forsythe & Redmond, 1974). Untreated enuresis is reported to remit spontaneously in approximately 15% of the remaining cases between ages 5 to 19 each year (Forsythe & Redmond, 1974).

While less than 10% of childhood enuresis is attributable to an organic etiology (Pierce, 1967), a medical examination should be conducted to determine whether organic factors are present. Among the organic or physical causes of enuresis are bladder or urinary tract infections, neurological problems such as central nervous system impairment, and anatomical problems in the genitourinary system (Novello & Novello, 1987).

Micturition, or the process of urination, is a complex act requiring the child to establish cognitive control over the bladder reflex. The child must be able to (1) inhibit bladder contractions until the bladder is full, (2) demonstrate an awareness of bladder distention as a need to void, and (3) postpone or initiate micturition at varying degrees of bladder fullness (Muellner, 1960; Yeates, 1973). Numerous theories have been suggested for a delay in control over micturition. A common assumption that enuresis is a symptom of psychological or emotional disturbance has not received support in the research literature (Schaefer, 1979; Walker & Shaw, 1988; Werry, 1967). Wagner, Smith, and Norris (1988) report, however, that while enuretic children exhibited no overall adjustment problems relative to nonenuretic children, there was evidence that children who had both diurnal and nocturnal enuresis reported lower self-esteem than children with only nocturnal enuresis. This finding is further supported by a study by Moffat, Kato, and Pless (1987), who found improvements in self-concept in children and adolescents following successful conditioning treatment of nocturnal enuresis. Further studies are needed to clarify the direction of causality in this area (e.g., do psychological factors such as lower self-esteem contribute to enuresis or do repeated enuretic episodes lead to lower self-esteem?). Research findings pertaining to the notion that depth of sleep is associated with enuresis are also equivocal (Doleys, 1979). Finally, it has been suggested that the volume of urine that enuretic children can retain before voiding is smaller than that of nonenuretic children; this could also account for their more frequent micturition (Muellner, 1960). While there is some evidence for this latter view (Esperanca & Gerrard, 1969; Starfield, 1967), research has not found all enuretic children to have smaller bladder capacities (Doleys, 1977).

Overview of Treatment Approaches

It is generally recognized that learning plays a significant role in the process of bringing the bladder reflex under cognitive control (Lovibond & Coote, 1970; Mowrer & Mowrer, 1938). From this perspective, enuresis is regarded as a behavioral deficit that results from faulty learning. The acquisition of bladder control is regarded as a high-level skill that may not develop because the particular behaviors necessary for initiating and inhibiting micturition were not learned. An enuretic child has not learned to exercise adequate control of the bladder's sphincter muscles and therefore, when the bladder is distended, fails to inhibit the bladder reflex controlling urination. Both classical and instrumental conditioning mechanisms are presumed to play a role in this learning process.

A wide variety of approaches to the treatment of childhood enuresis have been reported, including special diets, fluid restrictions, nighttime awakening, psychotherapy, and medication (Doleys & Ciminero, 1976; Johnson, 1980). However, there is little or no evidence for the efficacy of these methods (Johnson, 1980; Walker, Milling, & Bonner, 1988).

Behavioral approaches to childhood enuresis have received the most systematic research attention. Both operant and respondent conditioning procedures have been employed with varying degrees of success. The most frequently used procedures have included the urine-alarm or bell-and-pad procedure, techniques to directly increase functional bladder capacity, and approaches involving a combination of procedures.

Bell-and-Pad Procedure. To date, the most effective and frequently used behavioral method for treating enuresis in children is the bell-and-pad or urine-alarm conditioning procedure. This device was first used in the treatment of enuresis by Mowrer and Mowrer (1938) to help children learn nighttime bladder control. Although the bell-and-pad procedure was originally based on a respondent conditioning paradigm, the exact mechanism of its operation remains to be clearly determined (Lovibond, 1963). The systematic use of this procedure in the treatment of enuresis did not occur until 30 years after it was initially developed.

In the bell-and-pad procedure, the child sleeps on a specially constructed pad. It is made of two foil outer sheets, the top one having holes, which are separated by an absorbent paper connected to a buzzer. As soon as the child begins to urinate, the paper sheet becomes wet, completing an electric circuit that activates a bell or buzzer. The noise from the buzzer is presumed to inhibit further urination in bed by causing the bladder muscles to contract reflexively (automatically). The noise awakens the child at the time when his or her bladder is full. After a number of pairings of the noise with the full bladder, the child learns to wake up to the cues for bladder fullness and the need to urinate. Eventually the child learns to respond to the bladder cues without the help of the bell and pad, so that bladder distension automatically elicits contraction of the sphincter muscles and wakes up the child. More recently, a modification of the bell-and-pad device was introduced; it comprises a sensor electrode that reacts to only a few drops of urine and is attached directly to the child's underwear (Walker et al., 1988).

Despite beliefs that drinking before bedtime should be curtailed, in this procedure the child is encouraged to drink fluids before bedtime to ensure that sufficient pairings of the bell and the act of micturition will occur. The child and parents should be informed that the alarm will most likely sound at least several times in the first several nights of treatment (it is often incorrectly assumed that if treatment is working appropriately, the child will not be wetting the bed so frequently).

The child is asked to sleep without pajama bottoms or in light underclothing, so that the alarm is triggered at the exact moment that urination begins. When the alarm is activated, the child is instructed to turn it off and to go immediately to the bathroom to finish urinating. If the child has difficulty awakening, the parents are asked to rouse him or her, making sure the child is completely awake before going to the bathroom by washing his or her face with cold water. After returning to the bedroom, the device is reset, the pad is washed off, and a dry sheet is placed on the pad. The child typically is given primary responsibility to remake the bed before going back to bed.

The parents are asked to keep a record of the number of times that the bell rings each night and the diameter of the wet spot on the sheet. As the procedure begins to take effect, the size of the spot and the number of times that the bell rings should decrease. The child is rewarded with praise and sometimes with tangible reinforcers for each dry night, and parents are instructed not to make negative comments about any wetting incidents.

To maintain parental motivation and make sure that the procedure is being followed correctly, weekly contact with the parents and child is essential, particularly during the first several weeks of treatment. It should be explained to the parents and child that within 3 weeks after starting treatment, some reduction in wetting patterns should be noted. Use of the bell and pad is typically discontinued following 2 weeks of consecutive dry nights. Parents are told that relapses (typically defined as 2 or more wet nights a week) may occur and are asked to reinstate the bell-and-pad procedures if this happens. Most enuretic children require 4 to 8 weeks with the bell-and-pad method before treatment can be terminated. More detailed descriptions of the bell-and-pad procedure are presented by

Lovibond and Coote (1970), Walker (1978), and Werry (1967).

The bell-and-pad device can be purchased at several national catalogue stores at a modest price, or it can be rented from several commercial firms (Mountjoy, Ruben, & Bradford, 1984). Instructions for constructing this equipment are also available (Fried, 1974; Kashinsky, 1974). Despite the ready availability of this apparatus to nonprofessionals, it should not be used without professional consultation, as it is likely to be used incorrectly and result unnecessarily in treatment failure.

Research has revealed a high degree of effectiveness for the bell-and-pad procedure for children who remain in treatment. The bell-and-pad conditioning procedure has been found superior to traditional psychotherapy (DeLeon & Mandell, 1966; Werry & Cohressen, 1965) and drug therapy (Forrester, Stein, & Susser, 1964; Young & Turner, 1965) for the treatment of childhood enuresis. This procedure has demonstrated an initial success of between 75% and 80% (Doleys, 1977; Lovibond & Coote, 1970).

One problem in the use of this procedure has been the relapse rate, which has ranged from 20% to 30% (Doleys, 1977; O'Leary & Wilson, 1975). Several procedural modifications of the bell and pad have been found to effectively reduce the relapse rate. One of these procedures involves the reintroduction of the bell and pad immediately after a relapse occurs. An overlearning procedure—whereby the child increases fluid intake before bedtime and uses the bell-and-pad apparatus beyond the criterion point where it is normally withdrawn—has been effective in reducing the relapse rate (Houts, Peterson, & Whelan, 1986; Jehu, Morgan, Turner, & Jones, 1977; Young & Morgan, 1972). Doleys (1979a) has cautioned that excessive fluid intake prior to bedtime might result in renewed bedwetting and therefore discourage the parents and child. He suggests that some children may benefit from a delay in the use of the overlearning technique for several weeks after the initial training period and suggests a gradual increase in the quantity of liquids given.

A final method for reducing the rate of relapse is the use of intermittent reinforcement. In this method the alarm is activated during a variable number of wetting incidents (usually 50% to 70%) rather than after each wetting has occurred. According to learning theory, this procedure should be effective in reducing relapse rate because an intermittent schedule of reinforcement should make the trained response (i.e., bladder control) more resistant to extinction. Use of an intermittent reinforcement schedule has shown promise as a technique for reducing the relapse rate with the bell and pad (Finley, Besserman, Bennett, Clapp, & Finley, 1973; Finley & Wansley, 1976).

Bladder Retention Control Training. Based on the observation that enuretic children tend to urinate more frequently during the day and with a smaller volume of urine than nonenuretic children (Starfield & Mellitis, 1968; Zaleski, Gerrard, & Shokier, 1973), Muellner (1960) suggested a treatment program to increase bladder capacity and to reduce frequency of urination to weak bladder cues. Zaleski et al. (1973) have outlined several simple methods for assessing functional bladder capacity in children. In one method, the child drinks 30 milliliters of water for each kilogram of body weight. The child inhibits urination until discomfort is felt; then two consecutive voids are measured, the larger specimen being regarded as representing the maximum functional bladder capacity. In the second method, the parent is instructed to measure the volume of urine each time the child voids over the course of a week. The largest volume during the week is recorded as the maximum functional capacity of the child.

Kimmel and Kimmel (1970) have developed a systematic treatment program based on the method proposed by Muellner (1960), in which the child is taught to increase his bladder capacity through a daytime shaping procedure. At the point where bladder tension is sufficiently strong to stimulate urination, the child is taught to delay urination voluntarily for increasingly longer periods of time. It is assumed in this procedure that increased bladder control during the waking hours will generalize to nighttime retention of urine.

In the bladder retention training procedure, the child is encouraged to drink as many liquids as he or she wants during the day. When the child experiences the need to urinate, he or she is asked to "hold it" for an initial 5-minute period and then is permitted to go to the bathroom. This period of refraining from voiding is gradually increased several minutes each day until the child is able to delay urination for 30 to 45 minutes. Kimmel and Kimmel report that most children are able to reach this criterion in 3 weeks or less. Following each withholding period, parents are instructed to reinforce the child with praise and tangible reinforcers. Parents are also instructed to keep a record of the child's frequency of daytime urinations, the volume of urine, and the number of dry nights.

Paschalis, Kimmel, and Kimmel (1972) investigated the use of the daytime retention control procedure with 31 children between 6 and 11 years of age who had never experienced a dry night. At the end of treatment, 15 of the children were no longer wetting their beds at night and 8 showed significant reductions in their nighttime bedwetting. These improvements were maintained at a 3-month follow-up assessment. This procedure also receives support from a case study in the treatment of a 13-year-old girl who had been enuretic all her life (Paschalis et al., 1972). Noteworthy in this case is the fact that parental involvement was not required in any aspect of the treatment. The adolescent was able to follow the procedure and keep records of her frequency of urination during the day and the number of times she wet the bed at night. By the end of 3 months, she was no longer wetting the bed. A 3-month follow-up indicated that she had had only four wetting incidents.

Using the retention training procedure, Miller (1973) was able to eliminate bedwetting completely in two adolescents with secondary enuresis. During a 3-week baseline period, the adolescents kept a record of the number of times they wet their beds each week and the frequency of daytime urination. Retention control training was initiated subsequent to the baseline condition. The adolescents were instructed to delay urination an additional 10 minutes each week, so that by the third week of treatment they had held back urination for 30 minutes. Fluid intake was also increased during this treatment period. Following 3 weeks of treatment, the baseline condition was reinstated (i.e., the urination-delay procedure was discontinued). During the final phase of the program, the adolescents returned to the retention control training, which continued until they achieved 3 consecutive weeks of dry nights. A 7-month follow-up evaluation revealed that both adolescents had remained dry at night, with no relapses reported. There was a concomitant decrease in both the frequency of enuretic episodes and daily urinations when retention control training was in effect. These results suggest that this procedure also increased bladder capacity, since little urination occurred during the waking hours. Despite these positive results, there are some data to suggest that this procedure may not be effective with all children (Doleys, 1977; Hunsaker, 1976).

Combination of Procedures. Azrin, Sneed, and Foxx (1974) have recently presented a treatment procedure for enuresis referred to as "dry-bed training." This method is a multicomponent, complex treatment program which includes the use of both the bell-and-pad and retention-control training procedures. In addition, a number of other techniques, primarily operant procedures, are incorporated into the treatment program, including hourly wakenings, positive practice in going to the toilet, punishment for wetting the bed, and positive reinforcement for going to the bathroom at night. The treatment program as originally outlined by Azrin et al. (1974) involves one night of intensive training by a therapist-trainer who comes to the child's home. Dramatic results using this program were reported by Azrin et al. (1974), with all of the 24 children achieving the criterion of 7 consecutive dry nights. A relapse rate of 29% was noted, necessitating a brief reinstatement of the treatment program. Furthermore, they found dry-bed training to be more effective in eliminating enuresis than the bell-and-pad procedure alone.

Similar results are reported by Bollard and Woodroffe (1977) using the dry-bed training procedure. They achieved a 100% initial success rate with a 17% relapse rate. In this study, parents instead of professional trainers administered the intensive training program. In contrast, Doleys, Ciminero, Tollison, Williams, and Wells (1977) found that only 38% of the children achieved criterion for success within a 6-week period. In addition, one-third of these children relapsed. However, they did find that the dry-bed training procedure was more effective than retention training alone.

More recently, Azrin and his colleagues (Azrin, Hontos, & Besalel-Azrin, 1979; Azrin & Theines, 1978) reported modification of the dry-bed training program in which the bell-and-pad conditioning apparatus was eliminated from the procedure. Ninety-four children 3 to 15 years old were treated using a procedure that was less complicated to implement than the program ini-

tially developed by Azrin et al. (1974). These investigators reported that all the children who received this training were successfully treated, using a 2-week criterion of consecutive dry nights despite the elimination of the bell-and-pad procedure. Less than 20% of the children evidenced relapses, and these were reversed by a second training session. This reduction in wetting was greater than that in children in the group receiving the bell-and-pad procedure alone. Despite these very positive results, Ross (1981) suggests that the dry-bed training procedure appears to be less effective when the bell and pad is removed from treatment. He notes that more relapses were reported with the modified dry-bed procedure in the follow-up period than were reported in the Azrin et al. (1974) study, in which the bell-and-pad training method was included in the treatment program. Bollard and Woodroffe (1977) and Bollard, Nettelbeck, and Roxbee (1982) also found that dry-bed training without the bell-and-pad procedure was less effective, suggesting that the bell and pad may be an essential component in the treatment of some children with enuresis.

Finally, Houts, Liebert, and Padawer (1983) examined the efficacy of the bell-and-pad procedure combined with cleanliness training, retention training, and overlearning in the treatment of 60 children with primary enuresis. These investigators found that 81% of the children responded to the treatment program by achieving the initial criterion of 14 consecutive dry nights. At a 1-year follow-up assessment, 24% of the sample had relapsed. This treatment program was carried out with a limited amount of professional time per each child and family.

Discussion

Several procedures have been shown to be effective in decreasing the frequency of bed wetting. There are, however, no definitive guidelines to assist the therapist in choosing a particular method for a given child. Ciminero and Doleys (1976) have noted several factors that should be considered in selecting an appropriate treatment method for enuresis. One of the most important factors to consider is the degree of motivation and cooperation that can be expected from the parents and child, since the success of any treatment procedure depends on how accurately and consistently it is applied. For example, retention training places fewer demands on the parents or child, and it might, therefore, be considered for use where cooperation of the participants is judged to be less than optimal. In contrast, dry-bed training is considerably more complex to implement and requires a great deal of parental time and involvement.

The child's age should also be considered in choosing a treatment strategy. Younger children may have more difficulty understanding the retention training procedure than the other approaches, which depend to a greater extent on parental management. For older children and adolescents who can monitor their own voiding behavior and for whom parental involvement can be minimal, retention training or the bell-and-pad methods may be preferable. Finally, where motivation is assessed to be high and where severity of the problem seems to warrant it, multiple procedures might effectively be used.

Because parental cooperation is essential to treatment success, especially in the bell-and-pad and dry-bed training procedures, the motivation and capabilities of the parents and child should be assessed in the early phases of treatment. To assist in this endeavor, Morgan and Young (1975) have developed the Tolerance Scale for Enuresis, which measures parental attitudes and tolerance toward bed-wetting. Morgan and Young (1975) found that parents who were more intolerant were more likely to discontinue treatment with the bell-and-pad procedure prematurely. A measure like the Tolerance Scale might be useful in identifying families in need of greater support and supervision throughout the treatment program.

Another method for evaluating the family's capabilities for complying with the treatment program is to use an extended baseline period in which the parents and child are asked to keep records of the volume and frequency of urination during the day and the number of dry nights. If the family is unable to comply with these simple requests, it is unlikely that they will be able to adhere to the demands of a multifaceted treatment approach such as dry-bed training.

To date, few therapeutic interventions, including other behavioral methods, can claim as dramatically positive results as the bell-and-pad procedure (Sorotzkin, 1984). In fact, this procedure is the best-researched and documented approach for the treatment of enuresis. While the dry-bed training procedure and retention training show considerable promise, there are significantly fewer studies evaluating their treatment efficacy compared to the bell-and-pad method.

Johnson (1980) has aptly noted that children with enuresis represent a heterogenous group and that therefore one method is unlikely to prove equally effective with every child. She has also pointed to the almost complete lack of integration between the assessment of factors contributing to enuresis in a particular child and the choice of a treatment procedure. In this regard, there has been little research attention to individual differences that might lead to a more systematic set of guidelines for selecting the most effective method of intervention for each child. For example, there has been little attempt to document, before treatment is initiated, whether children have appropriate functional bladder capacity. Children who exhibit deficient bladder capacity might benefit from retention training in addition to the bell-and-pad procedure. On the other hand, where functional bladder capacity is within normal limits, the focus of the treatment program might be on training in bladder control or appropriate toileting skills rather than on bladder capacity training (Doleys, 1979). These issues have yet to be systematically investigated.

Another area that has received limited attention is the treatment of children who exhibit daytime wetting. The major focus in the literature has been on the treatment of nocturnal enuresis. To date, only a few studies have examined methods of treatment for children with daytime enuresis (Fielding, 1980; Halliday, Meadow, & Berg, 1987).

Finally, the treatment program should include plans for treating relapses after formal contact with the therapist has terminated. It is inevitable that bed-wetting will recur in some children after initial treatment. Parents and children need to be informed of this possibility so that they do not become discouraged when it happens. They need to be reassured that relapses can be managed effectively by reinstating the treatment program for a brief period of time as soon as the problem recurs.

Headaches

A common complaint during childhood is the occurrence of headache pain. While it is not a life-threatening disorder, chronic headache is associated with a number of physiological, psychological, and social consequences (Blanchard

& Andrasik, 1985). Extensive epidemiological studies indicate that almost 40% of children have had headaches by age 7 and that this rate increases to 75% by age 15 (Billie, 1962; Sillanpaa, 1983). The preventive implications of focusing on the management of headaches in children and adolescents is underscored by research, which demonstrates that as many as 60% continue to experience chronic headaches into adulthood (Billie, 1981; Sillanpaa, 1983).

The two most frequently diagnosed headaches are the muscle-contraction or tension headache and the vascular or migraine headache. A third type, the mixed or combined headache, includes features of both migraine and muscle-contraction headaches (Ad Hoc Committee on Classification of Headache, 1962). As the names suggest, each type of headache is presumed to originate from a different pathophysiological source. Muscle-contraction headaches are assumed to result from sustained contraction of muscles of the face, scalp, and neck. Migraine headaches, on the other hand, are thought to result from an excessive response (vasoconstriction and vasodilation) of the cranial and cerebral arteries (Bakal, 1975).

Recent evidence from psychophysiological investigations of headache patients suggests that there are little data to support the distinction between muscle-contraction and vascular headaches. More specifically, the literature indicates that high levels of tension in the head and neck and vasoconstriction of the scalp arteries have been observed in both types of headaches. Interestingly, a wide range of muscle tension in the head and neck has been found in some patients suffering from tension headaches, whereas others show normal levels of muscle activity (Cohen, 1978; Philips, 1978). Further research is needed to determine what, if any, differences exist between tension and migraine headaches. The etiology of both types of headaches appears to be varied and often difficult to specify (Feuerstein & Gainer, 1982).

Overview of Treatment Approaches

Treatment should begin with a comprehensive evaluation of the headaches including a thorough medical and neurological examination to ensure that neurological problems such as tumors, hematomas, and seizures are not present. This step is necessary despite the fact that less than 5% of headaches in children represent underlying organic problems (Shinnar & D'Souza,

1981). Once the physical examination has ruled out potential organic factors, further assessment is needed to ascertain the characteristics of the headache and environmental events that may precipitate or maintain headache episodes. Such an assessment is typically accomplished with the help of a headache diary, in which the patient is instructed to monitor the daily frequency, duration, and intensity of headache pain as well as the quantity and type of medication used. In addition, information regarding when and where the headache occurred and who was present at the time is recorded. The assessment information is subsequently used to develop appropriate treatment plans and provides an ongoing record regarding the effectiveness of the treatment program.

At present, there is no truly adequate treatment for chronic headaches, particularly the migraine type. The clinical approach to chronic headache is, therefore, directed at the *management* of the acute headache episodes rather than the elimination of headaches per se (Blanchard & Andrasik, 1985). The most common treatment for both migraine and muscle-contraction headaches is medication (Turner & Stone, 1979). However, aggressive treatment of headaches in children and adolescents is discouraged because of potential problems and risks, such as the occurrence of side effects, problems with patient compliance, and the potential for drug dependence and drug abuse. The issues of drug dependence and abuse are particularly important, given the evidence for the continued occurrence of headaches into adulthood (Medina & Diamond, 1977; Shinnar & D'Souza, 1981). Because of these problems, there is a strong impetus for the development of effective nonpharmacological treatment approaches for headaches in children.

Specific Psychological Treatment Approaches. Several psychological approaches to the treatment of headaches in children and adolescents have been reported. The most widely used nonpharmacological treatment strategies for vascular and muscle-contraction headaches have been relaxation techniques, biofeedback, and various combinations of these strategies (Andrasik, Blake, & McCarren, 1986).

A variety of relaxation techniques have been used in the management of headaches, ranging from more passive forms of relaxation (such as meditation and autogenic phrases) to more active forms (such as progressive muscle relaxation) (Feuerstein & Gainer, 1982). Autogenic training is a relaxation technique involving a passive, suggestive type of relaxation in which the individual covertly repeats phrases involving suggestions of warmth and body heaviness (Schultz & Luthe, 1969). The primary goal of each of these relaxation techniques is the modification of the overactive sympathetic nervous system and a reduction in skeletal muscle activity. Following treatment, it is presumed that the individual has learned to elicit a relaxation response simply through recall. The relaxation response is practiced daily and is used as an active coping skill in situations that might increase autonomic arousal. In addition, it is suggested that the relaxation response can serve to reduce the severity of a headache when it is elicited during an attack.

When relaxation techniques have a more global effect on the body, biofeedback techniques are directed at more specific physiological responses. In biofeedback training, the individual is taught a physiological response that is incompatible with the pathophysiological response presumed to underlie the headache (Melamed & Siegel, 1980). Given the widely held assumption that sustained muscle contraction of the head and neck is the major component of tension headaches, a primary goal of treatment is to reduce muscle activity through relaxation and thereby reduce headache pain. Electromyographic (EMG) biofeedback to assist the person to achieve deep levels of muscle relaxation has been used as the primary nonpharmacological treatment for muscle-contraction headaches. Typically, the individual receives feedback from muscles of the forehead area (frontalis muscle) and is trained to voluntarily reduce the frontalis EMG to increasingly lower levels.

Despite this accepted practice, research indicates that there is no consistent relationship between frontalis EMG levels and self-reports of frequency and intensity of headache pain (Blanchard & Andrasik, 1985). These findings suggest that for some headache patients, factors other than muscle tension may account for subjective reports of pain. In particular, environmental and social factors may be important in influencing headache pain behaviors such as verbal complaints, avoidance of usual activities, medication use, and so on (Fordyce, 1976). Therefore, the treatment procedures may differentially affect the physiological, subjective, and behavioral components of the headache pain, resulting in different rates of change in these three response systems (Melamed & Siegel, 1980).

While the specific pathophysiology of migraine headaches is unknown, a disturbance of the circulation in the cranial arteries is most often implicated as the cause of the debilitating pain accompanying this type of headache (Bakal, 1975). To modify this presumed abnormal response of the cranial arteries, a thermal biofeedback procedure has been used. In this procedure, the individual is trained to exercise voluntarily control over the blood flow in a specific area of the periphery of the body (usually the hands), producing a concomitant increase in the skin temperature of that area. It is thought that since migraine headaches are a result of excessive dilation of cranial arteries, temperature biofeedback functions to increase blood flow away from the forehead, thereby decreasing arterial dilation (Feuerstein & Garner, 1982). By teaching patients to increase the temperature of their hands, migraine attacks might then be reduced or prevented. At the present time, the mechanisms for the clinical effectiveness of thermal biofeedback in the treatment of migraine headaches remains highly speculative (Shapiro & Surwit 1976). More recently, a more direct approach to modifying arterial blood flow has been introduced in the form of blood-volume pulse (BVP) biofeedback. In this form of biofeedback, the individual learns to decrease blood flow directly in the temporal artery as a means of aborting a headache (Blanchard & Andrasik, 1985).

One of the earliest treatment studies is reported by Diamond and Franklin (1975). Thirty-two children and adolescents (9 to 18 years old) with migraine headaches were treated by a combination of thermal biofeedback using autogenic phrases, frontalis EMG biofeedback, and home practice of muscle relaxation and hand warming. Twenty-six of the patients were reported to show a good response to this treatment program (defined as a decrease in the frequency and severity of migraine). Only 2 patients were found to be completely nonresponsive to treatment. These findings are particularly impressive considering that all of these children had not responded to medication.

A more methodologically adequate study of treatment outcome of 7- to 16-year-old children with migraines is reported by Labbe and Williamson (1984). Twenty-eight children were randomly assigned to thermal biofeedback combined with autogenic training or a waiting-list control group. At the end of a 7-week period and at a 1-month follow-up, 88% of the subjects were either symptom-free or considerably improved. At a 6-month follow-up, 62% maintained significant improvement.

The efficacy of EMG biofeedback combined with meditative relaxation training and meditative relaxation alone in the treatment of pediatric migraine was investigated with 18 children between 8 and 12 years old (Fentress, Masek, Mehegan, & Benson, 1986). Subjects were randomly assigned to either of the two treatment groups or to a waiting-list control group. The results indicated that both treatment groups exhibited a significant reduction in headache symptoms and were significantly improved compared to the control group. There were no differences in effectiveness between the two treatment conditions. These findings were maintained 1 year following treatment.

In a study by McGrath et al. (1988), 99 children and adolescents between 9 and 17 years of age who had been diagnosed with frequent migraine headaches were randomly assigned to one of three groups: progressive muscle relaxation, attention-placebo control (recognizing and discussing feelings), or a control group consisting of a single-session contract by a therapist who helped each patient identify factors that might trigger migraine attacks. The findings indicated that all three groups showed a significant reduction in headaches following treatment. These improvements were maintained at a 1-year follow-up. The investigators conclude from these data that the important ingredient in effective treatment programs for migraine headaches in this population may be suggestions of techniques for self-control of headaches.

Feuerstein and Adams (1977) report the use of BVP biofeedback of the temporal artery in a 15-year-old with migraine headaches. Using a single-subject research design, EMG biofeedback was found to increase measures of headache activity, whereas BVP biofeedback significantly reduced headache activity. At a 9-week follow-up, headache frequency decreased 85%, duration decreased 68%, and intensity decreased 53% from baseline levels.

In an interesting study by Olness, MacDonald, and Uden (1987), the effectiveness of a psychological treatment program (self-hypnosis) was compared to the effectiveness of medication (propranolol) in the treatment of migraine head-

ache. The children were randomly assigned to a propranolol or placebo condition for 3 months and then crossed over for 3 months to the other condition. Following this phase of the study, all children were taught a self-hypnosis procedure that involved progressive muscle-relaxation exercises combined with pleasant imagery. The self-hypnosis treatment was found to reduce significantly the number of headaches reported by the children compared to the medication and placebo conditions. No significant changes in subjective or objective measures of headache severity were obtained with either treatment condition.

High school students were treated for either tension headaches or headaches of the mixed type (tension and migraine) in their school setting in a study reported by Larson, Melin, Lamminen, and Ullstedt (1987). Thirty-six adolescents were randomly assigned to one of three conditions: self-help relaxation (audiotaped progressive muscle relaxation); a problem-discussion group in which students discussed common problems that they were experiencing and possible solutions to these problems; or a self-monitoring condition in which the adolescents simply kept a headache diary throughout the course of the study. The self-help relaxation treatment resulted in significant improvements in all dimensions of headache activity following the 5-week treatment period. In addition, the relaxation treatment was found to be more effective than the problem-discussion group in reducing headache activity. These treatment effects were maintained at a 5-month follow-up.

Discussion

While the research on psychological approaches to the treatment of headaches in children is limited compared to the studies with adult populations, the findings are highly encouraging. Most of the research has focused on the treatment of childhood migraine. Only a few studies have been reported in the treatment of muscle-contraction headaches in this group. Both biofeedback and relaxation techniques are emerging as promising alternatives to the pharmacological treatment of chronic headaches in children. The relative safety of these psychological approaches and their avoidance of the problems associated with long-term medication use makes these strategies a particularly appealing alternative.

A number of methodological shortcomings in research in this area must be addressed before more definitive conclusions can be drawn regarding the efficacy of relaxation techniques, biofeedback, and other behavioral techniques (Hoelscher & Lichstein, 1984). Most of the reports in the literature represent anecdotal or systematic case reports, single-subject experimental designs, and single-group outcome studies. Definitive outcome studies are needed that compare the treatment techniques with waiting-list and attention-placebo control groups. In addition, the ultimate effectiveness of a treatment program for chronic headaches can only be judged over an extended period of time. To date, most investigations in this area have reported relatively short follow-up evaluations.

The treatment programs reported in the literature typically have used a variety of techniques simultaneously, making it difficult to isolate the components most responsible for the treatment effects. In addition, there is a need to identify those patient characteristics that are predictive of response to a particular treatment program; this would enhance the effectiveness of the intervention techniques. The lack of convincing evidence for the superiority of one technique over another provides little guidance to the clinician as to which treatment approach to use. At the present time, factors such as practicality and the personal bias of the therapist play a major role in the decision process for selecting a treatment method.

Another fruitful area of research that has received almost no attention with children is the monitoring of the physiological responses that are the focus of the intervention. For example, studies using thermal biofeedback have rarely reported changes in skin temperature over the course of the treatment program, so that there is no evidence that blood flow was in fact modified. Similarly, Blanchard and Andrasik (1985) have discussed the importance of evaluating psychophysiological responses both during a headache-free period as well as during a headache episode. Such information will provide useful data regarding some of the etiological factors associated with chronic headache in children.

SUMMARY

The somatic disorders presented in this chapter are only a sample of many that could have been included. In treating these disorders, it is important to reiterate that collaboration between physician and mental-health professional is nec-

essary to provide optimal care for the child. As can be surmised, individual cases will differ in the degree to which there is identifiable organic pathology that can be treated medically, but this must always be assessed. Although medical evaluation is imperative when a somatic disorder is suspected, it is also advisable to schedule a psychological assessment early in the diagnostic process. This can help the child and family begin to understand that psychological factors may play a role in somatic symptomatology and that treatment may have to include psychological intervention. This is an important point, as all too often psychological assessment and intervention are included as a last resort after other treatment approaches have failed to alleviate the problem.

As an alternative intervention strategy or as an adjunctive procedure to augment medical treatment, behavioral techniques offer several advantages for individuals who provide health-care services to children. First, behavioral methods of treatment can eliminate or avoid the use of other procedures that may have serious drawbacks or that can be highly aversive for the child. For example, tube feeding, which is often required in cases of anorexia nervosa to ensure nutritional intake, carries with it the risk of infection and the potential for aspiration of food into the lungs (Browning & Miller, 1968). In addition, behavioral treatment programs have effectively reduced or eliminated symptomatic behaviors that had previously necessitated pharmacological intervention. As a result, it has been possible to reduce significantly or to discontinue the use of medication that the child was taking. These findings have considerable implications for the child, because many problems may result from repeated, long-term use of certain medications. For instance, several drugs that are often used in treating the disorders presented in this chapter can result in undesirable physical side effects that may, in some instances, be permanent. Furthermore, there is some evidence to suggest that the learning process may be affected adversely by certain drugs. That is, research findings have indicated that learning that occurs while the child is taking the drug may not transfer to the nondrug state (Overton, 1966; Turner & Young, 1966). These suggestive findings are of particular concern when the goal of the treatment program is to help the child with somatic problems to *learn* more appropriate and adaptive behaviors. That is, behaviors acquired during a behavioral treatment program while a child is on certain medications may not persist following the withdrawal of the medication.

One of the significant features of behavioral treatment programs for somatic problems in children has been the extent to which parents and other significant persons in the child's environment, such as teachers, have been enlisted as primary change agents. With professional guidance and support, these individuals were trained to modify a variety of somatic disorders while the child was in its natural environment. Since it was clearly demonstrated in some cases that social contingencies were contributing to the maintenance of the symptomatic behaviors, the success of the behavioral procedures was dependent, to a considerable degree, on the participation and cooperation of significant persons in the child's world. Such individuals have been trained to use a wide variety of behavioral techniques for treating many somatic disturbances and to ensure that newly acquired adaptive behaviors would be maintained following treatment. Because behavioral procedures provide a systematic and explicit approach to treatment, many intervention programs can be effectively implemented by persons with little training and experience under professional supervision (Gordon & Davidson, 1981; O'Dell, 1974). Finally, this model of treatment has important implications for *preventing* the development of other somatic problems by training significant members of the child's environment in behavioral techniques.

The efficacy of any treatment approach must be judged not only for its ability to initiate behavior change but also for its potential to promote the maintenance of the behavior change after treatment (O'Leary & Wilson, 1975). The research evidence presented in this chapter supports the efficacy of psychological interventions for producing short-term changes in a number of somatic disorders in children. However, once desired changes in behavior have been achieved, these gains are often not maintained over longer periods of time. As Marholin, Siegel, and Phillips (1976) note in this regard, "research directed at providing techniques to assure transfer and maintenance [of treatment effects] has lagged significantly behind efforts to demonstrate the functional relationships between behavior change and the manipulation of pertinent variables in the treatment setting" (p. 331). In addition, long-term follow-up studies in the psychological

treatment of somatic disorders are at present clearly an exception. Because somatic disorders present in childhood are often carried into adulthood, methods for achieving long-term changes in behavior remains a research priority in this area.

While a number of effective psychological interventions are now available to modify dysfunctional somatic behaviors in children, until recently this area has lacked empirically validated assessment strategics. Children present a unique challenge in the assessment process as their participation in this process is often limited by developmental factors, particularly cognitive and language development. Given these constraints, mental health professionals working with children in health-related settings have made considerable progress in the development of reliable and valid instruments for assessing a variety of somatic problems (Karoly, 1988). Multiple sources of information (e.g., child, parent, teacher) are often helpful in providing a detailed picture of factors contributing to the child's somatic disorder which can then be used to develop an effective treatment approach.

Progress in the development of effective methods for changing dysfunctional somatic behaviors in children rests on the accumulation of rigorous research. However, notably lacking at this time are systematic, well-controlled investigations directed at isolating the critical variables in the psychological treatment of childhood somatic disorders. Many interventions include multicomponent approaches, and it is not always known which of these components account for the changes found. Unfortunately, many somatic disorders are not readily amenable to group research designs, and only these can assess the comparative effects of various approaches. Furthermore, several disorders are highly disruptive or present serious, life-threatening dangers to the child. As a result, many of these disorders require immediate and complete intervention, often at the expense of an adequate experimental design. However, well-controlled single-subject experimental designs can still enable the investigator to tell whether a change in the child's behavior can be attributed to the treatment program or to some other events that might have occurred at the same time (cf. Hersen & Barlow, 1976; Kratochwill, 1978).

Despite these problems, the preliminary results are sufficiently encouraging to warrant continued efforts in the psychological treatment of somatic disorders. The integration of behavioral scientists into health-care settings and the collaborative efforts of these individuals with various health-related disciplines, represents one of the significant developments in the field of health care. This collaboration between medicine and behavioral science has led to the development of many innovative treatment approaches with a wide array of somatic problems in children. In addition to those disorders presented in this chapter, other somatic problems that have been the focus of behavioral methods of intervention include sleep disorders, seizure disorders, chronic pain, recurrent abdominal pain, and cardiovascular problems, to name just a few. There are many exciting opportunities in developing new and effective approaches to the treatment of somatic problems in children. It is anticipated that, in the future, we shall see a systematic expansion of theory, research, and practice in this area.

REFERENCES

Ad Hoc Committee on Classification of Headache. (1962). Classification of headache. *Journal of the American Medical Association, 179,* 717–718.

Agras, W. S., Barlow, D. H., Chapin, H. N., Abel, G. G., & Leitenberg, H. (1974). Behavior modification of anorexia. *Archives of General Psychiatry, 30,* 279–285.

Ahles, T. A., Cassens, H. L., & Stallings, R. B. (1983). Private body consciousness, anxiety, and the perception of pain. *Journal of Behavior Therapy and Experimental Psychiatry, 18,* 215–222.

American Psychiatric Association. (1968). *Diagnostic and statistical manual of mental disorders* (2nd ed.). Washington, DC: Author.

American Psychiatric Association. (1980). *Diagnostic and statistical manual of mental disorders* (3rd ed.). Washington, DC: Author.

American Psychiatric Association. (1987). *Diagnostic and statistical manual of mental disorders* (3rd ed. rev.). Washington, DC: Author.

Anderson, A. E. (1986). Inpatient and outpatient treatment of anorexia nervosa. In K. D. Brownell & J. P. Foreyt (Eds.), *Handbook of eating disorders* (pp. 331–350). New York: Basic Books.

Andrasik, F., Blake, D., & McCarren, M. S. (1986). A biobehavioral analysis of pediatric headache. In N. A. Krasnegor, J. D. Arasteh, & M. F. Cataldo (Eds.), *Child health behavior: A behavioral pediatrics perspective* (pp. 394–434). New York: John Wiley & Sons.

Azrin, N. H., Hontos, P. T., & Besalel-Azrin, V. (1979). Elimination of enuresis without a conditioning apparatus: An extension by office instruction of the child and parents. *Behavior Therapy, 10,* 14–19.

Azrin, N. H., Sneed, T. J., & Foxx, R. M. (1974). Dry-bed: Rapid elimination of childhood enuresis. *Behavior Research and Therapy, 12,* 147–156.

Azrin, N. H., & Thienes, P. M. (1978). Rapid elimination of enuresis by intensive learning without a conditioning apparatus. *Behavior Therapy, 9,* 342–354.

Bakal, D. A. (1975). Headache: A biopsychological perspective. *Psychological Bulletin, 82,* 369–382.

Baller, W. R. (1975). *Bedwetting: Origins and treatment.* Elmsford, NY: Pergamon Press.

Bandura, A. (1977). Self-efficacy: Toward a unifying theory of behavioral change. *Psychological Review, 83,* 191–215.

Banji, S., & Thompson, J. (1974). Operant conditioning in the treatment of anorexia nervosa: A review and retrospective study of 11 cases. *British Journal of Psychiatry, 14,* 267–276.

Barsky, A. J., Goodson, J. D., Lane, R. S., & Cleary, P. D. (1988). The amplification of somatic symptoms. *Psychosomatic Medicine, 50,* 510–519.

Barsky, A. J., & Klerman, G. L. (1983). Overview: Hypochondriasis, bodily complaints, and somatic styles. *American Journal of Psychiatry, 140,* 273–283.

Basmajian, J. V. (1977). Learned control of single motor units. In G. E. Schwartz & J. Beatty (Eds.), *Biofeedback: Theory and research* (pp. 176–195). New York: Academic Press.

Beatty, J. (1977). Learned regulation of alpha and theta frequency activity in the human electroencephalogram. In G. E. Schwartz & J. Beatty (Eds.), *Biofeedback: Theory and research* (pp. 142–156). New York: Academic Press.

Bemis, K. (1978). Current approaches to the etiology and treatment of anorexia nervosa. *Psychological Bulletin, 85,* 593–617.

Bemis, K. (1987). The present status of operant conditioning for the treatment of anorexia nervosa. *Behavior Modification, 11*, 432–463.

Billie, B. (1962). Migraine in school children. *Acta Paediatrica, 51*, 1–51.

Billie, B. (1981). Migraine in childhood and its prognosis. *Cephalalgia, 1*, 71–75.

Birch, L. L., & Marlin, D. W. (1982). I don't like it; I never tried it: Effects of exposure on two-year-old children's food preferences. *Appetite: Journal of Intake Research, 3*, 353–360.

Blackburn, G. L., Lynch, M. E., & Wong, S. L. (1986). The very–low-calorie diet: A weight-reduction technique. In K. D. Brownell, & J. P. Foreyt (Eds.), *Handbook of eating disorders* (pp. 198–212). New York: Basic Books.

Blanchard, E. B., & Andrasik, F. (1985). *Management of headaches: A psychological approach.* Elmsford, NY: Pergamon Press.

Blanchard, E. B., & Young, L. D. (1974). Clinical applications of biofeedback training: A review of evidence. *Archives of General Psychiatry, 30*, 573–589.

Blinder, B. J., Freeman, D. M., & Stunkard, A. J. (1970). Behavior therapy of anorexia nervosa: Effectiveness of activity as a reinforcer of weight gain. *American Journal of Psychiatry, 126*, 1093–1098.

Bollard, J., Nettlebeck, T., & Roxbee, L. (1982). Dry-bed training for childhood bedwetting: A comparison of group with individually administered parent instruction. *Behavior Research and Therapy, 20*, 209–217.

Bollard, R., & Woodroffe, P. (1977). The effect of parent-administered dry-bed training on nocturnal enuresis in children. *Behavior Research and Therapy, 15*, 159–165.

Bonato, D. P., & Boland, F. J. (1983). Delay of gratification in obese children. *Addictive Behavior, 8*, 71–74.

Bouchard, C., Perusse, L., LeBlanc, C., Tremblay, A., & Theriault, G. (1988). Inheritance of the amount and distribution of human body fat. *International Journal of Obesity, 12*, 205–215.

Brener, J. A. (1974). A general model of voluntary control applied to the phenomena of learned cardiovascular change. In P. A. Obrist, A. H. Black, J. Brener, & L. V. DiCara (Eds.), *Cardiovascular psychophysiology* (pp. 206–239). Chicago: Aldine.

Brownell, K. D. (1982). Obesity: Understanding and treating a serious, prevalent, and refractory disorder. *Journal of Consulting and Clinical Psychology, 50*, 820–840.

Brownell, K. D., & Jeffrey, R. W. (1987). Improving long-term weight loss: Pushing the limits of treatment. *Behavior Therapy, 18*, 353–374.

Brownell, K. D., & Kaye, F. S. (1982). A school-based behavior modification, nutrition education, and physical activity program for obese children. *The American Journal of Clinical Nutrition, 35*, 277–283.

Brownell, K. D., Kelman, M. S., & Stunkard, A. J. (1983). Treatment of obese children with and without their mothers: Changes in weight and blood pressure. *Pediatrics, 71*, 515–523.

Brownell, K. D., & Stunkard, A. J. (1980). Physical activity in the development and control of obesity. In A. J. Stunkard (Ed.), *Obesity* (pp. 300–324). Philadelphia: W B Saunders.

Brownell, K. D., & Stunkard, A. J. (1980). Exercise in the development and control of obesity. In A. J. Stunkard (Ed.), *Obesity* (pp. 300–324). Philadelphia: W B Saunders.

Browning, C. H., & Miller, S. I. (1968). Anorexia nervosa: A study in prognosis and management. *American Journal of Psychiatry, 124*, 1128–1132.

Bruch, H. (1974). Perils of behavior modification in the treatment of anorexia nervosa. *Journal of American Medical Association, 230*, 1419–1422.

Bruch, H. (1977). Psychological antecedents of anorexia nervosa. In R. A. Vigersky (Ed.), *Anorexia nervosa* (pp. 1–10). New York: Raven Press.

Casper, R. C., Eckert, E. D., Halmi, K. A., Goldberg, S. C., & Davis, J. M. (1980). Bulimia: Its incidence and clinical importance in patients with anorexia nervosa. *Archives of General Psychiatry, 37*, 1030–1034.

Chiumello, G., del Guercio, M. J., Carnelutti, M., & Bidone, G. (1969). Relationship between obesity, chemical diabetes, and beta pancreatic function in children. *Diabetes, 18*, 238–243.

Ciminero, A. R., & Doleys, D. M. (1976). Childhood enuresis: Considerations in assessment. *Journal of Pediatric Psychology, 4*, 17–20.

Coates, T. J., Jeffrey, R. W., Slinkard, L. A., Killen, J. D., & Danaher, B. G. (1982). Frequency of contact and monetary reward in weight loss, lipid change, and blood pressure reduction with adolescents. *Behavior Therapy, 13,* 175–185.

Cohen, E. A., Gelfand, D. M., Dodd, D. K., Jensen, J., & Turner, C. (1980) Self-control practices associated with weight loss maintenance in children and adolescents. *Behavior Therapy, 11,* 26–37.

Cohen, M. J. (1978). Psychophysiological studies of headache: Is there similarity between migraine and muscle contraction headache? *Headache, 18,* 189–196.

Cohen, R. Y., & Stunkard, A. J. (1983). Behavior therapy and pharmacotherapy of obesity: A review of the literature. *Behavior Medicine Update, 4,* 7–12.

Crisp, A. H. (1980). *Anorexia nervosa: Let me be.* New York: Grune & Stratton.

Crisp, A. H., Hsu, L. K., Harding, B., & Hartshorn, J. (1980). Clinical features of anorexia nervosa: A study of a consecutive series of 120 female patients. *Journal of Psychosomatic Research, 24,* 171–191.

Dally, P. (1969). *Anorexia nervosa.* New York: Grune & Stratton.

Davison, G. C., & Neal, J. M. (1974). *Abnormal psychology: An experimental clinical approach.* New York: John Wiley & Sons.

DeLeon, G., & Mandell, W. A. (1966). A comparison of conditioning and psychotherapy in the treatment of functional enuresis. *Journal of Clinical Psychology, 22,* 326–330.

Diamond, S., & Franklin, M. (1975). Biofeedback: Choice of treatment in childhood migraine. In W. Luthe & F. Antonelli (Eds.), *Therapy in psychosomatic medicine: Vol. 4* (pp. 118–123). Rome: Autogenic Therapy.

Dietz, W. H., & Gortmaker, S. L. (1985). Do we fatten our children at the TV set? Obesity and television viewing in children and adolescents. *Pediatrics, 75,* 807–812.

Doleys, D. M. (1977). Behavioral treatment of nocturnal enuresis in children: A review of the recent literature. *Psychological Bulletin, 84,* 30–54.

Doleys, D. M. (1979). Assessment and treatment of childhood enuresis. In A. J. Finch & P. C. Kendall (Eds.), *Treatment and research in child psychopathology* (pp. 207–233). New York: Spectrum.

Doleys, D. M., & Ciminero, A. R. (1976). Childhood enuresis: Considerations in treatment. *Journal of Pediatric Psychology, 4,* 21–23.

Doleys, D., Ciminero, A., Tollison, J. W., Williams, C. L., & Wells, K. C. (1977). Dry-bed training and retention control training: A comparison. *Behavior Therapy, 8,* 541–548.

Duncker, K. (1938). Experimental modification of children's food preferences through social suggestion. *Journal of Abnormal and Social Psychology, 33,* 489–507.

Elder, S. T., Ruiz, Z. R., Deabler, H. L., & Dillenkoffer, R. L. (1973). Instrumental conditioning of diastolic blood pressure in essential hypertensive patients. *Journal of Applied Behavior Analysis, 6,* 377–382.

Engle, B. T. (1972). Operant conditioning of cardiac functioning: A status report. *Psychophysiology, 9,* 161–177.

Epstein, L. H. (1986). Treatment of childhood obesity. In K. D. Brownell & J. P. Foreyt (Eds.), *Handbook of eating disorders* (pp. 159–179). New York: Basic Books.

Epstein, L. H., Masek, B. J., & Marshall, W. R. (1978). A nutritionally based school program for control of eating in obese children. *Behavior Therapy, 9,* 766–788.

Epstein, L. H., Wing, R. R. (1987). Behavioral treatment of childhood obesity. *Psychology Bulletin, 101,* 331–342.

Epstein, L. H., Wing, R. R., Koeske, R., Andrasik, F., & Ossip, D. J. (1981). Child and parent weight loss in family-based behavior modification programs. *Journal of Consulting and Clinical Psychology, 49,* 674–685.

Epstein, L. H., Wing, R. R., Koeske, R., Ossip, D., & Beck, S. (1982). A comparison of lifestyle change and programmed exercise on weight and fitness changes in obese children. *Behavior Therapy, 13,* 651–665.

Epstein, L. H., Wing, R. R., Koeske, R., & Valoski, A. (1985). A comparison of lifestyle exercise, aerobic exercise, and calisthenics on weight loss in obese children. *Behavior Therapy, 16,* 345–356.

Epstein, L. H., Wing, R. R., Koeske, R., & Valoski, A. (1987). Long-term effects of family-based treatment of childhood obesity. *Journal of Consulting and Clinical Psychology, 55,* 91–95.

Epstein, L. H., Wing, R. R., Valoski, A., & Gooding, W. (1987). Long-term effects of parent weight on child weight loss. *Behavior Therapy, 18,* 219–226.

Epstein, L. H., Woodall, K., Goreczny, A. J., Wing, R. R., & Robertson, R. J. (1984). The modification of activity patterns and energy expenditure in obese young girls. *Behavior Therapy, 15,* 101–108.

Esperanca, M., & Gerrard, J. (1969). A comparison of the effect of imipramine and dietary restriction on bladder capacity. *Canadian Medical Association Journal, 101,* 324–327.

Fentress, D. W., Masek, B. J., Mehegan, J. E., & Benson, J. (1986). Biofeedback and relaxation-response training in the treatment of pediatric migraine. *Developmental Medicine and Child Neurology, 28,* 139–146.

Feuerstein, M., & Adams, H. E. (1977). Cephalic vaso motor feedback in the modification of migraine headaches. *Biofeedback and Self-Regulation, 2,* 241–254.

Feuerstein, M., & Garner, J. (1982). Chronic headache: Etiology and management. In D. M. Doleys, R. L. Meredith, & A. R. Ciminero (Eds.), *Behavioral medicine: Assessment and treatment strategies* (pp. 199–249). New York: Plenum Press.

Fielding, D. (1980). The response of day and night wetting in children and children who only wet at night to retention control training and the enuresis alarm. *Behavior Research and Therapy, 18,* 305–317.

Finley, W. W., Besserman, R. L., Bennett, L. F., Clapp, R. K., & Finley, P. M. (1973). The effect of continuous intermittent, and "placebo" reinforcement on the effectiveness of the conditioning treatment of enuresis nocturna. *Behavior Research and Therapy, 11,* 289–297.

Finley, W. W., & Wansley, R. A. (1976). Use of intermittent reinforcement in a clinical-research program for the treatment of enuresis nocturnal. *Journal of Pediatric Psychology, 4,* 24–27.

Flanery, R. C., & Kirschenbaum, D. S. (1986). Dispositional and situational correlates of long-term weight reduction in obese children. *Addictive Behaviors, 11,* 249–261.

Foch, T. T., & McClearn, G. E. (1980). Genetics, body weight, and obesity. In A. J. Stunkard (Ed.), *Obesity* (pp. 48–71). Philadelphia: W B Saunders.

Fordyce, W. (1976). *Behavioral methods for chronic pain and illness.* St. Louis: Mosby.

Forrester, R., Stein, Z., & Susser, M. A. (1964). A trial of conditioning therapy in nocturnal enuresis. *Developmental Medicine and Child Neurology, 6,* 158–166.

Forsythe, W., Merrett, J., & Redmond, A. A. (1972). A controlled study of trimipramine and placebo in the treatment of enuresis. *British Journal of Clinical Practice, 26,* 119–121.

Forsythe, W. I., & Redmond, A. (1974). Enuresis and spontaneous cure rate: Study of 1129 enuretics. *Archives of Diseases of Childhood, 49,* 259–276.

Fosson, A., Knibbs, J., Bryant-Waugh, R., & Lask, B. (1987). Early onset anorexia nervosa. *Archives of Disease in Childhood, 62,* 114–118.

Foster, G. D., Wadden, T. A., & Brownell, K. D. (1985). Peer-led program for the treatment and prevention of obesity in the schools. *Journal of Consulting and Clinical Psychology, 53,* 538–540.

Fried, R. (1974). A device for enuresis control. *Behavior Therapy, 5,* 682–684.

Garfinkel, P. E., & Garner, D. M. (1982). *Anorexia nervosa: A multidimensional perspective.* New York: Brunner/Mazel.

Garfinkel, P. E., & Kaplan, A. S. (1986). Anorexia nervosa: Diagnostic conceptualizations. In K. D. Brownell & J. P. Foreyt (Eds.), *Handbook of eating disorders* (pp. 266–282). New York: Basic Books.

Garfinkel, P. E., Kline, S. A., & Stancer, H. C. (1973). Treatment of anorexia nervosa using operant conditioning techniques. *Journal of Nervous and Mental Disease, 157,* 428–433.

Garfinkel, P. E., Moldofsky, H., & Garner, D. M. (1977). The outcome of anorexia nervosa: Significance of clinical features, body image, and behavior modification. In R. Vigersky (Ed.), *Anorexia nervosa* (pp. 315–329). New York: Raven Press.

Garner, D. M. (1986). Cognitive therapy for anorexia nervosa. In K. D. Brownell & J. P. Foreyt (Eds.), *Handbook of eating disorders* (pp. 301–327). New York: Basic Books.

Garner, D. M., Garfinkel, P. E., & Olmstead, M. (1983). An overview of sociocultural factors in the development of anorexia nervosa. In P. L. Darby, P. E. Garfinkel, D. M. Garner, & D. V. Coscina (Eds.), *Anorexia nervosa: Recent developments in research* (pp. 65–82). New York: Alan R. Liss.

Garner, D. M., Rocket, W., Olmstead, M. P., Johnson, C., & Coscina, D. V. (1985). Psychoeducational principles in the treatment of bulimia and anorexia nervosa. In D. M. Garner & P. E. Garfinkel (Eds.), *A handbook of psychotherapy for anorexia and bulimia* (pp. 513–572). New York: Guilford Press.

Garrow, J. S. (1986). Physiological aspects of

obesity. In K. D. Brownell & J. P. Foreyt (Eds.), *Handbook of eating disorders* (pp. 45–62). New York: Basic Books.

Geller, J. L. (1975). Treatment of anorexia nervosa by the integration of behavior and psychotherapy. *Psychotherapy and Psychosomatics, 26,* 167–177.

Geller, S. E., Keane, T. M., & Scheirer, C. J. (1981). Delay of gratification, locus of control, and eating patterns in obese and nonobese children. *Addictive Behavior, 6,* 9–14.

Gershon, E. S., Schreiber, J. L., Hamovit, J. R., Dibble, E. D., Kaye, W. H., Nurnberger, J. I., Anderson, A., & Ebert, M. H. (1983). Anorexia nervosa and major affective disorders associated in families: A preliminary report. In S. B. Guze, F. J. Earls, & J. E. Barrett (Eds.), *Childhood psychopathology and development* (pp. 279–284). New York: Raven Press.

Gillum, R. F., Prineas, R. J., Sopko, G., Koga, Y., Kubicek, W., Robitarlle, N. M., Bass, J., Sinaiko, A. (1983): Elevated blood pressure in school children—prevalence, persistence, and hemodynamics: The Minneapolis children's blood pressure study. *American Heart Journal, 105,* 316–322.

Gordon, S. B., & Davidson, N. P. (1981). Behavioral parent training. In A. Gurman & D. Kniskern (Eds.), *Handbook of family therapy* (pp. 326–387). New York: Brunner/Mazel.

Gortmaker, S. L., Dietz, W. H., Jr., Sobol, A. M., & Wehler, C. A. (1987). Increasing pediatric obesity in the United States. *American Journal of Diseases of Children, 141,* 535–540.

Group for the Advancement of Psychiatry. (1966). *Psychopathological disorders in childhood: Theoretical considerations and a proposed classification* (Vol. 6, Report No. 62).

Haggerty, J. J. (1983). The psychosomatic family: An overview. *Psychosomatics, 24,* 615–623.

Halliday, S., Meadow, S. R., & Berg, I. (1987). Successful management of daytime enuresis using alarm procedures: A randomly controlled trial. *Archives of Disease in Childhood, 62,* 132–137.

Hallsten, E. A. (1965). Adolescent anorexia nervosa treated by desensitization. *Behavior Research and Therapy, 32,* 87–91.

Halmi, K. A. (1974). Anorexia nervosa: Demographic and clinical features in 94 cases. *Psychosomatic Medicine, 36,* 18–25.

Halmi, K. A., Powers, P., & Cunningham, S. (1975). Treatment of anorexia nervosa with behavior modification. *Archives of General Psychiatry, 32,* 93–96.

Harper, L. V., & Sanders, K. M. (1975). The effects of adults' eating on young children's acceptance of unfamiliar food. *Journal of Experimental Child Psychology, 20,* 206–214.

Heald, F. P. (1971). Biochemical aspects of juvenile obesity. *Practitioner, 206,* 223–226.

Hersen, M. H., & Barlow, D. H. (1976). *Single case experimental designs: Strategies for studying behavior change.* Elmsford, NY: Pergamon Press.

Hoelscher, T. J., & Lichstein, K. L. (1984). Behavioral assessment and treatment of child migraine: Implications for clinical research and practice. *Headache, 24,* 94–103.

Holland, A. J., Hall, A., Murrary, R., Russell, G. F. M., & Crisp, A. H. (1984). Anorexia nervosa: A study of 34 twin pairs. *British Journal of Psychiatry, 145,* 414–419.

Holmes, T. H., & Rahe, R. A. (1967). The Social Readjustment Rating Scale. *Journal of Psychosomatic Research, 11,* 213–218.

Houts, A. C., Liebert, R. M., & Padawer, W. (1983). A delivery system for the treatment of enuresis. *Journal of Abnormal Child Psychology, 11,* 513–520.

Houts, A. C., Peterson, J. K., & Whelan, J. P. (1986). Prevention of relapse in full-spectrum home training for primary enuresis: A components analysis. *Behavior Therapy, 17,* 462–469.

Howat, P. M., & Saxton, A. M. (1988). The incidence of bulimic behavior in a secondary and university school population. *Journal of Youth and Adolescence, 17,* 221–231.

Humphrey, L. L. (1988). Relationships within subtypes of anorexic, bulimic, and normal families. *Journal of the American Academy of Child and Adolescent Psychiatry, 27,* 544–551.

Hunsaker, J. H. (1976). A two-process approach to nocturnal enuresis: Preliminary results. *Behavior Therapy, 6,* 560–561.

Israel, A. C., Stolmaker, L., & Andrian, C. A. (1985). The effects of training parents in general child management skills on a behavioral weight loss program for children. *Behavior Therapy, 16,* 169–180.

Jehu, D., Morgan, R. T. T., Turner, A., & Jones, A. (1977). A controlled trial of the treatment of nocturnal enuresis in residential homes for children. *Behavior Research and Therapy, 15,* 1–16.

Johnson, C. (1984). The initial consultation for patients with bulimia and anorexia nervosa. In D. M. Garner & P. E. Garfinkel (Eds.), *A handbook of psychotherapy for anorexia and bulimia* (pp. 9–51). New York: Guilford Press.

Johnson, S. B. (1980). Enuresis. In R. Daitzman (Ed.), *Clinical behavior therapy and behavior modification* (pp. 81–142). New York: Garland Press.

Johnson, C., Conners, M., & Tobin, D. L. (1987). Symptom management of bulimia. *Journal of Consulting and Clinical Psychology, 55,* 668–676.

Johnson, J. H., & Bradlyn, A. S. (1988). Assessing stressful life events in children and adolescents. In P. Karoly (Ed.), *Handbook of child health assessment: Biopsychosocial assessment* (pp. 303–331). New York: John Wiley & Sons.

Kanner, A. D., Coyne, J. C., Schaefer, C., & Lazarus, R. S. (1980). Comparison of two modes of stress measurement: Daily hassles and uplifts versus major life events. *Journal of Behavioral Medicine, 4,* 1–39.

Karoly, P. (1988). *Handbook of child health assessment: Biopsychosocial perspectives.* New York: John Wiley & Sons.

Kashinsky, W. (1974). Two low cost micturition alarms. *Behavior Therapy, 5,* 698–700.

Katz, R. C., & Zlutnick, S. (Eds.), (1975). *Behavior therapy and health care: Principles and applications.* Elmsford, NY: Pergamon Press.

Keesey, R. E. (1986). A set-point theory of obesity. In K. D. Brownell, & J. P. Foreyt (Eds.), *Handbook of eating disorders* (pp. 61–87). New York: Basic Books.

Keicolt-Glaser, J. K., & Glaser, R. (1988). Behavioral influences on immune function: Evidence for the interplay between stress and health. In T. M. Field, P. M. McCabe, & N. Schneidman (Eds.), *Stress and coping across development* (pp. 189–205). Hillsdale, NJ: Lawrence Erlbaum Associates.

Keys, A., Brozek, J., Henschel, A., Mickelsen, O., & Taylor, H. L. (1950). *The biology of human starvation.* Minneapolis: University of Minnesota Press.

Kimball, C. P. (1970). Conceptual developments in psychosomatic medicine: 1939–1969. *Annals of Internal Medicine, 73,* 307–316.

Kimmel, H. K., & Kimmel, E. (1970). An instrumental conditioning method for the treatment of enuresis. *Journal of Behavior Therapy and Experimental Psychiatry, 1,* 21–123.

Kirschenbaum, D. S., Harris, E. S., & Tomarken, A. J. (1984). Effects of parental involvement in behavioral weight loss therapy for preadolescents. *Behavior Therapy, 15,* 485–500.

Kirschner, M. A., Schneider, G., Ertel, N. H., & Gorman, J. (1988). An eight-year experience with a very low calorie formula diet for control of major obesity. *International Journal of Obesity, 12,* 69–80.

Klesges, R. C., Coates, T. J., Brown, G., Sturgeon-Tillisch, J., Moldenhauer-Klesges, L. M., Holzer, B., Woolfrey, J., & Vollmer, J. (1983). Parental influences on children's eating behavior and relative weight. *Journal of Applied Behavioral Analysis, 16,* 371–378.

Klesges, R. C., Malott, J. M., Boschee, P. F., & Weber, J. M. (1986). Parental influences on children's food intake, physical activity, and relative weight: An extension and replication. *International Journal of Eating Disorders, 5,* 335–46.

Kral, J. G., & Kissileff, H. R. (1987). Surgical approaches to the treatment of obesity. *Annals of Behavioral Medicine, 9,* 15–19.

Kratochwill, T. R. (1978). *Single subject research.* New York: Academic Press.

Labbe, E. L., & Williamson, D. A. (1984). Treatment of childhood migraine using autogenic feedback training. *Journal of Consulting and Clinical Psychology, 52,* 968–976.

Lagos, J. M. (1981). Family therapy in the treatment of anorexia nervosa: Theory and technique. *International Journal of Psychiatry in Medicine, 11,* 291–302.

Lansky, D., & Brownell, K. D. (1982). Comparison of school-based treatments for adolescent obesity. *The Journal of School Health, 52,* 384–387.

Larson, B., Melin, L., Lamminen, M., & Ullstedt, F. (1987). A school-based treatment of chronic headaches in adolescents. *Journal of Pediatric Psychology, 12,* 553–566.

Laskarzewski, P., Morrison, J. A., deGroot, I., Kelly, K. A., Mellies, M. J., Khoury, P., & Glueck, C. J. (1979). Lipid and lipoprotein tracking in 108 children over a four-year period. *Pediatrics, 64,* 584–591.

Lauer, R. M., Conner, W. E., Leaverton, P.

E., Reiter, M. A., & Clarke, W. R. (1975). Coronary heart disease risk factors in school children. *Journal of Pediatrics, 86,* 697–706.

Lazarus, R. S. (1966). *Psychological stress and the coping process.* New York: McGraw-Hill.

Leitenberg, H., Agras, W. S., & Thomson, L. E. (1968). A sequential analysis of the effect of selective positive reinforcement in modifying anorexia nervosa. *Behaviour Research and Therapy, 6,* 211–218.

Liebman, R., Minuchin, S., & Baker, L. (1974). An integrated treatment program for anorexia nervosa. *American Journal of Psychiatry, 131,* 432–436.

Lipowski, Z. J. (1977). Psychosomatic medicine in the seventies: An overview. *American Journal of Psychiatry, 134,* 233–244.

Lipton, E. L., Sternschneider, A., & Richmond, J. B. (1966). Psychophysiological disorders in children. In L. W. Hoff & M. L. Hoffman (Eds.), *Review of child development research: Vol. 2* (pp. 132–146). New York: Russell Sage.

Londe, S., Bourgoignie, J. J., Robson, A. M., & Goldring, D. (1972). Hypertension in apparently normal children. *Journal of Pediatrics, 78,* 569–575.

Lovibond, S. H. (1963). The mechanism of conditioning treatment of enuresis. *Behaviour Research and Therapy, 1,* 17–21.

Lovibond, S. H., & Coote, M. A. (1970). Enuresis. In C. G. Costello (Ed.), *Symptoms of psychopathology* (pp. 373–390). New York: John Wiley & Sons.

Magrab, P. R. (Ed.). (1978). *Psychological management of pediatric problems, Vol. 1.* Baltimore: University Park Press.

Marcus, M. D., & Wing, R. R. (1987). Binge eating among the obese. *Annals of Behavioral Medicine, 9,* 23–27.

Marholin, D., Siegel, L. J., & Phillips, D. (1976). Treatment and transfer: A search for empirical procedures. In M. Hersen, R. M. Eisler, & P. M. Miller (Eds.), *Progress in behavior modification, Vol. 3,* (pp. 293–342). New York: Academic Press.

McGrath, P. J., Humphrey, P., Goodman, J. T., Keene, D., Fireston, P., Jacob, P., & Cunningham, S. J. (1988). Relaxation prophylaxis for childhood migraine: A randomized placebo-controlled trial. *Developmental Medicine and Child Neurology, 30,* 626–631.

Mechanic, D. (1983). Adolescent health and illness behavior: A review of the literature and a new hypothesis for the study of stress. *Journal of Human Stress, 9,* 4–13.

Medina, J. L., & Diamond, S. (1977). Drug dependency in patients with chronic headache. *Headache, 17,* 12–14.

Meisner, W. W. (1974). Family process and psychosomatic disease. *International Journal of Psychiatry in Medicine, 5,* 411–430.

Melamed, B. G., & Siegel, L. J. (1980). *Behavioral medicine: Practical applications in health care.* New York: Springer.

Merrit, R. J. (1978). Treatment of pediatric and adolescent obesity. *International Journal of Obesity, 2,* 207–214.

Miller, N. E. (1969). Learning of visceral and glandular responses. *Science, 163,* 434–445.

Miller, P. M. (1973). An experimental analysis of retention control training in the treatment of nocturnal enuresis in two institutionalized adolescents. *Behavior Therapy, 4,* 288–294.

Millman, M. (1980). *Such a pretty face: Being fat in America.* New York: W W Norton.

Minuchin, S., Baker, L., Liebman, R., Milman, L., & Todd, T. C. (1975). A conceptual model of psychosomatic illness in children. *Archives of General Psychiatry, 32,* 1031–1038.

Minuchin, S., Rosman, B. L., & Baker, L. (1978). *Psychosomatic families: Anorexia nervosa in context.* Cambridge, MA: Harvard University Press.

Moffatt, M. E., Kato, C., & Pless, I. B. (1987). Improvements in self-concept after treatment of nocturnal enuresis: Randomized controlled trial. *Journal of Pediatrics, 110,* 647–652.

Morgan, R., & Young, G. (1975). Parental attitudes and the conditioning treatment of childhood enuresis. *Behaviour Research and Therapy, 13,* 197–199.

Mountjoy, P. T., Ruben, D. H., & Bradford, T. S. (1984). Recent technological advances in the treatment of enuresis: Theory and commercial devices. *Behavior Modification, 8,* 291–315.

Mowrer, O. H., & Mowrer, W. M. (1938). Enuresis: A method for its study and treatment. *American Journal of Orthopsychiatry, 8,* 436–459.

Muellner, S. R. (1960). The development of urinary control in children: A new concept in cause, prevention and treatment of primary enuresis. *Journal of Urology, 84*, 714–716.

Munford, P. R. (1980). Haloperidol and contingency management in a case of anorexia nervosa. *Journal of Behavior Therapy and Experimental Psychiatry, 11*, 67–71.

Murray, J. B. (1986). Psychological aspects of anorexia nervosa. *Genetic Psychological Monographs, 112*, 7–40.

Novello, A. C., & Novello, J. R. (1987). Enuresis. *Pediatric Clinics of North America, 34*, 719–733.

O'Brien, T. P., Walley, P. B., Anderson-Smith, S., & Drabman, R. S. (1982). Naturalistic observation of the snack selecting behavior of obese and non-obese children. *Addictive Behavior, 7*, 75–77.

O'Dell, S. (1974). Training parents in behavior modification: A review. *Psychological Bulletin, 81*, 418–433.

O'Leary, K. D., & Wilson, G. T. (1975). *Behavior therapy: Application and outcome.* Englewood Cliffs, NJ: Prentice-Hall.

Olness, K. O., MacDonald, J. T., & Uden, D. L. (1987). Comparison of self-hypnosis and propranolol in the treatment of juvenile classic migraine. *Pediatrics, 79*, 593–597.

Oppel, W., Harper, P., & Rowland, V. (1968). The age of attaining bladder control. *Journal of Pediatrics, 42*, 614–626.

Overton, D. A. (1966). State-dependent learning produced by depressant and atropineline drugs. *Psychopharmacologia, 10*, 6–31.

Palla, B., & Litt, I. (1988). Medical complications of eating disorders in adolescents. *Pediatrics, 81*, 613–623.

Paschalis, A., Kimmel, H. D., & Kimmel, E. (1972). Further study of diurnal instrumental conditioning in the treatment of enuresis nocturna. *Journal of Behavior Therapy and Experimental Psychiatry, 3*, 253–256.

Payne, B., & Norfleet, M. A. C. (1986). Chronic pain and the family: A review. *Pain, 26*, 1–22.

Pennebaker, J. W., & Skelton, J. A. (1978). Psychological parameters of physical symptoms. *Personality and Social Psychology Bulletin, 4*, 524–530.

Perri, M. G., Shapiro, R. M., Ludwig, W. W., Twentyman, C. T., & McAdoo, W. G. (1984). Maintenance strategies for the treatment of obesity: An evaluation of relapse prevention training and posttreatment contact by mail and telephone. *Journal of Consulting and Clinical Psychology, 52*, 404–413.

Philips, C. (1978). Tension headache: Theoretical problems. *Behaviour Research and Therapy, 16*, 249–261.

Pierce, C. M. (1967). Enuresis. In A. M. Freedman & H. I. Kaplan (Eds.), *Comprehensive textbook of psychiatry* (pp. 2780–2788). Baltimore: Williams & Wilkins.

Polivy, J., & Herman, C. P. (1987). Diagnosis and treatment of normal eating. *Journal of Consulting and Clinical Psychology, 55*, 635–644.

Premack, D. (1965). Reinforcement theory. In D. Levine (Ed.), *Nebraska symposium on motivation: 1965* (pp. 224–256). Lincoln, NE: University of Nebraska Press.

Roberts, A., Kewan, D. G., & Macdonald, H. (1973). Voluntary control of skin temperature: Unilateral changes using hypnosis and feedback. *Journal of Abnormal Psychology, 82*, 163–168.

Rogers, M. P., Dubey, D., & Reich, P. (1979). The influence of the psyche and the brain on immunity and disease susceptibility: A critical review. *Psychosomatic Medicine, 41*, 147–164.

Rosen, J. C., & Gross, J. (1987). Prevalence of weight reducing and weight gaining in adolescent girls and boys. *Health Psychology, 6*, 131–147.

Ross, A. O. (1981). *Child behavior therapy: Principles, procedures and empirical basis.* New York: John Wiley & Sons.

Russell, G. F., Szmukler, G. I., Dare, C., & Eisler, I. (1987). An evaluation of family therapy in anorexia nervosa and bulimia nervosa. *Archives of General Psychiatry, 44*, 1047–1056.

Sallade, J. (1973). A comparison of psychological adjustment of obese vs. non-obese children. *Journal of Psychosomatic Research, 17*, 89–96.

Sargent, J. D., Greene, E. E., & Walters, E. D. (1973). Preliminary report on the use of autogenic feedback training in the treatment of migraine and tension headaches. *Psychosomatic Medicine, 35*, 129–135.

Schaefer, C. E. (1979). *Childhood enuresis and encopresis: Causes and therapy.* New York: Van Nostrand.

Schaefer, C. E., Millman, H. L., & Levine, G. F. (1979). *Therapies for psychosomatic dis-*

orders in children. San Francisco: Jossey-Bass.

Schultz, J. H., & Luthe, U. (1969). *Autogenic training.* New York: Grune & Stratton.

Schwab, J. J., McGinnis, N. H., Morris, L. B., & Schwab, R. B. (1970). Psychosomatic medicine and the contemporary social scene. *American Journal of Psychiatry, 126,* 1632–1642.

Schwartz, G. E. (1973). Biofeedback as therapy: Some theoretical and practical issues. *American Psychologist, 28,* 666–673.

Seyle, H. (1956). *The stress of life.* New York: McGraw-Hill.

Shapiro, D., & Surwit, R. S. (1976). Learned control of psychological function and disease. In H. Leitenberg (Ed.), *Handbook of behavior modification and behavior therapy* (pp. 442–485). Englewood Cliffs, NJ: Prentice-Hall.

Shapiro, D., Tursky, B., & Schwartz, G. E. (1970). Control of blood pressure in man by operant conditioning. *Circulation Research (Supplement 1), 27,* 27–32.

Shinnar, S., & D'Souza, B. J. (1981). Diagnosis and management of headaches in childhood. *Pediatric Clinics of North America, 29,* 79–94.

Siegel, L. J. (1983). Psychosomatic and psychophysiological disorders. In R. J. Morris & T. R. Kratochwill (Eds.), *The practice of child therapy* (pp. 253–286). Elmsford, NY: Pergamon Press.

Siegel, L. J., & Richards, C. S. (1978). Behavioral interventions with somatic disorders in children. In D. Marholin (Ed.), *Child behavior therapy* (pp. 339–394). New York: Gardner Press.

Sillanpaa, M. (1983). Changes in the prevalence of migraines and other headaches during the first seven school years. *Headache, 23,* 15–19.

Sjostrom, L. (1980). Fat cells and body weight. In A. J. Stunkard (Ed.), *Obesity* (pp. 72–100). Philadelphia: W B Saunders.

Sobhany, M. S., & Rogers, C. S. (1985). External responsiveness to food and non-food cues among obese and non-obese children. *International Journal of Obesity, 9,* 99–106.

Sorotzkin, B. (1984). Nocturnal enuresis: Current perspectives. *Clinical Psychology Review, 4,* 293–316.

Staffieri, J. R. (1967). A study of social stereotype of body image in children. *Journal of* *Personality and Social Psychology, 7,* 101–104.

Starfield, B. (1967). Functional bladder capacity in enuretic and non-enuretic children. *Journal of Pediatrics, 70,* 777–782.

Starfield, B., & Mellitis, E. D. (1968). Increase in functional bladder capacity and improvement in enuresis. *Journal of Pediatrics, 72,* 483–487.

Strober, M. (1980). A cross-sectional and longitudinal analysis of personality and symptomological features in young non-chronic anorexia nervosa patients. *Journal of Psychosomatic Research, 24,* 353–359.

Strober, M. (1981). The significance of bulimia in juvenile anorexia nervosa: An exploration of possible etiologic factors. *International Journal of Eating Disorders, 1,* 28–43.

Strober, M. (1986). Anorexia nervosa: History of psychological concepts. In K. D. Brownell & J. P. Foreyt (Eds.), *Handbook of eating disorders* (pp. 231–246). New York: Basic Books.

Strober, M., & Humphrey, L. L. (1987). Familial contributions to the etiology and course of anorexia nervosa and bulimia. *Journal of Consulting and Clinical Psychology, 55,* 654–659.

Strober, M., Morrell, W., Burroughs, J., Salkin, B., & Jacobs, C. (1985). A controlled family study of anorexia nervosa. *Journal of Psychiatric Research, 19,* 239–246.

Stunkard, A. J., Sorensen, T. I. A., Hanis, C., Teasdale, T. W., Chakraborty, R., Schull, W. J., & Schulsinger, F. (1986). An adoption study of human obesity. *New England Journal of Medicine, 314,* 193–198.

Szmuckler, G. I., & Russell, G. F. M. (1986). Outcome and prognosis of anorexia nervosa. In K. D. Brownell & J. P. Foreyt (Eds.), *Handbook of eating disorders* (pp. 283–300). New York: Basic Books.

Turk, D. C., & Kerns, R. D. (eds.). (1985). Health, illness, and families: A life-span perspective. New York: John Wiley & Sons.

Turner, D. B., & Stone, A. J. (1979). Headache and its treatment: A random survey. *Headache, 19,* 74–77.

Turner, R. K., & Young, G. C. (1966). CNS stimulant drugs and conditioning treatment of nocturnal enuresis: A long term follow-up study. *Behaviour Research and Therapy, 4,* 225–228.

Uzark, K. C., Becker, M. H., Dielman, T. E.,

Rocchini, A. P., Katch, V. (1988). Perceptions held by obese children and their parents: Implications for weight control intervention. *Health Education Quarterly, 15,* 185–198.

Van Buskirk, S. S. (1977). A two-phase perspective in the treatment of anorexia nervosa. *Psychological Bulletin, 84,* 629–538.

Wadden, T. A., Foster, G. D., Brownell, K. D., & Finley, E. (1984). Self-concept in obese and normal-weight children. *Journal of Consulting and Clinical Psychology, 52,* 1104–1105.

Wagner, W. G., Smith, D., & Norris, W. R. (1988). The psychological adjustment of enuretic children: A comparison of two types. *Journal of Pediatric Psychology, 13,* 33–58.

Walen, S., Hauserman, N. M., & Lavin, P. J. (1977). *Clinical guide to behavior therapy.* Baltimore: Williams & Wilkins.

Walker, C. E. (1978). Toilet training, enuresis, encopresis. In P. R. Magrab (Ed.), *Psychological management of pediatric problems: Vol. 1* (pp. 129–189). Baltimore: University Park Press.

Walker, C. E., Milling, L. S., & Bonner, B. L. (1988). Incontinence disorders: Enuresis and encopresis. In D. Routh (Ed.), *Handbook of pediatric psychology* (pp. 363–397). New York: Guilford Press.

Waxman, M., & Stunkard, A. J., (1980). Caloric intake and expenditure of obese boys. *Journal of Pediatrics, 96,* 187–193.

Werry, J. (1967). Enuresis nocturna. *Medical Times, 95,* 985–991.

Werry, J., & Cohressen, J. (1965). Enuresis— an etiologic and therapeutic study. *Journal of Pediatrics, 67,* 423–431.

Werry, J. S., & Bull, D. (1975). Anorexia nervosa—A case study using behavior therapy. *Journal of the American Academy of Child Psychiatry, 14,* 646–651.

Whitehead, W. E., Fedoravicius, A. S., Blackwell, B., & Wooley, S. (1979). A behavioral conceptualization of psychosomatic illness: Psychosomatic symptoms as learned responses. In J. R. McNamara (Ed.), *Behavioral approaches to medicine: Application and analysis* (pp. 65–99). New York: Plenum Press.

Wolfle, J. A., Farrier, S. C., & Rogers, C. S. (1987). Children's cognitive concepts of obesity: A developmental study. *International Journal of Obesity, 11,* 73–83.

Woodall, K., & Epstein, L. H. (1983). The prevention of obesity. *Behavioral Medicine Update, 5,* 15–21.

Wooley, S. C., Blackwell, B., & Winget, C. (1978). The learning theory model of chronic illness behaviors: Theory, treatment, and research. *Psychosomatic Medicine, 40,* 379–401.

Worsley, A., Coonan, W., Leitch, D., & Crawford, D. (1984). Slim and obese children's perceptions of physical activities. *International Journal of Obesity, 8,* 201–211.

Worsley, A., Peters, M., Worsley, A. J., Coonan, W., & Baghurst, P. A. (1984). Australian 10-year-olds' perceptions of food: III. The influence of obesity status. *International Journal of Obesity, 8,* 327–340.

Yeates, W. K. (1973). Bladder function in normal micturition. In I. Kolvin, R. C. MacKeith, & S. R. Meadow (Eds.), *Bladder control and enuresis* (pp. 28–36). Philadelphia: W B Saunders.

Young, G., & Turner, R. (1965). CNS stimulant drugs and conditioning treatment of nocturnal enuresis. *Behaviour Research and Therapy, 3,* 93–101.

Young, G. C., & Morgan, R. T. T. (1972). Overlearning in the conditioning treatment of enuresis: A long-term follow-up study. *Behaviour Research and Therapy, 10,* 419–420.

Zaleski, A., Gerrard, J. W., & Shokier, M. H. K. (1973). Nocturnal enuresis: The importance of a small bladder capacity. In I. Kolvin, R. C. MacKeith, & S. R. Meadow (Eds.), *Bladder control and enuresis.* Philadelphia: W B Saunders.

CHAPTER 9

CHILDHOOD AUTISM

Marjorie H. Charlop
Laura Schreibman
Patricia F. Kurtz

In 1943, Leo Kanner described a group of 11 children who displayed a strikingly similar pattern of specific symptoms while differing from children with other childhood disorders. Kanner identified this severe form of child psychopathology as "early infantile autism" (Kanner, 1943, 1944). The children he described were, from early in life, markedly withdrawn and aloof. As infants, these children were not cuddly, disliked being held, and did not mold to their parents' bodies. They much preferred to be alone. These children were unresponsive to people as well as to their environment. They often manipulated objects in a rigid, stereotyped manner and lacked appropriate play. Kanner also noted that these children failed to acquire normal speech; in addition, many of the children displayed delayed echolalia and had difficulties with pronoun use. The children described also demonstrated an anxious insistence upon sameness in their environment, excellent rote memories, a normal

physical appearance, and good cognitive potential. In a subsequent paper, Eisenberg and Kanner (1956) reduced the essential symptoms for diagnosis to two primary characteristics: (1) extreme aloneness and (2) an obsessive insistence on the preservation of sameness. Thus, the language abnormalities that had previously been considered major symptoms of the syndrome were excluded.

More than four decades have passed since Kanner's (1943) identification of autism; much more is now known about the syndrome. Autism occurs in approximately 4.5 per 10,000 live births (Lotter, 1966; Schreibman, 1988). Among autistic children, boys outnumber girls 3 or 4 to 1 (Dunlap, Koegel, & O'Neill, 1985; Kanner, 1954; Lotter, 1966). Autism is characterized by extreme withdrawal; pervasive deficits in language, social behavior, and attention; and the presence of bizarre and/or repetitive behaviors. Typically, autism is diagnosed between the ages

The preparation of this chapter was supported in part by U.S.P.H.S. Research Grant MH39434 from the National Institute of Mental Health.

of 2 and 5. Presently there is no dominant theory of etiology; however, most researchers agree that autism is caused by organic factors and is present from birth.

BEHAVIORAL CHARACTERISTICS OF AUTISM

The diagnosis of autism is based on the manifestation of the behaviors (symptoms) characteristic of the syndrome. A child must display the majority but not necessarily all of the following characteristics in order to be diagnosed as autistic. While Eisenberg and Kanner (1956) reduced the essential symptoms to extreme aloneness and preservation of sameness, Rutter (1978) brought back the emphasis on language and defined autism in terms of four essential criteria: onset before the age of 30 months, impaired social development, delayed and deviant language development, and insistence on sameness. The behaviors discussed below have been described by Kanner (1943) and Rutter (1978) as well as other researchers (e.g., Ritvo & Freeman, 1978; Schreibman, Charlop, & Britten, 1983) and are those characteristics typically displayed by most autistic children.

Social Behavior

Autistic children display profound deficits in social behavior (Kanner, 1943; Rimland, 1964; Rutter, 1978). These children generally fail to develop relationships with other people. Autistic children rarely interact with others; they often do not express affection (Charlop & Walsh, 1986) and may actively resist physical contact (Kanner, 1943). Autistic children also tend to avoid eye contact (Rimland, 1964). As infants, they may not reach out in anticipation of being picked up or mold to their parents' bodies when held; rather, they may remain quite rigid when picked up or may "go limp." When older, autistic children typically will not seek out attention or comfort from parents, preferring instead to be alone. Indeed, they may appear to be quite indifferent to the arrival or departure of a parent (Kanner, 1943). This detachment contrasts sharply with the children's intense attachments to inanimate objects such as credit cards or pieces of string. Autistic children also generally do not play appropriately with toys or with other children (e.g., Charlop, Owen, Tan, & Milstein, 1988).

Speech and Language

Approximately 50% of autistic children fail to acquire functional speech (Rimland, 1964; Rutter, 1978). Although the structural or physiological components necessary for language are intact, some children may emit only a few sounds. These children who do not speak may resort to gestures as a means to communicate in a very limited manner (Ornitz & Ritvo, 1976; Rutter, 1978). For example, an autistic child may point with his or her hand or lead a person by the hand to the desired object.

Additionally, of the children who do acquire speech (50%), particular speech abnormalities characteristic of autism are typical. The verbal autistic children tend to display echolalia, the repetition of words or phrases spoken by others (Fay, 1969; Carr, Schreibman, & Lovaas, 1975). There are two broad categories of echolalia. Immediate echolalia occurs when the child repeats something he or she has just heard; for example, an autistic child may repeat in a parrotlike manner, "How was school today?" when asked this question, rather than answering appropriately. Immediate echolalia often interferes with learning and communication, as demonstrated by the child who echoes the task instructions rather than performing the task. Autistic children's immediate echolalia will likely increase in unfamiliar learning settings with unfamiliar task stimuli (Carr et al., 1975; Charlop, 1986) as well as when difficult or incomprehensible questions are presented (Schreibman & Carr, 1978). With delayed echolalia, the child echoes words or phrases he or she has heard in the past, a few hours, days, or months ago. Such echolalic speech is generally noncommunicative and contextually inappropriate. For example, an autistic child might sing a jingle from a TV commercial he or she had heard a few hours earlier or repeat part of a conversation from a few days before. It has been suggested that the occurrence of delayed echolalia may increase in the presence of aversive or fearful stimuli (Miller, 1969) or during high arousal situations (Charlop, Gonzalez, & Cugliari, 1987). For example, when one child was verbally reprimanded by his therapist for grabbing a cookie, the child shook a finger at the therapist and shouted, "Don't poke that dog!"—something his teacher had said a week before.

Autistic children who do use speech to communicate commonly display pronominal reversal (Kanner, 1943; Rutter, 1978). These children often use I–you pronouns incorrectly, as by saying, "Can you have a cookie?" when requesting a cookie. Or the child may simply refer to himself by name (e.g., "Johnny wants a drink, please."). This phenomenon appears to be closely related to echolalia (Bartak & Rutter, 1974).

Autistic children's comprehension of language is severely impaired (Kanner, 1943; Rutter, 1978). The children may interpret language quite literally (Kanner, 1943). For example, when one autistic child was instructed by a sibling to finish a sentence by a request to "Spit it out," the child then spit across the room. Autistic children may also have great difficulty following instructions. Additionally, these children may use language in a self-stimulatory manner, repeating sounds or words over and over again (e.g., "Strawberries, strawberries, strawberries!"). Typically, autistic children do not engage in the to-and-fro interaction characteristic of conversational speech (Charlop & Milstein, 1989). The prosodic features of their speech are often abnormal; autistic children's speech is characterized by unusual intonation and inaccurate rhythm, inflection, pitch, and articulation (e.g., Baltaxe, 1981; Baltaxe & Simmons, 1975; Schreibman, Kohlenberg, & Britten, 1986). In summary, these deficits in speech and language profoundly affect the child's ability to learn, to communicate, and to develop relationships with others.

Ritualistic Behavior and the Insistence on Sameness

This category is delineated into four common behaviors (Rutter, 1978). First, autistic children may display limited or rigid play. That is, they may repeatedly line up blocks or other household objects (e.g., bottles of salad dressing on the floor in order of size) or collect objects of a particular texture or shape. Second, autistic children frequently develop intense attachments to specific objects. They may be "obsessed" with such unusual things as business cards, vacuum cleaners, Honda cars, specific toys, pine cones, or particular letters of the alphabet. The child may talk repetitively about the object or insist on carrying it everywhere; if the object is lost or taken away, the child may become extremely upset. Such obsessions with objects may change suddenly or may last for years. Third, autistic children may also develop preoccupations with concepts such as colors, bus routes,

numbers, and geometric patterns. Fourth, many autistic children develop rigid routines that must be followed exactly. For example, one child would sleep only in the family room in front of the television set, surrounded by a semicircle of plastic pegs sorted by color and with all the television sets in the house turned on all night. Any slight deviation from an established routine, such as rearranging the furniture or changing a regularly scheduled therapy appointment, may be extremely agitating to an autistic child.

Abnormalities in Response to the Physical Environment

Autistic children exhibit an unusual responsiveness to environmental events or stimuli (Kanner, 1943; Ritvo & Freeman, 1978; Wing, 1976). Typically, these children are described by their parents as "living in a shell" or "lost in their own world." They may not seem to hear their names being called or see a person standing right before their eyes (Schreibman, 1988). Indeed, autistic children are often incorrectly suspected of being deaf or blind. They may not react when a door is slammed, yet they can hear a crinkling candy wrapper across the room. Thus, they are said to exhibit an "apparent" sensory deficit. Additionally, some children may overreact to certain stimuli, as by covering their ears when the rustling of a newspaper is heard.

Autistic children also display what has been termed "stimulus overselectivity." This is defined as the failure to respond to the simultaneous presentation of multiple cues (Koegel & Wilhelm, 1973; Lovaas, Koegel, & Schreibman, 1979; Lovaas, Schreibman, Koegel, & Rehm, 1971; Schreibman, Charlop, & Koegel, 1982). For example, to learn to discriminate the letters E and F, a normal child will note that the letters are identical except for the bottom horizontal line (the relevant feature or cue). In contrast, an autistic child may "overselect," or attend only to, an irrelevant cue of the stimulus (such as the top horizontal line) or respond to a very restricted number of cues, thereby failing to learn to discriminate the letters. Because of this failure to attend to multiple cues, the use of extrastimulus prompts (e.g., finger prompts) typically used to aid learning will be unsuccessful (Schreibman, 1975; Schreibman, Charlop, & Koegel, 1982). Autistic children's consistent failure to respond to complex multiple cues in the environment may account in part for the children's difficulty in learning speech (Lovaas, Litrownik, & Mann, 1971) and appropriate social behavior (Schreibman & Lovaas, 1973) as well as for their poor generalization of newly acquired skills (Rincover & Koegel, 1975).

Self-Stimulatory Behavior

Autistic children frequently display bizarre, repetitive behaviors (Kanner, 1943; Rutter, 1978). These stereotyped movements appear to serve no other purpose than to provide sensory input and are thus deemed self-stimulatory (Lovaas, Litrownik, & Mann, 1971; Lovaas, Newsom, & Hickman, 1987; Wing, 1972). Self-stimulatory behaviors may involve motor movements, such as rhythmic body rocking, arm or hand flapping, body arching or posturing, darting, toe walking, and spinning the body around; or these may involve objects, such as tapping, mouthing, or twirling objects, or flapping an object in front of the eyes. More subtle forms of the behavior may be exhibited, including rubbing hands on surfaces, squinting eyes, gazing at lights, or sniffing objects. Generally, each child will have his or her own repertoire of self-stimulatory behaviors.

Self-stimulatory behavior is a highly preferred activity of autistic children; indeed, if permitted, autistic children may engage in such bizarre behaviors for hours at a time, to the exclusion of all other activities. Autistic children's occurrence of self-stimulation is highest when they are alone in an unstructured setting (i.e., free play) (Runco, Charlop, & Schreibman, 1986). During structured learning situations, self-stimulatory behaviors occur significantly more often in the presence of an unfamiliar rather than a familiar therapist (Runco et al., 1986). Importantly, when engaging in self-stimulation, autistic children are particularly unresponsive to their environment. Self-stimulatory behaviors have been demonstrated to interfere with learning discrimination tasks (Koegel & Covert, 1972) and with engaging in appropriate play (Koegel, Firestone, Kramme, & Dunlap, 1974) and social behavior (Wing, 1972). Unfortunately, generalized, durable elimination of these bizarre interfering behaviors has not yet been achieved (Foxx & Azrin, 1973; Lovaas, Schaeffer, & Simmons, 1965; Mulhern & Baumeister, 1969; Rincover & Koegel, 1977a, b).

Self-Injurious Behavior

Self-injurious behavior (SIB) may be the most dangerous and dramatic behavior exhibited by autistic children. SIB is the infliction of physical damage by the child upon his or her own body (Tate & Baroff, 1966). The most common forms of SIB are head banging and self-biting (Rutter & Lockyer, 1967); other examples include hair pulling, eye gouging, face or head slapping, and arm and leg banging. Some children may run head-first into walls, repeatedly scratch their faces, or progressively bite their fingertips. The intensity of self-injury may vary, ranging from slight (where bruises, redness, or callouses result) to severe injury (in which broken bones, skull fractures, or removal of portions of skin may occur). In cases where there is risk of physical injury to the child, physical restraint (e.g., camisole) or protective equipment (e.g., padded gloves or helmet) may be necessary. However, extended use of restraints may lead to structural changes, such as arrested motor development, shortening of tendons, and demineralization of bones (Lovaas & Simmons, 1969) as well as the restriction of opportunities to learn and to engage in appropriate behaviors.

Inappropriate Affect

Autistic children commonly display affect that is contextually inappropriate (Kanner, 1943; Wing, 1976). For example, if frightened or hurt, an autistic child may laugh or giggle uncontrollably; similarly, an autistic child may cry or have a tantrum for no apparent reason. That is, these emotions are inappropriate to the situation. Other children may display flattened affect, rarely displaying extremes of joy or sorrow; or, conversely, they may exhibit mood swings ranging from uncontrollable laughing to prolonged crying and tantrums.

Additionally, autistic children may display irrational fears of commonplace objects or situations (Wing, 1976). They may appear terrified by the presence of such things as ferns, tortillas, particular toys, shadows, bandages, or objects of a particular color. Furthermore, these children may appear quite fearless in dangerous situations such as crossing a busy intersection or climbing to very high places (Schreibman & Charlop, 1987b).

Intellectual Functioning

It was originally thought that autistic children possessed normal intelligence, due to their excellent rote memory, clever and manipulative behavior, serious facial expression, and absence of physical abnormalities (Kanner, 1943). Later research, however, has not supported this hypothesis. The majority of autistic children are functionally mentally retarded (Ritvo & Freeman, 1978). It is estimated that 60% of autistic children have IQs below 50, 20% measure between 50 and 70, and 20% have IQs of 70 or more (Ritvo & Freeman, 1978).

Intellectual assessment of autistic children is often difficult (e.g., Schreibman & Charlop, 1987a). First, the children display many inappropriate behaviors, which interfere with test taking (e.g., SIB, self-stimulation). Second, due to their language impairment, these children tend to perform poorly on tests of abstract thought and symbolic or sequential logic; they tend to do best on tests assessing manipulative or visual–spatial skills and rote memory (Ritvo & Freeman, 1978). Thus, autistic children's performance on IQ tests may be quite variable.

Rutter (1978) suggested that IQ scores have the same properties in autistic children as they do in other children. Studies have consistently found that the IQ scores of autistic children remain quite stable throughout middle childhood and adolescence (e.g., Gittelman & Birch, 1967; Lockyer & Rutter, 1969). As with normal or retarded children, IQ also tends to be predictive of autistic children's educational performance (Rutter & Bartak, 1973). Thus, evidence suggests that autistic children are frequently functionally retarded.

Additional Characteristics

In addition to the above characteristics, some autistic children also display islets of superior ability, most commonly in the areas of music, mathematics, or mechanical skill (Applebaum, Egel, Koegel, & Imhoff, 1979; Rimland, 1978). One child may be able to dismantle and assemble complex machinery; another may remember and repeat complex musical melodies (Schreibman, 1988). Some autistic children can calculate on what day of the week a particular calendar date will fall. Such isolated "savant" skills often appear in children who concomitantly display low levels of functioning in other areas. One child, for example, could read a college-level psychology textbook but was not toilet trained.

Additionally, it has been suggested that autistic children tend to be extremely attractive and are healthier than children with other childhood disorders (Kanner, 1943). Autistic children also commonly display behavior problems, including feeding, toileting, and sleeping problems; pica (ingestion of inedible objects, such as rocks or buttons); noncompliance; tantrums; and aggression. These children are typically described by their parents as clever and very manipulative. Often, parents have difficulty controlling these behavior problems and are reluctant to take their child out in public. In view of the behavior problems—the severe deficits in language, social behavior, and other areas—and the bizarre behaviors typically displayed by these children, it is clear that autism has a profound effect on the family.

ETIOLOGY AND TREATMENT PARADIGMS

Although there has been a recent emphasis on exploring neurological and biochemical etiologies of autism (e.g., Freeman & Ritvo, 1984; Ornitz, 1985), the focus of this chapter is on treatment and therefore only the etiological theories that have led to a treatment protocol will be discussed. For a detailed discussion of additional theories of etiology, the reader is referred to Schreibman (1988).

Psychoanalytic Model and Treatment

The psychoanalytic model proposed that autism is caused by inadequate mothering and the child's extreme reaction to this destructive relationship (Bettelheim, 1967; O'Gorman, 1970). The most well-known proponent of the parental causation hypothesis is Bettelheim (e.g., Bettelheim, 1967). He suggested that the parents of autistic children provide inadequate, pathological responses to the child's normal behaviors during critical developmental periods (e.g., nursing, toilet training), resulting in the infant's emotional withdrawal. The mother–infant bond thus fails to develop and the mother responds by rejecting the infant. In such a threatening, rejecting environment, the child withdraws further from the parents and subsequently from the rest of the world; the "chronic autistic disease" thus results. This extreme withdrawal is the child's adaptive response to a hostile, rejecting world (Bettelheim, 1967; O'Gorman, 1970; Ruttenberg, 1971). Additionally, the classic autistic behaviors (e.g., echolalia, insistence on sameness) are indicative of hostility toward the parents (Kugelmass, 1970) and are considered to be an attempt to control the environment (Bettelheim, 1967).

The psychodynamic model of treatment consists of providing a supportive and accepting environment for autistic children in which they may express themselves in any manner and begin to reach out to the world. This setting contrasts sharply with the hostile, rejecting environment provided by the parents, which this model proposes to be the precipitating factor in autism. Typically, a mother substitute or therapist in a residential setting will encourage the child to engage in any activity without fear or frustration and will respond to any child behaviors—including, for example, aggressive or destructive behavior—with love and acceptance. According to Bettelheim (1967), the autistic child will gradually develop trust and autonomy in this supportive environment. In time, the child will begin to perceive the world as supportive and nonthreatening and will no longer need his or her autistic defenses.

Although Bettelheim (1968) claimed a high rate of success for psychodynamically oriented treatment, the theoretical assumptions on which this approach is based have been criticized. There is no empirical evidence to support the claim that the parents of these children display deviant personality characteristics (Cantwell, Baker, & Rutter, 1978; Cox, Rutter, & Newman, 1975; Rimland, 1964). Parents of autistic children do not differ from parents of normal children or children with other conditions (Cantwell et al., 1978; Cox et al., 1975; Freeman & Ritvo, 1984; Pitfield & Oppenheim, 1964; Koegel, Schreibman, O'Neill, & Burke, 1983). Indeed, in contrast to the psychodynamic view, experts today view the involvement of the parents and family in the treatment of autistic children as crucial to the success of treatment programs (Baker, 1984; Lovaas, Koegel, Simmons, & Long, 1973; Schreibman, 1988). Additionally, research has failed to support the hypothesized occurrence of extremely negative events that lead to autistic withdrawal (Cox et al., 1975).

Bettelheim's treatment procedures and outcome claims have also been challenged. Much criticism stems from the fact that the theoretical assumptions and resulting treatment procedures are based on subjective case studies rather than empirical data (Rimland, 1964; Schopler & Reichler, 1971; Wing, 1976). Bettelheim's (1968) reports of successful outcomes have also been questioned because of ambiguous outcome criteria (Rimland, 1964; Rutter, 1978; Schopler & Reichler, 1971). Finally, studies comparing autistic children in psychoanalytically oriented treatment to children receiving no treatment found that the children in therapy did not make greater gains than those with no treatment (Kanner & Eisenberg, 1955; Levitt, 1957, 1963). Other studies that systematically compared psychoanalytic treatment programs to more structured educational programs have demonstrated that children receiving psychoanalytic treatment make significantly fewer educational gains (e.g., reading, math) and display significantly more inappropriate behaviors (e.g., self-stimulation) (Bartak & Rutter, 1973; Rutter & Bartak, 1973).

Neurological Dysfunction Model and Treatment

Findings from several areas of research suggest the role of neurological factors in the etiology of autism (e.g., Mesibov & Dawson, 1986). Typically, neurological pathology may be inferred by the appearance of "soft signs" such as hypotonia, poor coordination, and toe walking, behaviors considered by some to be indicative of neurological damage, immaturity, and/or poor organization of the brain (Mesibov & Dawson, 1986). Although a few studies have reported the presence of these soft signs (e.g., DeMyer et al., 1973; Goldfarb, 1961; Knoblock & Pasamanick, 1975), no definitive relation between autism and neurological soft signs has yet been demonstrated.

One area of research has investigated autistic children's impaired sensory functioning as a possible etiological factor. As previously mentioned, many autistic children display a fluctuating overresponsiveness and underresponsiveness to sensory stimuli (Kanner, 1943; Schreibman & Mills, 1983; Wing, 1976). Ornitz and Ritvo (1968) thus proposed the perceptual inconstancy hypothesis, which suggests that due to a neurological defect in the homeostatic regulation of sensory input and motor output, autistic children fail to gain a stable inner representation of their environment. As a result of this inability to regulate sensory input, their ability to interact with others and to use communicative speech is impaired (Ritvo, 1976). Other behavioral symptoms of autism (e.g., disturbed relatedness to objects) are considered secondary (Ritvo, 1976).

Finally, a number of electrophysiological studies of the vestibular system in the brainstem suggested that autistic children differ from normal children in duration of nystagmus, or ocular motor response, following vestibular stimulation (e.g., being whirled in a chair) (e.g., Ornitz, 1985; Ornitz, Brown, Mason, & Putnam, 1974; Ornitz, Forsythe, & de la Pena, 1973; Ritvo et al., 1969). Such diminished vestibular reactivity is believed to be a result of abnormal interaction between the visual and vestibular systems (Ornitz et al., 1974). Additionally, studies of autistic children's rapid eye movements (REM) during sleep indicated an immature pattern of REM bursts (Ornitz et al., 1973), and an abnormal decrease in REM burst duration following mild vestibular stimulation during sleep (Ornitz et al., 1974). These authors suggest a theory of brainstem dysfunction involving the central connections of the vestibular system (Ornitz, 1974; Ornitz & Ritvo, 1976).

An alternative theory of sensory dysfunction based on a developmental model of receptor preference has been proposed (e.g., Goldfarb, 1956; Schopler, 1965; Stroh & Buick, 1964). These researchers hypothesize that autistic children display a preference for tactile, olfactory, and gustatory stimulation (near or proximal receptors) over auditory and visual stimulation (distal receptors). Developmentally, a preference hierarchy for normal persons proceeds from near receptor preference to distal receptor preference. Thus, the failure of autistic children to progress to distal receptor preference (Schopler, 1965) is believed to be an etiological factor in autism.

This theory has been given support by Ritvo and Provence (1953), who observed that autistic children generally explored their environment through touching and mouthing objects. Also, Hermelin and O'Connor (1970) demonstrated that autistic children preferred tactile stimulation and responded abnormally to auditory stimuli. Indeed, Prior (1984) argued that these perceptual abnormalities were in evidence from a very early age (e.g., Prior & Gajzago, 1974) and also preceded or coincided with other behavioral symptoms (e.g., Ornitz, 1969). This may have important implications for the organic etiology of the disorder but may also lead to questions of uncertainty as to whether these abnormalities cause the behavioral characteristics or whether they result from them.

The most comprehensive treatment program based on the neurological dysfunction model was developed by Schopler and Reichler (1971) and emphasizes the utilization of proximal receptors to facilitate development and organize sensory information. This developmental therapy focuses on four general areas. First, to increase responsiveness to others, a therapist participates in all the child's activities. The therapist provides proximal receptor stimulation such as bouncing, swinging, tickling, or cuddling. As the child begins to respond to the therapist, demands to engage in more appropriate behaviors are increased. Second, to enhance motivation, the child is encouraged by the therapist to explore toys and educational materials. As the child becomes more interested in such activities, he or she is encouraged to use materials in an appropriate manner and to explore new materials. Third, to stimulate cognitive development, the child is taught receptive and expressive communication skills. Nonverbal imitation, colors, shapes, and other discriminations are also taught. Some concepts may be taught through the use of sensory stimulation (e.g., teaching "up" and "down" by swinging the child up and down). Finally, to improve perceptual motor function, exercises to improve the child's body awareness and motor coordination are developed. The use of proximal and distal modalities is emphasized during these activities. Exercises are practiced to develop skills such as hand–eye coordination, jumping, and balancing.

This treatment philosophy has evolved into a comprehensive treatment and education program for autistic children (the TEACCH model). Despite reports of improvements from sensory integration-oriented treatment, empirical research assessing the efficacy of such programs is lacking. Additionally, conflicting evidence has been reported with regard to the etiological theories of sensory dysfunction (e.g., Lovaas, Schreibman, Koegel, & Rehm, 1971; Schopler, 1966).

Biochemical Model and Pharmacotherapy

Most research in biochemical processes in the etiology of autism has focused on the neurotransmitter serotonin. Serotonin is used by the body's arousal system. High levels of blood serotonin that are measured in normal infants have been found to decrease throughout childhood and stabilize in adulthood (Mesibov & Dawson, 1986; Ritvo et al., 1970). However, approximately 30% to 40% of autistic individuals show hyperserotonemia, an elevated level of blood serotonin, throughout life (Freeman & Ritvo, 1984). This failure to show the expected maturational decrease suggests immaturity in the neurological system. Additionally, Campbell and her colleagues (Campbell et al., 1976) have provided some evidence of a relationship between hyperserotonemia and poor intellectual functioning.

Based on the serotonin theory, Ritvo and his colleagues treated autistic children by administering fenfluramine (an anorectic agent) to reduce the levels of blood serotonin (e.g., Geller, Ritvo, Freeman, & Yuwiler, 1982). Importantly, improvements following administration of fenfluramine were reported. These included increased eye contact, social awareness, and attention to schoolwork; improved IQ scores; decreased hyperactivity and repetitive behaviors (e.g., hand flapping); and improved sleep patterns (e.g., August, Raz, & Baird, 1985; Klykylo, Feldis, O'Grady, Ross, & Halloran, 1985; Ritvo, Freeman, Geller, & Yuwiler, 1983; Ritvo et al., 1984, 1986). However, a recent study (Beisler, Tsai, & Stiefel, 1986) demonstrated that fenfluramine had no significant effects on autistic children's communication behaviors (e.g., expressive and receptive speech; echolalia). Also, mild side effects such as increased irritability and lethargy and decreased appetite have been observed (Ritvo et al., 1983, 1984, 1986). Additionally, Piggott, Gdowski, Villanueva, Fischhoff, and Frohman (1986) reported the occurrence of confusion and increased isolation and hand flapping. Finally, it is not certain whether the amount of serotonin in the blood is identical to that in the brain. Although these studies have begun to establish the safety and efficacy of fenfluramine as a treatment for autistic persons, the findings must be interpreted with extreme caution, as the precise manner by which fenfluramine acts to modify autistic children's symptoms is un-

known. Additional research is needed to critically assess long-term effects and side effects of fenfluramine before more definite conclusions may be drawn.

Generally, drug therapy has been criticized for improper usage (e.g., high dosages over long periods of time; no drug holidays), poor drug monitoring, and side effects (e.g., excessive sedation) that interfere with learning. Importantly, when drug treatment is withdrawn, behavioral symptoms often reappear. Finally, there is a lack of methodologically sound studies that demonstrate the efficacy of pharmacological treatment, particularly when used in combination with other behavioral treatments (Schreibman, 1988).

The pharmacological treatment of autistic children has, for the most part, had limited success. As no specific cause for autism has been identified, drug treatments have focused on alleviating some of the more disruptive symptoms. A wide variety of drugs have been used to treat these children, including antipsychotics and major tranquilizers such as haloperidol (Haldol) (Anderson et al., 1984; Campbell et al., 1978; Cohen et al., 1980), chlorpromazine (Thorazine) (Korein, Fish, Shapiro, Gerner, & Levidow, 1971), and trifluoperazine (Stelazine) (Campbell, Green, & Deutsch, 1985), L-dopa (Ritvo et al., 1971), and megavitamins (Rimland, Callaway, & Dreyfus, 1978). However, many studies have yielded conflicting findings. Amphetamines, for example, may reduce autistic children's overactivity and improve their attention span, but a worsening of other symptoms often occurs (Mesibov & Dawson, 1986). Thus, drugs are not commonly administered to autistic children.

BEHAVIORAL APPROACH TO AUTISM

Behavioral Model

The behavioral approach views the syndrome of autism as a cluster of specific behaviors and has promoted measurable and observable changes in such behaviors. This model suggests that child development consists primarily of the acquisition of behaviors and of stimulus functions, or aspects of the environment that acquire "meanings" for the child (Lovaas & Newsom, 1976; Lovaas, Schreibman, & Koegel, 1974). The behavioral perspective therefore suggests that manipulation of antecedents and consequences to make aspects of the environment meaningful to autistic children. In general, behavioral *deficits* are increased by teaching and systematically reinforcing occurrences, while behavioral *excesses* are the targets of reduction and elimination. The behavioral view of autism thus differs from the traditional conceptualization of the disorder as a "disease." Historically, autism (and other forms of psychopathology) has been viewed as a diagnostic entity. However, this traditional view has not proved useful in that a diagnosis of autism per se does not (1) lead to a specific treatment, (2) facilitate communication between professionals, or (3) predict a specific prognosis.

The failure of the diagnosis to suggest a specific treatment is primarily due to the tremendous heterogeneity in the population labeled as autistic. Because the syndrome, by any definition, comprises several behaviors, children referred to as "autistic" may individually appear quite different. For example, both a verbal echolalic child and a mute, self-injurious child may have a diagnosis of autism, although they manifest quite different levels of functioning. Thus, there is substantial variability in the meaning of autism, and this diagnosis communicates little about any particular child. Consequently, there may be agreement regarding treatment techniques for particular behaviors (e.g., removal of attention for tantrums), but there is a lack of consensus among professionals as to how to treat the *syndrome* of autism as a whole. Finally, the diagnosis of autism does not suggest a differential prognosis. It is known that without treatment, most autistic children will not improve (Rutter, 1968), and the general prognosis for these children is very poor. However, some research has demonstrated that many autistic children will improve greatly with treatment (e.g., Lovaas, 1987; Lovaas et al., 1973). Therefore, a diagnosis of autism does not suggest which children will improve and which ones will not.

Behavioral Definition of Autism

In view of these problems, behaviorists have deemphasized the importance of focusing on the entire syndrome and instead have emphasized the assessment and understanding of individual behavioral excesses and deficits. Through the use of behavioral assessment (e.g., Schreibman & Koegel, 1981), a functional definition of the syndrome specific to an individual child can be arrived at. This procedure involves operationally defining individual behaviors, identifying variables controlling behaviors, and grouping behaviors according to common controlling variables. This, in turn, leads to appropriate treatment procedures.

The use of a behavioral definition of autism has several advantages that alleviate some of the problems previously discussed. Heterogeneity becomes less of a problem, because the behavioral characteristics of each child are specified. Specific behavioral excesses and deficits are described in precise detail, allowing for reliable observation and measurement. Agreement on the presence or absence of specific behaviors in a specific child also enhances communication among professionals. Furthermore, a behavioral description of autistic children suggests a treatment. The identification of specific excesses and deficits indicates to the therapist which of a variety of identified treatment techniques may be effective. For example, if the child displays echolalia, the therapist may choose from a number of available treatment procedures (discussed below) to remediate it. Additionally, a behavioral definition of autism suggests a prognosis. Because some behaviors are better understood than others, one may assume that a child who displays behaviors that are well understood and for which effective treatments have been demonstrated would have a better prognosis than a child who manifests behaviors that are as yet poorly understood or considered difficult to remediate. Finally, the behavioral approach to diagnosis is not limited to persons with autism. As this perspective views a disorder in terms of specific behaviors, it is clearly appropriate for other disorders as well. Similarly, the treatment techniques to be discussed in this chapter, which are based on a behavior modification technology of treatment, are applicable not only to autistic children but also to other children with similar behavioral deficits or excesses. The following section discusses current research in the treatment of autistic children.

Treatment

The literature suggests that the behavioral approach is the only treatment model empirically demonstrated to be effective with autistic children (cf. Egel, Koegel, & Schreibman, 1980; Lovaas et al., 1974; Schreibman & Koegel, 1981).

Indeed, a recent study by Lovaas (1987) reports quite striking and optimistic findings regarding autistic children's progress as a result of intensive behavioral treatment. In this study, two groups of very young (less than 46 months of age) autistic children were provided with either more than 40 hours weekly (experimental group) or less than 10 hours weekly (control group) of intensive one-to-one behavioral intervention. Treatment was provided in all environments (e.g., home, school, community) by trained student therapists and parents; it generally consisted of reducing self-stimulatory, aggressive, and self-injurious behaviors and teaching imitation, compliance to requests, social behavior, appropriate play, language, preacademic tasks, and observational learning. Both groups received a minimum of 2 years of treatment; a second control group which did not receive treatment was also included in the study to guard against a sampling or referral bias. Results of this study indicated that 47% of the children receiving the long-term intensive treatment achieved normal intellectual and educational functioning, with normal-range IQ scores and successful first-grade performance in regular public schools. Another 42% of the subjects in this group were placed in aphasia classes and scored in the mildly retarded range. In contrast, subjects in the control groups fared rather poorly. Only 2% of these children achieved normal functioning; 45% scored in the mildly retarded range and were assigned to aphasia classes, and 53% scored in the severely retarded range and were placed in classes for the autistic/retarded. While these results are promising in that they suggest that some autistic children may become "normal" through comprehensive behavioral therapy, they must be interpreted with caution. These findings need to be replicated; additionally, certain methodological problems (e.g., use of contingent aversives in the experimental group but not in the control group) must be addressed. However, these findings clearly demonstrate that autistic children may make significant progress with behavioral-oriented treatment.

Behavioral techniques have a broad basis in the literature, and many have been studied extensively. Because of this strong empirical evidence documenting the effectiveness of the behavioral model, the remainder of this chapter will be devoted to a description and discussion of behavioral intervention with autistic children.

BEHAVIORAL EXCESSES

The three major categories of behavioral excesses include self-injurious behavior, self-stimulatory behavior, and disruptive behavior. As these maladaptive behaviors interfere with learning and thus may hinder the child's progress, it is often necessary to decrease or eliminate these behaviors through the use of reductive procedures. Importantly, the use of nonaversive procedures in the treatment of inappropriate behaviors has recently been emphasized in the literature. This issue will be addressed in more detail later.

Self-Injurious Behavior

As previously described, many autistic children display self-injurious behavior (SIB). SIB involves any behavior in which an individual inflicts physical damage to his or her own body (Tate & Baroff, 1966). Episodes of SIB may vary in intensity from mildly disruptive (e.g., redness resulting from leg slapping) to life-threatening (e.g., skull fractures caused by running head-first into walls). In addition to the apparent physical damage, there are also indirect effects of SIB, since potentially serious infections may result from open wounds. In severe cases where the SIB is intense and life-threatening, physical restraints may be used to prevent further occurrence of the behavior. Devices such as arm splints or camisoles have been used, or the child may be tied down to a chair or bed. However, some forms of prolonged restraint can cause structural changes such as shortening of tendons, bone demineralization, and arrested motor development secondary to nonuse of limbs (Lovaas & Simmons, 1969). Another indirect effect of SIB is that the behavior may interfere with the child's psychological and educational development. Use of physical restraints may further restrict participation in social and educational activities. Finally, a common occurrence is that parents and staff members may be reluctant to place demands on the child for fear of precipitating an SIB episode (Carr, 1977).

Early treatment approaches to SIB have included drugs, reassurance and affection and, as previously mentioned, physical restraints. These treatments have been ineffective in eliminating SIB (Carr, 1977). Indeed, the use of reassuring affection has been shown to worsen SIB (Lovaas & Simmons, 1969). The application of operant techniques such as extinction and punishment has been more successful.

The least intrusive treatment approach for SIB is extinction. This procedure involves removal of positive reinforcement (e.g., attention) for the undesired behavior (SIB). Several early studies by Lovaas and his colleagues (Lovaas, Freitag, Gold, & Kassorla, 1965; Lovaas & Simmons, 1969) demonstrated that self-injurious behavior was an operant behavior maintained by positive social consequences (i.e., attention). Lovaas and Simmons (1969) demonstrated that when a self-injurious child was placed alone in a room and thus deprived of attention, SIB decreased and, after repeated sessions, eventually ceased. This effect has been replicated numerous times and extinction continues to be a popular behavioral procedure.

Extinction may also be effective in cases where the SIB is maintained by negative reinforcement. For example, Carr, Newsom, and Binkoff (1976) described the case of Tim, whose self-injury was particularly severe when he was working with a teacher. Not wanting to provide attention for the SIB, the teacher would turn away from him when he engaged in the behavior. However, this only served to increase the SIB. In a systematic analysis, the authors noted that Tim's self-injury was maintained by the avoidance of teacher demands; thus, an appropriate extinction procedure would be to continue the teacher demands even though self-injury occurred. As reinforcement (escape from demand situation) is no longer provided, the child's self-injurious behavior should extinguish.

When considering the use of an extinction procedure, one important caveat must be noted. During an extinction "run," the target behavior will continue to occur for a period of time. Also, there is an initial temporary increase in intensity (the extinction "burst") before the behavior decreases. If the child's SIB is particularly intense, extinction may not be the treatment of choice, as the child may inflict severe damage in an extinction burst before treatment is completed.

An alternative treatment is the use of punishment, in which an unpleasant stimulus is contingently applied. Punishment procedures provide immediate results (if an effective punisher is used) and thus may be indicated in cases where self-injury is severe and must be stopped quickly.

Punishment has been successful in reducing SIB and a variety of punishers have been studied, including electric shock (Lovaas & Simmons, 1969), water mist (Dorsey, Iwata, Ong, & McSween, 1980), and aromatic ammonia (Tanner & Zeiler, 1975). For example, Lovaas and Simmons (1969) reported complete elimination of severe SIB in three children by applying electric shock contingent upon the behavior. In most cases, only a few short, localized shocks were necessary to eliminate the behavior.

The use of these and other physical aversives (e.g., spanking) has raised ethical concerns due to the potential for misuse. Their use is also not permitted in many settings; therefore, less intrusive procedures have been explored. One reductive procedure which has been shown to be effective in reducing SIB is overcorrection. This procedure requires that the child engage in tiring, effortful behavior contingent upon the occurrence of SIB. For example, contingent upon face slapping, the child would have to engage in appropriate hand clapping, but for 50 claps. Azrin, Gottlieb, Hughart, Wesolowski, and Rahn (1975) devised a successful procedure that consisted of four components: (1) positive reinforcement was provided for appropriate, incompatible behaviors; (2) upon the occurrence of SIB, the client was required to "rest" in bed in a restricted position for 2 hours ("required relaxation"); (3) when self-injury occurred, the client spent 20 minutes practicing holding his hands away from his body; and (4) the client was required to practice other behaviors, such as holding onto armrests or clasping his hands behind his back.

Although the overcorrection procedure avoids the use of painful stimuli, its disadvantages include a high cost in terms of staff time and energy, thus limiting its applicability in some treatment settings, and the possibility of negative effects (e.g., Charlop, Burgio, Iwata, & Ivancic, 1988). Additional research is needed to determine the parameters of the maximally efficient application of the overcorrection procedure.

When using any punishment procedure, several concerns must be noted. It is recommended that the least intrusive procedures be attempted first. Also, to maintain treatment effects, the child should be taught a new, appropriate behavior to replace the SIB. Importantly, positive reinforcement for appropriate behaviors should always be used in conjunction with a reductive procedure. A differential reinforcement of other behavior (DRO) procedure is typically used. For example, positive reinforcement would be provided when the child was *not* engaging in SIB, thus strengthening appropriate behaviors and weakening SIB. Finally, because treatment effects may not generalize to other settings, persons, or over time (e.g., Lovaas & Simmons, 1969), it may be necessary to have the procedure implemented in different settings by different people, with "booster" sessions programmed at future intervals.

In concordance with the recent emphasis on nonaversive procedures, a stimulus control approach to the treatment of SIB has been proposed by Touchette and his colleagues. Touchette, MacDonald, and Langer (1985) suggest that SIB is controlled by certain stimulus conditions. That is, SIB may occur in some situations (e.g., upon presentation of difficult tasks) but not during others (e.g., during mealtime). Using a scatterplot diagram, the environmental conditions that provoke SIB may be identified and subsequently changed to eliminate SIB. To illustrate, Touchette et al. (1985) described the case of Jim, a mute autistic adolescent who displayed severe head banging and face slapping. Reductive procedures (e.g., water mist) had been ineffective in reducing the frequency of the behavior. By reprogramming Jim's daily activity schedule to exclude activities that were likely to elicit SIB, the occurrence of self-injury was dramatically reduced and eventually eliminated.

Along the same line, a functional analysis of problem behavior has been advocated (e.g., Carr & Durand, 1985). Such an analysis allows a determination of the variables that set the occasion for or reinforce the behavior. In an extensive review of the literature on SIB, Carr (1977) identified three general motivations for the occurrence and maintenance of self-injury. First, the child may engage in SIB in order to obtain social attention or some other positive consequence. In other cases, a child may engage in SIB in order to avoid or escape an aversive situation or event, such as task demands. In this instance, self-injury may be maintained by negative reinforcement. Or the child may engage in SIB as a form of self-stimulation. That is, the child appears to engage in the self-injury because he or she enjoys it. Importantly, a systematic analysis of specific variables that serve to

maintain a specific child's SIB thus suggests an effective treatment approach.

One such assessment and nonaversive treatment strategy was proposed by Carr and Durand (1985). In this study, four children who displayed SIB and other disruptive behaviors participated in work sessions in which task difficulty and adult attention were systematically varied. Sessions of three conditions were presented: (1) easy task, adult attention during 100% of specified time intervals; (2) easy task, adult attention during 33% of intervals; and (3) difficult task, adult attention during 100% of intervals. Using a reversal design, it was demonstrated that the controlling variables for disruptive behavior varied across children. That is, children 1 and 2 displayed increased disruptive behavior when task demands increased (difficult task, 100% attention condition); child 3's behavior problems became more frequent when adult attention was reduced (easy task, 33% attention condition); and child 4 exhibited increased disruptive behavior when both increased task difficulty and reduced adult attention occurred (difficult task, 33% attention condition). Thus, in a second experiment, the children were taught verbal communicative phrases that served to elicit either adult assistance or adult attention during work sessions. For example, to solicit help with difficult tasks, children 1, 2, and 4 were taught to say, "I don't understand." Similarly, to solicit praise during low attention conditions, children 3 and 4 were taught to ask "Am I doing good work?" After appropriate communicative phrases, the experimenter provided appropriate consequences (i.e., assistance or praise). Irrelevant communicative phrases were also taught in each condition to assess effects of nonfunctional phrases on frequency of disruptive behavior. Results indicated that for both groups of children, the establishment of functional communicative responses was effective in reducing disruptive behaviors to low levels; unrelated communicative phrases were ineffective in reducing these behaviors. Importantly, these findings suggest that inappropriate behaviors such as SIB may serve a communicative function (e.g., to elicit attention); but it may effectively be eliminated by teaching a functionally equivalent phrase (e.g., "Am I doing good work?"). In summary, the findings reported by Touchette et al. (1985) and Carr and Durand (1985), although not without limitation, provide much promise for the continued development of effective, nonaversive treatment procedures for this hurtful behavior.

Self-Stimulatory Behavior

Self-stimulation (e.g., rocking, flapping hands or arms, sniffing objects) is a prominent feature of autism. These children typically engage in high rates of stereotyped behaviors. They not only appear bizarre when engaged in self-stimulation but are also unresponsive to the environment (Lovaas, Litrownik, & Mann, 1971; Schreibman, Charlop, & Britten, 1983). Lovaas and his colleagues (1971) demonstrated that autistic children's responding to auditory stimuli was disrupted when the auditory cues were presented while the child was engaging in self-stimulation. Similarly, Koegel and Covert (1972) found that autistic children failed to acquire a simple discrimination task; yet, when self-stimulation was suppressed, correct responding increased and the discrimination was acquired. These findings clearly demonstrate that self-stimulation interferes with learning. Subsequent studies have repeatedly demonstrated this inverse relationship between self-stimulatory behavior and performance of appropriate behaviors (e.g., Foxx & Azrin, 1973; Koegel et al., 1974; Lovaas et al., 1987). However, a recent study by Chock and Glahn (1983) suggests that some echolalic, higher-functioning autistic children may learn a discrimination task when engaging in self-stimulation.

A wide variety of behavioral procedures have been applied to self-stimulation. To reduce body rocking, Mulhern and Baumeister (1969) reinforced two retarded children for sitting still, a behavior incompatible with self-stimulation. The children's self-stimulatory behavior was reduced by about one-third. Although studies using DRO have reported similar decreases (e.g., Deitz & Repp, 1973; Herendeen, Jeffrey, & Graham, 1974), others (e.g., Foxx & Azrin, 1973; Harris & Wolchik, 1979) have not observed such reductions in self-stimulation.

Punishment procedures have been much more successful in suppressing self-stimulatory behaviors. Initial studies demonstrated the efficacy of aversive stimuli such as electric shock (Lovaas et al., 1965), physical restraint (Koegel et al., 1974), and slaps on the hand or thigh (Bucher & Lovaas, 1968; Foxx & Azrin, 1973; Koegel

& Covert, 1972). However, for many children, the use of less intrusive reductive procedures has been effective (e.g., Charlop, Burgio, Iwata, & Ivancic 1988; Favell, McGimsey, & Jones, 1978).

One relatively "mild" punishment procedure that has proved quite effective is overcorrection (Foxx & Azrin, 1973). This procedure consists of a period of "positive practice" in the correct form of the behavior contingent upon the occurrence of self-stimulatory behavior in the same topography. For example, one child who displayed repetitive head weaving was forced repetitively to practice appropriate head movements (e.g., "head up"). In a comparison with other procedures used to reduce self-stimulation (e.g., DRO, contingent spanking) overcorrection was the only procedure that completely eliminated the children's self-stimulatory behaviors. Additionally, these researchers suggest the use of verbal reprimands in conjunction with the overcorrection procedure, so as to maintain reduced levels of self-stimulation. Subsequent investigations (e.g., Azrin, Kaplan, & Foxx, 1973; Harris & Wolchik, 1979; Herendeen et al., 1974) have confirmed and extended these findings. However, as previously discussed, there are some problems associated with overcorrection; the procedure is demanding in terms of staff time, and the functional components of the package have not been clearly identified.

In spite of the success of these procedures, the generalized, durable elimination of self-stimulatory behavior has not been achieved (Rincover & Koegel, 1977a, b). Several studies suggest that the perceptual or sensory reinforcers provided to the child when engaging in self-stimulation serve as highly salient reinforcers that maintain the behavior (e.g., Lovaas et al., 1987; Rincover, 1978; Rincover, Newsom, Lovaas, & Koegel, 1977). For example, self-stimulatory hand flapping may be maintained by the proprioceptive feedback it generates. If self-stimulation is conceptualized as operant behavior maintained by its sensory consequences, it may therefore be possible to remove the positive consequences and the behavior should extinguish. Indeed, this rationale is the basis of the sensory extinction procedure devised by Rincover (1978). This treatment procedure was designed to eliminate self-stimulation by removing its auditory, visual, or proprioceptive sensory consequences. For example, for a child who twirled objects on a table, the procedure entailed removing auditory feedback by carpeting the table surface. Rincover (1978) empirically demonstrated the effectiveness of this method by eliminating the self-stimulatory behaviors of several children. Importantly, since self-stimulatory behaviors are idiosyncratic, specific maintaining sensory consequences had to be identified for each child. Different sensory extinction procedures were therefore necessary for different self-stimulatory behaviors. While this approach is effective, it may not be applicable in all environments or to more complex self-stimulatory behaviors.

In a recent study, Durand and Carr (1987) suggested that some children's self-stimulatory behavior may have a communicative function. In a functional analysis of four children's self-stimulatory behaviors, these researchers demonstrated that while easy tasks were presented, self-stimulation occurred infrequently; however, introduction of difficult tasks resulted in increases in self-stimulation. Furthermore, removal of the task materials (time out) occasioned increases in the behavior. Thus, removal of the difficult tasks served as a negative reinforcer for self-stimulation, which maintained the escape behavior. To provide an appropriate means for reducing task difficulty, the children were taught a communicative alternative ("Help me") to request teacher assistance; subsequently, substantial reductions in the children's self-stimulation occurred. Although self-stimulation generally remains a treatment-resistant behavior, the findings of these two studies are promising in that they suggest an effective treatment for the reduction of these behaviors and will stimulate further research interest in this area.

Disruptive Behaviors

Disruptive behaviors (e.g., tantrums, aggression, destruction of property) are often major obstacles to the treatment of autistic children. These children may frequently cry, scream, hit, bite, kick, or throw objects. Because these behaviors are displayed by other children as well as autistic ones, the treatment alternatives discussed below are not designed specifically for autistic children.

One frequently used procedure is extinction. For example, children often engage in tantrums to gain adult attention, or to get adults to "give in" to their demands. Ignoring the tantrum and not acquiescing to the child's demands is often effective in eliminating the behavior. However, as discussed in the section on SIB, initiation of an extinction procedure frequently results in a temporary increase in the strength of the behavior. Therefore, this procedure may not be the treatment of choice with some forms of disruptive behavior (e.g., severe aggression). An additional concern is that extinction results in a gradual reduction rather than a sharp decrement in the behavior (Lovaas & Simmons, 1969). These concerns must be anticipated and addressed prior to using an extinction procedure.

Punishment procedures have also proven to be effective in dealing with disruptive behavior (e.g., Lovaas & Simmons, 1969; Matson & DiLorenzo, 1984; Tate & Baroff, 1966). Such procedures have the advantage of providing rapid results, which may be especially important with a severely disruptive behavior. Additionally, positive side effects have been reported (Lichstein & Schreibman, 1976). A wide variety of punishment procedures have been evaluated, ranging from a loud "No" to physical aversives such as water mist or electric shock. Again, the previously mentioned concerns regarding punishment are relevant here. More intrusive reductive procedures are often not necessary for some disruptive behaviors, or they may not be permitted in some settings. These concerns have led to the development of other, less intrusive procedures.

One procedure which has been very effective is "time out." Time out is an arrangement in which the occurrence of a behavior is followed by a period of time during which a variety of reinforcers are no longer available (White, Nielsen, & Johnson, 1972). That is, contingent upon the inappropriate behavior, the child does not have the opportunity to obtain reinforcement. For example, contingent upon an aggressive act, the child would be placed in a small, barren room for a certain period of time. This relatively mild procedure has been shown to be effective with a variety of disruptive behaviors (e.g., Barton, Guess, Garcia, & Baer, 1970; Bostow & Bailey, 1969; Foxx & Shapiro, 1978; Rolider & Van Houten, 1985; White et al., 1972). The first empirical demonstration of the effectiveness of time out with an autistic child was provided by Wolf, Risley, and Mees (1964), who reduced the child's tantrum and self-injurious behaviors by placing it alone in a room each time the behavior occurred.

There are several important parameters to consider when implementing a time-out procedure. First, there is no consensus in the literature on the optimal duration for time out. Studies report the successful use of time-out intervals ranging from 2 minutes (Bostow & Bailey, 1969) to 3 hours (Burchard & Tyler, 1965). White et al. (1972) noted that most investigators have used intervals from 5 to 20 minutes. Second, the effectiveness of the time-out procedure may be influenced by the nature of the "time-in" environment (Solnick, Rincover, & Peterson, 1977). If the time-in setting is impoverished, time out may serve as a negative reinforcer in that the child's behavior may remove him or her from an undesirable situation. To alleviate this problem, an enriched (i.e., highly reinforcing) time-in setting should be provided (Solnick et al., 1977); under these conditions, the time-out procedure should be effective in reducing disruptive behavior (Carr et al., 1976; Solnick et al., 1977). Third, some investigators have reported that time out may have reinforcing as well as punishing effects. For example, Solnick et al. (1977) found that the use of time out resulted in an increase in one child's tantrums. Upon further analysis, it was found that the time-out period was used by the child to engage in self-stimulatory behavior. The suppression of movement in time out has proven effective in eliminating this problem. (e.g., Solnick et al., 1977; Rolider & Van Houten, 1985). Finally, a major concern in using a time-out procedure is that it may decrease the child's educational time, since it requires that he or she be removed from the teaching environment each time the behavior occurs. In this case, the use of an intermittent schedule of time out may be useful (e.g., Clark, Rowbury, Baer, & Baer, 1973; Dunlap, Koegel, Johnson, & O'Neill, 1987). Clark et al. (1973) demonstrated that the use of time out after every third or fourth occurrence of a disruptive behavior was nearly as effective as a continuous schedule.

Overcorrection has also been used to eliminate disruptive behavior. The objectives of the procedure, as proposed by Foxx and Azrin (1972), are (1) to overcorrect the environmental effects of an inappropriate act; and (2) to require the disrupter (i.e., the child) to thoroughly practice overly correct forms of appropriate behavior. The first objective is achieved through restitutional overcorrection, which requires the disrupter to return the disturbed scene to a greatly improved state. Thus, the individual must assume personal responsibility for the disruptive act. For example, a child who smears paint on the floor rather than on his or her paper might be required to clean up the paint, then wash and wax the entire floor. To achieve the second objective, positive practice overcorrection is used. In the previous example, the child who spilled paint on the floor would be required to practice painting appropriately on paper. If no environmental disruption then occurs, the restitutional overcorrection is not applicable and only the positive practice is used. In a comparison of the overcorrection procedure, time out, and social disapproval, Foxx and Azrin (1972) demonstrated that overcorrection was most effective in reducing aggressive behavior. Overcorrection has the advantages of not using painful physical stimuli and of teaching the individual an appropriate behavior. However, further research is necessary to determine the specific parameters for the effectiveness of the procedure.

While the use of less intrusive punishment procedures has been emphasized in the current literature, such procedures may be ineffective because of previous inconsistent or incorrect use. One means of enhancing the effects of less intrusive punishers has been proposed by Charlop, Burgio, Iwata, and Ivancic (1988). These researchers compared the effects of mild punishers presented in a single format to the use of varied punishers (presentation of one of three punishers) on the occurrence of disruptive behavior. Their results indicated that the varied-punisher format was most effective in reducing the children's disruptive behaviors. The authors discussed the advantageous use of these mild punishers in a varied format, suggesting that more intrusive procedures would not be necessary.

BEHAVIORAL DEFICITS

The general categories of behavioral deficits are speech and language, attention, motivation, and social behavior and play. A voluminous amount of research addressing these areas has been conducted in the past decade, and a variety of prompting procedures and other methods of aiding acquisition have been developed and have greatly improved our effectiveness in remediating these deficits.

Speech and Language

The failure of autistic children to acquire language and to use speech in a communicative manner is one of the most debilitating aspects of autism. As mentioned earlier, approximately 50% of autistic children are functionally mute (Rimland, 1964). These children lack receptive as well as expressive speech. Because research has indicated that the acquisition of speech prior to age 5 suggests a more favorable clinical prognosis for the autistic child (e.g., Eisenberg & Kanner, 1956; Lovaas, 1987; Rutter, 1968), most therapy time is often spent on language acquisition. Detailed descriptions of behavioral techniques for teaching functionally mute autistic children have been provided by Fay and Schuler (1980), Lovaas (1977), and Lovaas, Berberich, Perloff, and Schaeffer (1966). The reader is referred to these references for more detailed information, as a comprehensive discussion of language training is beyond the scope of this chapter. Following is a brief description of the initial steps of such language training.

An early procedure that continues to be used to teach speech is based on imitation. The child is taught to imitate vocalizations until a verbal imitative repertoire is acquired. Initially, the speech-training program consists of a series of steps in which finer discriminations are required of the child. Described below are the initial steps developed by Lovaas et al. (1966) for teaching vocal imitation.

Step 1. Any vocalizations made by the child are reinforced so as to increase the frequency of vocalizations.

Step 2. When vocalizations are occurring at a high rate, the child's vocalizations are reinforced only if emitted within 5 seconds of the therapist's vocalization. For example, the therapist might say "ah," to which the child must emit *any* sound within 5 seconds. This establishes a temporal discrimination, and for the first time the child's vocal behavior is under the control of the therapist's vocal behavior.

Step 3. Through shaping, the child is required to imitate the therapist's vocalization more and more closely until the child repeats the therapist's vocalization exactly. Initially, any sound that resembles the verbal stimulus is reinforced. Across progressive trials, only sounds that more closely approximate the therapist's model are reinforced. When the child consistently imitates the therapist's vocalization exactly for several trials, Step 4 is initiated.

Step 4. A new sound is acquired through the same procedure as Step 3. The presentation of that new sound is then interspersed with the first sound, so as to teach the child to discriminate between sounds. Eventually more and more sounds, then words and phrases, are added to extend the child's imitation repertoire.

Once such a repertoire is acquired, it is then necessary to transfer stimulus control of the imitated vocalization from the therapist's model to the appropriate object. That is, rather than imitate the therapist's model "ball," the child is taught to say "ball" when the appropriate referent (ball) is presented. Thus, the meaning of the verbal response is taught. The child is taught to label objects both receptively and expressively. With receptive labeling, the child must provide a nonverbal response but is not required to verbalize the label (i.e., "Give me the ball"). Expressive labeling requires the child to actually say the label (i.e., "What is this?" "Ball"). Initially, prompting procedures are used. Prompting procedures for receptive labeling tasks usually consist of a therapist pointing at or manually guiding the child's hand to the requested object; the prompt is gradually faded out over successive trials. For expressive labeling tasks, prompts typically consist of providing the child with the correct answer (the therapist's model) and allowing him or her to imitate the vocalization in the presence of the object. This prompt is gradually faded until the presence of the object elicits the vocalization. For example, the therapist would provide the answer to the question (e.g., "What is this?" "Ball") and then gradually fade out the presentation of the prompt "Ball" to the presentation of the /b/ sound. The therapist may then whisper the /b/ sound until it is no longer necessary. This prompting technique is also used to teach the child to speak in full sentences (e.g., "What is this?" "This is a ball."). Prompts may be similarly faded out until the child can answer "This is a ball" when asked, "What is this?"

Despite the success of these procedures, many autistic children remain without vocal speech. Researchers have explored the use of sign language as an alternative communication system for these children. The interested reader is referred to a series of studies by Carr and his colleagues (Carr, 1979, 1982a, 1982b; Carr, Binkoff, Kologinsky, & Eddy, 1978; Carr & Kologinsky, 1983; Carr, Kologinsky, & Leff-Simon, 1987).

Another language intervention program for autistic children is the natural language paradigm (NLP), developed by Koegel and his colleagues (e.g., O'Dell & Koegel, 1981; Koegel, O'Dell, & Koegel, 1987). NLP is conducted during short play sessions in which the therapist and child play together with a variety of toys and activities. During a session, the therapist models a variety of appropriate responses and provides numerous oportunities for the child to imitate. All attempts to communicate verbally are reinforced with access to a toy and with praise. Thus, this program incorporates specific variables that closely approximate normal language interactions (e.g., turn taking, sharing, natural consequences) and increase autistic children's motivation to respond (e.g., novel stimuli, task variation, direct reinforcers). Koegel et al. (1987) report that while the traditional discrete-trial language-training procedure, similar to the one previously described, resulted in a low level of imitative and spontaneous speech in two nonverbal autistic children, NLP training led to rapid increases in imitation and spontaneous speech. Importantly, generalization to settings outside the clinic occurred following NLP training.

An extension of these findings has been reported by Laski, Charlop, and Schreibman (1988). As a means to further enhance generalization, parents of verbal and nonverbal autistic children were trained to use NLP during play sessions at home. Specifically, parents were trained to criterion on four dimensions of NLP: (1) reinforcing the child's attempts (i.e., praising child's vocal attempts and providing contingent access to toys); (2) turn taking (i.e., exchanging toys back and forth); (3) task variation (i.e., frequently changing toys or words/phrases); and (4) shared control (permitting child to choose toy and or words to be used). Parents were instructed to conduct daily 15-minute sessions

of NLP at home. Following training in a clinic (experimental) setting, generalization probes were conducted in three nontraining settings: structured free-play settings at the clinic and at home, and in a less structured setting in the clinic waiting room. The results of this investigation indicated that parents readily learned to use NLP to teach their children speech. Additionally, following NLP training, both nonverbal and verbal children increased the frequency of their imitations, answers, and spontaneous speech. Importantly, generalization of speech gains across nontraining settings was observed. These findings are important in that they demonstrate (1) the efficacy of NLP as a speech and language training program and (2) the feasibility of teaching parents to use the program to teach their children speech and improve generalization.

As mentioned earlier, many autistic children do speak. However, their speech is predominantly echolalic, the meaningless repetition of words previously heard. Because of the presence of such speech, the procedures for teaching speech to echolalic children differ from those described for teaching mute children. In the case of the echolalic child, the goal of speech training is to teach the child to discriminate between appropriate and inappropriate echolalic utterances and to use speech in a communicative fashion (Fay & Schuler, 1980).

Several prompting procedures have been designed to eliminate echolalic speech (e.g., Lovaas et al., 1977; Risley & Wolf, 1967). For example, the therapist can present a picture of a ball, say "That's a ball," and wait until the child echoes, "That's a ball." Over successive trials, the prompt would gradually be faded out (e.g., "That's a b——") until stimulus control was transferred from the verbal prompt to the picture of the ball; thus, upon presentation of the picture, the child says, "That's a ball." In another procedure, Freeman, Ritvo, and Miller (1975) provided an answer-first/question-last paradigm to take advantage of the child's echolalia while teaching appropriate speech. For example, the therapist would present a picture and say, "Sitting. What is the boy doing?" When the child started to echo, he or she would be presented with reinforcers immediately after saying "Sitting," but before he or she had a chance to continue and echo the question.

In a functional analysis of echolalia, Carr and his colleagues (1975) determined that one factor that influenced the occurrence of echolalia was the "comprehensibility" of the verbal stimulus. In this study, when verbal autistic children were presented with nonsense phrases, they would echo the verbal stimulus; however, when presented with a stimulus for which they had a response (discriminative stimulus), the child would respond appropriately. Additionally, when the children were taught the appropriate responses to verbal stimuli, their echolalia ceased. As it would be impossible to teach responses to every novel verbal stimulus, Schreibman and Carr (1978) taught the children a generalized verbal response to previously echoed questions. When asked such a question, the children were taught to say, "I don't know," an appropriate verbal response common in nonhandicapped children.

Although the above procedures are designed to decrease autistic children's echolalic speech, one study has demonstrated how echolalia may be used to advantage to teach autistic children appropriate speech. Instead of eliminating echolalia, Charlop (1983) designed a procedure that utilized echolalia to teach receptive labeling. In this procedure, the therapist verbally labeled one of two objects. The child was then allowed the opportunity to echo this verbalization. The experimenter then placed the objects before the child and labeled the object again, and the child handed the experimenter an object. For example, the therapist would say, "boat," wait for the child to echo "boat," then present the toy boat and car and again say "boat" and allow the child to select the correct object. Charlop (1983) suggests that by echoing the word "boat," the children provided their own discriminative stimulus before responding manually, thus facilitating acquisition and generalization of object labels. These findings suggest that echolalia may be a useful tool in the treatment of autistic children.

The techniques for language acquisition and remediation described above are typically employed in a highly structured therapeutic environment. Although these techniques have been successful, speech remains an extremely difficult and complex behavior to teach. Language responses acquired in therapeutic training settings are often used in a rote, mechanical manner, and may be nonfunctional in more natural environments (Halle, 1982; Hart & Rogers-Warren, 1978). Additionally, language use often fails to occur outside of the training environment. Therefore, an important and promising area of

research has focused on teaching language under more natural conditions to promote spontaneous, generalized language use. Importantly, these procedures are designed to refine and naturalize the children's speech. Thus, these procedures focus not only on the natural environment per se but also on the use of the natural environment to facilitate more sophisticated and generalized use of speech.

One such procedure that has been very effective in teaching spontaneous speech is time delay (e.g., Halle, Baer, & Spradlin, 1981; Halle, Marshall, & Spradlin, 1979). This procedure consists of transferring stimulus control of an appropriate response from the therapist's prompt (e.g., saying "cookie") to the presentation of a stimulus (i.e., a cookie). Generally, this is accomplished by presenting the stimulus and modeling the correct verbal response; gradually, the presentation of the prompt is delayed (e.g., in 2-second increments), until the child anticipates the prompt and speaks spontaneously.

The effectiveness of this procedure was demonstrated by Charlop, Schreibman, and Thibodeau (1985), who taught 7 autistic children to request desired items spontaneously. In this study, the experimenter presented a highly preferred object (e.g., held up a cookie) and immediately said, "I want a cookie." If the child correctly imitated this model, the object was provided as a reinforcer. After three consecutive trials of correct imitation, a graduated time-delay procedure was implemented. Specifically, after the presentation of the object, a 2-second delay occurred before the experimenter modeled the appropriate request. Child requests made prior to the model and imitative responses were considered correct and were reinforced by providing the preferred object. Contingent upon three correct responses, the delay was increased by 2-second increments until a 10-second delay had been reached. Following time delay, generalization probes were presented. Results of this investigation indicated that all children learned to request items spontaneously using the time delay procedure. Also, generalization of spontaneous speech was demonstrated across unfamiliar settings, persons, situations, and untrained objects, thus providing additional support for the efficacy of this procedure. A series of studies by Charlop and Schreibman and their colleagues have assessed the transfer of stimulus control using more obvious physical referents (e.g., cookie) to less obvious cues such as certain actions, settings, or temporal cues. In one such study, the time-delay procedure was also successfully used to teach autistic children to provide verbal expressions of affection spontaneously (e.g., "I love you") in the presence of an action (a hug) (e.g., Charlop & Walsh, 1986).

This procedure has also been effective in promoting setting-cued speech. For example, autistic children were successfully taught to make spontaneous requests in appropriate environments, such as "I want to swing" at the playground, or requesting a cookie in the kitchen (Schreibman, Charlop, & Tryon, 1981). In another study, Charlop and Bieber (1988) taught parents of autistic children to implement the time-delay procedure at home so as to increase their children's spontaneous speech. In this study, autistic children were taught to speak spontaneously in response to temporal cues. That is, parents implemented the time-delay procedure at specific times throughout the day to teach contextually appropriate speech. For example, the children were taught to say "Good morning, Mom" upon waking; "May I have a snack please?" after school; and "Goodnight, Mom" at bedtime. Results indicated that parents effectively employed the procedure to increase their children's spontaneous speech. Importantly, the children's spontaneous speech occurred at the appropriate times of day but in a variety of settings, suggesting that the children's behavior was not dependent upon a specific location.

Another promising line of research has investigated the effects of modeling in facilitating autistic children's speech and language. While conflicting findings regarding the efficacy of modeling have been reported (e.g., Charlop & Walsh, 1986; Varni, Lovaas, Koegel, & Everett, 1979), a few studies (e.g., Charlop, Schreibman, & Tryon, 1983; Coleman & Stedman, 1974; Egel, Richman, & Koegel, 1981) have demonstrated that autistic children can benefit from observation of peer models. In one study, 4 low-functioning autistic children learned to receptively label objects through observation of an autistic peer model (Charlop et al., 1983). Results indicated that peer modeling was an effective procedure; additionally, as compared to a traditional discrete-trial approach, generalization and maintenance of correct responding were superior in the peer-modeling condition. This line of research has recently been extended by Charlop and Milstein (1989), who assessed the efficacy of using video modeling to increase autistic chil-

dren's conversational speech. In this study, verbal autistic children observed a videotape of two adult models engaging in conversations about specific toys. Results indicated that the children learned appropriate conversations through video modeling and generalized these skills to other topics of conversation than those that were modeled. In general, the results of these studies suggest that modeling may be an effective procedure for improving autistic children's speech.

As is evident, much progress has been made in increasing autistic children's severe deficits in speech and language. The studies and procedures described in this section provide a solid foundation for researchers to continue to develop means to further improve autistic children's ability to communicate.

Attention

One of the most serious problems displayed by autistic children is their lack of responsiveness to the environment. These children may not appear to notice salient features of their environment, such as comings and goings of people; indeed, as discussed earlier, these children often have early histories of suspected blindness or deafness. Conversely, autistic children may be overly sensitive to low-level stimulation (e.g., shadows from sunlight; turning of a book page). The failure of these children to effectively utilize environmental stimulation plus their great difficulty in learning new behaviors has led to extensive research in the area of attentional deficits; it is hoped that effective treatment procedures will ultimately be developed.

As previously discussed, when autistic children are presented with a learning situation in which response to multiple cues is required, they characteristically respond to a very restricted number of the available cues. This unique pattern of responding, deemed "stimulus overselectivity," was first identified by Lovaas and his colleagues (Lovaas, Schreibman, Koegel, & Rehm, 1971). In this study, autistic, retarded, and nonhandicapped children were trained to respond to a complex stimulus comprising a visual, an auditory, and a tactile component. Following this training, each component was presented separately to determine how much control it had acquired over the children's responses. Surprisingly, results indicated that while the nonhandicapped children responded equally to all three component cues, the autistic children responded to only one (either auditory or visual). The retarded children responded between these two extremes. Furthermore, subsequent training demonstrated that the autistic children could learn to respond to previously nonfunctional cues, thus suggesting that the problem lay in responding to the cues in the context of other cues rather than in a particular sensory modality. The phenomenon of stimulus overselectivity has been demonstrated to occur across different sensory modalities (e.g., Lovaas, Litrownik, & Mann, 1971; Lovaas & Schreibman, 1971) and within a single modality (e.g., Koegel & Wilhelm, 1973; Reynolds, Newsom, & Lovaas, 1974). Additionally, the presence of overselectivity may be more a function of low mental age than of autism per se (Wilhelm & Lovaas, 1976; Schreibman, Kohlenberg, & Britten, 1986).

The implications of overselective responding are serious. Consider, for example, the fact that most learning situations require a response to multiple cues. The inability of autistic children to respond accurately in these situations severely interferes with learning. Overselectivity has been implicated as a variable influencing language acquisition (Lovaas, Schreibman, Koegel & Rehm, 1971; Reynolds et al., 1974; Schreibman et al., 1986), social behavior (Schreibman & Lovaas, 1973), observational learning (Varni et al., 1979), prompting (Koegel & Rincover, 1976; Schreibman, 1975), and generalization (Rincover & Koegel, 1975).

Having identified the existence and parameters of stimulus overselectivity, researchers have focused on ameliorating the effects of this attentional deficit. One approach has involved attempting to directly remediate the overselectivity by teaching the children to respond to multiple cues. A second approach has involved developing teaching strategies that allow the children to learn despite the overselective attention. Both of these approaches will be discussed in turn.

As research suggested that, under some conditions, the overselectivity effect disappeared (e.g., Schreibman, Koegel, & Craig, 1977), it thus appeared likely that overselective responding could be changed. Indeed, studies by Koegel and Schreibman (1977) and Schreibman, Charlop, and Koegel (1982) demonstrated that overselective autistic children could learn to respond to multiple cues if trained on a conditional discrimination. For example, Schreibman, Charlop, and Koegel (1982) demonstrated that overselective autistic children failed to learn difficult

discrimination tasks when provided with a pointing prompt; however, after the children were trained to respond to multiple cues on several consecutive conditional discriminations, they could learn from such a prompt. The conditional discriminations used in this investigation are presented in Figure 9.1. Upon failure to use a pointing prompt, each child was presented with a training stimulus set until criterion was reached. Testing stimuli were then introduced to determine whether the training discrimination had been learned on the basis of only one cue (i.e., overselective responding). If this was the case, training on the test discrimination continued until the child was responding on the basis of multiple cues. Training then began on the next set of training stimuli until the child learned two consecutive training discriminations without demonstrating overselective responding. Results indicated that although the children had previously "overselected" to the pointing prompt and failed to attend to the stimulus materials, they were able, after multiple-cue training, to benefit from the prompting procedure. Importantly, these findings suggested that autistic children could learn from a more traditional teaching technique, and may be generally able to respond to their environment in a manner more similar to that of nonhandicapped children.

Although the above approach is encouraging in that it suggests a treatment for overselectivity, this procedure has not been successful with all autistic children. Thus, special techniques have been developed for these children so that they may learn despite their overselective responding. As mentioned above, one frequently used teaching technique is prompting. This involves adding an extra cue to guide the child to the correct response. Examples of such "extra-stimulus" prompts (Schreibman, 1975) include pointing to the correct answer, underlining, or using different colors. These prompts are commonly used and then gradually faded out until the child responds correctly without the prompt. Unfortunately, in the case of overselective autistic children, the total removal of an extra-stimulus prompt can be problematic in that the child may overselect to the prompt and fail to respond to the training stimulus.

Schreibman (1975) developed a "within-stimulus" prompting procedure, a prompting strategy that essentially took advantage of the children's tendency toward overselective responding. A within-stimulus prompt involves exaggerating

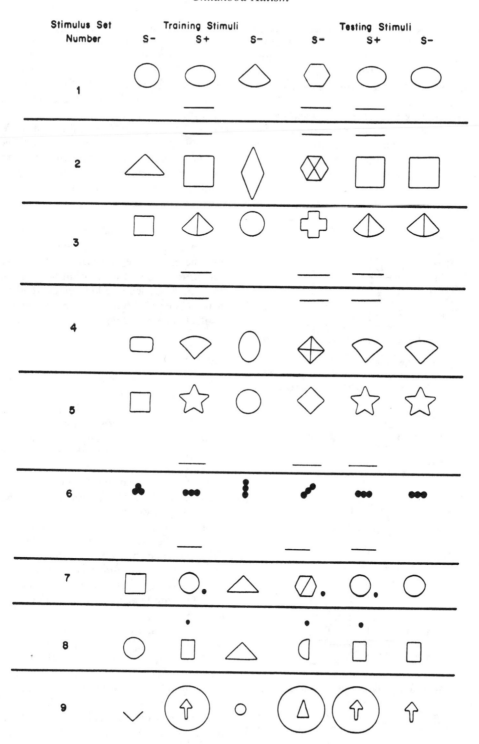

Figure 9.1. Examples of training and testing stimulus sets to teach response to multiple cues. From ''Teaching autistic children to use extra-stimulus prompts'' by L. Schreibman, M. H. Charlop, and R. L. Koegel, 1982, *Journal of Experimental Child Psychology, 33,* pp. 475–491. Copyright 1982 by Academic Press. Reprinted by permission.

a relevant feature of the S+ (correct) choice in a discrimination; this exaggeration is then gradually faded until the feature is again in the normal form (Schreibman, 1975). Thus, the child need only attend to the relevant component and not to multiple cues. For example, a within-stimulus prompting procedure for teaching the discrimination of "·X· versus X̣" is presented in Figure 9.2. The relevant cue for the discrimination of these two stimuli is the vertical versus horizontal dots. The X is redundant. Thus, the

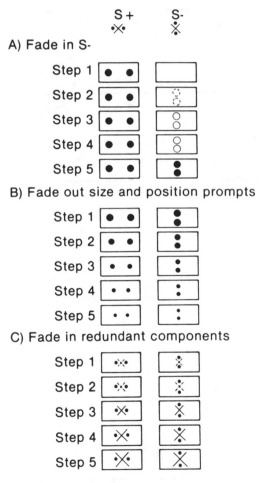

first step in within-stimulus prompting is to pretrain using an exaggerated presentation of the S+, the horizontal dots (Figure 9.2, Part A, Step 1). Only the horizontal dots are presented in this step to ensure that the child responds only on the basis of this cue. Once the child learns this step, the vertical dots (S−) are slowly faded in (Steps 2 through 5). The child is now reliably discriminating S+ from S−. The exaggerated size of the dots is then gradually faded to their normal size (Fig. 9.2, Part B). Finally, the redundant component of the discrimination (X) is slowly faded in (Part C).

There has been a good deal of research on improving autistic children's attentional deficit. Although results of these studies are encouraging, the procedures described are tedious and limited in potential use. Additional research in this area is needed to effect widespread changes in the children's functioning by eliminating overselective responding to the environment.

Motivation

One of the major obstacles in the treatment of autistic children is their pervasive lack of motivation to learn. These children seem to be motivated only by the most primary of reinforcers, such as food or avoidance of pain. As these children rarely respond to reinforcers such as praise or achievement, teachers and therapists have typically resorted to the use of primary reinforcers to increase motivation. There are several limitations to this approach, however.

Importantly, reinforcers such as food or drink may become artificial for some older children, since they may be only used in certain settings (e.g., a clinic environment) (Lovaas & Newsom, 1976). Also, generalization of treatment effects may be limited because these reinforcers are not available in settings outside of therapy (generalization). Finally, a common problem is that the children may quickly become satiated and cease to work. As a result of these problems, one area of research has focused on identifying ways to enhance the effectiveness of available food reinforcers.

One approach, suggested by Egel (1981), is to prevent or delay satiation by presenting a variety of food reinforcers, rather than the same reinforcer, during learning of new tasks. Egel (1981) demonstrated that autistic children satiated more rapidly when constant reinforcers were presented for correct responding than when-reinforcers were varied. Further, the children responded more rapidly when varied reinforcers were presented. Litt and Schreibman (1981) found that in addition to varying reinforcers, reinforcer effectiveness was further enhanced by pairing a particular reinforcer to a particular training stimulus. For example, during a receptive labeling task, correct responses to "Point to the ball" were always reinforced with a piece of cookie, while correct responses to "Point to the car" were always reinforced with a raisin. Compared to a varied condition (e.g., Egel, 1981), this stimulus-specific reinforcement led to faster learning (as measured by trials to criterion).

Another method designed to increase food reinforcer effectiveness was suggested by Koegel and Williams (1980). These investigators demonstrated that if a reinforcer was obtained as a natural part of the correct response sequence, it was more effective than if it was presented in an independent manner. For example, when the concepts "in" and "under" were being taught, the reinforcers were placed in the box and under the box, respectively, thus leading directly to acquisition of the reinforcer. This direct response–reinforcer relationship resulted in faster learning than an indirect response–reinforcer relationship, where the child was handed a food reinforcer following a correct response. Thus, a number of efficient methods for enhancing the effectiveness of available food reinforcers have been devised.

An alternative approach to increasing autistic children's motivation has been to develop new, salient reinforcers. As previously discussed, the sensory or perceptual reinforcers provided by autistic children's self-stimulation have been demonstrated to be highly salient reinforcers (e.g., Lovaas et al., 1987; Rincover et al., 1977). Rincover and his colleagues (1977) studied the properties of sensory stimulation for these children. The preferred sensory stimulus for each child was identified and then used as a reinforcer for correct responding on a learning task. For example, contingent upon correct response, brief presentations of the child's preferred sensory event (e.g., music) were presented. Results indicated that the use of sensory reinforcers produced high levels of responding that were durable over time. Importantly, if some satiation to a specific sensory event (e.g., a certain song) occurred, a minor change in that event (e.g., a different song) led to the recovery of a high rate of responding.

Along the same line, several studies have assessed the efficacy of using autistic children's self-stimulatory behavior as reinforcing events. Hung (1978), for example, used such behaviors as body rocking and object spinning as reinforcers to increase spontaneous appropriate sentences in two autistic children. Rincover and Devany (1979) and Wolery, Kirk, and Gast (1985) also reported positive findings when using self-stimulation as a reinforcer in learning situations. In another study, Charlop and Greenberg (1985) compared the use of food, self-stimulation, and varied (food or self-stimulation) reinforcers in a multielement design. Interestingly, sessions in which self-stimulation was briefly permitted contingent upon correct response were associated with the highest task performance. Poorest task performance occurred during sessions of the food condition. Importantly, ancillary measures of the occurrence of self-stimulatory and off-task behaviors demonstrated that there were no negative side effects of using self-stimulation as a reinforcer.

These findings were recently extended by Charlop and Kurtz (1987), who assessed the reinforcing properties of autistic children's obsessions with specific objects (e.g., certain catalogs, pine trees, Honda cars). In this study, autistic children were presented with difficult tasks during one-on-one work sessions of three reinforcement conditions: food, self-stimulation, or obsession as a reinforcer. For example, in the obsession condition, each child was allowed brief access (3 to 5 seconds) to his or her preferred object (e.g., picture of a Honda car) contingent upon a correct task response. Similarly, in the self-stimulation condition, each child was permitted to engage briefly in a preferred form of self-stimulation (e.g., twirling twig in front of eyes for 3 to 5 seconds). A variety of food reinforcers were available in the food condition. In addition to task performance, measures of the children's inappropriate behaviors (e.g., occurrence of self-stimulatory or obsessive behavior) were collected both during and after work sessions and at each child's home to assess potential side effects of using aberrant behaviors as reinforcers. Results indicated that for all children, task performance was highest during sessions of the obsession condition. Percent correct was also high when self-stimulation was available as a reinforcer. Edibles were least preferred, as evidenced by the children's poor task performance during these sessions. Importantly, the use of these aberrant behaviors as reinforcers was not associated with increases in inappropriate behaviors; indeed, for some children, the occurrence of such behaviors decreased when self-stimulation or obsessions were used as reinforcers. Thus, researchers have begun to identify new, highly salient reinforcers for these children. Furthermore, these reinforcers have the advantages of being relatively easy to identify and to use (e.g., providing pictures of a Honda or books on nature), and may be made available in a variety of settings, thus facilitating generalization of treatment gains (Rincover & Koegel, 1977a, 1977b).

Another approach to the motivation problem has focused on the effects of repeated failure experiences. That is, autistic children's frequent incorrect responding when they attempt a learning task may be a significant factor in their deficient motivation. To assess this effect, Koegel and Egel (1979) investigated the influence of correct versus incorrect task completion on autistic children's motivation to respond. Importantly, they found that autistic children responded in a manner similar to normal children. When autistic children worked on tasks at which they were typically unsuccessful, their attempts to respond (i.e., motivation) generally decreased. However, when procedures designed to maximize correct responding (and the receipt of reinforcers) were implemented, the children's attempts to respond on these tasks increased. This study demonstrated the importance of success-induced motivation.

In a desire to further increase autistic children's motivation to learn new tasks, subsequent studies have carefully analyzed and manipulated various features of the learning situation. Dunlap and Koegel (1980), for example, demonstrated that the presentation of new tasks interspersed with the presentation of previously learned (maintenance) tasks resulted in better performance than when the traditional format of massed trials of a single new task was used. Dunlap (1984) further demonstrated that learning of a new task was facilitated by the interspersal of maintenance tasks only—not by acquisition tasks. Although these studies manipulated antecedent variables as a means of improving the children's motivation to respond, Charlop, Kurtz, and Milstein (1986) assessed the effects of reinforcement contingencies in conjunction with task interspersal procedures on the acquisition of new tasks. These research-

ers suggested that when food reinforcers were presented for interspersed maintenance tasks (a typical motivation-enhancing procedure), the density of reinforcement favored the maintenance tasks rather than the new one. Thus, children presented with many more food reinforcers for previously acquired tasks may not be motivated to learn a new, more difficult behavior. In a comparison of various reinforcement contingencies for interpersed tasks, these researchers demonstrated that the learning of new tasks occurred more rapidly when either praise or no reinforcers were presented for interspersed maintenance tasks. Thus, performance was further enhanced by providing schedules of reinforcement that favored the acquisition task.

An additional means of enhancing autistic children's motivation to respond is to allow them to have some control over the learning situation. Specifically, by giving autistic children some choice as to topic of conversation, stimulus materials to be used, or activities to be engaged in, interest and motivation may be increased (Dyer, Bell, & Koegel, 1983; O'Dell & Koegel, 1981). For example, Koegel et al. (1987) demonstrated that allowing autistic children to select instructional stimuli and share materials and tasks with the therapist resulted in more spontaneous communication by the children and decreased avoidance. Similarly, incidental teaching procedures (e.g., Hart & Risley, 1968, 1974, 1975), which consist of arranging the natural environment to attract children to desired materials and activities, rely on child-initiated interactions to obtain access to desired reinforcers. When modified for autistic children, these procedures have been successful in teaching the children sign language (Carr & Kologinsky, 1983), receptive object labels (McGee, Krantz, Mason, & McClannahan, 1983), preposition use (McGee, Krantz, & McClannahan, 1985), and reading skills (McGee, Krantz, & McClannahan, 1986). Thus, these studies suggest that the sharing of control, topics, and materials in learning situations may serve to increase autistic children's motivation to respond or participate in various activities.

Social Behavior and Play

One of the hallmark features of autism is the children's severe withdrawal from the social environment. Characteristically, these children avoid eye contact, affection, and interaction with others; they also engage in solitary, stereotyped play. Many researchers (e.g., Ferster, 1961; Lovaas, Schaeffer, & Simmons, 1965; Lovaas & Newsom, 1976) have noted the difficulty involved in establishing meaningful social reinforcers for many autistic children. Generally, the failure of people to become meaningful to these children is attributed to a problem in the acquisition of secondary reinforcers (in this case, social reinforcers). Apparently, the mechanism that allows normal (and other) children to become dependent on social reinforcers (e.g., praise; hugs, approval) does not work for autistic children. Importantly, the failure of these children to acquire social reinforcers has serious implications for their overall development, as such reinforcers appear to support so much behavior in normal individuals. Two studies, however, have demonstrated that social stimuli can be established as reinforcers for autistic children. In one study, Lovaas, Freitag, Kinder, Rubenstein, Schaeffer, & Simmons, 1966, established a social reinforcer (the word "good") as a discriminative stimulus for the acquisition of a primary reinforcer (food). Once this was accomplished, the word "good" became functional as a secondary reinforcer, as demonstrated by its effectiveness in maintaining another learned response upon which it was contingent. In another study, Lovaas, Schaeffer, and Simmons (1965) used a negative reinforcement paradigm in which an appropriate approach response to the therapist's request "Come here" was required to terminate an aversive stimulus (mild electric shock to the feet).

Although these early studies demonstrated that autistic children could be taught to respond to social stimuli, the focus of more recent research has been on structuring the natural environment to teach autistic children behaviors that may lead to more social responsiveness and the establishment of social reinforcers. One area of research, for example, has sought to reduce the social avoidance typically displayed by autistic youngsters. In one study, Dyer et al. (1983) demonstrated that by allowing autistic children in educational settings to select their preferred activities and thus direct the social situation, the children's motivation to engage in social approach behavior increased. Also, the children's social approach behavior was maintained by natural contingencies; thus generalization and maintenance of the behavior occurred.

Researchers have also focused on integrating autistic children with handicapped and nonhandicapped peers in natural settings. A series of studies by Strain and his colleagues (e.g., Odom, Hoyson, Jamieson, & Strain, 1985; Odom & Strain, 1984, 1986; Strain, 1983; Strain, Kerr, & Ragland, 1979) have demonstrated the efficacy of this approach as a means of increasing the initiations and social interactions of autistic children. Typically, socially competent peers are taught to initiate interactions by saying, for example, "Let's go play," and handing the autistic child a toy. Using such forms of peer-mediated social initiations, large increases in autistic children's positive social behavior have been observed. Additionally, methods of increasing autistic children's initiations of social interactions through the use of teacher prompts have been explored (Odom & Strain, 1986).

While our understanding and remediation of autistic children's social withdrawal has certainly increased in the past decade, much work is still needed. These children's severe deficits in social interaction are among the most difficult behaviors to treat. A related area that has received relatively little attention in the literature is autistic children's social play.

As previously described, autistic children typically ignore toys or, if they play with them, it is generally in an inappropriate, self-stimulatory, or compulsive manner (Schreibman & Mills, 1983). For example, an autistic child may sniff a toy truck, spin its wheels repetitively, throw it across the room, or simply ignore it. Or the child may line up blocks or other objects by color or order of size for hours at a time. In one of the few systematic investigations of autistic children's toy play, Koegel and his colleagues (1974) studied the relationship between appropriate toy play and self-stimulation. They found that toys made available to the children were ignored; instead, the children engaged in a variety of self-stimulatory behaviors (e.g., eye crossing, repetitive vocalizations). Although the children had previously been taught to play appropriately with the toys, they did not do so until subsequent sessions in which self-stimulation was suppressed by the experimenters. Thus, self-stimulation and appropriate play were demonstrated to be inversely related.

Two subsequent studies have attempted to increase autistic children's appropriate play directly. In one study, Rincover, Cook, Peoples, and Packard (1979) identified the sensory reinforcers for each child's self-stimulation and then taught the children to play with toys that provided such stimulation. For example, if the child's preferred self-stimulatory behavior provided auditory stimulation (e.g., tapping blocks), then a musical toy would be provided to reinforce and maintain appropriate play. In another study, Charlop, Owen, Tan, and Milstein (1988) taught autistic children to play games that involved sharing and turn taking. After training with a therapist, the autistic children played appropriately with other trained autistic peers and also generalized the newly acquired play skills to novel, untrained games. Thus, while it appears likely that autistic children can acquire appropriate social-play skills, these results are preliminary and additional work is needed in this area.

GENERALIZATION

The previous section described treatment procedures that have been successful in teaching autistic children appropriate behaviors and decreasing inappropriate behaviors. However, treatment gains do not always generalize to settings other than the treatment environment or to untreated behaviors. Often, improvement is setting- and task-specific (Schreibman, 1988). Clearly, treatment is of only limited value if behavioral gains do not generalize. Because generalization does not tend to occur automatically, many treatment procedures now being explored incorporate provisions to promote generalization. A number of strategies discussed by Stokes and Baer (1977) have been added to the treatment of autistic children to facilitate generalization.

One approach to promoting generalized treatment gains is to implement procedures that directly occasion generalization. Sequential modification is a procedure in which generalization is programmed in every condition (e.g., across persons, settings, stimuli) where generalization has not occurred. For example, if an autistic child learned speech in a clinic setting but did not use speech at home, parents would be taught to teach speech to their child in the home (see section on parent training below).

Sequential modification can often be a tedious process, especially in situations where generalization must occur across many stimuli (e.g., each time the child sees a different printed version of the letter "A" when learning the alphabet) or across many settings (e.g., home, school,

peer's home, day care). In this situation, a more feasible approach would be to train sufficient exemplars (Stokes & Baer, 1977). For example, Stokes, Baer, and Jackson (1974) demonstrated that when greeting responses were being taught to mentally retarded children, the children did not generalize such behavior to any other persons besides the experimenter. However, when two persons (exemplars) served as experimenters, generalization occurred and the children greeted more than 20 other persons.

Another strategy for promoting generalization is to make the treatment setting more similar to the natural environment (Stokes & Baer, 1977). The use of intermittent schedules of reinforcement during treatment provides an atmosphere that is more similar to the natural environment, where behaviors are seldom reinforced on a continuous (CRF) basis. Results from several studies (e.g., Koegel & Rincover, 1974, 1977; Rincover & Koegel, 1977a, 1977b) have suggested that intermittent schedules have increased the durability of treatment gains by reducing the discriminability of the reinforcement schedules used in therapy settings and settings outside of therapy. Additionally, intermittent schedules have served to maintain treatment gains, allowing naturally occurring intermittent reinforcers to "take over" easily in natural environments.

The use of naturally maintaining contingencies (natural reinforcers) during treatment will also liken the treatment setting with other, more natural environments. Reinforcers should be similar to those that could be encountered in natural settings; additionally, specific behaviors that are more likely to acquire such reinforcers should be taught. Several studies have provided encouraging results with autistic children. For example, Carr (1980) taught autistic children to use sign language to request items that are easily found outside the treatment setting. The children were taught to spontaneously request their most preferred foods and toys as opposed to common but nonfunctional items (e.g., pictures of farm animals). Thus, when the children signed for a favorite food, they were likely to receive that food at home or school. In another study, Charlop and her colleagues (1985) taught verbal autistic children through time-delay procedures to spontaneously request their preferred food item. The children not only acquired the target behavior (spontaneous requests for preferred foods) but generalized such requests to environments other than the training setting. Additionally, this approach incorporates the use of common stimuli, those found in both treatment settings and extratherapy environments (Stokes & Baer, 1977).

Finally, a technique that has also proved useful is mediated generalization. This is the use of behaviors that are likely to occur in both treatment and nontreatment settings that occasion the occurrence of the target response. The most common mediator is language. Mediated generalization is advantageous over other procedures such as sequential modification and training sufficient exemplars, as those procedures can often be tedious when many examples are needed. Also, it is difficult to determine a priori how many exemplars will be necessary. Mediated generalization, then, is a more parsimonious approach to facilitating generalization.

Although few studies have addressed mediated generalization with autistic children, there is some indication that this may be a promising avenue to pursue. Charlop (1983) used autistic children's immediate echolalia as a verbal mediator. Recall that in this study, the verbal autistic children who were permitted to echo the experimenter's request (the object's label) before handing the experimenter the object learned the receptive labeling tasks faster and displayed generalized treatment gains. Charlop (1983) suggested that mediated generalization occurred for the echolalic children because, unlike the nonverbal children, they provided their own self-imposed discriminative stimulus (echo of the object's label), which was easily transported to the generalization setting. As another example, Koegel, Koegel, and Ingham (1986) suggested that teaching self-monitoring procedures to autistic children may also function to mediate generalization. Generally, the child is taught to self-record the occurrence of a specific target behavior, then to self-evaluate after a predetermined time period and self-administer reinforcers. When the child correctly self-monitors in a training setting, the program is introduced in the natural setting (e.g., classroom, home). In the final step, the self-monitoring procedures is gradually faded out.

Recently, in an attempt to incorporate many of the above procedures, researchers have explored the use of the natural environment for treatment. As a result, several promising techniques have emerged. These include time delay (previously described), NLP, and incidental

teaching. Recall that the time-delay procedure uses natural stimuli in natural settings. Additionally, this procedure incorporates a natural prompt (a time period) that can easily be transferred in a variety of settings and can be used for a variety of behaviors (Charlop & Walsh, 1986; Charlop et al., 1985; Touchette, 1971).

Incidental teaching procedures embed teaching trials with the child's daily activities. In one study, for example, autistic children were taught receptive labels of objects used in meal preparation (McGee et al., 1983). The training took place in the kitchen of the children's residential group home, when they were preparing the day's lunch with their care provider. In addition to enhancing motivation (see previous section), incidental teaching provides several techniques that enhance generalization. The "loose structure" in the teaching situation helps promote generalization (Stokes & Baer, 1977). Additionally, the behaviors taught are maintained by naturally occurring daily events in the individual's environment. Incidental teaching has been effective in facilitating generalization of a variety of behaviors such as sign language (Carr & Kologinsky, 1983), preposition use (McGee et al., 1985), and reading skills (McGee et al., 1986).

A third promising procedure, used specifically to teach speech, is the natural language paradigm (NLP). NLP has been designed to incorporate procedures to increase motivation (e.g., child-initiated episodes; turn taking; reinforcing attempts) with procedures for promoting generalization (loose structure; common stimuli; natural environment). During NLP, child and therapist interact in a play setting with a variety of toys. The child initially selects the toy he or she would like to "talk about" and play with. The therapist then models an appropriate verbalization for the child to imitate (e.g., "I want ball"). When the child makes any communicative attempt (e.g., imitates phrase or part of phrase; gestures toward the toy), the toy is given to the child as a reinforcer. After a short interval, it is the therapist's "turn" to play with the toy; the therapist then either models a different verbalization (e.g., "Catch the ball") or provides a new referent for the initial verbalization. NLP has been shown to facilitate acquisition and generalization as compared to traditional speech protocols (Koegel et al., 1987). Recently, the efficacy of this procedure has been demonstrated with parents using NLP in their homes

(Laski et al., 1988). Thus, in summary, the inclusion of strategies that promote generalization into the development of treatment procedures for autistic children may lead to a better understanding and more efficacious treatment of this most complex disorder.

TREATMENT ENVIRONMENTS

A majority of the specific treatment procedures described in this chapter have been developed in research and clinic settings. Increasingly, the trend has been to apply such procedures in more natural environments, such as the home, classroom, and specialized community settings. This broadening of treatment environments has been a result of three major factors. First, the problem of limited generalization of treatment gains from the clinic setting to other environments must be addressed. Clinic treatment is of little utility if improvement is not produced in the natural environment. Second, clinic treatment may be extremely costly in terms of staff time and money, and few such clinics are available for autistic children. Finally, the decentralization of mental-health care (e.g., phasing out of institutions) and the increasing emphasis on community resources has prompted utilization of other treatment environments.

Classroom Treatment

Prior to the 1970s, most autistic children were institutionalized before reaching adolescence (Schreibman, 1988). Typically, parents and teachers were unable to cope with the children's severely disruptive behavior and profound learning deficits; thus the children were frequently expelled from classrooms or never admitted. However, with the passage in 1972 of federal legislation (PL 94-142) mandating public education for autistic and other handicapped children, classrooms for autistic children were established. Since this time, a voluminous amount of research has addressed the topic of educating autistic children in the classroom. While major topics in the area will be discussed in this section, the reader is referred to Horner, Meyer, and Fredericks (1986) and Koegel, Rincover, and Egel (1982) for a more detailed description.

One major area of research that has emerged is the development of educational programs. Importantly, the development of "functional" curricula (e.g., Brown et al., 1979a, 1979b; Dun-

lap, Koegel, & Egel, 1979; Halle, 1982) has had a strong impact on educational planning for autistic children. Generally, a functional curriculum requires the educator to assess the student's behaviors and environments (e.g., home, vocational, community) and to target for instruction those skills that will be most useful in those settings. Thus, the emphasis of the functional curriculum is on teaching behaviors that are frequently required in the natural environment (e.g., using kitchen appliances, public transportation), are age-appropriate, and have long-term functional use (e.g., Johnson & Koegel, 1982).

Another important area of research has addressed the specific skills necessary for teachers of autism classrooms. It has been noted that autistic children, rather than their teachers' skills, are often blamed for their poor academic progress (Koegel, Russo, Rincover, & Schreibman, 1982). However, one group of researchers (Koegel, Russo, & Rincover, 1977) demonstrated that when teachers did not correctly implement behavior-modification procedures in learning situations, the children did not acquire the tasks; whereas when prompts, consequences, and other procedures were correctly used, the teachers were effective in improving the students' performance.

Significantly, researchers have also identified the skills necessary for autistic children to learn in classrooms and have devised procedures to teach these skills. According to Koegel and his colleagues (Koegel & Rincover, 1977; Rincover & Koegel, 1977a, 1977b; Rincover, Koegel, & Russo, 1978), if autistic children are to benefit from classroom instruction, they must be taught two specific skills: to learn while in a large group and to work on an individualized task without constant teacher supervision. The importance of these skills was made dramatically evident in a study by Koegel and Rincover (1974), which demonstrated that when eight autistic children were taught some basic classroom tasks on a one-to-one basis, the introduction of even one other child (i.e., to form a group) was enough to disrupt performance. Furthermore, after several weeks in a classroom group, no new learning occurred. This failure of autistic children to generalize individually taught behaviors to a larger group setting has often been reported (e.g., Bijou, 1972; Peterson, Cox & Bijou, 1971).

Koegel and Rincover (1974) thus developed a procedure that would allow the children to learn in a large group. First, the children were taught in 1:1 training sessions. Then, two children were brought together with one teacher and two aides. When these two children were responding proficiently, additional children were gradually faded in until the children would perform in a group of eight. Importantly, the children not only responded correctly on tasks which were individually taught but also continued to learn new behaviors when one teacher instructed the children in a group.

While learning in a classroom group is important, the fact that the children must learn some tasks individually at their own pace requires that children also learn to work individually, without constant teacher supervision, within the classroom context. To accomplish this goal, Rincover and Koegel (1977a) designed a shaping procedure to teach the children to work on long sequences of behaviors (preacademic readiness tasks) after a teacher instruction. Specifically, teachers initially provided reinforcers after the child made only one written response; then, the response requirement was increased to two, then three, etc., until the child completed the task on his or her own. These studies have demonstrated the importance of teaching autistic children the prerequisite skills that will permit them to benefit from classroom education.

While many autistic children are placed in such classrooms designed specifically to meet the needs of autistic children, PL 94-142 states that all children have a right to education in the least restrictive environment. Therefore, the public school system should provide as normal a classroom situation as possible while serving the child's educational needs. Indeed, many autistic children have made the transition into less structured classrooms with other handicapped children or into mainstreamed classrooms with normal children. Many people have also argued the importance of integrating autistic children with nonautistic and normal children (e.g., Koegel, Rincover, & Russo, 1982; Schreibman, 1988). By including autistic children in classrooms with these children, the autistic children are exposed to the many benefits associated with integrated classrooms, including the opportunity to learn from appropriate role models. Thus, much research has necessarily addressed the facilitation of autistic children's transition into less restrictive or mainstream environments. Generally, the focus in this area has been on teaching autistic children to work in classroom environments (e.g., Dunlap et al., 1979; Koegel & Rincover, 1974;

Rincover & Koegel, 1977a, b) teaching the teachers to effectively use behavioral techniques (e.g., Koegel, Rincover, & Russo, 1982), and programming for generalization and maintenance (e.g., Koegel & Rincover, 1977; Strain, 1983). Also, as previously discussed, the facilitation of social integration of autistic and nonhandicapped peers has received much attention in the literature (e.g., Odom et al., 1985; Odom & Strain, 1984, 1986).

The outlook for continued improvement in the area of education for autistic children is positive. The identification of functional curricula, and the development and refinement of effective procedures to teach critical skills to both students and teachers has greatly improved the quality of autistic children's education.

Parent Training

In recent years, there has been an increasing emphasis on training parents of autistic children (e.g., Harris, Wolchik, & Weitz, 1981; Koegel, Schreibman, Johnson, O'Neill, & Dunlap, 1984; Koegel, Schreibman, Britten, Burke, & O'Neill, 1982; Wing, 1972). Indeed, the literature addressing this important topic is quite extensive (cf. reviews by Baker, 1984; Moreland, Schwebel, Beck, & Wells, 1982). Generally, parents are trained by a therapist to implement the principles and procedures of behavior modification and thus may act as the primary contingency managers for their child.

The advantages to parent training are several (Schreibman, Koegel, Mills, & Burke, 1981). First, parents have the most contact with their children and thus are in the ideal position to effect behavior change. In addition to providing a constant treatment environment, parents may target aspects of the child's behavior (e.g., self-care) that would not otherwise be addressed by schools or clinics. Thus, parents may take an active role in their children's education. Second, parents' participation in the children's treatment may facilitate generalization of treatment gains, which has been demonstrated to be a significant problem with autistic children (e.g., Rincover & Koegel, 1975). Third, schools and clinics for autistic children are scarce, and/or limited in the number of treatment hours they may provide. Thus, training parents to be their child's primary therapist may be essential to achieving significant gains as well as being cost-efficient. Finally, teaching parents general treatment procedures will allow the parents to teach new skills and handle any new behavior problems that may arise.

In addition to the above reasons, a study by Lovaas et al. (1973) demonstrated the critical importance of parent training as a part of the autistic child's treatment. In this follow-up study, it was found that children who participated in one year of clinic treatment and whose parents had been trained in behavior-modification techniques maintained gains or improved further, while children who had participated in clinic treatment alone had lost the previously acquired skills. Thus, parent training is an essential component of autistic children's treatment.

There are numerous studies addressing the manner in which parents are trained. Methods of training parents to work with their autistic children have included individual or group training through lectures, written instruction, behavioral rehearsal, feedback, and live and videotape modeling (cf. Schreibman & Britten, 1984; Schreibman, Koegel, Mills, & Burke, 1984). In a recent study, siblings of autistic children were also successfully taught these general principles (Schreibman, O'Neill, & Koegel, 1983). More recently, one important line of research has addressed the effects of parent training on the parents and other family members. For example, Koegel, Schreibman, Britten, Burke, and O'Neill (1982) compared parent training to direct clinic treatment of autistic children. They found that parents who were trained reported a more positive family environment, an increase in leisure time, more time devoted to teaching their child, and less time devoted to custodial care. Parents in the clinic treatment group reported no such changes (Koegel et al., 1984). These results suggest that both parents and children can benefit from parent training programs.

While the efficacy of training parents to teach their autistic children has been clearly demonstrated, a number of issues must continue to be addressed. Importantly, the development of procedures to further enhance generalization of treatment gains is needed. One previously mentioned example of this is the teaching of NLP to parents of autistic children (Laski et al., 1988). Additionally, the social validation of the efficacy of behavior therapy with autistic children (e.g., Runco & Schreibman, 1983; Schreibman et al., 1981; Schreibman, Runco, Mills, & Koegel, 1982) as it pertains to parent training is a topic that merits additional research. Continued research

in these and other issues in the area of parent training can only improve the outlook for autistic children.

Residential Environments

The establishment of community-based treatment programs for autistic children has provided these individuals with living environments that may promote the use of various community resources to develop academic, social, and vocational skills. The trend toward deinstitutionalization and the phasing out of large institutions has led to the development of a number of different types of group homes for the developmentally disabled (e.g., Lovaas et al., 1981; McGee et al., 1983). These residential facilities typically provide professional treatment within a family-style context. Usually, 5 to 7 individuals, together with professionally trained counselors or "teaching parents," reside in the home on a 24-hour basis. Having a small group allows staff members to interact extensively with each individual and thus to reduce problem behaviors as well as teach alternative, appropriate behaviors. Importantly, these residential treatment facilities emphasize individual behavioral treatment in group settings. Each autistic resident's treatment program is designed to address his or her specific behavioral problems or needs. Furthermore, these facilities are generally small enough to permit objective behavioral measurements for each individual, thus providing feedback to staff to determine the success of various interventions. Finally, a critical component of residential treatment facilities is that the contingencies in the home are made as natural as possible and as similar to those likely to be encountered in the natural community, thus maximizing generalization across environments.

Finally, an important aspect of these community treatment programs is that the cost of treatment is substantially less than that of programs provided by large institutions (Lovaas et al., 1981; Phillips, Phillips, Fixsen, & Wolf, 1974). Indeed, after such residential treatment facilities are opened and operating, they cost about half as much to maintain than do institutions (Phillips et al., 1974). As these community treatment programs are a relatively new alternative for autistic individuals, the task of assessing their overall effectiveness as compared to other living arrangements (e.g., institutions, foster care, natural home with and without parent training) remains for future researchers to explore.

CONCLUDING COMMENTS

We have attempted to provide the reader with not only the most recent findings on treatment procedures but also some sense of the history of treatment research for autistic children. Clearly, the number of pages of the chapter has imposed a limitation, preventing us from covering in detail such a complex area. We hope, however, that our readers will seek additional information from the references provided.

Although autism remains a difficult-to-treat syndrome, we have come far in what we have learned about it and project a future of active research that will continue to enlighten us. While as yet there is no cure for autism, we believe that the future outlook is bright in that we will continue to improve the quality of care and, ultimately, the quality of life for these children.

REFERENCES

Anderson, L. T., Campbell, M., Grega, D. M., Perry, R., Small, A. M., & Green, W. H. (1984). Haloperidol in infantile autism: Effects on learning and behavioral symptoms. *American Journal of Psychiatry, 141,* 1195–1202.

Applebaum, E., Egel, A. L., Koegel, R. L., & Imhoff, B. (1979). Measuring musical abilities of autistic children. *Journal of Autism and Developmental Disorders, 9,* 279–285.

August, G. J., Raz, N., & Baird, T. D. (1985). Brief report: Effects of fenfluramine on behavioral, cognitive, and affective disturbances in autistic children. *Journal of Autism and Developmental Disorders, 15,* 97–107.

Azrin, N. J., Gottlieb, L., Hughart, L., Wesolowski, M. D., & Rahn, T. (1975). Eliminating self-injurious behavior by educative procedures. *Behaviour Research and Therapy, 13,* 101–111.

Azrin, N. J., Kaplan, S. J., & Foxx, R. M. (1973). Autism reversal: Eliminating stereotyped self-stimulation of retarded individuals. *American Journal of Mental Deficiency, 18,* 241–248.

Baker, B. L. (1984). Intervention with families with young severely handicapped children. In J. Blacher (Ed.), *Severely handicapped young children and their families: Research in review* (pp. 319–375). Orlando, FL: Academic Press.

Baltaxe, C. A. (1981). Acoustic characteristics of prosody in autism. In P. Mittler (Ed.), *Frontiers of knowledge in mental retardation* (pp. 223–233). Baltimore: University Park Press.

Baltaxe, C. A., & Simmons, J. Q. (1975). Language in childhood psychosis: A review. *Journal of Speech and Hearing Disorders, 30,* 439–458.

Bartak, L., & Rutter, M. (1973). Special educational treatment of autistic children: A comparative study. I. Design of study and characteristics of units. *Journal of Child Psychology and Psychiatry, 14,* 151–179.

Bartak, L., & Rutter, M. (1974). The use of personal pronouns by autistic children. *Journal of Autism and Childhood Schizophrenia, 4,* 217–222.

Barton, E. S., Guess, D., Garcia, E., & Baer, D. M. (1970). Improvement of retardates' mealtime behavior by timeout procedures using multiple baseline techniques. *Journal of Applied Behavior Analysis, 3,* 77–84.

Beisler, J. M., Tsai, L. Y., & Stiefel, B. (1986). Brief report: The effects of fenfluramine on communication skills in autistic children. *Journal of Autism and Developmental Disorders, 16,* 227–233.

Bettelheim, B. (1967). *The empty fortress.* New York: Free Press.

Bettelheim, B. (1968). Reply to G. G. Merritt's book review of "The Empty Fortress." *American Journal of Orthopsychiatry, 38,* 930–933.

Bijou, S. W. (1972). The technology of teaching young handicapped children. In S. W. Bijou & E. Ribes-Inesta (Eds.), *Behavior modification: Issues and extensions* (pp. 28–44). New York: Academic Press.

Bostow, D. E., & Bailey, J. B. (1969). Modification of severe disruptive and aggressive behavior using brief timeout and reinforcement procedures. *Journal of Applied Behavior Analysis, 2,* 31–37.

Brown, L., Branston, M. B., Hamre-Nietupski, S., Pumpian, I., Certo, N., & Gruenewald, L. (1979a). A strategy for developing chronological age appropriate and functional curricular content for severely handicapped adolescents and young adults. *Journal of Special Education, 13,* 81–90.

Brown, L., Branston-McClean, M. B., Baumgart, D., Vincent, L., Falvey, M., & Schroeder, J. (1979b). Utilizing the characteristics of a variety of current and subsequent least restrictive environments as factors in the development of curricular content for severely handicapped students. *AAESPH Review, 4,* 407–424.

Bucher, B., & Lovaas, O. I. (1968). Use of aversive stimulation in behavior modification. In M. R. Jones (Ed.), *Miami symposium on the prediction of behavior, 1967: Aversive stimulation* (pp. 77–140). Coral Gables, FL: University of Miami Press.

Burchard, J. D., & Tyler, V. O. (1965). The modification of delinquent behavior through operant conditioning. *Behaviour Research and Therapy, 2,* 245–250.

Campbell, M., Anderson, L. T., Meier, M., Cohen, I. L., Small, A. M., Samit, C., & Sachar, E. J. (1978). A comparison of haloperidol and behavior therapy and their interaction in autistic children. *Journal of the American Academy of Child Psychiatry, 17,* 640–655.

Campbell, M., Green, W., & Deutsch, S. (1985). *Child and adolescent psychopharmacology.* Beverly Hills, CA: Sage Publications.

Campbell, M., Small, A., Collins, P., Friedman, E., David, R., & Genieser, N. (1976). Levodopa and levoamphetamine: A crossover study in young schizophrenic children. *Current Therapeutic Research, 19,* 70–86.

Cantwell, D. P., Baker, L., & Rutter, M. (1978). Family factors. In M. Rutter & E. Schopler (Eds.), *Autism: A reappraisal of concepts and treatment* (pp. 269–286). New York: Plenum Press.

Carr, E. G. (1977). The motivation of self-injurious behavior: A review of some hypotheses. *Psychological Bulletin, 84,* 800–816.

Carr, E. G. (1979). Teaching autistic children to use sign language: Some research issues. *Journal of Autism and Developmental Disorders, 9,* 345–359.

Carr E. G. (1980, November). Generalization of treatment effects following educational intervention with autistic children and youth. In B. Wilcox & A. Thompson (Eds.), *Critical issues in educating autistic children and youth* (pp. 118–134). U.S. Department of Education, Office of Special Education.

Carr, E. G. (1982a). *How to teach sign language*

to developmentally disabled children. Lawrence, KS: H & H Enterprises.

Carr, E. G. (1982b). Sign language. In R. L. Koegel, A. Rincover, & A. L. Egel (Eds.), *Educating and understanding autistic children* (pp. 142–157). San Diego: College-Hill Press.

Carr, E. G., Binkoff, J. A., Kologinsky, E., & Eddy, M. (1978). Acquisition of sign language by autistic children. I. Expressive labeling. *Journal of Applied Behavior Analysis, 11,* 489–501.

Carr, E. G., & Durand, V. M. (1985). Reducing behavior problems through functional communication training. *Journal of Applied Behavior Analysis, 18,* 111–126.

Carr, E. G., & Kologinsky, E. (1983). Acquisition of sign language by autistic children. II. Spontaneity and generalization effects. *Journal of Applied Behavior Analysis, 16,* 297–314.

Carr, E. G., Kologinsky, E., & Leff-Simon, S. (1987). Acquisition of sign language by autistic children. III. Generalized descriptive phrases. *Journal of Autism and Developmental Disorders, 17,* 217–230.

Carr, E. G., Newsom, C. D., & Binkoff, J. A. (1976). Stimulus control of self-destructive behavior in a psychotic child. *Journal of Abnormal Child Psychology, 4,* 139–153.

Carr, E. G., Schreibman, L., & Lovaas, O. I. (1975). Control of echolalic speech in psychotic children. *Journal of Abnormal Child Psychology, 3,* 331–351.

Charlop, M. H. (1983). The effects of echolalia on acquisition and generalization of receptive labeling in autistic children. *Journal of Applied Behavior Analysis, 16,* 111–126.

Charlop, M. H. (1986). Setting effects on the occurrence of autistic children's immediate echolalia. *Journal of Autism and Developmental Disorders, 16,* 473–483.

Charlop, M. H., & Bieber, J. (1988). *Teaching parents to increase their autistic children's speech using a time delay procedure.* Paper presented at the meeting of the Association for Behavior Analysis, Philadelphia.

Charlop, M. H., Burgio, L. D., Iwata, B. A., & Ivancic, M. T. (1988). Stimulus variation as a means of enhancing punishment effects. *Journal of Applied Behavior Analysis, 21,* 89–95.

Charlop, M. H., Gonzalez, J., & Cugliari, C. P. (1987). *Environmental effects on the func-*

tional aspects of the delayed echolalia of autistic children. Unpublished manuscript.

Charlop, M. H., & Greenberg, F. (1985). *The use of self-stimulation as a reinforcer: A close look at a feasible approach.* Paper presented at the meeting of the Association for Behavior Analysis, Columbus, Ohio.

Charlop, M. H., Kurtz, P. F. (1987). *Using aberrant behaviors as reinforcers with autistic children.* Paper presented at the meeting of the Association for Behavior Analysis, Nashville, Tennessee.

Charlop, M. H., Kurtz, P. F., & Milstein, J. P. (1986). *Too much reinforcement, too little behavior: An analysis of reinforcement contingencies with autistic children.* Paper presented at the meeting of the Association for Behavior Analysis, Milwaukee, Wisconsin.

Charlop, M. H., & Milstein, J. P. (1989). Teaching autistic children conversational speech using video modeling. *Journal of Applied Behavior Analysis, 22,* 275–285.

Charlop, M. H., Owen, G., Tan, N., & Milstein, J. P. (1988, November). *Teaching autistic children cooperative play.* Paper presented at the annual meeting of the Association for the Advancement of Behavior Therapy, New York.

Charlop, M. H., Schreibman, L., & Thibodeau, M. G. (1985). Increasing spontaneous verbal responding in autistic children using a time delay procedure. *Journal of Applied Behavior Analysis, 18,* 155–166.

Charlop, M. H., Schreibman, L., & Tryon, A. S. (1983). Learning through observation: The effects of peer modeling on acquisition and generalization in autistic children. *Journal of Abnormal Child Psychology, 11,* 355–366.

Charlop, M. H., & Walsh, M. E. (1986). Increasing autistic children's spontaneous verbalizations of affection: An assessment of time delay and peer modeling procedures. *Journal of Applied Behavior Analysis, 19,* 307–314.

Chock, P. N., & Glahn, T. J. (1983). Learning and self-stimulation in mute and echolalic autistic children. *Journal of Autism and Developmental Disorders, 13,* 365–381.

Clark, H. B. Rowbury, T., Baer, A. M., & Baer, D. M. (1973). Timeout as a punishing stimulus in continuous and intermittent schedules. *Journal of Applied Behavior Analysis, 6,* 443–455.

Cohen, I., Campbell, M., Posner, D., Small, A.,

Triebel, D., & Anderson, L. (1980). Behavioral effects of haloperidol in young autistic children: An objective analysis using a within-subjects reversal design. *Journal of the American Academy of Child Psychiatry, 19,* 655–677.

Coleman, S. G., & Stedman, J. M. (1974). Use of a peer model in language training in an echolalic child. *Journal of Behavior Therapy and Experimental Psychiatry, 5,* 275–279.

Cox, A., Rutter, M., & Newman, S. (1975). A comparative study of infantile autism and specific developmental receptive language disorder. *British Journal of Psychiatry, 126,* 146–159.

Deitz, S. M., & Repp, A. L. (1973). Decreasing classroom misbehavior through the use of DRL schedules of reinforcement. *Journal of Applied Behavior Analysis, 6,* 457–463.

DeMyer, M. K., Barton, S., DeMyer, W. E., Norton, J. A., Allen, J., & Steele, R. (1973). Prognosis in autism: A follow-up study. *Journal of Autism and Childhood Schizophrenia, 3,* 199–246.

Dorsey, M. F., Iwata, B. A., Ong, P., & McSween, T. E. (1980). Treatment of self-injurious behavior using a water mist: Initial response suppression and generalization. *Journal of Applied Behavior Analysis, 13,* 343–353.

Dunlap, G. (1984). The influence of task variation and maintenance tasks on the learning and affect of autistic children. *Journal of Experimental Child Psychology, 37,* 41–64.

Dunlap, G., & Koegel, R. L. (1980). Motivating autistic children through stimulus variation. *Journal of Applied Behavior Analysis, 13,* 619–627.

Dunlap, G., Koegel, R. L., & Egel, A. L. (1979). Autistic children in school. *Exceptional Children, 45,* 552–558.

Dunlap, G., Koegel, R. L., Johnson, J., & O'Neill, R. E. (1987). Maintaining performance of autistic clients in community settings with delayed contingencies. *Journal of Applied Behavior Analysis, 20,* 185–191.

Dunlap, G., Koegel, R. L., & O'Neill, R. O. (1985). Pervasive developmental disorders. In P. H. Bornstein & A. E. Kazdin (Eds.), *Handbook of clinical behavior therapy with children* (pp. 499–540). Homewood, IL: Dorsey Press.

Durand, V. M., & Carr, E. G. (1987). Social influences on self-stimulatory behavior: Analysis and treatment application. *Jour-*

nal of Applied Behavior Analysis, 20, 119–132.

Dyer, K., Bell, L. K., & Koegel, R. L. (1983). *Generalized reduction of social avoidance behaviors in autistic children.* Paper presented at the American Psychological Association Annual Convention, Anaheim, California.

Egel, A. L. (1981). Reinforcer variation: Implications for motivating developmentally disabled children. *Journal of Applied Behavior Analysis, 14,* 345–350.

Egel, A. L., Koegel, R. L., & Schreibman, L. (1980). A review of educational treatment procedures for autistic children. In L. Mann & D. Sabatino (Eds.), *Fourth review of special education* (pp. 109–149). New York: Grune & Stratton.

Egel, A. L., Richman, G., & Koegel, R. L. (1981). Normal peer models and autistic children's learning. *Journal of Applied Behavior Analysis, 14,* 3–12.

Eisenberg, L., & Kanner, L. (1956). Early infantile autism. *American Journal of Orthopsychiatry, 26,* 556–566.

Favell, J. E., McGimsey, J. F., & Jones, M. L. (1978). The use of physical restraint in the treatment of self-injury and as positive reinforcement. *Journal of Applied Behavior Analysis, 11,* 225–241.

Fay, W. H. (1969). On the basis of autistic echolalia. *Journal of Communication Disorders, 2,* 38–47.

Fay, W. H., & Schuler, A. L. (1980). *Emerging language in autistic children.* Baltimore: University Park Press.

Ferster, C. B. (1961). Positive reinforcement and behavioral deficits of autistic children. *Child Development, 32,* 437–456.

Foxx, R. M., & Azrin, N. H. (1972). Restitution: A method for eliminating aggressive disruptive behavior of retarded and brain damaged patients. *Behaviour Therapy, 10,* 15–27.

Foxx, R. M., & Azrin, N. H. (1973). The elimination of autistic self-stimulatory behavior by overcorrection. *Journal of Applied Behavior Analysis, 6,* 1–14.

Foxx, R. M., & Shapiro, S. T. (1978). The timeout ribbon: A non-exclusionary timeout procedure. *Journal of Applied Behavior Analysis, 11,* 125–136.

Freeman, B. J., & Ritvo, E. R. (1984). The syndrome of autism: Establishing the diagnosis and principles of management. *Pediatric Annals, 13,* 284–305.

Freeman, B. J., Ritvo, E. R., & Miller, R. (1975). An operant procedure to teach an echolalic, autistic child to answer questions appropriately. *Journal of Autism and Childhood Schizophrenia, 5,* 169–176.

Geller, E., Ritvo, E. R., Freeman, B. J., & Yuwiler, A. (1982). Preliminary observations on the effect of fenfluramine on blood serotonin and symptoms in three autistic boys. *New England Journal of Medicine, 307,* 165.

Gittelman, M., & Birch, J. G. (1967). Childhood schizophrenia: Intellect, neurological status, perinatal risk, prognosis and family pathology. *Archives of General Psychiatry, 17,* 16–25.

Goldfarb, W. (1956). Receptor preferences in schizophrenic children. *Archives of Neurology and Psychiatry, 33,* 643–652.

Goldfarb, W. (1961). *Childhood schizophrenia.* Cambridge, MA: Harvard University Press.

Halle, J. W. (1982). Teaching functional language to the handicapped: An integrative model of the natural environment teaching techniques. *Journal of the Association for the Severely Handicapped, 7,* 29–36.

Halle, J. W., Baer, D. M., & Spradlin, J. E. (1981). Teachers' generalized use of delay as a stimulus control procedure to increase language use in handicapped children. *Journal of Applied Behavior Analysis, 14,* 389–409.

Halle, J. W., Marshall, A. M., & Spradlin, J. E. (1979). Time delay: A technique to increase language use and facilitate generalization in retarded children. *Journal of Applied Behavior Analysis, 12,* 431–439.

Harris, S. L., & Wolchik, S. A. (1979). Suppression of self-stimulation: Three alternative strategies. *Journal of Applied Behavior Analysis, 12,* 185–198.

Harris, S. L., Wolchik, S. A., & Weitz, S. (1981). The acquisition of language skills by autistic children: Can parents do the job? *Journal of Autism and Developmental Disorders, 11,* 373–384.

Hart, B., & Risley, T. R. (1968). Establishing use of descriptive adjectives in the spontaneous speech of disadvantaged preschool children. *Journal of Applied Behavior Analysis, 1,* 109–120.

Hart, B., & Risley, T. R. (1974). Using preschool materials to modify the language of disadvantaged children. *Journal of Applied Behavior Analysis, 7,* 243–256.

Hart, B., & Risley, T. R. (1975). Incidental teaching of language in the preschool. *Jour-*

nal of Applied Behavior Analysis, 8, 411–420.

Hart, B., & Rogers-Warren, A. (1978). Milieu teaching approaches. In R. I. Schiefelbusch (Ed.), *Bases for language intervention* (Vol. 2, pp. 193–235). Baltimore: University Park Press.

Herendeen, D. L., Jeffrey, D. B., & Graham, M. C. (1974). *Reduction of self-stimulation in institutionalized children: Overcorrection and reinforcement for nonresponding.* Paper presented at the eighth annual meeting of the Association for Advancement of Behavior Therapy, Chicago.

Hermelin, B., & O'Connor, N. (1970). *Psychological experiments with autistic children.* Elmsford, NY: Pergamon Press.

Horner, R. H., Meyer, L. H., & Fredericks, H. D. (1986). *Education of learners with severe handicaps: Exemplary service strategies.* Baltimore: Paul H. Brookes.

Hung, D. W. (1978). Using self-stimulation as reinforcement for autistic children. *Journal of Autism and Childhood Schizophrenia, 8,* 355–366.

Johnson, J., & Koegel, R. L. (1982). Behavioral assessment and curriculum development. In R. L. Koegel, A. Rincover, & A. L. Egel (Eds.), *Educating and understanding autistic children* (pp. 1–32). San Diego, CA: College Hill Press.

Kanner, L. (1943). Autistic disturbances of affective contact. *Nervous Child, 2,* 217–250.

Kanner, L. (1944). Early infantile autism. *Journal of Pediatrics, 25,* 211–217.

Kanner, L. (1954). To what extent is early infantile autism determined by constitutional inadequacies? *Research Publication of the Association of Nervous Mental Disorders, 33,* 378–385.

Kanner, L., & Eisenberg, L. (1955). Note on the follow-up studies of autistic children. In P. H. Hoch & J. Bubin (Eds.), *Psychopathology of childhood* (pp. 227–240). New York: Grune & Stratton.

Klykylo, W. M., Feldis, D., O'Grady, D., Ross, D. L., & Halloran, C. (1985). Brief report: Clinical effects of fenfluramine in ten autistic subjects. *Journal of Autism and Developmental Disorders, 15,* 417–423.

Knoblock, H., & Pasamanick, B. (1975). *Etiologic factors in "early infantile autism" and "childhood schizophrenia."* Paper presented at the 10th International Congress of Pediatrics, Lisbon.

Koegel, L. K., Koegel, R. L., & Ingham, J. M. (1986). Programming rapid generalization of correct articulation through self-monitoring procedures. *Journal of Speech and Hearing Disorders, 51,* 24–32.

Koegel, R. L., & Covert, A. (1972). The relationship of self-stimulation to learning in autistic children. *Journal of Applied Behavior Analysis, 5,* 381–387.

Koegel, R. L., & Egel, A. L. (1979). Motivating autistic children. *Journal of Abnormal Psychology, 88,* 418–426.

Koegel, R. L., Firestone, P. B., Kramme, K. W., & Dunlap, G. (1974). Increasing spontaneous play by suppressing self-stimulation in autistic children. *Journal of Applied Behavior Analysis, 7,* 521–528.

Koegel, R. L., O'Dell, M. C., & Koegel, L. K. (1987). A natural language teaching paradigm for nonverbal autistic children. *Journal of Autism and Developmental Disorders, 17,* 187–200.

Koegel, R. L., & Rincover, A. (1974). Treatment of psychotic children in a classroom environment: I. Learning in a large group. *Journal of Applied Behavior Analysis, 7,* 45–59.

Koegel, R. L., & Rincover, A. (1976). Some detrimental effects of using extra stimuli to guide learning in normal and autistic children. *Journal of Abnormal Child Psychology, 4,* 59–71.

Koegel, R. L., & Rincover, A. (1977). Research on the difference between generalization and maintenance in extra-therapy responding. *Journal of Applied Behavior Analysis, 10,* 1–12.

Koegel, R. L., Rincover, A., & Egel, A. L. (1982). *Educating and understanding autistic children.* San Diego, CA: College Hill Press.

Koegel, R. L., Rincover, A., & Russo, D. C. (1982). Classroom management: Progression from special to normal classrooms. In R. L. Koegel, A. Rincover, & A. L. Egel (Eds.), *Educating and understanding autistic children* (pp. 203–241). San Diego, CA: College Hill Press.

Koegel, R. L., Russo, D. C., & Rincover, A. (1977). Assessing and training teachers in the generalized use of behavior modification with autistic children. *Journal of Applied Behavior Analysis, 10,* 197–205.

Koegel, R. L., Russo, D. C., Rincover, A., & Schreibman, L. (1982). Assessing and training teachers. In R. L. Koegel, A. Rincover,

& A. L. Egel (Eds.), *Educating and understanding autistic children* (pp. 178–202). San Diego, CA: College Hill Press.

Koegel, R. L., & Schreibman, L. (1977). Teaching autistic children to respond to simultaneous multiple cues. *Journal of Experimental Child Psychology, 24,* 299–311.

Koegel, R. L., Schreibman, L., Britten, K. R., Burke, J. C., & O'Neill, R. E. (1982). A comparison of parent training to direct child treatment. In R. L. Koegel, A. Rincover, & A. L. Egel (Eds.), *Educating and understanding autistic children* (pp. 260–279). San Diego, CA: College Hill Press.

Koegel, R. L., Schreibman, L., Johnson, J., O'Neill, R. E., & Dunlap, G. (1984). Collateral effects of parent training on families with autistic children. In R. F. Dangel & R. A. Polster (Eds.), *Parent training: Foundations of research and practice* (pp. 358–378). New York: Guilford Press.

Koegel, R. L., Schreibman, L., O'Neill, R. E., & Burke, J. C. (1983). The personality and family-interaction characteristics of parents of autistic children. *Journal of Consulting and Clinical Psychology, 51,* 683–692.

Koegel, R. L., & Wilhelm, H. (1973). Selective responding to the components of multiple visual cues by autistic children. *Journal of Abnormal Child Psychology, 4,* 536–547.

Koegel, R. L., & Williams, J. (1980). Direct vs. indirect response-reinforcer relationships in teaching autistic children. *Journal of Abnormal Child Psychology, 4,* 337–347.

Korein, J., Fish, B., Shapiro, T., Gerner, E. W., & Levidow, L. (1971). EEG and behavioral effects of drug therapy in children: Chlorpromazine and diphenhydramine. *Archives of General Psychiatry, 24,* 552–563.

Kugelmass, N. I. (1970). *The autistic child.* Springfield, IL: Charles C Thomas.

Laski, K. E., Charlop, M. H., & Schreibman, L. (1988). Training parents to use the natural language paradigm to increase their autistic children's speech. *Journal of Applied Behavior Analysis, 21,* 391–400.

Levitt, E. E. (1957). The results of psychotherapy with children: An evaluation. *Journal of Consulting and Clinical Psychology, 21,* 189–196.

Levitt, E. E. (1963). Psychotherapy with children: A further evaluation. *Behaviour Research and Therapy, 1,* 45–51.

Lichstein, K. L., & Schreibman, L. (1976). Employing electric shock: A review of the side effects. *Journal of Autism and Childhood Schizophrenia, 6,* 163–174.

Litt, M. D., & Schreibman, L. (1981). Stimulus specific reinforcement in the acquisition of receptive labels by autistic children. *Analysis and Intervention in Developmental Disabilities, 1,* 171–186.

Lockyer, L., & Rutter, M. (1969). A five to fifteen year follow-up study of infantile psychosis. III. Psychological aspects. *British Journal of Psychology, 115,* 865–882.

Lotter, V. (1966). Epidemiology of autistic conditions in young children. I. Prevalence. *Social Psychiatry, 1,* 163–173.

Lovaas, O. I. (1977). *The autistic child.* New York: Irvington.

Lovaas, O. I. (1987). Behavioral treatment and normal educational and intellectual functioning in young autistic children. *Journal of Consulting and Clinical Psychology, 55,* 3–9.

Lovaas, O. I., Berberich, J. P., Perloff, B. F., & Schaeffer, B. (1966). Acquisition of imitative speech in schizophrenic children. *Science, 151,* 705–707.

Lovaas, O. I., Freitag, G., Gold, V. J., & Kassorla, I. C. (1965). Experimental studies in childhood schizophrenia. I. Analysis of self-destructive behavior. *Journal of Experimental Child Psychology, 2,* 67–84.

Lovaas, O. I., Freitag, G., Kinder, M. I., Rubenstein, B. D., Schaeffer, B., & Simmons, J. Q. (1966). Establishment of social reinforcers in two schizophrenic children on the basis of food. *Journal of Experimental Child Psychology, 4,* 109–125.

Lovaas, O. I., Glahn, T. J., Russo, D. C., Chock, P. N., Kohls, S., & Mills, D. L. (1981). *Teaching homes for autistic and retarded persons. I. Basic rationale.* Unpublished manuscript.

Lovaas, O. I., Koegel, R. L., & Schreibman, L. (1979). Stimulus overselectivity in autism: A review of research. *Psychological Bulletin, 86,* 1236–1254.

Lovaas, O. I., Koegel, R. L., Simmons, J. Q., & Long, J. S. (1973). Some generalization follow-up measures on autistic children in behavior therapy. *Journal of Applied Behavior Analysis, 6,* 131–166.

Lovaas, O. I., Litrownik, A., & Mann, R. (1971). Response latencies to auditory stimuli in autistic children engaged in self-stimulatory behavior. *Behaviour Research and Therapy, 9,* 39–49.

Lovaas, O. I., & Newsom, C. D. (1976). Behavior modification with psychotic children. In H. Leitenberg (Ed.), *Handbook of behavior modification and behavior therapy* (pp. 303–360). Englewood Cliffs, NJ: Prentice Hall.

Lovaas, I., Newsom, C., & Hickman, C. (1987). Self-stimulatory behavior and perceptual reinforcement. *Journal of Applied Behavior Analysis, 20,* 45–68.

Lovaas, O. I., Schaeffer, B., & Simmons, J. Q. (1965). Building social behavior in autistic children by use of electric shock. *Journal of Experimental Research and Personality, 1,* 99–109.

Lovaas, O. I., & Schreibman, L. (1971). Stimulus overselectivity of autistic children in a two stimulus situation. *Behaviour Research and Therapy, 9,* 305–310.

Lovaas, O. I., Schreibman, L., & Koegel, R. L. (1974). A behavior modification approach to the treatment of autism. *Journal of Autism and Childhood Schizophrenia, 4,* 111–129.

Lovaas, O. I., Schreibman, L., Koegel, R. L., & Rehm, R. (1971). Selective responding by autistic children to multiple sensory input. *Journal of Abnormal Psychology, 77,* 211–222.

Lovaas, O. I., & Simmons, J. Q. (1969). Manipulation of self-destruction in three retarded children. *Journal of Applied Behavior Analysis, 2,* 143–157.

Lovaas, O. I., Varni, J., Koegel, R. L., & Lorsch, N. L. (1977). Some observations on the non-extinguishability of children's speech. *Child Development, 48,* 1121–1127.

Matson, J. L., & DiLorenzo, T. M. (1984). *Punishment and its alternatives.* New York: Springer.

McGee, G. G., Krantz, P. J., Mason, D., & McClannahan, L. E. (1983). A modified incidental-teaching procedure for autistic youth: Acquisition and generalization of receptive object labels. *Journal of Applied Behavior Analysis, 16,* 329–338.

McGee, G. G., Krantz, P. J., & McClannahan, L. E. (1985). The facilitative effects of incidental teaching on preposition use by autistic children. *Journal of Applied Behavior Analysis, 18,* 17–31.

McGee, G. G., Krantz, P. J., & McClannahan, L. E. (1986). An extension of incidental teaching procedures to reading instruction for autistic children. *Journal of Applied Behavior Analysis, 19,* 147–157.

Mesibov, G. B., & Dawson, G. (1986). Pervasive developmental disorders and schizophrenia. In J. M. Reisman (Ed.), *Behavior disorders in infants, children, and adolescents* (pp. 117–152). New York: Random House.

Miller, L. N. (1969). *A preliminary report: The effect of fear on echolalic speech in autistic children.* Unpublished manuscript.

Moreland, J. R., Schwebel, S. B., Beck, S., & Wells, R. (1982). Parents as therapists: A review of the behavior therapy parent training literature—1975 to 1981. *Behavior Modification, 2,* 250–276.

Mulhern, I., & Baumeister, A. A. (1969). An experimental attempt to reduce stereotypy by reinforcement procedures. *American Journal of Mental Deficiency, 74,* 69–74.

O'Dell, M., & Koegel, R. L. (1981, November). *The differential effects of two methods of promoting speech in non-verbal autistic children.* Paper presented at the annual meeting of the American Speech-Language-Hearing Association, Los Angeles.

Odom, S. L., Hoyson, M., Jamieson, B., & Strain, P. S. (1985). Increasing handicapped preschoolers' peer social interactions: Cross-setting and component analysis. *Journal of Applied Behavior Analysis, 18,* 3–16.

Odom, S. L., & Strain, P. S. (1984). Classroom-based social skills instruction for severely handicapped preschool children. *Topics in Early Childhood Special Education, 4,* 97–116.

Odom, S. L., & Strain, P. S. (1986). A comparison of peer-initiation and teacher-antecedent interventions for promoting reciprocal social interaction of autistic preschoolers. *Journal of Applied Behavior Analysis, 19,* 59–71.

O'Gorman, G. (1970). *The nature of childhood autism.* London: Butterworths.

Ornitz, E. M. (1969). Disorders of perception common to early infantile autism and schizophrenia. *Comprehensive Psychiatry, 10,* 259–274.

Ornitz, E. M. (1974). The modulation of sensory input and motor output in autistic children. *Journal of Autism and Childhood Schizophrenia, 4,* 197–215.

Ornitz, E. M. (1985). Neurophysiology of infantile autism. *Journal of the American Academy of Child Psychiatry, 24,* 251–262.

Ornitz, E. M., Brown, M. B., Mason, A., & Putnam, N. H. (1974). The effect of visual input on vestibular nystagmus in autistic children. *Archives of General Psychiatry, 31,* 369–373.

Ornitz, E. M., Forsythe, A. B., & de la Pena, A. (1973). The effects of vestibular and auditory stimulation on the REMS of REM sleep in autistic children. *Archives of General Psychiatry, 29,* 785–791.

Ornitz, E. M., & Ritvo, E. R. (1968). Perceptual inconstancy in early infantile autism. *Archives of General Psychiatry, 18,* 76–98.

Ornitz, E. M., & Ritvo, E. R. (1976). The syndrome of autism: A critical review. *The American Journal of Psychiatry, 133,* 609–621.

Peterson, R. F., Cox, M. A., & Bijou, S. W. (1971). Training children to work productively in classroom groups. *Exceptional Children, 27,* 491–500.

Phillips, E. L., Phillips, E. A., Fixsen, D. L., & Wolf, M. M. (1974). *The teaching family handbook.* Lawrence, KS: University Printing Service.

Piggott, L., Gdowski, C., Villanueva, D., Fischhoff, J., & Frohman, C. (1986). Side effects of fenfluramine in autistic children. *Journal of the American Academy of Child Psychiatry, 25,* 287–289.

Pitfield, M., & Oppenheim, A. N. (1964). Child rearing attitudes of mothers of psychotic children. *Journal of Child Psychology and Psychiatry and Allied Disciplines, 5,* 287–289.

Prior, M. (1984). Developing concepts of childhood autism: The influence of experimental cognitive research. *Journal of Consulting and Clinical Psychology, 52,* 4–16.

Prior, M., & Gajzago, C. (1974). Recognition of early signs of autism. *Medical Journal of Australia, 8,* 153.

Reynolds, B. S., Newsom, C. D., & Lovaas, O. I. (1974). Auditory overselectivity in autistic children. *Journal of Abnormal Child Psychology, 2,* 253–263.

Rimland, B. (1964). *Infantile autism.* New York: Appleton-Century-Crofts.

Rimland, B. (1978). Inside the mind of an autistic savant. *Psychology Today, 12,* 68–80.

Rimland, B., Callaway, E., & Dreyfus, P. (1978). The effect of high doses of vitamin B-6 on autistic children: A double-blind crossover study. *American Journal of Psychiatry, 135,* 472–475.

Rincover, A. (1978). Variables affective stimulus-fading and discriminative responding in psychotic children. *Journal of Abnormal Psychology, 87,* 541–553.

Rincover, A., Cook, R., Peoples, A., & Packard, D. (1979). Sensory extinction and sensory reinforcement principles for programming multiple behavior change. *Journal of Applied Behavior Analysis, 12,* 221–233.

Rincover, A., & Devany, J. M. (1979). *The nature and role of side-effects in research on ethics.* Paper presented at the annual meeting of the Association for Behavior Analysis, Dearborn, Michigan.

Rincover, A., & Koegel, R. L. (1975). Setting generality and stimulus control in autistic children. *Journal of Applied Behavior Analysis, 8,* 235–246.

Rincover, A., & Koegel, R. L. (1977a). Classroom treatment of autistic children: II. Individualized instruction in a group. *Journal of Abnormal Child Psychology, 5,* 133–126.

Rincover, A., & Koegel, R. L. (1977b). Research on the education of autistic children: Recent advances and future directions. In B. B. Lahey & A. E. Kazdin (Eds.), *Advances in clinical child psychology.* (Vol. 1, pp. 329–361). New York: Plenum Press.

Rincover, A., Koegel, R. L., & Russo, D. C. (1978). Some recent behavioral research on the education of autistic children. *Education and Treatment of Children, 1,* 31–45.

Rincover, A., Newsom, C. D., Lovaas, O. I., & Koegel, R. L. (1977). Some motivational properties of sensory stimulation in psychotic children. *Journal of Experimental Child Psychology, 24,* 312–323.

Risley, T. R., & Wolf, M. (1967). Establishing functional speech in echolalic children. *Behaviour Research and Therapy, 5,* 73–88.

Ritvo, E. R. (Ed.). (1976). *Autism: Diagnosis, current research and management.* New York: Spectrum Publications.

Ritvo, E. R., & Freeman, B. J. (1978). National Society for Autistic Children definition of the syndrome of autism. *Journal of Autism and Childhood Schizophrenia, 8,* 162–167.

Ritvo, E. R., Freeman, B. J., Geller, E., & Yuwiler, A. (1983). Effects of fenfluramine on 14 outpatients with the syndrome of autism. *Journal of the American Academy of Child Psychiatry, 22,* 549–558.

Ritvo, E. R., Freeman, B. J., Sheibel, A. B., Duong, T., Robinson, R., Guthrie, D., &

Ritvo, A. (1986). Lower Purkinje cell counts in the cerebella of four autistic subjects: Initial findings of the UCLA-NSAC autopsy research report. *American Journal of Psychiatry, 143,* 862–866.

Ritvo, E. R., Freeman, B. J., Yuwiler, A., Geller, E., Yokota, A., Schroth, P., & Novak, P. (1984). Study of fenfluramine in outpatients with the syndrome of autism. *The Journal of Pediatrics, 105,* 823–828.

Ritvo, E. R., Ornitz, E. M., Eviatar, A., Markham, C. H., Brown, M. B., & Mason, A. (1969). Decreased postrotatory nystagmus in early infantile autism. *Neurology, 19,* 653–658.

Ritvo, E. R., Yuwiler, A., Geller, E., Kales, A., Rashkis, S., Schicor, A., Plotkin, A., Axelrod, R., & Howard, C. (1971). Effects of L-dopa on autism. *Journal of Autism and Childhood Schizophrenia, 1,* 190–205.

Ritvo, E. R., Yuwiler, A., Geller, E., Ornitz, E. M., Saeger, K., & Plotkin, S. (1970). Increasing blood serotonin and platelets in early infantile autism. *Archives of General Psychiatry, 23,* 566–572.

Ritvo, S., & Provence, S. (1953). Form perception and imitation in some autistic children. *Psychoanalytic Study of the Child, 8,* 115–161.

Rolider, A., & Van Houten, R. (1985). Movement suppression time-out for undesirable behavior in psychotic and severely developmentally delayed children. *Journal of Applied Behavior Analysis, 18,* 275–288.

Runco, M. A., Charlop, M. H., & Schreibman, L. (1986). The occurrence of autistic children's self-stimulation as a function of familiar versus unfamiliar stimulus conditions. *Journal of Autism and Developmental Disorders, 16,* 31–44.

Runco, M. A., & Schreibman, L. (1983). Parental judgments of behavior therapy efficacy with autistic children: A social validation. *Journal of Autism and Developmental Disorders, 13,* 237–248.

Ruttenberg, B. (1971). A psychoanalytic understanding of infantile autism and its treatment. In D. Churchill, G. Alpern, & M. K. DeMyer (Eds.), *Infantile autism: Proceedings, Indiana University colloquium* (pp. 145–184). Springfield, IL: Charles C Thomas.

Rutter, M. (1968). Concepts of autism: A review of research. *Journal of Child Psychology and Psychiatry, 9,* 1–25.

Rutter, M. (1978). Diagnosis and definition of childhood autism. *Journal of Autism and Childhood Schizophrenia, 8,* 139–161.

Rutter, M., & Bartak, L. (1973). Special educational treatment of autistic children: A comparative study. II. Follow-up findings and implications for services. *Journal of Child Psychology and Psychiatry, 14,* 241–270.

Rutter, M., & Lockyer, L. (1967). A five to fifteen year follow-up study of infantile psychosis. I. Description of sample. *British Journal of Psychiatry, 113,* 1169–1182.

Schopler, E. (1965). Early infantile autism and receptor processes. *Archives of General Psychiatry, 13,* 327–335.

Schopler, E. (1966). Visual versus tactile receptor preference in normal and schizophrenic children. *Journal of Abnormal Psychology, 71,* 108–114.

Schopler, E., & Reichler, R. J. (1971). Developmental therapy by parents with their own autistic child. In M. Rutter (Ed.), *Infantile autism: Concepts, characteristics and treatment* (pp. 206–227). London: Churchill Livingstone.

Schreibman, L. (1975). Effects of within-stimulus and extra-stimulus prompting on discrimination learning in autistic children. *Journal of Applied Behavior Analysis, 8,* 91–112.

Schreibman, L. (1988). *Autism.* Newbury Park, CA: Sage Publications.

Schreibman, L., & Britten, K. R. (1984). Training parents as therapists for autistic children: Rationale, techniques, and results. In W. P. Christian, G. T. Hannah, & T. J. Glahn (Eds.), *Programming effective human services* (pp. 295–314). New York: Plenum Press.

Schreibman, L., & Carr, E. G. (1978). Elimination of echolalic responding to questions through the training of a generalized verbal response. *Journal of Applied Behavior Analysis, 11,* 453–463.

Schreibman, L., & Charlop, M. H. (1987a). Autism. In V. B. Van Hasselt & M. Hersen (Eds.), *Psychological evaluation of the developmentally and physically disabled* (pp. 155–177). New York: Plenum Press.

Schreibman, L., & Charlop, M. H. (1987b). Infantile autism. In T. J. Ollendick & M. Hersen (Eds.), *Handbook of child psychopathology* (pp. 105–129). New York: Plenum Press.

Schreibman, L., Charlop, M. H., & Britten, K. R. (1983). Childhood autism. In R. Morris &

T. Kratochwill (Eds.), *The practice of child therapy* (pp. 221–251). Elmsford, NY: Pergamon Press.

Schreibman, L., Charlop, M. H., & Koegel, R. L. (1982). Teaching autistic children to use extra-stimulus prompts. *Journal of Experimental Child Psychology, 33,* 475–491.

Schreibman, L., Charlop, M. H., & Tryon, A. S. (1981, August). *The acquisition and generalization of appropriate spontaneous speech in autistic children.* Paper presented at the American Psychological Association Annual Convention, Los Angeles.

Schreibman, L., & Koegel, R. L. (1981). A guideline for planning behavior modification programs for autistic children. In S. M. Turner, K. S. Calhoun, & H. E. Adams (Eds.), *Handbook of clinical behavior therapy* (pp. 500–526). New York: John Wiley & Sons.

Schreibman, L., Koegel, R. L., & Craig, M. S. (1977). Reducing stimulus overselectivity in autistic children. *Journal of Abnormal Child Psychology, 5,* 425–436.

Schreibman, L., Koegel, R. L., Mills, D. L., & Burke, J. C. (1984). Training parent-child interactions. In E. Schopler & G. B. Mesibov (Eds.), *The effects of autism on the family* (pp. 187–206). New York: Plenum Press.

Schreibman, L., Koegel, R. L., Mills, J. I., & Burke, J. C. (1981). The social validation of behavior therapy with autistic children. *Behavior Therapy, 12,* 610–624.

Schreibman, L., Kohlenberg, B. S., & Britten, K. R. (1986). Differential responding to content and intonation components of a complex auditory stimulus by non-verbal and echolalic autistic children. *Analysis and Intervention in Developmental Disabilities, 6,* 109–125.

Schreibman, L., & Lovaas, O. I. (1973). Overselective response to social stimuli by autistic children. *Journal of Abnormal Child Psychology, 1,* 152–168.

Schreibman, L., & Mills, J. I. (1983). Infantile autism. In T. J. Ollendick & M. Hersen (Eds.), *Handbook of child psychopathology* (pp. 123–148). New York: Plenum Press.

Schreibman, L., O'Neill, R. E., & Koegel, R. L. (1983). Behavioral training for siblings of autistic children. *Journal of Applied Behavior Analysis, 16,* 129–138.

Schreibman, L., Runco, M. A., Mills, J. I., & Koegel, R. L. (1982). Teachers' judgements of improvements in autistic children in behavior therapy: A social validation. In R. L.

Koegel, A. Rincover, & A. L. Egel (Eds.), *Educating and understanding autistic children* (pp. 78–89). San Diego, CA: College Hill Press.

Solnick, J. V. Rincover, A., & Peterson, C. R. (1977). Determinants of the reinforcing and punishing effects of time-out. *Journal of Applied Behavior Analysis, 10,* 415–428.

Stokes, T. F., & Baer, D. M. (1977). An implicit technology of generalization. *Journal of Applied Behavior Analysis, 10,* 349–368.

Stokes, T. F., Baer, D. M., & Jackson, R. L. (1968). Programming the generalization of a greeting response in four retarded children. *Journal of Applied Behavior Analysis, 1,* 599–610.

Strain, P. S. (1983). Generalization of autistic children's social behavior change: Effects of developmentally integrated and segregated settings. *Analysis and Intervention in Developmental Disabilities, 3,* 23–34.

Strain, P. S., Kerr, M. M., & Ragland, E. U. (1979). Effects of peer-mediated social initiations and prompting/reinforcement procedures on the social behavior of autistic children. *Journal of Autism and Developmental Disorders, 9,* 41–54.

Stroh, G., & Buick, D. (1964). Perceptual development and childhood psychoses. *British Journal of Medical Psychology, 37,* 291–299.

Tanner, B. A., & Zeiler, M. (1975). Punishment of self-injurious behavior using aromatic ammonia as the aversive stimulus. *Journal of Applied Behavior Analysis, 8,* 53–57.

Tate, B. G., & Baroff, G. S. (1966). Aversive control of self-injurious behavior in a psychotic boy. *Behaviour Research and Therapy, 4,* 281–287.

Touchette, P. (1971). Transfer of stimulus control: Measuring the moment of transfer. *Journal of the Experimental Analysis of Behavior, 15,* 347–354.

Touchette, P. E., MacDonald, R. F., & Langer, S. N. (1985). A scatterplot for identifying stimulus control of problem behavior. *Journal of Applied Behavior Analysis, 18,* 343–351.

Varni, J., Lovaas, O. I., Koegel, R. L., & Everett, N. L. (1979). An analysis of observational learning in autistic and normal children. *Journal of Abnormal Child Psychology, 7,* 31–43.

White, G. D., Nielsen, G., & Johnson, S. M. (1972). Time-out duration and the suppression of deviant behavior in children. *Journal of Applied Behavior Analysis, 5,* 111–120.

Wilhelm, H., & Lovaas, O. I. (1976). Stimulus overselectivity: A common feature in autism and mental retardation. *American Journal of Mental Deficiency, 81,* 227–241.

Wing, L. (1972). *Autistic children: A guide for parents.* New York: Brunner/Mazel.

Wing, L. (1976). Diagnosis, clinical description and prognosis. In L. Wing (Ed.), *Early childhood autism: Clinical, educational and social aspects* (2nd ed., pp. 15–64). Elmsford, NY: Pergamon Press.

Wolery, M., Kirk, K., & Gast, D. L. (1985). Stereotypic behavior as a reinforcer: Effects and side effects. *Journal of Autism and Developmental Disorders, 15,* 149–161.

Wolf, M. M., Risley, T., & Mees, H. (1964). Application of operant conditioning procedures to the behaviour problems of an autistic child. *Behaviour Research and Therapy, 1,* 305–312.

CHAPTER 10

MENTALLY RETARDED CHILDREN

Johnny L. Matson
David A. Coe

HISTORICAL PERSPECTIVES

In ancient Greece and Rome, mentally retarded persons were objects of scorn and persecution. They were considered a burden to society, and it was not uncommon for parents to kill mentally retarded children for "the betterment of society." Attitudes towards mentally retarded persons began to change with the dawn of Christianity. During this period, limited attempts were made to provide comfort and support. By the time of the Middle Ages, however, the concept of these persons as fools, hardly worthy of society's care, had reemerged. This orientation persisted over hundreds of years in both Europe and the Orient as well as among American Indians (Rosen, Clark, & Kivitz, 1976). While mentally retarded persons were not intentionally killed during this period, no attempts were made to educate or care for them (Kanner, 1967).

With the Renaissance and the Reformation came the renewed interest in scientific inquiry, education, and humanitarianism that eventually brought about new approaches to the care of mentally retarded persons. In one of the earliest sustained and systematic programs on record, Itard, an 18th-century French physician, educated Victor, the "wild boy of Aveyron" (Rosen et al., 1976). Testing and placement considerations provided impetus for much of the early work done with mentally retarded individuals. In the early 1900s, Binet developed the first standardized intellectual assessment tests to identify and separate "feeble-minded" people from the general populace.

Interest in the care and habilitation of developmentally disabled individuals has grown, however, by easily the most substantial amount in the last 20 years, fueled by the growth of deinstitutionalization and advances in medical and behavior modification technology. A voluminous and ever-expanding literature on treatment, classification, etiology, and epidemiology stands as testament to the progress made in recent years. Most of what will be discussed in this chapter will be based on recent developments, historically speaking.

CLASSIFICATION, ETIOLOGY, AND INCIDENCE

In the United States, mental retardation is increasingly conceptualized as a broad range of behaviors, including social competence, educational capability, and intellectual level. Since 1959, the American Association on Mental Deficiency (AAMD) has defined mental retardation in terms of current levels of functioning in both intellectual and adaptive behavior (AAMD, 1983). This conceptualization has been adopted by the American Psychiatric Association (APA) in its most recent classification system outlined in the *Diagnostic and Statistical Manual of Mental Disorders* (American Psychiatric Association, 1987). Both the AAMD and APA classify mental retardation according to five categories: mild, IQ range 50–55 to approximately 70; moderate, IQ 35–40 to 50–55; severe, 20–25 to 35–40; profound, below 20 or 25; and unspecified, or a strong presumption of mental retardation in the absence of standard intelligence test assessment (AAMD, 1983; APA, 1987). To be classified as having mental retardation, an individual must exhibit significant subaverage performance on standardized measures of both intellectual and adaptive behavior (AAMD, 1983). Moreover, these impairments must be evident during the developmental period (i.e., between the time of conception and the individual's 18th birthday).

Estimates are that 90% to 96% of mentally retarded persons are mildly to moderately impaired (National Association for Retarded Citizens, 1972). In this group, organic pathology can be identified only infrequently, and social deprivation is generally believed to be the principal factor in creating the handicap. Thus, prevention in the form of education and behavior modification methods geared toward enriching the environment should be emphasized.

Individuals who fall in the severe and profound ranges of mental retardation suffer primarily from demonstrable organic disease or pathology (Berg, 1975). Causes range from predispositional factors prior to birth (e.g., fetal alcohol syndrome) to later physical trauma and disease. Aided by knowledge of the personal and family history, these pathological conditions may sometimes be detected prenatally (Milunsky, 1973).

Environmental and organic factors are not mutually exclusive. For example, the cognitive development of a person with considerable physiological damage may vary depending on the amount and type of environmental stimulation presented. An assortment of environmental and organic factors may result in mental retardation, including lack of educational and social stimulation. Organic factors including head injury (Rune, 1970), postnatal injury (Crome, 1960), and genetic difficulties such as neurofibromatosis (Canale, Bebin, & Knighton, 1964), acrocephalosyndactyly (Blank, 1960), craniofacial dysotosis (Vulliamy & Normandale, 1966), and phenylketonuria (Coutts & Fyfe, 1971). Berg (1975) provides a thorough review of these and other etiological considerations. The precision, however, with which such factors can be identified, particularly with less impaired individuals (i.e., mildly as opposed to severely and profoundly mentally retarded children) remains unsatisfactory (Berg, 1975). Clinical evidence of cerebral abnormalities, such as paralyses of the limbs and epilepsy, is demonstrable at postmortem examination in most grossly impaired persons. This finding is in stark contrast to findings with mildly and moderately mentally retarded persons.

Incidence and prevalence rates for mental retardation can be calculated along at least two lines. One is statistical, the second epidemiological. Epidemiological surveys have been infrequently employed in the United States, with statistical methods being more typically used. The statistical approach involves plotting intellectual functioning along a normal probability curve. Those individuals who are two or more standard deviations below the mean, roughly 3% of the population, are classified as mentally retarded. Epidemiological studies have been conducted with greater frequency in European countries, providing more precise data on frequency and types of mental retardation. Although cultural differences among different countries are readily apparent, there is considerable overlap in the prevalence rates of mental retardation yielded by various studies. Among studies with children 5 to 14 years of age, prevalence of persons with IQs below 50 range from 3.45 to 5.8 per thousand. These studies included England (Goodman & Tizard, 1962; Kushlick, 1961, 1964), America (Lemkau, Tietze, & Cooper, 1943), Sweden (Akesson, 1959), Scotland (Birch, Richardson, Baird, Harobin, & Illsby, 1970), and Northern Ireland (Drillien, Jameson, &

Wilkinson, 1966). In all cases except Sweden, these epidemiological studies were conducted in urban areas. Frequency rates are generally highest where compulsory universal education exists (Kushlick & Blunden, 1975). The most likely explanation for this finding is that most mentally retarded persons can perform at lower levels, having the skills needed for dressing, eating, and nonacademic work (such as janitors do); but they are more obviously impaired when they attempt higher-level academic tasks.

For those persons in the mild- and high-moderate ranges of mental retardation (50 to 70 IQ), the prevalence in England is 20/1,000, with the greatest number identified in the age range of 15 to 19. This is probably due to social-environmental factors and the fact that higher-order intellectual skills are required at more advanced educational levels (Kushlick & Blunden, 1975).

In recent years, there has been increasing recognition of the psychiatric problems of mentally retarded persons. Several studies indicate a higher prevalence of psychiatric disorders among those with subaverage intellectual functioning (e.g., Corbett, 1979). Despite this, there is evidence that mentally retarded individuals are actually less likely to be recognized as having mental-health problems distinct from intellectual and adaptive behavior deficits (Reiss, Levitan, & Szysko, 1982; Reiss & Szysko, 1983). Critically needed at this time is some consensus on an appropriate diagnostic system and suitable instruments for identifying and quantifying psychiatric problems in this population.

CHAPTER OUTLINE

In a single review chapter it would be impossible to consider the entire gamut of behavior change procedures that have been employed with mentally retarded children. The basic procedures of reinforcement, punishment, and social learning have been used over the years to develop an extensive array of programs for mentally retarded children. The present chapter therefore provides only a brief overview of available and empirically validated techniques. Apart from the addition of studies that have appeared since the first edition of this book was published, the present chapter also includes sections on topic areas that have received increasing attention from researchers and clinicians recently.

Our coverage begins with a brief discussion of behavior assessment. While the focus of this chapter is treatment, assessment has assumed greater importance in the behavior therapy literature in recent years (Frame & Matson, 1987). This belated attention has come with the realization that assessment is an integral part of any intervention program. Successful treatment relies not only on identifying variables that may foster and maintain desirable behavior but also on identifying conditions that presently control behavioral excesses and deficits. The basic paradigms of reinforcement (primary and secondary) and punishment (physical aversives, time out, physical restraint, and overcorrection) are next considered. Two additional classes of procedures receiving increasing attention and reviewed here are social learning and self-control methods. Our coverage concludes with a look at several of the more important concerns and developments in intervention technology of late, including (1) errorless discrimination and prompt procedures, (2) generalization and maintenance, and (3) parent, staff, and peer training.

ASSESSMENT

One of the most encouraging developments in recent years has been the increased interest in behavioral assessment. Our intention is not to discuss the assessment of mentally retarded children in depth, because a number of excellent sources already exist (e.g., McGrath & Kelly, 1987). Rather, we wish to provide a reminder of its integral relationship to treatment. Thorough assessment should cover life history; medical history; environmental factors; standardized intellectual, achievement, and adaptive behavior measures; and behavioral observations (McGrath & Kelly, 1987). At present, normative assessment of psychopathology is impeded by a lack of standard instruments. It is hoped that downward extensions of scales developed for use with mentally retarded adults (e.g., Aman, Singh, Stewart, & Field, 1985; Senatore, Matson, & Kazdin, 1983) will become available in the next few years.

Perhaps the most significant of recent developments in behavioral assessment have been related to the evaluation of self-injurious and other maladaptive behaviors. Touchette, MacDonald, and Langer (1985), for example, have demonstrated the use of scatter plots to identify temporal patterns in self-injurious and assaultive behaviors. This method makes it possible to identify patterns of behavior that are evident at given times or places. Similarly, Axelrod (1987) developed an extension of the scatter-plot approach incorporating analogue conditions to identify situational determinants of aberrant behaviors. Axelrod (1987) recently has demonstrated the use of analogue environments to identify controlling variables for stereotypies. Some are sure to balk at the extra time and effort required to complete assessments of the sort outlined in these two papers. In the long run, however, thorough assessments are likely to save clinicians all the time and effort that are often wasted in conducting ineffectual treatments. Also, with the emphasis on positive treatment alternatives, this may be one way of avoiding more intrusive treatments. In the case of self-injurious and other aberrant behaviors, improved assessment may decrease the need for using more restrictive and/or intrusive treatments.

POSITIVE REINFORCEMENT PROCEDURES

"Positive reinforcement" refers to any operation or intervention that increases the likelihood of a response by making the presentation of a stimulus contingent upon the occurrence of that response. Positive-reinforcement methods for increasing and decreasing rates of behavior have a long tradition in the care of mentally retarded children. The types of systems vary greatly, but the three principal methods are (1) reinforcement of positive behaviors with edibles or social behavior, (2) reinforcement of positive behaviors with secondary reinforcers in the form of tokens for accelerating behavior, and (3) differential reinforcement of appropriate behavior incompatible with aberrant behavior targeted for deceleration.

Positive reinforcers are generally divided into two types: primary and secondary. Primary reinforcers strengthen behavior in and of themselves. Examples include edibles and toys. Secondary reinforcers strengthen behavior by virtue of their association with primary reinforcers. Tokens are perhaps the most common example of a secondary reinforcer. Although secondary reinforcers are often easier to dispense and cause less interruption of ongoing programs, they may fail to exert control over the behavior of younger and more intellectually handicapped individuals. Consequently, primary reinforcers are typically employed with individuals who are younger, with lower intelligence levels, and severe problems.

One typical use of primary reinforcers with mentally retarded children is described by Hopkins (1968). He treated a 10-year-old mentally retarded boy for abnormally low rates of smiling by using candy (candy-coated chocolate or candy corn) as reinforcement. These primary reinforcers were dispensed on a regularly scheduled walk each time the child smiled within 5 seconds of a verbal exchange. These exchanges might take place with any person he met during the walk. Hopkin's results provided a convincing demonstration of the effectiveness of positive reinforcement for increased appropriate behavior.

Prescription

Eye contact and smiling are just two of the appropriate behaviors that can be increased with primary reinforcers. Procedure 1 is used to establish a response and procedure 2 is a means of maintaining the response once the appropriate behavior has been established.

Procedure 1

A contingency can be established by having the therapist give the child a piece of candy or other edible whenever he or she smiles. If the child smiles during the first 5 seconds of an encounter, the therapist immediately gives the child a piece of candy. If the child fails to smile, the therapist does not respond in any way for at least 15 seconds. Such reinforcers are most effective when given in a one-to-one training session after the target behavior has been adequately explained and demonstrated to the child.

Procedure 2

The same reinforcement procedure is used but the candy is to be presented only after the child emits a variable but predetermined number of smiles. Initially this could be after every two smiles, then every three and so on. The therapist will know that the contingencies are being increased too quickly if the number of reinforcers earned suddenly decreases (e.g., 30% to 50%). As a guide, 15 to 20 reinforcers should be earned before reinforcement schedules are changed.

An example of a secondary or token reinforcement approach that proved effective is described by Jackson and Wallace (1974). In their study, a 15-year-old girl who emitted few verbal responses was treated. She had been in classes for the mentally retarded since age 7 (IQ 75), and was described as severely disturbed and withdrawn. Her lack of speech extended to failing to answer questions posed by school personnel. Instead, she nodded or shrugged. Training sessions were of two types and were differentiated primarily by the presence or absence of an experimenter. In the "shaping" sessions the child was seated in a cubicle with a microphone lavaliere around her neck and 100 word cards in a pile. She read each of these words, with 5 seconds for each. Sensitivity of the voice-operated relay could be adjusted on the basis of voice volume. A word spoken above the sound threshold resulted in the automated delivery of a poker chip (token), which could be used to buy books, beauty aids, a photo album, and other items. Whenever 80% of the responses resulted in reinforcement, the sound threshold was increased.

After near-normal voice volume was achieved, a systematic program of promoting generalization of treatment effects to the classroom was begun. Procedures introduced by increments to shape appropriate speech in the classroom included the following: (1) reading polysyllabic words from a book rather than monosyllables from cards, (2) placing other students' desks next to the subject's study cubicle, (3) gradually extending responses to a criterion of two polysyllables, (4) opening the side of the subject's booth at a 45 degree angle to greatly reduce privacy, (5) increasing the reading criterion, (6) removing the side of the subject's cubicle, and, (7) conducting a study session in the room with a greater number of children and the teacher. The procedure resulted in greatly improved speech and was achieved with the sessions in the cubicle alone.

A major problem with mentally retarded children that has received attention for years is language acquisition (McCoy & Buckwalt, 1981). Although nonhandicapped children acquire language from naturally occurring interactions with their respective language environments, many mentally retarded children, particularly those functioning in the severe and profound range of mental retardation, fail to acquire even the most rudimentary language skills. This problem is compounded by many physical as well as cognitive deficits, which impede speech (e.g., hearing deficits, cleft palate). McCoy and Buckwalt (1981) provide an extensive review of the topic,

which includes both receptive and expressive skills. For the present review, a brief discussion of means for teaching expressive skills will be highlighted, since most procedures place a heavy emphasis on reinforcement.

The most desirable prerequisite skill for expressive-language training is generalized vocal imitation. With this procedure, the child demonstrates the ability to imitate sounds the first time they are modeled. This method, which McCoy and Buckwalt (1981) consider most useful in the acquisition of vocal imitation, was developed by Lovaas and his colleagues (Lovaas, 1977; Lovaas & Newsom, 1976), and variations of this treatment have been replicated by others (Matson, Esveldt-Dawson, & O'Donnel, 1979). They describe four steps to their procedure, which includes a variety of attempts to elicit vocalizations (e.g., tickling, verbal prompting), reinforcement of vocalizations, reinforcing approximations to a sound, and training imitation of sounds. A prescriptive explanation of this procedure follows.

A number of reviews have been published recently that provide a rundown of training procedures aimed at language-skill acquisition. For a detailed account the reader is referred to Guess, Sailor, and Keogh (1977); McLean and Snyder (1977); and McMorrow, Foxx, Faw, and Bittle (1986). Approaches include traditional learning theory for content and instructional method and also the incorporation of knowledge of the structure and sequence of normal child language development (Bricker, Dennison, & Bricker, 1976; Carrier & Peak, 1973). Thus, treatment approaches, none of which follow "purely" one approach, vary from behavioral to developmental psycholinguistics.

Behaviorally oriented programs almost always involve the use of tangible reinforcers (McCoy & Buckwalt, 1981), primarily portions of meals or treats such as soda pop, ice cream, sugar cereals, potato chips, or fruit. Aversive consequences (social disapproval or brief time outs for incorrect responding) are less frequently employed.

A few operant studies in addition to those already mentioned are worthy of review. Sailor (1971), for example, working with institutionalized severely mentally retarded children, showed that imitation and differential reinforcement of plural morphemes for pairs of objects produced pluralization for pairs of objects not already trained. Baer and Guess (1973) extended this work to noun suffixes. Four severely mentally retarded children (ages 11, 13, 16, and 16) were treated; they had modest expressive vocabularies but no expressive use of noun suffixes. Pictures depicting a person engaging in activities were used as training stimuli according to a standardized format. The experimenter showed a picture to the child while labeling, for example, "This man farms. He is a _____." Initially the response "farmer" was modeled, and imitation was differentially reinforced. The children began rapidly applying the /er/ and /ist/ suffix to new verbs and used the suffix currently undergoing training.

Similarly, Wheeler and Sulzer (1970) investigated imitation and reinforcement procedures in establishing use of articles and auxiliary verbs to form complete sentences. An 8-year-old mentally retarded boy was studied; he had the vocabulary to express himself in sentences but failed to do so. Training consisted of modeling and reinforcing responses of complete sentence forms. Results showed increased use of articles and auxiliary verbs, which also generalized to nontrained probe pictures. Clarke and Sherman (1975), whose unit of analysis was also complete sentences, employed training focused on approximately grammatical usage. In these cases, the reinforcement and modeling procedures proved to be highly useful.

Prescription

Morris (1978) provides some useful procedures for speech training. He describes two procedures as means of establishing functional speech (procedure 1) and the acquisition of functional language (procedure 2) that are similar to the methods of Lovaas and his colleagues.

Procedure 1
For a child with some speech, an imitation program for sounds is suggested. During one-to-one therapy sessions, the child should be reinforced for emitting any sound within a specified time period following the therapist's demonstration of the proper response. Closer approximations to other sounds should be tried as the initial sound is acquired. This shaping procedure should be continued until the terminal response (specific syllables or sounds) can be noted on a consistent basis. Daily sessions of 30 minutes are generally the best, but less frequent sessions can also prove effective (2 or 3 sessions weekly).

Procedure 2
For training functional speech, it must be assumed that the child has a stable level of vocal imitation and eye contact. Since a more complex skill is required and the child will have greater prerequisite skills, stimuli such as pictures can be shown to the child concurrent with the therapist naming the picture (e.g., "dog"). Social and, if necessary, tangible reinforcers can be given for imitating the therapist within a defined but brief period (e.g., a few seconds). After the child is imitating the therapist's words at a heightened stable rate, the therapist should begin to gradually fade out his or her naming of the picture. A second step is to get the child to use trained words as responses to questions posed by the therapist. Finally, persons other than the therapist should join the sessions and ask questions. These questions should be asked in naturalistic settings after the criteria for success on the previously noted skills has been achieved.

A second set of prescriptions applies with persons who have more rudimentary skills.

Prescription

Loud or very low verbalizations may be modified in a number of ways. The token reinforcement method, if used, should follow one of two procedures.

Procedure 1
Where no speech is present in a particular setting (elective mutism), a shaping procedure should be used along with token reinforcement. Initially the client should be reinforced with tokens for making audible noises in the setting where speech has not been present. Next, the child should be required to say words before a token reinforcer is earned. Finally, the child should be required to say these words in the company of others before receiving a reinforcer. (This reinforcer should always be given by the person to whom the verbalization is directed.)

Procedure 2
For a person already demonstrating unintelligible speech, the emphasis should be on increasing volume to audible levels, improving the clarity of speech, or standing closer and directly facing the person being spoken to as a means of increasing understanding. These methods are also applicable in cases where the child is saying

socially inappropriate words. These behaviors can be shaped by successive approximations using modeling, instructions, performance feedback, tokens, and social reinforcement. One method that has been commonly employed involves role-play scenes of past instances where the child displayed the inappropriate target behavior. Based on the child's response to the scenario, new alternative behavior would be described—or, if the response was correct, the answer would be reinforced.

The last few years have seen so many exciting developments in the use of positive reinforcement that it would be impossible to do full justice to them all here. Their implications for improving the efficacy of education and training procedures by bolstering motivation and response strength should not be underestimated. Table 10.1 presents some examples of positive reinforcement procedures. Recent studies have demonstrated the efficacy of varying reinforcement type (Egel, 1981), employing sensory as opposed to edible reinforcers (Rincover & Newson, 1985; Sandler & McLain, 1987), and using multimodal sensory reinforcement (Dewson & Whiteley, 1987). Among the most important developments has been the work on identifying viable reinforcers for severely and profoundly mentally retarded persons. Murphy, Callias, and Carr (1985), for example, found that traditional operant shaping failed to significantly increase the interaction of profoundly mentally retarded subjects with toys. In contrast, toy contact was increased when subjects interacted with spe-

cially designed toys that emitted vibratory, visual, or auditory stimulation when appropriately handled (Murphy, Carr, & Callias, 1986). Such studies reflect a growing realization that behavior therapy may be made more effective by identifying the relevant dimensions of reinforcement that actually strengthen behavior rather than relying on adventitious combinations of dimensions in naturally occurring reinforcers. Individuals interested in these as well as other uses of and variations on positive reinforcement are encouraged to examine some of the major journals publishing behavior therapy studies of mentally retarded children (*Behavior Therapy, Journal of Applied Behavior Analysis, Behaviour Research and Therapy, Journal of Mental Deficiency Research, Mental Retardation, American Journal of Mental Deficiency, Journal of Behavior Therapy and Experimental Psychiatry,* and *Research in Developmental Disabilities*).

PUNISHMENT

Punishment is any operation or intervention that decreases the frequency of a response by arranging the presentation or removal of a stimulus contingent upon the occurrence of that response. In recent years, considerable divisiveness has arisen in the mental-health and special-education fields between proponents and opponents of the use of punishment in eliminating life-threatening and other aberrant behavior. Although it is important to discuss and define ethical standards for research and treatment, it

Table 10.1. Sample Treatment Studies With Reinforcement Procedures

AUTHORS	TYPES OF PERSON(S) TREATED	BEHAVIOR TREATED	TREATMENT METHOD
Butz & Hasazi (1973)	1 mildly mentally retarded boy	Perseverative speech	Edible reinforcement
Jackson & Wallace (1974)	1 borderline mentally retarded female adolescent	Voice loudness	Token reinforcement
Dewson & Whiteley (1987)	6 nonambulatory profoundly mentally retarded children	Head turning	Sensory reinforcement
Murphy, Carr, & Callias (1986)	20 profoundly mentally retarded children and adolescents	Use of toys, stereotypies	Prompts; sensory reinforcement
Egel (1981)	3 moderately to mildly mentally retarded autistic boys (6 to 7 years old)	Use of adjectives, action verbs	Variations in edible reinforcers
Fabry, Mayhew, & Hanson (1984)	6 moderately to severely mentally retarded adolescents and young adults	Reading	Incidental teaching

is equally important to base dialogue on an impartial examination of treatment effectiveness. This has not always been the case. Constructive efforts, however, have been made in recent years to develop guidelines, with which practitioners should be well acquainted, for the use of aversives in clinical populations. Morris and Brown (1983), for example, recommended a three-tier system for implementing treatment programs. In their system, a patient would be exposed to treatments in a systematic, database fashion in order of least intrusiveness. Level-I procedures are the least intrusive and include extinction and differential reinforcement operations. Those on Level II are nonseclusionary time out and response-cost procedures. Level III includes overcorrection, seclusion time out, and physical aversives. Various states and courts have established variants of this approach. This system is probably workable in most cases. However, it should also be pointed out that where very serious, life-threatening situations exist, client safety may dictate skipping less intrusive but probably minimally effective alternatives.

Evident in the recent literature pertaining to the use of punishment is increased emphasis on evaluating the relative effectiveness of different aversive procedures (Barrett, McGonigle, Ackles, & Burkhart, 1987; Paniagua, Braverman, & Capriotti, 1986; Singh, Watson, & Winton, 1986; Watson, Singh, & Winton, 1986) and their effectiveness for different behaviors (Singh, Winton, & Ball, 1984). Several promising procedures that suppress aberrant behaviors while minimizing stimulus intensity have also been developed in recent years, including movement suppression (Rolider & Van Houten, 1985), screening (Watson, Singh & Winton, 1986), and combinations of two or more aversives (e.g. Barrett et al., 1987; Paniagua et al., 1986).

Physical Punishment

The term "physical punishment" has been used by Baumeister and Röllings (1976) to refer to noxious stimuli such as contingent electric shocks (Risley, 1968), loud noises (Sajwaj & Hedges, 1971), restraint (Sapasnek & Watson, 1974), noxious odors (Tanner & Zeiler, 1975), hair pulling (Banks & Locke, 1966), slapping (Bucker & Lovaas, 1968), and tickling (Greene & Hoats, 1971). Physical punishment is typically admin-

istered in a one-to-one situation by a highly trained therapist who has taken all necessary precautions to ensure the safety and general well-being of the client. Also, because of the controversial nature of this treatment, its lack of popularity among some professionals, and the associated danger, considerable emphasis on safeguards against misuse of the procedure are needed. Given the relative frequency with which punishment procedures are applied to mentally retarded individuals (Matson, 1982), the practitioner must be well versed in applying them.

Today, physical punishment procedures are typically used for decelerating only the most inappropriate behaviors. These may include chronic life-threatening rumination, severe self-injury, or serious incidents of aggression. Typically these methods are used in combination with reinforcement. The administration of noxious substances is generally straightforward and involves application of the substance immediately after the occurrence of the operationally defined behavior targeted for deceleration. Typically, a verbal warning is paired with the aversive substance, the latter being faded out gradually as the warning takes on increasingly aversive properties. Substantial amounts of the aversive substance are used immediately, rather than building up to gradually noxious levels. This approach is taken since persons will acclimate to punishment procedures and can withstand more aversive stimuli if they are introduced gradually to increasingly more severe levels.

Various physical punishment procedures have been used. A number of examples are presented in Table 10.2. One interesting application of physical punishment with mentally retarded children involves the use of lemon juice (Cook, Altman, Shaw, & Blaylock, 1978). In this study, a 7½-year-old boy with moderate spastic hemiplegia, microcephaly, and severe mental retardation was treated. Prior to treatment, the child had engaged in public masturbation in an institution, at home, and at school. He had done this frequently for a period of 4 years, much to his parents' consternation. (Private masturbation was considered appropriate and was encouraged rather than discouraged during the study.)

Treatment consisted of squirting 5 to 10 ml of unsweetened lemon juice into the child's mouth with a plastic squirt bottle whenever masturbation in a public place was observed. During the initial phase of treatment, he was under the

Table 10.2. Sample Studies With Physical Punishment

AUTHORS	TYPES OF PERSON(S) TREATED	BEHAVIOR TREATED	TREATMENT METHOD
Lovaas & Simmons (1969)	2 severely and profoundly mentally retarded children (8 to 11 years old)	Head banging	Contingent electric shock
Cook, Altman, Shaw, & Blaylock (1978)	1 severely mentally retarded boy	Masturbation	Lemon juice in mouth
Kauffmann, LaFleur, Hallahan, & Chanes (1985)	1 moderately mentally retarded girl (7 years old)	Sloppy eating	Verbal reprimand
Reichlich, Spooner, & Rose (1984)	1 severely or profoundly mentally retarded girl (10 years old)	Stereotypy	Water-mist spray
Paniagua, Braverman, & Capriotti (1986)	1 profoundly mentally retarded girl (4 years old)	Pica	Reprimand, response prevention, physical restraint, DRO
Barrett, McGonigle, Ackles, & Burkhart (1987)	1 profoundly mentally retarded girl	Aerophagia	Auditory cue, nose press, and visual screening

nearly constant supervision of a parent, teacher, or teacher's aide. Trained observers made sure that lemon juice was always readily available. Positive effects occurred rapidly and were maintained at 6-month follow-up.

The use of lemon juice as a noxious stimulus exemplifies the trend toward the use of stimuli carrying a lesser social stigma than slaps, contingent electric shock, and other procedures. Nonetheless, there are those who also oppose these less extreme aversives. The use of noxious stimuli is likely to continue, but the range of situations in which it will be permitted will depend on society's attitudes. Another of the commonly used methods, overcorrection, will be reviewed next.

Prescription

Unless a dire emergency dictates otherwise, the first course of action in the treatment of self-injurious behavior or any other behavior targeted for deceleration should be reinforcement of the behavior's omission, either by direct reinforcement of omission (DRO) or differential reinforcement of behavior incompatible with the behavior (DRI). Should a purely reinforcement-oriented program prove out of the question, however, an additional punishment contingency may then be warranted. Application of a physical aversive is one alternative.

For a case of severe hand biting, several types of aversives can be used. Ideally, one uses the least aversive or least intrusive contingency available that will decrease the behavior's frequency. All presentations of an aversive, moreover, should be paired with a concise verbal reprimand, in the expectation that the reprimand will eventually exert control over behavior as a conditioned punishment. Initially, lemon juice might be applied to the child's tongue contingent upon hand biting. This application should be made consistently and promptly. Punishment, in fact, should be delivered as early in the behavioral sequence as possible, taking care not to extinguish adaptive behavior in the process. Simultaneously, a reinforcement contingency should be in force for omission of biting (for example, reinforcing manipulation of toys or adaptive use of hands). If deceleration is not evident within a short time or the effectiveness of the punishment diminishes (over 30 to 40 presentations), use of a more intrusive aversive may be needed. For cases where the most effective intervention of several is unknown, an alternating treatment design may be useful. Here one applies different aversives under different circumstances to determine which is most effective. For example, comparing application of lemon juice, contingent restraint, or spanking to reduce hand biting might be considered. Finally, throughout the course of the intervention, general mood and behavior should be monitored to guard against undesirable side effects. This monitoring should cover assessment of withdrawal, tantrums, and changes in eating or sleeping patterns.

Overcorrection

Overcorrection is a punishment technique first described by Foxx and Azrin (1973). With this procedure, the child is required to correct the environmental consequences of the targeted response (restitution overcorrection) and/or practice acceptable or overly correct forms of that response (positive practice). In cases of restitution overcorrection, the child is frequently required to provide more than adequate compensation. For example, throwing food at the dinner table may be punished by demanding not only that the food be picked up but also that the floor and table be washed. Positive practice, in contrast, consists of practicing alternative behavior subsequent to the occurrence of inappropriate behavior. In the case of the child who overturned furniture, he or she could be instructed in appropriate use of furniture and be required to practice sitting in a chair several times. Positive practice also applies to behaviors such as toilet training, where appropriate behavior may be practiced several times in situations where accidents are routinely observed. Table 10.3 outlines several studies that have employed overcorrection procedures.

The range of techniques comprised by overcorrection are as varied as the behaviors treated. A variety of overcorrection procedures can, in fact, exist for the same target behavior. A number of persons have questioned the conceptual basis of overcorrection (Doke & Epstein, 1975; Forehand & Baumeister, 1976). Much less theoretically oriented research has appeared on this method as opposed to the other techniques discussed in this chapter. Despite this criticism, overcorrection can be a highly effective clinical procedure, one strongly worth considering because it is effective and has been more positively received than physical punishment by advocates for mentally retarded persons and by clinical staff.

One example of overcorrection's effectiveness is described by Stimbert, Minor, and McCoy (1977). They treated 3 boys and 3 girls between 3½ and 13½ years of age for poor feeding skills. Four of the children were profoundly mentally retarded, one was severely mentally retarded, and one was moderately mentally retarded. Meals were doubled by dividing each in half and training was limited to one utensil. These methods maximized the likelihood of obtaining some proficiency in socially appropriate eating. Complex behaviors such as meat cutting and bread buttering were not included, and children were not taken from the room to clean up. In addition, all meals were limited to 15 minutes and the entire six-meal-per-day schedule was adhered to until a maintenance phase was begun. Children on this intensive feeding program were served regular, nutritionally balanced meals prepared at the direction of a registered dietician.

Training included manual guidance, praise for correct responses, restitutional and positive-practice overcorrection, and time out. Manual guidance, which is frequently used as part and parcel of overcorrection, consisted of hand-on-hand guidance to aid the child in feeding until pressure cues indicated that the child could adequately be guided through the steps of the procedure by holding his or her hand. The location of the manual guidance was gradually

Table 10.3. Sample Treatment Studies With Overcorrection

AUTHORS	TYPES OF PERSON(S) TREATED	BEHAVIOR TREATED	TREATMENT METHOD
Stimbert, Minor, & McCoy (1977)	4 profoundly to moderately mentally retarded children	Eating	Overcorrection, time out
Matson, Kazdin, & Esveldt-Dawson (1980)	3 mildly or borderline mentally retarded children	Spelling	Overcorrection
Foxx & Azrin (1973)	3 severely mentally retarded girls (7 to 8 years old)	Self-stimulation	Overcorrection
Stewart & Singh (1986)	4 moderately mentally retarded adolescents (16 to 18 years old)	Spelling	Overcorrection, positive reinforcement
Halpern & Andrasik (1980)	1 profoundly mentally retarded male (23 years old)	Self-injury	Positive practice, overcorrection, DRO

shifted from the wrist, to the forearm, to the elbow, to the upper arm, and finally to the shoulder.

When an eating error or inappropriate behavior occurred, it was pointed out to the child. Restitution overcorrection was then used and consisted of guiding him or her through the clean-up of spilled food. Positive-practice overcorrection required three practice loadings of the spoon. The trainer then guided the child's hand to the mouth on the third trial so that he or she could eat.

Tray time out (authors' term) consisted of pushing the food tray out the child's reach for 30 seconds and was used when disruption occurred. Two trainers were present, with the primary trainer standing just behind and on the side of the subject's preferred hand. The other trainer sat beside the subject's nonpreferred arm and physically prevented the use of that arm or hand in eating or in any type of disruptive behavior.

After training, a maintenance phase was begun. This procedure consisted of monitoring the child's eating behavior and praising correct eating less frequently while employing the same training procedures. Positive effects of training were rapid and maintained at follow-up, which varied from 4 to 12 months. Another aspect of this study, characteristic of much of the overcorrection research, is that a large variety of behavioral techniques such as time out, instructions, and reinforcement were used in conjunction with overcorrection. This complicates assessment of the effectiveness and utility of overcorrection itself.

Prescription

A number of eating methods have been devised for mentally retarded adults and children. With some modifications, most of these are applicable for all ages and levels of intellectual ability. The type of treatment will also change on the basis of the degree of eating impairment and number of noncompliant behaviors the child displays. For more compliant children, Procedure 1 is recommended; for less compliant children, Procedure 2 is likely to be more effective.

Procedure 1. For the relatively compliant child, graduated guidance should prove highly useful, along with modeling, in demonstrating to the child proper eating skills. An example of how these procedures might be applicable would be the case of a 10-year-old mildly mentally retarded boy who does not know how to load a spoon and get the contents in his mouth. In this instance the therapist could model or demonstrate the steps involved in this task from dipping the spoon (correct side up) into soup to bringing it to the mouth without tilting the spoon to either side, thereby avoiding spillage of the contents until it reached the mouth. The child would then be required to practice the response until the therapist placed his or her hand on the child's as necessary to ensure that the various responses were carried out correctly.

Procedure 2. For children who manifest more socially inappropriate behavior, additional methods may be required beyond modeling and graduated guidance. The removal of food for a brief period (e.g., 30 seconds) would be one effective procedure to consider when the child refuses to follow instruction and/or becomes aggressive. In extreme cases of aggression, the child might also be removed from the table until agitation subsides. (The first author has observed instances when children have thrown food, hit other children, knocked dishes from the table, and overturned tables and chairs.)

A second example of overcorrection's effectiveness is described by Foxx and Azrin (1973) in the treatment of head weaving, hand clapping, and the mouthing of objects. They treated 5 children, 4 severely mentally retarded and 1 autistic. In this particular study, they described how overcorrection was more effective than a number of alternative treatments such as differential reinforcement of other behavior, noncontingent reinforcement, and physical punishment (slapping the child on the thigh for mouthing).

The experimenter concluded that mouthing an object would result in exposure to potentially harmful microorganisms through unhygienic oral contact. Thus, a restitution overcorrection method called "oral hygiene training" was used. Initially, the child was told no in a firm voice. Then her gums and teeth were brushed with mouthwash. Next, the child's lips were washed with a cloth dampened with the mouthwash. During the 2-minute training period, the child was periodically encouraged (by verbal instructions and the tickling of the tongue) to spit the cleansing solution into a cup. After administration of restitution overcorrection, the toothbrush and washcloth were rinsed in water and soaked in fresh mouthwash.

The two self-stimulatory behaviors treated in this study were head waving and hand clapping. They were described by the experimenters as nonfunctional, since the behaviors were independent of external control. Because environmental disruption did not occur, restitution overcorrection was considered inappropriate. Therefore, the rationale of positive-practice overcorrection was to teach and motivate the child to hold her head immobile and to move only when instructed to do so (this was considered functional). Thus, the positive-practice overcorrection was called functional movement training. The authors concluded that overcorrection was educative, since the individual learned specific head movements to specific directions.

The same rationale for treatment was used for hand clapping. When the boy clapped his hands, he was immediately overcorrected. The boy was instructed to move his hands in one of five positions: above his head, straight out in front of him, into his pockets, held together, and held behind his back. He was to assume these various hand postures based on the teacher's commands.

These descriptions are representative of the many uses of overcorrection. The programs for stereotyped behavior, which have also been used for self-injurious behavior, are perhaps the most commonly reported. Maintenance of treatment effects has been noted in a number of studies and has been found to be good (Marholin, Luiselli, & Townsend, 1980; Ferretti & Cavaliere, 1983). Similarly, some attempts at systematically programming generalization effects have been found (Marholin et al, 1980). Generalization by means of observing persons being overcorrected has been noted in children of normal intelligence (Epstein, Doke, Sajwaj, Sorrell, & Rimmer, 1974) and in mentally retarded adults (Ollendick, Matson, & Martin, 1978). These effects are not as great as when behaviors are directly treated.

Time Out

Another procedure that has frequently been used with mentally retarded children is time out. This technique is defined as a punishing consequence associated with the removal of reinforcing stimuli. It is aimed at decelerating aberrant behavior and presupposes that the child is in a high-reward situation (Drabman, Spitalnik, & O'Leary, 1973). Time out may vary widely in form, from sitting at a desk for a few minutes to more severe forms in which the child may be placed in a room devoid of reinforcing materials for short periods, generally 2 to 30 minutes (Drabman et al., 1973). In these instances, release from time out is based on the performance of socially desirable behavior. Table 10.4 gives examples of the broad array of uses for time out.

One interesting time-out procedure was described by Barton (1970). His subject was an 11-year-old profoundly mentally retarded hydrocephalic boy with a seizure disorder. The child vacillated between periods of withdrawal and aggression. His speech was described as clear, and he displayed a large, primarily inappropriate vocabulary. In addition, he frequently perseverated on particular responses, and his answers were typically unrelated to questions.

The training goal was to increase the frequency of socially appropriate replies. Inappropriate responses were irrelevant comments or those where a lack of verbal responding was noted. During treatment the child was presented with 50 pictures from a magazine and asked a question about each. Appropriate responses resulted in the award of a piece of candy-coated chocolate. The next question was then presented. Inappropriate responses resulted in time out. This latter procedure consisted in having the experimenter close the magazine and turn away from the child for a period of 10 seconds as a means of social isolation. At the end of the 10-second time out, the experimenter turned back to face the child, reopened the magazine to the next picture, and asked a new question. Negative responses were ignored. Treatment sessions were held twice daily three times a week.

A generalized component of the treatment program consisted initially of a situation similar to the initial training situation. The task was similar and was administered by the same therapist. No direct treatment was provided in this latter situation, but this could be easily done. A methodology of shaping by successive approximation similar to that described in the Jackson and Wallace (1974) study might be applicable.

Prescription

When properly implemented, time out can be a simple yet highly effective intervention. To decelerate a behavior of low to moderate intensity

Table 10.4. Sample Treatment Studies With Time Out

AUTHORS	TYPES OF PERSON(S) TREATED	BEHAVIOR TREATED	TREATMENT METHOD
Barton (1970)	1 profoundly mentally retarded boy	Bizarre speech	Time out, edible reinforcement
Vukelich & Hake (1971)	1 profoundly mentally retarded adolescent	Grabbing and choking staff and patients	Time out, contingent attention
Sisson & Dixon (1986)	6 severely to mildly mentally retarded boys (6 to 15 years old)	Eating skills	Time out, modeling, manual guidance, rehearsal
Foxx & Shapiro (1978)	5 profoundly to severely mentally retarded boys (8 to 18 years old)	Tantrums, self-injury, out of seat	Nonexclusionary time out, reinforcement
Rolider & Van Houten (1985)	6 autistic and/or mentally retarded children and adolescents	Self-injury, mouthing, poking others, self-stimulation	Movement-suppression time out, DRO

such as noncompliance, the following guidelines should be adhered to. First, as with any intervention, the key is to act early and consistently. Any act of noncompliance should be dealt with immediately. A short reprimand should be provided, indicating disapproval and the reason for implementing time out. The child is directed to time out with as little fanfare as possible. To maximize discrimination of contingencies, time out is implemented in one particular spot for a specific and fixed duration. Finally, for maximal effectiveness, time out is employed in the context of a program concurrently providing reinforcement and feedback for appropriate behavior.

SOCIAL-LEARNING METHODS

Social-learning methods stress the treatment of internal processes as covert events that can be measured and manipulated. These mediating processes are extensively controlled by external stimuli (Bandura, 1969). Unlike operant and classical conditioning models of learning, however, a much broader range of events and treatment techniques are associated with social-learning procedures. Techniques that typify these methods include modeling, role playing, and other forms of vicarious learning and social reinforcement.

Perhaps the area that has received the most attention by professionals using social-learning methods is social-skills training (the authors are employing the definition of Hersen and Bellack, 1976, which also encompasses assertion). Other important areas (they have involved largely nonretarded populations) include explosive rage (Foy, Eisler, & Pinkston, 1973), aggression (Goodwin & Mahoney, 1975), language training for autistic children (Coleman & Stedman, 1974), enuresis (Johnson & Thompson, 1974), anxiety in children and adults (Matson, 1981a, 1981b; Murphy & Bootzin, 1973), obsessions and compulsions (Matson, 1982; Roeper, Rachman, & Mark, 1975), extreme social withdrawal (Ross, Ross, & Evans, 1971), and covert modeling for a wide range of behaviors (Cautela, 1971; Hay, Hay, & Nelson, 1977; Nietzel, Martorano, & Melnick, 1977). These studies exemplify primarily modeling and social reinforcement. Many other methods are often involved, including instructions given prior to the implementation of a program and performance feedback on specific appropriate and inappropriate ways in which behavior was carried out during different variations of practice. Another commonly employed social-learning strategem is role playing (the acting out of a specific task being trained).

Instructions, performance feedback, role playing, and social reinforcement (e.g., praise) are relatively straightforward. Modeling, as Rimm and Masters (1979) point out, is more complex, however, and deserves a brief explanation, since imitation and observational learning are closely related techniques that are sometimes used interchangeably. In this chapter, Rimm and Master's (1979) definitions are used. They use "modeling" as a general term denoting learning that occurs from the observation of others and any imitative change in behavior that may follow. "Imitation" refers to the observer's behavior displayed after modeling. It reflects performance and not necessarily enduring learning by the observer. Observational learning is the product of viewing others. Of these three, modeling has been used more frequently in treatment research with mentally retarded children. As noted, modeling and other social-learning methods are frequently used in combination. The use of a standard training stimulus is generally found in such procedures. With social-skills research, scenes that depict situations in which the client displays social excesses or deficits are used.

A package of procedures that might be characterized as social-learning-oriented is described by Mahoney, Van Wagenen, and Meyerson (1971) for toilet training. They treated 3 normal-IQ children between 20 and 21 months of age and 5 severely to profoundly mentally retarded children between 4 and 9 years of age in an attempt to help them void in the toilet rather than in their clothing. All the children could follow simple instructions. One mentally retarded child had a severe hearing loss and paralysis of the right hand.

Parents were asked to withhold liquid and food for the hour preceding training to increase their effectiveness as reinforcers. While in training, each child wore a pants alarm apparatus that provided an auditory signal when urination occurred. The training procedures consisted of modeling, instructions, performance feedback, primary and social reinforcers, shaping, and taking advantage of manipulations of the physical environment in a six-stage process. In phase one, the child was trained to walk to the commode in response to the auditory signal, a task accomplished by placing toys near the entrance to the lavatory to enhance the probability that the child would wish to be in this area. Practice of an appropriate response then began, with the experimenter activating the transmitter signal for 5 seconds while telling the child it was time to go to the potty. Then the trainer took the child's hand and led him or her to the toilet. On subsequent trials, the speed of walking was increased, the experimenter moved further and further ahead of the child, and toys were placed at increasing distances from the commode. Walking to the lavatory was reinforced by the experimenter, who placed food in the child's mouth while praising him or her.

The second aspect of training in phase one consisted of fading out the physical intervention and verbal prompts of the experimenter when the auditory signal occurred. The trainer still activated the pants alarm but gradually reduced the use of verbal prompts and hand gestures. In the process, the trainer progressively moved to a position behind the child so that he or she

eventually entered the lavatory first (within 3 seconds after the onset of the alarm). These same procedures were used for the ensuing phases, which included teaching the child to lower his or her pants, sit on the toilet seat (or take the proper male stance while facing the commode), and exposing the child to the appropriate receptacle. Later phases included inducing the consumption of liquids, teaching the child to pull up his or her pants, and practicing behavior chains without the support of the auditory signal. These procedures proved effective.

Another social-learning package that exemplifies the diversity of behaviors trained and procedures used is represented by a program devised by Matson, Kazdin, and Esveldt-Dawson (1980). They treated two African-American boys (ages 11 and 12) diagnosed as anxiety reaction with psychotic features and conduct disorder, respectively. On the basis of behavioral observations, school records, and parent reports, both children were considered chronically antisocial and highly aggressive by school personnel and unit staff. Prior to hospitalization, each child had been seen by counselors and outpatient mental-health personnel. These children were selected for treatment because of gross and chronic deficits in social behavior.

Behaviors selected for treatment included physical gestures, facial mannerisms, eye contact, number of words spoken, voice intonation, verbal content, and overall social skill. To provide an estimate of performance of these behaviors among children not identified as deficient in the areas of interpersonal performance, children attending a university laboratory school were assessed. This normal-IQ, appropriate-social-behavior group was matched on age and sex with treated children. Performance of these normative children served as a basis for social validation or clinical significance of change.

Treatment consisted of practicing situations where the children frequently displayed poor social skills. Each scene consisted of the narrator's description of particular circumstance that might occur, the delivery of a prompt to the child by the trainer that was to be answered as if the child were in the circumstances described by the narrator, and the child's direct response to the trainer's prompt. The training occurred every weekday, with six scenes presented each session. Individual scenes were presented from one to three times based on the accuracy of the child's response. Following the presentation of a scene and the child's response, the therapist provided feedback regarding the appropriateness of the target behavior being trained. For behaviors performed incorrectly, the scene was represented with the trainer modeling the appropriate response. Following this training phase, the same scene was practiced a third time—a procedure used for each scene presented.

As can be seen in Figures 10.1 through 10.4, effects for the two children treated, Jack and Tom, were rapid and were maintained at follow-up sessions 4 to 6 weeks later. Additionally, generalization to untrained scenes was noted. Many other uses of social-learning procedures have been made, some of which are outlined in Table 10.5.

Prescription

Social-learning approaches differ considerably, but all are aimed primarily at the acquisition of new responses. Supervision of inappropriate behavior is handled primarily by ensuring that alternative incompatible responses are trained. The level of cognitive functioning dictates the variety of methods that are applicable. Some of the possibilities are now described.

Procedure 1

For those with lower cognitive ability, participant modeling is useful. Treatment should be carried out in the setting where the behavior is expected to occur naturally, thus eliminating problems relative to generalization. The therapist walks through the treatment procedure with the client, and reinforcement and feedback about performance is given immediately after the behavior is exhibited. A more detailed description of the procedure to train pedestrian skills is presented by Matson (1980).

Procedure 2

Vicarious learning, or learning by observation, has proved of considerable value with children of normal intelligence but has more limited applicability with mentally retarded children. However, since this is a much more cost-effective and time-efficient procedure than participative modeling, it will be described briefly. In this procedure, the child observes live or taped performances of appropriate behavior. Based on these performances, the child alters his or her behavior to match that of the role model. A typical method would be to have the therapist demonstrate specific behaviors (e.g., socially appropriate statements). The child would merely observe the behavior performed by the therapist. Over time, the same skill may be repeated on a number of occasions.

Generalization and maintenance have not been systematically evaluated. These initial studies do seem to suggest some promising findings in respect to these issues. A clearer delineation of the conditions under which generalization and maintenance are more likely to occur awaits further research.

SELF-CONTROL PROCEDURES

Over the past few years, self-control procedures have begun to increase in popularity, as evinced by the proliferation of studies describing the effective implementation of programs in this area. In Shapiro's (1981) review of this topic with mentally retarded individuals, he states that it is typically implied in the development of self-control techniques that increased independence is a desired outcome. Despite the possible utility of self-control as a means of increasing independent behavior (Mahoney & Mahoney, 1976), little has been done with mentally retarded persons as opposed to persons of normal intelligence. This situation is unfortunate, since clinicians may find these strategies useful. Some of the techniques that have been found effective are described below.

When self-control procedures are being used with mentally retarded persons, particularly children, some limitations arise. The potential problems include limited cognitive capacity, expectations by society that such techniques will not generally be applicable to this population, and developmental issues, such as poor impulse control and psychomotor skill, which could further compromise effectiveness. Certainly, these factors should be considered in skill development, but they should not be considered exclusionary.

The literature on self-control contains a number of inconsistencies in regard to terminology. For example, Karoly (1977) distinguishes between regulation (maintenance) and self-control (change) as methods of self-management, while others use the terms "self-management" and "self-control" indiscriminately (O'Leary & Dubey, 1979; Rosenbaum & Drabman, 1979).

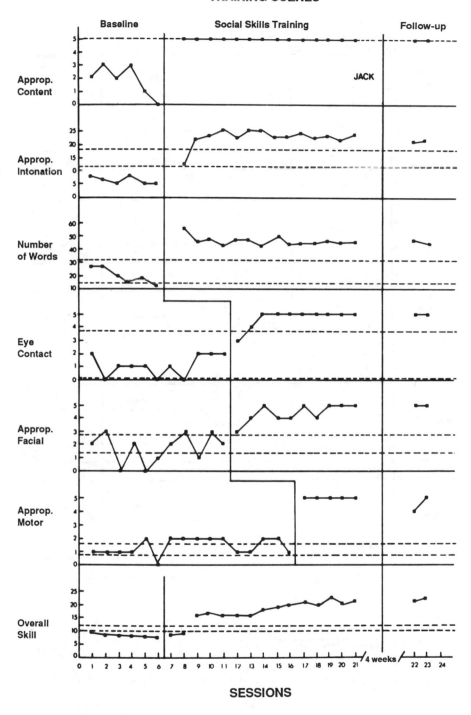

Figure 10.1. Multiple baseline analysis of the effects of training on specific target behaviors and overall rating of social skill for Jack. The horizontal lines depict the range delineated by the mean plus and minus one standard deviation for the validation sample. Due to equipment failure on day 7, audiotaped data for the first three behaviors were not recorded.

TRAINING SCENES

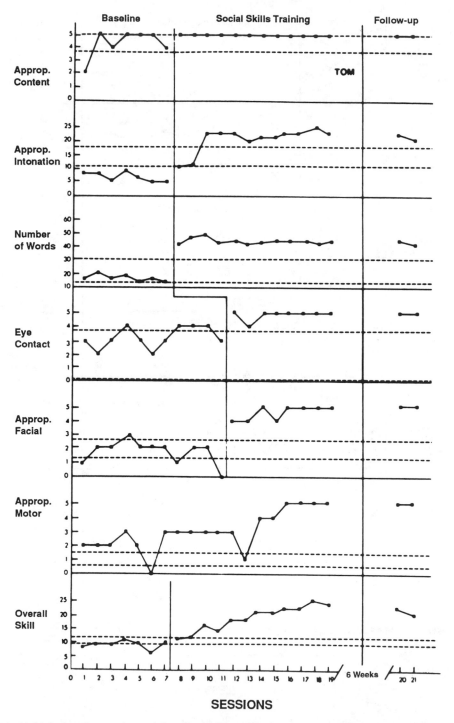

Figure 10.2. Multiple baseline analysis of the effects of training on specific target behaviors and overall rating of social skill for Tom. The horizontal lines depict the range delineated by the mean plus and minus one standard deviation for the validation sample.

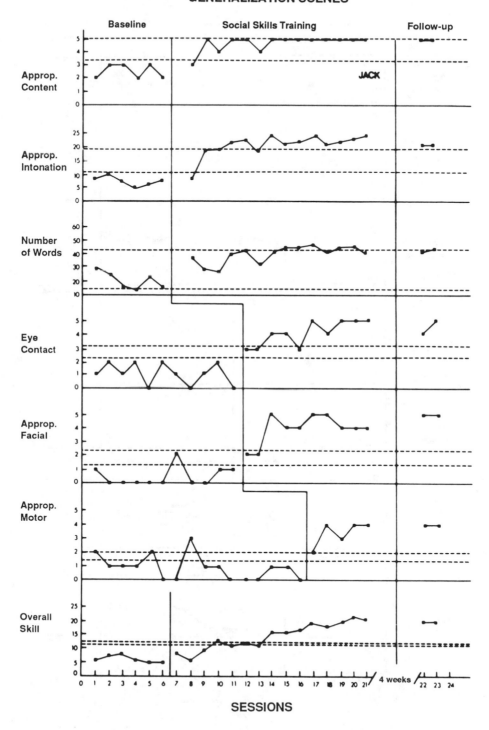

Figure 10.3. Multiple baseline analysis of generalization of training to specific behaviors and overall rating of social skill for Jack. The horizontal lines depict the range delineated by the mean plus and minus one standard deviation for the validation sample.

GENERALIZATION SCENES

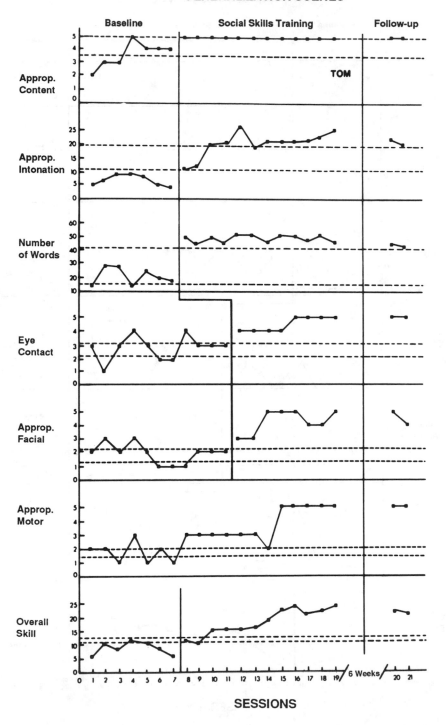

Figure 10.4. Multiple baseline analysis of generalization of training to specific behaviors and overall rating of social skill for Tom. The horizontal lines depict the range delineated by the mean plus and minus one standard deviation for the validation sample.

Table 10.5. Sample Treatment Studies With Social-Learning Methods

AUTHORS	TYPES OF PERSON(S) TREATED	BEHAVIOR TREATED	TREATMENT METHOD
Mahoney, Van Wagenen, & Meyerson (1971)	3 normal-IQ and 5 profoundly to severely mentally retarded children	Toilet training	Modeling, social & edible reinforcers, verbal and physical prompts
Matson, Kazdin, & Esveldt-Dawson (1980)	2 moderately mentally retarded boys (11 and 12 years old)	Verbal and nonverbal social behavior	Modeling, reinforcers, instructions, performance feedback, role playing
Matson (1981b)	3 moderately mentally retarded girls (8 to 10 years old)	Excessive fear of strange adults	Participant modeling, edible and social reinforcers
Egel, Richman, & Koegel (1981)	3 moderately mentally retarded and 1 normal-IQ autistic child	Concept discrimination	Peer modeling, social and edible reinforcers
Matson et al. (1988)	2 profoundly and 1 undetermined mentally retarded adolescent	Verbal and nonverbal social behavior	Modeling, edible and social reinforcers, prompts

Whatever the procedures are called, however, function seems to be generally the same (Shapiro, 1981).

Self-monitoring is generally defined as discriminating the occurrence of one's behavior and recording its occurrence (Nelson, 1977). Self-observation, self-assessment, and self-evaluation, however, are all synonymous terms referring to the initial portion of self-monitoring, with the individual determining whether specific behaviors have occurred. This procedure is followed by the other portion of self-monitoring, recording.

Initial research on self-control with mentally retarded children was conducted by Litrownik and his colleagues. In the first of their studies (Litrownik, Freitas, & Franzini, 1978), the researchers assessed and then trained self-monitoring in moderately mentally retarded children. Thirty children in the moderate-to-severe range of mental retardation were selected for study. Rule-out criteria included inability to draw lines between penciled objects or to discriminate between simple objects and numbers and marked visual and/or motor impairments. Training was in how to self-monitor the number of times the children were able to match body parts (as opposed to geometric shapes) or make appropriate scores on a bowling game by placing a red ring over a peg, thereby ringing a bell.

Training, in the form of verbal and physical prompts, consisted of providing instructions on how to self-monitor. Live demonstrations of appropriate self-monitoring on both tasks was followed by viewing of a color videotape in which self-monitoring for each task was demonstrated. During training, the discriminations needed for accurate self-monitoring were shaped via the modeling and prompting procedures described. It was found that, using the procedures just described, moderately mentally retarded children who could initially self-monitor accurately—after receiving instruction only—could learn this skill in only 1 hour.

As noted earlier, a second step in self-management is evaluation of self-monitored behavior. This skill was the focus of a study by Litrownik, Cleary, Lecklitner, and Franzini (1978). In this study, 24 moderately mentally retarded children 9 to 10 years of age were studied. Two treatment conditions and a control group were employed. The treatment groups differed only in whether they first received live demonstrations or films of a self-evaluation task. The film consisted of five clowns playing the bowling game mentioned in the previous study. Before bowling, each clown announced the score that they were trying to attain. Scores were predetermined and each clown met their standard. The groups were then given an opportunity to set their own standards before bowling. Trained children set their scores at the same level as those observed in training, while controls did not.

In a third study, Litrownik, Lecklitner, Cleary, and Franzini (1978) divided 16 moderately mentally retarded children 9 to 10 years of age into either a treatment or a control group. The simple matching task mentioned in the first study of this series was trained. When children being treated finished the task before a timer bell rang, they were instructed to put a "happy face" on the scoreboard in front of them as a positive self-assessment. If they did not finish before the bell rang, a green square was to be placed on the scoreboard to reflect a negative self-assessment. Following a positive self-assessment, children were to take one edible available from the cup in front of them. A generalization task required the children to match a block design constructed by the experimenter within an allotted time period. Students were then to self-assess and self-reinforce as before.

The results of these studies showed that mentally retarded children could learn to self-monitor and set appropriate criteria (evaluate performance) and that these skills would generalize. These initial results should encourage practitioners and researchers alike to attempt their own variations of these procedures in the future.

Other studies, more applied in focus, that have been conducted using self-management procedures are noted in Table 10.6. One good example of the use of self-management procedures with mentally retarded children is described by Robertson, Simon, Pachman, and Drabman (1979). In their study, 12 mild to moderately mentally retarded children with diagnoses from Down's syndrome to autism were treated for classroom disruption. Behavior was recorded once in the morning and once in the afternoon.

The purpose of training was to establish high levels of appropriate classroom behavior through external controls and then to maintain the behavior by self-management. Training progressed in phases. Initially, a timer was set by the teacher for 10 minutes, and the teacher would tell each child individually whether he or she had been "good," "OK," or "not good" during the preceding 10 minutes. Next, a token program was begun, with the students being rewarded at the end of five 10-minute periods daily. The tokens could be exchanged later for edibles. Self-management followed after these phases; students rated themselves using the three-point scale and tried to match the teacher's ratings. Successful matching was rewarded with points, with no penalty for failure to match. During the next series of phases, the matching requirements were faded to eliminate external evaluation by gradually reducing the number of children allowed to match the teacher. Those not selected to match were given the number of points they awarded themselves. When fading was complete, the students engaged in a complete self-evaluation phase for 13 days in which all self-management procedures were in effect without teacher control. Finally, the use of points was gradually faded out. All this training occurred with considerable success.

Prescription

Training self-control is best attempted for a simple behavior or one that is already in the child's repertoire but exhibits a variable outcome. By employing a response demanding relatively little effort on the child's part, greater attention can be directed toward training self-control. Variable outcome, on the other hand, provides opportunity for practicing monitoring and adjusting of behavior. Checking a school or work assignment provides an important training opportu-

Table 10.6. Sample Treatment Studies With Self-Management Procedures

AUTHORS	TYPES OF PERSON(S) TREATED	BEHAVIOR TREATED	TREATMENT METHOD
Litrownik, Freitas, & Franzini (1978)	30 moderately to severely mentally retarded children (7 to 11 years old)	Self-monitoring of games and perceptual motor tasks	Modeling, prompts, social reinforcement
Litrownik, Cleary, Lecklitner, & Franzini (1978)	24 moderately mentally retarded children (9 to 10 years old)	Self-monitoring of games and perceptual motor tasks	Modeling, instructions
Johnston, Whitman, & Johnston (1980)	3 mildly mentally retarded children	Accuracy on academic tasks	Modeling, verbal prompts, self-instruction
Whitman & Johnston (1983)	9 mildly mentally retarded and borderline children	Math computation skills	Modeling, verbal prompts, edible and social reinforcement, self-instruction
Sowers, Verdi, Bourbeau, & Sheehan (1985)	4 severely to moderately mentally retarded adolescents (18 to 21 years old)	Self-monitoring of task completion	Self-monitoring picture cues

nity. To maintain adequate performance, reinforcement of self-control should be distinguished from reinforcement of performance quality. The trainer should initially model checking the assignment and having the child imitate this sequence. Gradually the trainer provides less and less modeling and feedback. Periodic checks on a random basis are recommended to ensure continued accuracy. Once the self-control behavior is established for the monitoring of one skill, generalization to other skills can be specifically programmed by training and reinforcing monitoring of these other skills.

RECENT DEVELOPMENTS

Errorless Discrimination and Prompt Procedures

Earlier sections on reinforcement and punishment procedures outlined recent advances in behavior modification due to progress in programming consequences. Sensory reinforcement and punishment procedures are prime examples. While continued improvements in treatment outcome may come from increasing reinforcement and punishment effectiveness, it is more likely that developments in instruction methods will provide greater breakthroughs in the long run.

Indicative of this thinking is an increasing interest in manipulating antecedent events to control behavior. Singh and Singh (1984), for example, demonstrated how reading errors by moderately mentally retarded children could be reduced by providing previews of target words just prior to reading exercises. In another study, Katz and Singh (1986) used prompting procedures to increase the recreational activities of an entire school of 45 severely and moderately mentally retarded children and adolescents. Prompts were provided in the form of written and pictorial signs in combination with feedback. Using a multiple-baseline design, the researchers demonstrated increases in both ball-play and jungle-gym activities.

Other programs have employed manipulations of stimulus dimensions to bring behavior under control of appropriate stimuli while minimizing incorrect responses. Mosk and Bucher (1984) tested three procedures: (1) manipulation of stimulus dimensions (stimulus shaping), (2) external prompts, and (3) a combination of these two procedures to determine the most effective

means of teaching pegboard insertion and cleaning skills to moderately and severely mentally retarded individuals. The combination procedure proved most effective. Strand and Morris (1986) compared the relative efficacies of graded stimulus fading, graded prompt fading, and simple trial-and-error learning. Stimuli were presented on a computer monitor and manipulated in size for the graded-stimulus-fading condition. The prompt procedure consisted of a combination of physical, gestural, and verbal cues. Strand and Morris (1986) observed stimulus and prompt fading to be equally effective and both significantly better than trial-and-error learning. In contrast, Richmond and Bell (1983) reported criterion-related prompts to be more effective than trainer prompts in training size discrimination by profoundly mentally retarded adults. Further investigation is needed to determine the relative merits of different prompt and cue procedures.

Generalization and Maintenance Procedures

In the original edition of this book, Matson (1983) commented on the serious lack of research dealing with generalization and maintenance of treatment outcome for mentally retarded persons. While this criticism may apply to much of the behavior therapy literature, it is especially a problem in regard to the behavior of mentally retarded children and adults, who are often under restricted stimulus control. Those studies that have addressed generalization and maintenance of behavior have generated among the most stimulating findings of recent years in the mental retardation field. Van den Pol et al. (1981) and Haring (1985) are two examples of this line of research.

Van Den Pol and his associates (1981) taught restaurant dining skills to three mentally retarded individuals using a program that specifically programmed generalization. The subjects were first taught to perform the skills in a classroom and then prompted to perform these skills at actual restaurants. More recently, Haring (1985) looked at the effects of teaching generalization in one response class on the development of unprogrammed generalization in other response classes. Mentally retarded children were taught to apply play responses to new exemplars of certain toy classes. Assessment was then conducted to see if different responses taught to specific exemplars of other toy classes generalized to new exemplars of those classes. Haring found that limited generalization across classes did in fact occur.

Despite the difficulty of studying and programming generalization and maintenance, their importance cannot be overstated. If behavior therapy is to substantially expand its impact upon the lives of mentally retarded children and their families, future breakthroughs in generalization and maintenance research are absolutely essential.

Parent, Staff, and Peer Training

Over the last few years, a number of researchers have realized the value of teaching individuals who commonly interact with the child how to themselves modify the antecedents and consequences of the child's behavior. Such an approach increases the probability of generalization and maintenance of behavior outside the laboratory and clinic. Given its cost-effectiveness, we expect to see more of this training in the years to come.

Early studies of parent training have indicated the need to specifically train general as opposed to task-specific skills to parents in order to obtain generalization (Koegel, Glahn, & Nieminen, 1978; Miller & Sloane, 1976). One recent study by Cowart, Iwata, and Poynter (1984) demonstrated that the parents of three severely mentally retarded adolescents and adults could teach different tasks when exposed to a program including written instructions, slides, role plays, and performance feedback. Parents practiced training the skills to confederates in a clinical setting and then were assessed teaching different skills to their child in the home.

Other studies have focused on improving how staff interact with and train mentally retarded residents. Ivancic, Reid, Iwata, Faw, and Page (1981) used a combination of procedures to improve staff members' use of antecedent vocalization, descriptive praise, sound imitations, and sound prompts. The subjects of this program were the evening staff in a hospital responsible for the care of 5 profoundly mentally retarded children between the ages of 3 and 7 who were also nonambulatory. Prior to the study's onset, none of the children made identifiable requests, imitated others, or followed commands. Ivancic and his associates began the intervention with an initial in-service, followed by a prompt and

feedback program. This included use of public postings, instructions, and modeling with generalization probes in a second hospital setting. They found that the most significant benefits accrued to increasing antecedent vocalizations with smaller effects for descriptive praise, imitations, and prompts.

Burgio, Whitman, and Reid (1983) evaluated the effectiveness of a participative management approach to improve staff performance. The subjects in this study were 15 severely and profoundly mentally retarded children and adolescents with a mean age of 15 and their 10 direct-care staff. Staff behaviors assessed included (1) the use of contingencies in interactions with residents, (2) staff-to-staff interactions, (3) absence from unit, and (4) nonwork activity. Resident behaviors assessed included (1) appropriate and inappropriate toy contact, (2) interactions with other residents, (3) interactions with staff, (4) disruptive/aggressive behavior, and (5) self-stimulation. The participative-management program consisted of setting of daily goals, self-monitoring, data graphs, and self-praise. The results of this study included an increase in contingent interactions by staff and increased use of toys by residents. Moreover the program was rated high in effectiveness and acceptability.

A Dutch study by Seys and Duker (1986) reported significant increases in staff training and decreases in custodial care and off-task behavior when a program of scheduled activities and supervision—(1) self-recording and public posting, (2) daily staff meetings, and (3) feedback and prompting—was introduced on a ward of a residential facility for severely and profoundly mentally retarded individuals. The combination of scheduled activities and supervision, moreover, was found to be more effective than a program of scheduled activities alone.

Finally, several studies have demonstrated the utility of using peers as confederates to shape the behavior of mentally retarded children. James and Egel (1986) used direct prompting and modeling to increase reciprocal interactions between handicapped and nonhandicapped siblings. The three handicapped siblings ranged in age from 4 years two months to 4 years 6 months. All were severely mentally retarded. The nonhandicapped siblings ranged in age from 6 years 10 months to 8 years one month. Training proceeded in four steps. In the first, a trainer modeled for the nonhandicapped child how to initiate interactions, prompt responses, and then reinforce intiations and responses provided by his or her sibling. In the second step, the nonhandicapped child attempted interaction while the trainer provided cues and feedback. In the third step, the nonhandicapped child was taught how to elicit interaction by controlling access to toys. Finally response priming was used in generalization probes to prompt interactions. Generalization probes differed from training conditions by (1) the addition of untrained peers and (2) the presence of the children's mother rather than a trainer. Subsequently, stimulus control was evaluated by removing the mother from the situation. Follow-up probes were conducted 3 months later. Increases in reciprocal social interaction were noted in all conditions. Odom and Strain (1986) also reported success in increasing social responses by children who were both mentally retarded and autistic, using peers as confederates. The success of such programs warrants their continued investigation.

CONCLUSION

Considerable advances in the interventions available for mentally retarded children have occurred in the last 20 years with the introduction of procedures based on operant conditioning principles. Assessment, particularly as it pertains to identification of antecedents—as well as exciting variations and combinations of basic reinforcement, punishment, and social-learning procedures—have made it possible to modify an ever-wider range of behaviors in a variety of settings. New interest in evaluating the relative efficacies of different interventions should lead to even greater treatment advances. Some reasons for concern, however, exist. Much more research and evaluation are needed, especially with regard to generalization and maintenance of behavior changes. In addition, the present outcry against the use of aversive procedures threatens the availability of interventions that have repeatedly been shown to be effective against a range of life-threatening and debilitating behaviors. There is an urgent need for high-quality early assessment and intervention to permit identification and treatment of deficits early in a child's life. Long-term and systematic intervention should also receive greater priority than has been the case. Findings from the biological and developmental sciences may provide

useful guidance. In turn, future developments in services for mentally retarded children and adults should benefit other populations—for example, infants and individuals incurring brain damage later in life.

REFERENCES

Akesson, H. (1959). *Epidemiology and genetics of mental deficiency in a southern Swedish population.* Sweden: University of Uppsala.

Aman, M. G., Singh, N. N., Stewart, A. W., & Field, C. J. (1985). The Aberrant Behavior Checklist: A behavior rating scale for the assessment of treatment effects. *American Journal of Mental Deficiency, 89,* 485–491.

American Association on Mental Deficiency. (1983). *Classification in Mental Retardation.* Washington, DC: Author.

American Psychiatric Association. (1987). *Diagnostic and statistical manual of mental disorders.* (3rd. ed. rev.). Washington, DC: Author.

Axelrod, S. (1987). Functional and structural analyses of behavior: Approaches leading to reduced use of punishment procedures. *Research in Developmental Disabilities, 8,* 165–178.

Baer, D. M., & Guess, D. (1973). Teaching productive noun suffixes to severely retarded children. *American Journal of Mental Deficiency, 77,* 498–505.

Bandura, A. (1969). *Principles of behavior modification.* New York: Holt, Rinehart & Winston.

Banks, M., & Locke, B. J. (1966). *Self-injurious stereotypes and mild punishment with retarded subjects* (Working Paper No. 123). Parsons, KS: Parsons Research Center.

Barrett, R. P., McGonigle, J. J., Ackles, P. K., & Burkart, J. E. (1987). Behavioral treatment of chronic aerophagia. *American Journal of Mental Deficiency, 91,* 620–625.

Barton, E. S. (1970). Inappropriate speech in a severely retarded child: A case study in language conditioning and generalization. *Journal of Applied Behavior Analysis, 3,* 399–407.

Baumeister, A. A., & Rollings, J. P. (1976). Self-injurious behavior. In N. R. Ellis (Ed.), *International review of research in mental retardation: Vol. 8* (pp. 1–34). New York: Academic Press.

Berg, J. M. (1975). Aetiological aspects of mental subnormality: Pathological factors. In A. M. Clark & A. D. B. Clarke (Eds.), *Mental deficiency: The changing outlook* (pp. 81–117). New York: The Free Press.

Birch, H. G., Richardson, S. A., Baird, D., Harobin, G., & Illsby, R. (1970). *Mental subnormality in the community: A clinical and epidemiological study.* Baltimore, MD: Williams & Wilkins.

Blank, C. E. (1960). Apert's syndrome (a type of acrocephalosyndactyly) observations on a British series of thirty-nine cases. *Annals of Human Genetics, 24,* 151–164.

Bricker, D., Dennison, L., & Bricker, W. A. (1976). A language intervention program for developmentally young children. *MCCD Monograph Series* (No. 1).

Bucker, B., & Lovaas, O. I. (1967). Use of aversive stimulation in behavior modification. In M. R. Jones (Ed.). *Miami symposium on the prediction of behavior, 1967: Aversive stimulation* (pp. 77–145). Coral Gables, FL: University of Miami Press.

Burgio, L. D., Whitman, T. L., & Reid, D. H. (1983). A participative management approach for improving direct-care staff performance in an institution setting. *Journal of Applied Behavior Analysis, 16,* 37–53.

Butz, R. A., & Hasazi, J. E (1973). The effects of reinforcement on perseverative speech in a mildly retarded boy. *Journal of Behavior Therapy and Experimental Psychiatry, 4* 167–170.

Canale, D., Bebin, J., & Knighton, R. S. (1964). Neurologic manifestations of von Recklinghausen's disease of the nervous system. *Confin. Neurology, 24,* 359–403.

Carrier, J. K., & Peak, T. (1973). *Nonspeech language imitation program.* Lawrence, KS: H & H Enterprises.

Cautela, J. R. (1971). Covert extinction. *Behavior Therapy, 2,* 192–200.

Clarke, H. B., & Sherman, J. A. (1975). Teaching generative uses of sentence answers. *Journal of Applied Behavior Analysis, 8,* 321–330.

Coleman, S. L., & Stedman, J. M. (1974). Use of a peer model in language training in an echolalic child. *Journal of Applied Behavior Analysis, 5,* 275–279.

Cook, J. W., Altman, K., Shaw, J., & Blaylock, M. (1978). Use of contingent lemon juice to eliminate public masturbation by a severely

retarded boy. *Behaviour Research and Therapy, 16,* 131–133.

Corbett, J. A. (1979). Psychiatric morbidity and mental retardation. In F. E. James & R. P. Snaith (Eds.), *Psychiatric illness and mental handicap* (pp. 11–25). London: Gaskell.

Coutts, N. A., & Fyfe, N. M. (1971). Classical and mild phenylketonuria in a family. *Archives of Disturbed Childhood, 46,* 550–552.

Cowart, J. D., Iwata, B. A., & Poynter, H. (1984). Generalization and maintenance in training parents of the mentally retarded. *Applied Research in Mental Retardation, 5,* 233–244.

Crome, L. (1960). The brain and mental retardation. *British Medical Journal, 1,* 550–552.

Dewson, M. R. J., & Whiteley, J. H. (1987). Sensory reinforcement of head turning with nonambulatory, profoundly mentally retarded persons. *Research in Developmental Disabilities, 8,* 411–426.

Doke, L. A., & Epstein, L. H. (1975). Oral overcorrection: Side-effects and extended applications. *Journal of Experimental Child Psychology, 88,* 194–202.

Drabman, R. S., Spitalnik, R., & O'Leary (1973). Teaching self-control to disruptive children. *Journal of Abnormal Psychology, 82,* 110–116.

Drillien, C. M., Jameson, S., & Wilkinson, E. M. (1966). Studies in mental handicap. Part I: Prevalence and distribution by clinical type and severity of defect. *Archives of Disturbed Children, 41,* 528–538.

Egel, A. L. (1981). Reinforcer variation: Implications for motivating developmentally disabled children. *Journal of Applied Behavior Analysis, 14,* 345–350.

Egel, A. L., Richman, G. S., & Koegel, R. L. (1981). Normal peer models and autistic children's learning. *Journal of Applied Behavior Analysis, 14,* 3–12.

Epstein, L. H., Doke, L. A., Sajwaj, T. E., Sorrell, S., & Rimmer, B. (1974). Generality and side effects of overcorrection. *Journal of Applied Behavior Analysis, 7,* 385–390.

Fabry, R. D., Mayhew, G. L., & Hanson, A. (1984). Incidental teaching of mentally-retarded students within a token system. *American Journal of Mental Deficiency, 89,* 29–36.

Ferretti, R. P., & Cavalier, A. R. (1983). Critical assessment of overcorrection procedures with mentally retarded persons. In J. L. Matson & F. Andrasik (Eds.), *Treatment issues and innovations in mental retardation* (pp. 241–301). New York: Plenum Press.

Forehand, R., & Baumeister, A. A. (1976). Deceleration of aberrant behavior among retarded individuals. In M. Hersen, R. M. Eisler, & P. M. Miller (Eds.), *Progress in behavior modification: Vol. 2* (pp. 223–278). New York: Academic Press.

Foxx, R. M., & Azrin, N. H. (1973). The elimination of self-stimulatory behavior by overcorrection. *Journal of Applied Behavior Analysis, 6,* 1–14.

Foxx, R. M., & Shapiro, S. T. (1978). The timeout ribbon: A nonexclusionary time-out procedure. *Journal of Applied Behavior Analysis, 11,* 125–136.

Foy, E. W., Eisler, R. M., & Pinkston, S. (1975). Modeling assertion in a case of explosive rages. *Journal of Behavior Therapy and Experimental Psychiatry, 6,* 135–138.

Frame, C. L., & Matson, J. L. (1987). *Handbook of assessment in childhood psychopathology: Applied issues in differential diagnosis and treatment outcome.* New York: Plenum Press.

Goodman, N., & Tizard, J. (1962). Prevalence of imbecility and idiocy among children. *British Medical Journal, 1,* 216–219.

Goodwin, J. E., & Mahoney, M J. (1975). Modification of aggression through modeling: An experimental probe. *Journal of Behavior Therapy and Experimental Psychiatry, 6,* 200–202.

Greene, R. J., & Hoats, D. L. (1971). Aversive tickling: A simple conditioning technique. *Behavior Therapy, 2,* 289–293.

Guess, D., Sailor, W., & Keogh, W. (1977). *Language intervention programs and procedures for handicapped children: A review of the literature.* Final Project Report, U.S. Office of Education, Division of Mental Health and Mental Retardation of the Social and Rehabilitation Services Department of the State of Kansas.

Halpern, L. F., & Andrasik, F. (1980). The immediate and long-term effectiveness of overcorrection in treating self-injurious behavior in a mentally retarded adult. *Applied Research in Mental Retardation, 7,* 59–65.

Haring, T. G. (1985). Teaching between-class generalization of toy play behavior to handicapped children. *Journal of Applied Behavior Analysis, 18,* 127–139.

Hay, W. M., Hay, L. R., & Nelson, R. O. (1977). The adaptation of covert modeling procedures to the treatment of chronic alcoholism and obsessive-compulsive behavior. Two cases reports. *Behavior Therapy, 8,* 70–76.

Hersen, M., & Bellack, A. S. (1976). A multiple baseline analysis of social skills training in chronic schizophrenics. *Journal of Applied Behavior Analysis, 9,* 239–245.

Hopkins, B. L. (1968). Effects of candy and social reinforcement, instruction, and reinforcement schedule learning on the modification and maintenance of smiling. *Journal of Applied Behavior Analysis, 1,* 121–129.

Ivancic, M. T., Reid, D. H., Iwata, B. A., Faw, G. D., & Page, T. J. (1981). Evaluating a supervision program for developing and maintaining therapeutic staff-resident interactions during institutional care routines. *Journal of Applied Behavior Analysis, 14,* 95–107.

Jackson, D. A., & Wallace, R. F. (1974). The modification and generalization of voice loudness in a fifteen-year-old retarded girl. *Journal of Applied Behavior Analysis, 7,* 461–471.

James, S. D., & Egel, A. L. (1986). A direct prompting strategy for increasing reciprocal interactions between handicapped and nonhandicapped siblings. *Journal of Applied Behavior Analysis, 19,* 173–186.

Johnson, J. H., & Thompson, D. J. (1974). Modeling in the treatment of enuresis: A case study. *Journal of Behavior Therapy and Experimental Psychiatry, 5,* 93–94.

Johnson, M. B., Whitman, T. L., & Johnson, M. (1980). Teaching addition and subtraction to mentally retarded children: A self-motivational program. *Applied Research in Mental Retardation, 1,* 141–160.

Kanner, L. (1967). *A history of the care and study of the mentally retarded.* Springfield, IL: Charles C Thomas.

Karoly, P (1977). Behavioral self-management in children: Concepts, methods, issues and directions. In M. Hersen, R. M. Eisler, & P. M. Miller (Eds.), *Progress in behavior modification* (Vol. 5, pp. 197–262). New York: Academic Press.

Katz, R. C., & Singh, N. Y. (1986). Increasing

recreational behavior in mentally retarded children. *Behavior Modification, 10,* 508–519.

Kauffman, J. M., LaFleur, K. L., Hallahan, D. P., & Chanes, C. M. (1975). Imitation as a consequence for children's behavior: Two experimental case studies. *Behavior Therapy, 6,* 535–542.

Koegel, R. L., Glahn, T. J., & Nieminen, G. S. (1978). Generalization of parent-training results. *Journal of Applied Behavior Analysis, 11,* 95–109.

Kushlick, A. (1961). Subnormality in Salford. In M. W. Susser & A. Kushlick (Eds.), *A report on the mental health services of the city of Salford for the year 1960.* Salford Health Department.

Kushlick, A. (1964). *The prevalence of recognized mental subnormality of I.Q. under 50 among children in the south of England, with reference to the demand for places for residential care.* Paper presented at the International Copenhagen Conference on the Scientific Study of Mental Retardation, Copenhagen.

Kushlick, A., & Blunden, R. (1975). The epidemiology of mental subnormality. In A. M. Clarke & A. D. B. Clarke (Eds.), *Mental deficiency: The changing outlook* (pp. 31–81). New York: The Free Press.

Lemkau, P., Tietze, L., & Cooper, M. (1943). Mental-hygiene problems in an urban district. Fourth paper. *Mental Hygiene, 27,* 279–295.

Litrownik, A. H., Cleary, C. P., Lecklitner, G. L., & Franzini, L. R. (1978). Self-regulation in retarded persons: Assessment and training of self-monitoring skills. *American Journal of Mental Deficiency, 86,* 86–89.

Litrownik, A. H., Freitas, J. L., & Franzini, L. R. (1978). Self-regulation in retarded persons: Acquisition of standards for performance. *American Journal of Mental Deficiency, 82,* 499–506.

Litrownik, A. H., Lecklitner, G. L., Cleary, C. P., & Franzini, L. R. (1978). *Acquisition of self-evaluation and self-reward skills and their effects on performance.* Unpublished manuscript, San Diego University.

Lovaas, O. I. (1977). *The autistic child.* New York: Irvington.

Lovaas, O. I., & Newsom, C. D. (1976). Behavior modification with psychotic children. In H. Leitenberg (Ed.), *Handbook of behavior modification and behavior therapy* (pp. 303–360). Englewood Cliffs, NJ: Prentice-Hall.

Lovaas, O. I., & Simmons, J. Q. (1969). Manipulation of self-destruction in three retarded children. *Journal of Applied Behavior Analysis, 2,* 143–157.

Mahoney, M. J., & Mahoney, R. (1976). Self-control techniques with the mentally retarded. *Exceptional Children, 42,* 338–339.

Mahoney, K., Van Wagenen, R. K., & Meyerson, L. (1971). Toilet training of normal and retarded children. *Journal of Applied Behavior Analysis, 4,* 173–181.

Marholin, D., Luiselli, J. K., & Townsend, N. M. (1980). Overcorrection: An evaluation of its rationale and treatment effectiveness. In M. Hersen, R. M. Eisler, & R. M. Miller (Eds.), *Progress in behavior modification* (Vol. 9, pp. 49–80). New York: Academic Press.

Matson, J. L. (1981a). A controlled outcome study of phobias in mentally retarded adults. *Behavior Research and Therapy, 19,* 101–107.

Matson, J. L. (1981b). Assessment and treatment of clinical phobias in mentally retarded children. *Journal of Applied Behavior Analysis, 14,* 141–152.

Matson, J. L. (1982). Treatment of obsessive-compulsive behavior in mentally retarded adults. *Behavior Modification, 6,* 551–567.

Matson, J. L. (1983). Mentally retarded children. In R. J. Morris & T. R. Kratochwill (Eds.), *The practice of child therapy* (pp. 287–309). Elmsford, NY: Pergamon Press.

Matson, J. L., Esveldt-Dawson, K., & O'Donnel, D. (1979). Overcorrection, modeling and reinforcement procedures for reinstating speech in a mute boy. *Child Behavior Therapy, 1,* 363–371.

Matson, J. L., Kazdin, A. E., & Esveldt-Dawson, K. (1980). Training interpersonal skills among mentally retarded and socially dysfunctional children. *Behavior Research and Therapy, 18,* 419–427.

Matson, J. L., Manikam, R., Coe, D., Raymond, K., Taras, M., & Long. N. (1988). Training social skills to severely mentally retarded multiply handicapped adolescents. *Research in Developmental Disabilities, 9,* 195–208.

McCoy, J. F., & Buckwalt, L. A. (1981). Language acquisition. In J. L. Matson and J. R. McCartney (Eds.), *Handbook of behavior modification with the mentally retarded* (pp. 281–330). New York: Plenum Press.

McGrath, M. L., & Kelly, J. A. (1987). Mental retardation. In C. L. Frame & J. L. Matson (Eds.), *Handbook of assessment in childhood psychopathology* (pp. 511–529). New York: Plenum Press.

McLean, J. E., & Snyder. L. K. (1977). *A transactional approach to early language training. Derivation of a model system* (Final Project Report). Nashville, TN: George Peabody College for Teachers.

McMorrow, M. J., Foxx, R. M., Faw, G. D., & Bittle, R. G. (1986). *Looking for the words: Teaching functional language strategies.* Champaign, IL: Research Press.

Miller, S. J., & Sloane, H. N., Jr. (1976). The generalization effects of parent training across stimulus settings. *Journal of Applied Behavior Analysis, 9,* 355–370.

Milunsky, A. (1973). *The prenatal diagnosis of hereditary disorders.* Springfield, IL: Charles C Thomas.

Morris, R. J. (1978). Treating mentally retarded children: A prescriptive approach. In A. P. Goldstein (Ed.), *Prescriptions for child health and education.* Elmsford, NY: Pergamon Press.

Morris, R. J., & Brown, D. K. (1983). Legal and ethical issues in behavior modification with mentally retarded persons. In J. L. Matson & F. Andrasik (Eds.), *Treatment issues and innovations in mental retardation* (pp. 61–95). New York: Plenum Press.

Mosk, M. D., & Bucher, B. (1984). Prompting and stimulus shaping procedures for teaching visual-motor skills to retarded children. *Journal of Applied Behavior Analysis, 17,* 23–24.

Murphy, C. M., & Bootzin, R. R. (1973). Active and passive participation in the contact desensitization of snake fear in children. *Behavior Therapy, 4,* 203–211.

Murphy, G., Callias, M., & Carr, J. (1985). Increasing simple toy play in profoundly mentally handicapped children. I. Training to play. *Journal of Autism and Developmental Disorders, 15,* 375–388.

Murphy, G., Carr, J., & Callias, M. (1986). Increasing simple toy play in profoundly mentally handicapped children: II. Designing special toys. *Journal of Autism and Developmental Disorders, 16,* 45–58.

National Association for Retarded Citizens.

(1972). Residential programming mentally retarded persons. Prevailing attitudes and practice in mental retardation. Grant 56-p-20771-6-01(RI), *Division of Developmental Disabilities, Social Rehabilitation Services,* U.S. Department of Health, Education, and Welfare.

Nelson, R. O. (1977). Assessment and therapeutic functions of self-monitoring. In M. Hersen, R. M. Eisler, & P. M. Miller (Eds.), *Progress in behavior modification* (Vol. 5, pp. 264–308). New York: Academic Press.

Nietzel, M. T., Martorano, R. D., & Melnick, J. (1977). The effects of covert modeling with and without reply training on the development and generalization of assertive responses. *Behavior Therapy, 8,* 183–192.

Odom, S. L., & Strain, P. S. (1986). A comparison of peer-initiation and teacher-antecedent interventions for promoting reciprocal social interaction of autistic preschoolers. *Journal of Applied Behavior Analysis, 19,* 59–71.

O'Leary, S. G., & Dubey, D. R. (1979). Applications of self-control procedures by children: A review. *Behavior Therapy, 9,* 830–842.

Ollendick, T. H., Matson, J. L., & Martin, J. E. (1978). Effectiveness of hand overcorrection for topographically similar and dissimilar self-stimulatory behavior. *Journal of Experimental Child Psychology, 25,* 396–403.

Paniagua, F. A., Braverman, C., & Capriotti, R. M. (1986). Use of a treatment package in the management of a profoundly mentally retarded girl's pica and self-stimulation. *American Journal of Mental Deficiency, 90,* 550–557.

Reichlich, L. L., Spooner, F., & Rose, T. L. (1984). The effects of contingent water mist on the stereotypic responding of a severely handicapped adolescent. *Journal of Behaviour Therapy and Experimental Psychiatry, 15,* 165–170.

Reiss, S., Levitan, G. W., & Szyszko, J. (1982). Emotional disturbance and mental retardation: Diagnostic overshadowing. *American Journal of Mental Deficiency, 86,* 567–574.

Reiss, S., & Szyszko, J. (1983). Diagnostic overshadowing and professional experience with mentally retarded persons. *American Journal of Mental Deficiency, 87,* 396–402.

Richmond, G., & Bell, J. (1983). Comparison of three methods to train a size discrimination with profoundly mentally retarded students. *American Journal of Mental Deficiency, 87,* 564–576.

Rimm, D. C., & Masters, J. C. (1979). *Behavior therapy: Techniques and empirical findings.* New York: Academic Press.

Rincover, A., & Newsom, C. D. (1985). The relative motivational properties of sensory and edible reinforcers in teaching autistic children. *Journal of Applied Behavior Analysis, 18,* 237–248.

Risley, T. (1968). The effects and side effects of punishing the autistic behaviors of a deviant child. *Jounal of Applied Behavior Analysis, 1,* 21–31.

Robertson, S. J., Simon, S. J., Pachman, J. S., & Drabman, R. J. (1979). Self-control and generalization procedures in a classroom of disruptive retarded children. *Child Behavior Therapy, 1,* 347–362.

Roeper, G., Rachman, S., & Mark, I. (1975). Passive and participant modeling in exposure treatment of obsessive-compulsive neurotics. *Behaviour Research and Therapy, 13,* 271–279.

Rolider, A., & Van Houten, R. (1985). Movement suppression time-out for undesirable behavior psychotic and severely developmentally delayed children. *Journal of Applied Behavior Analysis, 18,* 275–288.

Rosen, M., Clark, G. R., & Kivitz, M. S. (1976). *The history of mental retardation* (Vol. 1). Baltimore: University Park Press.

Rosenbaum, M. S., & Drabman, R. S. (1979). Self-control training in the classroom: A review and critique. *Journal of Applied Behavior Analysis, 12,* 467–485.

Ross, D. M., Ross, S. A., & Evans, T. A. (1971). The modification of extreme social withdrawal by modeling with guided participation. *Journal of Behavior Therapy and Experimental Psychiatry, 2,* 273–279.

Rune, V. (1970). Acute head injuries in children: An epidemiologic, child psychiatric and electrocephalographic study of primary school children in Vmean. *Acta Paediatrica Scandinavia* (Suppl. 209), 1–222.

Sailor, W. (1971). Reinforcement and generalization of productive plural allomorphs in two retarded children. *Journal of Applied Behavior Analysis, 4,* 305–310.

Sajwaj, T., & Hedges, D. (1971, April). "Side effects" of a punishment procedure in an oppositional, retarded child. Paper presented at the meeting of the Western Psychological Association, San Francisco.

Sandler, A. G., & McLain, S. C. (1987). Sensory reinforcement: Effects of response-contingent vestibular stimulation on multiply handicapped children. *American Journal of Mental Deficiency, 91,* 373–378.

Sapasnek, D. T., & Watson, L. S., Jr. (1974). The elimination of the self-destructive behavior of a psychotic child: A case study. *Behavior Therapy, 5,* 79–89.

Senatore, V., Matson, J. L., & Kazdin, A. E. (1983). An inventory to assess psychopathology of mentally retarded adults. *American Journal of Mental Deficiency, 89,* 459–466.

Seys, D. M., & Duker, P. C. (1986). Effects of a supervisory treatment package on staff-mentally retarded resident interactions. *American Journal of Mental Deficiency, 90,* 388–394.

Shapiro, E. S. (1981). Self-control procedures with the mentally retarded. In M. Hersen, R. M. Eisler, & P. Miller (Eds.), *Progress in behavior modification* (Vol. 2, pp. 265–297). New York: Academic Press.

Singh, N. N., & Singh, J. (1984). Antecedent control of oral reading errors and self-correction by mentally retarded children. *Journal of Applied Behavior Analysis, 17,* 111–119.

Singh, N. N., Watson, J. E., & Winton, A. S. W. (1986). Treating self-injury: Water mist spray versus facial screening or forced arm exercise. *Journal of Applied Behavior Analysis, 19,* 403–410.

Singh, N. N., Winton, A. S. W., & Ball, P. M. (1984). Effects of physical restraint on the behavior of hyperactive mentally retarded persons. *American Journal of Mental Deficiency, 89,* 16–22.

Sisson, L. A., & Dixon, M. J. (1986). Improving mealtime behaviors through token reinforcement—A study with mentally retarded behaviorally disordered children. *Behavior Modification, 10,* 333–354.

Sowers, J. A., Verdi, M., Bourbeau, P., & Sheehan, M. (1985). Teaching job independence and flexibility to mentally-retarded students through the use of a self-control package. *Journal of Applied Behavior Analysis, 18,* 81-85.

Stewart, C. A., & Singh, N. N. (1986). Overcorrection of spelling deficits in moderately mentally-retarded children. *Behavior Modification, 10,* 355–365.

Simbert, V. E., Minor, J. W., & McCoy, J. F. (1977). Intensive seeding training with retarded children. *Behavior Modification, 1,* 517–529.

Strand, S. C., & Morris, R. C. (1986). Programmed training of visual discriminations: A comparison of techniques. *Applied Research in Mental Retardation, 7,* 165–181.

Tanner, B. A., & Zeiler, M. (1975). Punishment of self-injurious behavior using aromatic ammonia as the aversive stimulus. *Journal of Applied Behavior Analysis, 8,* 53–57.

Touchette, P. E., MacDonald, R. F., & Langer, S. N. (1985). A scatter plot for identifying stimulus control of problem behavior. *Journal of Applied Behavior Analysis, 18,* 343–351.

van Den Pol, R. A., Iwata, B. A., Ivancic, M. T., Page, T. J., Neef, N. A., & Whiteley, F. P. (1981). Teaching the handicapped to eat in public places: Acquisition, generalization and maintenance of restaurant skills. *Journal of Applied Behavior Analysis, 14,* 61–69.

Vukelich, R., & Hake, D. F. (1971). Reduction of dangerously aggressive behavior in a severely retarded person through a combination of positive reinforcement procedures. *Journal of Applied Behavior Analysis, 4,* 215–225.

Vulliamy, D. G., & Normandale, P. A. (1966). Cranio-facial dysostosis in a Dorset family. *Archives of Disturbed Childhood, 41,* 375–382.

Watson, J., Singh, N. N., & Winton, A. S. W. (1986). Suppressive effects of visual and facial screening on self-injurious finger-sucking. *American Journal of Mental Deficiency, 90,* 526–534.

Wheeler, A. J., & Sulzer, B. (1970). Operant training and generalization of a verbal response form in a speech-deficient child. *Journal of Applied Behavior Analysis, 3,* 139–147.

Whitman, T., & Johnston, M. B. (1983). Teaching addition and subtraction with regrouping to educable mentally-retarded children—a group self-instructional training-program. *Behavior Therapy, 14,* 127-143.

CHAPTER 11

CHILDREN MEDICALLY AT RISK

Lawrence J. Siegel
Karen E. Smith
Thomas A. Wood

DEFINITION

Children who would have died a number of years ago are now reaching adolescence and/or young adulthood as a result of advances in biomedical science and medical technology. These children live with chronic medical conditions. Mattsson (1972) has defined a chronic illness as "a disorder with a protracted course which can be fatal or associated with a relatively normal life span despite impaired physical or mental functioning. Such a disease frequently shows a period of acute exacerbations requiring intensive medical attention" (p. 801). Chronic medical conditions of childhood are diverse and include many disease categories such as juvenile rheumatoid arthritis, diabetes, asthma, phenylketonuria, sickle cell disease, leukemia, cystic fibrosis, congenital heart disease, hemophilia, and chronic kidney disease.

Many pediatric chronic diseases individually have a low incidence. However taken together, they represent disproportionate numbers in terms of their use of the health-care system. It is estimated that 10% to 15% of children in the United States will experience one or more chronic medical conditions by 18 years of age (Gortmaker, 1985; Pless & Roghmann, 1971). Medically, most chronic medical conditions are mild in terms of functional limitations. Yet approximately 10% of children with chronic diseases are so severely affected by their medical condition that they exhibit major functional limitations in their daily activities (Haggerty, Roghmann, & Pless, 1975; Hobbs, Perrin, & Ireys, 1985).

A chronic medical condition in childhood is generally assumed to be a major life stressor. These diseases and the various approaches used in their medical management place systematic and unpredictable stresses on the lives of the children and their families. Among other things, these individuals must cope with frequent and painful invasive medical procedures, repeated hospitalizations and clinic visits, surgery, periodic and unpredictable exacerbation of symptoms, physical discomfort, bodily disfigurement, side effects of medication, and the potential for a shortened life expectancy (Mattsson, 1972; Travis, 1976).

A chronic disease can seriously disrupt a family's routines and life-style. In many conditions, children and their families must adhere to complex, long-term regimens that may involve dietary and activity modifications, medication taking, and other daily care routines and medical treatments, such as dialysis for children with chronic kidney disease. Such regimens contribute to a child's feeling of being "different" and can interfere with his or her autonomy needs. This can present a particular problem for adolescents, who want to maintain some degree of independence from their families (Magrab & Calcagno, 1978).

Another factor that contributes to this experience of "feeling different" from one's healthy peers is the physical changes that often occur as a result of the disease process and/or medical treatment. For example, growth failure, facial hair and weight gain from steroids, loss of hair from chemotherapy and radiation treatment, amputations, and crippling of joints in arthritis and hemophilia can all result in reduced self-esteem and can deter normal peer socialization. Peer relationships are also affected by the frequent school absences that these children may experience as a result of numerous hospitalizations and exacerbations of their disease symptoms. Problems associated with academic achievement often are an additional consequence of numerous disruptions in school attendance.

In addition to the impact of the chronic medical condition on the affected child, the condition also imposes a potential strain on other family members and can disrupt family roles and relationships. Conflicts may arise over competing demands imposed by the child's medical condition and the needs of other family members. Each family member shares in the child's suffering and may be affected by the redirecting of physical, emotional, and financial resources necessary for the care of the ill child (Hobbs, Perrin, & Ireys, 1985). Siblings may be particularly vulnerable to the stresses that result from the burdens of caring for a child with a chronic medical condition.

Because of the pervasive stressors to which these children are exposed throughout their lives, it is intuitively appealing to assume that this population is at greater risk for developing considerable problems in psychological adjustment. Early researchers in this area generally concluded that children with chronic diseases were seriously maladjusted compared to their healthy peers and that their families tended to cope poorly (Pless & Pinkerton, 1975). However, the research on which these findings are based had a number of serious methodological problems, including retrospective reports, subjective evaluations and clinical case material, the use of measures with questionable reliability and validity, and a lack of appropriate control groups. Recent, better-designed investigations tend to suggest that children with chronic medical conditions are considerably less deviant when compared with normative groups than was initially noted (Drotar, Owens, & Gotthold, 1980; Gayton, Friedman, Tavormina, & Tucker, 1977; Kellerman, Zeltzer, Ellenberg, Dash, & Rigler, 1980; Kupst & Schulman, 1988; Tavormina, Kastner, Slater, & Watt, 1976).

Current research suggests that although a chronic medical condition can be a life stressor for children and place them at greater risk for adjustment problems than physically healthy children, the disease itself does not appear to be the *primary* cause of more serious emotional and behavioral problems. Rather, it has been suggested that the adjustment problems that these children face (including feelings of anxiety, depression, and anger) are best regarded as normal responses to stressful experiences associated with long-term illness and/or treatment regimens; that is, they cannot be seen as psychiatric disorders (Drotar, 1981; Varni, 1983).

Research has not demonstrated a consistent relationship between objective measures of severity of illness and the occurrence of adjustment problems. Instead, there are many potential determinants of the impact of the child's chronic medical condition on his or her overall adjustment, including age of disease onset, degree of disability, the course of the illness (i.e., progressive, stable, relapsing), life-threatening nature of the disease, visibility of the disease, family dysfunction, level of social support, family resources, and the coping skills of the child and family (Drotar & Bush, 1985; Hobbs et al., 1985; Perrin & Gerrity, 1984; Pless & Pinkerton, 1975). These factors can influence a child's reaction to a chronic medical condition regardless of the specific disease. As a result, researchers have proposed that there are many common aspects to having a chronic condition that cut across diverse physical disease processes. These commonalities have led to a general agreement among researchers to view the psychosocial aspects of chronic medical conditions in children within a noncategorical framework (Hobbs et al., 1985; Pless & Perrin, 1985; Stein & Jessop, 1982, 1984).

The purpose of this chapter is to present an overview of a wide range of psychological approaches used to manage various problem areas that are common to children with chronic medical conditions. As noted earlier, the child who exhibits serious adjustment problems is the exception rather than the rule. Most of these children show considerable resilience in the face of stressful experiences associated with their illness and require minimal psychological intervention (Drotar & Bush, 1985). Most of the problems presented by the child with a chronic medical condition pertain to coping with their disease and medical treatments—problems that affect the tasks of daily living and age-appropriate developmental tasks. The focus of this chapter is on interventions that address these developmental and disease-related tasks.

OVERVIEW OF ASSESSMENT ISSUES

The reasons for assessing children who are medically at risk are generally multifaceted and can be prompted by general as well as specific, acute concerns. An assessment can be used to provide diagnostic information regarding the child's current medical status, level of psychosocial functioning, and how these factors may interact so that appropriate interventions can be initiated. A second purpose could be to document the impact of medical and psychological interventions. Similarly, assessment information may be used to determine the effect of the medical condition over time, irrespective of interventions. Evaluations may be needed to address very specific concerns raised by health-care providers, the child, and/or parents. Finally, assessments can be an important tool in terms of prevention by helping to identify strengths and vulnerabilities that may shake the child's overall adjustment.

There are particular times during the treatment of a medical condition that may be more stressful or anxiety-provoking than others. These include the period of initial diagnosis as well as transition points in the medical treatment and the child's own development. Therefore, the context in which the evaluation is made and the timing with regard to duration of illness, stage of medical treatment, and general physical and emotional growth and development should be considered in collecting data and interpreting results.

Assessment must cover both medical and psychosocial areas, with particular attention as to how they influence each other. The scope of areas assessed will depend upon whether a question has been raised about a specific area of functioning or whether a more general picture of the child's adjustment is needed. Leventhal (1984) has posed six questions that can be used to guide a global clinical assessment:

> What is the extent of the disease and its complications in the child? What are the physical effects of the illness on the child? How has the illness affected the child's performance at home, with peers, and at school? How has the child adjusted to the illness, including an understanding of the disease, a view of self, and relationships with important people in the child's life? What impact does the child's illness have on the family and its members? How has the family adjusted to the special impact or burden of the illness? (p. 71–72)

These questions outline the importance of understanding the impact of a medical condition on the child, his or her family system, and his or her functioning in other important systems like school. In addition, answers to these questions depend, in part, upon a comparison with the child's previous level of psychological adjustment and development. Given that a child's understanding of his or her medical condition is often essential to adjustment and, in some cases, to medical management, a careful evaluation of the child's cognitive-developmental level is essential (Elkind, 1985). Although intellectual functioning as assessed by standardized intellectual tests is one means to ascertain cognitive-developmental level, an assessment using a Piagetian framework may be more useful in this regard. If the child is reasonably intelligent, one may first want to know how he or she is making sense of the world; then one can try to offer help by explaining his or her medical condition and its treatment. This will be particularly important if the child is expected to participate in the ongoing medical management of the condition, as with insulin-dependent diabetes (Ingersoll, Orr, Herrold, & Golden, 1986). Age is often inappropriately used as a measure of cognitive development; tools are available for a more individualized assessment (Burbach & Peterson, 1986).

In adjusting to the diagnosis of a chronic medical condition, both child and parents bring to this situation coping behaviors learned through various life experiences (Lazarus & Folkman, 1984; Siegel & Smith, 1989). Therefore, it may be helpful to ask children and their parents directly how they have coped with previous stressful situations, so as to gain some idea of their experience with prior stressful events, types of coping strategies used, and their perceived success. (Melamed, Siegel, & Ridley-Johnson, 1988). This offers the health-care provider an opportunity to reinforce coping behaviors that are likely to facilitate successful adjustment to the current medical condition and all that it involves. In addition, strategies that might have a negative effect on adjustment can be identified and discussed.

Just as knowledge of previous stressful situations can help identify and anticipate the use of various coping strategies by the child and parent, a careful assessment of parenting style can aid in the identification of families who may be at risk for parent–child problems or health-care provider–child problems. For example, is this a child whose parents have been inconsistent in their expectations for responsibilities and limit setting when appropriate? Are these parents who, prior to the medical diagnosis, typically were more protective of the child, being reluctant to let him or her engage in age-appropriate activities away from home?

A variety of paper-and-pencil measures are available to assess a number of psychological constructs that may be relevant to the child with a chronic medical condition. These include anxiety, depression, self-esteem, behavior problems, hospital-related fears, impact of illness on family, family adaptability and cohesion, parenting stress, and coping strategies (Karoly, 1988). The majority of these measures include some normative references as to how children of different ages and/or gender typically respond to the questionnaire. Yet with few exceptions, the normative samples comprise children without any significant medical conditions. Questions have been raised as to the appropriateness of these norms for children with significant medical conditions (Beck & Smith, 1988).

Instruments for intellectual and academic assessment can be used to address specific concerns regarding changes in cognitive functioning and/or academic progress. These tools are often used to determine the impact of a chronic med-ical condition (Franceschi et al., 1984; Ryan, 1988) or a medical treatment (Copeland, et al., 1985; Stehbens, Kisker, & Wilson, 1983) on cognitive abilities. As can be surmised, assessment of the child who is medically at risk can be complex, requiring expertise in a variety of areas. Therefore, it is important that the assessment process involve an interdisciplinary team (Varni & Babani, 1986). Children with medical conditions receive periodic evaluation of the condition itself; some level of ongoing psychosocial assessment should be included to facilitate optimal total health care (Drotar & Bush, 1985). Assessments for specific, acute problems may be handled quickly and intervention initiated promptly. An evaluation of current psychological functioning and the impact a medical condition may have on the child and family will require more time and can become very complex.

INTERDISCIPLINARY APPROACH TO TREATMENT

Given the diversity of physical, psychological, and social issues that may be involved in the treatment of children and adolescents with medical conditions, the experts involved in the health care of this population must reflect this same diversity (Hobbs et al., 1985; Klerman, 1985; Magrab & Calcagno, 1978; Varni & Babani, 1986). The ideal approach to total health care in this population calls for an interdisciplinary team composed of a physician, mental-health professional, and other allied health-care professionals. The advantage to this system is the collaboration that can occur in the assessment of children with medical conditions and in the development of treatment plans that are sensitive to both medical and psychosocial needs. An additional advantage for the mental-health professional in working within a team framework is that his or her involvement in the child's treatment may be more readily accepted. If the mental-health professional is perceived by the child and family as "another team member," there is often less resistance to needed psychological intervention. Families or individual family members do not have to feel "singled out" when a psychological intervention is suggested, as this type of intervention is "routine." In this vein, Cameron (1978) has suggested that simultaneous medical and psychological assessment and treatment, as opposed to a sequential one, may help minimize patient's negative reactions to a psychological referral. Since coping with a medical condition is an ongoing, dynamic process, the continuity of having a psychological expert on the team—one who is known to the family—can facilitate the therapeutic relationship when psychological interventions are needed.

The concept of an interdisciplinary team must include the child and family as active, participating members. This philosophy is crucial for medical conditions such as insulin-dependent diabetes mellitus, cystic fibrosis, and others, where the child and family are actively involved in medical management of the condition on a daily basis. As will be noted later, the inclusion of patients in the development of a treatment plan will contribute to greater adherence and feelings of personal responsibility for self-care (Meichenbaum & Turk, 1987). Involvement in decision making may promote a greater sense of perceived control in parents and older children and enhance feelings of self-efficacy in managing what oftentimes can be a rigorous treatment plan.

MEDICAL CONDITION AND TREATMENT

Acquisition of Information

Education of medically-at-risk children and families regarding the medical condition and necessary treatment is important for a variety of practical and psychological reasons. Informed consent by the parent and/or child, if of legal age, is necessary to provide appropriate medical assessment and treatment as with chemotherapy for cancer patients or a kidney biopsy in a child with end-stage renal disease. With some medical conditions—such as insulin-dependent diabetes mellitus, cystic fibrosis, or spina bifida—active participation in medical management is required of the child and parent. Without accurate knowledge, such participation is not possible. Psychologically, providing information can facilitate adjustment to the medical condition and treatment by decreasing anxiety (Melamed, 1982; Shaw, Stephens, & Holmes, 1986) and in some instances by increasing perceptions of control (Jamison, Lewis, & Burish, 1986; Nannis, Susman, Strope, & Woodruff, 1982). Given that the patient's knowledge is related to obtaining informed consent, to increasing active participation in medical care or adherence, and to facil-

itating psychological adjustment, it is important to consider factors that may affect how children and their parents acquire information. Cognitive-developmental level, coping style, and timing are all variables that can affect the acquisition of information.

A number of investigations have documented the relationship between cognitive-developmental level and conception of illness in children both with and without a significant medical condition (Bibace & Walsh, 1979; Brewster, 1982; Perrin & Gerrity, 1981; Shagena, Sandler, & Perrin, 1988; Susman, Dorn, & Fletcher, 1987). In general these studies indicate that the child's conception of illness becomes more sophisticated as his or her cognitive abilities mature through the preoperational, concrete operational, and formal operational levels of development (Piaget, 1929). Through systematic investigations, Bibace and Walsh (1979) have identified six levels of understanding of illness: (1) phenomenism, (2) contagion (preoperational), (3) contamination, (4) internalization (concrete operational), (5) physiological, and (6) psychophysiological (formal operational), which are briefly summarized in Table 11.1.

The documented relationship between children's cognitive reasoning abilities and their ability to understand the concept of illness has direct clinical implications when one is trying to teach children about their own medical conditions and management. As noted by Brewster (1982), providing accurate information to children does not necessarily result in accurate knowledge for several reasons: ". . . children have their own conceptions of what has happened to them, their ability to assimilate the information is limited and they often distort what they are told, and other factors, unrelated to cognition, may have a greater bearing on their responses to treatment" (p. 355). At the very minimum, educational programs must be developmentally based. They should incorporate instruction geared to the child's developmental level or one stage above, as it has been suggested that children can understand explanations one level beyond their current level of cognitive reasoning (Kohlberg, 1963; Turiel, 1969). Educational programs should routinely elicit the child's current understanding about how he or she came to have the medical condition and what he or she thinks will need to be done to manage it. Attempts to correct any misperceptions or distortions in the child's

Table 11.1. Developmental Stages of Children's Conceptualizations of Illness

APPROXIMATE AGE RANGE	PIAGETIAN STAGE	CAUSAL UNDERSTANDING OF ILLNESS
3 to 7	Preoperational	*Phenomenism:* illness due to magical process or an event that happened at same time as symptom occurred. *Contagion:* illness the result of some event that was linked spatially or temporally; direct contact not required.
8 to 12	Concrete operational	*Contamination:* illness the result of contact through germs, dirt, or misbehavior. *Internalization:* illness due to an external contaminant that has entered the body in some observable manner.
13 and older	Formal operational	*Physiological:* illness due to the malfunctioning of internal body parts or processes. *Psychophysiological:* illness can have psychological causes and symptoms in addition to physiological.

Adapted from Bibace & Walsh (1979).

thinking should again be geared toward his or her current level of reasoning or one stage beyond. An understanding of the child's level of cognitive reasoning will also allow the health-care provider to respond more effectively to fears and concerns related to the medical condition and treatment (Bibace & Walsh, 1979). For example, a child at the preoperational level may feel that the bone marrow aspiration she has to undergo is a punishment for some imagined or real misdeed, resulting in even greater pretreatment anxiety. The health-care provider can listen emphathetically and reassure her that the procedure is not intended to punish her but to see if the "special medicine" (chemotherapy) is doing its job. Concerns regarding the long-term implications of having a medical condition are unlikely to be reported until the child has achieved the formal operational reasoning level. At this point, concerns regarding how the medical condition or treatment may affect relationships with others—as well as plans for the future—should be expected (Allen, Affleck, Tennen, McGrade, & Ratzan, 1984).

Understanding something about cognitive reasoning can help clinicians in developing appropriate expectations for adherence to a prescribed treatment regimen. For children at the preoperational stage, incorporating the necessary behaviors into the current daily routine—with appropriate praise and rewards from parents when the behavior is performed—is likely to result in greater adherence than discussing the benefits of such behavior with the child. Informational statements about how certain adherence behaviors, like taking medication, will make the child feel better are more likely to have a beneficial effect on children as they reach the concrete operational stage of internalization.

Using a cognitive-developmental framework to foster adherence during adolescence can be of particular importance. Yet it should be remembered that even though an adolescent may be capable of more complex cognitive reasoning, this skill may not always be used. Since the child is "older," health-care providers and parents can automatically raise their expectations regarding independent adherence behaviors; a step which may not always be appropriate. For example, with more complicated treatment programs, such as those required of a child with diabetes, the ability to make adjustments in insulin dose has been associated with cognitive maturity (Ingersoll, Orr, Herrold, & Golden, 1986), which does not necessarily correlate with age. In addition, greater cognitive maturity, which theoretically should enable greater independent adherence, comes at a time when other concerns, such as peer relationships and social activities, may take priority over caring for one's medical condition. Therefore, a decrease in adherence may actually be observed, especially when the behavior must be performed in a social setting (e.g., for an adolescent with diabetes, following a meal plan; or, for an adolescent with spina bifida, excusing oneself to catheterize). In addition, greater cognitive sophistication enables the adolescent to think about his or her medical condition and the impact it has had on his or her life in a more complex manner. The adolescent can begin to think about what life would have been like *without* the condition and treatment. As a result, an adolescent who previously appeared to have adjusted well to having a chronic medical condition may experience feelings of depression, anger, or other psychological reactions to these cognitions (Elkind, 1985).

Acquisition of information may also be affected by the child's style of coping with medical procedures and the medical condition. The assessment of preferred coping style is a relatively new area of investigation that has taken several approaches. One of these has been to identify specific behavioral coping strategies that children use when confronted with medical procedures or other stressful events (Siegel, 1983). Another approach has been to investigate children's preferences for obtaining or avoiding information related to required medical procedures and disease states (Peterson & Toler, 1986; Levenson, Pfefferbaum, Copeland, & Silberberg, 1982; Smith, Ackerson, & Blotcky, 1989). These initial investigations suggest that children, like adults, differ, even after controlling for age, in how much information they prefer (Peterson & Toler, 1986). For children with cancer, the preferred coping style regarding information appears to be related to duration of illness (Smith et al., 1989; Levenson et al., 1982). Children who have had their disease for a shorter period of time are less likely to want additional information regarding it or detailed information during the invasive medical procedures necessary for treatment. For these patients, an avoidant coping style may be the means of dealing with this potentially life-threatening disease.

If children have preferred coping styles regarding the level of information they receive about their medical condition and treatment, an important question is raised. Should health-care providers attempt to offer detailed information to those children who would prefer not to have that level of information? For medical conditions that require life-style changes and active participation by the child in medical management, it would be difficult to honor the child's desire not to have detailed information. For medical conditions where these factors are not an issue, the question posed must be addressed empirically, as one may hypothesize that providing information to a child who prefers an avoidant coping style may result in negative repercussions such as adjustment difficulties. One study has addressed this question in pediatric cancer patients undergoing invasive medical

procedures (Smith, et al., 1989). Children who preferred to avoid information but were given detailed information about what was happening and what they might think and feel during the medical procedures actually gave lower subjective reports of experienced pain than did those who were offered verbal distraction during the procedures. Therefore, it may not always be detrimental to provide an intervention that seems inconsistent with a child's preferred coping style. Certainly further information is needed across a variety of medical conditions and settings before definitive statements can be made.

When patient education is necessary to facilitate adherence, it is important to remember that the timing of that education in relation to the diagnosis is important. Patients and their families typically react emotionally upon hearing a diagnosis of a chronic medical condition, and this may well interfere with their ability to process additional information (Meichenbaum & Turk, 1987). It may be prudent to provide basic skills initially, with the timing of further education dependent upon when the family has had an opportunity to work through emotions generated by the diagnosis.

In summary, there are multiple factors that health-care providers need to consider in developing educational approaches to enhance parents' and children's knowledge about medical conditions and treatment. These factors should also be considered when professionals involved in medical care speculate about what children "should" or "need to know." In those situations where children need information to participate in their own care, it is extremely important to remember that adequate knowledge does not necessarily translate into adequate adherence or performance of necessary self-care. The application of knowledge may be inhibited by a variety of factors, including the child's emotional adjustment, level of self-control, and perceptions of self-efficacy.

Management of Pain and Discomfort

Pain is a special source of stress for a number of children with diseases such as arthritis, hemophilia, sickle cell disease, kidney disease, and cancer (Travis, 1976). Many children with chronic medical conditions must endure chronic pain associated with the disease process. Much of the stress that occurs with chronic pain results from the unpredictability of painful episodes and their degree of severity. Chronic pain not only results in considerable discomfort for these children but it can interfere with the activities of daily living. It can cause social isolation and lead to dependence on analgesic medications as well as on the medical care system (Varni & Gilbert, 1982; Walco & Dampier, 1987).

Chronic pain, longstanding and intractable, is caused by severe injury or progressive disease (Bonica, 1977). Fordyce (1976) has noted that although pain may result from underlying organic pathology, environmental consequences can modify and further maintain various aspects of chronic pain behaviors. These include a number of observable pain responses such as complaining, grimacing, restricted body movement, inactivity, and medication use. They may, in turn, be affected by socioenvironmental consequences. Thus, the patient's family and medical staff may actually help him or her to learn chronic pain behaviors by inadvertently reinforcing overt manifestations of pain. Consequences such as attention and sympathy from others, rest, and the avoidance of unpleasant duties and responsibilities, for example, can eventually maintain the pain behaviors independent of disease-related factors (Bonica, 1977).

Because pain is a private, subjective experience, it is important to evaluate factors that may affect individual differences in pain perception and pain behavior (Varni, 1983). For children, these factors include the child's cognitive-developmental level, attitude toward the pain, previous experiences with pain events, perceived ability to handle pain (i.e., self-efficacy), and repertoire of coping skills, as well as family influences that which may provide reinforcement and models for pain behavior (Siegel & Smith, 1989). Given the complex nature of pain in children, an adequate assessment of pain problems in this population calls for an interdisciplinary approach that includes an evaluation of self-report, cognitive, behavioral, social-environmental, and medical factors (Lavigne, Schulein, & Hahn, 1986a, 1986b; Thompson & Varni, 1986; Varni, 1983).

A variety of behavioral intervention strategies have been used in the management of chronic pain in children (Masek, Russo, & Varni, 1984). Varni (1983) has noted that behavioral techniques used in the management of pain can be classified as being methods that regulate either pain *perception* or pain *behavior*. In the former approaches, the child is taught to regulate or modify his or her perception of pain through self-regulatory methods such as hypnosis, guided imagery, relaxation, and biofeedback training. Techniques to regulate pain behavior involve the manipulation and modification of environmental events that are seen as maintaining pain behaviors. In this latter approach, environmental events such as social attention, entertainment, and special activities are systematically controlled and made to occur contingent on age-appropriate, adaptive behaviors. Family members are taught to respond to the child in ways that reduce pain-related disability and to maximize healthy behaviors.

Zeltzer, Dash, and Holland (1979) describe a treatment program for helping adolescents with sickle cell disease to deal with painful vasoocclusive crises that occur when misshapen sickle cells block the flow of blood in small blood vessels. These adolescents were taught to use a self-hypnosis procedure that involved eye fixation and progressive muscle relaxation. Following this induction procedure, the subjects were instructed in guided imagery involving a pleasant scene and given suggestions for body warmth and dilation of their blood vessels. After learning these techniques, the adolescents were told to use these procedures at the onset of a painful crisis. Using thermal biofeedback equipment, this intervention was found to increase peripheral skin temperature significantly (indicating that they had learned to produce vasodilation) and to reduce the frequency and intensity of pain crises and analgesics used over an 8-month period. Reductions in outpatient visits and total number of days of hospitalization were also noted.

Varni and his associates (Varni, 1981; Varni & Gilbert, 1982) have investigated the use of self-regulation techniques in the control of chronic arthritic pain in children with hemophilia. This pain typically results from repeated bleeding episodes in the joints. The treatment program involved progressive muscle relaxation training, meditative breathing, and guided imagery. The patients were instructed to imagine themselves in a scene associated with warmth and pain relief. These techniques were effective in reducing the number of days of perceived chronic pain and analgesic medication use. Improvements were also noted in the patients' mobility and sleep. Monitoring by means of thermal biofeedback equipment indicated that skin temperature increased over the targeted joints.

Adherence to Therapeutic Regimens

No discussion of medically at-risk children would be complete without specific attention to the issue of adherence to medical and/or behavioral therapeutic regimens. Therapeutic regimens vary—depending upon the medical condition—in the specific components involved (e.g., taking medication, dietary changes, exercise, etc.), the complexity of the regimen, and the duration of treatment. Typically the purpose of the regimen is to facilitate optimal physiological functioning in the child via management of the medical condition, though with some diseases, such as leukemia and other cancers, the purpose of treatment is curative. More often than not, the regimen must be adhered to over longer period of time, often years, whereas more acute problems such as infections may call for briefer treatments.

In keeping with current nomenclature, the term "adherence" rather than "compliance" is being used. Often these terms have been used interchangeably, though recent discussions in the literature have argued for consistent use of "adherence" (Kasl, 1975; Varni & Wallender, 1984), as this term connotes a more active, collaborative patient role. "Compliance," on the other hand, connotes a passive, obedient, "do what the doctor says" role that no longer seems to apply to patient–physician relationships. In addition, the term "noncompliance" has a negative connotation often implying that the patient alone is to blame for not following a therapeutic regimen (Meichenbaum & Turk, 1987). In fact, some treatment prescriptions may be too vague, too complex, or misunderstood due to poor communication between patient and physician. Therefore, the term "adherence" is recommended and is used throughout this chapter.

Studies of adherence to medical regimens indicate that a significant number of patients do not adhere, with estimates ranging from 10% to 60% in pediatric practice (La Greca, 1988). Typically, adherence to treatment for chronic medical condtions is lower than that for acute problems (Haynes, 1976). In general, studies that attempt to assess adherence are faced with several methodological issues that can affect the results. Adherence is often difficult to operationalize (e.g., at what point is a person classified as nonadherent?) (La Greca, 1988). It is a difficult concept to assess adequately (Rudd, 1979; La Greca, 1988), and results obtained may be biased in that people who are not adherent are less likely to participate in these studies (Cluss & Epstein, 1985).

Of particular concern to the clinician is the ability to assess adherence. A variety of methods have been used, including self- or parent monitoring, interviews and 24-hour recall, biochemical markers, pill counts, and clinical outcome or health status (Johnson, Silverstein, Rosenbloom, Carter, & Cunningham, 1986; Meichenbaum & Turk, 1987; Parrish, 1986). Each method has its disadvantages, though Parrish (1986) has noted that while self- or parent report may overestimate adherence, it may be the most efficient means of obtaining the data. Good interviewing skills can enhance the accuracy of reporting nonadherent behaviors. Interviews can be advantageous in that information regarding obstacles to adherence can often be gleaned from parents' and patients' responses (Parrish, 1986). Interviews that focus on recent periods of time and ask specifically what the patient did or did not do will enhance the accuracy of patient or parent reports (Johnson et al., 1986).

Czajkowski and Koocher (1986) have developed an instrument that predicts nonadherence in patients with cystic fibrosis. The Medical Compliance Incomplete Stories Test is composed of five stories where the main character is faced with the decision of whether or not to follow medical recommendations. The patient is required to complete the story and note what the outcome for the character will be. Responses to the story are scored for compliance/coping, optimism, and self-efficacy. This innovative approach to predicting adherence seems easily adaptable to other situations and may be another means of identifying patients at risk for nonadherence.

The use of clinical outcome or health status as a measure of adherence represents a significant tautological problem and requires the assumption that the most effective treatment for that individual has been prescribed (Johnson, 1988; Pickering, 1979). Therefore, until more is known regarding the relationship between clinical outcome and adherence, the use of the former to assess the latter is discouraged (Johnson, 1988). Moreover, in future investigations, it will be more helpful to include both adherence and health-status measures to facilitate a greater understanding of the relationship among these measures and variables that may affect one or both of them (La Greca, 1988; Johnson, 1988).

A variety of factors have been correlated with adherence, including duration and complexity of treatment, health beliefs regarding the medical condition and treatment, patient's level of knowledge and skill, presence of symptoms and effect of treatment on symptoms, and patient satisfaction with medical treatment and relationship with the health-care provider. A comprehensive review of this extensive literature is beyond the scope of this chapter; the reader is referred to other sources for a more thorough discussion (Haynes, 1976; Janis, 1984; La Greca, 1988; Meichenbaum & Turk, 1987). It is important to conceptualize adherence as a dynamic rather than a static process as adherence is apt to change over time, particularly for chronic conditions (Meichenbaum & Turk, 1987). In addition, adherence is not an "all or none" situation in that, with more complex regimens, adherence to one aspect of the treatment is not necessarily related to adherence to others (Johnson, et al., 1986; Schafer, Glasgow, McCaul, & Dreher, 1983). For example, an adolescent may almost always take his insulin injections at the appropriate time, although he may rarely follow an appropriate meal plan. Therefore, adherence must be assessed periodically over time and adherence to different treatment components should be assessed separately.

The complexity of a regimen and the specificity of recommendations made by the health-care provider are two factors, related to the treatment regimen itself, which have been associated with adherence (Haynes, 1976; Meichenbaum & Turk, 1987). One practical guideline is to keep treatment demands that are placed on patients and their families as simple as possible. Therefore, if a medication can be administered in one dose each day versus two or three, then the simpler regimen is more likely to facilitate adherence. Yet some treatment regimens, such as those typically prescribed for diabetes or cystic fibrosis, are quite complex and/or require multiple steps that can interfere with day-to-day functioning. In these cases in particular, adherence may be enhanced by trying to fit the regimen into the patient's life-style rather than the reverse (Meichenbaum & Turk, 1987).

Specific guidelines as to the particular behaviors a patient should follow and when these should be performed is another practical step that can improve adherence. While this is a seemingly simple guideline, in some instances health-care providers may be unaware that their recommendations lack specificity. Zola (1981) provides multiple examples of treatment prescriptions that may sound clear to the health-care provider yet can be confusing to the patient. For example, " 'Take the drug 4 times a day.' Does this mean every 6 hours? That is, must the patient wake up in the middle of the night? What if the patient forgets; should he or she take twice the dose when he or she remembers?" (p 247).

Obviously patients and their families must possess knowledge about the disease and be able to perform the behaviors necessary to follow the appropriate treatment plan. Although issues related to patient education were reviewed in a previous section, it should be remembered that knowledge and skill are necessary but not sufficient conditions to promote adherence (Lorenz, Christensen, & Pichert, 1985; McCaul, Glasglow, & Schafer, 1987). Varni and Babani (1986) provide a cogent review of behavioral methods used to facilitate education and implementation of treatment regimens, with specific attention to antecendents and consequences that may interfere with adherence. Reduction of symptoms has been associated with greater adherence to health-care-provider recommendations (Arnhold et al., 1970; Shope, 1981). Yet with some chronic medical conditions, following a prescribed treatment regimen may have no obvious, immediate effect; due to this, many children do not adhere to therapeutic regimens. In some situations adherence may result in aversive symptoms, such as nausea or hair loss with chemotherapy or increased weight due to prednisone therapy in children with renal transplants. Therefore the immediate consequence of adherent behavior may be unnoticeable or aversive. For example, Dolgin, Katz, Doctors, and Siegel (1986) found greater nonadherence associated with more treatment side effects and visible physical changes in one sample of children and adolescents with cancer. Moreover, some health-care providers and/or parents may feel that maintaining good health or preventing future complications should be sufficient motivators to ensure adherence in children and adolescents. Cognitive developmental level and concerns about feeling different are often not taken into consideration when this perception is held. To facilitate adherence over longer periods of time, Varni and Babani (1986) suggest that external positive reinforcers may be necessary to increase motivation to engage in adherent behaviors.

One of the primary means of promoting adherence is to foster a collaborative relationship between the health-care provider, the patient, and his or her family (Korsch, Gozzi, & Francis, 1968; Korsch, & Negrete, 1972; Meichenbaum & Turk, 1987). In dealing with the chronic medical problems over time, the relationship between the family and the medical care system is particularly important if obstacles to adherence or dissatisfaction with treatment are to be uncovered and if the health-care provider is to be an effective motivator for adherent behaviors. Good communication skills and rapport as well as continuity of care appear to be important ingredients to fostering such a relationship (Meichenbaum & Turk, 1987). The Health Belief Model (Becker & Rosenstock, 1984; Rosenstock, 1985) may be a useful heuristic device to aid the health-care provider in understanding current adherence or nonadherence (DiMatteo & DiNicola, 1982). A patient's perceived susceptibility to such things as future complications, availability of reminders to engage in the necessary adherent behaviors, perceived obstacles and the costs/benefits ratio of engaging in the required behaviors, and beliefs regarding one's ability to perform the required behaviors (e.g., self-efficacy) should all be assessed to more clearly understand why a patient may not adhere to a prescribed treatment regimen (Becker & Rosenstock, 1984; Rosenstock, 1985). In addition, the patient's beliefs regarding the treatment's effectiveness should be addressed.

Several studies with children and adolescents with chronic medical conditions highlight the importance of these factors. McCaul, Glasglow, and Schafer (1987) found that self-efficacy beliefs were the strongest predictors across adherence behaviors in adolescents with diabetes. Brownlee-Duffeck et al. (1987) found that perceived costs was significantly predictive of adherent behaviors in adolescents with IDDM. Yet Czajkowski and Koocher (1986) sensitively note that some patients may not express their beliefs regarding the medical condition and or treatment in a direct manner. Using the Medical Compliance Incomplete Stories described earlier, patients' responses revealed negative and depressing feelings regarding the future that had not been directly expressed.

The role of the family and other sources of social support in facilitating adherence has been addressed (see reviews by La Greca, 1988; Meichenbaum & Turk, 1987; Parrish, 1986). Specific examples include the finding that in adolescents with diabetes, negative interactions with parents were associated with less adherence to diet and less frequent blood sugar monitoring (Schafer et al., 1983). Beck et al. (1980) noted that "family instability" (e.g., parents divorced, parent did not accompany child to clinic, child responsible for medication) was associated with less adherence in children who had kidney transplants.

Though current studies are limited by the complex methodology required to investigate interactional patterns (La Greca, 1988), an additional guideline for the clinician is to assess not only the patient's beliefs regarding the medical condition and treatment but those of all significant family members as well. Some family interactional patterns, such as overprotection, may inadvertently reinforce unnecessary sick-role behavior. In addition, parents—out of care and concern—may do too much for the child and decrease the child's opportunity to gain experience and develop feelings of mastery in dealing with his or her medical condition.

In reviewing different factors that may facilitate or impede adherence to treatment, the health-care provider should not lose sight of the fact that nonadherence may be the end result of a decisional process. Deaton (1985) is one of the few to study the adaptability of nonadherence in pediatric patients with a chronic medical condition: asthma. Others have suggested that a decision to not adhere to prescribed treatment regimen is a means by which patients may exert control (Hayes-Bautista, 1976; Stinson, 1974) or, even less adaptive, that it is a form of indirect self-destruction behavior (Faberow, 1986).

Adjustment to Hospitalization and Medical Procedures

Children with chronic medical conditions often require numerous hospitalizations for diagnostic procedures, surgery, medical treatments, and the management of exacerbations of their disease process. Hospitalization, for example, may be necessary to treat a diabetic child in ketoacidosis, to manage joint pain in a child with sickle cell disease, to give highly toxic drugs to children with leukemia, or to manage joint bleeding in a child with hemophilia. For some of these children, extended periods of hospitalization will occur throughout their lives.

While children with chronic medical conditions encounter many experiences in the hospital similar to those of acutely ill children or children admitted for elective treatment, the stresses of a chronic diagnosis present special problems and challenges in adjustment. Long-term and/or repeated hospitalizations have significant consequences for the development of children and adolescents (Hobbs et al., 1985). School absences, separation from family members and peers, isolation from normal childhood activities and experiences, immobility, and loss of control over daily events are among these consequences. In addition, frequent medical procedures that are often distressing and painful have to be endured (Siegel, 1983).

For those children with potentially life-threatening chronic medical conditions, admission to the hospital may have a considerably different meaning than it does for children who are hospitalized with less serious illnesses or for elective surgeries. Thus, while all hospitalized children may encounter similar experiences while in the hospital, the nature of their medical problems and the purpose of the admission can present different challenges to the child's adaptation (Siegel, 1988).

There is substantial literature documenting the stressful effects of hospitalization and surgery in normal children (Thompson, 1985; Vernon, Foley, Sipowicz, & Schulman, 1965). Short- and long-term emotional and behavioral problems have been reported in as many of 30% of children both during and following the period of hospitalization (Siegel, 1976). There is evidence that repeated and prolonged hospitalizations are risk factors for the development of behavioral disturbances in children and adolescents (Thompson, 1985)—a common situation for many children with chronic medical diagnoses.

In one of the few studies in this area, Wells and Schwebel (1987) investigated the effects of hospitalization and surgery on children from infancy through 13 years of age who had chronic medical conditions. They found that children with chronic conditions were no more likely to exhibit behavioral disturbances than children

without chronic diagnoses. Approximately 44% of the medically at-risk children showed some signs of posthospitalization adjustment problems.

A child's response to the hospital experience is influenced by a number of factors. One of the most important is the child's cognitive-developmental level (Siegel, 1983, 1988). In general, the literature consistently supports the finding that younger children tend to be at greater risk for developing emotional and behavioral problems both during and following hospitalization (Melamed & Siegel, 1980). These findings are consistent with the developmental literature, which indicates that younger children have a lower level of conceptual understanding of illness and medical procedures which, in turn, contributes to their higher level of anxiety and fearful behavior.

While there is some disagreement about the ideal timing for the preparation of children for the hospital experience, particularly when this is accompanied by surgery or other medical procedures, there is almost universal agreement in the literature about the necessity for some form of preparation to reduce the stress associated with hospitalization (Peterson & Brownlee-Duffeck, 1984; Siegel, 1976). Most of the work in this area has been in the preparation of children for surgery or invasive diagnostic procedures. There is considerable evidence for the effectiveness of various preparation programs in reducing anxiety before, during, and after hospitalization, in minimizing posthospitalization behavioral disturbance, and in facilitating adaptive coping during hospitalization (Siegel, 1976; Thompson, 1985).

There are five major components that are the focus of most preparation programs with children, including (1) giving information, (2) encouraging emotional expression, (3) establishing a trusting relationship between the child and hospital staff, (4) providing the parents with information, and (5) providing coping strategies to the child an/or parents (Elkins & Roberts, 1983; Vernon, Foley, Sipowicz, & Shulman, 1965). Several interventions that include one or more of these components have received empirical support. One has been the use of film models. In this method, the child is exposed to various aspects of the hospital experience through the perspective of another child. During various medical procedures, the model typically responds in a manner that demonstrates relatively nonanxious and cooperative behaviors. Various types of information are also provided in film modeling. In this regard, Cohen and Lazarus (1980) have identified four specific types of information that can be provided in the context of medical treatment, including the reasons for medical treatment, the actual medical procedures that will be used, the sensations that will be experienced, and specific coping strategies that the patient might use. Film modeling has been shown to be effective in reducing anxiety and facilitating cooperation behavior in children undergoing hospitalization for surgery (Ferguson, 1979; Melamed & Siegel, 1975) and anesthesia induction (Vernon & Bailey, 1974).

Another method of preparing children for hospitalization and surgery involves training children in specific coping skills. For example, Peterson and Shigetomi (1981) taught children to use several cognitive-behavioral coping strategies comprising cue-controlled relaxation; they paired deep muscle relaxation with the cue word "calm." In addition, the subjects instructed to use distracting imagery (i.e., imaging a pleasant scene) and calming self-instructional phrases. The children were encouraged to use these techniques during particularly stressful or painful experiences in the hospital. This intervention was effective in reducing distress and increasing cooperative behaviors in children 2 to 10 years of age who were hospitalized for elective surgery.

Some investigators have focused on the parents of hospitalized children, usually the mother, as the primary point of intervention in facilitating adjustment to the hospital. This is based on the assumption that parents who are anxious might communicate their anxiety to their child and would therefore be less effective in supporting the child during the hospitalization (Siegel, 1976). Skipper and his colleagues (Skipper & Leonard, 1968; Skipper, Leonard, & Rhymes, 1968) found a reduction in stress responses by others and less emotional distress for their children when a supportive nurse provided mothers with information about hospital routines and medical procedures and informed the mothers of their role in caring for their child in the hospital. Wolfer and Visintainer (1975) developed a preparation program that focused on both the child and the parents. In the experimental condition, the mother and child received preparation and supportive care at six "stress points"

throughout the hospitalization. The child's preparation included procedural and sensory information, rehearsal of appropriate behaviors, and emotional support. Mothers were provided with support by a nurse, including individual attention at stress points, an opportunity to clarify their feelings and thoughts, accurate information, and an explanation regarding ways in which they could help care for their children. This comprehensive program was found to reduce distress-related behaviors to and facilitate cooperation in the children, decrease self-reported maternal anxiety, and increase satisfaction with the care the children received.

Children with chronic medical conditions must sometimes receive medical care in unusually stressful settings within the hospital, such as intensive care units and protected environments. A child in a pediatric intensive care unit (PICU) is typically immobilized and confronted with periods of overstimulation alternating with periods of sensory deprivation (Rothstein, 1980). Cataldo, Bessman, Parker, Pearson, and Rogers (1979) describe an intervention program designed to improve patient's overall psychosocial functioning in the PICU. Children were given the opportunity to interact with a child-life worker while playing with age appropriate toys. This brief and relatively simple intervention resulted in an increase in the children's interactions, attention to activities, and positive affect and a reduction in inappropriate and nonadaptive behaviors.

Where the risk of infections must be minimized, some children need to be confined, often for extended periods of time, to a room where the air is continuously cleaned. The use of such protected environments is particularly common with pediatric cancer patients undergoing chemotherapy or bone marrow transplants, where the medication they receive significantly increases the risk of infection by affecting the child's immune system. Prolonged isolation can have a potentially deleterious effect on the child's adjustment because of potential sensory deprivation as a result of confinement and exposure to a limited number of persons.

Kellerman and his colleagues (Kellerman, Rigler, Siegel, & McCue, 1976; Kellerman, Rigler, & Siegel, 1979) developed a comprehensive intervention program designed to mitigate the effects of prolonged isolation for children in protected environments. This approach included the provision of access to window views and clocks, the establishment of daily schedules, regular visits from family members, the services of a play therapist and schoolteacher, and counseling for the family. These investigators found that while some children experienced transitory periods of depression, this comprehensive psychosocial program was effective in preventing significant or prolonged psychological adjustment problems.

As noted earlier, these children must often endure painful and highly aversive medical procedures. A number of intervention programs have been developed to help them to cope with this more effectively. For example, pediatric cancer patients experience frequent diagnostic and treatment procedures such as bone marrow aspirations and lumbar punctures. Children, particularly younger ones, can become so distressed during these that they require physical restraint to permit the procedures to be performed (Jay, Ozolins, Elliott, & Caldwell, 1983). Hypnosis—involving progressive muscle relaxation, focused attention, and imagery—has been used to help these children to manage the acute distress they often experience (Kellerman, Zeltzer, Ellenbery, & Dash, 1983; Zeltzer & LeBaron, 1982).

Jay, Elliott, Ozolins, Olson, and Pruitt (1985) describe a multicomponent treatment program for reducing behavioral distress in preadolescent cancer patients undergoing bone marrow aspirations and lumbar punctures. This program involved a number of cognitive-behavioral techniques including filmed modeling, breathing exercises, emotive imagery (fantasies in which superhero figures are used to help the child cope), behavioral rehearsal, and positive reinforcement of cooperative behavior. After each child practiced these techniques, the therapist accompanied the child into the treatment room and "coached" him or her in the use of these coping techniques. The results indicated that this program was effective in reducing behavioral distress and self-reported pain.

Cardiac catheterization is a highly invasive and stressful diagnostic procedure used to evaluate the cardiac status of children with congenital heart disease. Naylor, Coates, and Kan (1984) examined the efficacy of a preparation program in reducing the distress experienced by 40 children 3 to 6 years of age undergoing cardiac catheterization. The intervention included behavioral rehearsal in the catheterization lab (including distraction techniques) and the provision of procedural and sensory information. Children who received this intervention cried less, had fewer pain complaints, and exhibited less motor activity than did children who were not exposed to this intervention. The experimental group children also exhibited fewer behavior problems at home following the catheterization.

A major source of distress for children with cancer is the side effects of the chemotherapy agents typically used in the treatment of these diseases. Toxic anticancer medications often cause nausea and vomiting, which typically occur within hours of the drugs' administration. In addition to this, some patients develop nausea and vomiting *prior* to the administration of the drugs. Research with pediatric populations suggests that anticipatory nausea and vomiting (ANV) occurs in approximately 20% to 30% of these patients (Dolgin, Katz, McGinty, & Siegel, 1985).

There is a general consensus that ANV is a conditioned response whose etiology can be attributed to a classical conditioning paradigm (Carey & Burish, 1988). According to this learning model, chemotherapy serves as an unconditioned stimulus that elicits drug-induced nausea and vomiting (the unconditioned response). Previously neutral stimuli preceding the chemotherapy and associated with the treatment environment (i.e., clinic odors, sights of the hospital, tastes, and thoughts), through pairing with the unconditioned response, may become conditioned stimuli capable of eliciting ANV.

Anticipatory and posttreatment nausea and vomiting have been particularly refractory to treatment with antiemetic drugs (Oliver, Simon, & Aisner, 1986). A number of behavioral treatment approaches have been investigated as alternative methods for reducing these side effects. Zeltzer and her colleagues (LeBaron & Zeltzer, 1984; Zeltzer, LeBaron, & Zeltzer, 1984) found that compared to a supportive counseling group, hypnosis helped to reduce nausea and vomiting—as well as anxiety associated with chemotherapy—in children 6 to 17 years of age. The hypnosis procedure consisted of helping the children to become as intensely involved as possible in imagery and fantasy. Another intervention used with children involves attention-diversion/cognitive-distraction techniques. In a multiple-baseline design with 3 adolescent cancer patients, Kolko and Richard-Figueroa (1988) investigated the use of video games as a means of diverting attention away from the chemotherapy experience and potential conditioned stimuli in the treatment environment. This procedure resulted in a reduction in the number of anticipatory symptoms and a decrease in the aversiveness of the postchemotherapy side effects. Similar findings are reported by Redd et al. (1987) using the same treatment approach. While the effectiveness of interventions such as progressive muscle relaxation training, systematic desensitization, and biofeedback in ameliorating the stress-related side effects of chemotherapy with adult cancer patients has been demonstrated, the use of these procedures has not been reported with children (Carey & Burish, 1988; Morrow & Dobkin, 1988).

Terminal Illness and the Dying Child

Despite the improved outlook for the medical treatment of children with life-threatening diseases such as cancer and cystic fibrosis, many of them die from their disease. Few experiences are more challenging and require greater emotional sensitivity on the part of health-care professionals than working with children and their families during the terminal stage of illness. Meeting the needs of these individuals requires not only special professional and interpersonal skills but also self-awareness on the part of the caregivers with regard to their own values and attitudes toward death and dying (Weiner, 1970).

One of the most difficult situations that the families of children with life-threatening illnesses face is the emotional "roller coaster" that results from episodes of relapse and critical illness that are interspersed with periods of improvement and a temporary return of normal functioning (Bronheim, 1978; Travis, 1976). Multiple medical crises contribute to the family's "anticipatory mourning." While this anticipatory process can help family members prepare for the child's impending death, it can also have a negative effect by causing the family to withdraw from the child emotionally long before the child's actual death. As a result, the child may experience a profound sense of abandonment and isolation at a time when he or she most needs support (Bronheim, 1978; Koocher & Sallan 1978).

Children with life-threatening illnesses and their families require emotional support throughout the course of illness. This should begin at the time of diagnosis and continue through the terminal phase of illness (Koocher, 1977; Stehbens,

1988). Repeated supportive contacts with the family by various members of the health-care team help to establish these individuals as a supportive resource for the family during the crisis period of the child's impending death. It is a difficult task, at best, for caregivers to build an effective supportive relationship during the terminal phase of a child's illness when a prior relationship with the family has not been established.

In addition to the medical management of the child's illness, there are several major tasks that health-care professionals must confront in their work with the terminally ill child and his or her family. One of the most basic therapeutic goals is to help to normalize the life of the child and family as much as may be possible within the constraints of the child's illness (Blake & Paulsen, 1981). Another basic goal is to facilitate effective coping with stressful events that are associated with the disease and its treatment (Stehbens, 1988). The methods for achieving these goals include facilitating communication among family members, encouraging the expression of feelings and concerns, and fostering a sense of mastery and control (Koocher & Sallan, 1978).

One of the most important and difficult tasks facing caregivers who work with critically ill children involves the process and content of informing children about their disease and communicating about the issue of death. It is the general consensus among clinicians that children should receive an honest, factual, and age-appropriate explanation of their disease and the seriousness of their illness (Koocher & Sallan, 1978; Spinetta, 1980; Stehbens, 1988). This information can be provided to the child in a sensitive and supportive manner and in a way that does not deprive the child of hope for the future. Specifically, Koocher and his colleagues (Koocher & O'Malley, 1981; Koocher & Sallan, 1978) recommend that a child with a life-threatening illness be told the name of the disease, given accurate information about the nature of the illness within the child's level of conceptual understanding, and be told that it is a serious illness from which children sometimes die.

It is important for those professionals who work with critically ill children to be familiar with the development of children's concepts of death. Research in this area suggests that children's abilities to conceptualize death and to comprehend its irreversibility are related to

Piagetian stages of cognitive development similar to those presented earlier in this chapter in a discussion of children's concepts of illness (Koocher, 1973; Spinetta, 1974).

In general, research with physically healthy children has shown that children under 5 years of age do not understand either the permanence or the universality of death. Children between the ages of 6 to 9 tend to view death as a process of physical harm that may result from some wrongdoing. Older children and adolescents attain an idea of death as a gradual cessation of bodily functioning that is permanent and irreversible (White, Elsom, & Prawat, 1978). Some authors, based on clinical observations, have suggested that the development of a more advanced understanding of death can be accelerated in younger children who personally experience a life-threatening illness (Bluebond-Langer, 1977; Spinetta, 1974). A study by Jay, Green, Johnson, Caldwell, and Nitschke (1987), however, found no evidence that children with cancer demonstrated more mature concepts of death than did physically well children.

Communication with children about illness or death should be determined by the child's needs and desire for information. Health-care professionals need to be sensitive to the child's need to communicate when he or she is ready to do so. In order to facilitate communication with terminally ill children, it is important to accept their feelings, avoid putting off questions, and provide honest, simple explanations.

Koocher and Sallan (1978) note that children's failure to ask questions about their illness should not be interpreted as an indication that they do not want to "know." Often children will not ask questions because they perceive barriers that interfere with attempts at open communication. These perceptions may stem from the actions of parents and health-care workers, who unwittingly provide verbal and nonverbal cues that they feel uncomfortable discussing this subject (Koocher, 1977; Stehbens, 1988). Typically children need to feel that they have "permission" to talk about these difficult topics (Spinetta, 1980).

Support for this open approach to communication with terminally ill children comes from a number of different sources. Clinical observations indicate that even when children are not directly informed about the seriousness of their illness, they obtain information from others (e.g., medical staff and parents who are overheard talking, other patients, and from nonverbal communication). Thus, despite the intentions of adults to "protect" children from knowledge of their illness, even young children are often well informed about the nature of their disease and their impending death (Bluebond-Langer, 1974; Spinetta & Maloney, 1975; Vernick & Karon, 1965).

Spinetta (1980) offers several practical considerations that the clinician must address when communicating with children about the possibility of death. In addition to developmental factors, he notes that it is important to understand the parents' own philosophy of death so that death can be discussed with the child within this context. One must also assess the family's emotional responses and personal experiences with death, since each family expresses its fears and griefs differently. The child's views of death can best be understood in relation to the family's patterns of coping with death and other stressful situations. Finally, Spinetta (1980) suggests that the child's emotional response to a serious illness depends more on *how* information is provided than on the *content* of the information.

In addition, Spinetta (1980) has provided practical advice on how to talk with children about their own impending death in a sensitive and reassuring manner. He suggests that the basic messages to communicate to the child include the following: (1) the child will not be alone at death or after death; (2) children should know that they have done all that they could do with their lives; (3) it is all right to cry and feel sad and angry and not want to talk at times about the illness or death; (4) when it comes, death will not hurt and there will be no pain after death; (5) they will be able to say good-bye to friends and family if they want to; (6) adults do not always understand why children die, and they too sometimes cry because they do not want to lose their child; and (7) the parents will always remember the child after he or she dies and will be happy for the good times that they shared together.

Several studies indicate that the level of adjustment of terminally ill children, survivors of life-threatening disease, and family members following a child's death is related to their level of communication regarding the child's illness. There is evidence that failure to communicate honestly with children about their disease can lead to a sense of isolation, depression, and mistrust (Spinetta, 1974; Spinetta & Maloney,

1975; 1978). Families who are able to communicate openly about the child's illness have consistently been found to achieve a better adjustment, whether they are surviving patients or families of children who have died from their disease. In a study of childhood cancer survivors, children who had been told about their diagnosis early in the course of their illness were found to be better adjusted than children from whom such information was deliberately withheld (Slavin, O'Malley, Koocher, & Foster, 1981). Similarly, parents who were able to communicate openly with their child tended to exhibit better adaptation to his or her eventual death than did parents who were unable to talk honestly with their child (Spinetta, Swarner, & Sheposh, 1981).

Following a child's death, continued contact with the family is essential in order to monitor parental and sibling reactions and to assess their adjustment. The hospital where the child has been treated and a familiar caregiver can serve as a supportive resource during the period of mourning and periodically thereafter (Koocher & Sallan, 1978). If ongoing support has been provided to the family while the child was alive, it is likely that the extent of psychological intervention required after the child's death will be minimal (Bronheim, 1978; Koocher & O'Malley, 1981).

Over the past decade, as a means of assisting parents in their efforts to cope with the stresses of their child's life-threatening illness and/or the death of their child, numerous self-help groups have developed. The primary purpose of these groups is to enhance the social support available to parents by providing a network of people who are experiencing similar stresses in their lives (Borman, 1985). The Candlelighters Foundation is an international network of parent groups who have experienced childhood cancer and other life-threatening illnesses. This group was founded in order to help parents deal with their fears and frustrations through the sharing of feelings and experiences, thus reducing their sense of isolation. The group also provides educational information regarding the illness, treatment approaches, and side effects. Compassionate Friends is a group for parents whose child has died irrespective of the cause. The focus of the group is on preventing family dysfunction and maladaptive grieving responses. Group discussions include methods for maintaining relationships with friends and relatives,

who often withdraw from the bereaved parents (Borman, 1985).

A recent trend in the treatment of terminally ill children has been home or hospice care during the terminal stage. Home care of the dying child maximizes the quality of the child's life during his or her final days and has a number of psychological advantages compared with hospitalization. Children do not have to be separated from parents, siblings, and friends and they can participate in family activities until they die. Parents can be trained to provide care at home, which can help to reduce the sense of helplessness that parents often feel when they relinquish their parental role in the hospital setting. Nurses are available on a 24-hour basis at the parents' request. Advocates of home care for the terminally ill child acknowledge that this approach is not appropriate for all families, since some may not have the necessary emotional or physical resources (Armstrong & Martinson, 1980). Such families require the security of the hospital, and hospitalization is always available even for families that elect to use home care.

An alternative to home care for the terminally ill is the hospice. The hospice concept includes both home care or inpatient care in a health-care facility that is more like a home environment and is staffed by specially trained medical and mental-health personnel (Davidson, 1985; National Hospice Organization, 1984).

Martinson, Nesbit, and Kersey (1984) investigated the adaptation of 68 families who cared for their children at home during the terminal stage of cancer, following them for more than 5 years after their child's death. The findings from this study indicate a high level of satisfaction and good adjustment among family members. Families of 37 children who had died of cancer were studied by Mulhern, Lauer, and Hoffman (1983). The investigators found that the parents of 13 children who had died in the hospital were more anxious and had more somatic problems than were parents whose children had received terminal care at home. Siblings of children who had died in the hospital were also found to be more emotionally inhibited, withdrawn, and fearful than siblings who had participated in the home-care program.

The emotional impact of a child's life-threatening illness is not limited to the child and his or her family. Members of the health-care team must also cope with the painful reality of the dying child (Martin & Mauer, 1982; Vernick &

Karon, 1965). Koocher and Sallan (1978) refer to the difficulties experienced by professionals who provide care for children with life-threatening illnesses over extended periods of time, develop close personal relationships with these children and their families, and then must face the eventual death of some of these children. "Burnout" is, therefore, a risk for these caregivers (Kolotkin, 1981). Various approaches to facilitating adaptive coping among health-care professionals who work with these children have been described, including professional support groups (Stuetzer, 1980) and course work for training caregivers to cope with death and dying (Barton, 1972; Woolsey, 1985).

TASKS OF DAILY LIVING

Education Management

Since schooling is the main occupation of children, the interruption of the educational process by illness and its treatment should be minimized (Perrin, Ireys, Shayne, & Moynihan, 1984). The importance of integrating the child with a chronic medical condition into the regular school program has implications for the social development of the child, the quality of education received by the child, and the child's later integration into the adult work force and the community. The continuum-of-services model as proposed by Deno (1973) includes four levels of regular classroom placement, including the regular classroom plus consultation, itinerant teaching, and resource-room services. More restrictive settings include hospital or homebound instruction, self-contained classrooms, and special day or residential schools. In keeping with the requirement of Public Law 94-142, the Mandatory Education of the Handicapped Act, the child must be educated in the least restrictive environment (LRE). Therefore, every effort should be made to place children in the least intensive/most integrated setting possible. If a child must be placed in a more intensive/less integrated program, consideration for a more integrated placement should occur at the earliest possible date.

Children with chronic medical conditions often have special educational needs that can be met if the child qualifies for special education placement under one of three labels: orthopedically handicapped, other health-impaired, or multiply handicapped. In some cases, certain related services such as occupational and physical therapy and transportation must also be provided, as required by Public Law 94-142. In 1986, this law was extended to children aged 3 to 5; it is to be implemented in all states by the 1990-91 school year. In addition, funding incentives will be made available to states to develop early intervention programs for handicapped and medically at-risk children under the age of 36 months. However, if a child's impairment does not interfere with his or her ability to function in the regular classroom setting, he or she may not qualify for special education services. In order to provide the related services (e.g., transportation, physical therapy, etc.) special education placement is a prerequisite.

A number of service delivery options are utilized to provide educational services to children with chronic medical conditions or physical handicaps. For some children, no special administrative arrangements are needed aside from providing time and a place to take care of daily treatment needs, such as monitoring blood sugars (for children with diabetes) or self-catheterization (in minimally affected children with spina bifida). Other medical conditions may be so severe or hospitalizations so frequent that a homebound program is required. With this program, the special teacher provides all the instruction the child needs at home until the child is able to return to school. If hospitalized for long periods of time, the child may receive instruction through a hospital school. Home and hospital programs, while often the only educational option for students with chronic medical conditions, may vary in quality and instructional time allotted. For example, some states require only 3 hours per week (Perrin et al., 1984).

In addition to the traditional academic areas, children who are medically at risk may have specialized educational needs such as vocational and career preparation, disease management, nutrition, use of leisure time, care of medical equipment, and adaptive physical education. Supportive services needed may involve transportation and physical therapy for children with physical disabilities (juvenile rheumatoid arthritis, spina bifida, or muscular dystrophy), special diets for children with endocrine disorders (diabetes, cystic fibrosis), in-school administration of medications, special treatments such as catheterization, counseling, and liaison services (Baird & Ashcroft, 1984). The individualized educational program (IEP) is the planning and management tool utilized to deliver special education and related services to handicapped children under Public Law 94–142. Although there is no clear role for physicians and health professionals in the development of an IEP, their participation may be critical for children with certain chronic conditions who require related services. Though provision of related services, when necessary, is required by Public Law 94–142, some school systems have tended to avoid listing all of a child's needs and the necessary services on an IEP, fearing that they may ultimately be responsible for the cost of these services. If parents feel that their child's educational rights have been violated, they may appeal to their state's department of education for a "due process hearing." Parents have the right to an independent evaluation if they have reason to believe that their child's needs have not been accurately diagnosed by the school system. In addition, each state has an advocacy office for children with special needs.

Some children with chronic medical conditions may be considered "temporarily handicapped" and have a need for special education services for brief periods only while out of school. These children also have a right to a free and appropriate public school while they are temporarily impaired. Their right to educational access is protected by Section 504 of the Rehabilitation Act of 1973 (National Association of State Directors of Special Education and National Association of State Boards of Education, 1979).

A number of approaches have been suggested to help school systems meet the needs of children with chronic medical conditions. Nader and Parcel (1978) recommend that schools develop health education programs that will meet the needs of certain target groups, such as asthmatic children. Certain disease-oriented voluntary associations (American Cancer Society, Arthritis Foundation, National Association for Sickle Cell Disease) have developed educational materials that may be helpful to school programs. Baird and Ashcroft (1984) have suggested that the itinerant-teacher, resource-room, and consultant-teacher models frequently utilized to provide educational services to handicapped children could be expanded to provide programs for those with chronic medical needs. Grandstaff (1981) suggested a model that would allow for flexible arrangements for children; it included both full- and part-time teachers to provide services to hospitalized and home-bound

children. In addition, he suggested hourly employees for very specialized curricular areas.

A few programs across the country have developed innovative practices to serve school-aged children with chronic illnesses. The Chronic Health Impaired Project (CHIP) of the Baltimore City Schools has full-time teachers who visit chronically ill children every day they are out of school, beginning with the first day of absence. CHIP personnel also provide additional services, including child and family counseling, career guidance, and peer tutoring programs (Baird & Ashcroft, 1984). The School Health Corporation developed by the Robert Wood Johnson Foundation in Commerce City, Colorado, offers a program designed to provide health-care services within the school system. As a separate entity, the corporation protects the school district from liability, allows for third-party reimbursement, and maintains separation between educational and medical dollars (Clark, 1982).

Technological models have also been utilized in meeting the educational needs of chronically ill children at home or in the hospital—for example, telephone devices that, even though costly, provide two-way communication between the child and the classroom (Grandstaff, 1981). Computer technology will undoubtedly allow for sophisticated teaching models for these children in the near future.

The efficacy of a comprehensive program for facilitating the school and social reintegration of newly diagnosed children and adolescents with cancer was investigated by Katz, Rubenstein, Hubert, and Bleu (1989). Specific components of the School Reintegration Project included preparing the child and parents for a return to school as soon as possible after diagnosis and maintaining contact with the school and teachers until the child returned to school; in-service training for school personnel to provide information about the child's medical diagnosis, treatment, and plans for school absences; providing classmates (with the child present) with age-appropriate information about the child's diagnosis and treatment; maintaining continued contact with the school to facilitate communication between the family, medical staff, and school; and keeping the school informed of the child's medical status. Compared to a control group, children in the School Reintegration Project exhibited fewer behavior problems, were less depressed, and showed higher levels of social competence and self-esteem. There were no differences between groups on school grades or absenteeism.

This project highlights ways to overcome many of the barriers that can be met in trying to reintegrate the child at school. Parental concerns regarding the child's safety can be a problem, particularly in the case of younger children. Another is finding someone who can help the child with daily care needs. The teacher's attitude about educating the child with a chronic medical condition in a regular classroom setting can pose another dilemma. Teachers may not know enough about chronic medical conditions (Eiser & Town, 1987), or they may feel ill equipped to handle medical emergencies (Bradbury & Smith, 1983). Teachers may believe that children with serious illnesses will create emotional difficulties for healthy children; few may perceive it as their responsibility to inform all the children about the sick child's medical condition. Some teachers may even isolate a child in the belief that his or her illness might be contagious (Eiser & Town, 1987).

Within the classroom, teachers may have mistaken ideas about the academic skills and capacities of children with chronic medical diagnoses. For example, a teacher may be too willing or too reluctant to excuse poor achievement because a child has been frequently absent for medical treatment or was unusually tired as a result of a particular treatment (Baird & Ashcroft, 1984). Teachers may also have goals that differ or are incompatible with those of healthcare professionals working with the child. For example, the physician of an asthmatic child may request limited exercise while the school is interested in helping the child to achieve certain goals in physical education.

A study by Deasy-Spinetta and Spinetta (1980) investigated how regular classroom teachers view the school functioning of children with cancer. Teachers of 42 children in grades K through 12 responded to a questionnaire comparing children with cancer to their peers in the same classroom. The results indicated significantly different views of certain behaviors in the children with cancer as opposed to the controls. Children with cancer were seen as having more difficulty concentrating, being underactive, and lacking in energy. They were also viewed as more inhibited and less willing to try new things. Children with cancer were also seen as less able to express positive or negative emotions.

Several studies have suggested that some chronic medical conditions and medical treatments have a negative effect on cognitive functioning in children (Fowler et al., 1988; Fennel, Rasbury, Fennel, & Morris, 1984; Peckman, Meadows, Bastil, & Marrero, 1988). These findings have important implications for a child's academic achievement as well as parental and teacher expectations. At present, these results should be interpreted cautiously, as important variables such as parental occupation and social class have not always been considered (Trantman et al., 1988). Moreover, frequent school absences and a learned adaptational style secondary to having a chronic medical condition are potential confounding variables which are not typically considered. For the clinician trying to reintegrate the child into school, it may be helpful to obtain a baseline of cognitive functioning early in the diagnosis and prior to treatments (e.g., chemotherapy, radiation) so as to determine whether the medical condition and/or treatment has a significant impact on cognitive functioning in each given instance.

Aside from the impact on academic achievement, frequent school absences can significantly affect the child's socialization experiences and the development of normal peer relationships. Embarrassment over their disease may further increase the social isolation of these children. As a result, maladaptive social behaviors and social-skills deficits may appear. Absenteeism may be directly related to the chronic illness, or it may be related to adjustment problems that lead to school avoidance (Pless & Roghman, 1971). A recent study of children with cardiac conditions hypothesized that school absence would be related to the severity of the cardiac disease, psychosocial factors, and family functioning (Fowler, Johnson, Welshimer, Atkinson, & Loda, 1987). Results indicated that absenteeism was indeed related to medical factors such as necessary clinic visits, hospitalization, limitations imposed by a physician, or keeping a child out of school due to a minor illness. However, in comparison to the control group, who were not ill, no significant differences related to psychosocial factors or family functioning were found. While these findings are encouraging, investigations of other types of medical conditions are needed to answer the question of how psychological factors and family functioning affect school attendance in children with chronic medical diagnoses.

Effect of Child's Illness on Family Functioning

For all children, whether ill or well, the family is the most important social milieu and a major locus of experience. Although, previously, the primary focus of care for chronically ill children was the hospital, such children now receive much of their treatment in the community, with the family as the primary provider.

The impact of a chronic illness on the family is best understood through a systems and developmental perspective. The family is conceptualized as a semiclosed system (Hill & Rogers, 1964) in which all members interact and events affecting one member will touch all the others within the system. A chronic medical condition will, therefore, not only change the life of the affected child, parents, and siblings but also impair the development of intrafamily relationships. The onset of a chronic condition can create a crisis for the family and disrupt the stability of the family system.

It is also important to consider the stages of the family life cycle in seeking to understand the impact of a chronic medical condition. For example, those families into which a child is born with a chronic medical condition will need to cope with the grief of not having the "ideal" child. For the family with a toddler, a chronic medical condition may present difficulties in trying to obtain day care. The usual stress related to transition periods such as school entrance, adolescence, and school exit may be intensified by the presence of a chronic medical condition.

A family may react to the initial diagnosis of a chronic illness in a variety of ways. The reaction of some families may follow a series of stages, such as those suggested by Drotar, Baskiewicz, Irvin, Kennel, and Klaus (1975). These stages include initial shock (at time of birth/diagnosis), denial, sadness, anger, and anxiety. In dealing with these families, stage theory should be applied with caution, since all families may not experience each stage or go through them in a systematic manner. Also, since some medical conditions may intensify at certain intervals, families may reexperience various stressors and reactions at either periodic or unpredictable times. For example, each time a child with cancer relapses, the family may experience a new shock or grief reaction.

The impact of a chronic medical diagnosis on a particular family depends upon a number of factors that include the limitations imposed by the medical condition and its treatment, tangible family resources (e.g., financial resources, transportation, job stability), the social support system both within and outside the family itself, coping resources, and the general psychological functioning of the family prior to the onset of the illness. For example the severity of a certain illness may require more frequent physician visits, intermittent or prolonged hospital stays, and greater demands on the child's primary caregivers. In addition, a family may not have insurance or sufficient funds to cover medical expenses or the cost of specialized equipment. In a study of chronic medical conditions in families, Pless and Satterwhite (1975) reported that 66% of the families mentioned financial difficulty as a major concern. So called "middle-class" families may already be overextended, and even families on public assistance may lack basic resources such as transportation.

In today's society, where the single-parent and dual-career nuclear family are more common and increased mobility has resulted in greater distances from extended family, a social support system that will help in caring for siblings or provide respite care for the medically at-risk child is not always available. Moreover, a family's current support network may be affected when care demands interfere with previous social opportunities. Parents may have little or no time to participate in community activities. The parents, and in particular a nonworking mother, may feel extremely isolated.

The effects of having a child with a chronic medical condition on the parent's marital relationship have been investigated. A number of studies suggest that either the marital relationship faces a greater risk of divorce or that intact relationships are brought closer together by the experience (McAndrew, 1976). Friedrich and Friedrich (1981) conducted a study with families of 34 handicapped children. When their responses were compared to those of a control group, the parents of the handicapped children reported a less satisfactory marriage, less social support, less religiousness, and less psychological well-being. The handicapped parents' group not only appeared to be under greater stress but also had fewer psychological assets to cope with the stress. Conversely, Markova, MacDonald, and Forbes (1979) stated that half of the 16 families they studied felt the child's illness had brought them closer together. In a study of terminally ill children, Obetz, Swenson, Mc-Carthy, Gilchrist, and Burgert (1980) found that many parents had altered their values and priorities and experienced personal growth as a result of having a child with leukemia in the family. A more recent study by Wood, Siegel, and Scott (1989) compared the effects of stress and martial satisfaction in families of chronically ill, handicapped, and not ill/not handicapped children. While families of chronically ill and handicapped children reported greater stress, parents of chronically ill children indicated greater martial satisfaction than either parents of handicapped or not ill/not handicapped children. Sabbath and Leventhal (1984) suggest that couples with a chronically ill child are no more likely to divorce than couples with healthy children but are more likely to be dissatisfied and argumentative than parents of healthy children. A chronic illness that has a high probability of genetic recurrence may indirectly threaten a marriage through a rational decision to have no more children. However, in a review of the literature on families attending genetic counseling clinics, Begleiter, Burry, and Harris (1976) found that the divorce rate for these families was lower than the overall national average.

The evidence regarding the impact on siblings' adjustment is mixed as well. Some studies have found more adjustment problems in siblings of a child with a chronic medical condition than in the siblings of healthy children (Breslau, Weitzman, & Messenger, 1981; Lavigne & Ryan, 1979; Spinetta & Deasy-Spinetta, 1981; Tew & Lawrence, 1975). These adjustment problems may be related to lack of personal attention from parents, increased demands for siblings to assume adult responsibilities, and from extreme feelings of repressed anger and guilt. Research with siblings of handicapped and chronically ill children has consistently shown significant interaction effects with birth order and gender (Breslau, 1982; Tew & Lawrence, 1975). Although younger children may assume roles that contradict birth order and older children may take on the responsibilities of teacher and caregiver (Brody & Stoneman, 1986), the greatest impact seems to be on younger brothers and older sisters.

Conversely, some studies have shown that having a sibling with a chronic medical condition can have a positive impact on peer relationships, social competence, interpersonal qualities such as compassion and sensitivity, and appreciation for one's own good health (Ferrari, 1984; Grossman, 1972). Siblings of chronically ill children have often attributed their own adjustment or reaction to their parents' communication pattern regarding the disease as well as their parents acceptance of the disease (Gogan & Slavin, 1981). Simensson and McHale (1981) have stated that the comprehensibility of the disease will affect the siblings' reactions and adjustment. Mother's mental and physical health has also been mentioned as a factor having an impact on sibling adjustment (Tew & Lawrence, 1975).

Mothers have been and continue to be viewed as the primary caregivers to the child with a chronic medical condition; consequently they have been the subject of a number of investigations, which suggest a negative impact on the mother's emotional and physical functioning (Breslau, Starvek, & Mortimer, 1982; Tew & Lawrence; 1975; Wallander et al., 1989). Very little research attention has been directed toward the fathers of these children or to comparisons between mothers and fathers. In a study of emotional well-being and communication styles, Shapiro and Shumaker (1987) found that fathers perceived the overall family environment more negatively than did their wives. Fathers communicated less openly and often with their ill child and generally rated their child's adjustment lower than did their wives. On the other hand, Wood, Siegel, and Scott (1989) obtained no significant differences in stress or marital satisfaction scores between fathers and mothers of children with chronic medical conditions.

Much of the difficulty encountered by families coping with chronic illness may be related to perceived stress and coping resources. Nevin and McCubbin (1979) found that those families of children with spina bifida who were perceived to be under low levels of stress were more cohesive, better organized, and lower in conflict than more highly stressed families. Shulman (1983) studied children with leukemia and found that 85% of their families coped well. Factors associated with good family adjustment included a history of prior good coping, good quality of marital and familial relationships, good support system, religious faith, and a trusting relationship with a physician.

Holiday (1984) has discussed three major coping strategies successfully utilized by parents of a child with a chronic medical diagnosis: (1) gaining as much information about the child's illness in order to understand it and assign meaning to the illness; (2) integrating the child into the mainstream of society to the maximum extent possible and thereby achieving normalization; and (3) establishing a social support system to share the burden of the illness. One of the most effective support systems cited by Holiday is the parent–to–parent support group. Parents who have had experience with chronic medical conditions in their own children can help other parents gain insight into their own situations. Mattsson (1977) outlined a number of suggestions to assist these families in the development of coping skills. These included parental attitudes and behaviors related to child discipline, utilizing cognitive techniques to maintain control, and becoming better informed about the child's condition. Parents were also urged to encourage their children in self-care, reasonable physical activities, and regular school attendance.

Support groups of various types have been of benefit to families of children with chronic medical conditions. Providing mutual support is often related to the members' stage of coping and integration. Toseland and Hacker (1982) conducted an investigation of self-help groups and emphasized that leadership, direction, and participation should come from within the target population. Frequently a group can serve as a forum for problem identification and solution, information sharing, and discussions related to medical treatment. The value of support groups for siblings of chronically ill children has not been thoroughly investigated; however, sibling groups may have particular value for adolescents (McKeever, 1983). Although support groups can be beneficial, families that appear to be dysfunctional because of the additional stress stemming from their child's illness may be candidates for a referral to family therapy.

Educational programs that provide information and/or skills training may also be beneficial to these families. Kirkham, Schilling, Norelius, and Schinke (1986) reported positive results of a training program designed to reduce stress, develop coping skills, and enhance social support in mothers of handicapped children. An educational program developed for parents of children with cancer was evaluated in six pediatric oncology centers (Wallace, Bakke, Hubbard, & Pendergrass, 1984). Gaining more knowledge about their child's disease promoted greater parental understanding toward the child and the overall effect of cancer on the family.

An additional benefit of the program was decreased parental feelings of isolation and greater opportunity for staff to interact with family members.

Minimizing "Sick Role" Behavior

Becoming or being sick has been recognized as a social-psychological as well as a physical process (Mechanic & Volkart, 1961; Parsons, 1951, 1958). Behaviors ascribed to the sick role are in part socially determined, as once the label of "sick" or "disabled" is applied, others' expectations for the sick person change. In addition, the expectations the person holds about his or her own behavior change as well. Changes in behavioral expectations by self and others are sanctioned by societal norms and often involve special privileges and reduction in day-to-day obligations such as work and/or school (Twaddle & Hessler, 1977). Furthermore, it is assumed that professional assistance is needed to recover from whatever condition has made the person sick. This places the sick person in a dependent and helpless role with respect to others. In short, the person behaves differently and others respond differently to the person who has been labeled sick (Melamed & Siegel, 1980).

The above conceptualization was developed during a time when acute, infectious illnesses were the primary source of illness. Today, chronic medical conditions have become more prominent and a question is raised as to whether these persons should be considered sick or healthy (Rosenstock & Kirscht, 1979). Individuals with a chronic medical condition such as diabetes or asthma typically have periods where they do not feel ill, yet a medical diagnosis still applies. When does or should the sick role apply for these children? What criteria should be used to legitimize periods of ill health and wellness? Such is the dilemma that faces children with a medical condition, their parents, and those who provide their health care.

Helping the child maintain a normal routine with respect to day-to-day functioning (e.g., attending school, chores, etc.), as discussed earlier in this chapter, is one means of minimizing the sick role in children with a chronic medical condition. Modifying expectations to match the child's physical state of health may be necessary from time to time. What complicates this seemingly simple picture is that these children may, as adults, later continue to perceive themselves as ill during periods of relatively good health and therefore may be more likely to try and remove themselves from routine activities and responsibilities associated with daily living (Twaddle, 1969). Moreover, receiving preferential treatment from others because of a medical condition can result in a greater display of sick-role behaviors. Such preferential treatment and removal of typical daily responsibilities can be highly reinforcing and result in significant secondary gain or benefit to the child. As a result of such powerful reinforcers, the child may continue to display behaviors or symptoms of being ill, and cooperation with treatments to improve the medical condition may be less than optimum (Melamed & Siegel, 1980).

For many children this sequence is a learned behavior that parents, friends, and health-care providers may inadvertently reach out of care and concern for the child's health and emotional adjustment. Creer and Christian (1976) have noted that family members and health-care providers are often caught in what is referred to as an "illness trap" when interacting with an individual who has a chronic medical condition or disability. Greater attention is paid to physical complaints, requests for assistance, and noncompliance with treatment than to more adaptive, independent behaviors, which may be overlooked. Yet, continued adoption of the sick role can also become a deliberate manipulation, particularly during the adolescent years (Elkind, 1985).

Aside from the above-mentioned learning model, very little empirical evidence is currently available to document factors that may contribute to the persistence of sick-role behavior. Family interactional styles and cognitive-perceptual styles are factors that have received some empirical attention.

Certain types of family interactional styles may promote and maintain sick-role behavior. Minuchin and his colleagues (Minuchin et al., 1975) have noted interactional styles between family members that appear to exacerbate symptoms in some types of chronic medical conditions such as asthma and diabetes. Interactional styles that appear problematic include those where family members are enmeshed, overprotective, and rigid and where conflict resolution skills are poor. In addition to citing maladaptive interactional styles, Minuchin and his colleagues (1975) propose that by maintaining a sick role the child may serve a homeostatic

function for the family. Focus on the sick child may help the family to avoid dealing with other areas of conflict, such as marital difficulties between the parents.

Research that has involved either direct observation of parent–child interactions or questionnaires regarding family interactional styles lends support to this above hypothesis. Several studies with adolescents who have diabetes indicate that poorer metabolic control is associated with greater family conflict (Anderson, Miller, Auslander, & Santiago, 1981) and greater difficulty in negotiating areas of conflict (Bobrow, AvRuskin, & Siller, 1985). Yet typically these studies are based on cross-sectional data, so it is impossible to discern cause and effect. Longitudinal studies that can map interactional patterns across time and status of medical condition, such as that by Hauser and his colleagues (cf. Hauser et al., 1986), are needed to more fully investigate these hypotheses regarding family interactional patterns and to guide the development of effective, family-based interventions.

Unfortunately, interactional styles with other systems (e.g., health-care providers, school system) with which the child and family interact have received even less empirical attention. It is conceivable that health-care providers may interact with patients and their families in similar ways to promote and maintain sick-role behavior, such as encouraging excessive dependency. Teachers may also promote excessive sick-role behavior by limiting activities unnecessarily (e.g., overprotectiveness). Future research focusing on interactional styles must expand to include other systems besides the family to further our understanding of how interactions within larger systems contribute to or minimize the occurrence of sick-role behavior.

Differences in perception and interpretation of bodily states is another factor that may contribute to sick-role behavior. Studies of the development of physical symptoms in generally healthy samples have shown that some children and adolescents have a heightened awareness of or preoccupation with bodily states which contributes to the development and persistence of physical symptoms (see Siegel & Smith, chapter 8). While the concepts of "introspection" (Mechanic, 1983) and "amplifying somatic style" (Barsky, Goodson, Lane, & Cleary, 1988; Barsky & Klerman, 1983) have not been studied in the context of a chronic medical condition, this may be a population at risk for such learned behavior. Most medical conditions involve some fluctuation in physical symptoms, which require attention so that appropriate medical treatment can be instituted. Yet this may result in heightened sensitivity to all bodily states and to the identification of benign physical sensations as signs of "not feeling well." Family members may inadvertently reinforce the report of these symptoms due to their own sensitivity to the fact that, at times, medical action is necessary, resulting in maintenance of the sick role.

Though specifics may vary depending upon medical diagnosis, several basic guidelines can help in minimizing sick-role behaviors in children with chronic medical conditions. Normalize the child's life by maintaining a regular routine and expectations regarding school and chores when medically possible (Perrin et al., 1984). This would apply to scheduled hospitalizations as well, where, when physically possible, the child should maintain a regular schedule (e.g., sleep–wake cycle, personal grooming, school, etc.). Guidelines regarding maintenance of a normal routine have been discussed at length in a previous section.

Use of the term medical "condition" vs. "illness" by health-care providers in conjunction with anticipatory guidance on how to discriminate illness episodes that need treatment or medical attention are two practical suggestions to help minimize sick role behavior. The term "medical illness' has obvious connotations that may not always apply to many children with a chronic medical condition. Even children with life-threatening diseases, such as leukemia and cystic fibrosis, are likely to experience some episodes of health. For other children with diagnoses such as diabetes or sickle cell anemia, periods of good health may be the norm, with only episodic illnesses. By using the term "medical condition," health-care providers can encourage an identification with health.

Given that the sick role may be reinforcing due to greater attention and decrease in responsibilities during illness episodes, it can be helpful for the health-care provider to work with the family in setting concrete guidelines as to when "sick day" rules apply. A particular problem may arise in trying to decide when a child should or should not go to school. The child may complain of not feeling well and the parent is faced with the task of trying to discern if the complaints are due to the medical condition, an acute illness, avoidance of school, wanting to remain home with the parent (e.g., separation issues), or some combination of these factors. In addition, for those days where it is deemed necessary that the child remain at home, adherence to bed rest the entire day as opposed to just school hours is recommended. Caretakers should carefully weigh the amount of increased attention given to the child when he/or she has to remain at home, particularly if there is a question regarding whether the child is trying to avoid school or is concerned with separating from the parent. If health-care providers have helped the family anticipate what to do when this situation arises, then the possibility of inadvertently reinforcing inappropriate sick-role behavior may be minimized. Of course, these general guidelines will need to be used flexibly, as, for example, a child who is required to remain home due to low white cell counts may benefit from extra attention to help structure the day at home. Yet extra attention for a child with sickle cell anemia who has had to remain home because of a painful crisis may result in an increase in pain complaints and/or increased duration of the crisis.

CONCLUSIONS

The methodological sophistication of psychosocial research with children diagnosed with chronic health problems has improved considerably over the past decade. There are a number of longitudinal studies across a wide range of medical conditions in children—studies that have used appropriate comparison groups and reliable and valid assessment procedures. The majority of these investigations have focused on identifying risk factors for problems of adjustment in the child and his or her family. As such, the preponderance of data in these predictive studies is correlational in nature. In contrast, there are considerably fewer intervention studies addressing the numerous tasks and stressful experiences with which these children and their families must cope over extended periods of time. Yet the effects of the interventions that have been studied with this population have generally been limited to several problem areas. For example, there is a comparatively large body of literature pertaining to treatment approaches for reducing the stresses associated with hospitalization and medical treatment and in helping children to manage pain associated with their disease or various diagnostic and medical procedures. On the other hand, there are a limited number of intervention studies in the areas of adherence to medical regimens, school programs for children with chronic health problems, and programs for facilitating the adjustment of family members. It is anticipated that treatment studies in these latter areas will increase in the future as research provides useful data on those factors which are predictive of adaptive behavior in these various situations.

One area that warrants further study is specific coping behaviors that differentiate children and families who experience few adjustment problems from those individuals who exhibit serious maladjustment in relation to the chronic medical condition and disease-related tasks and experiences. The coping skills that children and family members use in their attempts to manage the potential stresses imposed by the illness have received little research attention. It is suggested that specific coping skills are an important focus of study in order to understand the individual differences observed in children's and families' response to the disease in the face of comparable degrees of severity and type of illness (Melamed, Siegel, & Ridley-Johnson, 1988). In this regard, Drotar (1981) has noted that coping behavior in chronically ill children and their families is "best studied from an ipsative and/or developmental perspective . . . over time . . . with measures which link coping processes to adaptive outcome in life situations" (p. 219).

Coping strategies in children with chronic medical conditions need to be evaluated from two perspectives. First, one must study how children negotiate the normal tasks of childhood and adolescence. Whether or not a child is physically ill, adaptation and coping must be assessed within the context of age-appropriate developmental tasks that must be accomplished by all children. A long-term health problem may or may not increase the difficulty faced by a child in seeking to master the various developmental tasks.

The second level of assessment of coping in children with chronic medical conditions must also focus on disease-related tasks that are unique to a child's particular illness, such as adherence to a specific medication regimen or tolerating invasive medical procedures. This would permit the identification of specific behaviors associated with the child's attempts to meet the demands imposed by the various disease-related tasks.

Using this approach, it would be possible to determine whether these children differ from their physically healthy peers both in terms of accomplishing appropriate developmental tasks and using coping strategies. In addition, research in this area would permit investigators to assess whether children with different disease-related tasks show different levels of adjustment based on their use of particular coping strategies. By systematically identifying adaptive coping strategies, it will be possible to develop more effective intervention programs for children with chronic health problems. Building on the coping skills that are already in a child's repertoire will permit researchers to develop interventions that can be tailored to a particular child's specific needs to assist him or her in the efforts to negotiate key developmental and disease-related tasks.

Given that a chronic medical condition has the *potential* to disrupt a child's normal growth and development and to interfere with a family's relationships and tasks, *all* these children and their families should be followed periodically to monitor their ongoing psychological adjustment and adaptation. An interdisciplinary and comprehensive approach to the care of children with chronic health problems is recognized as essential for maximizing their physical, emotional, intellectual, and social potential (Magrab & Calcagno, 1978). This includes the provision of ongoing psychosocial support and educational interventions (Drotar & Bush, 1985; Hobbs, Perrin, & Ireys, 1985). Psychosocial services offered during the early stages of a child's illness provide an opportunity to prevent major psychological crises from occurring and enables the mental-health professional to assist the child and family in their adjustment to particularly difficult developmental and disease-related transition periods. In addition, the introduction of such services early in the course of a child's illness reduces the likelihood that the child and family will feel "singled out" for seeing a mental-health professional during periods of crisis or when experiencing severe adjustment problems.

Finally, a recent report by the Surgeon General of the United States (Koop, 1987) advocates a "family-centered, community-based approach" to the comprehensive care of children with special health-care needs. This report strongly recommends that parents and professionals collaborate at all levels of the child's care. In addition, community-based services are encouraged. Here children would receive the majority of medical, mental health, educational, and other supportive services in their local communities rather than going to tertiary care facilities that are often considerable distances from their homes. This approach would have a profound impact on normalizing the lives of children with chronic medical conditions and minimizing the pervasive disruptions experienced by their families.

REFERENCES

Allen, D. A., Affleck, G., Tennen, H., McGrade, B. J., & Ratzan, S. (1984). Concerns of children with a chronic illness: A cognitive-developmental study of juvenile diabetes. *Child Care, Health, and Development, 10,* 211–218.

Anderson, B. J., Miller, J. P., Auslander, W. F., & Santiago, J. V. (1981). Family characteristics of diabetic adolescents: Relationship to metabolic control. *Diabetes Care, 4,* 586–594.

Armstrong, G. D., & Martinson, I. M. (1980). Death, dying, and terminal care: Dying at home. In J. Kellerman (Ed.), *Psychological aspects of cancer in children* (pp. 295–311). Springfield, IL: Charles C. Thomas.

Arnhold, R. G., Adebonojo, F. O., Callas, E. R., Callas, J., Carte, E., & Stein, R. C. (1970). Patients and prescriptions: Comprehension and compliance with medical instructions in a suburban pediatric practice. *Clinical Pediatrics, 9,* 648–651.

Baird, S. M., & Ashcroft, S. C. (1984). Education and chronically ill children: A need-based policy orientation. *Peabody Journal of Education, 61,* 91–129.

Barsky, A. J., & Klerman, G. L. (1983). Overview: Hypochondriasis, bodily complaints, and somatic styles. *American Journal of Psychiatry, 140,* 273–283.

Barsky, A. J., Goodson, J. D., Lane, R. S., & Cleary, P. D. (1988). The amplification of somatic symptoms. *Psychosomatic Medicine, 50,* 510–519.

Barton, D. (1972). Death and dying: A course for medical students. *Journal of Medical Education, 47,* 945–951.

Beck, D. E., Fennell, R. S., Yost, R. L., Robinson, J. D., Geary, D., & Richards, G. A. (1980). Evaluation of an educational program on compliance with medication regimens in pediatric patients with renal transplants. *Journal of Pediatrics, 96,* 1094–1097.

Beck, S., & Smith, L. K. (1988). Personality and social skills assessment of children with special reference to somatic disorders. In P. Karoly (Ed.), *Handbook of child health assessment: Biopsychosocial perspectives* (pp. 149–172). New York: John Wiley & Sons.

Becker, M. H., & Rosenstock, I. M. (1984). Compliance with medical advice. In A. Steptoe & A. Mathews (Eds.) *Health care and human behavior* (pp. 175–208). New York: Academic Press.

Begleiter, M. L., Burry, V. F., & Harris, D. J. (1976). Prevalence of divorce among parents of children with cystic fibrosis and other chronic diseases. *Social Biology, 23,* 260–264.

Bibace, R., & Walsh, M. E. (1979). Developmental stages in children's conceptions of illness. In G. C. Stone, F. Cohen, & N. E. Adler (Eds.), *Health psychology* (pp. 285–301). San Francisco: Jossey-Bass.

Blake, S., & Paulsen, K. (1981). Therapeutic interventions with terminally ill children: A review. *Professional Psychology, 12,* 655–663.

Bluebond-Langer, M. (1974). I know, do you? A study of awareness, communication and coping in terminally ill children. In B. Schoenberg, A. C. Curr, A. H. Kutscher, D. Perets, & I. Goldenberg (eds.), *Anticipatory grief* (pp. 171–181). New York: Columbia University Press.

Bobrow, E. S., AvRuskin, T. W., & Siller, J. (1985). Mother–daughter interaction and adherence to diabetes regimens. *Diabetes Care, 8,* 146–151.

Bonica, J. J. (1977). Neurophysiologic and pathologic aspects of acute and chronic pain. *Archives of Surgery, 112,* 750–761.

Borman, L. D. (1985). Self-help and mutual aid groups. In N. Hobbs & J. M. Perrin (Eds.). *Issues in the care of children with chronic illnesses* (pp. 771–789). San Francisco: Jossey-Bass.

Bradbury, A. J., & Smith, C. S. (1983). An assessment of the diabetic knowledge of school teachers. *Archives of Disease in Childhood, 58,* 692–696.

Breslau, N. (1982). Siblings of disabled children: Birth order and age-spacing effects. *Journal of Abnormal Child Psychology, 10,* 85–96.

Breslau, N., Weitzman, M., & Messenger, K.

(1981). Psychologic functioning of siblings of disabled children. *Pediatrics, 67,* 344–353.

Brewster, A. B. (1982). Chronically ill hospitalized children's concept of their illness. *Pediatrics, 69,* 355–362.

Brody, G., & Stoneman, L. (1986). Contextual issues in the study of sibling socialization. In J. J. Gallagher & P. M. Vietze (Eds.), *Families of handicapped persons: Research, programs, and policy issues* (pp. 123–136). Baltimore: Paul H. Brooks.

Bronheim, S. P. (1978). Pulmonary disorders: Asthma and cystic fibrosis. In P. Magrab (Ed.), *Psychological management of pediatric problems: Vol. 1. Early life conditions and chronic diseases* (pp. 309–344). Baltimore: University Park Press.

Brownlee-Duffeck, M., Peterson, L., Simonds, J. F., Goldstein, D., Kilo, C., & Hoette, S. (1987). The role of health beliefs in the regimen adherence and metabolic control of adolescents and adults with diabetes mellitus. *Journal of Consulting and Clinical Psychology, 55,* 139–144.

Burbach, D. J., & Peterson, L. (1986). Children's concepts of physical illness: A review and critique of the cognitive-developmental literature. *Health Psychology, 5,* 307–325.

Cameron, R. (1978). The clinical implementation of behavior change techniques: A cognitively oriented conceptualization of therapeutic "compliance" and "resistance." In J. P. Foreyt & D. P. Rathjen (Eds.), *Cognitive behavior therapy: Research and application* (pp. 233–250). New York: Plenum Press.

Carey, M. P., & Burish, T. G. (1988). Etiology and treatment of the psychological side effects associated with cancer chemotherapy: A critical review and discussion. *Psychological Bulletin, 104,* 307–325.

Cataldo, M. F., Bessman, C. A., Parker, L. H., Pearson, J. E., & Rogers, M. C. (1979). Behavioral assessment for pediatric intensive care units. *Journal of Applied Behavior Analysis, 12,* 83–97.

Clark, D. (1982). *Colorado school health program.* Unpublished manuscript, Vanderbilt University, Chronically Ill Child Project, Nashville, TN.

Cluss, P. A., & Epstein, L. H. (1985). The measurement of medical compliance in the treatment of disease. In P. Karoly (Ed.), *Measurement strategies in health psychology.* New York: John Wiley & Sons.

Cohen, F., & Lazarus, R. S. (1980). Coping with the stress of illness. In G. C. Stone, F. Cohen & N. E. Adler (Eds.), *Health psychology: A handbook* (pp. 217–254). San Francisco: Jossey-Bass.

Copeland, D. R., Fletcher, J. M., Pfefferbaum-Levine, B., Jaffe, N., Ried, H., & Maor, M. (1985). Neuropsychological sequelae of childhood cancer in long-term survivors. *Pediatrics, 75,* 745–753.

Creer, T. L., & Christian, W. P. (1976). *Chronically ill and handicapped children: Their management and rehabilitation.* Champaign, IL: Research Press.

Czajkowski, D. R., & Koocher, G. P. (1986). Predicting medical compliance among adolescents with cystic fibrosis. *Health Psychology, 5,* 297–305.

Davidson, G. W. (Ed.). (1985). *The hospice: Development and administration* (2nd ed.). Washington, DC: Hemisphere Publishing.

Deasy-Spinetta, P., & Spinetta, J. J. (1980). The child with cancer in school. *American Journal of Pediatric Hematology/Oncology, 2,* 89–94.

Deaton, A. V. (1985). Adaptive noncompliance in pediatric asthma. The parent as expert. *Journal of Pediatric Psychology, 10,* 1–14.

Deno, E. (1973). *Instructional alternatives for exceptional children.* Reston, VA: Council for Exceptional Children.

DiMatteo, M. R., & DiNicola, D. D. (1982). *Achieving patient compliance: The psychology of the medical practitioner's role.* Elmsford, NY: Pergamon Press.

Dolgin, M. J., Katz, E. R., McGinty, K., & Siegel, S. E. (1985). Anticipatory nausea and vomiting in pediatric cancer patients. *Pediatrics, 75,* 547–552.

Dolgin, M. J., Katz, E. R., Doctors, S. R., & Siegel, S. (1986). Caregivers' perceptions of medical compliance in adolescents with cancer. *Journal of Adolescent Health Care, 7,* 22–27.

Drotar, D. (1981). Psychological perspectives in chronic childhood illness. *Journal of Pediatric Psychology, 6,* 211–228.

Drotar, D., Baskiewicz, A., Irvin, N., Kennell, J., & Klaus, M. (1975). The adaptation of parents to the birth of an infant with a congenital malformation: A hypothetical model. *Pediatrics, 56,* 710–717.

Drotar, D., & Bush, M., (1985). Mental health issues and services. In N. Hobbs & J. M.

Perrin (Eds.), *Issues in the care of children with chronic illnesses: A sourcebook on problems, services, and politics* (pp. 514–550). San Francisco: Jossey-Bass.

Drotar, D., Owens, R. & Gotthold, J. (1980). Personality adjustment of children and adolescents with hypopituitarism. *Child Psychiatry and Human Development, 11,* 59–66.

Eiser, C., & Town, C. (1987). Teacher's concern about chronically sick children: Implications for pediatricians. *Developmental Medicine and Child Neurology, 29,* 56–63.

Elkind, D. (1985). Cognitive development and adolescent disability. *Journal of Adolescent Health Care, 6,* 84–89.

Elkins, P. D., & Roberts, M. C. (1983). Psychological preparation for pediatric hospitalization. *Clinical Psychology Review, 3,* 1–21.

Faberow, N. L. (1986). Noncompliance as indirect self-destructive behavior. In K. E. Gerber & A. A. Nehemkis (Eds.), *Compliance: The dilemma of the chronically ill* (pp. 24–43). New York: Springer.

Fennell, R. S., Rasbury, W. C., Fennell, E. B., & Morris, M. K. (1984). The effects of kidney transplantation on cognitive performance in a pediatric population. *Pediatrics, 74,* 273–278.

Ferguson, B. F. (1979). Preparing young children for hospitalization. A comparison of two methods. *Pediatrics, 64,* 656–664.

Ferrari, M. (1984). Chronic illness: Psychosocial effects on siblings: I. Chronically ill boys. *Journal of Child Psychology and Psychiatry, 25,* 459–476.

Fordyce, W. E. (1976). *Behavioral methods for chronic pain and illness.* St. Louis: C. V. Mosby.

Fowler, M. G., Johnson, M. P., Welshimer, K. J., Atkinson, S. S., & Loda, F. A. (1987). Factors related to school absence in children with cardiac factors. *American Journal of Diseases in Children, 141,* 1317–1320.

Fowler, M. G., Whitt, J. K., Lallinger, R. R., Nash, K. B., Atkinson, S. S., Wells, R. J., & McMillan, C. (1988). Neuropsychologic and academic functioning of children with sickle cell anemia. *Developmental and Behavioral Pediatrics, 9,* 213–220.

Franceschi, M., Cecchetto, R., Minicucci, F., Smizne, S., Baio, G., & Canal, N. (1984). Cognitive processes in insulin-dependent diabetes mellitus. *Diabetes Care, 7,* 228–231.

Friedrich, W. N., & Friedrich, W. L. (1981).

Psychosocial assets of parents of handicapped and nonhandicapped children. *American Journal of Mental Deficiency, 85,* 551–553.

Gogan, J. L., & Slavin, L. (1981). Interviews with brothers and sisters. In G. P. Koocher & J. E. O'Malley (Eds.), *The Damocles syndrome: Psychosocial consequences of surviving childhood cancer* (pp. 101–111). New York: McGraw-Hill.

Gortmaker, S. L. (1985). Demography of chronic childhood diseases. In N. Hobbs & J. M. Perin (Eds.), *Issues in the care of children with chronic illness: A sourcebook on problems, services, and policies* (pp. 135–154). San Francisco: Jossey-Bass.

Gayton, W. F., Friedman, S. B., Tavormina, J. F., & Tucker, F. (1977). Children with cystic fibrosis: 1. Psychological test findings of patients, siblings, and parents. *Pediatrics, 59,* 888–894.

Grandstaff, C. L. (1981). Creative approaches to compliance with P. L. 94-142 and home/hospital programs. *Journal of the Division of the Physically Handicapped, Council for Exceptional Children, 5,* 37–44.

Grossman, F. K. (1972). *Brothers and sisters of retarded children: An exploratory study.* New York: Syracuse University Press.

Haggerty, R. J., Roghmann, K. J., & Pless, I. B. (1975). *Child health and the community.* New York: John Wiley & Sons.

Hauser, S. T., Jacobson, A. M., Wertlieb, D., Weiss-Perry, B., Follansbee, D., Wolfsdorf, J. I., Herskowitz, R. D., Houlihan, J., & Rajapark, D. C. (1986). Children with recently diagnosed diabetes: Interactions within their families. *Health Psychology, 5,* 273–296.

Hayes-Bautista, D. E. (1976). Modifying the treatment: Patient compliance, patient control, and medical care. *Social Science & Medicine, 10,* 233–238.

Haynes, R. B. (1976). A critical review of the "determinants" of patient compliance with therapeutic regimens. In D. L. Sackett & R. B. Haynes (Eds.), *Compliance with therapeutic regimens* (pp 26–39). Baltimore: The John Hopkins University Press.

Hill, R., & Rogers, R. H. (1964). The developmental approach. In H. T. Christensen (Ed.), *Handbook of marriage and the family* (pp. 171–211). Chicago: Rand McNally.

Hobbs, N., Perrin, J. M., Ireys, H. T. (1985).

Chronically ill children and their families. San Francisco: Jossey-Bass.

Holiday, B. (1984). Challenges of rearing a chronically ill child: Caring and coping. *Nursing Clinics of North America, 19,* 361–368.

Ingersoll, G. M., Orr, D. P., Herrold, A. J., & Golden, M. P. (1986). Cognitive maturity and self-management among adolescents with insulin-dependent diabetes mellitus. *Journal of Pediatrics, 108,* 620–623.

Jamison, R. N., Lewis, S., & Burish, T. (1986). Psychological impact of cancer on adolescents: Self-image, locus of control, perception of illness, and knowledge of cancer. *Journal of Chronic Diseases, 39,* 609–617.

Janis, I. L. (1984). Improving adherence to medical recommendations: Prescriptive hypotheses derived from recent research in social psychology. In A. Baum, S. E. Taylor, & J. E. Singer (Eds.), *Handbook of psychology and health: Vol. 4. Social psychology of aspects of health* (pp. 113–148). Hillsdale, NJ: Lawrence Erlbaum Associates.

Jay, S. M., Elliott, C. H., Ozolins, M., Olson, R. A., & Pruitt, S. D. (1985). Behavioral management of children's distress during painful medical procedures. *Behavioural Research and Therapy, 23,* 513–520.

Jay, S. M., Green, V., Johnson, S. Caldwell, S., & Nitschke, R. (1987). Differences in death concepts between children with cancers and physically healthy children. *Journal of Clinical Child Psychology, 16,* 301–306.

Jay, S. M., Ozolins, M., Elliott, C. H., & Caldwell, S. (1983). Assessment of children's distress during painful medical procedures. *Health Psychology, 2,* 133–147.

Johnson, S. B. (April, 1988). *Compliance in pediatric psychology.* Paper presented at the Florida Conference on Child Health Psychology, Gainesville, FL.

Johnson, S. B., Silverstein, J., Rosenbloom, A., Carter, R., & Cunningham, W. (1986). Assessing daily management in childhood diabetes. *Health Psychology, 5,* 545–564.

Karoly, P. (1988). *Handbook of child health assessment: Biosocial perspectives.* New York: John Wiley & Sons.

Kasl, S. V. (1975). Issues in patient adherence to health care regimens. *Journal of Human Stress, 1,* 5–18.

Katz, E. R., Rubinstein, C. L., Hubert, N. C.,

& Bleu, A. (1989). School and social reintegration of children with cancer. *Journal of Psychosocial Oncology, 6,* 123–140.

Kellerman, J., Rigler, D., & Siegel, S. E. (1979). Psychological responses of children to isolation in a protected environment. *Journal of Behavioral Medicine, 2,* 263–274.

Kellerman, J., Rigler, D., Siegel, S. E., McCue, K., Pospisil, J., & Uno, R. (1976). Pediatric cancer patients in reverse isolation utilizing protected environments. *Journal of Pediatric Psychology, 1,* 21–25.

Kellerman, J., Zeltzer, L., Ellenberg, L., & Dash, J. (1983). Adolescents with cancer: Hypnosis for the reduction of the acute pain and anxiety associated with medical procedures. *Journal of Adolescent Health Care, 4,* 85–90.

Kellerman, J., Zeltzer, L., Ellenberg, L., Dash, J., & Rigler, D. (1980). Psychological effects of illness in adolescence: Anxiety, self-esteem and the perception of control. *Journal of Pediatrics, 97,* 126–131.

Kirkham, M. A., Schilling, R. F., Norelius, K., & Schinke, S. P. (1986). Developing coping styles and social networks: An intervention. *Child Care Health and Development, 12,* 313–323.

Klerman, L. V. (1985). Interprofessional issues in delivering services to chronically ill children and their families. In N. Hobbs & J. M. Perrin (Eds.), *Issues in the care of children with chronic illness* (pp. 420–440). San Francisco: Jossey-Bass.

Kolhberg, L. (1963). Development of children's orientations toward a moral order: I. Sequence in development of moral thought. *Vita Humana 6,* 11–33.

Kolko, D. J., & Richard-Figueroa, J. L. (1985). Effects of video games on the adverse corollaries of chemotherapy in pediatric oncology patients: A single-case analysis. *Journal of Consulting and Clinical Psychology, 53,* 223–228.

Kolotkin, R. A. (1981). Preventing burn-out and reducing stress in terminal care: The role of assertiveness training. In H. J. Sobel (Ed.), *Behavioral therapy in terminal care: A humanistic approach* (pp. 229–252). Cambridge, MA: Ballinger.

Koocher, G. P. (1973). Childhood, death, and cognitive development. *Developmental Psychology, 9,* 369–374.

Koocher, G. P. (Ed.). (1977). Death and the

child [Special issue]. *Journal of Pediatric Psychology, 2*(2).

Koocher, G. P., & O'Malley, J. E. (1981). *The Damocles syndrome: Psychological consequences of surviving childhood cancer*. New York: McGraw-Hill.

Koocher, G. P., & Sallan, S. E. (1978). Pediatric oncology. In P. Magrab (Ed.), *Psychological management of pediatric problems: Vol. 1. Early life conditions and chronic diseases* (pp. 283–307). Baltimore: University Park Press.

Koop, C. E. (1987). *Surgeon General's report: Children with special health care needs*. Washington, DC: United States Public Health Service.

Korsch, B., & Negrete, V. (1972). Doctor–patient communication. *Scientific American, 227*, 66–74.

Korsch, B., Gozzi, E., & Francis, V. (1968). Gaps in doctor–patient interaction and patient satisfaction. *Pediatrics, 42*, 855–871.

Kupst, M. J., & Schulman, J. L. (1988). Long-term coping with pediatric leukemia: A six-year follow-up study. *Journal of Pediatric Psychology, 13*, 7–22.

LaGreca, A. (1988). Adherence to prescribed medical regimens. In D. K. Routh (Ed.), *Handbook of pediatric psychology* (pp. 229–320). New York: Guilford Press.

Lavigne, J. V., & Ryan, M. (1979). Psychologic adjustment of siblings of children with chronic illness. *Pediatrics, 63*, 616–627.

Lavigne, J. V., Schulein, M. J., & Hahn, Y. S. (1986a). Psychological aspects of painful medical conditions in children. I. Developmental aspects and assessment. *Pain, 27*, 133–146.

Lavigne, J. V., Schulein, M. J., & Hahn, Y. S. (1986b). Psychological aspects of painful medical conditions in children. II. Personality factors, family characteristics and treatment. *Pain, 27*, 147–169.

Lazarus, R. S., & Folkman, S. (1984). *Stress, appraisal, and coping*. New York: Springer.

LeBaron, S., & Zeltzer, L. (1984). Behavioral intervention for reducing chemotherapy related nausea and vomiting in adolescents with cancer. *Journal of Adolescent Health Care, 5*, 178–182.

Levenson, P. M., Pfefferbaum, B. J., Copeland, D., & Silberberg, Y. (1982). Information preferences of cancer patients ages 11–20 years. *Journal of Adolescent Health Care, 3*, 9–13.

Leventhal, J. M. (1984). Psychosocial assessment of children with chronic physical disease. *Pediatric Clinics of North America, 31*, 71–86.

Lorenz, R. A., Christensen, N. K., & Pichert, J. W. (1985). Diet-related knowledge, skill, and adherence among children with insulin dependent diabetes mellitus. *Pediatrics, 75*, 872–876.

Magrab, P. R., & Calcagno, P. L. (1978). Psychological impact of chronic pediatric conditions. In P. R. Magrab (Ed.), *Psychological management of pediatric problems: Vol. 1. Early life conditions and chronic diseases* (pp. 3–14). Baltimore: University Park Press.

Markova, I., MacDonald, K., & Forbes, C. (1979). Impact of haemophilia on child-rearing practices and parental cooperation. *Journal of Child Psychology and Psychiatry, 21*, 153–161.

Martin, G. W., & Mauer, A. M. (1982). Interactions of health-care professionals with critically ill children and their parents. *Clinical Pediatrics, 21*, 540–544.

Martinson, I. M., Nesbit, M., & Kersey, J. (1984). Home care for the child with cancer. In A. E. Christ & K. Flomenhaft (Eds.), *Childhood cancer: Impact on the family* (pp. 177–198). New York: Plenum Press.

Masek, B. J., Russo, D. C., & Varni, J. W. (1984). Behavioral approaches to the management of chronic pain in children. *Pediatric Clinics of North America, 31*, 1113–1131.

Mattsson, A. (1972). Long-term physical illness in childhood: A challenge to psychosocial adjustment. *Pediatrics, 50*, 801–810.

Mattsson, A. (1977). Long-term physical illness in childhood: A challenge to psychosocial adaptation. In R. J. Moos (Ed.), *Coping with physical illness* (pp. 183–199). New York: Plenum Press.

McAndrew, I. (1976). Children with a handicap and their families. *Child Care, Health, and Development, 2*, 213–218.

McCaul, K. D., Glasgow, R. E., & Schafer, L. C. (1987). Diabetes regimen behaviors: Predicting adherence. *Medical Care, 25*, 868–881.

McKeever, P. (1983). Siblings of chronically ill children: A literature review with implications for research and practice. *American Journal of Orthopsychiatry, 53*, 209–218.

Mechanic, D. (1983). Adolescent health and illness behavior: A review of the literature and a new hypothesis for the study of stress. *Journal of Human Stress, 9,* 4–13.

Mechanic, D., & Volkart, E. H. (1961). Stress, illness behavior, and the sick role. *American Sociological Review, 26,* 51–58.

Meichenbaum, D., & Turk, D. C. (1987). *Facilitating treatment adherence: A practitioner's guidebook.* New York: Plenum Press.

Melamed, B. G. (1982). Reduction of medical fears: An information processing analyses. In J. Boulougouris (Ed.), *Learning theory approaches to psychiatry* (pp. 205–218). New York: John Wiley & Sons.

Melamed, B. G., & Siegel, L. J. (1980). *Behavioral medicine: Practical applications in health care.* New York: Springer.

Melamed, B. G., & Siegel, L. J. (1975). Reduction of anxiety in children facing hospitalization and surgery by use of filmed modeling. *Journal of Consulting and Clinical Psychology, 43,* 411–521.

Melamed, B. G., Siegel, L. J., & Ridley-Johnson, R. R. (1988). Coping behaviors in children facing medical stress. In T. Fields, P. McCabe, & N. Schneiderman (Eds.), *Stress and coping across development* (pp. 109–137). Hillsdale, NJ: Lawrence Erlbaum Associates.

Minuchin, S., Baker, L., Rosman, B. L., Liebman, R., Milman, L. & Todd, T. C. (1975). A conceptual model of psychosomatic illness in children. *Archives of General Psychiatry, 32,* 1031–1038.

Morrow, G. R., & Dobkin, P. L. (1988). Anticipatory nausea and vomiting in cancer patients undergoing chemotherapy treatment: Prevalence, etiology, and behavioral interventions. *Clinical Psychology Review, 8,* 517–556.

Mulhern, R., Lauer, M. E. & Hoffman, R. G. (1983). Death of a child at home or in the hospital: Subsequent psychological adjustment of the family. *Pediatrics, 71,* 743–747.

Nader, P. R., & Parcel, G. S. (1978). Competence: The outcome of health and education. In P. R. Nader (Ed.), *Options for school health: Meeting community needs* (pp. 1–17). Germantown, MD: Aspen Systems Corporation.

Nannis, E., Susman, E. J., Strope, B. E., & Woodruff, P. J. (1982). Correlates of control in pediatric cancer patients and their families. *Journal of Pediatric Psychology, 7,* 75–84.

National Association of State Directors of Special Education and National Association of State Boards of Education. (1979). *Answering your questions about Public Law 94-142 and Section 504.* Washington, DC: Authors.

National Hospice Organization. (1984). *Fact sheet.* Arlington, VA: Author.

Naylor, D., Coates, T. J., & Kan, J. (1984). Reducing distress in pediatric cardiac catheterization. *American Journal of Diseases of Children, 138,* 726–729.

Nevin, R. S., & McCubbin, H. (1979). Parental coping with physical handicaps: Social policy implications. *Spina Bifida Therapy, 2,* 151–164.

Obetz, S. W., Swenson, W. M., McCarthy, C. A., Gilchrist, G. S., & Burgert, E. O. (1980). Children who survive malignant disease: Emotional adaptation of the children and their families. In J. L. Schulman, & M. J. Kupst (Eds.), *The child with cancer: Clinical approaches to psychosocial care-research in psychosocial aspects* (pp. 194–210). Springfield, IL: Charles C Thomas.

Oliver, I. N., Simon, R. M., & Aisner, J. (1986). Antiemetic studies: A methodological discussion. *Cancer Treatment Reports, 20,* 555–563.

Parrish, J. M. (1986). Parent compliance with medical and behavioral recommendations. In N. A. Krasnegor, J. D. Arasteh, & M. F. Cataldo (Eds.), *Child health behavior: A behavioral pediatrics perspective* (pp. 453–501). New York: John Wiley & Sons.

Parsons, T. (1951). *The social system.* Glencoe, IL: Free Press.

Parsons, T. (1958). Definitions of health and illness in light of American values and social structure. In E. Jaco (Ed.), *Patients, physicians, and illness* (pp. 165–187). New York: Free Press.

Peckman, V. C., Meadows, A. T., Bastil, N., & Marrero, O. (1988). Educational late effects in long-term survivors of childhood acute lymphocytic leukemia. *Pediatrics, 81,* 127–133.

Perrin, E., & Gerrity, P. S. (1981). There's a demon in your belly: Children's understanding of illness. *Pediatrics, 67,* 841–849.

Perrin, E. C., & Gerrity, P. S. (1984). Development of children with a chronic illness.

Pediatric Clinics of North America, 31, 19–31.

Perrin, J. M., Ireys, H. T., Shayne, M. W. & Moynihan, L. C. (1984). Children and schools: The special issues of chronically ill children. In S. C. Ashcraft (Ed.), Education and chronically ill children: A need-based policy orientation. *Peabody Journal of Education, 61*, 10–15.

Peterson, L., & Brownlee-Duffeck, M. (1984). Prevention of anxiety and pain due to medical and dental procedures. In M. C. Roberts & L. Peterson (Eds.), *Prevention of problems in childhood: Psychological research and applications* (pp. 266–308). New York: John Wiley & Sons.

Peterson, L., & Shigetomi, C. (1981). The use of coping techniques to minimize anxiety in hospitalized children. *Behavior Therapy, 12*, 1–14.

Peterson, L., & Toler, S. M. (1986). An information seeking disposition in child surgery patients. *Health Psychology, 4*, 343–358.

Piaget, J. (1929). *The child's conception of the world*. New York: Harcourt Brace Jovanovich.

Pickering, G. (1979). Therapeutics: Art or science. *Journal of the American Medical Association, 242*, 649–653.

Pless, I. B., & Perrin, J. M. (1985). Issues common to a variety of illnesses. In N. Hobbs & J. M. Perrin (Eds.), *Issues in the care of children with chronic illness: A sourcebook on problems, services, and policies* (pp. 41–60). San Francisco: Jossey-Bass.

Pless, I. B., & Pinkerton, P. (1975). *Chronic childhood disorder: Promoting patterns of adjustment*. Chicago: Year Book Medical Publishers.

Pless, I. B., & Roghmann, K. J. (1971). Chronic illness and its consequences: Some observations based on three epidemiological surveys. *Journal of Pediatrics, 79*, 351–359.

Pless, I. B., & Satterwhite, B. B. (1975). Chronic illness. In R. Haggerty, K. Roghmann, & I. B. Pless (Eds.), *Child health and the community* (pp. 78–94). New York: John Wiley & Sons.

Redd, W. H., Jacobsen, P. B., Die-Trill, M., Dermatis, H., McEvoy, M., & Holland, J. C. (1987). Cognitive/attentional distraction in the control of conditioned nausea in pediatric cancer patients receiving chemotherapy. *Journal of Consulting and Clinical Psychology, 55*, 391–395.

Rosenstock, I. M. (1985). Understanding and enhancing patient compliance with diabetic regimens. *Diabetes Care, 8*, 610–616.

Rosenstock, I. M., & Kirscht, J. P. (1979). Why people seek health care. In G. C. Stone, F. Cohen, & N. Adler (Eds.), *Health psychology* (pp. 161–188). San Francisco: Jossey-Bass.

Rothstein, R. (1980). Psychological stress in families of children in a pediatric intensive care unit. *Pediatric Clinics of North America, 27*, 613–620.

Rudd, P. (1979). In search of the gold standard for compliance measurement. *Archives of Internal Medicine, 139*, 627–628.

Ryan, C. M. (1988). Neurobehavioral complications of Type 1 diabetes: Examination of possible risk factors. *Diabetes Care, 11*, 86–93.

Sabbath, B. F., & Leventhal, J. M. (1984). Marital adjustment to chronic childhood illness: A critique of the literature. *Pediatrics, 73*, 762–768.

Schafer, L. C., Glasgow, R. E., McCaul, K. D., & Dreher, M. (1983). Adherence to IDDM regimens: Relationship to psychosocial variables and metabolic control. *Diabetes Care, 6*, 493–498.

Shagena, M. M., Sandler, H. K., & Perrin, E. C. (1988). Concepts of illness and perception of control in healthy children and in children with chronic illnesses. *Developmental and Behavioral Pediatric, 9*, 252–256.

Shapiro, J. & Shumaker, S. (1987). Differences in emotional well-being and communication styles between mother and fathers of pediatric cancer patients. *Journal of Psychosocial Oncology, 5*, 121–131.

Shaw, S. N., Stephens, L. R., & Holmes, S. S. (1986). Knowledge about medical instruments and reported anxiety in pediatric surgery patients. *Children's Health Care, 14*, 134–141.

Shope, J. T. (1981). Medication compliance. *Pediatric Clinics of North America, 28*, 5–21.

Shulman, J. L. (1983). Coping with major disease—child, family, and pediatrician. *Pediatrics, 102*, 988–991.

Siegel, L. J. (1976). Preparation of children for hospitalization: A selected review of the research literature. *Journal of Pediatric Psychology, 1*, 26–30.

Siegel, L. J. (1983). Hospitalization and medical care of children. In E. Walker & M. Roberts

(Eds.), *Handbook of clinical child psychology* (pp. 1089–1108). New York: John Wiley & Sons.

Siegel, L. J. (1988). Measuring children's adjustment to hospitalization and to medical procedures. In P. Karoly (Ed.), *Handbook of child health assessment: Biosocial perspectives* (pp. 265–302). New York: John Wiley & Sons.

Siegel, L. J., & Smith, K. S. (1989). Children's strategies for coping with pain. *Pediatrician: International Journal of Child and Adolescent Health, 16,* 110–118.

Simensson, R. J., & McHale, S. M. (1981). Review: Research on handicapped children: Sibling relationships. *Child Care Health and Development, 7,* 153–171.

Skipper, J. K., & Leonard, R. C. (1968). Children, stress, and hospitalization: A field experiment. *Journal of Health and Social Behavior, 9,* 275–287.

Skipper, J. K., Leonard, R. C., & Rhymes, J. (1968). Child hospitalization and social interaction: An experimental study of mother's feelings of stress, adaptation, and satisfaction. *Medical Care, 6,* 496–506.

Slavin, L., O'Malley, J. E., Koocher, G. P., & Foster, D. J. (1981). Communication of the cancer diagnoses to pediatric patients: Impact on long-term adjustment. *American Journal of Psychiatry, 139,* 179–183.

Smith, K. E., Ackerson, J. D., & Blotcky, A. D. (1989). Reducing distress during invasive medical procedures: Relating behavioral interventions to preferred coping style in pediatric cancer patients. *Journal of Pediatric Psychology, 14,* 405–419.

Spinetta, J. J. (1974). The dying child's awareness of death: A review. *Psychological Bulletin, 81,* 256–260.

Spinetta, J. J. (1980). Disease-related communication. How to tell. In J. Kellerman (Ed.), *Psychological aspects of childhood cancer* (pp. 257–269). Springfield, IL: Charles C. Thomas.

Spinetta, J. J., & Deasy-Spinetta, P. (Eds.). (1981). *Living with childhood cancer.* St. Louis: C. V. Mosby.

Spinetta, J. J., & Maloney, L. J. (1975). Death anxiety in the outpatient leukemic child. *Pediatrics, 65,* 1034–1037.

Spinetta, J. J. & Maloney, L. J. (1978). The child with cancer: Patterns of communication and denial. *Journal of Consulting and Clinical Psychology, 46,* 1540–1541.

Spinetta, J. J., Swarner, J. A., & Sheposh, J. P. (1981). Effective parental coping following the death of a child from cancer. *Journal of Pediatric Psychology, 6,* 251–263.

Stehbens, J. A., Kisker, C. T., & Wilson, B. K. (1983). Achievement and intelligence test–retest performance in pediatric cancer patients at diagnosis and one year later. *Journal of Pediatric Psychology, 8,* 47–56.

Stehbens, J. A. (1988). Childhood cancer. In D. K. Routh (Ed.), *Handbook of pediatric psychology* (pp. 135–161). New York: Guilford Press.

Stein, R. E. K. & Jessop, D. J. (1982). A non-categorical approach to chronic childhood illness. *Public Health Reports, 97,* 354–362.

Stein, R. E. K. & Jessop, D. J. (1984). Relationship between health status and psychological adjustment among children with chronic conditions. *Pediatrics, 73,* 169–174.

Stinson, G. V. (1974). Obeying doctor's orders: A view from the other side. *Social Science & Medicine, 8,* 97–104.

Stuetzer, C. (1980). Support systems for professionals. In J. L. Schulman & M. J. Kupst (Eds.), *The child with cancer: Clinical approaches to psychosocial care research in psychosocial aspects* (pp. 63–71). Springfield, IL: Charles C. Thomas.

Susman, E. J., Dorn, L. D., Fletcher, J. C. (1987). Reasoning about illness in ill and healthy children and adolescents: Cognitive and emotional developmental aspects. *Developmental and Behavioral Pediatrics, 8,* 266–273.

Tavormina, J., Kastner, L. S., Slater, P. M., & Watt, S. L. (1976). Chronically ill children: A psychologically and emotionally deviant population? *Journal of Abnormal Child Psychology, 4,* 99.

Tew, B., & Lawrence, K. M. (1975). Some sources of stress in mothers of spina bifida children. *British Journal of Prevention and Social Medicine, 29,* 27–30.

Thompson, R. H. (1985). *Psychosocial research on pediatric hospitalization and health care: A review of the literature.* Springfield, IL: Charles C. Thomas.

Thompson, K. L., & Varni, J. W. (1986). A developmental cognitive-biobehavioral approach to pediatric pain assessment. *Pain, 25,* 283–296.

Toseland, R., & Hacker, L. (1982). Self-help groups and professional development. *Social Work, 27,* 341–347.

Trantman, P. D., Erickson, C., Shaffer, D., O'Conner, P. A., Sitarz, A., Correra, A., & Schonfeld, I. S. (1988). Prediction of intellectual deficits in children with acute lymphoblastic leukemia. *Journal of Developmental and Behavioral Pediatrics, 9,* 122–128.

Travis, G. (1976). *Chronic illness in children: Its impact on child and family.* Stanford, CA: Stanford University Press.

Turiel, E. (1969). Developmental processes in the child's moral thinking. In P. Mussen, J. Langer, M. Covington (Eds.), *New directions in developmental psychology* (pp. 92–133). New York: Holt, Rinehart, & Winston.

Twaddle, A. C. (1969). Health decisions and sick role variations: An exploration. *Journal of Health and Social Behavior, 10,* 105–115.

Twaddle, A. C., & Hessler, R. M. (1977). *A sociology of health.* St. Louis: C. V. Mosby.

Varni, J. W. (1981). Self-regulation techniques in the management of chronic arthritic pain in hemophilia. *Behavior Therapy, 12,* 185–194.

Varni, J. W. (1983). *Clinical behavioral pediatrics: An interdisciplinary biobehavioral approach.* Elmsford, NY: Pergamon Press.

Varni, J. W., & Babani, L. (1986). Long-term adherence to health care regimens in pediatric chronic disorders. In N. A. Krashegor, J. D. Arasteh, & M. F. Cataldo (Eds.), *Child health behavior: A behavioral pediatrics perspective* (pp. 502–520). New York: John Wiley & Sons.

Varni, J. W., & Gilbert, A. (1982). Self-regulation of chronic arthritic pain and long-term analgesic dependence in a hemophilia. *Rheumatology and Rehabilitation, 21,* 171–174.

Varni, J. W., & Wallender, J. L. (1984). Adherence to health-related regimens in pediatric chronic disorders. *Clinical Psychology Review, 4,* 585–596.

Vernick, J., & Karon, M. (1965). Who's afraid of death on a leukemia ward? *American Journal of Diseases of Children, 109,* 393–397.

Vernon, D. T. A., & Bailey, W. C. (1974). The use of motion pictures in the psychological preparation of children for induction of anesthesia. *Anesthesiology, 40,* 68–74.

Vernon, D. T. A., Foley, J. M., Sipowicz, R. R., & Schulman, J. L. (1965). *The psychological responses of children to hospitalization and illness.* Springfield, IL: Charles C. Thomas.

Walco, G. A., & Dampier, C. D. (1987). Chronic pain in adolescent patients. *Journal of Pediatric Psychology, 12,* 215–225.

Wallace, M. H., Bakke, K., Hubbard, A., & Pendergrass, T. W. (1984). Coping with childhood cancer: An educational program for parents of children with cancer. *Oncology Nursing Forum, 11,* 30–35.

Wallander, J. L., Varni, J. W., Babani, L., Banis, H. T., Dehaan, C. B., & Wilcox, K. T. (1989). Disability parameters, chronic strain, and adaptation of physically handicapped children and their mothers. *Journal of Pediatric Psychology, 14,* 23–42.

Wells, R. D., & Schwebel, A. I. (1987). Chronically ill children and their mothers: Predictors of resilience and vulnerability to hospitalization and surgery stress. *Developmental and Behavioral Pediatrics, 8,* 83–89.

White, E., Elsom, B., & Prawat, R. (1978). Children's conceptions of death. *Child Development, 49,* 307–310.

Wiener, J. M. (1970). Response of medical personnel to the fatal illness of a child. In B. Schoenberg, A. Carr, D. Perets, & A. Kutscher (Eds.), *Loss and grief: Psychological management in medical practice.* New York: Columbia University Press.

Wolfer, J. A., & Visintainer, M. A. (1975). Pediatric surgical patients' and parents' stress responses and adjustment. *Nursing Research, 24,* 244–255.

Wood, T. A., Siegel, L. J., & Scott, R. L. (April, 1989). *A comparison of marital adjustment and stress with parents of chronically ill, handicapped, and non-handicapped children.* Paper presented at the Second Florida Conference on Child Health Psychology, Gainesville, FL.

Woolsey, S. (1985). A medical school course in coping with death: An opportunity to consider some basic health care issues. *Developmental and Behavioral Pediatrics, 6,* 91–99.

Zeltzer, L. K., Dash, J., & Holland, J. P. (1979). Hypnotically induced pain control in sickle cell anemia. *Pediatrics, 64,* 533–536.

Zeltzer, L., & LeBaron, S. (1982). Hypnoses and nonhypnotic techniques for reduction of pain and anxiety during painful procedures in children and adolescents with cancer. *Journal of Pediatrics, 101,* 1032–1035.

Zeltzer, L., LeBaron, S., Zeltzer, P. M. (1984). The effectiveness of behavioral intervention for reduction of nausea and vomiting in children and adolescents receiving chemotherapy. *Journal of Clinical Oncology, 2,* 683–690.

Zola, I. K. (1981). Structural constraints on the doctor–patient relationship: The case of noncompliance. In L. Eisenberg & A. Kleinman (Eds.), *The relevance of social science for medicine* (pp. 241–252). New York: D. Reidel.

PART III

ISSUES AND CONCERNS REGARDING INTERVENTION

CHAPTER 12

AN OVERVIEW OF PSYCHOPHARMACOTHERAPY FOR CHILDREN AND ADOLESCENTS

Kenneth D. Gadow
John C. Pomeroy

INTRODUCTION

Drug therapy for emotional and behavioral problems is a contentious issue that produces widely divergent opinions on its appropriate applications. Child and adolescent disorders commonly have an intermingling of developmental, biological, and environmental factors, which necessitates a broad orientation to assessment and intervention. Psychopharmacotherapy is but one part of the full armamentarium of effective treatments available, but it is apparent that the increasingly sophisticated scientific investigation of this treatment has been one of the major advances for child psychiatrists. Earlier in this century, relatively few psychotropic drugs were available for clinical application (see Darrow, 1929; Meyer, 1922), but this situation began to change in the late 1930s with the discovery that amphetamine was a useful intervention for the management of behavior disorders. The most important developments, however, came in the 1950s with the appearance of the neuroleptics, antianxiety agents, antidepressants, and antimanic drugs. The significance of this era (the late 1930s to the late 1950s) is attested to by the fact that today the most commonly prescribed medication (or its chemical equivalent) from each category of psychotropic drugs was "discovered" (often serendipitously) during this time. Ironically, the wealth of data that exists for some of these therapeutic agents is due in no small part to the hiatus in the discovery of major new psychotropic drugs. This is not to say that there is any dearth of new products but simply that safer and more effective substitutes for established medications have been slow to appear.

Pediatric psychopharmacotherapy has moved from being characterized as "islands of understanding in a sea of ignorance" (Taylor, 1983, p. 322) and as lagging behind adult psychopharmacology (Werry, 1982) to showing the early signs of significant progress, mainly because of advances in diagnosis and research methodology as well as an increasing understanding of the neurochemistry of childhood psychopathology (Campbell & Spencer, 1988). In spite of significant progress in certain areas of psychotropic drug therapy, there has been much less advance

367

in the development and evaluation of practical treatment procedures for application in typical clinical settings (Gadow, 1988a) or in the formulation and critical examination of theories of treatment.

This chapter presents an overview of pharmacotherapy for mood, thought, and behavior disorders in children and adolescents. The specific disorders that are covered (and the drugs that are characteristically used to treat them) are presented in alphabetical order in Table 12.1. In keeping with the organization of this text, drug therapy is discussed by diagnostic category instead of drug class. This organization plan, unfortunately, creates some redundancy because many psychoactive agents have multiple therapeutic applications, often at comparable doses. It was therefore decided to limit more detailed discussions of therapeutic and untoward effects to a particular diagnostic category, generally the one for which the drug is most commonly prescribed. Information about general clinical management is also presented, but space limitations preclude a thorough discussion of this topic. For the same reason, only brief mention is made of drug therapy for mentally retarded people. Readers who are specifically interested in this clinical population may find *Pharmacotherapy and Mental Retardation* (Gadow & Poling, 1988) to be a useful reference. Little attention is given to diagnostic procedures or alternative treatments because they are addressed in other chapters in this book. Specific drugs are referred to by trade names, because professionals from nonmedical backgrounds are generally more familiar with these than with generic names. For readers more accustomed to the latter, the generic name appears in parentheses following the first mention of each trade name product. A list of many psychotherapeutic drugs in current use is presented in the Appendix. Deciding upon the most appropriate label for each disorder is also a problem, because diagnostic nomenclature has changed repeatedly over the years. So as not to imply uniformity in subject-selection criteria in drug studies conducted over the past several decades, we use more general terms to refer to the various childhood and adolescent disorders discussed in this chapter. However, the American Psychiatric Association's (1987) categorical label appears in parentheses following the subheading for each disorder.

The material presented in this chapter is based upon the two-volume series *Children On Medication* (Gadow, 1986a, 1986b) and has been updated to reflect current developments in psychopharmacology. Readers interested in more comprehensive discourses on pediatric psychopharmacology are referred to the following and other sources (Aman & Singh, 1988; Barkley, 1981; Ross & Ross, 1982; Werry, 1978; Wiener, 1985).

ACADEMIC UNDERACHIEVEMENT (ACADEMIC SKILLS DISORDERS)

Although no drug in therapeutic use in the United States is approved specifically for enhancing academic performance, many psychotropic agents can affect academic functioning, and underachievement is a pervasive problem in children referred for psychiatric evaluation. When academic performance is enhanced, this is generally considered to be a good thing, particularly for children and adolescents who are underachieving prior to drug exposure. There are, of course, many disorders for which academic underachievement is a commonly associated problem. In some cases underachievement is expected, because the child is of below-average mental ability. For other youngsters, the symptoms of their behavioral disability are an impediment to learning. When academic performance (measured by a standardized achievement test) is significantly below what would be predicted on the basis of innate ability (determined by an individually administered IQ test) and not the consequence of another educationally recognized disorder (e.g., mental retardation), the condition is referred to as a learning disability.

Caregiver and peer reactions to academic performance are hypothesized to play an important role in the formation of self-concept and personal happiness; hence underachievement is believed to have important psychosocial sequelae. Academic achievement is also believed to be an extremely important contributor to success and happiness in adult life (particularly for people from middle- and upper-class backgrounds), in spite of a truly compelling literature to the contrary. This is even true for learning disabled children, whose primary disability is academic underachievement. When evaluating the effect of a psychotropic drug on academic functioning and its potential role in treatment, it is important for the clinician to be cognizant of patient characteristics, the exact nature of the academic

Table 12.1. Psychoactive Drugs Currently Being Used (or Under Investigation) for the Treatment of Childhood and Adolescent Disorders

DISORDER	DRUG CLASS	REPRESENTATIVE TRADE PRODUCTS[a]
Academic underachievement and learning disabilities[b]	Stimulants	Ritalin, Dexedrine, Cylert
Affective		
Bipolar	Antimanics	Eskalith, Lithane, Lithobid
	Neuroleptics	Mellaril, Haldol, Thorazine
	Antiepileptics	Tegretol
Depression	Antidepressants	
	Tricyclics	Tofranil, Elavil, Norpramin
	MAOIs	Nardil, Parnate
Anxiety		
Anxiety states	Antianxiety agents	Valium, Ativan, Xanax
	Beta blockers	Inderal
Obsessive compulsive	Antidepressants	
Panic disorder	Tricyclics	Anafranil, Tofranil, Norpramin
	MAOIs	Nardil, Parnate
Separation anxiety	Tricyclic antidepressants	Tofranil
Autism	Neuroleptics	Haldol
	Stimulants	Ritalin
	Anorectics	Pondimin
	Opioid antagonists	Trexan
Conduct problems		
Aggression	Neuroleptics	Mellaril, Thorazine, Haldol
	Stimulants	Ritalin, Dexedrine
	Antimanics	Eskalith, Lithane, Lithobid
	Beta blockers	Inderal
	Antiepileptics	Tegretol
Oppositional behavior	Stimulants	Ritalin, Dexedine, Cylert
Enuresis	Tricyclic antidepressants	Tofranil, Norpramin, Elavil
	Stimulants	Ritalin
Hyperactivity	Stimulants	Ritalin, Dexedrine, Cylert
	Neuroleptics	Mellaril, Haldol
	Tricyclic antidepressants	Tofranil, Norpramin, Elavil
Schizophrenia	Neuroleptics	Mellaril, Navane, Haldol, Loxitane
Self-injurious behavior	Neuroleptics	Mellaril, Haldol, Thorazine
	Opioid antagonists	Narcan, Trexan
	Antimanics	Eskalith, Lithane, Lithobid
Speech and language	Stimulants	Benzedrine, Dexedrine, Ritalin
	Neuroleptics	Haldol
Stereotypies	Neuroleptics	Mellaril, Haldol, Thorazine
Tourette syndrome	Neuroleptics	Haldol, Prolixin, Orap
	Antihypertensives	Catapres

[a] Only trade-name products marketed in the United States are listed. In the case of drugs no longer protected by patent laws, the inclusion of trade names other than the original was arbitrary.
[b] At the present time, academic underachievement is not a recognized indication for any approved psychoactive drug.

performance problem, and the personal and social implications of underachievement.

The adverse effects of medication on academic progress is a primary clinical concern. Although many psychoactive drugs are known to induce behavior and cognitive changes that would likely result in impaired school performance (reviewed by Aman, 1978; Gadow, 1986a; Reynolds, 1983), academic productivity and achievement are rarely used in research or clinical settings to assess behavioral toxicity. In spite of the logistical problems that one often encounters in trying to obtain such information, an effort should be made to elicit reports from caregivers about changes in schoolwork.

In his seminal paper on Benzedrine (amphetamine) in behavior-disordered children, Bradley (1937) observed that treatment with stimulant medication led to improvement in schoolwork as demonstrated by increased productivity, comprehension, and accuracy, which was attributed to a " 'drive' to accomplish as much work as possible during the school period" (p. 578). Bradley conducted additional research and concluded that the drug did accelerate academic progress by increasing the number of pages of arithmetic "thoroughly learned" during a 1-month period (Bradley & Bowen, 1940). However, the effect upon the number of lists of spelling words thoroughly learned was less dramatic. Another important finding from this study was the fact that response to stimulants is variable. Some children showed vast improvement on medication, whereas others actually became worse.

Molitch and Sullivan's (1937) investigation into the effects of a single dose of Benzedrine on juvenile delinquents who were housed in a state-operated residential facility was the first stimulant drug study to employ a standardized achievement test. Although their data were not analyzed statistically, Molitch and Sullivan concluded that the drug group clearly outperformed the placebo group in enhancing academic achievement test performance. Nevertheless, the magnitude of the drug effect was modest.

It is a curious fact, but nevertheless true, that our understanding of stimulant drug effects on academic performance has progressed very little since these early efforts. Academic productivity (e.g, amount of correct work completed) is still the most popular measure of academic performance, and the size of the treatment effect is relatively large, at least for some types of academic skills. Standardized achievement tests are also occasionally used; but because they are generally more suitable for longer periods of drug exposure, their value for understanding treatment effects in short-term studies (which dominate the literature) is limited. Collectively, the findings from a number of investigations suggest that the academic achievement test gains associated with stimulant drug treatment are not particularly robust, long-lasting, or cumulative, which is not to say that they are nonexistent.

Reading

The research findings on stimulants and reading performance in hyperactive children are mixed. Medication does enhance the amount of accurate reading-related seat work that is completed during the school day (e.g., Pelham, Bender, Caddell, Booth, & Moorer, 1985; Pelham, Swanson, Bender, & Wilson, 1980; Rapport, Stoner, DePaul, Birmingham, & Tucker, 1985), but the mechanism of action is entirely un-

known. Standardized achievement test performance, however, is affected much less dramatically. This is not to suggest that everyone shares this interpretation of the research literature or that the findings from all studies are equally discouraging. For example, Richardson, Kupietz, Winsberg, Maitinsky, and Mendell (1988) reported a study of Ritalin (methylphenidate) in hyperactive children who were underachievers in reading and who were participating in a special after-school reading program. Although the size of the drug effect was very small after 6 months of treatment, a subgroup of "good" responders (determined on the basis of teacher ratings of classroom behavior) were said to have benefited much more. Methodological and other considerations aside, the clinical implications of these findings for school-labeled learning disabled hyperactive children is unclear.

Within the last few years, three studies have been published on the use of stimulant medication with *nonhyperactive* learning disabled children (Aman & Werry, 1982; Gittelman-Klein & Klein, 1976; Gittelman, Klein, & Feingold, 1983). In their first study, Gittelman-Klein and Klein (1976) randomly assigned children to either Ritalin or placebo conditions. All subjects were selected on the basis of being 2 years below reading grade level despite average intelligence, and most were receiving academic remediation in school. At the end of 12 weeks, differences in achievement test scores for arithmetic and spelling were trivial, but the difference in reading scores approached statistical significance. Teachers' global ratings of reading and arithmetic performance did not discriminate between the two treatment groups. On the basis of these and other findings, Gittelman-Klein and Klein concluded that Ritalin was not an effective agent for the remediation of reading deficits in non-hyperactive learning disabled children. They also noted, however, that medication effects may be manifested only in the presence of a specialized academic intervention.

To test this hypothesis, Gittelman et al. (1983) conducted a second study in which nonhyperactive reading-retarded children were randomly assigned to one of three groups: (1) reading remediation (phonics program) and placebo, (2) academic tutoring (without reading instruction) and placebo, and (3) reading remediation and Ritalin. The results indicted that although medication did enhance cognitive task performance, it did not facilitate academic achievement. Some reading achievement measures, however, did show drug effects or trends favoring the medication-treated group, suggesting that the impact of Ritalin on reading instruction was not a strong one. Quite unexpectedly, medication markedly enhanced other areas of academic performance (e.g., social studies), which were not part of the reading program. However, a retest of these academic skills 8 months after the termination of pharmacotherapy failed to show residual benefits. In other words, gains in achievement test scores appeared to fade over time after medication was stopped.

Aman and Werry (1982) administered Ritalin, Valium (diazepam), and placebo for 1 week each to 15 children diagnosed as being severely reading-retarded (but with normal IQ). Medication was not found to improve cognitive functions presumed to be associated with reading disability.

In sum, although stimulant medication does not appear markedly to improve reading achievement in hyperactive (Barkley & Cunningham, 1978) or nonhyperactive learning disabled children (Gittelman-Klein & Klein, 1976; Gittelman et al., 1983) or to correct the underlying problem that is causing the reading disability (Aman & Werry, 1982), it does increase the amount of reading-related workbook assignments in underachieving hyperactive children. One would predict that if medication helped students to pay attention and complete more schoolwork, their reading levels would improve. At the present time, however, it is difficult to say with certainty whether this conclusion is true or false.

Arithmetic

Since Bradley's (1937, Bradley & Bowen, 1940) early studies were published, a number of other investigators have also shown that stimulant medication enhances academic productivity on classroom and laboratory arithmetic tasks (e.g., Douglas, Barr, O'Neill, & Britton, 1986; Pelham et al., 1985; Rapport et al., 1985; see also Sprague's study in Gadow and Swanson, 1985). In spite of these encouraging reports, improvement in academic achievement test performance is less dramatic. For example, of the 11 short-term studies in Barkley and Cunningham's (1978) review that employed measures of arithmetic achievement, statistically significant drug effects were reported in only one instance (Conners,

Rothschild, Eisenberg, Stone, & Robinson, 1969). Interestingly, the Gittelman et al. (1983) study found significant Ritalin-induced gains on the arithmetic subtests of the Stanford Achievement Test in nonhyperactive learning disabled children, even though arithmetic skill development was not part of the intervention program.

The findings from studies of stimulant medication and arithmetic productivity are fairly consistent. Drug therapy appears to increase work output without sacrificing accuracy; however, there are only a few reports of improved performance on standardized achievement tests (Conners et al., 1969; Gittelman et al., 1983). Nothing is known about the effects of stimulants on children who have a specific arithmetic disability with or without a concurrent behavior or learning disorder.

Spelling

There were 11 short-term drug studies included in the review by Barkley and Cunningham (1978) that employed either measures of spelling achievement ($n = 10$) or productivity ($n = 1$); significant drug effects were demonstrated in only two instances (Conners, Taylor, Meo, Kurz, & Fournier, 1972; Weiss, Minde, Douglas, Werry, & Sykes, 1971). Pelham et al. (1985) reported a modest Ritalin-related increase in the proportion of words correct on weekly spelling tests, which consisted of words that the hyperactive children could not spell correctly. In a similar study, however, Cylert (pemoline) failed to enhance spelling performance (Pelham et al., 1980). Another investigation (Stephens, Pelham, & Skinner, 1984) of Ritalin, Cylert, and placebo revealed that stimulant drugs produced a 25% reduction in spelling errors (nonsense words) compared with placebo. In view of these conflicting findings, no definite conclusions can be drawn about stimulant medication and spelling. Furthermore, there is no drug research on spelling disability per se.

Handwriting

A number of investigators have reported that stimulant drugs can enhance handwriting ability in hyperactive children and adolescents. Moreover, there are a number of published handwriting samples (e.g., Levy, 1973; Schain & Reynard, 1975; Taylor, 1979) that compellingly demonstrate the magnitude of this effect. Nevertheless, poor handwriting is rarely the basis for medical referral, nor is it a clinical indication for treatment. The only published study that selected children (diagnosed as having minimal brain dysfunction) on the basis of poor handwriting was conducted by Lerer, Lerer, and Artner (1977). They found that handwriting improved in 52% of those initially receiving Ritalin and in only 4% of those initially receiving placebo. In general, handwriting deteriorated subsequent to drug withdrawal, but improvement was maintained for months in those children who remained on medication.

Although these findings seem exciting, neatness is only one small component of what people generally refer to as written communication skills. The latter include spelling, sentence structure, grammar, the ability to express and organize ideas, and so forth. It is important not to underestimate neatness and legibility, but we must also realize that little is known about the effect of stimulant drugs on more serious forms of written communication disorders.

Clinical Considerations

Stimulant drugs do increase academic productivity in hyperactive (and, in all probability, learning disabled) children. Moreover, treated children are aware of this change in their academic behavior (see Gadow, 1988b), which may lead to less stress in their lives. As Bradley (1957) noted, "medication is at best a crutch, but if in the long run it enables the child to experience success and a sense of being loved and appreciated, it is well justified" (p. 1051). It seems plausible that for some children a dramatic improvement in productivity and proficiency may even be more clinically meaningful than a modest increase in standardized achievement test performance. In addition, one of the commonly associated reasons for treatment in the first place is that the child does not complete his or her schoolwork and subsequently may not make satisfactory academic progress. Some clinicians, therefore, believe that if medication makes a child more responsive to educational instruction, then it is clinically useful. After all, the education literature is replete with scientific studies that document how various strategies designed to increase task motivation improve academic productivity. Nevertheless, careful consideration must be given to the seriousness of academic underachievement, the magnitude of the treatment effect, and the safety of the drug.

If one were seriously to consider the clinical implications of learning disabilities, the clear focus is on reading. The other areas of skill performance are simply not that essential to satisfactory adjustment in a typical employment setting (Chandler, 1978). Snyder (1979, 1983) even makes a compelling case for the questionable necessity of reading skills in most areas of employment because, when they are necessary, there is usually some way to compensate. The real problem with learning disabilities is that they are handicaps with regard to obtaining most traditional postsecondary education (e.g., college, trade school). The tragedy is that most jobs require very little academic ability; however, in order to get them, one must run the gauntlet of traditional academic instruction. Fortunately, follow-up studies of learning disabled children generally show a favorable adult outcome (Horn, O'Donnell, & Vitulano, 1983). The same can be said for many clinically diagnosed and treated cases of hyperactivity, but there is some disagreement on this point.

With regard to nonpharmacological interventions, research indicates that certain academically oriented behavioral interventions are clearly superior to stimulant medication in facilitating academic performance in hyperactive, learning disabled, and hyperactive–learning disabled children (Gadow, 1985). Moreover, although stimulant drugs enhance a variety of learning-related behaviors (e.g., attention span) and have been shown to increase academic productivity, they do not appear markedly to facilitate academically oriented behavioral interventions unless the latter are ineffective. These findings are fairly consistent across a number of studies that vary greatly, which suggests that if a clinically significant combination treatment effect does exist, it is not particularly robust.

AFFECTIVE DISORDERS (MOOD DISORDERS)

The primary disorders of affect are an abnormally lowered (depression) or elevated (mania) mood. Although mania is considerably less common, it does occur in adolescents (and possibly, but less clearly, in children) and is part of a special type of mood disorder known as bipolar affective disorder (or manic-depressive illness). In such cases, phases or cycles of illness are seen in which either mania or depression are manifested. Bipolar and some unipolar disorders have characteristics which suggest that the individual is genetically or, in some way, biologically predisposed.

In preadolescents there is little doubt that the full range of depressive syndromes can be observed, but the relationship between the depressive symptoms in children and disorders observed in adults is not fully understood. For example, biological characteristics and treatment response appear to be different in the two age groups. There is a rapid increase in the rate and discreteness of affective disorders following puberty. Adolescents who experience these problems suffer recurring, intermittent disturbances that may or may not be related to external precipitants (e.g., death in the family, poor school grades); but the disorder itself is believed to have a physiological component. Diagnosis is complicated by the fact that the associated symptoms of mood disorders vary so greatly in children and teenagers and include such behaviors as refusal to go to school, social withdrawal, deteriorating academic performance, unexplained conduct disturbance, and antisocial activities.

Depression (Depressive Disorders)

Depression in prepubertal children has generated much interest, and most of the research on this disorder has appeared within the last decade. Once considered a vary rare condition, more recent surveys show that the prevalence of major depressive disorder in prepubertal children in the United States is approximately 1.8% (Kashani & Simonds, 1979). Many of the children who fit the criteria for depression are not taken for psychological or psychiatric help, and few are currently treated with medication (Kovacs, Feinberg, Crouse-Novak, Paulaukas, & Finkelstein, 1984). Children with major depressive disorder are unlikely to recover within the first 3 months of the depressive episode, but remission generally occurs within 6 to 18 months. If the child does not recover by that time, the illness is likely to be protracted. The more early the age of onset of the disorder, the longer the recovery period.

Antidepressant medication consists largely of two major groups of drugs: the tricyclics and MAOIs (monoamine oxidase inhibitors). Newer antidepressants have been developed, but at this time none seem likely to replace the tricyclics as the primary agents for the management of mood disorders.

Children

There are several reports (uncontrolled or case studies) on the use of tricyclic antidepressants for the treatment of major depressive disorder in children, a few of which are noted here. Tofranil (imipramine) has been used to treat this condition (Petti & Law, 1982; Puig-Antich, 1982; Puig-Antich et al., 1979), with dosages of 5 mg/kg per day or higher if necessary (Puig-Antich, 1982). Elavil (amitriptyline) at a dosage of 1.5 mg/kg per day (45 to 110 mg) may be effective in improving mood and level of interest, as evidenced by a greater desire to play with other children, and purportedly produces few side effects (Kashani, Shekim, & Reid, 1984). Other tricyclics that have been used for depression in children are Aventyl (nortriptyline) and Norpramin/Pertofrane (desipramine) (Freeman, Poznanski, Grossman, Buchsbaum, & Banegas, 1985; Geller, Cooper, Chestnut, Abel, & Anker, 1984). Depressed children who respond best to these medications are more likely to have higher concentrations of the drug in their blood (regardless of dose) and family members who have a history of depressive illness. In spite of these somewhat encouraging reports, several placebo-controlled studies all failed to show that tricyclics were superior to placebo in diminishing depressive symptoms (reviewed by Ambrosini, 1987; also Puig-Antich, Perel, & Lupatkin, 1987). Therefore, caution is warranted in prescribing drug therapy for this disorder; appropriate child- and family-oriented psychological interventions are the treatments of choice.

Children who meet the diagnostic criteria for major depressive disorder may also experience other psychiatric problems. Many have conduct disorders (Carlson & Cantwell, 1980; Puig-Antich, 1982) or exhibit antisocial behavior (Geller, Chestnut, Miller, Price, & Yates, 1985), anxiety disorder (Kovacs et al., 1984), separation anxiety (Geller et al., 1985), school phobia (Kolvin, Berney, & Bhate, 1984), or psychotic symptoms such as hallucinations or delusions (Freeman et al., 1985). For these children, the total treatment plan is complicated by the presence of multiple target behaviors, some of which may become the reason for pharmacotherapy.

Adolescents

The commonest pharmacological treatment of adolescent depression is also tricyclic medication, particularly Tofranil. In adolescents, the therapeutic dose of Tofranil, Elavil, and Norpramin ranges up to 5 mg/kg per day, whereas the average dose of Aventyl is 1 to 2 mg/kg per day (Ryan & Puig-Antich, 1987). Tofranil can safely be administered as a single dose at night, particularly once a steady state has been achieved (Ryan et al., 1987). It is possible to measure the amount of tricyclic medication in the blood, if required, to ensure a therapeutic level (see Table 12.2). This can be particularly helpful in ruling out the possibility that individual variation in medication causes (1) drug failure at high doses because of a subtherapeutic level of medication in the blood or (2) side effects at low doses due to an unexpectedly high level of drug in the blood (Preskorn, Bupp, Weller, & Weller, 1989). Because there is a delay in the onset of the antidepressant effect, it may take from 4 to 7 weeks before the response to medication can be adequately evaluated. The best indicators that a depressed adolescent will respond to antidepressant medication are the presence of so-called vegetative (biological) symptoms such as sleep disturbance, change in eating patterns, and lack of drive, particularly if there is also a family history of depression.

Many of our present assumptions about the use of tricyclics in depressed adolescents depends on an extrapolation of information from adult studies and clinical experience. Peculiarly, the controlled studies of drug treatment in adolescents have not been compelling. Kramer and Feiguine (1981) showed no advantage for Elavil 200 mg per day over placebo in 10 adolescent inpatients with major depression. Ryan et al. (1986) found that less than half of their sample of 34 depressed adolescents had a complete recovery within 4 weeks of a final weight-adjusted dose of Tofranil (mean = 234 mg per day), but all had at least a partial response. No relationship was found between plasma level and clinical response.

Tricyclic antidepressants often produce unwanted side effects that are troublesome but rarely dangerous. These include dry mouth, drowsiness, lethargy, nausea, blurred vision, constipation, and—very rarely—an inability to pass urine (urinary retention). Another major complication is its effect on electrochemical conduction within the heart muscle (Biederman et al., 1989). Therapeutic levels of the tricyclics can produce changes in heart function that register on EKG records, and susceptible individuals may develop unusual heart rhythms or a "racing" of the heart (tachycardia). During treatment, therefore, it is imperative for the physician to assess heart function thoroughly. It is recommended that an EKG be obtained prior to the beginning of treatment, to determine whether there is a preexisting heart disorder, and after each increase in dosage (Ryan & Puig-Antich, 1987). The effect on the heart is one of the main reasons why these drugs can be lethal in overdose (accidental or not), which is an important consideration when treating children or adolescents, particularly those with suicidal ideas. The risk to the heart is also the reason why a single nighttime dose may be ill advised in preadolescent children, because they are more likely than adolescents to develop toxic blood

TABLE 12.2. Antidepressants Used in Children and Adolescents

DRUG	TRADE NAME	PLASMA LEVEL	ANTICHOLINERGIC SYMPTOMS	DEGREE OF SEDATION
Imipramine	Tofranil	150–240 ng/mL[b]	4+	2+
Desipramine[a]	Norpramine Pertofrane	115 ng/mL	1+	1+
Amitriptyline[a]	Elavil	100–300 ng/mL	4+	4+
Nortriptyline[a]	Aventyl[c] Pamelor	50–100 ng/mL	3+	2+

[a] Not currently approved by the Food and Drug Administration for use with children under 12 years of age.
[b] Based on studies conducted with children.
[c] Available in liquid form.
From "Depression: Pharmacotherapies" by G. A. Carlson in *Handbook of treatment approaches in childhood psychopathology* (p. 355) edited by J. L. Matson, 1988, New York: Plenum Press. Copyright 1988 by Plenum Press. Reprinted by permission.

levels. A rarer adverse reaction to tricyclics is the development of epileptic seizures, which appears to be associated with higher doses of medication.

The effects of tricyclic medication on cognitive and academic performance have not been studied extensively, but most reports with children are encouraging. The tricyclics have some actions that are similar to those of the stimulants, which probably accounts for their beneficial effect, such as increasing attention span and decreasing impulsivity, on some hyperactive children (Rapoport, Quinn, Bradbard, Riddle, & Brooks, 1974; Yepes, Balka, Winsberg, & Bialer, 1977). There is also evidence that long-term tricyclic treatment does not cause deterioration in academic performance (Quinn & Rapoport, 1975). Nevertheless, some depressed children treated with tricyclics appear forgetful, perplexed, or confused.

When adolescents respond to tricyclic antidepressants, there is a need to consider how long treatment should be continued. Mood disorders carry a risk of recurrence; the evidence from studies of depressed adults suggests that treatment should be maintained for 3 to 6 months after full recovery. This policy also seems practical for adolescents. Reduction of the medication should be gradual, because withdrawal symptoms (sleep disturbance, nightmares, nausea, headache, and other physical complaints) may occur if medication is stopped abruptly. Occasionally, adolescents predisposed to bipolar disorder "switch" to mania or even a rapid cycling process (continuous bouts of mania and depression; Wehr & Goodwin, 1979, 1987) during the course of treatment with an antidepressant (Strober & Carlson, 1982; Van Scheyen & Van Kamman, 1979). This is an indication to withdraw the antidepressant medication and use an antimanic drug. At the present time there is some controversy as to whether the "switch" is due to the pharmacologic properties of the antidepressant drug or purely a part of the illness process (Lewis & Winokur, 1982). Because the tricyclics are among the more commonly used drugs for attempted suicide in this age group (Fazen, Lovejoy, & Cone, 1986), medication should be administered and safely stored by the parent.

Adolescents who do not respond favorably to an adequate trial of tricyclic medication may show improvement with the addition of lithium carbonate to the treatment regimen. Research on this practice is limited but nevertheless encouraging (Ryan, Meyer, Dachille, Mazzie, & Puig-Antich, 1988a).

Several MAOIs are available for medical use, of which Nardil (phenelzine) is one of the more commonly prescribed. They are considered to act as antidepressants because they inhibit an enzyme that breaks down certain chemical transmitters within the nervous system. The MAOIs are more commonly used in adults as the drug of second choice for depression, and there are few, if any, indications for their use in adolescence except in intractable (difficult to control) depressions (Ryan et al., 1988b) and severe emotional disorders.

The side effects of the MAOIs are usually few but include nausea, dizziness, and sleep disturbance, particularly if given later in the day. The main concern is the potential for life-threatening reactions when treated individuals eat food containing tyramine (e.g., matured cheeses, yeast products) or are given a number of different medications. The combination of MAOIs and these substances can produce a rapid rise in blood pressure because the normal biochemical mechanism for breaking down these chemicals has been inhibited by the drug. It is therefore important that the adolescent who is given an MAOI (1) takes medication in the prescribed manner, (2) follows all dietary restrictions, and (3) avoids illicit drugs, particularly cocaine and amphetamine (speed).

Mania and Bipolar Affective Disorder (Bipolar Disorders)

Children

Bipolar affective disorder is considered to be a rare condition in prepubertal children, and there is no consensus of opinion about its diagnostic features. It has been described by DeLong (1978) as a condition characterized by "cyclic or periodic hostile aggressiveness; extremes of mood including manic excitement, depression, and angry irritability; distractibility; neurovegetative disorders (hyperdipsia, hyperphagia, encopresis, salt or sugar craving, excess sweating); and a family history of affective disorder" (DeLong & Aldershof, 1987, p. 389). Children exhibiting such symptoms may be responsive to treatment with lithium, implying but not confirming a continuity with adult bipolar disorder. Weller, Weller, and Fristad (1986) provide guidelines for adjusting lithium dosage in prepubertal children (see Table 12.3). Many young patients with bipolar disorder show both manic and depressive symptoms simultaneously, which is referred to as mixed bipolar disorder.

Adolescents

The existence and treatment of mania is somewhat better documented in adolescents (Carlson, 1983, 1986). Antimanic agents that are most commonly used are of two major types, the neuroleptics and lithium salts (e.g., Eskalith, Lithane, Lithobid). Both groups of drugs are efficacious in treatment of the acute state of mania, although the neuroleptics generally have a more rapid calming effect. Lithium is also effective in reducing the recurrence of mood disorder in individuals prone to bipolar affective disorder.

The increasing use of lithium in adolescent psychiatry is attested to by a number of recent review articles on this topic (e.g., Campbell, Perry, & Green, 1984b; Steinberg, 1980). Although noted in the 1940s to be a possible treatment for manic excitement (Cade, 1949), it was not until the 1960s in Scandinavia that the beneficial effects of lithium were really tested. One of the difficulties of using the drug is that there is a narrow range between therapeutic and toxic drug blood levels; consequently regular measurements of the level of lithium in the blood are necessary.

Lithium is effective in treating mania. In the initial phase of the illness, however, it is commonly given in combination with a neuroleptic, because the latter helps the adolescent calm down. Haldol (haloperidol) is *not* recommended for use in combination with lithium, because

there are a few reports of brain damage in patients taking both these drugs (Tyrer & Shopsin, 1980). Long-term pharmacotherapy with lithium is considered appropriate when (1) there is clear evidence of frequently recurring episodes of mood disorder and (2) the manic episodes are disruptive enough to warrant the risks of such treatment. Dosage is generally in the range of 1,000 to 1,600 mg per day, but the true measure of dosage is the amount of lithium necessary to keep the level in the blood within the known therapeutic range (0.6 to 1.2 mg/mL). Adolescents reportedly tolerate larger doses of lithium than older adults because they tend to excrete lithium through their kidneys more rapidly.

The side effects of lithium include nausea, headache, fine tremor (slight trembling or shaking, usually of the hands), thirst, excessive need to urinate (polyuria), and loose stools. Signs of toxicity are vomiting, diarrhea, shaking, sleepiness, slurred speech, and dizziness. Concerns about long-term adverse reactions include potentially irreversible effects on the kidney, thyroid, and possibly bone (Birch, 1980). None of these problems has proven to be common and all can be easily watched for by regular testing of chemical and hormonal levels in the blood. Because there is a risk of birth defects with lithium treatment (Weinstein, 1980), it should be used with caution for females who may become pregnant.

The effects of lithium on cognitive function are unclear. In normal volunteers, lithium can induce apathy, impair word learning, and reduce performance on visual-motor tasks, but studies of patients on long-term lithium therapy have found no gross impairment on standardized in-

Table 12.3. Lithium Carbonate Dosage Guide for Prepubertal School-Aged Children[a]

WEIGHT (kg)	DOSAGE (mg)			
	8 A.M.	12 NOON	6 P.M.	TOTAL DAILY DOSE
<25	150	150	300	600
25–40	300	300	300	900
40–50	300	300	600	1,200
50–60	600	300	600	1,500

[a]Dose specified in schedule should be maintained at least 5 days with serum lithium levels drawn every other day 12 hours after ingestion of the last lithium dose until two consecutive levels apper in the therapeutic range (0.6–1.2 mEq/L). Dose may then be adjusted based on serum level, side effects, or clinical response. Do not exceed 1.4 mEq/L serum level. With mentally retarded children, lower doses are recommended.
From E. B. Weller, R. A. Weller, and M. A. Fristad, "Lithium dosage guide for prepubertal children: A preliminary report," *Journal of the American Academy of Child Psychiatry, 25,* p. 93, 1986. Copyright 1986 by American Academy of Child and Adolescent Psychiatry. Reprinted by permission.

telligence test performance (Judd, Squire, Butters, Salmon, & Paller, 1987). One study of conduct disordered children treated with lithium found no adverse effects on cognition at optimal doses (Platt, Campbell, Green & Grega, 1984). It seems reasonable, therefore, to conclude that for adolescents with severe recurrent mood disorder, neither side effects nor fear of cognitive deterioration are sufficient reasons not to use lithium in appropriate cases.

Initial reports of an antimanic effect of Tegretol (carbamazepine) (Ballenger & Post, 1978) have been followed by more rigorous studies that confirm that the drug is useful in the treatment of mania and rapid-cycling mood disorders (prolonged mood disturbance with rapid switches between mania and depression) as well as for long-term treatment to prevent mood disorder (Kishimoto, Ogura, Hazama, & Inoue, 1983; Roy-Byrne, Jaffe, Uhde, & Post, 1984a). In the study by Kishimoto et al. there was evidence that Tegretol was more effective in patients with an onset of bipolar affective disorder before the age of 20.

At present Tegretol is used largely for lithium-resistant patients (Post, 1987). Therapeutic dosages are similar to those for the treatment of seizure disorders and are usually based on measurement of drug level in the blood. Combination therapy with lithium and Tegretol has been reported as beneficial, but there remains uncertainty whether this combination can produce a toxic reaction in the nervous system (Shukla, Godwin, Long, & Miller, 1984).

Clinical Considerations

It is important to realize that depressive (and occasionally manic) symptoms are often observed in association with environmental stress (e.g., death of a loved one), drug and alcohol abuse, physical illness, and other psychiatric disorders. Focusing treatment on the depressive symptoms instead of a patient's life problems may be ineffective or even detrimental.

Medical treatment for serious mood disorders is recommended for all age groups. Although these disorders are self-limiting, appropriate medical management significantly reduces the length and severity of disturbance and the risk of harm either through self-neglect or suicide. Management consists of both therapy for the acute illness and long-term treatment for prevention of recurrence.

ANXIETY DISORDERS

Children

The American Psychiatric Association (1987) currently recognizes three childhood anxiety disorders (separation anxiety disorder, avoidant disorder, overanxious disorder) and several adult anxiety disorders that can occur in prepubertal children (simple phobia, social phobia, obsessive compulsive disorder, and post-traumatic stress disorder). There is very little research on the validity of these diagnostic constructs as separate entities in children (Gittelman & Koplewicz, 1986), and the position of obsessive compulsive disorder within the group of anxiety disorders is controversial (Elkins, Rapoport, & Lipsky, 1980). Nevertheless, there is some evidence that separation anxiety and overanxious disorder represent distinct conditions in children. For example, one investigation found that of children referred for evaluation on the basis of anxiety symptoms, those who were diagnosed as having overanxious disorder were older (pubertal) and more likely to have concurrent anxiety disorders (simple phobia, panic disorder) than patients with separation anxiety (Last, Hersen, Kazdin, Finkelstein, & Strauss, 1987). With regard to pharmacotherapy, the two conditions in children for which there is an empirical basis for treatment are separation anxiety and obsessive compulsive disorder.

One common symptomatic manifestation of separation anxiety disorder is school refusal, and Gittelman-Klein and Klein (1971; Gittelman-Klein, 1975) showed that Tofranil was superior to placebo in facilitating school attendance. Treatment with medication resulted in a considerable reduction in depression, severity of phobia, maternal dependence, physical complaints, and fear of going to school. British workers are less enthusiastic about this type of medication and have shown that behavioral treatments can be as effective for the therapy of school phobia (Berney et al., 1981).

The average dose of Tofranil for separation anxiety is 75 to 100 mg per day with a maximal upper limit of 200 mg per day. Although behavioral improvement may be evident immediately after the onset of treatment, it is more characteristically manifested sometime within the first 2 weeks. Unfortunately, many children who have a complete remission of symptoms with Tofranil later suffer relapses. Medication is often given before bed to avoid side effects (e.g., drowsiness, dry mouth). Total duration of treatment, including a gradual withdrawal period, lasts about 3 months. To be truly effective, treatment must include psychotherapy as well as the cooperation of the school, family, and child. Behavioral intervention strategies should be considered before a trial of medication.

The other childhood anxiety disorder shown to be responsive to medication is obsessive compulsive disorder. In children, symptoms commonly take the form of repetitive thoughts of violence, contamination, or doubt and ritualistic actions involving hand washing, counting, checking, or touching. Flament et al. (1985) found that Anafranil (clomipramine), which was recently approved for use in the United States, was effective for controlling these symptoms in children and adolescents. Unfortunately, most drug responders did not recover fully, and there was a relapse in symptoms after drug withdrawal. Patients with compulsions responded better than those with obsessions only. Doses ranged from 100 to 200 mg per day, and untoward reactions included tremor, dry mouth, dizziness, constipation, and acute dyskinesia. One patient experienced a tonic-clonic seizure.

The findings from one uncontrolled study indicate that Prozac (fluoxetine), an atypical antidepressant, is also effective for the control of obsessive compulsive disorder in children and adolescents (Riddle, Hardin, King, Scahill, & Woolston, 1990). Study doses ranged from 10 to 40 mg per day.

Many children experience appropriate anxiety about strange events and people as well as a natural development of certain types of fears (e.g., animals, abandonment, parents' health). However, by adolescence, continuing anxiety reactions are often related to familial, constitutional, and environmental factors and begin to differentiate into the more classical group of anxiety disorders described in adult psychiatry: phobic disorders (agoraphobia, social phobia, simple phobia), anxiety states (panic disorder, generalized anxiety disorder, obsessive compulsive disorder) and post-traumatic stress disorder.

Adolescents

Panic disorder, obsessive compulsive disorder, and social phobias commonly have their onset in adolescence, but all the aforementioned anxiety disorders can occur during this stage of development. Unfortunately, the anxiety disorders of adolescents, unlike those of younger children, are more chronic in nature. There is undoubtedly some overlap between anxiety disorders and depression in certain patients, and milder depressed states may have a predominance of anxiety symptoms. Early adolescent school refusers with severe anxiety symptoms often report depressive symptoms (dysphoria, low self-esteem, anhedonia, suicidal ideation); and it has been suggested that the co-occurrence of the two disorders may be a type of depression (Bernstein & Garfinkel, 1986).

Because adolescent anxiety disorders are similar to adult states, it is reasonable to apply the experience of adult psychiatrists to their management (reviewed by Brown, Mulrow, & Stoudemire, 1984). This is helpful because there have been few significant adolescent studies on the value of drug treatment. Some of the major advances in the treatment of anxiety and phobias have been in the area of cognitive behavioral therapy, which challenges the thinking patterns of the patient and incorporates relaxation techniques with internal imagery of fears and/or direct exposure to fears (reviewed by Hersov, 1985).

Inderal (propranolol) has been known to reduce the physical symptoms of anxiety since the 1960s, but controlled studies of the different anxiety disorders have produced discrepant results. Some clinicians suggest that Inderal is comparable to the benzodiazepines and (given fears about the dependency and abuse of the latter) may be a useful adjunct therapy (Hallstrom, Treasaden, Edwards, & Lader, 1981). Clinical experience suggests that although Inderal may block the physical aspects of anxiety, it, unlike most benzodiazepines, does not alter the perception of fear. Most benzodiazepines also have a central calming effect.

The benzodiazepines (e.g., Valium, Librium) have dominated the market for the management of anxiety symptoms; by the late 1970s the level of drug prescribing had reached staggering proportions. Until then, these drugs were considered safe (even in very large doses), the major complications being related to sedation and reduced coordination. Occasionally, a "paradoxical reaction" occurs when susceptible individuals become aggressive and hostile (Lion, Azcarate, & Koepke, 1975). However, concerns about the level of prescribing, the tendency to use the drugs to avoid more active psychological therapies, and reports of abuse and even physiological addiction has led to a reappraisal of their use.

At this time, short-term drug therapy (2 to 3 months) for anxiety states while at the same time also initiating psychological treatments seems to be the most common clinical practice. Many practitioners are using the more rapidly eliminated benzodiazepines, such as Ativan (lorazepam), or Xanax (alprazolam), but it is uncertain that this is of significant advantage. In situations where recurrent stress related to medical procedures leads to marked anticipatory or situational anxiety, Xanax has been shown to be an effective agent for children and adolescents (Pfefferbaum et al., 1987). Inderal and the benzodiazepines have been indicated for most anxiety states except obsessive compulsive disorder.

The antidepressant drugs, both tricyclics and MAOIs, have shown some specific benefits for agoraphobia, panic disorder, and obsessive compulsive disorder. One particular researcher has been interested in the usefulness of tricyclic antidepressants for the treatment of panic attacks in agoraphobic patients (Klein, 1981).

As previously noted, the tricyclic Anafranil (clomipramine) is of interest in the treatment of anxiety states because it has been shown to be an effective agent in some adolescents with obsessive compulsive disorder (reviewed by Elkins et al., 1980; Flament et al., 1985). Other drugs, including the MAOIs, have also been reported in uncontrolled studies to benefit patients with obsessional states. The MAOIs are useful for the treatment of panic attacks and may even be superior to tricyclics (Sheehan, Ballenger, & Jacobsen, 1980), but concerns about their safety prevent general acceptance as the drug of first choice.

AUTISM (AUTISTIC DISORDER)

Because autism can be extremely debilitating and difficult to treat, it is not an exaggeration to say that over the years investigators have examined the clinical efficacy of almost every psychotropic and antiepileptic drug for this condition (reviewed by Campbell & Deutsch, 1985; Campbell, Anderson, Deutsch, & Green, 1984a; Fish, 1976). Owing to the early onset of symptoms, pharmacotherapy may be initiated during the early childhood period. No drugs cure this disorder, but symptom suppression is achieved in some cases.

Children

Neuroleptics

At present, neuroleptics are considered to be the drugs of first choice for symptomatic improvement in autistic children. For some patients, they reduce withdrawal, hyperactivity, stereotypies, fidgetiness, emotional lability, and abnormal object relations. Haldol is superior to the phenothiazines (e.g., Mellaril, Thorazine, Stelazine) because it is less likely to cause sedation at optimal dosages. Haldol has also been shown to increase the effectiveness of a language-based behavioral therapy program (Campbell et al., 1978) and appears to facilitate discrimination learning (Anderson et al., 1984). The optimal dose for most preschoolers ranges between 0.5 to 1.0 mg per day. Hypoactive autistic children are not helped by treatment with Haldol; their symptoms may even become worse.

Campbell et al. (1984a) report the following adverse drug reactions to Haldol in autistic children:

> Unlike in adults, affectomotor side effects (e.g., irritability, alterations in level of motor activity) occur commonly with neuroleptic administration to children. On the other hand, parkinsonian side effects appear to be a function of age; the younger the child, the less frequent their occurrence. These side effects in children are best treated by dosage reduction. Antiparkinsonian medication is avoided because there is some evidence that they may reduce serum neuroleptic levels (Rivera-Calimlim et al., 1976) and contribute to worsening of behavioral symptoms and cognition due to central anticholinergic properties. Acute dystonic reactions are less frequent if drug is begun with very low doses and increases are gradual. However, should they occur, they are usually rapidly responsive to diphenhydramine (Benadryl), either orally or intramuscularly (25 mg). These dystonic reactions result from involuntary contractions of skeletal muscle groups and may be manifest as painful stiffening or arching of the back, neck, or tongue, and oculogyric crisis. (pp. 313)

Apart from acute dystonic reaction, preschoolers are also at risk for the development of other extrapyramidal symptoms. One long-term treatment study of Haldol found that 22%

of the children developed dyskinesias (like those associated with tardive dyskinesia) either during treatment or when switched to placebo (Campbell et al., 1983). In a few cases the dyskinesias were manifested as an aggravation of preexisting stereotypies. The dyskinesias appeared anywhere from 5 weeks to 16 months after the initiation of medication. The dyskinesias stopped within 16 days to 9 months after they first began. In some cases they ceased while the child was on medication, and in others after the child had been switched to a placebo or medication was discontinued.

Dosage guidelines for the neuroleptics are difficult to set because there is a great deal of variability across children. Titration is the recommended procedure, and the optimal dose in milligrams per kilogram may be higher than for adults. This can be explained in part by the fact that children metabolize many types of drugs at a faster rate than do adults. A Haldol dosing schedule of 5 days on medication and 2 days off was found to be just as effective as a 7-day on medication schedule (Perry et al., 1989).

The duration of treatment is determined in part by the degree to which the drug continues to produce a clinically meaningful therapeutic response. This can only be assessed with systematic dosage reductions and drug-free periods. One study has shown that Haldol remained clinically effective even after 2 ½ years of drug administration (Campbell et al., 1983). Nevertheless, other children in that same investigation no longer required drug therapy after several months of medication.

The clinical management of maladaptive behaviors in autistic children with medication can be a difficult process. Children who respond favorably to one type of drug at an early age may do much better on a different medication when older. Also, the search for an effective agent may be a long and tedious process of gradually adjusting the dose and assessing therapeutic benefits. It may also require trials of several different drugs. The duration of treatment varies depending upon the magnitude of the therapeutic response. Because relatively little is known about the use of neuroleptics with young children, careful monitoring is in order for this age group, and drug-free periods should be scheduled regularly to assess the continued need for treatment.

Stimulants

The usefulness of stimulants for the treatment of learning and behavioral disorders in autistic children is controversial. Campbell, Fish, Shapiro, Collins, and Koh (1972), for example, found that Dexedrine (dextroamphetamine) often exacerbated the symptoms of autism by increasing social withdrawal and stereotypies. Many youngsters also became more hyperactive and irritable. Their subject sample, however, was confined to preschoolers, who are known to be overly sensitive to these types of reactions (see Ounsted, 1955). Other investigators, however, report favorable treatment outcomes (reduction of hyperactivity symptoms and aggression) for elementary school–aged autistic children receiving Dexedrine (Geller, Guttmacher, & Bleeg, 1981) and Ritalin (Birmaher, Quintana, & Greenhill, 1988; Strayhorn, Rapp, Donina, & Strain, 1988; Vitriol & Farber, 1981). Our own experience in evaluating methylphenidate response in hyperactive and/or inattentive autistic children has been favorable, and we encourage clinicians to consider this drug in appropriate cases.

Pondimin

One of the newest drugs for the treatment of autism is Pondimin (fenfluramine). It is approved by the Food and Drug Administration for the treatment of obesity and is pharmacologically similar to the amphetamines. Pondimin was reported to decrease hyperactivity, distractibility, and stereotypies and to increase eye contact, social responsiveness, and language performance (reviewed by Aman & Kern, 1989; Campbell, 1988). The daily dosage employed in studies with children ranges from 1.2 to 2.1 mg/kg per day, which is divided into a morning and an afternoon dose. Side effects are generally mild and include decreased appetite, lethargy, and irritability, which may respond to dosage reduction (see also Piggott, Gdowski, Villaneuva, Fischhoff, & Frohman, 1986). Many children appear to experience a rebound effect (irritability, restlessness, aggressivity) upon drug withdrawal. For preschool-aged autistic children in a hospital setting, therapeutic benefits are much less noteworthy, and there is a risk of impairment of learning ability (Campbell et al., 1988). Furthermore, some investigators have found that Pondimin has little effect on reducing maladaptive behavior in older (9 to 28 years) autistic individuals in a residential treatment program and that side effects (tension, agitation, insomnia, sweating) can be troublesome (Yarbrough et al., 1987).

Trexan

There is some encouraging preliminary research on the opiate antagonist Trexan (naltrexone) as a treatment for autism. Clinicians are currently interested in the opiod antagonists because some autistic children appear to have abnormal levels of endogenous opiods, which may be related to elevated pain thresholds and self-injurious behavior. For example, Campbell et al. (1989) found that 0.5 to 2.0 mg/kg per day doses of Trexan reduced stereotypies, hyperactivity, and social withdrawal and increased verbal production in several preschool-aged autistic children.

Adolescents

Over the years, some symptoms of autism may change and new problems may arise. Those children who appear hyperactive may have a reduction in their extreme activity level in adolescence. However, new problems in adolescence are common. Seizures begin to occur in a third of the autistic population, and between 10% and 30% of autistic adolescents show a significant deterioration in performance and behavior (reviewed by Paul, 1987). This may include loss of verbal, social, and self-help skills, increased aloofness, and the development of stereotypic and self-injurious behaviors. Many of these children also show cyclic behavioral disturbance, with hyperactive and aggressive or more withdrawn, apathetic periods. It has been proposed that there is increased risk for this change in female patients and in the presence of a family history of affective disorder. Other problems that may be related to pubescence itself include adjustment to sexual development (which can lead to inappropriate public sexual behavior) and, for many higher-functioning autistic adolescents, increasing insight into their difference from nonautistic peers (which can lead to marked depression).

Therefore, in the adolescent years, pharmacotherapy may become more crucial, particularly for patients who show deterioration. Neuroleptics may be required for the control of behavior disorders; antidepressant treatment may help mood-related symptoms; and for periodic disorders, lithium or Tegretol may be considered. Inderal has reduced severe aggressive behavior disorders in some autistic adolescents.

Clinical Considerations

Autistic children require intense educational intervention to facilitate the acquisition of language and social skills and to suppress maladaptive behaviors (reviewed by Rutter, 1985). There exists a truly impressive literature on the effectiveness of behavioral therapy techniques with this population; these are routinely employed in exemplary intervention programs. As was previously noted, drug researchers have been emphatic about the adjunctive status of medication in the treatment of autistic children and adolescents. Although there are some data to suggest that neuroleptic medication may make educational interventions more effective (Campbell et al., 1978), the magnitude of the therapeutic benefit from medication is in general modest. In short, even on medication these children remain seriously handicapped. Because autistic children typically receive special education and other services, medication should be used only when it leads to more rapid cognitive, academic, or social development.

CONDUCT PROBLEMS (DISRUPTIVE BEHAVIOR DISORDERS)

Conduct problems involve a variety of aggressive (fighting), oppositional (noncompliant, defiant), antisocial (lying, stealing), and delinquent (status offenses, drug abuse) behaviors. They are commonly found in hyperactive children, especially those who are referred to special diagnostic and treatment facilities, youngsters in special education programs for the emotionally disturbed/behavior disordered, patients in psychiatric hospitals and residential community mental-health facilities, and mentally retarded people in institutions and community placements. Two DSM-III-R diagnostic constructs that are defined in terms of conduct problems are oppositional defiant disorder and conduct disorder. Under the current diagnostic plan, a child who has both oppositional defiant disorder and conduct disorder receives only one diagnosis, namely, conduct disorder. However, a child who exhibits both attention-deficit hyperactivity disorder (ADHD) and conduct disorder (or oppositional defiant disorder) is diagnosed as having both conditions.

Aggression (Conduct Disorder)

Aggression is manifest in a variety of ways: verbal aggression (cursing, threatening, malicious teasing), object aggression (breaking toys, destroying property), symbolic aggression (feigning physical attack, making offensive gestures), and physical aggression (striking, shoving, or tripping other people). Individuals can also aggress against or hurt themselves (self-injurious behavior), but this disorder is present primarily in children and adolescents who are moderately to profoundly mentally retarded or autistic and is treated as a separate topic in this chapter. Aggression is a poorly developed concept, at least in terms of its behavioral referents in the child psychopathology literature. It includes oppositional behavior, emotional lability, and norm-violating behaviors. This unweildy use of the term is also evident in the items constituting "Aggression" factors in some behavior rating scales. The popularity of these instruments in medication evaluation studies has resulted in a lack of precision in documenting and describing treatment effects. Aggressive behavior is a relatively common characteristic of many childhood and adolescent psychiatric disorders, and it is currently believed that the treatment of aggressive behavior in the absence of a thorough diagnostic evaluation can lead to inappropriate drug selection, or, equally disconcerting, divert attention away from the primary cause of the behavioral disturbance. Aggressive behavior is generally managed with a neuroleptic drug; however, recent interest has focused on tricyclic antidepressants and stimulants. In the case of intermittent outbursts of violence, three medications (Inderal, lithium, and Tegretol) have shown some early promise of efficacy.

Neuroleptics

When aggression is the primary target behavior, clinicians are most likely to prescribe a neuroleptic drug. This is particularly true for children and adolescents in residential treatment settings. Numerous studies have shown that neuroleptic drugs can suppress aggressive behavior in youngsters diagnosed as being mentally retarded (reviewed by Gadow & Poling, 1988), hyperactive (e.g., Gittelman-Klein, Klein, Katz, Saraf,

& Pollack, 1976; Werry & Aman, 1975), autistic (see Campbell et al., 1978), and conduct-disordered (e.g., Campbell et al., 1984c). The three most commonly prescribed neuroleptic drugs for severe conduct problems (especially children who are also hyperactive and/or impulsive) are Mellaril (thioridazine), Haldol (haloperidol), and Thorazine (chlorpromazine). In general, neuroleptics are prescribed only when necessary because they are associated with a greater risk of side effects than are the stimulants. Because Mellaril has been reported to have a favorable effect on seizure reduction, this drug can be used with some confidence in the treatment of behavior disorders in epileptic children (Kamm & Mandel, 1967).

There is a considerable range in the reported doses of neuroleptics across studies with children (see Table 12.4). The average daily dose of Mellaril and Thorazine ranges from 75 to 150 mg. Some clinicians prescribe one large dose at night to prevent daytime drowsiness, whereas others divide the total amount into two or three doses during the day (Katz et al., 1975; Winsberg & Yepes, 1978). Relative to body weight, the average dose is 3 to 6 mg/kg per day. The effective dose of haloperidol ranges from 2 to 5 mg per day, which is divided into three daily doses. It is noteworthy that, in hyperactive boys, significant improvements in cognitive performance have been reported with low (0.025 mg/kg) doses of Haldol (Werry & Aman, 1975).

The side effects of neuroleptics in children are similar to those reported in adults. Sedative effects (drowsiness, lethargy, and apathy) are common with Thorazine, but children usually develop a tolerance for this reaction within several days to a few weeks. Dosage reduction may be necessary in some cases. It is noteworthy that irritability and excitability are also possible. Skin reactions are infrequent. Also reported are diarrhea, upset stomach, dry mouth, blurred vision, constipation, urinary retention, and abdominal pain. A number of studies report increased appetite, weight gain, or both, during drug treatment.

Katz et al. (1975) stated that, in their experience with hyperactive children, the side effects of Mellaril were frequent and severe. Drowsiness was the most common adverse reaction and was difficult to manage. If the dose was reduced, the drowsiness was less severe, but the therapeutic response was weaker. Many children developed enuresis and had to be taken

**Table 12.4. Neuroleptic Drug Dosages for Children Under
12 Years of Age[a]**

GENERIC NAME	TRADE NAME	ORAL DOSE (mg/day)
chlorpromazine	Thorazine	10–200
fluphenazine[b]	Prolixin	0.25–16
haloperidol	Haldol	0.25–16
molindone[b]	Moban	1–40
pimozide[c]	Orap	1–7
thioridazine	Mellaril	10–200
thiothixene[b]	Navane	1–40
trifluoperazine[d]	Stelazine	1–15

[a]The most current issue of the *Physician's Desk Reference* should be consulted for dosage information.
[b]Not approved by the Food and Drug Administration for use with children under 12 years of age.
[c]Approved for use in the pediatric age range only for the treatment of Tourette syndrome.
[d]Recommended for use only with children who are hospitalized or under close supervision.

off medication. Increased appetite was also common, as was puffiness around the eyes and mild dry mouth. Stomachache, nausea, and vomiting necessitated dosage reduction in a number of children. Other side effects included nosebleed, mild tremor, and orthostatic hypotension. Some children who reacted well to Mellaril later developed changes in temperament. They became irritable, moody, and belligerent, and due to this, medication eventually had to be stopped.

Extrapyramidal syndromes are frequently reported in studies using Haldol to control behavior disorders in children. Clinicians manage these side effects by administering an anticholinergic agent either at the beginning of drug treatment (a practice that is controversial) or after symptoms appear. Although Haldol is usually not associated with sedative effects, drowsiness has sometimes been reported in studies of children. Other side effects include nausea, ataxia, slurred speech, and weight gain.

Perhaps the most controversial side effect of the neuroleptics is cognitive and academic impairment. This issue is controversial because the studies in this area have not been particularly well designed and are few in number (see Winsberg & Yepes, 1978). Nevertheless, there are good examples of research on the use of neuroleptics for hyperactive (e.g., Sprague, Barnes, & Werry, 1970; Werry & Aman, 1975) and mentally retarded (e.g., Wysocki, Fuqua, Davis, & Breuning, 1981) individuals, which strongly suggest that mental impairment is a definite possibility. It is important, therefore, to monitor adaptive behavior during dosage adjustment and to assess the extent to which desirable behaviors may be adversely affected.

Stimulants

Given the relative safety and pervasive use of stimulant medication, it is noteworthy that little is known about its effect on child and adolescent aggression. An aggression suppression effect is often inferred from rating-scale data (e.g., Campbell, Cohen, & Small, 1982); but, as previously noted, "Aggression" factor scores typically represent an amalgam of conduct problems. Allen, Safer, and Covi (1975) commented that a post hoc analysis of specific rating-scale items showed that stimulant drug treatment led to lower teacher ratings of aggressive behavior (fights; defiant). Similarly, Amery, Minichiello, and Brown (1984) reported that the administration of Dexedrine resulted in lower parent and teacher ratings of aggressiveness as well as decreased levels of fantasy and object aggression in a clinic playroom setting. Others have observed a reduction in the rate of negative verbal statements in the classroom for hyperactive children taking Ritalin (e.g., Abikoff & Gittelman, 1985; Whalen, Henker, Collins, Finck, & Dotemoto, 1979). Because acts of physical aggression are infrequent, particularly in classrooms and laboratory playrooms, less is known about drug effects on this behavior. An in-depth examination of the effect of Ritalin on aggressive children in public school settings (classroom, lunchroom, playground) using direct observation procedures was conducted by Gadow, Nolan, Paolicelli, Sverd, and Sprafkin (1990). They found that medication did, in fact, suppress physical aggression during school recess periods. Moreover, some of these same children also showed concurrently increased rates of appropriate social interaction.

Lithium

There is a growing number of reports on the efficacy of lithium treatment for aggressive behavior in prepubertal children. Campbell et al. (1984c), for example, conducted a thorough and well-controlled investigation into the effects of Haldol and lithium on hospitalized, conduct-disordered, undersocialized, aggressive children between 5 and 13 years of age. The optimal dose of Haldol ranged from 1.0 to 6.0 mg per day (0.04 to 0.21 mg/kg per day), and the optimal dose of lithium was 500 to 2,000 mg per day (or serum levels of 0.32 to 1.51 mEq/L). Both Haldol and lithium were highly effective in reducing aggressive behavior. Qualitatively, whereas Haldol rendered the children more manageable, lithium reduced the explosive nature of their aggressive behavior, which enabled other positive changes to take place. Subjectively, the children receiving Haldol felt "slowed down," and the youngsters getting lithium thought that medication "helped to control" them. It appeared that the optimal dose of Haldol interfered with daily functioning more than lithium.

Lithium has shown some effectiveness as an antiaggression agent for some mentally retarded people (reviewed by Gadow & Poling, 1988), epileptic patients, and neurologically normal male delinquents (reviewed by Sheard, 1978). Among the latter group, certain characteristics seem to be associated with the effectiveness of lithium treatment: mood lability (rapid changes between euphoria and depression), irritability, hostility, restlessness, impulsivity, distractibility, pressured speech (excessive, rapid talking), and a loud and provocative manner. Other workers have described a similar personality profile among adolescent girls, which they have called the emotionally unstable character disorder (Rifkin, Quitkin, Carillo, Blumberg, & Klein, 1972). Individuals with this disorder are also purported to show a response to lithium therapy. The doses of lithium recommended in these studies are the same as those used to control mania in adolescents.

Beta Blockers

A relatively new drug for the treatment of aggression and explosive aggressive outbursts is Inderal (propranolol), a beta-adrenergic blocking agent or "beta blocker" (Silver & Yudofsky, 1985). This drug is used primarily for the treatment of hypertension (high blood pressure), angina (intense chest pains), and cardiac arrhythmias (irregular heartbeat). An increasing number of studies (reviewed by Gualtieri, Golden, & Fahs, 1983) indicate that Inderal may be effective for a variety of psychiatric disorders; however, it is not yet approved by the Food and Drug Administration for use in the treatment of these conditions. Reports of Inderal's effectiveness for childhood behavior disorders have focused on children with some form of organic brain damage or brain dysfunction (e.g., Williams, Mehl, & Yudofsky, 1982). The average dose for children and adolescents is 160 mg/day, but the optimal range is 50 to 960 mg/day. (Maximal doses are considerably higher than for other medical uses.) Side effects include a reduction in blood pressure and pulse rate and, rarely, breathing difficulties, nightmares, and decreased motor coordination. When Inderal is used with the "right" children and dosage is gradually increased, side effects are not a major problem. A key point here is use with the right children. Inderal should be employed only in cases where conventional pharmacological and behavioral treatments have failed. The use of this drug is contraindicated for children and youths with a history of cardiac or respiratory disease (e.g., asthma), who have hypoglycemia, or who are taking MAOIs (Gualtieri et al., 1983).

A study of Inderal for the treatment of aggression and self-injurious behavior in severely and profoundly mentally retarded adults was conducted by Ratey et al. (1986). Over half the patients made pronounced therapeutic gains on Inderal, which was an especially important outcome because all "had undergone numerous trials of varying drug, educational, and behavioral regimens without benefit" (p. 103). The investigators employed doses (40 to 240 mg/day) lower than those used by others and cautioned that because the onset of therapeutic response may be gradual in some patients, there is a risk of increasing the dose prematurely. The primary side effects were hypotension and bradycardia (abnormally slow heart rate).

Tegretol

A number of reports show that Tegretol (carbamazepine) is helpful in reducing aggressive and impulsive behavior occurring in patients with various different diagnoses, including schizophrenia, personality disorder, and brain disorders such as trauma or seizures (reviewed by Roy-Byrne, Uhde, & Post, 1984b, 1984c), and this drug is currently receiving increasing application in child psychiatry (reviewed by Evans, Clay, & Gualtieri, 1987). The enthusiasm for Tegretol was tempered by early reports that it might worsen aggression in some children and adolescents, but Roy-Byrne et al. (1984b) have stated that the therapeutic effects of Tegretol are in many ways similar to those of lithium. This is particularly noticeable in one controlled study, which showed that Tegretol significantly reduced self-destructive behavior (overdosing, wrist cutting, and cigarette burning) in 13 girls who exhibited symptoms similar to those of the emotionally unstable character disorder.

The side effects of Tegretol include drowsiness, ataxia, nausea, anorexia, and visual disturbances. Although there is also a risk of blood and bone disorders, these adverse reactions are rare. Nevertheless, they could be fatal and therefore blood monitoring is mandatory. Tegretol has been reported to induce tics (Evans et al., 1987) and seizures (e.g., Lerman, 1986) in some children. Clinicians who prescribe Tegretol for the control of aggression and other behavior disorders should also conscientiously monitor for behavioral toxicity, the signs of which include irritability, hyperactivity, agitation, aggression, impulsivity, and manic symptoms (e.g., euphoria, pressured speech, grandiose ideas; Pleak, Birmaker, Gavrilescu, Abichandani, & Williams, 1988). The doses of Tegretol used for the control of aggression are generally the same as those used for the treatment of seizure disorders. However, Evans et al. (1987) note that little is known about the length of adequate drug trials, significance of blood levels, and degree of negative cognitive effects in psychiatric patients.

Oppositional Behavior (Oppositional Defiant Disorder)

DSM-III-R defines oppositional defiant disorder as a pattern of behavior characterized by "negativistic, hostile, and defiant behavior" with specific symptoms such as "loses temper, ar-

gues with adults, actively defies or refuses adult requests or rules, deliberately does things to annoy other people, blames other for . . . own mistakes" (American Psychiatric Association, 1987, pp. 56–57). To the best of our knowledge, there are no psychotropic drug studies of children or adolescents who were diagnosed as having "pure" oppositional defiant disorder. Nevertheless, these negativistic behaviors are common in hyperactive and conduct-disordered children and their responsiveness to stimulant and neuroleptic medication has been commented upon for many years (e.g., Bradley, 1937). More recently, psychopharmacologists have employed direct observation techniques in natural settings to examine changes in specific behaviors more precisely. The results of these investigations show that hyperactive children who are oppositional do become more compliant with regard to adult directives when receiving stimulant medication (e.g., Gadow, Nolan et al., 1990). Parents, in particular, see the treated child as being more manageable. Dramatic reductions in emotional liability (temper tantrums, irritability, argumentativeness) are also observed in children for whom this is a major clinical concern (e.g., Speltz, Varley, Peterson, & Beilke, 1988).

Antisocial Behavior (Conduct Disorder)

There is really no well-controlled research on drug therapy for nonconfrontational forms of antisocial behavior such as lying, stealing, illicit substance use, and so forth. Although it is certainly plausible that in some cases (particularly when impulsivity is a major factor) decreases in such behaviors might be expected subsequent to effective pharmacotherapy, these often low-frequency and sometimes secretive behaviors are difficult to study.

ENURESIS (FUNCTIONAL ENURESIS)

In an excellent review of the literature, Blackwell and Currah (1973) state that the tricyclic antidepressants are the only drugs that have consistently proved to be more effective than placebo for the treatment of nocturnal enuresis (bed wetting). Several different tricyclics are presently available, but Tofranil is the one most commonly used to treat this disorder. It was first reported effective for the treatment of enuresis by MacLean in 1960 and 13 years later was approved by the FDA for use with this disorder. Other tricyclics used for enuresis include Norpramin/Pertofrane and Elavil.

When Tofranil works, the response is immediate, usually during the first week of treatment. A complete cure (total remission of symptoms), however, is reported for less than half of the children on medication. It should be noted that if a less stringent criterion is used (e.g., 50% fewer wet nights), the "success" rate is much higher. Unfortunately, "relapse tends to occur immediately following withdrawal after short periods of treatment, and long-term followup studies suggest that total remission (no wet nights) occurs in only a minority of patients" (Blackwell & Currah, 1973, p. 253).

The total daily dose of Tofranil commonly reported in the literature is 25 to 50 mg given in one oral dose at bedtime. For children over 12 years of age, the dose may be increased to 75 mg if the smaller amount is unsuccessful. The FDA recommends that the dose of Tofranil not exceed 2.5 mg/kg per day because there is a risk of severe side effects at higher doses (Robinson & Barker, 1976).

Daytime wetting is referred to as diurnal enuresis. This condition is more common in girls and is often associated with behavior problems at home and at school (Meadow & Berg, 1982). It is a difficult disorder to treat successfully (i.e., no relapses). In one study that examined the utility of two different dosages of Tofranil (25 mg and 50 mg administered in the morning) for diurnal enuresis, Meadow and Berg (1982) found that medication was not more effective than placebo.

Although stimulant drugs are not generally prescribed for nocturnal enuresis, there have been numerous reports over the years of how hyperactive children with nocturnal enuresis became dry after taking stimulant medication for hyperactivity. Research on stimulants for enuresis has a long history (e.g., Molitch & Poliakoff, 1937), and it has recently been suggested that Ritalin may be an effective treatment for some enuretic patients who become dry and later relapse (Diamond & Stein, 1983).

DDAVP (desmopressin), an antidiuretic hormone used for the treatment of diabetes insipidus, has also been shown to diminish nocturnal enuresis in several placebo-controlled studies (reviewed by Klauber, 1989). It has a rapid onset of action and negligible side effects. Child patients are generally treated with doses ranging from 20 to 40 micrograms administered intra-

nasally at bedtime. DDAVP's efficacy in nocturnal enuresis is related to its ability to increase water reabsorption in the kidneys, which reduces the volume of water entering the bladder. The drawbacks of DDAVP treatment are the relatively high cost of the medication and the likelihood of relapse when medication is discontinued (Miller, Goldberg, & Atkin, 1989). Gradual tapering of the dose during the withdrawal period (which may last several months) reduces the probability of relapse.

The treatment of first choice for noctural enuresis is use of the pad-and-buzzer device, which may or may not be incorporated into a more elaborate behavioral therapy program (Shaffer, 1985). Medication should be considered only when proven behavioral interventions have failed or are not practical or when special circumstances warrant, such as vacations or highly stressful home settings. Studies comparing psychological and pharmacological treatments for enuresis have resulted in mixed findings. For example, Kolvin et al. (1972) examined the relative efficacy of Tofranil, conditioning, and placebo. Children in the study were separated into three groups, each receiving one of the aforementioned treatments. Therapy for each group lasted 2 months, with the results being evaluated 2 months later. Treatment was considered successful if there was an 80% decrease in wet nights. Using this criterion, 42% of the placebo group, 30% of the medication group, and 50% of the pad-and-buzzer group were considered improved. Conversely, Wagner, Johnson, Walker, Carter, and Wittner (1982) found tricyclic antidepressants to be superior to the pad and buzzer in a short-term study.

HYPERACTIVITY (ATTENTION-DEFICIT HYPERACTIVITY DISORDER)

The most common reason for psychiatric referral and for the prescription of psychotropic medication to children is for hyperactivity, a disorder that is now saddled with legion of labels (e.g., minimal brain dysfunction, hyperkinesis, hyperkinetic syndrome, hyperkinetic reaction of childhood, attention-deficit disorder with hyperactivity, attention-deficit hyperactivity disorder). The traditionally recognized symptoms of the disorder have been motor restlessness, short attention span, and impulsivity. However, the use of the term "hyperactivity" as a diagnostic construct is currently undergoing change. This is due in part to the idea that poor attending skills rather than excessive motor restlessness may be the essence of the problem (Douglas, 1972; Douglas & Peters, 1979), a notion that has been discussed for a number of years (e.g., Ounsted, 1955) and is now somewhat controversial (see, for example, Porrino et al., 1983). One consequence of the controversy concerning the "right" label, the primary symptoms, and the diagnostic criteria has been the obfuscation of target symptoms. Taylor (1985), for example, noted that it is unclear from the drug research literature exactly what is being treated: hyperactivity, aggression, or both. The fact that aggression is poorly operationalized also complicates matters. For some researchers and clinicians in the hyperactivity area, the primary reason for treatment is to render the child more manageable. Morever, the behavior problem is attributed to the child's abnormal activity level, attention deficits, impulsivity, or some combination of these problems. Because academic underachievement was considered to be "almost a hallmark of this syndrome" (Wender, 1973, p. 16), drug-induced improvement in academic productivity and associated cognitive deficits was widely embraced as a justification and a reason for treatment (Gadow, 1983). So as not to belabor the point, suffice it to say that with the notable exception of Charles Bradley (Bradley, 1957; Bradley & Bowen, 1941), few investigators in this area have either formulated or critically examined theories of treatment.

The associated features of hyperactivity are several and include oppositional behavior (defiance of authority figures, emotional lability), peer aggression (verbal, physical), conduct problems (delinquency, lying, stealing, physical violence), affective symptoms (anxiety, depression), and learning disabilities. Because these symptomatic concomitants of hyperactivity are also recognized as being distinct disorders (in the presence or absence of hyperactivity) and are addressed separately in this chapter, the present discussion focuses primarily but not exclusively on hyperactivity symptoms and interpersonal relations.

Stimulants

The stimulants (Ritalin, Dexedrine, and Cylert) are the most commonly prescribed drugs for hyperactivity, and Ritalin is by far the preferred drug and the most extensively studied. Because a number of comprehensive reviews of stimulant

drug therapy are available (Barkley, 1981; Cantwell & Carlson, 1978; Conners, 1971; Eisenberg & Conners, 1971; Gadow, 1986a; Ross & Ross, 1982; Safer & Allen, 1976; Sprague & Werry, 1974; Whalen, 1982; see also the chapter by DuPaul, Guerremont, & Barkley in this volume), only a few representative studies are noted here.

The effect of stimulant drugs on activity level is greatly influenced by task and setting variables. For example, Ellis, Witt, Reynolds, and Sprague (1974) found little effect of Ritalin on motor movement in the playroom, yet these same children were perceived by their teacher to be less active in school (Sleator & von Neumann, 1974) and to wiggle less in their chair while performing a laboratory task (Sprague & Sleator, 1973) when taking medication compared with placebo. Others have found that stimulants reduce activity during highly structured, task-oriented classroom situations (e.g., Gadow, Nolan et al., 1990; Whalen et al., 1979).

Stimulant drugs improve performance on a variety of cognitive tasks including measures of sustained attention (e.g., Conners & Rothschild, 1968; Sykes, Douglas, Weiss, Minde, 1971), impulsivity (e.g., Brown & Sleator, 1979), short-term memory (e.g., Sprague & Sleator, 1977; Weingartner et al., 1980), and paired-associate learning (e.g., Conners & Rothschild, 1968; Swanson & Kinsbourne, 1976). There is also research to suggest that problem-solving behaviors may be enhanced, as evidenced by studies of search strategies (Dykman, Ackerman, & McCray, 1980), flexible thinking (Dyme, Sahakian, Golinko, & Rabe, 1982), information processing (Reid & Borkowski, 1984), visual scanning patterns (Flintoff, Barron, Swanson, Ledlow, & Kinsbourne, 1982), and inspection strategy (Sprague, 1984). In spite of years of research on stimulant drugs and their effect on cognitive performance, the exact mechanism(s) by which these performance gains are achieved is poorly understood.

There are at least several ways in which stimulant-induced changes in a hyperactive child's behavior result in modifications of parent, teacher, and peer behavior. As hyperactive children become less disruptive and more compliant, others around them begin to react differently. For example, mothers become less controlling and less negative in response to the improvement in their child's behavior (e.g., Barkley & Cunningham, 1979; Humphries, Kinsbourne, & Swanson, 1978). Moreover, changes in the mother's behavior appear to be dose-related (Barkley, Karlsson, Strzlecki, & Murphy, 1984); that is, they are more evident at moderate (0.5 mg/kg twice a day) than low (0.15 mg/kg twice a day) doses. Teachers also may react to hyperactive children much differently depending on whether they are receiving medication or placebo. Whalen, Henker, and Dotemoto (1980) found that when the hyperactive child is receiving Ritalin, the teacher is less controlling (i.e., guidance, commands, and admonitions), less intense (i.e., vigor, loudness, rapidity, and emotionality), and less likely to call out the child's name. There are few studies of how the behavior of peers changes in response to stimulant-induced improvement in the hyperactive child's behavior. In one laboratory study, Cunningham, Siegel, and Offord (1985) found that Ritalin treatment resulted in decreased levels of controlling behavior in hyperactive children, and peers responded to this change by reacting to the hyperactive child in a less controlling manner. Another study by Gadow, Paolicelli et al. (1990) in public school classrooms found that peers engaged in less nonphysical aggression when an aggressive-hyperactive boy was receiving Ritalin than when he was taking placebo.

At moderate doses, stimulant drugs produce few serious side effects and are generally considered to be safe. At the onset of drug treatment, two of the more common adverse reactions are insomnia and anorexia (loss of appetite). Insomnia is typically not a problem if medication is administered only in the morning, but many children receive a dose at noon and some even get medication late in the day. If such a schedule is necessary, an additional drug may be prescribed to induce sleep. Anorexia can usually be managed by taking the pill just before or with meals. Other minor side effects include headache, stomachache, nausea, and increased talkativeness. Stimulant drugs can also produce mood changes such as dysphoria (withdrawal, lethargy, apathy, serious facial expression, unusual inactivity, weepiness), fearfulness, irritability, and euphoria (rare). Younger children appear to be more susceptible to mood changes. Children typically develop a tolerance for these side effects, but the dose may have to be reduced and gradually increased to lessen the degree of discomfort.

There are other possible side effects of stimulant medication that do not occur very often but should be monitored nevertheless. One such reaction is involuntary movement of muscles.

This would include a variety of actions such as protrusion of the tongue, grimacing, facial tics (spasm or twitching of the facial muscles), choreoathetoid (jerking and writhing) movements of arms or legs, and twisting of the head and neck (e.g., Denkla, Bemporad, & McKay, 1976; Husain, Chapel, & Malek-Ahmadl, 1980; Mattson & Calvery, 1968; Robbins & Sahakian, 1979). These drugs can also induce or exacerbate stereotypies such as nail biting (e.g., Robbins & Sahakian, 1979). In some cases, these side effects will abate by simple reduction of the dosage. In others, treatment may have to be discontinued or the child switched to a different drug.

There have been reports of stimulant-induced hallucinations (Lucas & Weiss, 1971) and psychosis (Greenberg, Deem, & McMahon, 1972), but this is considered a rare phenomenon. A child who experiences such a reaction may complain about "hearing things" or talk in a strange or bizzare manner. Discontinuation of medication is recommended.

The only long-term side effects of Ritalin or Dexedrine that have been reported so far are small changes in height and weight (e.g., Mattes & Gittelman, 1983; Safer & Allen, 1973). However, when drug treatment is stopped, children show a growth rebound, an increase in growth rate that compensates for the slower rate while on medication (Safer, Allen, & Barr, 1975). The Pediatric Advisory Panel of the FDA reviewed the available literature about stimulants and growth suppression (Roche, Lipman, Overall, & Hung, 1979) and concluded that "stimulant drugs, particularly in the 'high normal' dose range, moderately suppress growth in weight . . . [but] early growth suppression during treatment is no longer evident in adulthood" (p. 849). At present there is no evidence that long-term treatment with Ritalin (approximately 0.25 mg/kg given twice a day) adversely affects the functioning of the liver, the endocrine system, or the cardiovascular system (Satterfield, Schell, & Barb, 1980).

Stimulants are relatively short-acting drugs. Their behavioral effects can be observed within a half hour after being administered orally. A 10 mg tablet of Ritalin produces a therapeutic effect for approximately 3 to 4 hours, and a 20 mg tablet lasts for at least an hour longer (Carter, 1956; Safer & Allen, 1976). Dexedrine Spansules, a timed-release product, produce a longer-lasting effect (approximately 12 hours) than do Dexedrine tablets. Also, a long-lasting (approximately 8 hours) form of Ritalin called Ritalin-SR is now available. The SR stands for "sustained-release." According to one report, one 20 mg tablet of Ritalin-SR administered at breakfast produces a therapeutic effect equivalent to a 10 mg tablet of regular Ritalin given twice a day (Whitehouse, Shah, & Palmer, 1980). The findings from another study, however, indicate that standard Ritalin (10 mg twice a day) is superior to Ritalin-SR (20 mg) in suppressing certain forms of disruptive behavior (Pelham et al., 1987).

Children differ greatly in terms of optimal dose. Some do well on a low dose (0.1 mg/kg), whereas others appear unchanged unless the dose is very high (e.g., 1.0 mg/kg). For this reason, most clinicians start out with a small dose that is gradually increased until the desired effect is achieved. (The figures for milligrams per kilogram given here refer to individual doses of medication, which may or may not be administered more than once per day.) The average daily dose of methylphenidate is usually 20 to 30 mg, with a morning dose of 10 to 20 mg and a noon dose of 10 mg (Safer & Allen, 1976). Others have also found that the optimal dose (for paired-associate learning) is 10 to 15 mg for many, but certainly not all, elementary-school-aged children diagnosed with this disorder (Swanson, Kinsbourne, Roberts, & Zucker, 1978). It is not unusual, however, to find reports stating that the average daily dose of Ritalin is 55 mg or that some children are receiving as much as 120 to 140 mg per day (Gittelman-Klein & Klein, 1976; Renshaw, 1974).

It is common clinical lore that Dexedrine is twice as potent as Ritalin (Safer & Allen, 1976). However, in actual practice, the daily doses of these drugs prescribed by physicians appear to be comparable (Gadow, 1981).

The beginning dose of Cylert (pemoline) is usually 37.5 mg, which may be increased to 75 mg per day (Safer & Allen, 1976). The dosage ratio of Ritalin to Cylert ranges from 1:4 to 1:6 (Pelham, 1983; Stephens et al., 1984). In other words, the behavioral effect produced by 0.3 mg/kg of Ritalin administered twice a day is similar to the effect produced by 1.2 to 1.8 mg/kg of Cylert given once a day.

Nonstimulant Drugs

Not all hyperactive children can be effectively managed with stimulant medication, particularly those who exhibit severe behavior disorders or who are multiply handicapped. For such children clinicians are more likely to prescribe a neuroleptic (see the discussion of conduct problems), such as Mellaril (e.g., Gittelman-Klein et al., 1976) or Haldol (e.g., Werry & Aman, 1975), or a tricyclic antidepressant, such as Tofranil, which was once considered the drug of second choice for the treatment of hyperactivity on the basis of findings from several studies (e.g., Rapoport et al., 1974; Werry, Aman, & Diamond, 1980). Unfortunately, many children appear to develop a tolerance for the therapeutic response (Quinn & Rapoport, 1975). There are some data to suggest that hyperactive children who (1) are more difficult to manage in the evening hours, (2) have mood-disturbance symptoms, or (3) are highly anxious may be more responsive to Tofranil than to stimulant drugs (Pliszka, 1987). The total daily dose of Tofranil ranges from 50 mg to 200 mg, usually administered in divided doses. The primary side effects are drowsiness, dizziness, dry mouth, profuse sweating, nausea, increased appetite, weight gain, and weight loss. Tofranil may also lower the seizure threshold, especially in brain-damaged children (Brown, Winsberg, Bialer, & Press, 1973).

Another tricyclic antidepressant, desipramine, which is marketed as Norpramin and Pertofrane, was also found to be effective for hyperactive children and adolescents, many of whom were poor responders to stimulants (Biederman, Baldessarini, Wright, Knee, & Harmatz, 1989). The average daily dose used by Biederman et al. was 4.6 mg/kg, but they note that in clinical practice the average daily dose should be increased gradually with concurrent assessment of therapeutic and untoward effects.

Tourette Syndrome

In addition to motor and vocal tics, approximately half of all diagnosed cases of Tourette syndrome also experience the behavioral symptoms of hyperactivity (e.g., Comings & Comings, 1984; Sverd, Curley, Jandorf, & Volkersz, 1988). Our own preliminary research with stimulants in four hyperactive children with Tourette syndrome indicated that Ritalin was effective for hyperactivity symptoms (Sverd, Gadow, & Paolicelli, 1989). Furthermore, there was little or no worsening of tics at moderate dosages. Because stimulant drugs can induce tics and exacerbate the symptoms of Tourette syndrome (Bradley, 1950; Lowe, Cohen, Detlor, Kremenitzer, & Shaywitz, 1982), they should be used with extreme caution in hyperactive Tourette syndrome patients; the risks of treatment must be carefully explained to caregivers and, when appropriate, the child patient. Unfortunately, all of the commonly prescribed drugs for hyperactivity and for Tourette syndrome can induce or exacerbate tics (Gadow & Sverd, 1990). It is controversial whether stimulants can cause Tourette syndrome in children who would not otherwise develop it. For this reason, some clinicians have cautioned against the use of stimulants for hyperactivity with children who have a first-degree relative (parent, brother, or sister) with Tourette syndrome and recommend drug withdrawal for children who experience drug-induced tics (i.e, were tic-free before treatment). The latter is also controversial because tics may abate with dosage reduction.

Clinical Considerations

Although one can never overemphasize the idiosyncratic nature of stimulant drug response in terms of behavioral effects, dose, and dose-response relationships, the general pattern of treatment with Ritalin is as follows: The typical dose for elementary-school-aged children is 10 to 15 mg administered in the morning and at noon. Many (but certainly not all) clinicians believe that individual doses greater than 0.6 mg/kg are generally not necessary for adequate therapeutic response and clinical management. When possible, it is recommended that medication not be given at times when it is unnecessary (e.g., on weekends and during summer vacations). However, such breaks from medication are not in the best interests of some patients. In good responders, treatment typically lasts for several (2 to 4) years, but periodic drug-free periods (at least once a year) are recommended to ascertain the need for continued treatment. Multiple-drug regimens are almost always ill advised. Drug therapy is typically terminated before the child enters junior high, but this does not mean that medication is no longer effective. Quite the contrary; stimulants appear to be efficacious for symptom suppression in hyperactive patients of all ages (infancy to adulthood). The probability of success when withdrawing medication can be greatly increased by the concurrent or subsequent implementation of alternative interventions (e.g., behavior therapy).

Stimulant drug therapy is a palliative; to the best of our knowledge, no one has yet demonstrated that medication leads to the permanent alteration of neurological structures, imparts new learning, or is even instrumental in the acquisition of skills that would not develop had treatment been withheld. Serious, thoughtful consideration must therefore be given to all the patient's clinical needs and to those of his or her caregivers if the latter bear on the patient's well-being, and they often do.

SCHIZOPHRENIA

Children

Childhood schizophrenia is a rare disorder, and it does appear to be a separate diagnostic entity from infantile autism. Follow-up studies show that even during the elementary-school years, children with infantile autism remain distinguishable from youngsters with schizophrenia (Green et al., 1984). One important difference between the two groups is that autistic children, on clinical examination, do not have auditory or visual hallucinations or delusions, whereas most schizophrenic children do experience these symptoms.

There is relatively little psychotropic drug research on prepubertal schizophrenic children. Although they were no doubt included in early investigations of autism or psychosis, drug response has not been examined separately for this diagnostic entity as it is currently defined in DSM-III-R. Based upon the adolescent and adult literature, neuroleptics would be the drugs of choice. Neuroleptics that are more "stimulating" (e.g., Navane, Haldol) are generally preferred. Whether these drugs actually suppress hallucinations, delusions, and disordered thought in prepubertal schizophrenic children is not well documented, and cases of drug failure have been reported (e.g., Green et al., 1984). When treating this disorder with psychotropic medication, the same caveats and clinical management guidelines as for infantile autism apply.

Adolescents

There are few methodologically sound studies of the efficacy of neuroleptic medication for the treatment of schizophrenia in adolescents. One of the better studies, conducted by Pool, Bloom, Mielke, Roniger, and Gallant (1976), showed that Haldol and Loxitane (loxapine) were superior to placebo in controlling psychotic symptoms. Similarly, Realmuto, Erickson, Yellin, Hopwood, and Greenberg (1984) studied adolescents receiving Mellaril and Navane (thiothixene) and found that (compared with baseline) treatment with either medication was associated with decreased anxiety, tension, excitement, and hallucinations, and, to a modest extent, cognitive disorganization. The optimal doses of Mellaril and Navane were 3.3 mg/kg per day and 0.30 mg/kg per day, respectively. Unfortunately, despite the diminution of symptoms, the youths "continued to be quite impaired" (p. 441) and, by the end of the study, only half were considered to be improved. Particularly troubling was the finding that drug-induced drowsiness was a common side effect, not only for Mellaril (75%) but also for Navane (54%), which is a less sedating neuroleptic, at least for adults.

In adolescence, the unwanted effects of neuroleptic medication have to be weighed against the severity of psychiatric disturbance. For example, a minor deterioration in intellectual performance is much less clinically relevant in a patient who is experiencing hallucinations and delusions and who will be institutionalized unless treated with neuroleptic medication. The management of acute (short-term) psychosis raises few concerns about the use of neuroleptics. Most side effects are self-limiting and reversible or, in the case of the acute extrapyramidal syndromes, treatable with anticholinergic drugs. The major clinical problem is for adolescents who require chronic or long-term treatment. Unfortunately, the findings from one study suggest that adolescent schizophrenics have a poor response to neuroleptics (Welner, Welner, & Fishman, 1979). Moreover, long-term neuroleptic treatment may cause tardive dyskinesia in some patients (Gualtieri, Barnhill, McGinsey, & Schell, 1980; Gualtieri, Quade, Hicks, Mayo, & Schroeder, 1984) and also produce changes in hormone secretions (Apter et al., 1983) and deterioration in cognitive performance (Erickson, Yellin, Hopwood, Realmuto, & Greenberg, 1984).

At present, the use of long-term neuroleptic treatment should be carefully considered. If the adolescent disorder is significantly improved with medication, it may only be a matter of trying to maintain the lowest dose and using the low-dose–high-potency drugs (e.g., Haldol, Navane, Loxitane) when possible. The development of serious side effects (e.g., tardive dyskinesia) usually necessitates a withdrawal of medication and a review of other approaches to treatment. In the case of schizophrenia, social and vocational intervention are crucial aspects of treatment, and the sole reliance on medication is not likely to be effective.

SELF-INJURIOUS BEHAVIOR (STEREOTYPY/HABIT DISORDER)

Studies of mentally retarded people in institutions (e.g., Griffin, Williams, Stark, Altmeyer, & Mason, 1986; Schroeder et al., 1978) suggest that approximately 10 to 15% exhibit self-injurious behavior (generally referred to as SIB). The extent of this problem is often unappreciated. Schroeder, Bickel, and Richmond (1986), for example, estimated that as many as 34,000 severely and profoundly mentally retarded persons exhibit serious SIB, which may result in tissue damage, permanent impairment, and even death. Despite the seriousness of this disorder and our heartfelt reactions to it, there are few well-conducted studies that have examined the effectiveness of neuroleptics, even though these drugs are generally considered to be therapeutic (reviewed by Farber, 1987; Singh & Millichamp, 1985). Both the phenothiazines (e.g., Mellaril, Thorazine) and Haldol have been reported to reduce SIB.

The opiate antagonist Narcan (naloxone), which is used to treat respiratory depression resulting from narcotic overdose, has recently been shown to be effective for the control of SIB (Davidson, Kleene, Carroll, & Rockowitz, 1983; Richardson & Zaleski, 1983; Sandman et al., 1983). Narcan can be administered intravenously, intramuscularly, or subcutaneously, but not orally. Unfortunately, Narcan is not effective for all mentally retarded individuals (Beckwith, Conk, & Schumacher, 1986), and the necessity of administration by injection also limits the clinical utility of the drug. Trexan (naltrexone), however, is an opiate antagonist that can be administered orally, and it was shown to be effective for SIB in one controlled case study (Bernstein, Hughes, Mitchell, & Thompson, 1987).

Lithium may also be of some value in the treatment of SIB (reviewed by Farber, 1987). However, this suggestion is based primarily on uncontrolled studies.

Because SIB has multiple etiologies, both psychological (Durand, 1986) and biological

(Schroeder, Bickel, & Richmond, 1986), careful consideration should be given, in formulating a treatment plan, to the possibility that specific environmental events are maintaining this behavior. A variety of behavioral techniques can be used to suppress SIB (see Romanczyk, 1986). Durand (1982) showed that haloperidol in combination with mild punishment was more effective than either treatment used alone in reducing SIB in a profoundly mentally retarded adolescent.

SPEECH, LANGUAGE, AND COMMUNICATION DISORDERS

Although it is true that relatively little psychopharmacotherapy research has been conducted on speech, language, and communication disorders, there are a surprising number of case studies or anecdotes about how various psychotropic drugs affect the speech or language of specific children. Bender and Cottington (1942), for example, described a case of elective mutism that appeared to respond to Benzedrine. However, there were other children with developmental aphasia or organic brain damage for whom stimulant medication had no beneficial effect. Ginn and Hohman (1953) described the treatment of a 4-year-old hyperactive boy with 7.5 mg of Dexedrine in the morning. The boy "jabbered only a few words" and stuttered. Medication presumably made him talk more slowly.

Most of the research on the effects of drugs on verbal behavior pertains to hyperactive children; the nature of whatever speech and language problems they may have is generally not specified. Creager and VanRiper (1967), for example, administered Ritalin (20 mg twice a day) and placebo to 30 children with "cerebral dysfunction." The children were referred to a psychiatric clinic for a variety of reasons, including "hyperactivity, scholastic difficulty, unmanageable behavior, withdrawal, short attention span, and maturational delay" (p. 624). An analysis of their verbal behavior indicated that medication caused the children to talk more. The authors believed that this was important for children undergoing speech therapy, because the child must talk if therapy is going to work. Similarly, Ludlow, Rapoport, Brown, and Mikkelson (1979) found that Dexedrine increased verbal productivity and language complexity in hyperactive boys.

The observed effects of stimulant drugs on verbal behavior are determined to a considerable degree by the characteristics of the task and setting. This is obvious from the findings from two additional studies. In one of these, Barkley, Cunningham, and Karlsson (1983) administered Ritalin and placebo to hyperactive children who did not exhibit deficits in language complexity and found that medication reduced the number of vocalizations in both free and structured settings with no concurrent change in complexity. Whalen et al. (1978) also found that Ritalin significantly reduced task-irrelevant speech and verbal productivity to a more normal level.

Collectively, although these studies provide us with information about stimulants and hyperactive children, they tell us relatively little about the usefulness of stimulant medication for the treatment of communication disorders. Nevertheless, Cantwell and Baker's studies on speech and language impaired children clearly show that such children exhibit a variety of psychiatric disorders, most notably hyperactivity (Baker & Cantwell, 1985; Cantwell & Baker, 1985). Therefore, the successful management of behavior disorders may have direct bearing on the efficacy of speech and language therapy and possibly on language development.

There are several published reports on the effect of Haldol on stuttering (e.g., Burns, Brady, & Kuruvilla, 1978; Tapia, 1969). In general, the findings from these studies and case reports indicate that Haldol can suppress or diminish stuttering in some individuals. Why Haldol should have this effect on stutterers is unclear, and, as for all disorders for which this drug is prescribed, careful consideration must be given to the risks of treatment versus the benefits. Interestingly, in an uncontrolled study, Fisher, Kerbeshian, and Burd (1986) found that Haldol also had a marked effect on facilitating language development in nonautistic children with pervasive developmental disorder.

STEREOTYPIES (STEREOTYPY/HABIT DISORDER)

Stereotypic behaviors are of concern to caregivers because they interfere with educational and habilitative efforts. Moreover, they can be an impediment to normalization in that bizarre behaviors are generally perceived in a negative way by others. Surveys (e.g., Eyman & Call, 1977) show that approximately half of the mentally retarded children under 13 years of age in institutions have stereotypies (repetitive, often bizarre motor activity). In general, the figures are lower for those in community placements and for older, moderately retarded residents. Examples of such behavior are rhythmic rocking, head weaving, mouthing, hand or arm flapping, and rubbing parts of the body (see Baumeister & Forehand, 1973). There is now substantial evidence that Mellaril reduces levels of stereotypic behavior in mentally retarded people (e.g., Aman & White, 1988; Davis, 1971; Davis, Sprague, & Werry, 1969; Singh & Aman, 1981; Zimmerman & Heistad, 1982). Whether drug-induced reductions in stereotypies lead to performance gains in other areas is unknown. Singh and Aman (1981) found that a low dose (2.5 mg/kg) of Mellaril was as effective as higher therapeutic doses in controlling stereotypies. Interestingly, although Zimmermann and Heistad (1982) found that withdrawal from Mellaril led to a marked increase in stereotypic behavior (e.g., rocking, undirected repetitive vocalizations, masturbation, arm swinging, repetitive behaviors) in severely mentally retarded adults housed in a large state institution, stereotypies were rarely targeted as the reason for prescribing medication in the first place.

TOURETTE SYNDROME

At present, the only proven effective treatment for the control of motor and vocal tics associated with Tourette syndrome are psychotropic drugs. Because the symptoms of Tourette syndrome can produce a considerable degree of emotional anguish for a child, the benefits of treatment must be carefully weighed against the associated risks (e.g., adverse drug reactions, psychosocial aspects of taking medication). Several different drugs are currently being used in the pharmacological management of this disorder; each is briefly discussed. More detailed presentations of this disorder and its pharmacological treatment are available elsewhere (e.g., Cohen, Bruun, & Leckman, 1988; Shapiro, Shapiro, Young, & Feinberg, 1988).

Since the 1960s, the drug of first choice for the treatment of Tourette syndrome has been Haldol. Approximately 80% of all people show some initial benefit from medication, but—

owing primarily to side effects—far less (approximately 20% to 30%) take the drug for extended periods. Haldol is very effective at low doses. Children are generally started on a dose of 0.25 to 0.5 mg per day (administered at bedtime), which is increased every 4 or 5 days (at no more than 0.5 mg increments) to an average daily dose of 3 to 4 mg. At low doses, many patients experience a complete remission of symptoms and few adverse reactions.

The withdrawal of Haldol may lead to an exacerbation of symptoms to a level far worse than before, and this exacerbation can last up to 2 to 3 months. Conversely, some children may show improvement following drug discontinuation, only to get worse later and gradually improve again. The withdrawal of medication may also be greeted with some relief, because side effects such as cognitive blunting dissipate. For these reasons, evaluating the need to continue treatment is a complex process, and the patient and his or her family should be prepared for these possible outcomes. Drug-free periods or dosage reductions should be scheduled to assess the need to continue medication.

Although the results of early uncontrolled investigations (e.g., Cohen, Detlor, Young, & Shaywitz, 1980) indicated that Catapres (clonidine), an antihypertension drug, was an effective agent for the treatment of Tourette syndrome, more recent studies indicate that it is less effective than Haldol (e.g., Shapiro, Shapiro, & Eisenkraft, 1983) and no better than placebo for controlling tics (Goetz et al., 1987). It may, however, be useful in controlling the associated symptoms, such as hyperactivity and inattentiveness. Catapres is initiated at a small daily dose (0.05 mg) that is gradually increased over several weeks to 0.15 to 0.30 mg. Because Catapres has a short half-life, it is administered in small doses three to four times per day. Catapres has a slower onset of action than Haldol and may take 3 weeks or more to produce a therapeutic response. Tolerance to beneficial effects is a problem in some children.

The major side effect of Catapres is sedation, but this generally goes away after several weeks. Nevertheless even transient sedation can have significant consequences, as evidenced by one patient who was involved in a serious auto accident because of this reaction (Shapiro et al., 1983). Teenagers who drive (and their parents) must be warned of the risks associated with drug-induced sedation. Other reported side effects include impaired cognition, dry mouth, sensitivity of eyes to light, bradycardia, hypotension, dizziness, irritability, nightmares, and insomnia.

Orap is a powerful neuroleptic shown to be effective for the treatment of Tourette syndrome (e.g., Shapiro & Shapiro, 1984); uncontrolled studies suggest that it may be as effective as Haldol and less sedating. Treatment is typically initiated with a dose of 1 mg per day, which is gradually increased to 6 to 10 mg per day (0.2 mg/kg per day). Because Orap has a relatively long half-life, it is possible to administer medication once a day. The side effects of Orap are similar to those of Haldol. Because Orap can have an adverse effect on heart function, an EKG should be administered prior to treatment.

The behavioral concomitants of Tourette syndrome (e.g., hyperactivity, obsessions, compulsions) and its psychological sequelae (e.g., embarrassment, social rejection, anxiety from not being in control of one's own body) and associated academic impediments (both drug-induced and preexisting) relegate drug therapy to an adjunctive role in the treatment process. An effort should be made to ensure that the child is receiving an adequate educational program and that his or her emotional needs are being attended to (see Bauer & Shea, 1984).

SUMMARY

The discovery and empirical verification of clinically effective psychoactive drugs is one of the most significant developments in child and adolescent psychiatry. Many of the commonly prescribed agents in current use have been noted in the literature for over two decades. In prepubertal children, by far the most researched pharmacological treatments are for the management of hyperactivity, oppositional behavior, and aggression. There are well over a hundred published stimulant drug studies of hyperactive children alone. Collectively, research findings show that stimulant treatment can produce profound symptomatic improvement for these children. Other drugs, such as the neuroleptics and the tricyclic antidepressants, are also effective, but concerns about untoward reactions relegate them to the status of alternative agents. Much less is know about effective pharmacological interventions for affective and anxiety disorders in this age group. With the exception of Tofranil

for separation anxiety, drug therapy for these disorders is tentative. Medication can provide symptomatic relief for some individuals with developmental disabilities (e.g., autism, mental retardation), but prudence dictates that the benefits of treatment must clearly outweigh the risks. Programmatic pharmacological research on these disorders is currently limited to an extremely small number of clinics, and early studies in this area were not particularly laudatory with regard to methodological rigor. At the present time, neuroleptics, particularly Haldol, may be of some benefit for autistic children. Mild to moderately mentally retarded individuals appear to show the full spectrum of psychiatric disorders, and their response to medication is generally similar to that of nonretarded peers. However, the incidence of drug failure is reportedly higher in this population; diagnostic features may differ; and the evaluation of clinical response can be greatly complicated by the presence of multiple disabilities (see Gadow & Poling, 1988).

There are relatively few well-controlled drug studies of adolescent psychiatric disorders; consequently, evidence for drug efficacy and guidelines for clinical management must often be extrapolated from research on adults. Briefly, hyperactivity in adolescence is responsive to both the stimulants and the tricyclics, with child psychiatrists favoring the latter. Although antidepressant and antimanic drugs are routinely prescribed for adolescent affective disorders, evidence for their efficacy from rigorous clinical trials is somewhat discouraging. Neuroleptics are an important adjunctive treatment for adolescent schizophrenia, but even with medication, many patients are still seriously disabled.

This chapter has addressed the classical syndromes seen in child and adolescent psychiatry and the drugs that are generally used in their management. This does not, however, exhaust all the clinical psychiatric situations in which drug therapy or drug interactions may be of importance (e.g., sleep disorders, encopresis, drug and alcohol abuse, eating disorders). Although space constraints have precluded detailed discussion of the psychosocial aspects of these disorders and their management (e.g., patient–clinician interaction), it bears repeating that our intent is not to suggest that pharmacotherapy is necessarily appropriate or desirable for all or even most young patients with mood, thought, or behavior disorders. Child and adolescent psychiatric disorders can be extreme and volatile, and many different elements (biological, psychological, and environmental) interact to produce them. For this reason, different types of intervention might result in some improvement for the patient, but the social and personal pressures on the psychiatrist to successfully and rapidly "treat" the condition can lead to the use of medication before other therapeutic approaches have been tried.

Ideally, psychopharmacotherapy would be used only for those child and adolescent psychiatric disorders in which a biological disturbance is being specifically improved by the action of the drug itself. Many of the descriptions of drug use in this chapter have shown that although medication may improve target symptoms, it does not necessarily alter the overall course of illness. It is important, therefore, that the risks of drug therapy be clearly weighed against the benefits. It is not unusual for the side effects of a particular drug to lead to the use of additional medications to manage the side effects (e.g., the concomitant use of anticholinergic and neuroleptic drugs). For the severely disturbed patient, such treatment may be appropriate. However, the addition of tricyclic medication to treat drug-induced school phobia in children and adolescents receiving neuroleptic medication for Tourette syndrome creates a worrying precedent (Linet, 1985).

Perhaps the most difficult challenge lies in helping adolescents who have both physical illnesses and psychological problems. The importance of physical appearance and peer acceptance during adolescence can make physical illness a very traumatic and, at times, self-destructive experience. The psychiatrist's role is in helping the adolescent adjust to the effects and demands of managing the illness. Depressive reactions, often expressed as anger and hostility, can be common in these situations, but the psychiatrist must also be aware of the potential psychological reactions to the treatment itself or stemming directly from it. For example, steroid drug treatment (hormone therapy), commonly used in the management of immunological disorders, can cause severe psychological change, usually mimicking depression or mania.

In summary, therefore, it is important to realize the limitations of pharmacotherapy as well as the benefits. Medication can, at times, be crucial to recovery, but even in these situations, secondary social handicaps may remain after recovery that will require more intensive psychological therapies. Most child and adolescent psychiatric disorders respond to psychological interventions without medication and—except in rare circumstances, such as acute psychosis—these interventions are generally recommended as the first approach. However, when behavioral treatments are ineffective, impractical, or unavailable, drug therapy may produce marked symptomatic improvement, much to the relief of patient and caregiver.

Appendix: Selected Psychotherapeutic Drugs

GENERIC NAME	TRADE NAME*	GENERIC NAME	TRADE NAME*
ANTIANXIETY AGENTS		**ANTIANXIETY AGENTS** (*Continued*)	
Propanediols		*Azaspirodecanediones*	
meprobamate	Equanil, Miltown	buspirone	BuSpar
Diphenylmethane		**ANTIDEPRESSANTS**	
hydroxyzine	Atarax, Vistaril	*Tricyclics*	
Benzodiazepines		amitriptyline	Elavil, Endep
alprazolam	Xanax	camoxapine	Asendin
chlordiazepoxide	Librium	clomipramine	Anafranil
clorazepate	Tranxene	desipramine	Norpramin, Pertofrane
diazepam	Valium		
flurazepam	Dalmane	doxepin	Adapin, Sinequan
halazepam	Paxipam	imipramine	Janimine, SK-Pramine, Tofranil
lorazepam	Ativan		
oxazepam	Serax		
prazepam	Centrax		
temazepam	Restoril	maprotiline	Ludiomil
triazolam	Halcion		

*Only trade name products marketed in the United States are listed. In the case of drugs no longer protected by patent laws, the inclusion of trade names other than the original was arbitrary.

Appendix: Selected Psychotherapeutic Drugs (continued)

GENERIC NAME	TRADE NAME*	GENERIC NAME	TRADE NAME*
ANTIDEPRESSANTS *(Continued)*		**NEUROLEPTICS (ANTIPSYCHOTICS)**	
Tricyclics (Continued)		*(Continued)*	
nortriptyline	Aventyl, Pamelor	*Dibenzazepine*	
		clozapine	Clozaril
protriptyline	Vivactil	*Dibenzoxazepines*	
trimipramine	Surmontil	amoxapine	Asendin
Monoamine Oxidase Inhibitors		loxapine	Loxitane
isocarboxazid	Marplan	*Diphenylbutylpiperidine*	
phenelzine	Nardil	pimozide	Orap
tranylcypromine	Parnate		
Atypical		**SEDATIVE-HYPNOTICS**	
trazodone	Desyrel	*Barbiturates*	
fluoxetine	Prozac	amobarbital	Amytal
bupropion	Wellbutrin	aprobarbital	Alurate
		butabarbital	Butisol
		mephobarbital	Mebaral
ANTIMANIA AGENTS		pentobarbital	Nembutal
lithium carbonate	Eskalith, Lithane, Lithobid	phenobarbital	Luminal
		secobarbital	Seconal
		Nonbarbiturates	
		chloral hydrate	Noctec
		ethchlorvynol	Placidyl
NEUROLEPTICS (ANTIPSYCHOTICS)		ethinamate	Valmid
Phenothiazines		glutethimide	Doriden
Aliphatic		methyprylon	Noludar
chlorpromazine	Thorazine		
trifluopromazine	Vesprin	**STIMULANTS**	
Piperdine		amphetamine	Benzedrine
piperacetazine	Quide	deanol	Deaner
mesoridazine	Serentil	dextroamphet- amine	Dexedrine
thioridazine	Mellaril	methamphet- amine	Desoxyn
Piperazine		methylphenidate	Ritalin
acetophenazine	Tindal	pemoline	Cylert
fluphenazine	Prolixin, Permitil		
perphenazine	Trilafon	**MISCELLANEOUS**	
prochlorperazine	Compazine	carbamazepine	Tegretol
trifluoperazine	Stelazine	clonazepam	Klonopin
Thioxanthenes		clonidine	Catapres
chlorprothixene	Taractan	fenfluramine	Pondimin
thiothixene	Navane	naloxone	Narcan
Butyrophenone		naltrexone	Trexan
haloperidol	Haldol	propranolol	Inderol
Dihydroindolone		valproic acid	Depakene
molindone	Moban		

*Only trade name products marketed in the United States are listed. In the case of drugs no longer protected by patent laws, the inclusion of trade names other than the original was arbitrary.

REFERENCES

Abikoff, H., & Gittelman, R. (1985). The normalizing effects of methylphenidate on the classroom behavior of ADDH children. *Journal of Abnormal Child Psychology, 13,* 33–44.

Allen, R. P., Safer, D., & Covi, L. (1975). Effects of psychostimulants on aggression. *Journal of Nervous and Mental Disease, 160,* 138–145.

Aman, M. G. (1978). Drugs, learning, and the psychotherapies. In J. S. Werry (Ed.), *Pediatric psychopharmacology: The use of behavior modifying drugs in children* (pp. 79–108). New York: Brunner/Mazel.

Aman, M. G., & Kern, R. A. (1989). Review of fenfluramine in the treatment of the developmental disabilities. *Journal of the American Academy of Child and Adolescent Psychiatry, 28,* 549–565.

Aman, M. G., & Singh, N. N. (Eds.). (1988). *Psychopharmacotherapy of the developmental disabilities.* New York: Springer-Verlag.

Aman, M. G., & Werry, J. S. (1982). Methylphenidate and diazepam in severe reading retardation. *Journal of the American Academy of Child Psychiatry, 1,* 31–37.

Aman, M. G., & White, A. J. (1988). Thioridazine dose effects with reference to stereotypic behavior in mentally retarded residents. *Journal of Autism and Developmental Disorders, 18,* 355–366.

Ambrosini, P. J. (1987). Pharmacotherapy in child and adolescent major depressive disorder. In H. Y. Meltzer (Ed.), *Psychopharmacology: The third generation of progress* (pp. 1247–1254). New York: Raven Press.

American Psychiatric Association. (1987). *Diagnostic and statistical manual of mental disorders* (3rd ed. rev.). Washington, DC: Author.

Amery, B., Minichiello, M. D., & Brown, G. L. (1984). Aggression in hyperactive boys: Response to d-amphetamine. *Journal of the American Academy of Child Psychiatry, 23,* 291–294.

Anderson, L. T., Campbell, M., Grega, D. M., Perry, R., Small, A. M., & Green, W. H. (1984). Haloperidol in the treatment of infantile autism: Effects on learning and behavioral symptoms. *American Journal of Psychiatry, 141,* 1195–1202.

Apter, A., Dickerman, Z., Gonen, N., Assa, S., Prager-Lewin, R., Kaufman, H., Tyano, S., & Laroy, Z. (1983). The effect of chlorpromazine on hypothalamic-pituitary-gonadal function in 10 adolescent schizophrenic boys. *American Journal of Psychiatry, 140,* 1588–1591.

Baker, L., & Cantwell, D. P. (1985). Psychiatric and learning disorders in children with speech and language disorders: A critical review. In K. D. Gadow (Ed.), *Advances in learning and behavioral disabilities* (Vol. 4, pp. 1–27). Greenwich, CT: JAI Press.

Ballenger, J. C., & Post, R. M. (1978). Therapeutic effects of carbamazepine in affective illness: A preliminary report. *Communication in Psychopharmacology, 2,* 159–175.

Barkley, R. A. (1981). *Hyperactive children: A handbook for diagnosis and treatment.* New York: Guilford Press.

Barkley, R. A., & Cunningham, C. E. (1978). Do stimulant drugs improve the academic performance of hyperkinetic children? *Clinical Pediatrics, 17,* 85–92.

Barkley, R. A., & Cunningham, C. E. (1979). The effects of methylphenidate on the mother–child interactions of hyperactive children. *Archives of General Psychiatry, 36,* 201–208.

Barkley, R. A., Cunningham, C. E., & Karlsson, J. (1983). The speech of hyperactive children and their mothers: Comparison with normal children and stimulant drug effects. *Journal of Learning Disabilities, 16,* 105–110.

Barkley, R. A., Karlsson, J., Strzelecki, E., & Murphy, J. V. (1984). Effects of age and Ritalin dosage on the mother-child interactions of hyperactive children. *Journal of Consulting and Clinical Psychology, 52,* 750–758.

Bauer, A. M., & Shea, T. M. (1984). Tourette syndrome: A review and educational implications. *Journal of Autism and Developmental Disorders, 14,* 69–80.

Baumeister, A. A., & Forehand, R. (1973). Stereotyped acts. In N. R. Ellis (Ed.), *International review of research in mental retardation* (Vol. 6, pp. 55–96). Orlando, FL: Academic Press.

Beckwith, B. E., Conk, D. I., & Schumacher, K. (1986). Failure of naloxone to reduce self-injurious behavior in two developmentally disabled females. *Applied Research in Mental Retardation, 7,* 183–188.

Bender, L., & Cottington, F. (1942). The use of amphetamine sulfate (Benzedrine) in child psychiatry. *American Journal of Psychiatry, 99,* 116–121.

Berney, T. B., Kolvin, I., Bhate, S. R., Garside, R. F., Jeans, J., Kay, B., & Scarth, L. (1981). School phobia: A therapeutic trial with clomipramine and outcome. *British Journal of Psychiatry, 138,* 110–118.

Bernstein, G. A., & Garfinkel, B. D. (1986). School phobia: The overlap of affective and anxiety disorders. *Journal of the American Academy of Child Psychiatry, 25,* 235–241.

Bernstein, G. A., Hughes, J. R., Mitchell, J. E., & Thompson, T. (1987). Effects of narcotic antagonists on self-injurious behavior: A single case study. *Journal of the American*

Academy of Child and Adolescent Psychiatry, 26, 886–889.

Biederman, J., Baldessarini, R. J., Wright, V., Knee, D., & Harmatz, J. S. (1989). A double-blind placebo controlled study of desipramine in the treatment of ADD: I. Efficacy. *Journal of the American Academy of Child and Adolescent Psychiatry, 28,* 777–784.

Biederman, J., Baldessarini, R. J., Wright, V., Knee, D., Harmatz, J. S., & Goldblatt, A. (1989). A double-blind placebo controlled study of desipramine in the treatment of ADD: II. Serum drug levels and cardiovascular findings. *Journal of the American Academy of Child and Adolescent Psychiatry, 28,* 903–911.

Birch, N. J. (1980). Bone side-effects of lithium. In F. N. Johnson (Ed.), *Handbook of lithium therapy* (pp. 365–371). Lancaster, England: MTP Press.

Birmaher, B., Quintana, H., & Greenhill, L. L. (1988). Methylphenidate treatment of hyperactive autistic children. *Journal of the American Academy of Child and Adolescent Psychiatry, 27,* 248–251.

Blackwell, B., & Currah, J. (1973). The psychopharmacology of nocturnal enuresis. In I. Kalvin, R. C. MacKeith, & S. R. Meadow (Eds.), *Bladder control and enuresis* (pp. 231–257). London: Heinemann.

Bradley, C. (1937). The behavior of children receiving Benzedrine. *American Journal of Psychiatry, 94,* 577–585.

Bradley, C. (1950). Benzedrine and dexedrine in the treatment of children's behavior disorders. *Pediatrics, 5,* 24–37.

Bradley, C. (1957). Characteristics and management of children with behavior problems associated with organic brain damage. *Pediatric Clinics of North America, 4,* 1049–1060.

Bradley, C., & Bowen, M. (1940). School performance of children receiving amphetamine (Benzedrine) sulfate. *American Journal of Orthopsychiatry, 10,* 782–788.

Bradley, C., & Bowen, M. (1941). Amphetamine (Benzedrine) therapy of children's behavior disorders. *American Journal of Orthopsychiatry, 11,* 92–103.

Brown, D., Winsberg, B. G., Bialer, I., & Press, M. (1973). Imipramine therapy and seizures: Three children treated for hyperactive behavior disorders. *American Journal of Psychiatry, 130,* 210–212.

Brown, J. T., Mulrow, C. D., & Stoudemire, G. A. (1984). The anxiety disorders. *Annals of Internal Medicine, 100,* 558–564.

Brown, R. T., & Sleator, E. K. (1979). Methylphenidate in hyperkinetic children: Differences in dose effects on impulsive behavior. *Pediatrics, 64,* 408–411.

Burns, D., Brady, J. P., & Kuruvilla, K. (1978). The acute effect of haloperidol and apormorphine on the severity of stuttering. *Biological Psychiatry, 13,* 255–264.

Cade, J. F. J. (1949). Lithium salts in the treatment of psychotic excitement. *Medical Journal of Australia, 36,* 349–352.

Campbell, M. (1988). Fenfluramine treatment of autism. Annotation. *Journal of Child Psychology and Psychiatry, 29,* 1–10.

Campbell, M., Adams, P., Small, A. M., Curren, E. L., Overall, J. E., Anderson, L. T., Lynch, N., & Perry, R. (1988). Efficacy and safety of fenfluramine in autistic children. *Journal of the American Academy of Child and Adolescent Psychiatry, 27,* 434–439.

Campbell, M., Anderson, L. T., Deutsch, S. I., & Green, W. H. (1984a). Psychopharmacological treatment of children with the syndrome of autism. *Pediatric Annals, 13,* 309–316.

Campbell, M., Anderson, L. T., Meier, M., Cohen, I. L., Small, A. M., Samit, C., & Sachar, E. J. (1978). A comparison of haloperidol and behavior therapy and their interaction in autistic children. *Journal of the American Academy of Child Psychiatry, 17,* 640–655.

Campbell, M., Cohen, I. L., & Small, A. M. (1982). Drugs and aggressive behavior. *Journal of the American Academy of Child Psychiatry, 21,* 107–117.

Campbell, M., & Deutsch, S. I. (1985). Neuroleptics in children. In G. D. Burrows, T. Norman, & B. Davies (Eds.), *Drugs in psychiatry: Vol. 3. Antipsychotics* (pp. 213–238). New York: Elsevier Biomedical.

Campbell, M., Fish, B., Shapiro, T., Collins, P., & Koh, C. (1972). Response to triiodothyronine and dextroamphetamine: A study of preschool schizophrenic children. *Journal of Autism and Childhood Schizophrenia, 2,* 343–358.

Campbell, M., Overall, J. E., Small, A. M., Sokol, M. S., Spencer, E. K., Adams, P., Foltz, R. L., Monti, K. M., Perry, R., Nobler, M., & Roberts, E. (1989). Naltrexone in autistic children: An acute open dose range tolerance trial. *Journal of the American Academy of Child and Adolescent Psychiatry, 28,* 200–206.

Campbell, M., Perry, R., Bennett, W. G., Small, A. M., Green, W. H., Grega, D., Schwartz, V., & Anderson, L. (1983). Long-term therapeutic efficacy and drug-related abnormal movements: A prospective study of haloperidol in autistic children. *Psychopharmacology Bulletin, 19,* 80–83.

Campbell, M., Perry, R., & Green, W. H. (1984b). Use of lithium in children and adolescents. *Psychosomatics, 2,* 95–106.

Campbell, M., Small, A. M., Green, W. H., Jennings, S. J., Perry, R., Bennett, W. G., & Anderson, L. (1984c). Behavioral efficacy of haloperidol and lithium carbonate: A comparison in hospitalized aggressive children with conduct disorder. *Archives of General Psychiatry, 120,* 650–656.

Campbell, M., & Spencer, E. K. (1988). Psychopharmacology in child and adolescent psychiatry: A review of the past five years. *Journal of the American Academy of Child and Adolescent Psychiatry, 27,* 269–279.

Cantwell, D. P., & Baker, L. (1985). Psychiatric and learning disorders in children with speech and language disorders: A descriptive analysis. In K. D. Gadow (Ed.), *Advances in learning and behavioral disabilities* (Vol. 4, pp. 27–47). Greenwich, CT: JAI Press.

Cantwell, D. P., & Carlson, G. A. (1978). Stimulants. In J. S. Werry (Ed.), *Pediatric psychopharmacology: The use of behavior modifying drugs in children* (pp. 171–207). New York: Brunner/Mazel.

Carlson, G. A. (1983). Bipolar affective disorders in childhood and adolescence. In D. P. Cantwell & G. A. Carlson (Eds.), *Affective disorder in childhood and adolescence: An update* (pp. 61–83). New York: Spectrum.

Carlson, G. A. (1986). Classification issues of bipolar disorder in childhood. *Psychiatric Development, 6,* 273–285.

Carlson, G. A. (1988). Depression: Pharmacotherapies. In J. L. Matson (Ed.), *Handbook of treatment approaches in childhood psychopathology* (pp. 345–363). New York: Plenum Press.

Carlson, G. A., & Cantwell, D. P. (1980). Unmasking masked depression in children and adolescents. *American Journal of Psychiatry, 137,* 445–449.

Carter, C. H. (1956). The effects of reserpine and methylphenidate (Ritalin) in mental defectives, spastics, and epileptics. *Psychiatric Research Reports, 4,* 44–48.

Chandler, H. N. (1978). Confusion compounded: A teacher tries to use research results to teach math. *Journal of Learning Disabilities, 11,* 361–369.

Cohen, D. J., Bruun, R. D., & Leckman, J. F. (Eds.). (1988). *Tourette's syndrome and tic disorders.* New York: John Wiley & Sons.

Cohen, D. J., Detlor, J., Young, J. G., & Shaywitz, B. A. (1980). Clonidine ameliorates Gilles de la Tourette syndrome. *Archives of General Psychiatry, 37,* 1350–1357.

Comings, D. E., & Comings, B. G. (1984). Tourette's syndrome and attention deficit disorder with hyperactivity: Are they genetically related? *Journal of the American Academy of Child Psychiatry, 23,* 138–146.

Conners, C. K. (1971). Drugs in the management of children with learning disabilities. In L. Tarnopol (Ed.), *Learning disorders in children: Diagnosis, medication, education* (pp. 253–301). Boston: Little, Brown.

Conners, C. K., & Rothschild, G. H. (1968). Drugs and learning in children. In J. Hellmuth (Ed.), *Learning disorders* (Vol. 3). Seattle, WA: Special Child.

Conners, C., Rothschild, G., Eisenberg, L., Stone, L., & Robinson, E. (1969). Dextroamphetamine in children with learning disorders. *Archives of General Psychiatry, 21,* 182–190.

Conners, C. K., Taylor, E., Meo, G., Kurz, M. A., & Fournier, M. (1972). Magnesium pemoline and dextroamphetamine: A controlled study in children with minimal brain dysfunction. *Psychopharmacologia, 26,* 321–336.

Creager, R. O., & VanRiper, C. (1967). The effect of methylphenidate on the verbal productivity of children with cerebral dysfunction. *Journal of Speech and Hearing Research, 10,* 623–628.

Cunningham, C. E., Siegel, L. S., & Offord, D. R. (1985). A developmental dose-response analysis of the effects of methylphenidate on the peer interactions of attention deficit disordered boys. *Journal of Child Psychology and Psychiatry, 26,* 955–971.

Darrow, C. W. (1929). Psychological effects of drugs. *Psychological Bulletin, 26,* 527–545.

Davidson, P. W., Kleene, B. W., Carroll, M., & Rockowitz, R. J. (1983). Effects of naloxone on self-injurious behavior: A case study.

Applied Research in Mental Retardation, 4, 1–4.

Davis, K. V. (1971). The effect of drugs on stereotyped and nonstereotyped operant behavior in retardates. *Psychopharmacology, 22,* 195–213.

Davis, K. V., Sprague, R. L., & Werry, J. S. (1969). Stereotyped behavior and activity level in severe retardates: The effect of drugs. *American Journal of Mental Deficiency, 73,* 721–727.

DeLong, G. R. (1978). Lithium carbonate treatment of select behavior disorders in children suggesting manic-depressive illness. *Journal of Pediatrics, 93,* 689–694.

DeLong, G. R., & Aldershof, A. L. (1987). Long-term experience with lithium treatment in childhood: Correlation with clinical diagnosis. *Journal of the American Academy of Child and Adolescent Psychiatry, 26,* 389–394.

Denkla, M. B., Bemporad, J. R., & McKay, M. D. (1976). Tics following methylphenidate administration. *Journal of the American Medical Association, 235,* 1349–1351.

Diamond, J. M., & Stein, J. M. (1983). Enuresis: A new look at stimulant therapy. *Canadian Journal of Psychiatry, 28,* 395–397.

Douglas, V. I. (1972). Stop, look, and listen: The problem of sustained attention and impulse control in hyperactive and normal children. *Canadian Journal of Behaviour Science, 4,* 259–282.

Douglas, V. I., Barr, R. G., O'Neill, M. E., & Britton, B. G. (1986). Short term effects of methylphenidate on the cognitive, learning and academic performance of children with attention deficit disorder in the laboratory and the classroom. *Journal of Child Psychology and Psychiatry, 27,* 191–211.

Douglas, V. I., & Peters, K. G. (1979). Toward a clearer definition of the attention deficit of hyperactive children. In G. A. Hale & M. Lewis (Eds.), *Attention and cognitive development* (pp. 173–247). New York: Plenum Press.

Durand, V. M. (1982). A behavioral/pharmacological intervention for the treatment of severe self-injurious behavior. *Journal of Autism & Developmental Disorders, 12,* 243–251.

Durand, V. M. (1986). Self-injurious behavior as intentional communication. In K. D. Gadow (Ed.), *Advances in learning and behavioral disabilities* (Vol. 5, pp. 141–155). Greenwich, CT: JAI Press.

Dykman, R. A., Ackerman, P. T., & McCray, D. S. (1980). Effects of methylphenidate on selective and sustained attention in hyperactive, reading-disabled, and presumably attention-disordered boys. *Journal of Nervous and Mental Disease, 168,* 745–752.

Dyme, I. Z., Sahakian, B. J., Golinko, B. E., & Rabe, E. F. (1982). Perseveration induced by methylphenidate in children: Preliminary findings. *Progress in Neuropsychopharmacology & Biological Psychiatry, 6,* 269–273.

Eisenberg, L., & Conners, C. K. (1971). Psychopharmacology in childhood. In N. B. Talbot, J. Kagan, & L. Eisenberg (Eds.), *Behavioral science in pediatric medicine* (pp. 397–423). Philadelphia: Saunders.

Elkins, R, Rapoport, J. L., & Lipsky, A. (1980). Obsessive-compulsive disorder of childhood and adolescence. A neurobiologic viewpoint. *Journal of the American Academy of Child Psychiatry, 19,* 511–524.

Ellis, M. J., Witt, P. A., Reynolds, R., & Sprague, R. L. (1974). Methylphenidate and the activity of hyperactives in the informal setting. *Child Development, 45,* 217–220.

Erickson, W. D., Yellin, A. M., Hopwood, J. H., Realmuto, G. M., & Greenberg, L. M. (1984). The effects of neuroleptics on attention in adolescent schizophrenics. *Biological Psychiatry, 19,* 745–753.

Evans, R. W., Clay, T. H., & Gualtieri, C. T. (1987). Carbamazepine in pediatric psychiatry. *Journal of the American Academy of Child and Adolescent Psychiatry, 26,* 2–8.

Eyman, R. K., & Call, T. (1977). Maladaptive behavior and community placement of mentally retarded persons. *American Journal of Mental Deficiency, 82,* 137–144.

Farber, J. M. (1987). Psychopharmacology of self-injurious behavior in the mentally retarded. *Journal of the American Academy of Child and Adolescent Psychiatry, 26,* 296–302.

Fazen, L. E., Lovejoy, F. H., & Crone, R. K. (1986). Acute poisoning in a children's hospital. A 2-year experience. *Pediatrics, 77,* 144–151.

Fish, B. (1976). Pharmacotherapy for autistic and schizophrenic children. In E. R. Ritvo, B. J. Freeman, E. M. Ornitz, & P. E. Tanguay (Eds.), *Autism: Diagnosis, current research and treatment* (pp. 107–119). New York: Spectrum.

Fisher, W., Kerbeshian, J., & Burd, L. (1986). A treatable language disorder: Pharmacological treatment of pervasive developmental disorder. *Developmental and Behavioral Pediatrics, 7,* 73–76.

Flament, M. F., Rapoport, J. L., Berg, C. J., Sceery, W., Kilts, L., Mellstrom, B., & Linnoila, M. (1985). Clomipramine treatment of childhood obsessive-compulsive disorders. *Archives of General Psychiatry, 42,* 977–983.

Flintoff, M. M., Barron, R. W., Swanson, J. M., Ledlow, A., & Kinsbourne, M. (1982). Methylphenidate increases selectivity of visual scanning in children referred for hyperactivity. *Journal of Abnormal Child Psychology, 10,* 145–161.

Freeman, L. N., Poznanski, E. O., Grossman, J. A., Buchsbaum, Y. Y., & Banegas, M. E. (1985). Psychotic and depressed children: A new entity. *Journal of the American Academy of Child Psychiatry, 24,* 95–102.

Gadow, K. D. (1981). Drug therapy for hyperactivity: Treatment procedures in natural settings. In K. D. Gadow & J. Loney (Eds.), *Psychosocial aspects of drug treatment for hyperactivity* (pp. 13–76). Boulder, CO: Westview Press.

Gadow, K. D. (1983). Effects of stimulant drugs on academic performance in hyperactive and learning disabled children. *Journal of Learning Disabilities, 16,* 290–299.

Gadow, K. D. (1985). Relative efficacy of pharmacological, behavioral, and combination treatments for enhancing academic performance. *Clinical Psychology Review, 5,* 513–533.

Gadow, K. D. (1986a). *Children on medication: Vol. 1. Hyperactivity, learning disabilities, and mental retardation.* Austin, TX: PRO-ED.

Gadow, K. D. (1986b). *Children on medication: Vol 2. Epilepsy, emotional disturbance, and adolescent disorders.* Austin, TX: PRO-ED.

Gadow, K. D. (1988a). Attention deficit disorder and hyperactivity: Pharmacotherapies. In J. L. Matson (Ed.), *Handbook of treatment approaches in childhood psychopathology* (pp. 215–247). New York: Plenum Press.

Gadow, K. D. (1988b). Pharmacotherapy. In K. A. Kavale, S. R. Forness, & M. Bender (Eds.), *Handbook of learning disabilities: Vol. 2. Methods and interventions* (pp. 195–214). Boston: College-Hill Press.

Gadow, K. D., Nolan, E. E., Paolicelli, L. M., Sverd, J., & Sprafkin, J. (1990). Methylphenidate in aggressive-hyperactive boys: I. Effects on peer aggression in public school settings. *Journal of the American Academy of Child and Adolescent Psychiatry* (in press).

Gadow, K. D., Paolicelli, L. M., Sverd, J., Sprafkin, J., Nolan, E. E., & Schwartz, J. (1990). *Methylphenidate in aggressive-hyperactive boys: 2. Treatment spillover effects and behavioral normalization.* Manuscript submitted for publication.

Gadow, K. D., & Poling, E. (1988). *Pharmacotherapy and mental retardation.* Austin, TX: PRO-ED.

Gadow, K. D., & Sverd, J. (1990). Stimulants for child patients with Tourette syndrome. *Journal of Developmental and Behavioral Pediatrics* (in press).

Gadow, K. D., & Swanson, H. L. (1985). Assessing drug effects on academic performance. *Psychopharmacology Bulletin, 21,* 877–886.

Geller, B., Chestnut, E. C., Miller, M. D., Price, D. T., & Yates, E. (1985). Preliminary data on DSM III associated features of major depressive disorder in children and adolescents. *American Journal of Psychiatry, 142,* 643–644.

Geller, B., Cooper, T. B., Chestnut, E., Abel, A. S., & Anker, J. A., (1984). Nortriptyline pharmacokinetic parameters in depressed children and adolescents: Preliminary data. *Journal of Clinical Psychopharmacology, 4,* 265–269.

Geller, B., Guttmacher, L., & Bleeg, M. (1981). Coexistence of childhood onset pervasive developmental disorder and attention deficit disorder with hyperactivity. *American Journal of Psychiatry, 138,* 388–389.

Ginn, S. A., & Hohman, L. B. (1953). The use of dextroamphetamine in severe behavior problems of children. *Southern Medical Journal, 46,* 1124–1127.

Gittelman, R., Klein, D. F., & Feingold, I. (1983). Children with reading disorders-II. Effects of methylphenidate in combination with reading remediation. *Journal of Child Psychology and Psychiatry, 24,* 193–212.

Gittelman, R., & Koplewicz, H. S. (1986). Pharmacotherapy of childhood anxiety disorders. In R. Gittelman (Ed.), *Anxiety disorders of childhood* (pp. 188–203). New York: Guilford Press.

Gittelman-Klein, R. (1975). Pharmacotherapy and management of pathological separation anxiety. *International Journal of Mental Health, 4,* 255–271.

Gittelman-Klein, R., & Klein, D. F. (1971). Controlled imipramine treatment of school phobia. *Archives of General Psychiatry, 25,* 204–207.

Gittelman-Klein, R., & Klein, D. F. (1973). School phobia: Diagnostic considerations in the light of imipramine effects. *Journal of Nervous and Mental Disease, 156,* 199–215.

Gittelman-Klein, R., & Klein, D. F. (1976). Methylphenidate effects in learning disabilities. *Archives of General Psychiatry, 33,* 655–664.

Gittelman-Klein, R., Klein, D. F., Katz, S., Saraf, K., & Pollack, E. (1976). Comparative effects of methylphenidate and thioridazine in hyperactive children. *Archives of General Psychiatry, 33,* 1217–1231.

Goetz, C. G., Tanner, C. M., Wilson, R. S., Carroll, S., Como, P. G., & Shannon, K. M. (1987). Clonidine and Gilles de la Tourette's syndrome: Double-blind study using objective rating methods. *Annals of Neurology, 21,* 307–310.

Green, W. H., Campbell, M., Hardesty, A. S., Grega, D. M., Padron-Gayol, M., Shell, J., & Erlenmeyer-Kimling, L. (1984). A comparison of schizophrenic and autistic children. *Journal of the American Academy of Child Psychiatry, 23,* 399–409.

Greenberg, L. M., Deem, M. A., & McMahon, S. (1972). Effects of dextroamphetamine, chlorpromazine, and hydroxyzine on behavior and performance in hyperactive children. *American Journal of Psychiatry, 129,* 532–539.

Griffin, J. C., Williams, D. E., Stark, M. T., Altmeyer, B. K., & Mason, M. (1986). Self-injurious behavior: A state-wide prevalence survey of the extent and circumstances. *Applied Research in Mental Retardation, 7,* 105–116.

Gualtieri, C. T., Barnhill, J., McGinsey, J., & Schell, D. (1980). Tardive dyskinesia and other movement disorders in children treated with psychotropic drugs. *Journal of the American Academy of Child Psychiatry, 19,* 491–510.

Gualtieri, C. T., Golden, R. N., & Fahs, J. J. (1983). New developments in pediatric psychopharmacology. *Developmental and Behavioral Pediatrics, 4,* 202–209.

Gualtieri, C. T., Quade, D., Hicks, R. E., Mayo, J. P., & Schroeder, S. R. (1984). Tardive dyskinesia and other clinical consequences of neuroleptic treatment in children and adolescents. *American Journal of Psychiatry, 141,* 20–23.

Hallstrom, C., Treasaden, I., Edwards J. G., & Lader, M. (1981). Diazepam, propranolol and their combination in the management of chronic anxiety. *British Journal of Psychiatry, 139,* 417–421.

Hersov, L. (1985). Emotional disorders. In M. Rutter & L. Hersov (Eds.), *Child and adolescent psychiatry: Modern approaches* (rev. ed., pp. 368–381). Oxford: Blackwell.

Horn, W. F., O'Donnell, J. P., & Vitulano, L. A. (1983). Long-term follow-up studies of learning disabled persons. *Journal of Learning Disabilities, 16,* 542–555.

Humphries, T., Kinsbourne, M., & Swanson, J. (1978). Stimulant effects on cooperation and social interaction between hyperactive children and their mothers. *Journal of Child Psychology and Psychiatry, 19,* 13–22.

Husain, A., Chapel, J., & Malek-Ahmadl, P. (1980). Methylphenidate, neuroleptics and dyskinesia-dystonia. *Canadian Journal of Psychiatry, 25,* 254–258.

Judd, L. L., Squire, L. R., Butters, W., Salmon, D. P., & Paller, K. A. (1987). Effects of psychotropic drugs on cognition and memory in normal humans and animals. In H. Y. Meltzer (Ed.), *Psychopharmacology: The third generation of progress* (pp. 1467–1476). New York: Raven Press.

Kamm, I., & Mandel, A. (1967). Thioridazine in the treatment of behavior disorders in epileptics. *Diseases of the Nervous System, 28,* 46–48.

Kashani, J. H., Shekim, W. O., & Reid, J. C. (1984). Amitriptyline in children with major depressive disorder: A double-blind crossover pilot study. *Journal of the American Academy of Child Psychiatry, 23,* 348–351.

Kashani, J., & Simonds, J. F. (1979). The incidence of depression in children. *American Journal of Psychiatry, 136,* 1203–1205.

Katz, S., Saraf, K., Gittelman-Klein, R., & Klein, D. F. (1975). Clinical pharmacological management of hyperkinetic children. *Inter-*

national Journal of Mental Health, 4, 157–181.

Kishimoto, A., Ogura, C., Hazama, H., & Inoue, K. (1983). Long-term prophylactic effects of carbamazepine in affective disorder. *British Journal of Psychiatry, 143*, 327–331.

Klauber, G. T. (1989). Clinical efficacy and safety of desmopressin in the treatment of nocturnal enuresis. *Journal of Pediatrics, 114*, 719–722.

Klein, D. F. (1981). Anxiety reconceptualized. In D. F. Klein & J. G. Rabkin (Eds.), *Anxiety: New research and current concepts*. New York: Raven Press.

Kolvin, I., Berney, T. P., & Bhate, S. R. (1984). Classification and diagnosis of depression in school phobia. *British Journal of Psychiatry, 145*, 347–357.

Kolvin, I., Taunch, J., Currah, J., Garside, R. F., Nolan, J., & Shaw, W. B. (1972). Enuresis—a descriptive analysis and a controlled trial. *Developmental Medicine and Child Neurology, 14*, 715–726.

Kovacs, M., Feinberg, T. L., Crouse-Novak, M. A., Paulauskas, S. L., & Finkelstein, R. (1984). Depressive disorders in childhood: I. A longitudinal prospective study of characteristics and recovery. *Archives of General Psychiatry, 41*, 229–237.

Kramer, A. D., & Feiguine, R. J. (1981). Clinical effects of amitriptyline in adolescent depression: A pilot study. *Journal of the American Academy of Child Psychiatry, 20*, 636–644.

Last, C. G., Hersen, M., Kazdin, A. E., Finkelstein, R., & Strauss, C. C. (1987). Comparison of DSM-III separation anxiety and overanxious disorders: Demographic characteristics and patterns of comorbidity. *Journal of the American Academy of Child and Adolescent Psychiatry, 26*, 527–531.

Lerer, R. J., Lerer, M. P., & Artner, J. (1977). The effects of methylphenidate on the handwriting of children with minimal brain dysfunction. *Journal of Pediatrics, 91*, 127–132.

Lerman, P. (1986). Seizures induced or aggravated by anticonvulsants. *Epilepsia, 27*, 708–710.

Levy, H. B. (1973). *Square pegs, round holes: The learning-disabled child in the classroom and the home*. Boston: Little, Brown.

Lewis, J. L., & Winokur, G. (1982). The induction of mania. *Archives of General Psychiatry, 39*, 303–306.

Linet, L. S. (1985). Tourette syndrome, pimozide and school phobia: The neuroleptic sep-aration anxiety syndrome. *American Journal of Psychiatry, 142*, 613–615.

Lion, J. R., Azcarate, C. L., & Koepke, H. H. (1975). "Paradoxical rage reactions" during psychotropic medication. *Diseases of the Nervous System, 36*, 557–558.

Lowe, T. L., Cohen, D. J., Detlor, J., Kremenitzer, M. W., & Shaywitz, B. A. (1982). Stimulant medications precipitate Tourette's syndrome. *Journal of the American Medical Association, 247*, 1729–1731.

Lucas, A., & Weiss, M. (1971). Methylphenidate hallucinosis. *Journal of the American Medical Association, 217*, 1079–1081.

Ludlow, C., Rapoport, J., Brown, G., & Mikkelson, E. (1979). The differential effects of dextroamphetamine on the language and communicative skills of hyperactive and normal children. In R. Knights & D. Bakker (Eds.), *Rehabilitation, treatment, and management of learning disorders*. Baltimore: University Park Press.

MacLean, R. E. G. (1960). Imipramine hydrochloride and enuresis. *American Journal of Psychiatry, 117*, 551.

Mattes, J. A., & Gittelman, R. (1983). Growth of hyperactive children on maintenance regimen of methylphenidate. *Archives of General Psychiatry, 40*, 317–321.

Mattson, R. H., & Calverly, J. R. (1968). Dextroamphetamine-sulfate-induced dyskinesias. *Journal of the American Medical Association, 204*, 400–402.

Meadow, R., & Berg, I. (1982). Controlled trial of imipramine in diurnal enuresis. *Archives of Disease in Childhood, 57*, 714–716.

Meyer, M. F. (1922). The psychological effects of drugs. *Psychological Bulletin, 19*, 173–182.

Miller, K., Goldberg, S., & Atkin, B. (1989). Nocturnal enuresis: Experience with long-term use of intranasally administered desmopressin. *Journal of Pediatrics, 114*, 723–726.

Molitch, M., & Poliakoff, S. (1937). Effect of benzedrine sulfate on enuresis. *Archives of Pediatrics, 54*, 499–501.

Molitch, M., & Sullivan, J. P. (1937). Effect of benzedrine sulfate on children taking New Stanford Achievement Test. *American Journal of Orthopsychiatry, 7*, 519–522.

Ounsted, C. (1955). The hyperkinetic syndrome in epileptic children. *Lancet, 2*, 303–311.

Paul, R. (1987). Natural history. In D. J. Cohen,

A. M. Donnellan, & R. Paul (Eds.), *Handbook of autism and pervasive developmental disorders* (pp. 121–130). New York: John Wiley & Sons.

Pelham, W. E. (1983). The effects of psychostimulants on academic achievement in hyperactive and learning-disabled children. *Thalamus, 3,* 1–49.

Pelham, W. E., Bender, M. E., Caddell, J., Booth, S., & Moorer, S. H. (1985). Methylphenidate and children with attention deficit disorder: Dose effects on classroom academic and social behavior. *Archives of General Psychiatry, 42,* 948–952.

Pelham, W. E., Sturges, J., Hoza, J., Schmidt, C., Bijlsma, J. J., Milich R., & Moorer, S. (1987). The effects of Sustained Release 20 and 10 mg Ritalin b.i.d. on cognitive and social behavior in children with attention deficit disorder. *Pediatrics, 80,* 491–501.

Pelham, W. E., Swanson, J., Bender, M., & Wilson, J. (1980, September). *Effects of pemoline on hyperactivity: Laboratory and classroom measures.* Paper presented at the annual meeting of the American Psychological Association, Montreal.

Perry, R., Campbell, M., Adams, P., Lynch, N., Spencer, E. K., Curren, E. L., & Overall, J. E. (1989). Long-term efficacy of haloperidol in autistic children: Continuous versus discontinuous drug administration. *Journal of the American Academy of Child and Adolescent Psychiatry, 28,* 87–92.

Petti, T. A., & Law, W. (1982). Imipramine treatment of depressed children: A double-blind pilot study. *Journal of Clinical Psychopharmacology, 2,* 107–110.

Pfefferbaum, B., Overall, J. E., Boren, H. A., Frankel, L. S., Sullivan, M. P., & Johnson, K. (1987). Alprazolam in the treatment of anticipatory and acute situational anxiety in children with cancer. *Journal of the American Academy of Child and Adolescent Psychiatry, 26,* 532–535.

Piggot, L. R., Gdowski, C. L., Villanueva, D., Fischhoff, J., & Frohman, C. F. (1986). Side effects of fenfluramine in autistic children. *Journal of the American Academy of Child Psychiatry, 25,* 287–289.

Platt, J. E., Campbell, M., Green, W. H., & Grega, D. M. (1984). Cognitive effects of lithium carbonate and haloperidol in treatment-resistant aggressive children. *Archives of General Psychiatry, 120,* 657–662.

Pleak, R. R., Birmaker, B., Gavrilescu, A., Abichandani, C., & Williams, D. T. (1988). Mania and neuropsychiatric excitation following carbamazepine. *Journal of the American Academy of Child and Adolescent Psychiatry, 27,* 500–503.

Pliszka, S. R. (1987). Tricyclic antidepressants in the treatment of children with attention deficit disorder. *Journal of the American Academy of Child and Adolescent Psychiatry, 26,* 127–132.

Pool, D., Bloom, W., Mielke, D. H., Roniger, J. J., & Gallant, D. M. (1976). A controlled evaluation of Loxitane in seventy-five adolescent schizophrenic patients. *Current Therapeutic Research, 19,* 99–104.

Porrino, L. J., Rapoport, J. L., Behar, D., Sceery, W., Ismond, D. R., & Bunney, W. E. (1983). A naturalistic assessment of the motor activity of hyperactive boys. *Archives of General Psychiatry, 40,* 681–687.

Post, R. M. (1987). Mechanisms of action of carbamazepine and related anticonvulsants in affective illness. In H. Y. Meltzer (Ed.), *Psychopharmacology: The third generation of progress* (pp. 567–576). NY: Raven Press.

Preskorn, S. H., Bupp, S. J., Weller, E. B., & Weller, R. A. (1989). Plasma levels of imipramine and metabolites in 68 hospitalized children. *Journal of the American Academy of Child and Adolescent Psychiatry, 28,* 373–375.

Puig-Antich, J. (1982). Major depression and conduct disorder in prepuberty. *Journal of the American Academy of Child Psychiatry, 21,* 118–128.

Puig-Antich, J., Perel, J. M., & Lupatkin, W. (1987). Imipramine in prepubertal major depressive disorders. *Archives of General Psychiatry, 44,* 81–89.

Puig-Antich, J., Perel, J. M., Lupatkin, W., Chambers, W. J., Shea, C., Tabrizi, M. A., & Stiller, R. L. (1979). Plasma levels of imipramine (IMI) and desmethylimipramine (DMI) and clinical response in prepubertal major depressive disorder. *Journal of the American Academy of Child Psychiatry, 18,* 616–627.

Quinn, P. O., & Rapoport, J. L. (1975). One-year follow-up of hyperactive boys treated with imipramine or methylphenidate. *American Journal of Psychiatry, 132,* 241–245.

Rapoport, J. L., Quinn, P. O., Bradbard, G., Riddle, K. D., & Brooks, E. (1974). Imipramine and methylphenidate treatments of hyperactive boys. *Archives of General Psychiatry, 30,* 789–793.

Rapport, M. D., Stoner, G., DePaul, G. J., Birmingham, B. K., & Tucker, S. (1985). Methylphenidate in hyperactive children: Differential effects of dose on academic, learning, and social behavior. *Journal of Abnormal Child Psychology, 13,* 227–244.

Ratey, J. J., Mikkelsen, E. J., Smith, G. B., Upadhyaya, A., Zuckerman, H. S., Martell, D., Sorgi, P., Polakoff, S., & Bemporad, J. (1986). β blockers in the severely and profoundly mentally retarded. *Journal of Clinical Psychopharmacology, 6,* 103–107.

Realmuto, G. M., Erickson, W. D., Yellin, A. M., Hopwood, J. H., & Greenberg, L. M. (1984). Clinical comparison of thiothixene and thioridazine in schizophrenic adolescents. *American Journal of Psychiatry, 141,* 440–442.

Reid, M. K., & Borkowski, J. G. (1984). Effects of methylphenidate (Ritalin) on information processing in hyperactive children. *Journal of Abnormal Child Psychology, 12,* 169–185.

Renshaw, D. C. (1974). *The hyperactive child.* Chicago: Nelson-Hall.

Reynolds, E. H. (1983). Mental effects of antiepileptic medication: A review. *Epilepsia, 24* (Suppl. 2), S85–S95.

Richardson, E., Kupietz, S. A., Winsberg, B. G., Maitinsky, S., & Mendell, N. (1988). Effects of methylphenidate dosage in hyperactive reading-disabled children: II. Reading achievement. *Journal of the American Academy of Child and Adolescent Psychiatry, 27,* 78–87.

Richardson, J. S., & Zaleski, W. A. (1983). Naloxone and self-mutilation. *Biological Psychiatry, 18,* 99–101.

Riddle, M. A., Hardin, M. T., King, R., Scahill, L., & Woolston, J. L. (1990). Fluoxetine treatment of children and adolescents with Tourette's and obsessive compulsive disorders: Preliminary clinical experience. *Journal of the American Academy of Child and Adolescent Psychiatry, 29,* 45–48.

Rifkin, A., Quitkin, F., Carillo, C., Blumberg, A. G., & Klein, D. F. (1972). Lithium carbonate in emotionally unstable character disorder. *Archives of General Psychiatry, 27,* 519–523.

Robbins, T. W., & Sahakian, B. J. (1979). "Paradoxical" effects of psychomotor stimulant drugs in hyperactive children from the standpoint of behavioral pharmacology. *Neuropharmacology, 18,* 931–950.

Robinson, D. S., & Barker, E. (1976). Tricyclic antidepressant cardiotoxicity. *Journal of the American Medical Association, 236,* 2089–2090.

Roche, A. F., Lipman, R. S., Overall, J. E., & Hung, W. (1979). The effects of stimulant medication on the growth of hyperkinetic children. *Pediatrics, 63,* 847–850.

Romanczyk, R. G. (1986). Self-injurious behavior: Conceptualization, assessment, and treatment. In K. D. Gadow (Ed.), *Advances in learning and behavioral disabilities* (Vol. 5, pp. 29–56). Greenwich, CT: JAI Press.

Ross, D. M., & Ross, S. A. (1982). *Hyperactivity: Current issues, research, and theory.* New York: John Wiley & Sons.

Roy-Byrne, P. P., Joffe, R. T., Uhde, T. W., & Post, R. M. (1984a). Approaches to the evaluation and treatment of rapid-cycling affective illness. *British Journal of Psychiatry, 145,* 543–550.

Roy-Byrne, P. P., Uhde, T. W., & Post, R. M. (1984b). Carbamazepine for aggression, schizophrenia and nonaffective syndromes. *International Drug Therapy Newsletter, 19,* 9–12.

Roy-Byrne, P. P., Uhde, T. W., & Post, R. M. (1984c). Carbamazepine for hyperactivity, anxiety and withdrawal syndromes. *International Drug Therapy Newsletter, 19,* 25–26.

Rutter, M. (1985). The treatment of autistic children. *Journal of Child Psychology and Psychiatry, 26,* 193–214.

Ryan, N. D., Meyer, V., Dachille, S., Mazzie, D., & Puig-Antich, J. (1988a). Lithium antidepressant augmentation of TCA-refractory depression in adolescents. *Journal of the American Academy of Child and Adolescent Psychiatry, 27,* 371–376.

Ryan, N. D., & Puig-Antich, J. (1987). Pharmacological treatment of adolescent psychiatric disorders. *Journal of Adolescent Health Care, 8,* 137–142.

Ryan, N. D., Puig-Antich, J., Cooper, T. B., Rabinovich, H., Ambrosini, P., Davies, M., King, J., Torres, D., & Fried, J. (1986). Imipramine in adolescent major depression: Plasma level and clinical response. *Acta Psychiatrica Scandinavica, 73,* 275–288.

Ryan, N. D., Puig-Antich, J., Cooper, T. B., Rabinovich, H., Ambrosini, P., Fried, J.,

Davies, M., Torres, D., & Suckow, R. F. (1987). Relative safety of single versus divided dose imipramine in adolescent major depression. *Journal of the American Academy of Child and Adolescent Psychiatry, 26,* 400–406.

Ryan, N. D., Puig-Antich, J. Rabinovich, H., Fried, J., Ambrosini, P., Meyer, V., Torres, D., Dachille, S., & Mazzie, D. (1988b). MAOIs in adolescent major depression unresponsive to tricyclic antidepressants. *Journal of the American Academy of Child and Adolescent Psychiatry, 27,* 755–758.

Safer, D. J., & Allen, R. P. (1973). Factors influencing the suppressant effects of two stimulant drugs on the growth of hyperactive children. *Pediatrics, 51,* 660–667.

Safer, D. J., & Allen, R. P. (1976). *Hyperactive children: Diagnosis and management.* Baltimore: University Park Press.

Safer, D., Allen, R., & Barr, E. (1975). Growth rebound after termination of stimulant drugs. *Pediatrics, 86,* 113–116.

Sandman, C. A., Datta, P. C., Barron, J., Hoehler, F. K., Williams, C., & Swanson, J. M. (1983). Naloxone attenuates self-abusive behavior in developmentally disabled clients. *Applied Research in Mental Retardation, 4,* 5–11.

Satterfield, J. H., Schell, A. M., & Barb, S. D. (1980). Potential risk of prolonged administration of stimulant medication for hyperactive children. *Journal of Developmental and Behavioral Pediatrics, 1,* 102–107.

Schain, R. J., & Reynard, C. L. (1975). Observations on effects of central stimulant drug (methylphenidate) in children with hyperactive behavior. *Pediatrics, 55,* 709–716.

Schroeder, S. R., Bickel, W. K., & Richmond, G. (1986). Primary and secondary prevention of self-injurious behaviors: A lifelong problem. In K. D. Gadow (Ed.), *Advances in learning and behavioral disabilities* (Vol. 5, pp. 63–85). Greenwich, CT: JAI Press.

Schroeder, S. R., Schroeder, C. S., Smith, B., & Dalldorf, J. (1978). Prevalence of self-injurious behaviors in a large state facility for the retarded: A three-year follow-up study. *Journal of Autism and Childhood Schizophrenia, 8,* 261–269.

Shaffer, D. (1985). Enuresis. In M. Rutter & L. Hersov (Eds.), *Child and adolescent psychiatry* (2nd ed., pp. 465–481). London: Blackwell Scientific.

Shapiro, A. K., & Shapiro, E. (1984). Controlled study of pimozide vs. placebo in Tourette's syndrome. *Journal of the American Academy of Child Psychiatry, 2,* 161–173.

Shapiro, A. K., Shapiro, E., & Eisenkraft, G. J. (1983). Treatment of Gilles de la Tourette's syndrome with clonidine and neuroleptics. *Archives of General Psychiatry, 40,* 1235–1240.

Shapiro, A. K., Shapiro, E. S., Young, J. G., & Feinberg, T. E. (1988). *Gilles de la Tourette syndrome* (2nd ed.). New York: Raven Press.

Sheard, M. H. (1978). The effects of lithium and other ions on aggressive behavior. In L. Valzelli (Ed.), *Modern problems of pharmacopsychiatry* (Vol. 13, pp. 53–68). New York: Karger.

Sheehan, D. V., Ballenger, J., & Jacobsen, G. (1980). Treatment of endogenous anxiety with phobic, hysterical and hypochondrial symptoms. *Archives of General Psychiatry, 37,* 51–59.

Shukla, S., Godwin, C. D., Long, L. E. B., & Miller, M. (1984). Lithium-carbamazepine neurotoxicity and risk factors. *American Journal of Psychiatry, 141,* 1604–1606.

Silver, J. M., & Yudofsky, S. (1985). Propranolol for aggression: Literature review and clinical guidelines. *International Drug Therapy Newsletter, 20,* 9–12.

Singh, N. N., & Aman, M. G. (1981). Effects of thioridazine dosage on the behavior of severely mentally retarded persons. *American Journal of Mental Deficiency, 85,* 580–587.

Singh, N. N., & Millichamp, C. J. (1985). Pharmacological treatment of self-injurious behavior in mentally retarded persons. *Journal of Autism and Developmental Disorders, 15,* 257–267.

Sleator, E. K., & von Neumann, A. (1974). Methylphenidate in the treatment of hyperkinetic children. *Clinical Pediatrics, 13,* 19–24.

Snyder, R. D. (1979). The right not to read. *Pediatrics, 63,* 791–794.

Snyder, R. D. (1983). Coping strategies for inefficient readers. *Journal of Learning Disabilities, 5,* 261–263.

Speltz, M. L., Varley, C. K., Peterson, K., & Beilke, R. L. (1988). Effects of dextroamphetamine and contingency management on a preschooler with ADHD and oppositional defiant disorder. *Journal of the American Academy of Child and Adolescent Psychiatry, 27*, 175–178.

Sprague, R. L. (1984). Preliminary report of cross-cultural study and cognitive strategies of ADD children. In L. M. Bloomingdale (Ed.), *Attention deficit disorder: Diagnostic, cognitive, and therapeutic understanding* (pp. 211–219). New York: Spectrum.

Sprague, R. L., Barnes, K. R., & Werry, J. S. (1970). Methylphenidate and thioridazine: Learning, reaction time, activity, and classroom behavior in emotionally disturbed children. *American Journal of Orthopsychiatry, 40*, 615–628.

Sprague, R. L., & Sleator, E. K. (1973). Effects of psychopharmacologic agents on learning disorders. *Pediatric Clinics of North America, 20*, 719–735.

Sprague, R. L., & Sleator, E. K. (1977). Methylphenidate in hyperkinetic children: Differences in dose effects on learning and social behavior. *Science, 198*, 1274–1276.

Sprague, R. L., & Werry, J. S. (1974). Psychotropic drugs and handicapped children. In L. Mann & D. A. Sabatino (Eds.), *The second review of special education* (pp. 1–50). Philadelphia: JSE Press.

Steinberg, D. (1980). The use of lithium carbonate in adolescence. *Journal of Child Psychology and Psychiatry, 21*, 263–271.

Stephens, R. S., Pelham, W. E., & Skinner, R. (1984). The state-dependent and main effects of methylphenidate and pemoline on paired-associates learning and spelling in hyperactive children. *Journal of Consulting and Clinical Psychology, 523*, 104–113.

Strayhorn, J. M., Rapp, N., Donina, W., & Strain, P. (1988). Randomized trial of methylphenidate for an autistic child. *Journal of the American Academy of Child and Adolescent Psychiatry, 27*, 244–247.

Strober, M., & Carlson, G. A. (1982). Bipolar illness in adolescents with major depression. *Archives of General Psychiatry, 39*, 549–555.

Sverd, J., Curley, A. D., Jandorf, L., & Volkersz, L. (1988). Behavior disorder and attention deficits in boys with Tourette syndrome. *Journal of the American Academy of Child and Adolescent Psychiatry, 27*, 413–417.

Sverd, J., Gadow, K. D., & Paolicelli, L. M. (1989). Methylphenidate treatment of attention-deficit hyperactivity disorder in boys with Tourette syndrome. *Journal of the American*

Academy of Child and Adolescent Psychiatry, 28, 574–579.

Swanson, J. M., & Kinsbourne, M. (1976). Stimulant-related state-dependent learning in hyperactive children. *Science, 192*, 1354–1357.

Swanson, J., Kinsbourne, M., Roberts, W., & Zucker, K. (1978). Time-response analysis of the effect of stimulant medication on the learning ability of children referred for hyperactivity. *Pediatrics, 61*, 21–29.

Sykes, D. H., Douglas, V. I., Weiss, G., & Minde, K. K. (1971). Attention in hyperactive children and the effect of methylphenidate (Ritalin). *Journal of Child Psychology and Psychiatry, 2*, 129–139.

Tapia, F. (1969). Haldol in the treatment of children with tics and stutterers—and an incidental finding. *Psychiatric Quarterly, 43*, 647–649.

Taylor, E. (1979). The use of drugs in hyperkinetic states: Clinical issues. *Neuropharmacology, 18*, 951–958.

Taylor, E. (1983). Critical notice: From romance to ritual: The development of paediatric psychopharmacology. *Journal of Child Psychology and Psychiatry, 24*, 321–323.

Taylor, E. (1985). Drug treatment, In M. Rutter & L. Hersov (Eds.), *Child and adolescent psychiatry* (pp. 781–793). London: Blackwell Scientific.

Tyrer, S. P., & Shopsin, B. (1980). Neural and neurotransmitter effects of lithium. In F. N. Johnson (Ed.), *Handbook of lithium therapy* (pp. 289–309). Lancaster, England: MTP Press.

Van Scheyen, J. D., & Van Kamman, D. P. (1979). Clomipramine induced mania in unipolar depression. *Archives of General Psychiatry, 36*, 560–565.

Vitriol, C., & Farber, B. (1981). Stimulant medication in certain childhood disorders. *American Journal of Psychiatry, 138*, 1517–1518.

Wagner, W., Johnson, S. B., Walker, D., Carter, R., & Wittner, J. (1982). A controlled comparison of two treatments for nocturnal enuresis. *Journal of Pediatrics, 101*, 302–307.

Wehr, T. A., & Goodwin, F. K. (1979). Rapid cycling in manic-depressives induced by tricyclic antidepressants. *Archives of General Psychiatry, 36*, 555–559.

Wehr, T. A., & Goodwin, F. K. (1987). Can antidepressants cause mania and worsen the course of affective illness. *American Journal of Psychiatry, 144,* 1403–1411.

Weingartner, H., Rapoport, J. L., Buchsbaum, M. S., Bunney, W. E., Ebert, M. H., Mikkelsen, E. J., & Caine, E. D. (1980). Cognitive processes in normal and hyperactive children and their response to amphetamine treatment. *Journal of Abnormal Psychology, 89,* 25–37.

Weinstein, M. R. (1980). Lithium treatment of women during pregnancy and in the post-delivery period. In F. N. Johnson (Ed.), *Handbook of lithium therapy* (pp. 421–432). Lancaster, England: MTP Press.

Weiss, G., Minde, K., Douglas, V., Werry, J., & Sykes, D. (1971). Comparison of the effects of chlorpromazine, dextroamphetamine and methylphenidate on the behavior and intellectual functioning of hyperactive children. *Canadian Medical Association Journal, 104,* 20–25.

Weller, E. B., Weller, R. A., & Fristad, M. A. (1986). Lithium dosage guide for prepubertal children: A preliminary report. *Journal of the American Academy of Child Psychiatry, 25,* 92–95.

Weller, E. B., Weller, R. A., Fristad, M. A., Cantwell, M., & Tucker, S. (1987). Saliva lithium monitoring in prepubertal children. *Journal of the American Academy of Child and Adolescent Psychiatry, 26,* 173–175.

Welner, A., Welner, Z., & Fishman, R. (1979). Psychiatric adolescent inpatients: Eight to ten year follow-up. *Archives of General Psychiatry, 36,* 698–700.

Wender, P. (1973). *Minimal brain dysfunction in children.* New York: John Wiley & Sons.

Werry, J. S. (Ed.). (1978). *Pediatric psychopharmacology: The use of behavior modifying drugs in children.* New York: Brunner/Mazel.

Werry, J. S. (1982). An overview of pediatric psychopharmacology. *Journal of the American Academy of Child Psychiatry, 21,* 3–9.

Werry, J. S., & Aman, M. G. (1975). Methylphenidate and haloperidol in children. *Archives of General Psychiatry, 32,* 790–795.

Werry, J. S., Aman, M. G., & Diamond, E. (1980). Imipramine and methylphenidate in hyperactive children. *Journal of Child Psychology and Psychiatry, 21,* 27–35.

Whalen, C. K. (1982). Hyperactivity and psychostimulant treatment. In J. R. Lachenmeyer and M. S. Gibbs (Eds.), *Psychopath-*

ology in childhood* (pp. 375–402). New York: Gardner Press.

Whalen, C., Collins, B., Henker, B., Alkus, S., Adams, D., & Stapp, J. (1978). Behavior observations of hyperactive children and methylphenidate effects in systematically structured classroom environments: Now you see them, now you don't. *Journal of Pediatric Psychology, 3,* 177–187.

Whalen, C. K., Henker, B., Collins, B. E., Finck, D., & Dotemoto, S. (1979). A social ecology of hyperactive boys: Medication effects in structured classroom environments. *Journal of Applied Behavior Analysis, 12,* 65–81.

Whalen, C. K., Henker, B., & Dotemoto, S. (1980). Methylphenidate and hyperactivity: Effects on teacher behaviors. *Science, 208,* 1280–1282.

Whitehouse, D., Shah, U., & Palmer, F. B. (1980). Comparison of sustained release and standard methylphenidate in the treatment of minimal brain dysfunction. *Journal of Clinical Psychiatry, 41,* 282–285.

Wiener, J. M. (Ed.). (1985). *Diagnosis and psychopharmacology of childhood and adolescent disorders.* New York: John Wiley & Sons.

Williams, D. T., Mehl, R., & Yudofsky, S. (1982). The effect of propranolol on uncontrolled rage outbursts in children and adolescents with organic brain dysfunction. *Journal of the American Academy of Child Psychiatry, 21,* 129–135.

Winsberg, B. G., & Yepes, L. E. (1978). Antipsychotics (major tranquilizers, neuroleptics). In J. S. Werry (Ed.), *Pediatric psychopharmacology: The use of behavior modifying drugs in children* (pp. 234–273). New York: Brunner/Mazel.

Winsberg, B. G., Yepes, L. E., & Bialer, I. (1976). Pharmacologic management of children with hyperactive/aggressive/inattentive behavior disorders. *Clinical Pediatrics, 15,* 471–477.

Wysocki, T., Fuqua, W., Davis, V. J., & Breuning, S. E. (1981). Effects of thioridazine (Mellaril) on titrating delayed matching-to-sample performance of mentally retarded adults. *American Journal of Mental Deficiency, 85,* 539–547.

Yarbrough, E., Santat, U., Perel, I., Webster, C., & Lombardi, R. (1987). Effects of fenfluramine on autistic individuals residing in a state developmental center. *Journal of Autism & Developmental Disorders, 17,* 303–314.

Yepes, L., Balka, E., Winsberg, B., & Bialer, I. (1977). Amitriptyline and methylphenidate treatment of behaviorally disordered children. *Journal of Child Psychology and Psychiatry, 18,* 39–52.

Zimmermann, R. L., & Hcistad, G. T. (1982). Studies of the long term efficacy of antipsychotic drugs in controlling the behavior of institutionalized retardates. *Journal of the American Academy of Child Psychiatry, 21,* 136–143.

CHAPTER 13

PREVENTION

A. Dirk Hightower
Jeffrey Braden

Previous chapters have reviewed therapeutic methods and techniques designed for specific disorders. This chapter shifts focus from treatment to prevention. Although such clinical treatments are called "tertiary prevention" within a public-health model, using the term "prevention" to describe rehabilitation or treatment of individuals with established disorders is confusing. The goals of treatment are "neither unworthy nor unneeded; they simply are not prevention" (Cowen, 1983, p. 11). The term "prevention" as used here means secondary and primary prevention in mental health; tertiary prevention activities are called "treatment."

The essence of secondary prevention is early identification of problems and intervention before they become severe psychological disorders. Identifying and dealing with problems in their earliest stages, to shorten their duration and minimize the intensity, reduces the prevalence of disorders. Children are often targets of secondary prevention approaches because of their psychological malleability and flexibility. The younger the child, the less likely it is that problems or disorders will develop and become entrenched and the more favorable the prognosis for intervention.

Defining primary prevention has proved difficult; indeed a consensus among authors has still not been reached (e.g., Bloom, 1977, 1979; Bower, 1977; Caplan, 1964; Cowen, 1980, 1983; Felner, Jason, Moritsugu & Farber, 1983; Goldston, 1987; Kessler & Albee, 1975; Klein & Goldston, 1977; Rappaport, 1977; Roberts & Peterson, 1984). However, one convergent definitional characteristic of primary prevention efforts is that they seek to change the incidence of new cases by intervening proactively, *before* disorders occur. For example: (1) competencies may be increased through education; (2) training may be provided to help people develop coping strategies that will mitigate the negative effects of stressful life events and crises; (3) environments may be modified to reduce or counteract harmful circumstances; and (4) support systems may be developed more fully. Whole populations or groups considered at-risk, rather than individuals, are the targets for such interventions. In sum, primary prevention efforts do *not* attempt to reduce existing problems; rather, they call for proactive, preemptive efforts.

Some (e.g., Cowen, 1980, 1983; Goldston, 1987; Klein & Goldston, 1977; Prevention Task Panel Report, 1978) have proposed distinctive features of primary prevention programs, so that the effectiveness of preventive implementations can be thoroughly documented, evaluated, disseminated, and replicated. Others (e.g., Felner et al., 1983; Zax & Specter, 1974) have described secondary prevention as the application of treatment methodologies similar to those described in earlier chapters. In practice, however, it is sometimes difficult or impossible to differentiate among treatment or primary and secondary prevention efforts by the activities associated with them. For example, children from divorced families are at risk for developing serious dysfunction (see below). If such children are brought together as a group to (1) share common experiences, thoughts, and feelings in a warm, empathetic, supportive atmosphere; (2) observe and rehearse various behaviors through modeling and role playing; and (3) learn new ways of handling anger or anxiety, it may be possible to reduce the potential for stress or existing stress along the prevention–treatment spectrum.

In the last analysis, of course, the key issue both for treatment and prevention programs is how well they meet their desired goals. But most treatments have not convincingly reduced the prevalence of various disorders and disorders afflicting humans have never been eliminated or controlled through treatment, but only ameliorated by successful prevention (Albee, 1982, 1986; Kessler & Albee, 1975); therefore the argument for prevention becomes clearer.

There are 43 million people in need of mental health services in the United States (Price, Cowen, Lorion, & Ramos-McKay, 1988), five times as many as our present delivery system can serve. This problem has been stable since the 1950s (Albee, 1959). The echo that Albee started can still be heard today: "There will never be enough mental health professionals to provide help for such widespread distress" (Price et al., 1988). What is required is that more mental health professionals change their focus from individual treatment of the "diseased" to at-risk or population-oriented approaches—that is, from after-the-fact treatment to proactive prevention. Although rational arguments for prevention are well developed, the resources,

personnel, and research base for such programs are just beginning to be established (Albee, 1982; Albee & Joffe, 1977; Cowen, 1982a, 1982b, 1986; Lorion, 1983; Price et al., 1988).

The challenge of working with children before they experience problems can be put within the framework of this book. What if some of the techniques designed for treating individuals were intentionally modified, adapted, and evaluated for children before they struggled with substance use, parental divorce, delinquency, or school transitions? Those same techniques successfully used to treat entrenched symptoms and behaviors might also be effective with those individuals just starting to show signs of disturbances or who have a propensity to develop such conditions.

In sum, the paradigm shift from treatment to prevention can be a relatively small yet logical change for many mental health professionals. Whereas many intervention technologies are surprisingly similar, conceptual and philosophical distinctions between treatment and prevention are real. In essence, treatment and prevention differ primarily in terms of the *time* of intervention in relation to the period of onset of difficulties and the *target* of such interventions (i.e., individuals experiencing problems as opposed to the population at large or at-risk groups). The distinction among types of prevention may be less important than the demonstrated effectiveness of the interventions. The ever-present need for mental health services, the continuing shortage of professionals, and the relatively small gains made in treating or eliminating various behavioral conditions or mental disorders all point to the need for further development of prevention programs.

HISTORICAL CONTEXT

Because detailed developmental and historical analyses of the prevention movement are available in other sources (Albee, 1982; Albee & Joffe, 1977; Cowen, 1986; Felner et al., 1983; Joffe, Albee, & Kelly, 1984; Kessler & Goldston, 1986; Price et al., 1988; Roberts & Peterson, 1984; Spaulding & Balch, 1983), only a brief summary is provided here. Prevention in mental health for children has, like child therapy (reviewed earlier by Morris and Kratochwill), roots that go back to Clifford Beers's writings about the early mental hygiene movement and the establishment of child guidance clinics. Prevention's more unique history was triggered by the passage of the Mental Health Study Act in the 1950s. That act created the Joint Commission on Mental Health and Mental Illness and charged it to review and make recommendations about practices designed to reduce the number of new cases and the duration of mental illness. Using the Joint Commission Report as a foundation, President Kennedy (1963) cited the social, economic, and prognostic advantages of prevention.

Later in 1963 the Mental Retardation Facilities and Community Mental Health Centers Construction Act (PL 88-164) provided for five essential services. One of these—consultation and education—specified prevention as one indirect service to be provided. Unfortunately, community mental health centers have historically neglected prevention, concentrating instead on direct fee-for-service models based on traditional treatment approaches (Roberts & Peterson, 1984).

Shortly thereafter Caplan (1964) translated the public health concepts of primary, secondary, and tertiary prevention into the mental health arena. Caplan's effort provided a conceptual base for prevention in mental health.

Community psychology was born at the Swampscott Conference (Anderson et al., 1966; Iscoe & Spielberger, 1970). Prevention as a major focus of community psychology is reflected by the many articles published in its associated journals: the *American Journal of Community Psychology, Journal of Community Psychology, Community Mental Health Journal,* and *Prevention in Human Services.* Since 1974, the Vermont Conference on the Primary Prevention of Psychopathology (VCPPP) has been conducted annually and has produced a series of volumes reporting current prevention issues as well as research on programming, interventions, and training. This group has also maintained the *Journal of Primary Prevention.*

The federal role in developing prevention concepts and priorities stimulated an important expansion of prevention. Within the President's Commission on Mental Health (1978), two task panels (Prevention and Learning Failure and Unused Learning Potential) documented prevention needs, rationales, definitions, targets, barriers, and priorities for children. As direct outgrowths of the President's Commission, the National Institute of Mental Health created an Office of Prevention, developed a network of

Preventive Intervention Research Centers, and developed the Prevention Publication Series to disseminate, stimulate, and promote prevention activities in mental health.

In 1981, the American Psychological Association appointed a Task Force on Prevention Alternatives. Over the course of six years, this panel contacted 900 professionals knowledgeable about prevention, received 300 replies describing prevention efforts, and evaluated 52 programs with reasonable evidence of effectiveness. It chose 14 of these as model promotion, prevention, or intervention alternatives worthy of dissemination (Price et al., 1988). Of the 14 programs described, 5 were designed and targeted toward infancy and early childhood and an additional 5 for school-aged children and adolescents.

Although prevention in mental health for children has a history of several decades, it is still, relatively speaking, in its infancy. The growth of this field, which has been slow, is now steadily progressing. Many of its early efforts were relatively ineffective—a not uncommon situation in a discipline's infancy. But as the field matures or gets past the "terrible twos," it will increasingly challenge past practices and the status quo.

FACTORS INFLUENCING DEVELOPMENT OF PROGRAMS

Several factors, in combination, facilitate the development, evaluation, and dissemination of prevention programs. These include educating prevention professionals, understanding the needs of constituent groups, establishing baselines for problems or competencies, clarifying important interactions between personal and environmental dimensions, and developing a generative knowledge base of health-associated variables. Several of these factors are discussed in this section. Barriers to implementing prevention programs are reviewed later in the chapter.

Until very recently prevention professionals have been self-educated rather than formally trained (Price, 1986). Specifically, Price (1986) noted that many participants in the Vermont Conference of Primary Prevention of Psychopathology "did not initially identify themselves as prevention researchers. They were experts on specific problems and content areas, some of whom for the first time discovered that the knowledge they were developing could actually be applied to primary prevention efforts" (p. 292).

Indeed, the four roles Price (1983, 1986) specifically proposed for prevention professionals (i.e., problem analyst, innovation designer, field evaluator, and diffusion researcher) all have parallels in traditional graduate programs for preparing mental health professionals.

The problem-analyst role, for example, requires defining the issue, developing an understanding of a problem's etiology, and determining the needs of various populations (Price, 1983). These activities are no less important within traditional treatment paradigms. One perhaps distinguishing function of a prevention professional is to clarify risk factors associated with a problem or the development of competence.

Price (1983, 1986) defines innovative designers as "people with a broad knowledge of change methods" (p. 292). Existing graduate-training-program standards from organizations such as the American Psychological Association, the National Association of School Psychologists, and the National Association of Social Workers, and many state licensing boards include provisions to ensure that qualified professionals have a broad knowledge base. Although competent mental health practitioners and researchers qualify as innovative designers, their focus has not typically been directed to prevention activities.

Professionals involved in prevention use many competencies and skills already taught in current graduate training programs (Lorion, 1983; Lorion & Lounsbury, 1981). Program evaluation methods, experimental designs, and statistics are blind to the conceptual frame of a problem. True and quasi-experimental large-group designs (or ABAB) or multiple-baseline single-subject designs are equally appropriate, or inappropriate, for prevention research and practice as they are for treatment research and practice.

Theoretical orientations explaining behaviors, which are also similar across prevention and treatment paradigms and training programs, focus on the development of prevention programs. There are behavioral, psychodynamic, humanistic, developmental, ecological, and eclectically based preventive interventions. Characteristics or variables deemed important enough to attend to and manipulate may differ by theoretical persuasion, but working with people *before* significant problems become established is a consistent feature.

Prevention interventions should also rest on sound generative knowledge bases (Cowen, 1980, 1986; Lorion, 1983; Lorion, Tolan, & Wahler, 1987). Knowledge about the etiology of competencies and problems offers one source of valuable information on the timing and development of relevant interventions. Such information must come from "core" areas of psychology (e.g., social, developmental, organizational, clinical, school), social work, sociology, education, and medicine and must be integrated to avoid past mistakes and to develop realistic future plans (Cowen, 1980, 1986; Lorion, 1983; Price, 1983; Munoz, Snowden, & Kelly, 1979; Zins, Conyne, & Ponti, 1988).

One important body of generative information for the development and evaluation of prevention programs is knowledge about base rates for certain types of outcome conditions. Because most definitions of prevention are anchored by the reduction of problems or the increase of competencies, establishing the efficacy of primary prevention interventions is tied to changes in the incidence of these conditions. Much the same holds for determining the effectiveness of other types of mental health interventions (e.g., Cronbach & Meehl, 1955) and is no less important today in determining the validity of preventive interventions (Lorion et al., 1987).

Other chapters in this volume describe evaluation findings for treatment and reports of treatment effectiveness across settings, providers, times, and behaviors. Those types of evaluation yardsticks are just as important for prevention efforts (Cowen, 1980, 1983, 1986; Lorion, 1983; Lorion & Lounsbury, 1981; Price & Smith, 1985). Understanding the differential effectiveness and generalization of treatment approaches can provide insights for innovative development of prevention programs (Lorion et al., 1987). Knowledge of specific prevention models with associated steps and processes can be used to transfer, execute, and develop preventive interventions (Cowen, 1982b, 1986; Price, 1983, 1986).

Individual and environmental factors and interactions and transactions among them are parts of systems to which preventive interventions can be targeted. A significant change in any these factors can cause shifts in incidence or prevalence rates (Albee, 1982; Lorion et al., 1987; Sameroff & Chandler, 1975). Although genetic factors are obviously important in certain adverse outcomes, research has documented repeatedly the effects socioeconomic status (SES), community conditions such as poverty, the influence of schools and their staff, as well as various parental and familial characteristics on the incidence and prevalence of conditions (Bloom, 1977; Botvin & Tortu, 1988; Davidson & Redner, 1988; Gump, 1980; Insel & Moos, 1974; Kellam, Branch, Agrawal, & Ensminger, 1975; Learning Failure and Unused Learning Potential Task Panel, 1978; Lorion et al., 1987; Moos, 1974; Prevention Task Panel Report, 1978).

In sum, the generative knowledge base that informs prevention programs comes from diverse fields and orientations; from work with individuals, environments and their interactions; and from basic and applied research. This meaningful body of knowledge is available to all creative, innovative, competent mental health professionals. For it to be applied to prevention, however, a paradigm shift (Kuhn, 1970) away from treatment and toward preventive interventions is needed. Prevention by definition is an applied endeavor. Neither the prevalence nor the incidence of dysfunctional conditions can be changed toward greater health anywhere but in the real world. As such, all preventive work is subject both to the benefits and risks inherent to applied, in vivo program efforts.

OVERVIEW OF METHODS

Methods to prevent mental illness in children stem from several distinct traditions: medical, environmental, promotional-educational, and at-risk models, as well as eclectic syntheses of them. Those traditions share the goal of preventing illness and the assumption that prevention is, in principle, preferable to treatment. This section discusses the contexts and assumptions of these prevention models and gives examples of each. The medical model, presented first, provides a baseline against which the discriminating features of the other models are developed.

Medical Model

Context

The best-known of all prevention models is the medical model. The tradition of vaccination and inoculation has a history of accomplishment in medicine—the virtual elimination of smallpox, polio, and similar diseases. Medical prevention models typically have two focuses: (1) reduction of the spread of a disease (by isolation of infectious individuals) and (2) enhancement of the organism's ability to resist infection. Early efforts to prevent mental illness adopted the first focus, isolation of mentally ill individuals in institutions where they could not "infect" the general population. Beginning with the mental-hygiene movement of the late 1800s, efforts to prevent mental illness have attempted to enhance people's resistance to it.

Assumptions

The medical tradition assumes that the host organism can be altered to increase its resistance to illness, making the organism the primary focus of prevention efforts. The treatment is of individuals, not systems or environments. If one wishes to prevent a child from becoming mentally ill, the medical model suggests that it is best to change the child directly in some way. The anti-drug abuse campaign slogan "Just say no" assumes that this phrase "inoculates" children against the "infection" of drug use; that is, by saying no, children's ability to resist drug usage increases. The child is assumed to maintain resistance despite changes in environment, maturation, or other circumstances.

The medical model also assumes that specific causes bring about specific effects. Polio is caused by a virus; the immune system is strengthened by inoculation. Huntington's chorea is caused by a particular gene; genetic counseling is used to address the weakness. Mental-illness prevention programs often assume a similar linear, sequential relationship: A cause is ineffective coping coupled with a crisis. An appropriate intervention is stress-inoculation training.

A third assumption that permeates the medical tradition is the emphasis on illness rather than health. Illness is defined as a condition that interferes with the ability of the organism to maintain homeostasis and is identified by symptoms of discomfort. Health is assumed to be the absence of illness in medical prevention models. The increased ability by the organism to resist attacks becomes the goal. What the organism does between attacks is of little interest except as activities increase the host organism's defensive posture.

Example

The medical model of prevention is expressed in Caplan's (1965) work with children in schools. Caplan argues that children's crises are predictable, either in their timing (e.g., separation from home to begin school) or in their content (e.g., death of a grandparent, parental divorce). Because many children suffer as a result of inadequate crisis resolution, he proposes that psychologists work with teachers, parents, and children to assist with appropriate crisis resolution. In support of his position, Caplan (1964, 1965) puts forth the following arguments:

1. Crisis creates a time at which children are uniquely predisposed to change.
2. Unsuccessful resolution of a crisis increases the likelihood of mental illness.
3. Successful resolution of a crisis decreases the likelihood of mental illness.
4. Children will generalize coping strategies learned in the successful resolution of a crisis to future stressors.

These arguments clearly mirror the assumptions of the medical model. The child is the intervention's focus, the response directly addresses the cause of the illness, and illness prevention is the goal of the intervention. Furthermore, Caplan draws the analogy between timely crisis intervention and inoculation. In much the same way that inoculations introduce a virus in order to enhance the host organism's response to future contact with the virus, crises introduce stress, which can be used to enhance children's responses to current and future stressors.

Environmental-Manipulation Model

Context
The environmental-manipulation model grew from the medical model when it was realized that, for some diseases, control of the environment was more appropriate than inoculation of the organism. Two circumstances make environmental manipulation more attractive than the treatment of organisms: (1) the inability to identify an appropriate individualized preventative intervention or (2) the inability to deliver an appropriate preventative intervention. An example of the first circumstance is lead poisoning—children cannot be inoculated against lead poisoning, so the environment must be manipulated to reduce lead intake. An example of the second circumstance is vaccination against rabies—it is expensive, difficult to administer, and risky, so the environment is controlled to reduce exposure to rabies. In both examples, the focus of

change is the environment or context in which the host organism resides. Environmental- and medical-model prevention efforts are often complementary (e.g., vaccination against diphtheria is complemented by clean water supplies).

Assumptions
The environmental-manipulation model assumes that altering the environment rather than the organism can increase adaptation. Although this has the acknowledged limitation that environmental changes will not become permanent features of the organism, environmental changes do have the advantage of affecting many organisms, usually at less cost and greater convenience than individually based treatments.

Example
Just as the physical safety of children has received attention in recent years (Peterson, 1988), the psychological safety of the child may also be improved by removing potentially dangerous features from the child's psychological environment. The school curriculum has been found to contain psychologically harmful features, which may be removed or replaced with those that facilitate children's development.

One such feature identified by Gold (1978), is the "missing addend" problem (e.g., $3 + \_\_ = 7$) typically found in primary texts for the first and second grades. Children in these grades will usually add the two numbers, write "10" in the blank, and resist efforts to change their answer. They are typically at a preoperational cognitive level where the operation of reversibility required to solve the problem is not yet developed. Missing addend problems, because they conflict with most children's cognitive development, introduce failure into the classroom so that social rewards for industry, success, and mastery are likely to be withheld. When such problems are introduced in the third grade, where the developmental level is more appropriate, children solve missing addend problems with little trouble (Gold, 1978) and the problems associated with failure do not appear.

Promotional-Educational Model

Context
Two traditions are combined in the promotional-educational model of prevention. The first is a medical orientation that emphasizes health promotion rather than illness prevention; the sec-

ond is the educational tradition that emphasizes learning. The medical emphasis on health is relatively new to modern Western society. Its recent popularity may be traced to interests in diet and exercise, non-Western philosophies, cost-benefit emphasis on preventive health care, and perceived shortcomings of the traditional medical model for dealing with some diseases and conditions (e.g., cancer). Health-oriented efforts focus on life-styles and interrelated actions rather than on prevention or defense against disease.

The educational tradition complements the health-promotion orientation but does so from a different philosophical base. The application of learning theory to education has led to an emphasis on the acquisition of measurable behaviors as opposed to insight or knowledge as outcomes of instruction. In a learning-theory context, mental illness is viewed as inappropriate or insufficient learning. Therefore, mental health is promoted and mental illness prevented by teaching specific behaviors that replace inappropriate behaviors.

Assumptions

The health-promotion tradition has three premises: (1) linear cause-and-effect models are inappropriate for understanding the reciprocal interaction between the organism and the environment; (2) health is a facet of human potential, not simply a physical condition of homeostasis; and (3) health enhances the organism's ability to cope with a variety of stressors, of which illness is only one example. The first premise is a major departure from the medical model of prevention, which typically attempts to isolate causes of illness and then seeks specifically to attack those causes. In the reciprocal interaction approach, causality is contextual; the environment affects the organism, the organism affects the environment, and the interaction between the two defines the system when a change in one member necessarily introduces a change in the other.

The second premise rejects dualistic notions of mind–body and posits that emotional, social, and psychological forces cannot be separated from biological factors in defining illness or health. Thus, prevention emphasizes one aspect of the individual, whereas promotion emphasizes the whole person in conceiving of health and illness. The perspective that psychological development

is an active, constructive process rather than an absence of abnormality is compatible with a health-promotion orientation.

The third premise extends the holistic perspective to its logical conclusions: that health is incompatible with illness and that any particular illness is best understood as but one of many possible outcomes of unhealthy living. Unfortunately, this orientation conflicts with accountability models of human services that link specific outcomes (prevention of a particular problem) with specific processes (the prevention effort).

The educational premises are simple. First, behavior is learned; children learn "mentally ill" behaviors just as they learn "mentally healthy" behaviors. Second, the total behavior exhibited by an organism must sum to a finite amount. The educational tradition assumes that problems of mental illness are best understood as a failure to learn and spontaneously produce appropriate behaviors. When children increase appropriate behavior, inappropriate behavior must decrease in frequency, intensity, or duration. Therefore, mental illness is prevented by learning behaviors said to represent mental health. It is interesting to note that although the educational model contradicts the health orientation by assuming linear causality and accepting the isolation of target behaviors, both models agree that the best means of prevention is promotion.

Example

Myrick (1987) proposes the use of peer facilitators in schools as a means of reducing the psychological problems of children. This approach trains children in such facilitative behaviors as active listening and then creates circumstances for these facilitators to meet with and develop relationships with other children in a broad array of school-based activities such as welcoming new children to school or academic tutoring. These interactions, in turn, lead to the recruitment of other peer facilitators, and these behaviors become infused into the school climate. Some of these activities, arranged along a continuum, can be seen in Figure 13.1.

Aside from the economic advantage that children do not have to be paid for providing this service, the approach also capitalizes on the health-promotion and educational traditions. First, Myrick assumes that an emphasis on facilitation, friendship, and positive peer interac-

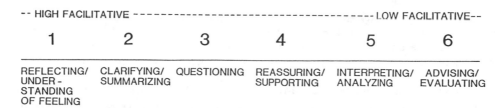

Figure 13.1. The facilitative continuum.

tion is a worthy goal and part of healthy living. The goal is not simply to stay out of trouble; rather, the goal is to promote ties among children that encourage social, cognitive, and academic development. Second, the frequency with which facilitative behaviors occur is a consequence of learning. Children can learn facilitative behaviors, and if they are taught and reinforced for such behaviors, they will exhibit facilitative actions, such as comments reflecting feelings or questions, to clarify meaning instead of nonfacilitative actions like ridicule or vandalism. This approach combines the health-promotional and educational traditions in a preventive program. (See Figure 13.2.)

At-Risk Models

Context

This promotion model focuses on particular individuals or groups that are "at risk" to develop problems. Democratic traditions, cost-benefit analyses, and the generalized notion of "Don't fix it if it ain't broke" are combined with models of public health to support the at-risk model. The democratic tradition of helping people in need of assistance and respecting the rights of the individual to privacy and freedom from intrusion encourage a targeted intervention focus. Cost-benefit accountability and the understandable reluctance of systems to change when there are no immediate problems also encourage a targeted approach to prevention. Consequently, the at-risk model of mental-illness prevention draws on the public-health model of secondary prevention (Bower, 1969) to identify and serve those individuals who are most likely to develop and maintain mental health disorders.

Assumptions

The at-risk model borrows liberally from other prevention models (medical, environmental, and educational-promotional) in developing the rationale and methods for prevention. The key

distinction is that the at risk model typically narrows the scope of the prevention effort to a particular group or groups. Target groups are often defined by demographic (e.g., income, residence), physical (e.g., low birth weight, disability), or behavioral (e.g., truant, low-achieving) characteristics. The link between the choice of targeting characteristic and the intervention is often empirical, not theoretical. For example, higher than expected rates of high-school dropouts and crime are reported for African-American males, but it is not assumed that their race or gender are causal characteristics. The atheoretical mandates that drive at-risk models do not encourage theoretical consistency or clarity of assumptions. As a consequence, some at-risk prevention models may be at risk for inadequate conceptual development and procedural design.

Example

A good example of at-risk prevention is provided by Feldman, Caplinger, and Wodarski (1983). They treated youths referred for antisocial behavior (higher risk) and nonreferred youths (lower risk) in a community-based agency. Most youths who participated in the program were from traditionally at-risk backgrounds (e.g., low SES, African-American males). Treatment to prevent antisocial behavior varied on three factors: (1) composition of group (referred, nonreferred, mixed), (2) theoretical orientation of treatment (social work, behavior modification, no explicit orientation), and (3) group leader's experience (experienced graduate students, inexperienced undergraduate students). Despite problems with treatment integrity and collection of follow-up data, Feldman et al (1983) found that treated children benefited from the program in that they exhibited less antisocial behavior one year after treatment than untreated cohorts.

The fact that individuals with characteristics that placed them at risk for antisocial behavior were targeted for the preventive treatment makes this effort an example of an at-risk model. The theoretical discipline and methodological rigor Feldman et al. (1983) bring to the treatment of youths at risk for antisocial behavior are exemplary in comparison to many other at-risk prevention efforts.

Eclectic Model

Context

The eclectic combinations of prevention models and traditions is the norm in mental-health prevention efforts. There are three reasons for the popularity of the eclectic model. First, the evi-

TO KEEP IN MIND

FACILITATIVE CONDITIONS

1. Caring
2. Understanding
3. Acceptance
4. Respect
5. Friendliness
6. Trustworthiness

CAREFUL LISTENING

1. Look at who is talking.
2. Pay attention to the person's words.
3. Be aware of the person's feelings.
4. Say something that shows you are listening.

PROBLEM SOLVING MODEL

1. What is the problem or situation?
2. What have you tried?
3. What else could you do?
4. What is your next step?

FACILITATIVE PROCESS

1. Self-disclosure
2. Feedback
3. Increased awareness and decision-making
4. Responsible action

FACILITATIVE RESPONSES

1. Feeling-focused response
2. Clarifying or summarizing response
3. Open question
4. Facilitative feedback: complimenting and confronting
   a. Be specific about the behavior
   b. Tell how the person's behavior makes you feel
   c. Tell what your feelings make you want to do
5. Simple acknowledgement
6. Linking

PLEASANT FEELINGS			UNPLEASANT FEELINGS		
Accepted	Free	Relaxed	Afraid	Dumb	Overwhelmed
Admired	Friendly	Relieved	Aggravated	Embarrassed	Picked-on
Amused	Grateful	Respected	Alone	Exhausted	Pressured
Appreciated	Happy	Satisfied	Angry	Fearful	Put-down
Calm	Hopeful	Secure	Annoyed	Frightened	Rejected
Certain	Important	Settled	Ashamed	Frustrated	Restless
Challenged	Included	Special	Bitter	Furious	Sad
Cheerful	Inspired	Stimulated	Bored	Gloomy	Scared
Close	Interested	Strong	Cheated	Hated	Shocked
Comfortable	Involved	Successful	Confused	Helpless	Shy
Confident	Joyful	Supported	Crazy	Hopeless	Startled
Contented	Liked	Supportive	Defeated	Horrible	Stupid
Cozy	Loved	Sure	Depressed	Hurt	Teased
Delighted	Needed	Touched	Desperate	Idiotic	Tense
Eager	Optimistic	Thrilled	Disagreeable	Insecure	Terrible
Enthused	Peaceful	Trusted	Disappointed	Irritated	Tired
Enthusiastic	Pleased	Trusting	Discouraged	Left-out	Unconfident
Excited	Powerful	Warm	Disgusted	Lonely	Uncomfortable
Fantastic	Proud		Disliked	May	Unloved
Fascinated	Refreshed		Distant	Miserable	Unwanted
			Disturbed	Mixed-up	Worried
			Down	Nervous	Worthless

Figure 13.2. Components of peer facilitation: an example of the promotional-educational model.

dence is inconclusive regarding the superiority of specific methods. Second, the lack of a generative knowledge base, such as the inability to isolate a specific cause of schizophrenia, argues against adoption of a specific philosophy. Third, the drive for the practitioner to serve children in the best way possible encourages multifaceted prevention programs that integrate many theories, interventions, and assumptions.

Assumptions

A critical assumption behind eclectic methods is that generative research results cannot simply be transferred to a new setting or problem. Instead, practitioners must consider the unique constellation of factors in a particular setting and select methods that best address these factors. Another assumption is that the problems to be prevented or competencies to be enhanced are usually caused by a number of cooccurring factors that call for the application of distinct preventative interventions. Finally, the lack of agreement regarding the basic tenets of psychological theory (e.g., competition between behavioral, developmental, and psychodynamic schools of thought) encourages prevention efforts to combine methods and theoretical disciplines.

The biggest danger in an eclectic model is the ambiguity and confusion that typically accompany a departure from orthodoxy. Tolstoy's criticism of science (namely, that "What is called science today consists of a haphazard heap of information, united by nothing") might well apply to many eclectic models of prevention. If the atheoretical force driving at-risk models fails to encourage conceptual clarity, eclectic models positively discourage clarity as well as consistency by mixing theories, methods, and outcome measures. Because most prevention efforts freely draw from various models of prevention, diverse schools of thought, and a wide range of treatment techniques, it is often difficult to separate truly eclectic models—those that systematically select the best features of various prevention approaches—from models that are poorly considered, ill planned, and inconsistently executed.

Example

Specific examples of successful preventive intervention approaches, most of which are eclectic in orientation, are considered in detail in the following section.

SPECIFIC INTERVENTIONS

To exemplify prevention programming possibilities for children and adolescents, six different interventions will be highlighted. Two examples of commonly considered secondary prevention efforts will be reviewed. They are the Primary Mental Health Project, which targets the reduction of school-adjustment problems in young children, and the Adolescent Diversion Project, which attempts to reduce delinquent acts in teenagers. Third, the Children of Divorce Intervention Program preventively targets along the preventive continuum at-risk children experiencing their parents' divorce. Consequently, it provides a transition to "purer" examples of primary prevention interventions.

Finally, three primary prevention projects are reviewed. They are (1) the School Transitional Environment Project, which assists middle and high school entrants to make the transition from less to more complex school environments; (2) the Life Skills Training program, which prevents substance use and abuse by targeting junior high students; and (3) the Interpersonal Cognitive Social Problem Solving program, which helps urban preschoolers develop social reasoning skills. For each program, a brief overview is provided, followed by "Background," "Program Description," and "Evaluation Results" sections. Since all these programs have existed for at least seven years and some for as long as three decades, interested readers should consult the references provided for more comprehensive information.

THE PRIMARY MENTAL HEALTH PROJECT

The Primary Mental Health Project (PMHP) is a secondary prevention program targeted at primary-school-aged children (K–3) who are at risk for developing school adjustment problems. By means of an early detection and screening process involving multiple sources of information and multiple methods, children at risk are identified and offered helping services individually or in small groups by paraprofessional child associates. Because direct services to children are being provided by the child associates, the role of the professional mental-health worker (e.g., psychologist, social worker, etc.) changes to that of providing indirect student services, such as child-associate training and supervision and consultation with parents and school staff. Detailed descriptions of PMHP are provided elsewhere (e.g., Cowen & Hightower, 1990; Cowen & Hightower, 1989; Cowen et al., 1975).

Background

PMHP began in one city school in Rochester, New York, in 1957, following two clinical observations: (1) teachers reported that relatively few students, from two to four, required approximately 50% of the teacher's disciplinary effort, and (2) children being referred for mental health services in later elementary and high school years typically experienced school adjustment difficulties in the primary grades. In fact, initial studies showed that at-risk students presented more school adjustment difficulties over time (Cowen et al., 1975; Cowen, Zax, Izzo, & Trost, 1966). Cowen and his colleagues recognized, as did others working in the area of early identification (e.g., Bower, 1977, 1978; Keogh & Becker, 1973), that identification without effective interventions may do more harm than good.

PMHP explored alternatives to providing services to children at risk, a historically underserved population (e.g., Glidewell & Swallow, 1969; Namir & Weinstein, 1982; Prevention Task Panel Report, 1978). Consultation was provided to teachers by the mental health team. Children's needs and associated individual plans were discussed, developed, and implemented. Other school personnel became involved as children's needs dictated. After-school activity groups were run by teachers selected for their natural caregiving characteristics of warmth, empathy, and genuineness. Mental health professionals provided discussion groups for teachers and parents. Although these earlier attempts did not significantly reduce school adjustment difficulties, they were the seeds from which PMHP developed.

Program Description

PMHP programs have four basic structural consistencies but vary in regards to specific program practices. A description of these consistencies are followed by a "least squares" program description.

PMHP programs involve an early detection-and-screening component. Specifically, screening is perceived as an ongoing process that continues throughout the school year. Therefore there is no single set of established procedures or criteria for student entry into the project. However, recommended practices include (1) using multiple sources of information, (2) involving multiple methods to obtain information, (3) using a multidisciplinary approach in reviewing screening information and making referral decisions, and (4) conducting various screening activities throughout the year. Screening is perceived as a necessary but not sufficient process for meeting children's needs.

Working with young children is another structural consistency of the program. Young children have been defined as children in kindergarten through third grades, but this has recently been modified to include children in preschool programs. Because PMHP is a prevention program for children at risk of developing school-adjustment problems, those who might receive PMHP services include older children who might experience various crisis situations, children diagnosed as having various learning disabilities, those who are termed mentally retarded, and others. Those children who are diagnosed as seriously emotionally disturbed or behaviorally disordered, however, are not appropriate for PMHP. PMHP is a prevention program targeted toward the population of young children at risk for school-adjustment difficulties.

A third and central component of PMHP is the use of nonprofessionals to provide direct, ongoing, support services to children. People used as nonprofessional child-associates include volunteers, (e.g., college students, foster grandparents, Mental Health Association members) and paid part-time employees (successful parents). Almost all child associates are recruited and selected for preexisting caregiving abilities and characteristics of warmth, empathy, and benevolent firmness that are typically associated with successful therapeutic outcomes. Initially, child associates were selected because of personnel shortages and because they were cheaper. However, recent research has noted consistently that nonprofessionals are as effective, if not more effective, as professionals in producing positive therapeutic outcomes (Berman & Norton, 1985; Durlack, 1979; Hattie, Sharpley, & Rogers, 1984). Therapeutic approaches child associates use when working with children vary by treatment unit (individual or group) and intervention orientation (nondirective to behavioral) of the supervising professional. Such variations are encouraged to meet the specific needs of school districts.

The fourth common structural strand includes changes in professional roles. Such activities include selection, training, and supervision of nonprofessional child associates and counsulative resource activities with school personnel and parents. Supervision is not a role for which training is typically provided in most graduate programs (Knoff, 1986), so further training may be necessary. Consultation, on the other hand, is frequently required as part of most graduate curricula. Professionals involved in PMHP typically have structured times specifically designated for consultation activities (i.e., assignment, progress, and end-of-program conferences), which lead to additional unstructured consultation meetings. In many ways, the structures of PMHP promote alternate professional roles for mental health professionals.

The following example summarizes how a PMHP program might operate during a school year. The program begins in September with an introduction or reintroduction of PMHP as a prevention program for children at risk for school-adjustment difficulties. For schools where additional training modules have been completed (e.g., crisis training, planned short-term intervention, working with children who act out), children appropriate for those services are also described. Time lines for completing various programmatic steps are provided. Behavior observations occur after 3 to 4 weeks, whereas teacher and child ratings and any direct testing occur at 4 to 6 weeks into the school year. Child associates assist with the screening process. After the initial screening procedures are completed, an assignment conference involving the PMHP team (mental health professionals, child associates, principal, and teacher) would meet to discuss and review the screening data and any other pertinent information. School professionals contact the parents, describe the program, indicate which goals have been suggested for the child, and request the parent's written permission for the child to become involved. During the assignment conferences, each and every student from each and every targeted grade is discussed, and at this time appropriate, specific goals are developed. While teachers are attending the assignment conferences, a substitute teacher rotates from class to class.

Following parent permission, child associates see children one to three times a week in a playroom stocked with various play materials. Professionals supervise child associates 1/2 to 1 hour per week either individually or in a group. Activities conducted in the playroom range from establishing behavioral contracts to active listening, depending upon the child's goals and the associate's training.

Formal progress conferences are held midway between assignment and program termination, while informal consultations occur as needed. During those meetings, goals are reviewed, intervention strategies may be changed, and significant others may become involved in the child's plan. Children who were not initially selected but show needs might enter the program, whereas those children meeting their goals would leave the program.

Evaluation Results

Both formative and summative program evaluations have occurred throughout PMHP's history of over 30 years. An array of studies involving various samples, dependent variables, sophistication of experimental design, and methods of analysis are reported by PMHP (Cowen et al., 1975; Cowen, Weissberg et al., 1983; Weissberg, Cowen, Lotyczewski, & Gesten, 1983) and by others (Durlak, 1977; Kirschenbaum, 1979; Kirschenbaum, DeVoge, Marsh & Steffen, 1980; Rickel, Dyhdalo, & Smith, 1984; Sandler, Duricko, & Grande, 1975). Consequently, all but a transistorized "main effects" summary is beyond the scope of this chapter. The preponderance of reported outcomes suggest that PMHP decreases school-adjustment problems and increases behaviors associated with school competence. Although long-term, (longer than 5 years) follow-up studies have yet to be done, a number of short- to intermediate-term follow-up studies have reported that early program gains are maintained over time (Chandler, Weissberg, Cowen, & Guare, 1984; Cowen, Dorr, Trost & Izzo, 1972; Lorion, Caldwell, & Cowen, 1976).

There are many PMHP formative evaluations. Terrell, McWilliams, and Cowen (1972) reported that child associates can work as effectively with small groups of children as they can with individuals. Lorion, Cowen, and Caldwell (1974) evaluated the relative effectiveness of PMHP in working with acting out or shy-withdrawn children and those referred for learning difficulties. They found that PMHP was more effective with shy-anxious than with acting out children. Following this result, a limit-setting method for dealing with acting-out youngsters was successfully developed and implemented (Cowen, Orgel, Gestin, & Wilson, 1979). Felner and his colleagues (e.g., Felner, Ginter, Boike, & Cowen, 1981; Felner, Stolberg, & Cowen, 1975) reported that children experiencing stressful life events, such as death of a family member or parental divorce, had more serious school-adjustment difficulties than noncrisis peers. A specific crisis intervention program successfully addressed the needs of students in crisis (Felner, Norton, Cowen, & Farber, 1981). Lorion, Cowen, and Kraus (1974) explored the regularities and efficacies of various program practices and discovered that multiple sessions during a week were no more effective than seeing children once a week. Although children tended to be seen for an entire school year (Lorion et al., 1974), Winer, Weissberg, and Cowen (1988) developed a short-term intervention and found it to be as effective as full-year interventions in reducing problem behaviors. In sum, many of the formative evaluations have guided changes within PMHP practices.

Generalization of results across settings, providers, and behaviors have been evaluated (e.g., Cowen, Weissberg, et al., 1983) and surveyed (Cowen, Davidson, & Gesten, 1980; Cowen, Spinell, Wright, & Weissberg, 1983). Highlights of these results include successful program implementations in large, small, urban, suburban, and rural districts with African-American, Hispanic, Asian, and Caucasian populations; successful use of a wide range of child associates; and the proliferation of diverse theoretical intervention perspectives across various treatment formats. In sum, the flexibility of the PMHP structural model accepts the infusion of local practices and procedures allowing for widespread application of PMHP.

PMHP is not without limitations, some of which have been described previously (Cowen et al., 1975). Most important is PMHP's lack of long-term longitudinal follow-up studies. Although short-term effectiveness has been repeatedly documented, there are no studies presently available that document long-term results. Differential outcomes of working with acting out or shy-anxious children have been documented,

but other at-risk children referred for poor interpersonal relationships, a lack of frustration tolerance, or poor self-esteem have not been evaluated. In part, no clear understanding of what constitutes a "child at risk for school-adjustment difficulties" has been operationalized. Although flexibility in targeting children at risk may facilitate program adaptation, a clear understanding of which children should and should not receive a PMHP-type of intervention is less than clear. PMHP has adopted a traditional medical model aimed at treating the child rather than working with other environmental factors, such as families and parents. As such, PMHP has not systematically explored the potential impact of environmental interventions focused on these factors. Finally, despite the fact that PMHP provides a structure by which mental health professionals may change their roles and gain a foothold from which further preventive efforts can be developed, it must be recognized that PMHP essentially recapitulates traditional treatment models of service delivery, but targeted toward young children. Therefore, the criticisms and limitations of PMHP could also be leveled at traditional treatment approaches and vice versa.

THE ADOLESCENT DIVERSION PROJECT

The Adolescent Diversion Project (ADP) is a secondary prevention program that attempts to divert juvenile offenders after they have been apprehended by police but before they have been adjudicated in juvenile court (Davidson, Gensheimer, Mayer, & Gottschalk, 1987; Davidson, & Rapp, 1976; Davidson & Redner, 1988; Davidson, Redner, Amdur, & Mitchell, 1988; Davidson, Redner, Blakely, Mitchell, & Emshoff, 1987; Davidson, & Seidman, 1974). This point for intervention was chosen due to the inability of previous research to adequately predict delinquent behavior before the occurrence of such behavior and the desire to minimize the negative labeling affects of the court adjudication process (Davidson et al., 1988; Davidson et al., 1987; Davidson & Redner, 1988).

Background

The development of ADP was prompted by (1) the observations that youthful offenders become adult criminals, (2) that the present juvenile justice system has failed to deal effectively with juvenile offenders, and (3) that the cost of present existing programs for juvenile offenders was high in terms of failed lives and dollars (e.g., $40,000 per year per offender) (Davidson & Redner, 1988). Thus, secondary prevention efforts were believed worthy of concerted efforts on social, ethical, and economic grounds.

Davidson and his colleagues systematically reviewed major theories relating to juvenile delinquency (e.g., Redner & Davidson, 1983), examined individual differences between delinquents and nondelinquents across many domains, and evaluated intervention attempts based on individual differences (Davidson & Redner, 1988; Redner, Snellman, & Davidson, 1983). Ecological theories and research regarding various environmental conditions indicative of delinquent development were reviewed. In addition, social labeling theory, which purports that society determines delinquent behavior by labeling such acts and actors, and rehabilitation programs based on social labeling theory were considered and merged into the ADP philosophy (Davidson et al., 1987).

Program Description

ADP has evolved through multiple phases encompassing 15 years (Davidson & Redner, 1988). The essence of the program, however, has remained relatively consistent. In all phases, juvenile offenders were referred to ADP after apprehension for relatively serious legal infractions, such as larceny or breaking and entering, but before petitioning or other formal involvements with the juvenile justice system. The average participant's age was approximately 14 years.

Common to the first three phases, volunteers (e.g., university or community college students, adult members of the community) provided individual contacts within the home milieu, behavioral contracting, and child advocacy intervention techniques designed to limit recidivism within the target population. Unique to the second phase, six interventions were evaluated. They were as follows: (1) the volunteer model described above (n = 77); (2) family-focusd behavioral program (n = 24); (3) a relationship-therapy intervention (n = 12); (4) an application of the volunteer model described above, but practiced within the juvenile court setting instead of the home milieu (n = 12); (5) an attention control placebo group (n = 29), and (6) a no-treatment control group (n = 60).

The last phase of the project involved translating the ADP volunteer model to a paid-employee model. Three conditions were tested: (1) paid professionals providing individual contacts within the home milieu, behavioral contracting, and child advocacy; (2) youthful offenders released to their parents; and (3) a control group being processed through the traditional juvenile court system.

Evaluation Results

In brief, recidivism rates across the project's phases and at 1- and 2-year reevaluations consistently and significantly showed the ADP group to have fewer subsequent arrests than those offenders who went through the traditional juvenile justice system. Volunteers and paid professional were equally successful, but there was differential effectiveness among treatments provided in the second phase. More specifically, the ADP volunteer model involving relationship development, behavioral contracting, and child advocacy; the family-focused behavioral contracting model that worked with family members instead of directly with youthful offenders; and the relationship group, which actively sought to develop relationships through empathy (unconditional positive regard) were found to be equivalent among themselves and superior to the control groups, who just received attention or the traditional juvenile justice treatment and the ADP volunteer model practiced at juvenile court instead of the offender's home milieu. In sum, recidivism rates of youthful offenders were reduced across all types of service providers who provided structured treatment interventions, but only when offenders were provided services within their home milieu.

ADP was evaluated across multiple settings, types of treatment, types of providers, various offenses, and multiple years. As Davidson and Redner (1988) and others (Price, 1983, 1986) note, program dissemination and replication of the ADP model in particular and after prevention programs in general is a difficult and complex process. Relatively strict adherence to a model appears necessary for results to be replicated. As such, Davidson and Redner (1988) suggest a detailed action plan which should be used to maximize the chance of a true ADP replication.

In sum, ADP may be one of the best-researched programs in the area of juvenile delinquency. Davidson and his colleagues have attended to methodological and research design issues and have conducted true experiments within the community. Although some questions remain unanswered, such as how effective this program may be for reducing the recidivism rate into adulthood or how effective it is with older or younger first-time offenders, this program documents how significant human and cost-benefit gains can be realized with a targeted prevention program (Price et al., 1988).

CHILDREN OF DIVORCE INTERVENTION PROGRAM

The Children of Divorce Intervention Program (CODIP) is a school-based prevention program for children of divorce. Targeted to elementary-school children, curricula have been developed and evaluated (Alpert-Gillis, 1987; Pedro-Carroll, 1985; Pedro-Carroll & Alpert-Gillis, 1987; Pedro-Carroll, Alpert-Gillis, & Sterling, 1987; Pedro-Carroll & Cowen, 1985, 1987; Pedro-Carroll, Cowen, Hightower, & Guare, 1986; Sterling, 1986; Wyman, 1987; Wyman, Cowen, Pedro-Carroll, & Hightower, 1988). for in-depth coverage, readers are referred to the above material.

Background

The Children of Divorce Intervention Project emerged from data indicating that (1) divorce rates have tripled since 1960, (2) divorce is a stressful life event which has short- and long-term debilitating effects on those involved, and (3) divorce is now one of the most frequently occurring life stressors for children (it will affect from 50% to 60% of all children before they reach adulthood). Armed with this information, Pedro-Carroll and her colleagues noted that few intervention programs for children of divorce had been systematically developed or evaluated. One exception was the Divorce Adjustment Program, where a support group was designed and implemented in an attempt to improve adjustment (Stolberg, Cullen, & Garrison, 1982; Stolberg, & Garrison, 1985). The CODIP program evolved from Stolberg's work, but it was modified to include (1) an effective component to enhance communication around identification and expression of feelings, (2) extensive use of hands-

on and experiential activities, and (3) incorporation of Wallerstein's (1983) six hierarchical divorce-related coping tasks (Pedro-Carroll, 1985; Pedro-Carroll et al., 1987; Pedro-Carroll & Cowen, 1985, 1987).

Program Description

CODIP's overarching goal is to prevent or ameliorate the academic, behavioral, and emotional problems that children often experience during or after their parents' divorce (Pedro-Carroll, 1985; Pedro-Carroll et al., 1987). (See Table 13.1.) Two program curricula have been developed for this purpose; one for older latency-aged children in the fourth through sixth grades and the other for early latency-aged children in the second and third grades. These group interventions typically involve 6 to 8 older children or 5 to 7 younger children equally distributed by sex. Both curricula emphasize the developing social support and learning how to cope with various thoughts, feelings, and perceptions of their parents, families, and themselves. Children are helped to differentiate between solving steps targeted toward realistic resolution of solvable versus unsolvable problems and taught specific problem-solving steps targeted toward the resolution of solvable ones. Active involvement in role playing skits as well as homework assignments in the real world provide opportunities for practicing new skills. Twelve sessions with specific goals, tasks, and materials are detailed for older children, 16 sessions with a similar format are provided for younger children. (See Table 13.2.)

Training for group leaders in the CODIP method involves four 2-hour training sessions in which background information and generative research pertaining to divorce is provided. Following this initial training, leaders have been given weekly training sessions in which the next week's curriculum materials have been reviewed and issues and questions about the previous week's lessons have been discussed.

Evaluation Results

Since its first implementation during the 1982 to 1983 school year, CODIP was evaluated for six consecutive cohorts (i.e., through the 1987–88 school year). In addition, a follow-up evaluation was conducted 3 years after the initial intervention year and 2 years after the second interven-

Table 13.1. Children of Divorce Intervention Program—Overview of Program Goals for Young Children

1. Provide a supportive group environment.
2. Facilitate identification and expression of divorce-related feelings.
3. Promote understanding of divorce-related concepts and encourage exploration and clarification of divorce-related misconceptions.
4. Teach relevant coping skills, including social problem-solving skills.
5. Enhance children's positive perceptions of themselves and their families.

From *Children of Divorce Intervention Program: Procedures manual for conducting support groups with 2nd and 3rd grade children* (p. 21) by J. L. Pedro-Carroll, L. J. Alpert-Gillis, and S. Sterling, 1987, Rochester, NY: Primary Mental Health Project. Copyright 1987 by the Primary Mental Health Project. Reprinted by permission.

tion year. The results of all evaluation efforts were used to evaluate the programs' overall effectiveness and to provide information needed to enhance and modify various program practices. A summary of these results follow.

The first (Pedro-Carroll & Cowen, 1985), second (Pedro-Carroll et al., 1986), and fifth (Pedro-Carroll, Alpert-Gillis, & Cowen, 1989) program years targeted fourth- through sixth-grade children. The first two cohorts were from suburban settings, whereas the fifth was from an urban setting. The first year's program evaluation started as a true experimental delay-treatment design. Children of divorce were initially matched on

various demographic variables and length of time since parental separation; then they were randomly assigned to either experimental or control groups. Years 2 and 5 used a two-group (experimental, control) quasi-experimental design and involved all children who returned parental permission. Children from divorced families received CODIP, while the comparison groups were either demographically matched with peers from intact families or matched with children from divorce families who had agreed to participate in a study not involving an intervention.

Data collected from teachers, parents, group leaders, and participants showed that CODIP

Table 13.2. Table of Contents of Children of Divorce Intervention Program: Procedures Manual for Conducting Support Groups With 2nd and 3rd Grade Children

From *Children of Divorce Intervention Program: Procedures manual for conducting support groups with 2nd and 3rd grade children* (p. 21) by J. L. Pedro-Carroll, L. J. Alpert-Gillis, and S. Sterling, 1987, Rochester, NY: Primary Mental Health Project. Copyright 1987 by the Primary Mental Health Project. Reprinted by permission.

participants improved over their respective comparison groups by exhibiting fewer school problems, greater gains in school competencies, decreased feelings of self-blame, better ability to solve divorce-related problems, and decreased anxiety. These results were consistent across all years.

Wyman et al. (1988) tracked the cohorts from the first two years. Over half of the CODIP participants from year 1 lost the gains they had evidenced over a control group when they were reevaluated 3 years later. Approximately 70% of the CODIP participants from year 2 maintained gains after 2 years. Wyman et al. (1988) suggest a number of reasons as to why follow-up results were different for the two cohorts including (1) improvements in the program's curriculum contents and delivery and (2) differential levels of social support. Those researchers also noted, however, that additional long-term follow-up studies are needed.

A second CODIP curriculum was developed and refined in urban and suburban settings during years 3, 4, and 6 (Alpert-Gillis, 1987; Alpert-Gillis, Pedro-Carroll, & Cowen, 1989; Sterling, 1986). Although the initial program evaluation (year 3) of the second- and third-grade CODIP participants showed no significant improvements in school-related behaviors across multiple raters, there were postprogram gains in children's divorce-related knowledge and concerns (Sterling, 1986). For year 4, Alpert-Gillis (1987) and Alpert-Gillis et al. (1989), reported school-adjustment gains similar to those observed in the fourth- through sixth-grade samples. Once again, CODIP participants were found to have fewer or less severe problems and more competencies both at home and at school. The evaluation results for year 6 are presently in process and not yet available.

CODIP has not been systematically evaluated outside the Rochester, New York, metropolitan area, which is a limitation. However, the approach appears to be successful with African-American children from inner-city urban settings and white children from affluent suburban settings. Group leaders of the CODIP program have ranged from school psychologists, school social workers, clinical psychologists, graduate students, teachers, principals, and trained nonprofessionals. To date, however, there are no efficacy comparisons of the various group leaders. The one follow-up study (i.e., Wyman et al., 1988) suggests that the CODIP program may

have some long-term efficacy, but more definitive studies are needed. Comparison among years is difficult due to enhancement of the curriculum based on formative evaluation results. Although minority students in Rochester, who are typically African-American, have successfully participated in the program, CODIP's efficacy with other minority groups is unknown. The investigators have attempted true experimental designs whenever possible, but, as with most fieldwork, such designs are more often idealized than realized.

In sum, CODIP's two curricula, one for fourth- through sixth-graders and the other for second- and third-graders, provide the means of intervening with those children who are at risk as a result of their parents' divorce. As a research-based program, CODIP has taken generative research results and applied that knowledge to a specific societal need. Both short- and long-term results are encouraging, but continued work is needed before CODIP's preventive efficacy can be more firmly established.

SCHOOL TRANSITIONAL ENVIRONMENT PROJECT

The School Transitional Environment Project (STEP) approaches a regularly occurring transitional event in the life of students—such as moving from elementary to middle or junior high schools or from middle and junior high schools to high school—and manipulates the school's environment to increase the school's ability to respond to children's individual needs by providing personalized social support (Felner, Ginter, & Primavera, 1982; Felner & Adan, 1988). The program's purpose is to reduce the incidence of school failure associated with unsuccessful transition.

Background

STEP is based on the premise that school transitions constitute major life transitions, which either enhance and facilitate or decrease and retard students' psychological, social, academic, and behavioral functioning. Felner and his colleagues (Felner & Adan, 1988; Felner et al., 1983; Felner, Primavera, & Cauce, 1981) have reported that school transitions are frequently followed by significant decreases in academic functioning and psychological health as well as by increased substance abuse, delinquency, and dropout rates. Recognizing these circumstances, Felner et al. (1982) and Felner and Adan (1988) focused on the transition of adequately coping students or on those not having difficulties before transition. Students with known difficulties in personal, social, or academic areas were *not* targets of the STEP program. In essence, STEP was designed for students who were reasonably successful as evidenced by past school functioning but who were presently entering a transition by moving from one school organizational pattern to another.

Specific school characteristics were considered in developing the STEP program. One was the school's environmental complexity. Schools with higher levels of disorganization, new student entrance from many feeder schools, and many new social demands were considered complex. Limited support service was a second feature indicative of a school in need of STEP. The larger the school, the less likely it will be that individualized attention is given to each student by the school staff.

STEP attempts to change this normal educational/developmental transition, which is associated with personal, social, academic, and other life difficulties. In addition, the complexity and level of social support provided by an environment are recognized as significant influences on children's resolution of life-transition crises.

Program Description

STEP has three major components. First, it organizes the school environment, for those participating students, into STEP units or subgroups of four to five home rooms. Students assigned to STEP units have the same home room and attend basic academic subjects—such as English, mathematics, social studies, science, and health—together. To facilitate familiarity with the school environment and to reduce the complexity of the setting, STEP classrooms are strategically placed near one another. Felner and Adan (1988) suggest that such an arrangement makes schools less overwhelming, more familiar, less stressful, and more comfortable to incoming students.

The second component restructures home-room periods. Home-room teachers have historically taken daily attendance. New responsibilities include follow-up of suspected truancy and major guidance responsibilities, as in as-

sisting students in the choice of classes and/or providing brief counseling for various problems. Home-room teachers are helped to assume these roles by brief training and ongoing consultation.

The third STEP component is an interdisciplinary team approach to solving problems. Teachers in a STEP unit meet regularly to coordinate assessment of students' functioning, provide appropriate referrals, and to request additional consultation and assistance from other school personnel.

In sum, the STEP program provides an instructional model, similar to that of many middle schools, in which students receive their primary educational training from a core group of four to five teachers. Teachers' academic responsibilities are maintained while administrative and counseling activities are increased. By making each STEP unit relatively small, responsibility for unit members is enhanced. Additional roles and responsibilities characterize the operation of a "small school" (Barker & Gump, 1964).

Evaluation Results

The initial STEP evaluation (Felner et al., 1982) assessed changes in academic performance, self-esteem, school absenteeism, perceptions of school environment, and social support over one school year. When compared with a matched no-treatment control group, STEP students obtained significantly better results for all the above variables. Thus, STEP prevented many typically occurring problems from occurring.

Felner and Adan (1988) summarized follow-up results from the initial STEP implementation described above and additional STEP implementations. Academic grades, achievement test data, attendance statistics, and information on those students who graduated, transferred, or dropped out of school were obtained for over 90% of the initial cohort. Results showed (1) that 43% of those students experiencing the regular education program (controls) versus 21% of the STEP students dropped out of school; (2) that STEP students had significantly higher grades and fewer absences than did controls; (3) and that the STEP program helped low-achieving students, those who would typically fail or drop out, to complete their high school education.

Replication and generalization studies using middle and high school students from large urban, suburban, and rural schools as well as lower, low-middle, working, semiskilled, or blue-collar SES backgrounds shared similar results (Felner & Adan, 1988). STEP enhanced the educational outcomes and simultaneously reduced school failure for many students.

STEP initially examined etiological and theoretical causes of school success and completion. By reducing the movement patterns of students and by increasing teachers' and students' responsibilities to each other, the school environment promoted successful school behavior patterns. Therefore, STEP alters a potentially harmful situation and provides additional social support to students during a particularly stressful life event—school transition. Although STEP has not been replicated with all potential target groups, the results of available studies suggest that the STEP process is an effective primary prevention intervention.

LIFE SKILLS TRAINING

Life Skills Training (LST) is example of a substance-abuse prevention program (Botvin, 1983, 1986; Botvin, Baker, Renick, Filazzola, & Botvin, 1984; Botvin & Eng, 1982; Botvin, Eng, & Williams, 1980; Botvin & McAlister, 1981; Botvin & Tortu, 1988) designed for junior high school students. Students are taught to resist peer pressures to smoke, drink, or use drugs and peer influences in general (Botvin, 1983; Botvin & Tortu, 1988).

Background

Botvin and his colleagues (Botvin & McAlister, 1981; Millman & Botvin, 1983) have concluded that factors indicative of high risk for alcohol and substance abuse include low self-esteem, aggression associated with shy-withdrawn behaviors, high anxiety and nervousness, passivity, lack of assertiveness, and an external locus of control. They also mention external social factors, including attitudes and behaviors of family and friends. Furthermore, positive portrayal of substance abuse in the popular media can influence young people (Botvin & Tortu, 1988). Low grades and associated school failure (e.g., dropouts) are associated with the above internal and social factors as well as with increased potential for substance use and abuse (Jessor, 1982). Botvin (1983) attempts to enhance students' resistance to factors associated with substance use and abuse by teaching them new intrapersonal and interpersonal skills.

Botvin and Tortu (1988) argue that seventh-, eighth-, and ninth-graders should be targeted for intervention because children in these grades actively experiment with various substances, behaviors, life-styles, and values. This experimentation is a predictable phenomenon that allows for the influence of positive and negative informational and experiential events. Furthermore, students at this age have a propensity to engage in risk-taking, health-compromising, peer-group patronizing, and cognitively challenging forms of behavior that increase their potential to ignore established rules and rationalize their self-serving behaviors (Botvin & Tortu, 1988). As a second arm to that of learning how to resist social pressures, the LST approach is designed to reduce the motivation to use various substances and to increase overall competence through the development and promotion of effective individual and peer social skills. Because the LST program uses positive information, extreme negative consequences or scare tactics are avoided and supplanted by knowledge appropriate to the "here-and-now" orientation of most young adolescents. Short-term, not long-term, substance-abuse consequences are stressed.

Program Description

Botvin and Tortu (1988) summarize LST's research results. The program has five major components. The first provides general information about the "gateway" substances: tobacco, alcohol, and marijuana. Lessons in this section are designed to increase students' knowledge regarding short-term effects of these commonly available substances. The second component offers strategies as to how to make responsible decisions and shows how advertisers attempt to persuade consumers to use their products. The third component explores self-perceptions and includes a short 8-week self-improvement project. This component provides new information on how to approach a goal, but it also provides direct life experiences in which to try this new information. Basic relaxation techniques, the fourth component, targets students' anxieties in various social situations. Once again, practice is encouraged in various settings to promote skill generalization. The component is designed to provide skills needed to establish and maintain relationships through the refinement of communication, initiation, and assertiveness training. The social-learning perspective, which is basic to the program, continues as the students are encouraged to practice the various behaviors in different situations and settings. In addition to the components outlined above, booster curricula are available for the eighth and ninth grades. Observation, practice, and continued learning of refusal and social skills are emphasized (Botvin & Tortu, 1988).

Evaluation Results

LST program evaluations have focused on cigarette smoking (Botvin et al., 1980; Botvin & Eng, 1982; Botvin et al., 1984), alcohol (Botvin & Tortu, 1988; Botvin, et al., 1984) and marijuana use (Botvin et al., 1984). These evaluations have taken place in suburban New York or New York City public schools. Botvin and his colleagues have had highly rigorous evaluation designs for their applied research. Random assignment to groups has been used frequently and control groups for comparison purposes have been used consistently. The research has relied not only on self-reports and other paper-and-pencil tasks but also on more "hard" data techniques, such as collecting saliva samples. Overall, the studies report treatment groups to have 40% to 75% fewer new cigarette smokers compared with no-treatment controls after initial, 3-month, and 1-year follow-up studies. In a large study, Botvin et al. (1984) found that peer-led LST group members, when compared to control groups, engaged in cigarette and marijuana smoking significantly less often. These results, however, did not generalize to teacher-led groups. One problem associated with the teacher-led groups was treatment integrity. Teachers did not always follow the curriculum as designed, which may have influenced the quality of their program implementation (Botvin & Tortu, 1988).

In summary, Botvin and his colleagues have systematically assessed the background and etiological factors related to substance abuse. From that generative research, they have developed the LST program for junior high school students. Although Botvin and his colleagues are continuing to research and evaluate their program (Botvin & Tortu, 1988), LST has not been replicated outside the New York area and only the incidence "getaway drugs," not "hard" drugs, have been tracked. Nonetheless, Botvin's work is an example of a well-conceived and well-researched primary prevention program.

INTERPERSONAL COGNITIVE PROBLEM SOLVING

Interpersonal Cognitive Problem Solving (ICPS) is a health-promotion strategy (i.e., increasing a population's incidence of mental health competencies instead of reducing the incidence of dysfunction). Health promotion has been a major emphasis of social problem solving as a primary prevention strategy. Although some would regard health promotion as separate from primary prevention (e.g., Lorion, 1983), others believe it to be one major emphasis of primary prevention (e.g., Cowen, 1980; Zins, et al., 1988). In fact, Durlak (1983) finds social problem solving to be "one of the most frequently cited approaches to primary prevention" (p. 31). Although many social problem-solving curricula have been developed, the work of Myrna Shure, George Spivack, and their colleagues at Hahnemann Medical College is seminal (Cowen, 1986; Durlack, 1983). Therefore, Shure and Spivack's work will be used to illustrate the basic social problem-solving strategy.

Background

ICPS is founded on the belief that children should be taught *how* to think, not *what* to think. Shure and Spivack believe that the ability to think allows for emotional relief, thus preventing psychopathological dysfunction and promoting mental health (Shure & Spivack, 1988; Spivack, Platt, & Shure, 1976; Spivack & Shure, 1974). Spivack and Shure (1974) maintain that such problem-solving skills as the ability to develop alternative ways to solve problems and to consider the consequences of various alternatives are key to facilitating social and psychological health. People who lack ICPS skills are more likely to be aggressive, unconcerned about others, and socially isolated. These conditions may result in poor school adjustment as well as academic, delinquency, and substance-abuse problems (Shure, 1979; Shure & Spivack, 1978; Shure and Spivack, & Jaeger, 1971; Spivack, Marcus, & Swift, 1986; Spivack & Swift, 1977; Spivack et al., 1976).

Shure & Spivack (1988) believe that ICPS is appropriate for young (preschool) children who have adequate verbal skills and for those who are at risk due to their low socio-economic status. Ideally, ICPS is offered to intact classes, so children do not feel singled out and "labeled."

Shure and Spivack believe that children who have adequate problem-solving skills will not be adversely affected by formal ICPS training and that they should be immersed in ICPS throughout a day's interaction with parents and/or teachers.

Program Description

ICPS is presented in formal program scripts or curricula divided into four participation units. A unit addresses each of the following: (1) prerequisite cognitive and linguistic concepts (e.g., "same-different," "if-then," "some-all"), (2) the identification of feelings (e.g., happy, sad), (3) problem-solving skills (e.g., developing alternative solutions, understanding consequences, and pairing various solutions with consequences), and (4) dialoguing (i.e., the coordination of problem-solving steps via a sequenced series of questions posed by a parent or teacher. Modeling, role playing, discussion, and other action-oriented activities are used throughout the curriculum.

Evaluation Results

Problem-solving programs have routinely shown increases in specific problem-solving skills when intervention groups were compared with control groups (Durlack, 1983; Shure & Spivack, 1988; Spivack et al., 1976; Urbain & Kendall, 1980; Work& Olsen, 1988). One successful target population has included disadvantaged 4-year-olds from an urban setting who were offered a formal program lasting approximately 20 minutes per day for 2 to 4 months (Spivack & Shure, 1974). Although Shure and Spivack have consistently found that children's development of problem-solving skills is associated with decreases in impulsivity, inhibition, aggression, and behavior difficulties at the end of training and at 1-year follow-up periods, others replicating ICPS with older children and adults have had equivocal results in relating the attainment of specific problem-solving skills to decreases in psychopathology (Durlack, 1983).

ICPS approaches have been applied to many diverse groups. Problem-solving curricula have been developed and evaluated for preschool children (Spivack & Shure, 1974), kindergartners (Winer, Hilpert, Gesten, Cowen, & Schubin, 1982), elementary-aged children (Weissberg, Gesten, Rapkin, et al., 1981), high school

students, and adults (Spivack et al., 1976). (See Table 13.3.) Curricula have also been applied to individuals from diverse socioeconomic groups, people with various handicapping conditions, and those exhibiting various types of dysfunctional behaviors (Durlack, 1983; Elias & Branden, 1988; Shure & Spivack, 1988; Urbain & Kendall, 1980). Successful trainers of problem-solving skills have included teachers, college students, undergraduate and graduate psychology students, therapists of various persuasions, and nonprofessionals (Durlack, 1983; Shure & Spivack, 1988; Spivack & Shure, 1974; Urbain & Kendall, 1980; Weissberg, Gesten, Carnike, et al., 1981; Work & Olson, 1988).

In sum, social problem-solving approaches have been developed for a wide array of subjects, trainers, and target populations. Almost all combinations increase the incidence of problem-solving abilities. However, the link between problem-solving skills and adjustment for school-aged and older children is not firmly established. In other words, the ICPS model effectively increases the incidence of ICPS skills, but it is not clear whether the promotion of ICPS skills reduces the incidence of social maladjustment.

BARRIERS TO SUCCESSFUL WORK WITH CHILDREN

Problems with Prevention

Despite the success of prevention efforts, psychologists still devote little energy to prevention. Certainly, prevention efforts are worthy and within the domain of psychological practice. Ethical standards and practice guidelines promulgated by professional associations (e.g., American Psychological Association, 1981; National Association of School Psychologists, 1985) place the welfare of the client (child) above all other concerns and consequently specify prevention programs as a major service to be delivered by psychologists. Why, then, do psychologists resist prevention-oriented activities? There are at least three sources of resistance to prevention: (1) effective factors influencing professional behavior; (2) the knowledge, skills, and abilities required for preventive work; and (3) system characteristics.

Effective Factors
Rational-emotive therapy (RET) and psychodynamic models have been used to account for the unwillingness of professionals to engage in

Table 13.3. Example of a Rochester Social Problem-Solving Lesson

---

Lesson 16:   Problem-solving skits—allow 20 minutes
Purpose: To provide children with the opportunity to develop skits and practice problem-solving steps 1–6
                       behaviorally.
Materials Needed: None
     Today we're going to make up problem-solving skits! But first, let's see if we can say the problem-solving steps. (Call
on a few volunteers to name them.)
     1. *Say exactly what the problem is.*
     2. *Decide on your goal.*
     3. *Stop to think before you act.*
     4. *Think of as many solutions as you can.*
     5. *Think ahead to what might happen next.*
     6. *When you have a really good solution, try it!*
     Very good class! Now we are going to break into small groups. In your groups, you should pick a problem to act out.
Try to make one up that we haven't talked about before.
     When your group has finished deciding how to act out the problem-solving steps, all groups will come together again
to watch the skits the other groups made up.

     Before children begin, it may be useful for the teacher and aide or selected child to act out a problem and model this
activity. Children may then divide into groups of 4 or 5 by counting off or some other method. Depending on the amount
of structure needed, you may wish either to assign a problem topic to each group or allow them to generate it independently. Regardless, problems should be group-oriented, i.e., playground difficulties, line cutting, etc., so that everyone
can be involved. It is also suggested that children be limited to two solution–consequence pairs in the interest of time and
simplicity. Finally, a structure-lending script which can be written on the board often helps to get children started.

Note. This table represents the first two pages of Lesson 16.
From *Rochester Social Problem Solving Manual. A training manual for teachers of 3rd & 4th grade children. 20 Lessons
Abbreviated Format* (p. 67) by W. C. Work, 1986, Rochester, NY: Primary Mental Health Project. Copyright 1986 by the
Primary Mental Health Project. Reprinted by permission.

professionally appropriate behaviors (e.g., prevention work). In the RET model (e.g., Ellis &
Bernard, 1985), irrational beliefs held by psychologists account for psychologists' avoidance
of rational, prevention-oriented activities. Irrational beliefs afflicting psychologists include (1)
the view that prevention programs might not
work (failure is intolerable), (2) the idea that the
system should ask psychologists to do prevention work (others should understand and respond to psychologists' needs), and (3) the belief
that psychologists do not have time (psychologists are not responsible for their own behavior,
the system is) (Braden, 1988). These beliefs
reduce the likelihood that psychologists will initiate and maintain prevention-oriented activities.

     Psychodynamic factors believed to influence
professional behaviors have been grouped into
two categories: (1) loss of objectivity and (2)
lack of self-confidence. Researchers with a psychodynamic orientation (e.g., Caplan, 1970;
McCready, 1985) typically emphasize loss of
objectivity as a source of professional impairment. Because prevention work does not usually
include case-specific features that would elicit a
loss of objectivity (e.g., transference, theme interference), the most likely obstacle for preven-

tion work is the psychologist's lack of self-
confidence. Although there is no empirical research linking self-confidence and prevention-
oriented behaviors among psychologists, these
practitioners may lack self-confidence in the
preventive arena due to their lack of understanding of the knowledge, skills, and abilities that
are needed for prevention work.

Knowledge, Skills, and Abilities (KSAs)
Despite the recommendation that psychologists
engage in prevention work, professional organizations do not mandate ''training'' in prevention KSAs (e.g., American Psychological Association, 1986; National Association of School
Psychologists, 1986). Consequently, most psychologists receive little or no formal training in
prevention. Although this lack of training may
be due in part to the problem of delimiting
prevention KSAs (i.e., prevention work typically draws on ''core'' knowledge in psychological theory, program evaluation methods, and
organizational behavior strategies), it may also
be due to the conflict inherent in training practitioners to ''do something'' versus training them
to ''do nothing'' even without sufficient empirical support. Prevention programs on occasion
fall between these alternatives by responding to

the needs of children based on the "best guess" about what will work (Garmezy, 1971).

The lack of specific training in prevention work, and the emphasis on individually-oriented models of service delivery (e.g., behavior modification, psychotherapy, individual assessment, case-centered consultation), leave psychologists with the belief, and sometimes correctly, that additional KSAs are needed to engage in prevention work. This, in turn, leads to two problems: (1) avoidance of prevention work and (2) prevention work with an unnecessarily high degree of failure. Psychologists avoid prevention work because of effective factors and because their perceived or actual lack of KSAs contribute to a unrealistic or realistic appraisal of their inability to fulfill a preventive role in children's lives. Their ignorance of prevention promotes "the mythology . . . that a technology of primary prevention is missing" (Zins et al., 1988). When psychologists do engage in prevention work, their lack of KSAs may lead to failure due to unrealistic time perspectives for intervention effects, inflated expectations for program goals, unrealistic demands on human and financial resources, and psychologically simplistic program content (Cowen, 1980, 1982b; Hightower, 1988; Lorion, 1983; Sarason, 1986).

System Factors

Funding mechanisms, reinforcement contingencies, and organizational structures also inhibit psychologists' involvement in prevention. In schools, categorically oriented funding mechanisms create an unrelenting demand for psychologists to declare children eligible for special education. Schools with many children in special education are given more money than schools with few children in special education. This funding method reinforces the psychologist's role as gatekeeper for special programs, and it discourages prevention programs by withholding resources from schools that successfully prevent school failure. Nonschool agencies, such as clinics, are also driven by funding mechanisms that reward treatment services (e.g., third-party payments for therapy) or symptom-specific interventions (e.g., grants or contracts for specific problems). Even research or demonstration programs suffer from a funding structure that discourages longitudinal work (i.e., most programs are funded in one-year cycles).

Behavioral reinforcement contingencies also discourage the psychologists from engaging in preventive efforts. By declaring children eligible for special programs and removing the child from the class, school psychologists negatively reinforce teacher requests to test and place the child. Conversely, prevention-oriented programs that keep problematic children in the regular class punish teachers by leaving a noxious stimulus (the problem child) in the environment. Agency-based psychologists also find themselves in a milieu where treatment of problems, rather than their prevention, are rewarded by personal interest, collegial support (e.g., case conferences), and the implicit promise of "fixing the child." Paradoxically, some successful prevention programs fail to garner reinforcement because they may result in nonevents. It is impossible to observe something that does not occur; consequently, it is difficult to attribute nonevents (e.g., the lack of depression, no suicides) to the presence of the prevention program, especially in situations where there is no prior history of maladaptive behaviors.

Mental health professionals are usually peripheral to children's lives and are typically found in nonschool settings rather than in schools. The physical distance between mental health professionals and children discourages prevention efforts, so that only children needing direct treatment who can have it paid for overcome the barriers and enter the agency. Even mental health professionals employed by school districts shuttle between many schools, spending a day a week at a school in borrowed space while also often having other primary roles to fulfill (e.g., testing). These factors erode the mental health professional's ability to influence prevention-oriented activities. Judicious use of expert and referent power may increase the ability of mental health professionals to create and maintain prevention programs, but it is an uphill battle that is complicated by limited physical proximity and a lack of administrative sanction.

Responses to Obstacles

The critique of obstacles to prevention activities implies a number of actions for the future. Training programs should consider explicitly training students in prevention activities. Appropriate coursework, practica, and supervised field experiences could be combined to promote mental health professionals' KSAs, self-confidence, and motivation to pursue prevention work. Professional organizations could help prevention work by developing appropriate training standards and by working with regulatory agencies, third-party providers, and legislative bodies to reduce prohibitions and increase incentives for prevention efforts.

On an individual level, psychologists can increase preventive work by recognizing already existing or acquiring new KSAs, increasing self-confidence, eliminating irrational beliefs, and altering their work system. Acquisition of KSAs might be addressed via continuing professional education. Effective factors might best be addressed via professional supervision. Systemic change may be brought about by advocating policies and practices consistent with prevention work and by communicating to school personnel how prevention work facilitates the common goal of children's welfare. All mental health professionals must mobilize a host of potential resources (i.e., effective factors, KSAs, and systems) if they are to prevent mental illness and promote mental health in children.

CONCLUSION

Prevention and treatment paradigms for children have several important and significant common elements. Both share a common heritage from the child guidance movement through the mid 1950s. Historically, the two approaches have had more similar than dissimilar years. Both approaches rest on common theories (e.g., learning, personality, social, and developmental systems), generative knowledge bases, experimental methodologies, and statistics. In that sense both share the goals of modifying perceptions, thinking, behaviors, environments, or systems that limit individuals functioning (Strayhorn, 1988). As such, various interventions have developed according to various theories and orientations. Finally, professionals in prevention or treatment must be able to define and/or diagnose problems, innovate designs to address those problems, evaluate the efficacy and effectiveness of interventions, and disseminate and/or use the acquired information in real-life situations.

Differences between prevention and treatment start with their definitions. Preventive interventions characteristically target populations rather than troubled individuals and do so earlier than treatment in the cycle of unfolding problems. Indeed, timing interventions to occur before significant difficulties are established is a hallmark that distinguishes prevention from treatment activities. Whereas the individual is the prime target for treatment, prevention programs are more likely to target combinations of individual, environmental, and systemic features. Whereas those involved in treating individuals must observe, diagnose, and implement treatment plans for them, prevention professionals must be able to diagnose, plan, and intervene with larger, more complex, systems. Finally, relevant intervention outcomes are different in the two approaches. Those who treat have the goal of "curing" a problem and thus reducing existing cases by at least one. For prevention, the goal is to change incidence either by enhancing competence or decreasing problems in a targeted population. In the societal sense, treatment has had and will continue to have limited potential; by contrast, prevention's potential has yet to be realized.

The intrinsic paradigm shift that prevention programs entail may create some threats to professional identity. Prevention activities also challenge an existing status quo. They can empower the disempowered; they can provide alternatives in situations that previously lacked alternatives. Nothing that has been said is intended to attach value judgments to prevention or treatment but rather reflect that the two approaches differ from each other and address issues at different ends of a service continuum. Although prevention interventions no longer need to justify their existence or theoretical potential, they, like treatment approaches, must document their effectiveness.

Prevention is a process. Whereas many interventions, methodologies, and theoretical orientations have the potential to be preventive, only those that demonstrate changes in incidence over time can be considered preventive. Demonstrating that an intervention has positive immediate impact on behaviors, thoughts, or feelings is worthwhile, but it is not enough. For an intervention to be truly preventive, it must also show changes in the incidence of targeted behaviors either by increasing competencies or decreasing problems. No single act or intervention can by itself be preventive; the process of bringing about and maintaining positive change is prevention.

REFERENCES

Albee, G. W. (1959). *Mental health manpower trends.* New York: Basic Books.

Albee, G. W. (1982). Preventing psychopathology and promoting human potential. *American Psychologist, 37,* 1043–1050.

Albee, G. W. (1986). Lessons from observations

on the primary prevention of psychopathology. *American Psychologist, 41,* 891–898.

Albee, G. W., & Joffe, J. M. (Eds.). (1977). *The primary prevention of psychopathology: The issues.* Hanover, NH: University Press of New England.

Alpert-Gillis, L. J. (1987). *Children of Divorce Intervention Program: Development, implementation, and evaluation of a program for young urban children.* Unpublished doctoral dissertation, University of Rochester, Rochester, NY.

Alpert-Gillis, L. J., Pedro-Carroll, J. P., & Cowen, E. L. (1989). *Children of Divorce Intervention Program: Development, implementation and evaluation of a program for young urban children.* Manuscript submitted for publication.

American Psychological Association. (1981). Ethical principles of psychologists. *American Psychologist, 36,* 633–638.

American Psychological Association. (1986). *Accreditation handbook.* Washington, DC: Author.

Anderson, L. S., Cooper, S., Hassol, L., Klein, D. C., Rosenblum, G., & Bennett, C. C. (1966). *Community psychology: A report of the Boston Conference on the Education of Psychologists for Community Mental Health.* Boston: Boston University.

Barker, R. G., & Gump, P. (1964). *Big school, small school.* Stanford, CA: Stanford University Press.

Berman, J. S., & Norton, N. C. (1985). Does professional training make a therapist more effective? *Psychological Bulletin, 98,* 401–407.

Bloom, B. L. (1977). *Community mental health: A general introduction.* Monterey, CA: Brooks/Cole.

Bloom, B. L. (1979). Prevention of mental disorders: Recent advances in theory and practice. *Community Mental Health Journal, 15,* 179–191.

Botvin, G. J. (1983). *Life Skills Training: Teacher's manual.* New York: Smithfield Press.

Botvin, G. J. (1986). Substance abuse prevention research: Recent developments and future directions. *Journal of School Health, 56,* 369–374.

Botvin, G. J., Baker, E., Renick, N., Filazzola, A. D., & Botvin, E. M. (1984). A cognitive-behavioral approach to substance abuse prevention. *Addictive Behaviors, 9,* 137–147.

Botvin, G. J., & Eng, A. (1982). The efficacy of a multicomponent approach to the prevention of cigarette smoking. *Preventive Medicine, 11,* 199–211.

Botvin, G. J., Eng, A., & Williams, C. L. (1980). Preventing the onset of cigarette smoking through Life Skills Training. *Preventive Medicine, 9,* 135–143.

Botvin, G. J., & McAlister, A. (1981). Cigarette smoking among children and adolescents: Causes and prevention. In C. B. Arnold (Ed.), *Annual review of disease prevention* (pp. 222–249). New York: Springer.

Botvin, G. J., & Tortu, S. T. (1988). Preventing adolescent substance abuse through Life Skills Training. In R. H. Price, E. L. Cowen, R. P. Lorion, & J. Ramos-McKay (Eds.), *Fourteen ounces of prevention: A casebook for practioners* (pp. 98–110). Washington, DC: American Psychological Association.

Bower, E. M. (1969). Slicing the mystique of prevention with Occam's razor. *American Journal of Public Health, 5,* 478–484.

Bower, E. M. (1977). Mythologies, realities and possibilities in primary prevention. G. W. Albee & J. M. Joffe (Eds.), *Primary prevention of psychopathology: Vol. I. The issues* (pp. 24–41). Hanover, NH: University Press of New England.

Bower, E. M. (1978). Early periodic screening diagnosis and treatment: Realities, risks, and possibilities. *American Journal of Orthopsychiatry, 48,* 114–130.

Braden, J. P. (1988). *Irrational beliefs of school psychologists: Why I can't (won't) do prevention work.* Paper presented at the annual convention of the National Association of School Psychologists, Chicago.

Caplan, G. (1964). *Principles of preventive psychiatry.* New York: Basic Books.

Caplan, G. (1985). Opportunities for school psychologists in the primary prevention of mental disorders in children. In N. M. Lambert (Ed.) *The protection and promotion of mental health in schools* (Public Health Service Publication No. 1226). Washington, DC: U.S. Government Printing Office.

Caplan, G. (1970). *The theory and practice of mental health consultation.* New York: Basic Books.

Chandler, C., Weissberg, R. P., Cowen, E. L., & Guare, J. (1984). The long-term effects of a school-based secondary prevention program for young maladapting children. *Jour-*

nal of Consulting and Clinical Psychology, 52, 165–170.

Cowen, E. L. (1980). The wooing of primary prevention. *American Journal of Community Psychology, 8,* 258–284.

Cowen, E. L. (Ed.). (1982a). Research in primary prevention in mental health [special issue]. *American Journal of Community Psychology, 10*(3).

Cowen, E. L. (1982b). Primary prevention research: Barriers, needs and opportunities. *Journal of Primary Prevention, 2,* 131–137.

Cowen, E. L. (1983). Primary prevention in mental health: Past, present and future. In R. D. Felner, L. Jason, J. Moritsugu, & S. S. Farber (Eds.), *Preventive psychology: Theory, research and practice in community interventions* (pp. 11–25). Elmsford, NY: Pergamon Press.

Cowen, E. L. (1986). Primary prevention in mental health: A decade of retrospect and a decade of prospect. In M. Kessler & S. E. Goldston (Eds.), *A decade of progress in primary prevention* (pp. 3–42). Hanover, NH: University Press of New England.

Cowen, E. L., Davidson, E. R., & Gesten, E. L. (1980). Program dissemination and the modification of delivery practices in school mental health. *Professional Psychology, 11,* 36–47.

Cowen, E. L., Dorr, D. A., Trost, M. A., & Izzo, L. D. (1972). A follow-up study of maladapting school children seen by non-professionals. *Journal of Consulting and Clinical Psychology, 39,* 235–238.

Cowen, E. L., & Hightower, A. D. (1989). The Primary Mental Health Project: Thirty years after. In R. E. Hess (Ed.). *Prevention in human services* (pp. 225–257). New York: Haworth Press.

Cowen, E. L., & Hightower, A. D. (1990). The Primary Mental Health Project: Alternative approaches in school-based prevention interventions. In T. B. Gutkin & C. R. Reynolds (Eds.), *The handbook of school psychology* (2nd ed.) (pp. 775–794). New York: John Wiley & Sons.

Cowen, E. L., Orgel, A. R., Gesten, E. L., & Wilson, A. B. (1979). The evaluation of an intervention program for young school children with acting-out problems. *Journal of Abnormal Child Psychology, 7,* 381–396.

Cowen, E. L., Spinell, A., Wright, S., & Weissberg, R. P. (1983). Continuing dissemination

of a school-based early detection and prevention model. *Professional Psychology, 14,* 118–127.

Cowen, E. L., Trost, M. A., Izzo, L. D., Lorion, R. P., Dorr, D., & Isaacson, R. V. (1975). *New ways in school mental health: Early detection and prevention of school maladaptation.* New York: Human Sciences Press.

Cowen, E. L., Weissberg, R. P., Lotyczewski, B. S., Bromley, M. E., Gilliland-Mallo, G., DeMeis, J. L., Farago, J. P., Guassi, R. J., Haffey, W. G., Weiner, M. J., & Woods, A. (1983). Validity generalization of school-based preventive mental health program. *Professional Psychology, 14,* 613–623.

Cowen, E. L., Zax, M., Izzo, L. D., & Trost, M. A. (1966). Prevention of emotional disorders in the school setting: A further investigation. *Journal of Consulting Psychology, 30,* 381–387.

Cronbach, L. J., & Meehl, P. F. (1955). Construct validity in psychological tests. *Psychological Bulletin, 52,* 281–302.

Davidson, W. S., Gensheimer, L. K., Mayer, J. P., & Gottschalk, R. G. (1987). Current status of rehabilitation programs for juvenile offenders. In C. Hampton (Ed.), *Antisocial behavior and substance abuse* (pp. 68–75). Washington, DC: U.S. Government Printing Office.

Davidson, W. S., & Rapp, C. (1976). A multiple strategy model of child advocacy. *Social Work, 21,* 225–232.

Davidson, W. S., & Redner, R. (1988). The prevention of juvenile delinquency: Diversion from the juvenile justice system. In R. H. Price, E. L. Cowen, R. P. Lorion, & J. Ramos-McKay (Eds.), *Fourteen ounces of prevention: A casebook for practitioners* (pp. 123–128). Washington, DC: American Psychological Association.

Davidson, W. S., Redner, R., Amdur, R., & Mitchell, C. (1988). *Alternative treatments for troubled youth.* New York: Plenum Press.

Davidson, W. S., Redner, R., Blakely, C. H., Mitchell, C. M., & Emshoff, J. G. (1987). Diversion of juvenile offenders: An experimental comparison. *Journal of Consulting and Clinical Psychology, 55,* 68–75.

Davidson, W. S., & Seidman, E. (1974). Studies of behavior modification and juvenile delinquency. *Psychological Bulletin, 81,* 998–1011.

Durlak, J. A. (1977). Description and evaluation

of a behaviorally oriented, school-based preventive mental health program. *Journal of Consulting and Clinical Psychology, 45,* 27–33.

Durlak, J. A. (1979). Comparative effectiveness of paraprofessional and professional helpers. *Psychological Bulletin, 86,* 80–92.

Durlak, J. A. (1983). Social problem-solving as a primary prevention strategy. In R. D. Felner, L. A. Jason, J. N. Moritsugu, & S. S. Farber (Eds.), *Preventive psychology: Theory, research and practice* (pp. 31–48). Elmsford, NY: Pergamon Press.

Elias, M. J., & Branden, L. R. (1988). Primary prevention of behavioral and emotional problems in school aged populations. *School Psychology Review, 17,* 581–592.

Ellis, A., & Bernard, M. E. (Eds.). (1985). *Clinical applications of rational-emotive therapy.* New York: Plenum Press.

Feldman, R. A., Caplinger, T. E., & Wodarski, J. S. (1983). *The St. Louis conundrum: The effective treatment of anti-social youths.* Englewood Cliffs, NJ: Prentice-Hall.

Felner, R. D., & Adan, A. M. (1988). The School Transition Environment Project: An ecological intervention and evaluation. In R. H. Price, E. L. Cowen, R. P. Lorion, & J. Ramos-McKay (Eds.), *Fourteen ounces of prevention: A casebook for practioners* (pp. 111–122). Washington, DC: American Psychological Association.

Felner, R. D., Ginter, M. A., Boike, M. F., & Cowen, E. L. (1981). Parental death or divorce and the school adjustment of young children. *American Journal of Community Psychology, 9,* 181–191.

Felner, R. D., Ginter, M., & Primavera, J. (1982). Primary prevention and school transitions: Social support and environmental structure. *American Journal of Community Psychology, 10,* 277–290.

Felner, R. D., Jason, L. A., Moritsugu, J. N., & Farber, S. S., (Eds.). (1983). *Preventive psychology: Theory, research and practice.* Elmsford, NY: Pergamon Press.

Felner, R. D., Norton, P. L., Cowen, E. L., & Farber, S. S. (1981). A prevention program for children experiencing life crisis. *Professional Psychology, 12,* 446–452.

Felner, R. D., Primavera, J., & Cauce, A. M. (1981). The impact of social transitions: A focus for preventive efforts. *American Journal of Community Psychology, 9,* 449–459.

Felner, R. D., Stolberg, A. L., & Cowen, E. L. (1975). Crisis events and school mental health referral patterns of young children. *Journal of Consulting and Clinical Psychology, 43,* 305–310.

Garmezy, N.(1971). Vulnerability research and the issue of primary prevention. *American Journal of Orthopsychiatry, 41,* 101–116.

Glidewell, J. C., & Swallow, C. S. (1969). *The prevalence of maladjustment in elementary schools: A report prepared for the Joint Commission on the Mental Health of Children.* Chicago: University of Chicago Press.

Gold, A. P. (1978). *Cumulative learning versus cognitive development: A comparison of two different treatment bases for planning remedial instruction in arithmetic.* Unpublished doctoral dissertation, University of California, Berkeley, CA.

Goldston, S. E. (1987). *Concepts of primary prevention: A framework for program development.* California Department of Mental Health, Office of Prevention.

Gump, P. V. (1980). The school as a social situation. In M. R. Rosenzweig & L. W. Porter (Eds.), *Annual Review of Psychology, 31,* 553–582.

Hattie, J. A., Sharpley, C. F., & Rogers, H. J. (1984). Comparative effectiveness of professional and paraprofessional helpers. *Psychological Bulletin, 95,* 534–541.

Hightower, A. D. (1988, April). Prevention program development: The pragmatics. In A. D. Hightower (Chair), *The nuts and bolts of implementing a prevention program.* Symposium conducted at the NASP annual meeting, Chicago.

Insel, P. M., & Moos, R. H. (1974). Psychosocial environments: Expanding the scope of human ecology. *American Psychologist, 29,* 179–188.

Iscoe, I., & Spielberger, C. D. (Eds.). (1970). *Community psychology: Perspectives in training and research.* New York: Appleton-Century-Crofts.

Jessor, R. (1982). Critical issues in research on adolescent health promotion. In T. Coates, A. Petersen, & C. Perry (Eds.), *Promoting adolescent health: A dialogue on research and practice* (p. 447). New York: Academic Press.

Joffe, J. M., Albee, G. N., & Kelly, L. D. (Eds.). (1984). *Readings in primary preven-*

tion of psychopathology. Hanover, NH: University Press of New England.

Kellam, S. G., Branch, J. D., Agrawal, K. C., & Ensminger, M. E. (1975). *Mental health and going to school: The Woodlawn program of assessment, early intervention, and evaluation.* Chicago: University of Chicago Press.

Kennedy, J. F. (1963). *Message from the president of the United States relative to mental illness and mental retardation* (88th Congress, 1st Session, U.S. House of Representatives Document #58). Washington, DC: U.S. Government Printing Office.

Keogh, B. K., & Becker, L. D. (1973). Early detection of learning problems: Questions, cautions and guidelines. *Exceptional Children, 40,* 5–11.

Kessler, M., & Albee, G. W. (1975). Primary prevention. In M. R. Rosenzweig & L. W. Porter (Eds.), *Annual review of psychology, 26,* 557–591.

Kessler, M., & Goldston, S. E. (Eds.). (1986). *A decade of progress in primary prevention.* Hanover, NH: University Press of New England.

Kirschenbaum, D. (1979). Social competence intervention and evaluation in the inner city: Cincinnati's Social Skills Development Program. *Journal of Consulting and Clinical Psychology, 47,* 778–780.

Kirschenbaum, D., DeVoge, J. B., Marsh, M. E., & Steffen, J. J. (1980). Multimodal evaluation of therapy vs. consultation components in a large inner-city early intervention program. *American Journal of Community Psychology, 8,* 587–601.

Klein, D. C., & Goldston, S. E. (Eds.). (1977). *Primary prevention: An idea whose time has come* (DHEW Publication No. ADM 77-447). Washington, DC: U.S. Government Printing Office.

Knoff, H. M. (1986). Supervision in school psychology: The forgotten or future path to effective services? *School Psychology Review, 15,* 529–545.

Kuhn, T. S. (1970). *The structure of scientific revolutions* (2nd ed.). Chicago: University of Chicago Press.

Lorion, R. P. (1983). Evaluating preventive interventions: Guidelines for the serious social change-agent. In R. D. Felner, L. A. Jason, J. N. Moritsugu, & S. S. Farber (Eds.), *Preventive psychology: Theory, research and practice* (pp. 251–268). Elmsford, NY: Pergamon Press.

Lorion, R. P., Caldwell, R. A., & Cowen, E. L. (1976). Effects of a school mental health project: A one-year follow-up. *Journal of School Psychology, 14,* 56–63.

Lorion, R. P., Cowen, E. L., & Caldwell, R. A. (1974). Problem types of children referred to a school based mental health program: Identification and outcome. *Journal of Consulting and Clinical Psychology, 42,* 491–496.

Lorion, R. P., Cowen, E. L., & Kraus, R. M. (1974). Some hidden "regularities" in a school mental health program and their relation to intended outcomes. *Journal of Consulting and Clinical Psychology, 42,* 346–352.

Lorion, R. P., & Lounsbury, J. W. (1981). Conceptual and methodological considerations in evaluating preventive interventions. In W. R. Task & G. Stahler (Eds.), *Innovative approaches to mental health evaluations.* New York: Academic Press.

Lorion, R. P., Tolan, P. H., & Wahler, R. G. (1987). Prevention. In H. C. Quay (Ed.), *Handbook of juvenile delinquency* (pp. 383–416). New York: John Wiley & Sons.

McCready, K. F. (1985). Differentiation of transference versus theme interference in consultee-centered case consultation. *School Psychology Review, 14,* 471–478.

Millman, R. B., & Botvin, G. J. (1983). Substance use, abuse, and dependence. In M. D. Levine, W. B. Carey, A. C. Crocker, & R. T. Gross, (Eds.), *Developmental-behavioral pediatrics* (pp. 683–708). Philadelphia: W. B. Saunders.

Moos, R. H. (1974). *Evaluating treatment environments: A social ecological approach.* New York: John Wiley & Sons.

Munoz, R. F., Snowden, L. F., & Kelly, J. G. (Eds.). (1979). *Social and psychological research in community settings.* San Francisco: Jossey-Bass.

Myrick, R. D. (1987). *Developmental guidance and counseling: A practical approach* (Chap. 9). Minneapolis, MN: Educational Media.

Namir, S., & Weinstein, R. S. (1982). Children: Facilitating new directions. In L. R. Snowden (Ed.), *Reaching the underserved: Mental health needs of neglected populations* (pp. 43–73). Beverly Hills, CA: Sage.

National Association of School Psychologists. (1985). *Professional conduct manual.* Washington, DC: Author.

National Association of School Psychologists. (1986). *Standards for training and credentialling in school psychology.* Washington, DC: Author.

Pedro-Carroll, J. L. (1985). *The Children of Divorce Intervention Program: Procedures manual.* Rochester, NY: University of Rochester Center for Community Study.

Pedro-Carroll, J. L., & Alpert-Gillis, L. J. (1987). Helping children cope: Preventive interventions for children of divorce. *The Community Psychologist, 20*(2), 11–13.

Pedro-Carroll, J. L., Alpert-Gillis, L. J., & Cowen, E. L. (1989). *A preventive intervention for 4th–6th grade urban children of divorce.* Manuscript submitted for publication.

Pedro-Carroll, J. L., Alpert-Gillis, L. J., & Sterling, S. (1987). *Children of Divorce Intervention Program: Procedures manual for conducting support groups with 2nd and 3rd grade children.* Rochester, NY: Primary Mental Health Project.

Pedro-Carroll, J. L., & Cowen, E. L. (1985). The Children of Divorce Intervention Project: An investigation of the efficacy of a school-based prevention program. *Journal of Consulting and Clinical Psychology, 53,* 603–611.

Pedro-Carroll, J. L., & Cowen, E. L. (1987). The Children of Divorce Intervention Program: Implementation and evaluation of a time limited group approach. In J. P. Vincent (Ed.), *Advances in family intervention, assessment, and theory* (Vol. 4) (pp. 281–307). Greenwich, CT: JAI Press.

Pedro-Carroll, J. L., Cowen, E. L., Hightower, A. D., & Guare, J. C. (1986). Preventive intervention with latency-aged children of divorce: A replication study. *American Journal of Community Psychology, 14,* 277–290.

Peterson, L. (1988). Preventing the leading killer of children: The role of the school psychologist in injury prevention. *School Psychology Review, 17,* 593–600.

President's Commission on Mental Health (1978). *Report to the President* (Vol. 1) (Stock No. 040-000-00390-8). Washington, DC: U.S. Government Printing Office.

Prevention Task Panel Report. (1978). *Task Panel reports submitted to the President's Commission on Mental Health* (Vol. 4, pp. 1822–1863) (Stock No. 040-000-00393-2). Washington, DC: U.S. Government Printing Office.

Price, R. H. (1983). The education of a preven-tion psychologist. In R. D. Felner, L. A. Jason, J. N. Moritsugu, & S. S. Farber (Eds.), *Preventive psychology: Theory, research and practice* (pp. 290–296). Elmsford, NY: Pergamon Press.

Price, R. H. (1986). Education for prevention. In M. Kessler & S. E. Goldston (Eds.), *A decade of progress in primary prevention* (pp. 289–306). Hanover, NH: University Press of New England.

Price, R. H., Cowen, E. L., Lorion, R. P., & Ramos-McKay, J. (Eds.). (1988). *Fourteen ounces of prevention: A casebook for practitioners.* Washington, DC: American Psychological Association.

Price, R. H., & Smith, S. S. (1985). *A guide to evaluating prevention programs in mental health.* Rockville, MD: National Institute of Mental Health.

Rappaport, J. (1977). *Community psychology: Values, research, and action.* New York: Holt, Rinehart & Winston.

Redner, R., Snellman, L. J., & Davidson, W. S. (1983). Juvenile delinquency. In R. Morris & T. R. Kratochwill (Eds.), *The practice of child therapy* (pp. 193–251). Elmsford, NY: Pergamon Press.

Rickel, A. U., Dyhdalo, L. L., & Smith, R. L. (1984). Prevention with preschoolers. In M. C. Roberts & L. Peterson (Eds.), *Prevention of problems in childhood: Psychological research and applications* (pp. 74-102). New York: John Wiley & Sons.

Roberts, M. C., & Peterson, L. (Eds.). (1984). *Prevention of problems in childhood: Psychological research and applications.* New York: John Wiley & Sons.

Sameroff, A. J., & Chandler, M. J. (1975). Reproductive risk and the continuum of caretaking casualty. In F. D. Horowitz, M. Heatherington, S. Scarr-Salapatek, & G. Siegel (Eds.), *Review of child development research* (Vol. 4, pp. 187–244). Chicago: University of Chicago.

Sandler, I. N., Duricko, A., & Grande, L. (1975). Effectiveness of an early secondary prevention program in an inner city elementary school. *American Journal of Community Psychology, 3,* 23–32.

Sarason, S. B. (1986, August). *And what is the public interest?* Paper presented at the American Psychological Association Annual Convention, Washington, DC.

Shure, M. B. (1979). Training children to solve

interpersonal problems: A preventive approach. In R. F. Munoz, L. F. Snowden, & J. G. Kelly (Eds.), *Social and psychological research in community settings* (pp. 50–68). San Francisco, CA: Jossey-Bass.

Shure, M. B., & Spivack, G. (1978). *Problem-solving techniques in childrearing*. San Francisco: Jossey-Bass.

Shure, M. B., & Spivack, G. (1988). Interpersonal cognitive problem solving (ICPS). In R. H. Price, E. L. Cowen, R. P. Lorion, & J. Ramos-McKay (Eds.), *Fourteen ounces of prevention: A casebook for practioners* (pp. 69–82). Washington, DC: American Psychological Association.

Shure, M. B., Spivack, G., & Jaeger, M. A. (1971). Problem solving thinking and adjustment among disadvantaged preschool children. *Child Development, 42,* 1791–1803.

Spaulding, J., & Balch, P. (1983). A brief history of primary prevention in the twentieth century. *American Journal of Community Psychology, 11,* 59–80.

Spivack, G., Marcus, J., & Swift, M. (1986). Early classroom behaviors and later misconduct. *Developmental Psychology, 22,* 124–131.

Spivack, G., Platt, J. J., & Shure, M. B. (1976). *The problem-solving approach to adjustment*. San Francisco: Jossey-Bass.

Spivack, G., & Shure, M. B. (1974). *Social adjustment of young children: A cognitive approach to solving real-life problems*. San Francisco: Jossey-Bass.

Spivack, G., & Swift, M. (1977). The Hahnemann High School Behavior (HHSB) Rating Scale. *Journal of Abnormal Child Psychology, 5,* 299–308.

Sterling, S. E. (1986). *School-based intervention program for early latency-aged children of divorce*. Unpublished doctoral dissertation, University of Rochester, Rochester, NY.

Stolberg, A. L., Cullen, P. M., & Garrison, K. M. (1982). Divorce Adjustment Project: Preventive programming for children of divorce. *Journal of Preventive Psychiatry, 1,* 365–368.

Stolberg, A. L., & Garrison, K. M. (1985). Evaluating a primary prevention program for children of divorce: The Divorce Adjustment Project. *American Journal of Community Psychology, 13,* 111–124.

Strayhorn, J. M. (1988). *The competent child: An approach to psychotherapy and pre-ventive mental health*. New York: Guilford Press.

Task Panel Report: Learning Failure and Unused Learning Potential. (1978). *Task panel reports submitted to the President's commission on mental health* (Vol. 3, pp. 661–704) (Stock No. 040-000-00392-4). Washington, DC. U.S. Government Printing Office.

Terrell, D. L., McWilliams, S. A., & Cowen, E. L. (1972). Description and evaluation of group-work training for nonprofessional aides in a school mental health program. *Psychology in the Schools, 9,* 70–75.

Urbain, E. S., & Kendall, P. C. (1980). Review of social-cognitive problem-solving interventions with children. *Psychological Bulletin, 88,* 109–143.

Wallerstein, J. S. (1983). Children of divorce: Stress and developmental tasks. In N. Garmezy & M. Rutter (Eds.), *Stress, coping and development in children* (pp. 265–302). New York: McGraw-Hill.

Weissberg, R. P., Cowen, E. L., Lotyczewski, B. S., & Gesten, E. L. (1983). The Primary Mental Health Project: Seven consecutive years of program outcome research. *Journal of Consulting and Clinical Psychology, 51,* 100–107.

Weissberg, R. P., Gesten, E. L., Carnrike, C. L., Toro, P. A., Rapkin, B. D., Davidson, E., & Cowen, E. L. (1981). Social problem-solving skills training: A competence building intervention with 2nd–4th grade children. *American Journal of Community Psychology, 9,* 411–424.

Weissberg, R. P., Gesten, E. L., Rapkin, B. D., Cowen, E. L., Davidson, E., Flores de Apodaca, R., & McKim, B. J. (1981). Evaluation of a social problem-solving training program for suburban and inner-city third-grade children. *Journal of Consulting and Clinical Psychology, 49,* 251–261.

Winer, J. I., Hilpert, P. L., Gesten, E. L., Cowen, E. L., & Schubin, W. E. (1982). The evaluation of a kindergarten social problem-solving program. *Journal of Primary Prevention, 2,* 205–216.

Winer, J. I., Weissberg, R. P., & Cowen, E. L. (1988). Evaluation of planned short-term intervention for school children with focal adjustment problems. *Journal of Child Clinical Psychology, 17,* 106–115.

Work, W. C. (1986). *Rochester social problem solving manual. A training manual for teach-*

ers of 3rd & 4th grade children. *20 Lessons Abbreviated Format*. Rochester, NY: Primary Mental Health Project.

Work, W. C., & Olsen, K. H. (1988). *Development and evaluation of a revised social problem solving curriculum for fourth graders*. Manuscript submitted for publication.

Wyman, P. A. (1987). *Follow-up evaluation of a school-based prevention program for children of divorce*. Unpublished doctoral dissertation, University of Rochester, Rochester, NY.

Wyman, P. A., Cowen, E. L., Pedro-Carroll, J.

L., & Hightower, A. D. (1988). *Follow-up evaluation of a school based prevention program for children of divorce*. Manuscript submitted for publication.

Zax, M., & Specter, G. A. (1974). *An introduction to community psychology*. New York: John Wiley & Sons.

Zins, J. E., Conyne, R. K., & Ponti, C. R. (1988). Primary prevention: Expanding the impact of psychological services in schools. *School Psychology Review, 17,* 542–549.

CHAPTER 14

LEGAL ISSUES IN THE CONDUCT OF CHILD THERAPY

Mark B. DeKraai
Bruce Sales

There are a great number of legal issues associated with therapy in general and child therapy specifically, but an in-depth analysis of them all is beyond the scope of this chapter. Thus, we will offer a detailed look at three topics that are particularly relevant to child therapy: informed consent, confidentiality, and child-abuse reporting requirements. Each of these legal topics has unique aspects associated with child therapy as opposed to therapy with adults. (Examples of issues encountered in child therapy but not addressed here include issues relating to involuntary confinement, such as use of restraint, right to refuse treatment, and wrongful discharge; issues involving certain types of professional malpractice such as suicide, improper therapy, and sexual activity with a client; and certain professional issues such as licensure and advertising. For the most part, these topics are common to both adult and child therapy and are discussed elsewhere [e.g., Brakal, Parry, & Weiner, 1985; Keith-Spiegel & Koocher, 1985].) In our discussion, we will not attempt to provide an exhaustive review of the relevant laws in each state and federal jurisdiction. Rather, our focus will be on the analysis of the critical legal issues that the topics raise.

INFORMED CONSENT

Informed consent is based on the notion that individuals should have the authority to decide what happens to their bodies. The doctrine originated and found its early refinement in the context of medical surgery (*Schloendorff v. Society of New York Hospital,* 1914; *Canterbury v. Spence,* 1972). With regard to psychotherapy, informed consent applies to client decisions regarding whether to engage in therapy, what happens during the course of therapy, and what information to allow the therapist to disclose to others. In other words, apart from certain exceptions such as emergency treatment or civil commitment, a client cannot be given therapy and cannot be required to engage in particular conduct or disclose particular information while in therapy without his or her informed consent. Furthermore, apart from the exceptions outlined in the next section, a therapist cannot legally disclose information obtained in therapy without the client's informed consent. Actions taken by the therapist, such as the release of confidential information, without the informed consent of the client may result in professional liability.

To satisfy the doctrine of informed consent, the consent must be *voluntary, knowing,* and *competent* (Brakal, Parry, & Weiner, 1985). To meet the criterion of voluntariness, the decision must be the product of free choice and cannot be the result of factors such as threat, fraud, or duress. Stricter standards are likely to apply to children as opposed to adults. For example, in an analogous situation involving waiver to the right against self-incrimination, the U.S. Supreme Court suggested that special care should be taken to ensure that a waiver by a child is voluntary (*In re Gault,* 1967). However, the Court has never articulated these special standards.

The second criterion, knowing, primarily concerns the type of information about therapy that the therapist should provide to the client. The therapist must disclose the nature of the proposed treatment and the foreseeable risks and benefits that may result from it. For example, the therapist should disclose the nature of the diagnosis or evaluation of the problem, the prognosis of the problem without therapy, the nature and goals of the specific treatment techniques, the efficacy of the treatment techniques when outcome studies are available, the projected length of treatment, and the limits of confidentiality (see Keith-Spiegel & Koocher, 1985; Simon, 1987).

Traditionally, the legal standard for meeting this criterion revolved around some standard measure of professional behavior. In other words, the information that a professional was required to disclose depended upon information normally disclosed by other professionals practicing the same type of treatment (see *Natanson v. Kline,* 1960). Under this rule, an aggrieved client who brought a malpractice action was required to show that professional standards were not met— a requirement that has proved difficult for client/ litigants to meet (Brakal, et al., 1985). Although this rule is still the law in some states, a new standard has emerged. The "reasonable patient or client" standard requires the professional to disclose information that a reasonable client would need in order to make informed decisions concerning the treatment procedure (*Canterbury*

v. Spence, 1972; *Largey v. Rothman,* 1988). The basis for this change in legal standards is the idea that it is the client, not the therapist, who has the prerogative of deciding what is in the best interests of the client. Under this standard, therapists must disclose the information that they know or reasonably should know would influence client decisions.

The third criterion, competency, is perhaps the most relevant to child therapy. In most cases, a person is presumed competent to consent; that is, they have the necessary cognitive capacity to give a legally valid consent to treatment. However, at common law, children were presumed incompetent to consent (Rozovsky, 1984). They were thought to lack the necessary mental capacity to consent because of the nature of their inexperience and immaturity.

Over the years, however, this blanket presumption has given way to various exceptions. One exception to the presumption of a minor's incompetency is the mature minor doctrine. This doctrine was initially carved out by courts, but a few states have codified the rule in statute. Generally the doctrine holds that in certain cases a minor may be deemed mature enough to give competent consent. The doctrine is typically applied to situations where the minor is near the age of majority and is able to comprehend the nature and impact of the treatment (Wadlington, 1983). The complexity of the therapy and the risks involved are also likely to be considered in applying the rule (Rozovsky, 1984). As Ehrenreich and Melton (1983) point out, the courts have not clearly articulated the standards used to determine whether a minor is mature.

A second exception is the emancipated minor doctrine. Under this doctrine, minors are deemed capable of consenting to treatment if they have become independent from their parents. Factors to consider in determining emancipation include marriage, service in the armed forces, head of a household, employment, and living on one's own (Rozovsky, 1984). Generally, emancipation is considered on a case-by-case basis; however, in many states the issue of emancipation is controlled by statute.

A third category of exceptions involves state statutes that vary in their relationship to therapy. Some of these laws allow minors to consent to most treatments (Ehrenreich, & Melton, 1983). Others are more restrictive and pertain only to specific types of therapy, such as treatment for substance abuse, or to certain aspects of therapy, such as consent for the release of confidential information. Still other statutes apply to informed consent for medical procedures that may include certain types of therapy; however, these medical-care consent statutes have their own restrictions and may apply only to specific situations such as emergency care, routine procedures, or where a guardian or parent is not immediately available (Rozovsky, 1984).

Finally, consent statutes generally provide an age limit above which a child can give valid consent. Generally, this age can range from 12 to 18. The Colorado statute illustrates this point: "[A] minor fifteen years of age or older who is living separate and apart from his parent, parents, or legal guardian, and is managing his own financial affairs, regardless of the source of income . . . may give consent" (Colorado Revised Statute of 1985).

Not only may a child be incompetent to consent because of age, he or she may be incapable of consenting because of mental illness or deficiency. This problem has been referred to as double incompetency (Koocher, 1983). Generally, a person is not deemed incapable of consenting merely because he or she is undergoing therapy for a mental illness (e.g., *Wilson v. Lehman,* 1964). An individual is usually presumed competent unless adjudicated incompetent. Therefore, if a child falls under an exception to the presumption of child incompetency (e.g., emancipation) the therapist can presume that the child can provide legal consent unless the child has been declared legally incompetent.

If a child is not legally competent, who can consent to the minor's treatment? Traditionally, parents have had the authority for consenting on behalf of their minor children, but many states have enacted laws that give other persons, such as guardians or relatives, the authority to consent on behalf of minors. The Georgia law (items b, c, g, and h of 1986 Georgia Code 88-2904) provides an example of a statute giving certain individuals the authority to consent to medical treatment:

(b) Any parent, whether an adult or a minor, for his minor child;

(c) Any person temporarily standing in loco parentis whether formally serving or not, for the minor under his care and any guardian for his ward; . . .

(g) In the absence of a parent, any adult, for his minor brother or sister;

(h) In the absence of a parent, any grandparent for his minor grandchild (Georgia Code of 1986)

Other states may require joint consent by parents and their children and may even involve the therapist in the consent process. An Illinois law regarding consent to disclosure of confidential information provides a unique example (Illinois Revised Statute of 1985). Under this statute, if the client is under 12 years of age, the parent may consent to disclosure on the child's behalf. If the client is over 18, he or she may consent unless determined to be incompetent. If the client is between 12 and 18 years old, the parents and the client must give consent to disclosure. However, if the parents consent but the minor client refuses, the therapist may reveal the information if he or she determines the disclosure to be in the best interests of the child.

The traditional standard for substitute consent is the best interests of the child. In other words, when a child is legally incapable of consenting to therapy or disclosure of information, a substitute decision maker, such as a parent or guardian, must make decisions that are in the child's best interests, which is defined by what a reasonable person would say. A second standard has developed in recent years: the standard of substituted judgment, which requires the substitute decision maker to act as the client would act if he or she were competent. A third and more recent standard is a combination of the best interests and substituted judgment standards (Parry, 1987a; 1987b).

In certain circumstances, there may be a conflict of interest between the substitute decision maker and the client, and the substitute decision maker may have difficulty acting in the best interests of the client or as the client would act if competent. Consider a case reported by Weinapple and Perr (1981), in which a mother directed the disclosure of her son's psychotherapeutic records for use in a child custody proceeding. In this case, the consent for disclosure was designed more for the benefit of the mother than of the child. Although the trial court held that the client, who was 14 years old, had the capacity to refuse to consent to disclosure, a similar situation could occur in which a client would be declared incompetent to consent. In such a case, where there is a conflict of interest on the part of the parent or guardian, courts tend to appoint a *guardian ad litem* (a person appointed by the court to represent the interests of the child in a litigation) to determine whether the directed disclosure is in the best interests of the client (Matter of J.C.G., 1976).

Occasionally, the state may intervene on behalf of a child when the substitute decision maker does not follow the legal standards. State intervention typically occurs when parents refuse to consent to a medical procedure necessary to save the life of their child. Less common are situations where the state intervenes because parents have refused to give consent for their children to undergo mental-health treatment (Ehrenreich & Melton, 1983).

In summary, apart from involuntary or emergency treatment, the therapist must obtain informed consent to provide therapy to a child. The consent must be voluntary, knowing, and competent. To ensure that the consent is voluntary, the therapist should assess whether the consent is a product of fraud, threat, or duress. To ensure that the decision is knowing, the therapist must reveal enough information to allow the child or substitute decision maker to make an informed decision. The therapist should discuss the potential benefits of therapy and the potential for alleviation of the presenting problem. Where outcome studies are available, they also should be discussed. Finally, risks attendant to therapy should be discussed, including the potential for disclosure of sensitive information, discussed in the next section.

To ensure that the consent is competent, the therapist must become informed about the relevant laws in the particular jurisdiction. In reviewing these laws, the therapist should determine (1) what is the age of majority, (2) whether the jurisdiction has mature minor or emancipated minor laws, and (3) whether the jurisdiction has enacted minor consent statutes and the scope of these statutes. The therapist should also attend to whether a substitute decision maker is using proper legal standards in consenting on behalf of a minor. In general, a therapist should not take action that would be contrary to the interests of the minor, even if requested to do so by a parent or guardian.

CONFIDENTIALITY

There are two primary arguments regarding the importance of confidentiality in the therapeutic process. First, some assert that the confidentiality of information disclosed in therapy is important to protect the interests of the client. Not to do so, for example, may result in therapeutic information subsequently being used against the client (Winslade, 1982); often information revealed in therapy, if disclosed, could adversely affect a client's legal status, relationships, and so forth. Another interest is the avoidance of embarrassment or stigmatization. Often, information revealed in therapy will be of such a nature that if disclosed to the public it would cause a devaluation of the person (Denkowski & Denkowski, 1982; Friedlander, 1982). Confidentiality of this information, then, maintains the client's autonomy and dignity (Applebaum, Kaken, Walters, Lidz, & Roth, 1984). Although some scholars have suggested that it is the therapist rather than the client who is interested in confidentiality (Slovenko, 1977), many recent studies show that clients are concerned about the release of stigmatizing confidential information (McGuire, Toal, & Blau, 1985; Applebaum, et al., 1984; Schmid, Applebaum, Roth, & Lidz, 1983; Lindenthal, & Thomas, 1982 a, b).

The second argument focuses on the effect confidentiality has on psychotherapy. Some argue that without confidentiality, psychotherapy is rendered less effective or possibly even ineffective (Shwed, Kuvin, & Baliga, 1979; Siegal, 1979; Laurence, 1984; Epstein, Steingarten, Weinstein, & Nashel, 1977; Hollender, 1965)—an assertion that is accepted by the majority of mental health professionals (Jagim, Wittman, & Noll, 1978; Suarez & Balcanoff, 1966; Wise, 1978). This argument is based on at least five assumptions. Absent confidentiality: (1) potential clients will not seek out psychotherapy; (2) potential clients will be reluctant to enter therapy, thus causing a delay in required assistance; (3) clients already in therapy will be more likely to terminate therapy prematurely; (4) clients will be reluctant to divulge essential information, thereby rendering therapy ineffectual; and (5) therapists will employ procedures that are detrimental to the therapeutic process (e.g., they may be reluctant to keep written records) (DeKraai & Sales, 1984; Shuman & Weiner, 1982). As Trempor (1988) points out, however, the first three assumptions are probably less relevant to younger children, who seldom initiate therapy or decide when to terminate.

Although most therapists agree that confidentiality is important, there are a number of threats to confidentiality of information revealed by clients in general and minor clients in particular. The major threats are searches, subpoenas, breach of confidence, and access requirements.

Search and Seizure

Searches and seizures present a significant threat to the privacy of psychotherapy, since "under existing law, valid warrants may be issued to search *any* property, whether or not occupied by a third party, at which there is probable cause to believe that fruits, instrumentalities, or evidence of a crime will be found" (emphasis in original) (*Zurcher v. Stanford Daily,* 1978, p. 554). Law enforcement officers may engage in such practices in a number of cases. First, the government might suspect the therapist of committing a crime against the state or a third party. For example, the therapist might be accused of submitting false insurance claims, thus attempting to defraud an insurance company (*Hawaii Psychiatric Society v. Ariyoshi,* 1979; *McKirdy v. Superior Court,* 1982; *People v. Blasquez,* 1985; *Reynaud v. Superior Court,* 1982). Second, the state might suspect the therapist of committing a crime against a client (e.g., *Burrows v. Superior Court,* 1974; *State v. Tsavaris,* 1980, 1981). Third, information given to the therapist during therapy may be considered evidence to a crime committed by the client which is unrelated to therapy (*In re Gartley,* 1985). Fourth, a client might be suspected of a crime in connection with the therapy, such as fraudulent collection of unemployment compensation (*Doe v. Harris,* 1982). Fifth, both the therapist and the client may be suspected of complicity in a crime (*Commonwealth v. Santner,* 1982; Nye, 1980). Sixth, a client in therapy might reveal information about criminal activities of a third party. This situation is particularly relevant to juveniles who reveal their parents' child-, spouse-, or grandparent-abusing activities. Hence, numerous scenarios exist for search and seizure in the therapist's office. But is a search of the therapeutic files truly pernicious?

Many factors exist which make the search more damaging than other forms of confidential information disclosure. Irrelevant but confidential information will be examined during a search in an effort to identify relevant documents. Bloom (1980) calls this examination of nonsuspect third-party files a "rummaging effect." A search also can disrupt normal business operations. Therapy sessions may have to be canceled, secre-

taries and other employees may be prevented from working, office space and files may be restricted from use. In addition, a search can damage a therapist's reputation. A search is a relatively public event; clients in the office and people on the street will be aware of it, with the result that the therapist may be stigmatized. Relatedly, the search may damage clients' reputations, since law enforcement officials will become aware of the names of various clients when a search is conducted. This result is particularly onerous to clients who are politicians, lawyers, or otherwise highly visible in the community. Finally, the disclosure is government-forced, with little or no opportunity for discussion. Unlike other court-ordered disclosures, no opportunity is allowed for adversarial dispute of the forced disclosure until after intrusion has occurred, the premises have been searched, and the materials have been seized.

Generally, when presented with a valid search warrant, the therapist has few options in attempting to safeguard the confidentiality of client information. However, there are some guidelines that can minimize the intrusion. First, the therapist should contact an attorney immediately, since he or she is in the best position to prevent a search or seek an injunction to stop a search in progress. Note, however, that there is no requirement for the searching officers to wait for an attorney to review the warrant, supervise the search, or take action to stop the search. Second, the therapist should offer to produce the requested documents. This action will protect the confidentiality of irrelevant client files from the rummaging effect. However, if searching officers believe the presented documents to be incomplete, they may search the irrelevant files anyway. Finally, the therapist should request that the documents be sealed until proceedings can be initiated to determine whether the information should be disclosed. In most states, however, the searching officers would not be required to comply with this request.

California is one of the few states to provide a system of search-and-seizure protections to assure the confidentiality of particularly sensitive information such as client files (California Penal Code, 1982). The state provides statutorily for a master (a person appointed by a court to act as its representative in some particular act) to be appointed to accompany the searching officers when the search involves evidence in the possession of an attorney, a physician, a psychotherapist, or a clergyman who is not suspected of engaging in illegal activities. The master is required to request that the desired items be relinquished voluntarily. Only upon refusal to comply with the request will a search be conducted. When the psychotherapist or other professional requests the maintenance of confidentiality for particular items, the master is required to seal those items. If the therapist is not present during the search and cannot be located, the master is given the discretion to decide which documents appear to be privileged and to seal those items. The California statute further provides for a hearing regarding return of seized documents on the ground that the warrant or search was constitutionally deficient or that the documents are privileged. The hearing is to be conducted within 3 days of service of the warrant unless this is impractical. These proceedings are required to be held in camera (closed to the public).

Subpoena

Therapists are frequently required by law to testify in court as to matters that would normally be considered confidential by both the therapist and his or her client. The most common method for courts to require such disclosure is through a subpoena. There are two types—the *subpoena ad testificandum,* which requires a witness to appear before the issuing court or magistrate and give testimony, and the *subpoena duces tecum,* which requires a witness to produce documents or records in his or her possession at a legal proceeding. The legal authority for a court's subpoena power is usually found in a statute or court rule of the jurisdiction. Generally, all persons within the court's jurisdiction are subject to this power. Failure to comply with a subpoena (i.e., to reveal client information to the court) may result in criminal sanction such as fine or imprisonment.

The most common defense available to a therapist when subpoenaed is that the information requested is privileged from disclosure under privileged communications law. In a jurisdiction with a privileged communications law that applies to communications between a therapist and a client, the disclosure of such communications may not be compelled in a legal proceeding unless a statutory or judicial exception to the privilege applies.

Nearly all states have enacted privileged communications laws for at least some types of

therapists (DeKraai & Sales, 1982). Which professions are covered by the privilege, however, varies across jurisdictions and is an issue of debate (Herlihy & Sheeley, 1987). While many states provide privileges for communications between clients and psychologists or psychiatrists, few provide privileges for other types of therapists. This is in contrast to much of the literature that proposes extending privileges to other therapists (Stroube, 1979) such as social workers (Delgado, 1973; Reynolds, 1976), school guidance counselors (Robinson, 1974), and rape crisis counselors (Applebaum & Roth, 1981; Laurence, 1984; Scarmeas, 1982; Stouder, 1982; Williamson, 1984). Even if all professionals that could be considered psychotherapists were included under a psychotherapist–client privilege (see Nye, 1979; Knapp & VandeCreek, 1985), however, there would still exist a serious threat to confidentiality. Nonprofessionals (e.g., secretaries, clerks, direct-care technicians, graduate student interns) often have access to psychotherapeutic information and could be compelled to reveal the information under most privileges (*Myers v. State,* 1984; *Lipsey v. State,* 1984; but see *Oregon v. Miller,* 1985). This had led some to suggest that the locus of the privilege and the responsibility for confidentiality should lie with the facility or program rather than a specific professional (Hague, 1983; Kenny, 1982).

Another issue concerns the type of information that is privileged. Generally, information must be confidential and revealed in the context of a professional relationship to be privileged. As Shah (1969) points out, this requirement would not cover the fact that the person has or is currently undergoing psychotherapy. Unfortunately, even in today's society where participation in psychotherapy is less stigmatizing than in the past, clients may be reluctant to seek out therapy if they believe this fact will be disclosed.

An additional problem is that, traditionally, courts did not consider communications confidential if made in the presence of third parties (e.g., *United States v. Blackburn,* 1971). Hence, group or family therapy communications might not be considered confidential. In recent years, however, courts that have been confronted with this issue have generally found the information to be confidential and privileged (e.g., *Sims v. Georgia,* 1984).

Even if the information meets the above requirements and thereby falls under the therapist–client privilege, the disclosure of such information may be required if it falls under an exception to the privilege. Many psychotherapists have argued that the privilege should be absolute; in other words, confidential communications made to a therapist in the context of a professional relationship should never be allowed to be revealed in a legal proceeding (Everstine et al., 1980). In most jurisdictions, however, this position has not been adopted, and exceptions have been carved out where the need for information is deemed to outweigh the privacy interests of clients. Some of the most common exceptions include the following situations: (1) where a therapist has been appointed by a court to examine a party to a legal proceeding, (2) where a client raises his or her mental state as a claim or defense in a legal proceeding, (3) where a therapist determines that a client requires hospitalization for a mental or emotional disorder, and (4) where a client brings an action for malpractice against the therapist.

Another exception that is gaining increasing popularity is the child-custody exception (see Beigler, 1972; *Dawes v. Dawes*, 1984; Guernsey, 1981; *In re Adoption of Embick*, 1986; Knapp & VandeCreek, 1985, 1987; *Morey v. Peppin*, 1984). The competing interests involved with this exception essentially revolve around assumptions that the interests in proper custody determinations on behalf of children outweigh the privacy of parents and children. This exception generally applies to communications made between either a therapist and parents or a therapist and child (*Matter of M.C.*, 1986).

A relevant issue to child therapy concerns who may assert the privilege and who may waive the privilege. Generally, the privilege belongs to the client and only the client may assert or waive the privilege (e.g., *Fitzgibbon v. Fitzgibbon*, 1984).

This principle is illustrated in the case of *Lora v. Board of Education of the City of New York* (1977). *Lora* involved a lawsuit by Black and Hispanic emotionally disturbed children alleging that the Board of Education standards and procedures pertaining to youths with emotional disorders were arbitrary and applied in a radically discriminating manner. As part of their case, the students attempted to introduce into evidence 50 randomly selected files which contained "the student's school history, teachers' observations, social workers' studies of the student and his family, results of psychological and psychiatric consultations or examinations, and other clinical and intensely personal information" (p. 568). To

maintain the confidentiality of the information, the students requested that all identifying information be deleted from the records.

The defendant school board sought to bar the introduction of the therapeutic information, arguing that disclosure of this information would violate the students' constitutional right to privacy and a federal evidentiary privilege. The court held that assuming the information is privileged, the privilege cannot be waived by the school district. Furthermore, a waiver by the children could not be assumed. As the court stated, "It is highly unlikely that the fifty students to be randomly selected from this group would acquiesce in the assertion of a privilege by the very individuals alleged to have fostered such system-wide bias."

Although the privilege is generally considered to be the client's, in the case of child therapy, parents rather than the minor client may have the authority to assert or waive the privilege. As a general rule, if a privilege statute gives a minor client the authority to assert the privilege (Ehrenreich & Melton, 1983) or if the child has the capacity to provide competent consent (Weinapple & Perr, 1981) then the privilege belongs to the child rather than the parents. However, minor clients should be informed that they may not have the ability to assert or waive the privilege.

In summary, therapists should become aware of the laws in their jurisdictions that safeguard confidential information from disclosure through subpoenaed testimony or record production. If presented with a subpoena, the therapist should consult an attorney. If a parent attempts to assert or waive the privilege on behalf of a minor client and the therapist disagrees with the decision, he or she should raise the issue of potential parental conflict of interest with the court. In such a situation, a court may appoint a guardian ad litem to represent the best interests of the child or the court may decide whether a privilege should be waived (Knapp & VandeCreek, 1987). It should be kept in mind that even in situations where the therapist believes information should remain confidential, if a court orders the therapist to testify, he or she must do so or face criminal penalties.

Breach of Confidence

Whereas the previously discussed threats to confidentiality pertained to forced disclosure, "breach of confidence" refers to voluntary disclosures or the threat that someone who has legitimate access to confidential information will wrongfully disclose that information.

In our complex society, a variety of individuals may have or may obtain legitimate access to psychotherapeutic information, including the therapist, the client, other consulting therapists, the client's family, student interns, treatment staff, clerical staff, government agencies, and insurance agencies. With the potentially wide dispersion of this information, the maintenance of confidentiality becomes increasingly problematic.

Many states have enacted laws that protect clients from voluntary disclosures (DeKraai & Sales, 1984). Most of these nondisclosure laws are found in the professional sections of state codes that cover specific psychotherapeutic professions (e.g., psychologists, psychiatrists, social workers). These provisions vary considerably, resulting in disparate protection among different types of therapists. Other nondisclosure laws are limited to specific types of clients (e.g., persons with developmental disabilities, persons treated for substance abuse) or to a specific type of agency (e.g., community mental-health programs, state supported mental retardation programs). In these states, the protection of confidentiality will vary across psychotherapeutic situations.

In addition to statutory remedies for voluntary disclosures, there are at least five common law tort remedies (see generally Lamb, 1983; Newman, 1981; Egar, 1976): (1) breach of confidence, which is an action for malpractice that requires the client to show the existence of a professional duty to maintain confidentiality, breach of that duty, and injury resulting from the breach (see generally, Vickery, 1983); (2) breach of contract, which is an action based on the theory that an implied or expressed contract exists between therapists and clients (Feldman & Ward, 1979); (3) breach of a fiduciary duty, which is an action based on the theory that clients have placed trust and reliance upon the therapist who is then obligated to act in the best interests of the client (Turner & Thomason, 1970); (4) breach of privacy, which is an action based on the right of the individual to be free from unwarranted disclosure of one's private life; and (5) defamation, which is an action that is available if the disclosure of information subjects the client to public ridicule or shame (DeKraai & Sales, 1984).

Concurrent with the variations in the laws found across different jurisdictions, the penalties for wrongful disclosure also vary by state. Some laws provide for license revocation for specific types of professions. Other laws allow civil damages including actual and punitive damages. Still other laws impose criminal sanctions for wrongful disclosure (i.e., fines and/or imprisonment).

Remember, however, that not all disclosures of psychotherapeutic information will result in sanctions since, as already noted, not all information can legally be kept confidential. For information to be protected from disclosure, it must be confidential. Information indicating that clients are participating in therapy is generally considered nonconfidential (Shah, 1970). In addition, for information to be considered confidential, it must have been disclosed in the context of a professional relationship. And laws designed to protect the confidentiality of psychotherapeutic information often allow persons with access to the information to disclose it to specified persons or entities without incurring liability. These laws allow disclosure to treatment professionals other than the treating therapist, treatment facilities, certain state agencies, law enforcement officials, insurance agencies, attorneys, guardians, and families or clients (DeKraai & Sales, 1984).

An interesting issue is raised with regard to reporting laws (discussed below). These laws require that therapists divulge certain information about their clients under certain situations. Failure to reveal the information may result in criminal or civil liability. For example, if a therapist fails to warn a third party of a client's dangerous intentions toward that party, the therapist may be liable for harm the client inflicts. Most child-abuse reporting laws provide immunity from liability for good-faith reporting (Knapp & VandeCreek, 1987). However, for reporting laws not based in statute (i.e., some dangerous person reporting laws), the issue is unsettled, although it is unlikely that the client would win an action against the therapist for disclosure of information that a law mandates the therapist to disclose.

Some psychotherapists have argued that all information disclosed in psychotherapy should be confidential even if the client consents to its release (Dubey, 1974). Others have argued that clients should have control over release of their records (Coleman, 1984; Keith-Spiegel &

Koocher, 1985; Rosen, 1977). This latter position reflects the law in most jurisdictions; it requires the therapist to release the information when the client gives consent (DeKraai & Sales, 1984).

With child therapy, however, the issue of the child's competency to waive confidential arises, just as it does with consent to treatment and with the assertion or waiver of privileged communications. Hence, the same guidelines apply as well. The easiest route for the therapist is to obtain consent from both the parents and the child before releasing confidential information. If this is not possible, the therapist must determine whether the child has the legal capacity to consent or whether a substitute decision maker must give consent.

In conclusion, in addition to knowing the laws governing consent, the therapist should know whether confidentiality statutes exist in the jurisdiction, the types of therapists and clients included in the statutes, the penalties for wrongful disclosure, and who may have access without client consent. In addition, therapists should inform others with access to confidential information (e.g., secretaries, interns, other clients) of their duty to protect the information. Finally, therapists should inform their clients of the potential for disclosure, including the persons who will have access to the information and the remedies for breach of confidences.

Access Requirements

In many cases persons outside of therapy, such as parents of a minor client, will desire access to therapeutic information. Often disclosure of this information will be beneficial to the therapeutic process (Simon, 1987). In such a case, the child's privacy interests are not compromised if the therapist explains the reason for disclosure and the child consents. A more difficult issue occurs when parents wish access to information and the child desires that his or her communications to the therapist remain confidential.

Generally, if parents are the legal substitute decision makers and have consented to treatment, they may have a right to access the child's therapeutic records (Ehrenreich & Melton, 1983). One rationale for parental access in this situation is that because parents have the authority to consent to release of the child's therapeutic records to other persons or entities (e.g., insur-

ance companies), the parents should be aware of the content of the records to make an informed decision about disclosure.

Where the child has the legal capacity to consent, the issue of parental access is less clear. As Ehrenreich and Melton (1983) point out, there is little statutory or case law on this matter. Given this lack of precedent, each situation is judged on a case-by-case basis. One of the few cases that have addressed this issue indicates that parents may be denied access where disclosure would be contrary to the interest of the child and where a child is promised confidentiality. In *State of New Jersey in the interest of D. G.* (1980), a father requested the therapeutic records of his 15-year-old daughter. The daughter had been adjudged as in need of supervision, placed in foster care, and provided mental health services. The daughter had been promised confidentiality and her therapist testified that it would not be in the child's best interests to allow the parents access to the records.

The parents, on the other hand, argued that they were interested in the welfare of their daughter and wanted the records so as to gain insight into their daughter's problems. The state appellate court denied access holding that in spite of state law which apparently allows access to parents, the decision to release the information rests with the discretion of the court. Because the client was promised confidentiality and the available evidence indicated hostility between the father and daughter, the court in its discretion would not allow disclosure to the parents.

When parents request access to their child's therapeutic records, the therapist should assess whether disclosure is in the best interests of the child. If the child has the capacity to consent but desires confidentiality or if the child does not have the capacity or consent and disclosure would not be in the best interests of the child, the therapist should deny parental access. There are a number of legal theories upon which parents may seek access in a court of law (e.g., Madden, 1982). The court will then determine whether access should be granted.

REPORTING LAWS

Reporting laws impose an affirmative duty on therapists to disclose specific knowledge obtained in therapy. Failure by the therapist to reveal information under these circumstances may lead to personal liability. These laws are based on the premise that the privacy of therapy is outweighed by the physical safety of citizens in society. There are two major types of reporting laws: dangerous-person reporting laws and child-abuse reporting laws.

Dangerous-Person Reporting Laws

The courts in some states have established a dangerous-person reporting requirement or a duty to warn for therapists. The most famous case to establish such a mandate was *Tarasoff v. Board of Regents* (1974, 1976). In this case the California Supreme Court held that when the therapist knows or reasonably should know that a client poses a threat to some third party, the therapist has a duty to take reasonable action to protect the potential victim. Although this action could include such measures as initiating emergency commitment procedures, the most common duty, as discussed in *Tarasoff* and subsequent court cases, includes warning the potential victim of the client's threats. Failure to warn the victim in these situations will result in civil liability if the client harms the victim. It is evident that the dangerous-person reporting or warning requirements directly conflict with confidentiality. In recognizing this conflict, the Court in Tarasoff found that the interests in effective treatment and individual privacy are outweighed by society's interest in the safety of its citizens. Subsequent cases in California and other states have followed the Tarasoff doctrine (Beck, 1985; George, 1985; Knapp & VandeCreek, 1982).

For the most part, the commentary on the duty-to-warn laws has been critical and has included the following observations: (1) the laws are based on the faulty presumption that psychotherapists can accurately predict dangerousness (Gurevitz, 1977; Latham, 1975; Merton, 1982; Stone, 1976) when, in fact, the evidence is to the contrary (e.g., Cocozza & Steadman, 1976; Monahan, 1981; APA ad hoc Committee on Legal Issues, 1985); (2) an incorrect judgment could lead to liability for breach of confidence (Cohen, 1978; Roth & Meisel, 1977); hence, therapists may overpredict or underpredict dangerousness to avoid liability (Bersoff, 1976; Stone, 1976); (3) therapists might become reluctant to engage in therapy with potentially dangerous clients and clients may become reluctant to reveal their dangerous urges to therapists; psy-

chotherapy will thereby become negatively affected, increasing the danger to society (Noll, 1976; Sloan & Klein, 1977; Stone, 1976); (4) warning a potential victim may cause unnecessary mental distress for the person (Griffith & Griffith, 1978); and (5) disclosure of a dangerous client's intentions may threaten the therapist's safety (Sloan & Klein, 1977).

Not all of the commentary concerning Tarasoff has been negative, however. For example, it has been argued that psychotherapists should have a duty to society and the potential victim as well as the client and that warning the potential victim may fulfill this duty by preventing injury or death (Fleming & Maximov, 1974; Glassman, 1975; Kaplan, 1975; Leonard, 1977). In fact, the legal duty to warn is in accordance with current ethical standards adopted by the psychotherapeutic professions (Kaplan, 1975). It has also been argued that dangerous-person reporting laws will benefit not only society but the psychotherapeutic process as well. Wexler (1979, 1981) suggests that these laws will facilitate the use of joint and family therapy where both the client and the potential victim are included.

Other scholars propose that the arguments against these laws are unconvincing. For example, Seligman (1977) points out that there is no clear evidence that these types of laws will have a negative impact on psychotherapy. Existing research tends to support this argument (Givelber, Bowers, & Blitch, 1984, 1985; Beck, 1982; but see Wise, 1978). It has also been noted that although therapists now contend that they cannot predict dangerousness, they contended just the opposite for years and, in fact, still are involved in the prediction of dangerousness in various legal arenas (e.g., civil commitment, termination of parental rights) (Ayres & Holbrook, 1975; Seligman, 1977).

Regardless of the academic commentary on this issue, the refinement of the legal principle has proceeded apace in courts throughout the country. These cases have established parameters to the duty to warn. One parameter found in the common law of negligence is that a special relationship must exist between the client and the therapist before a duty to warm arises. Generally a therapeutic relationship will satisfy this condition (*Tarasoff v. Board of Regents,* 1974, 1979; *McIntosh v. Milano,* 1979; *Abernathy v. United States,* 1985).

A second parameter concerns the type of threat

the client poses. Most cases have involved a threat to the physical safety of a third person (e.g., *Tarasoff v. Board of Regents*, 1974, 1976; *McIntosh v. Milano*, 1979; *Lipari v. Sears, Roebuck & Co.*, 1980; *Shaw v. Glickman*, 1980). Other cases have raised the issue of a duty to warn third persons when a client poses a physical danger to self (e.g., *Bellah v. Greenson*, 1978).

A recent case which may signal a trend, however, found a duty to warn even where the threat involved property damage. In *Peck v. Counseling Service of Addison County, Inc.* (1985), a therapist learned of a minor client's desire to burn down his father's barn. The therapist did not warn the father, and the client subsequently did in fact set fire to the barn. The Supreme Court of Vermont adopted the Tarasoff reasoning and held the therapist liable for failing to warn the father of his son's intentions. The Court failed to note the distinction between the harm inflicted in the Tarasoff case (murder) and the harm committed in the case before it (barn burning).

A third parameter concerns preexisting knowledge by the victim that the client is dangerous. In *Matter of Estate of Votteler* (1982), the Supreme Court of Iowa held that the Tarasoff doctrine should not extend to a situation where the potential victim is aware of the danger. Hence, in such a situation, the therapist does not have a duty to warn the potential victim.

A fourth parameter involves the therapist's knowledge of the danger. In Tarasoff the therapist had determined that his client posed a threat to a third party. But is actual knowledge of serious and imminent danger a requisite for the duty to arise? Courts have found that a duty to warn an intended victim exists even where the therapist may not have actual knowledge of the danger. Although a slight suspicion that the client may pose a threat will not create a duty to warn, the therapist will be held to the standards of the psychotherapeutic profession in determining whether he or she should have known of the danger (*Tarasoff v. Board of Regents*, 1976; *Davis v. Lhim*, 1983; *Lipari v. Sears, Roebuck & Co.*, 1980). Therefore, if actual knowledge cannot be shown, whether the therapist should have predicted the danger is a question of fact that must be determined at trial.

A fifth parameter concerns to whom the duty to warn should extend. Generally the duty ex-

tends to readily identifiable and foreseeable victims (*Doyle v. U.S.*, 1982; *Chrite v. U.S.*, 1983). Although the intended victim need not be specifically named, he or she must be a member of a distinct group or identifiable potential victims (*Mavroudis v. Superior Court*, 1980; *Jablonski v. U.S.*, 1983; *Hedlund v. Superior Court*, 1983). Courts have held that the duty to warn does not extend to members of a large amorphous public or to a potential victim who is in no greater danger than any other member of the public (*Brady v. Hopper*, 1983, 1984; *Cairl v. State*, 1982; *Leedy v. Hartnett*, 1981; *Thompson v. County of Alameda*, 1980). However, a recent case deviates from this line of authority and created a cause of action even for victims who were not readily identifiable. In *Schuster v. Attenberg* (1988), a minor client's family brought suit against a psychiatrist for failure to warn the client of a medication's side effects, failure to warn the client's family of her dangerousness, and failure to seek commitment. The plaintiffs sought damages for injuries and medical expenses resulting from a car accident in which the client was killed and her sister seriously injured. It was alleged that the medication's side effects caused the client to have the accident. The Wisconsin Supreme Court held that the duty to warn was not limited to specific threats against an identified person and that the cause of action is based on whether the therapist took action that conforms to accepted standards of care.

Should a civil lawsuit be brought against a therapist for failure to warn, the therapist may raise a defense based upon the five parameters. No duty will exist if the therapist can show that (1) no therapeutic relationship existed; (2) the client did not pose a serious threat to the safety of self or others (however, a recent trend may be to impose a duty where the client poses a threat to property); (3) the victim knew of the threat; (4) under existing professional standards, a therapist could not have predicted the danger; and (5) the victim was not a member of a readily identifiable and foreseeable group for which the threat of danger was significantly greater than for others.

In summary, the duty to warn is receiving increasing attention in the nation's courts as third-party victims bring suit against therapists for the actions of their clients. Unfortunately, in most jurisdictions therapists cannot know whether a duty to warn exists until a test case reaches the jurisdiction's court system and, in fact, therapists may be subject to liability for breach of confidentiality if they do warn a potential victim. To remedy the ambiguity in the law a number of states have introduced duty-to protect bills in their legislatures (APA, 1985).

Abuse Reporting Laws

Abuse reporting laws are designed to facilitate the detection of abuses toward persons who are unable or unlikely to report the abuse themselves. Although some abuse reporting laws apply to particularly vulnerable adults such as the elderly or persons with a developmental disability (DeKraai & Sales, 1984), the most visible of these laws apply only to children (see Fraser, 1978; Guyer, 1982).

Statutes vary across states regarding what type of abuse is reportable. Laws usually require specified persons to report to state authorities nonaccidental physical injury, neglect, sexual abuse, and mental or emotional harm of persons in the protected class. An individual must have a reasonable suspicion that the defined abuse has occurred for the reporting requirement to take effect (Smith & Meyer, 1984). Although early reporting laws required only physicians to report abuse, recent laws have increasingly included other persons such as therapists (Comment, 1985). Some laws are so broad that they require "any person" to report child abuse. These laws are particularly problematic for group or family therapy. In this situation, all of the participants in therapy may have a duty to report abuse (Smith & Meyer, 1984).

Legislators have attempted through various legal mechanisms to encourage therapists to comply with the law. Generally, reporting statutes provide immunity from civil or criminal liability for good-faith reporting; that is, a civil or criminal action may not be brought against a therapist for breaching a client's confidences by reporting the abuse (*Awkerman v. Tri-County Orthopedic Group, P.C.*, 1985). In addition, statutes impose civil or criminal liability for failure to report the abuse (DeKraai & Sales, 1984; Mazura, 1977; *Landeros v. Flood*, 1976). Thus, these laws are based on the belief that the interest in protecting the harmed individual outweighs the interest in therapeutic confidentiality (Cunningham, 1984; Weisberg & Wald, 1984).

Pesce v. Sterling Morton High School District 201, Cook County, Illinois (1987) illustrates the conflict between maintaining confidentiality and disclosing possible child abuse. This case involved the following facts. Student A contacted a school psychologist, therapist A, and expressed concerns about her friend, student B. She showed the therapist a note written by her friend which indicated suicidal thoughts and a confusion about his sexual preferences. Student A also informed the therapist that something sexual had occurred between student B and a male faculty member. The therapist encouraged student A to have student B come in for counseling.

Student B contacted the therapist, and the therapist informed student B that his communication would be confidential. Student B denied having suicidal thoughts and stated that nothing sexual had occurred with the teacher; however, he said that the teacher had shown him some "pictures" while he was at the teacher's house. The student told the school psychologist that he wanted assistance in resolving his confusion about sexual preferences, and therapist A arranged for counseling from therapist B.

In making a decision about whether to disclose the possible sexual abuse, therapist A contacted an attorney and a psychologist and consulted state laws, school guidelines, and professional/ethical guidelines. Therapist A decided not to disclose the information. Later, however, therapist A met with student B and therapist B and discussed the idea of revealing the information. During the discussion, student B disclosed that he had engaged in sex with the teacher. The student agreed that the information should be revealed, and therapist A contacted school authorities.

Subsequently, the school board held a hearing where it suspended and demoted therapist A for failing to promptly report the sexual abuse. Therapist A challenged the school board's action in state court, arguing that state child-abuse reporting requirements violated the constitutional right to privacy. The Court of Appeals held that the compelling interest of the state in preventing child abuse outweighed the privacy interests. As stated by the Court:

> Of critical importance here is the fact that the state is acting to protect one of the most pitiable and helpless classes in society—abused children. . . . The compelling interest of the state reflects several characteristics special to abused children: they often may be unaware of their own abuse or injury; they may often be unable

to report abuse; the effects of abuse may be invisible to third parties; abused children can carry physical and emotional scars for a lifetime; and of course the state bears a special responsibility to protect children who are considered unable voluntarily to choose their own course of action. (p. 798)

Many therapists have been critical of abuse reporting laws and have questioned their effectiveness. They first point out that to be effective, therapists must be aware of the existence of the law and its specific requirements. Research suggests, however, that this is not the case (Swoboda, Elwork, Sales, & Levine, 1978). Second, psychotherapists must be willing to breach the confidentiality of the clients' communications to report the abuse. Research suggests that this also might not be the case (Muehleman & Kimmons, 1981). Third, clients must be willing to testify against the abuser. This does not always occur (Thurman, 1984).

Even if effective, a major issue is whether abuse reporting laws or confidentiality requirements best meet society's interest in ultimately protecting children and dependent adults from abuse. Sherlock and Murphy (1984) point out that therapy for the abuser might more effectively protect society's interests in the long run than reporting the abuse. The assumption is that mandatory reporting will preclude beneficial therapy for the abuser.

Therapists should become aware of the laws in their jurisdiction regarding abuse reporting. They should know who has a duty to report, what types of abuse are required to be reported, to whom the case should be reported, and whether there is immunity for good-faith reporting. In addition, therapists should inform their clients that if they disclose child abuse during therapy, the therapist may have a duty to report.

CONCLUSION

The areas of informed consent, confidentiality of therapeutic information, and reporting laws are particularly relevant to the field of child therapy. Therapists have a duty to understand the laws in these areas so as to protect themselves from possible legal disabilities as well as to protect the interests of their clients. Although this chapter provides an analysis of the relevant legal issues pertaining to these areas, we recommend that psychologists become knowledgeable about the particular laws that apply in their

jurisdiction. We further recommend that should a legal issue arise, the therapist consult an attorney.

REFERENCES

Abernathy v. U.S., 773 F.2d 391 (8th Cir. 1985).

American Psychological Association. (1985, December). State legislative preview. *Executive Newsbulletin*, p. 1.

American Psychological Association, ad hoc Committee on Legal Issues (1985, August). *Duty to protect: Legislative alert*. Washington, DC: Author.

Applebaum, P. S., Kapen, G., Walters, B., Lidz, C. & Roth, L. H. (1984). Confidentiality: An empirical test of the utilitarian perspective. *Bulletin of the American Academy of Psychiatry and the Law, 12,* 109–116.

Applebaum, P. S. & Roth, L. H. (1981). In the matter of PAAR: Rape problems and matters of confidentiality. *Hospital and Community Psychiatry, 32,* 461–462.

Awkerman v. Tri-County Orthopedic Group, P.C., 373 N.W.2d 204 (Mich. App. 1985).

Ayers, R. J., Jr. & Holbrook, J. T. (1975). Law, psychotherapy, and the duty to warn: A tragic trilogy. *Baylor Law Review, 27,* 677–705.

Beck, J. C. (1982). When the patient threatens violence: An empirical study of clinical practice after *Tarasoff. Bulletin of the American Academy of Psychiatry and Law, 10,* 189–201.

Beck, J. C. (1985). *The potentially violent patient and the Tarasoff decision in psychiatric practice*. Washington, DC: American Psychiatric Press.

Beigler, J. S. (1972). The 1971 amendment of the Illinois statute on confidentiality: A new development in privilege law. *American Journal of Psychiatry, 129,* 311–315.

Bellah v. Greenson, 146 Cal. Rptr. 535 (App. 1978).

Bersoff, D. N. (1976). Therapists as protectors and policemen: New roles as the result of *Tarasoff? Professional Psychology, 7,* 267–273.

Bloom, L. H., Jr. (1980). The law office search: An emerging problem and some suggested solutions. *Georgetown Law Journal, 69,* 1–100.

Brakal, S. J., Parry, J., & Weiner, B. A. (1985). *The mentally disabled and the law*. Chicago, IL: American Bar Foundation.

Brady v. Hopper, 570 F.Supp. 1333(1983), aff'd 751 F.2d 329 (1984).

Burrows v. Superior Court, 13 Cal. 3d 238, 529 P.2d 590, 118 Cal. Rptr. 166 (1974).

Cairl v. State, 323 N.W.2d 20 (Minn. 1982).

California Penal Code § 1524 (West 1982).

Canterbury v. Spence, 464 F.2d 772 (D.C.Cir. 1972).

Chrite v. U.S., 564 F.Supp. 341 (E.D. Mich. 1983).

Cocozza, J. & Steadman, H. (1976). The failure of psychiatric predictions of dangerousness: Clear and convincing evidence. *Rutgers Law Review, 29,* 1048–1101.

Cohen, R. N. (1978). *Tarasoff v. Regents of the University of California:* The duty to warn: Common law and statutory problems for psychotherapists. *California Western Law Review, 14,* 153–182.

Coleman, V. (1984). Why patients should keep their own records. *Journal of Medical Ethics, 10,* 27–28.

Colorado Revised Statute. § 13-22-103(1985).

Comment (1985). Duties in conflict: Must psychotherapists report child abuse inflicted by clients and confided in therapy? *San Diego Law Review, 22,* 645.

Commonwealth v. Santner, 454 A.2d 24 (Pa. Super. 1982).

Cunningham, C. D., Jr. (1984). Vanishing exception to the psychotherapist–patient privilege: The child abuse reporting act. *Pacific Law Journal, 16,* 335–352.

Davis v. Lhim, 124 Mich. App. 291, 335 N.W.2d 481 (1983).

Dawes v. Dawes, 454 So.2d 311 (La. 1984).

DeKraai, M. B., & Sales, B. D. (1982). Privileged communications of psychologists. *Professional Psychology: Research and Practice, 13,* 372–388.

DeKraai, M. B., & Sales, B. D. (1984). Confidential communications of psychotherapists. *Psychotherapy, 21,* 293–318.

Delgado, R. (1973). Underprivileged communications: Extension of the psychotherapist privilege to patients of psychiatric social workers. *California Law Review, 61,* 1050–1071.

Denkowski, K. M., & Denkowski, G. C. (1982). Client–counselor confidentiality: An update of rationale, legal status, and implications. *The Personnel and Guidance Journal, 60,* 371.

Doe v. Harris, 696 F.2d 109 (D.C. Cir. 1982).

Doyle v. U.S., 530 F.Supp. 1278 (C.D. Cal. 1982).

Dubey, J. (1974). Confidentiality as a requirement of the therapist: Technical necessities for absolute privilege in psychotherapy. *American Journal of Psychiatry, 131,* 1093–1096.

Egar, D. L. (1976). Psychotherapist's liability for extrajudicial breaches of confidentiality. *Arizona Law Review, 18,* 1061–1094.

Ehrenreich, N. S., & Melton, G. B. (1983). Ethical and legal issues in the treatment of children. In C. E. Walker & M. C. Roberts (Eds.). *Handbook of clinical child psychology* (pp. 1285–1305). New York, NY: John Wiley & Sons.

Epstein, G. N., Steingarten, J., Weinstein, H. D., & Nashel, H. M. (1977). Panel report: Impact of law on the practice of psychotherapy. *Journal of Psychiatry and Law, 5,* 7–40.

Everstine, L., Everstine, D. S., Heymann, G. M., True, R. H., Frey, D. H., Johnson, H. G. & Seiden, R. H. (1980). Privacy and confidentiality in psychotherapy. *American Psychologist, 35,* 828–840.

Feldman, S. R., & Ward, T. M. (1979). Psychotherapeutic injury: Reshaping the implied contract as an alternative to malpractice. *North Carolina Law Review, 58,* 63–96.

Fitzgibbon v. Fitzgibbon, 484 A.2d 46 (N.J. 1984).

Fleming, J. G, & Maximov, B. (1974). The patient or his victim: The therapist's dilemma. *California Law Review, 62,* 1025–1068.

Fraser, B. G (1978). A glance at the past, a gaze at the present, a glimpse at the future: A critical analysis of the development of child abuse reporting statutes. *Chicago-Kent Law Review, 54,* 641–686.

Friendlander, W. J. (1982). A basis of privacy and autonomy in medical practice. *Social Science and Medicine, 16,* 1709–1718.

George, J. C. (1985). Hedlund paranoia. *Journal of Clinical Psychology, 41,* 291–294.

Georgia Code § 88-2904 (1986).

Givelber, D. J., Bowers, W. J., & Blitch, C. L. (1984). *Tarasoff,* myth and reality: An empirical study of private law in action. *Wisconsin Law Review, 1984,* 443–497.

Givelber, D. J., Bowers, W., & Blitch, C. L. (1985). The *Tarasoff* controversy: A summary of findings from an empirical study of legal, ethical, and clinical issues. In J. C. Beck (Ed.) *The potentially violent patient and the Tarasoff decision in psychiatric practice* (pp. 35–57). Washington, DC: American Psychiatric Press.

Glassman, M. S. (1975). Psychotherapist has a duty to warn an endangered victim whose peril was disclosed by communications between the psychotherapist and patient. *University of Cincinnati Law Review, 44,* 368–375.

Griffith, E. J., & Griffith, E. E. H. (1978). Duty to third parties, dangerousness, and the right to refuse treatment: Problematic concepts for psychiatrist and lawyer. *California Western Law Review, 14,* 241–274.

Guernsey, T. F. (1981). The psychotherapist–patient privilege in child placement: A relevancy analysis. *Villanova Law Review, 26,* 955–996.

Gurevitz, H. (1977). Tarasoff: Protective privilege versus public peril. *American Journal of Psychiatry, 134,* 289–292.

Guyer, M. J. (1982). Child abuse and neglect statutes: Legal and clinical implications. *American Journal of Orthopsychiatry, 52,* 73–81.

Hague, W. W. (1983). The psychotherapist-patient privilege in Washington: Extending the privilege to community mental health clinics. *Washington Law Review, 58,* 565–586.

Hawaii Psychiatric Society v. Ariyoshi, 481 F. Supp. 1028 (D. Hawaii 1979), aff'd CV79-0113 (D. Hawaii 1982).

Hedlund v. Superior Court, 34 Cal.3d 595, 194 Cal. Rptr. 805, 669 P.2d 41 (1983).

Herlihy, B., & Sheeley, V. L. (1987). Privileged communications in selected helping professions: A comparison among statutes. *Journal of Counseling and Development, 65,* 479–483.

Hollender, M. (1965). Privileged communications and confidentiality. *Diseases of the Nervous System, 26,* 169–175.

Illinois Revised Statute Ch 91 1/2 § 801 et seq. (1985 Supp.).

In re Adoption of Embick, 506 A.2d 455 (Pa. Super. Ct. 1986).

In re Gartley, 491 A.2d 851 (Pa. Super. 1985).

In re Gault, 387 U.S.1 (1967).

Jablonski v. U.S., 712 F.2d 391 (9th Cir. 1983).

Jagim, R. D., Wittman, W. D., & Noll, J. O.

(1978). Mental health professionals attitudes toward confidentiality, privilege, and third-party disclosure. *Professional Psychology, 9,* 458–466.

Kaplan, R. B. (1975). Tarasoff v. Regents of the University of California: Psychotherapists, policemen and the duty to ward—an unreasonable extension of the common law? *Golden Gate University Law Review, 6,* 229–248.

Keith-Spiegel, P., & Koocher, G. P. (1985). *Ethics in psychotherapy: Professional standards and cases.* New York: Random House.

Kenny, D. J. (1982). Confidentiality: The confusion continues. *Journal of Medical Ethics, 8,* 9–11.

Knapp, S. J., & VandeCreek, L. (1982). Tarasoff: Five years later. *Professional Psychology, 13,* 511–516.

Knapp, S. J., & VandeCreek, L. (1985). Psychotherapy and privileged communications in child custody cases. *Professional Psychology: Research and Practice, 16,* 398–407.

Knapp, S., & VandeCreek, L. (1987). *Privileged communications in the mental health professions.* New York, NY: Van Nostrand Reinhold Company.

Koocher, G. P. (1983). Competence to consent: Psychotherapy. In G. B. Melton, G. P. Koocher, & M. J. Saks (Eds.), *Children's competence to consent* (pp. 111–128). New York, NY: Plenum Press.

Landeros v. Flood, 17 Cal.3d 399, 551 P.2d 389, 131 Cal. Rptr. 69 (1976).

Largey v. Rothman, 540 A.2d 504 (N.J. Sup. Ct. 1988).

Lamb, L. E. (1983). To tell or not to tell: Physician's liability for disclosure of confidential information about a patient. *Cumberland Law Review, 13,* 617–637.

Latham, J. A., Jr. (1975). Liability of psychotherapists for failure to warn of homicide threatened by patient. *Vanderbilt Law Review, 28,* 631–640.

Laurence, M. (1984). Rape victim–crisis counselor communications: An argument for an absolute privilege. *University of California, Davis Law Review, 17,* 1213–1245.

Leedy v. Hartnett, 510 F.Supp. 1125 (1981).

Leonard, J. B. (1977). A therapist's duty to potential victims: A nonthreatening view of Tarasoff. *Law and Human Behavior, 1,* 309–317.

Lindenthal, J. J., & Thomas, C. S. (1982a).

Psychiatrists, the public and confidentiality. *The Journal of Nervous and Mental Disease, 170,* 319–323.

Lindenthal, J. J., & Thomas, C. S. (1982b). Consumers, clinicians, and confidentiality. *Social Science and Medicine, 16,* 333–335.

Lipari v. Sears, Roebuck & Co., 497 F.Supp. 185 (D.C. Neb. 1980).

Lipsey v. State, 170 Ga. App. 770, 318 S.E.2d 184 (1984).

Lora v. Board of Education of the City of New York, 74 F.R.D. 565 (1977).

Madden, J. M. (1982). Patient access to medical records in Washington. *Washington Law Review, 57,* 697–713.

Matter of Estate of Votteler, 327 N.W.2d 759 (Iowa, 1982).

Matter of J. C. G., 144 N.J. Super. 579; 366 A.2d 733 (1976).

Matter of M. C., 391 N.W.2d 674 (S.D. 1986).

Mavroudis v. Superior Court, 102 Ca. App.3d 594, 162 Cal. Rptr. 724 (1980).

Mazura, A. C. (1977). Physicians liability for failure to diagnose and report child abuse. *Wayne Law Review, 23,* 1187–1201.

McGuire, J. M., Graves, S., & Blau, B. (1985). Depth of self-disclosure as a function of assured confidentiality and video tape recording. *Journal of Counseling and Development, 64,* 259–263.

McGuire, J. M., Toal, P. & Blau, B. (1985). The adult client's conception of confidentiality in the therapeutic relationship. *Professional Psychology: Research and Practice, 16,* 375–384.

McIntosh v. Milano, 168 N.J. Super 466, 403 A.2d 500 (1979).

McKirdy v. Superior Court, 138 Cal. App. 3d 12, 188 Cal. Rptr. 143 (1982).

Merton, V. (1982). Confidentiality and the "dangerous" patient: Implications of *Tarasoff* for psychiatrists and lawyers. *Emery Law Journal, 31,* 261–343.

Monahan, J. (1981). *The clinical prediction of violent behavior.* Rockville, MD: National Institute of Mental Health.

Morey v. Peppin, 353 N.W.2d 179 (Minn. 1984).

Myers v. State, 251 Ga. 883, 310 S.E.2d 504 (1984).

Muehleman, T., & Kimmons, C. (1981). Psychologist's view on child abuse reporting, confidentiality, life, and the law: An explor-atory study. *Professional Psychology, 12,* 631–638.

Natanson v. Kline, 350 P.2d 1093 (Kan. 1960).

Newman, S. (1981). Privacy in medical information: A diagnosis. *University of Florida Law Review, 33,* 394–424.

Noll, J. O. (1976). The psychotherapist and informed consent. *American Journal of Psychiatry, 133,* 1451–1453.

Nye, S. (1979). Commentary on model law on confidentiality of health and social service records. *American Journal of Psychiatry, 136,* 145–147.

Nye, S. G. (1980). Patient confidentiality and privacy: The federal initiative. *American Journal of Orthopsychiatry, 50,* 649–658.

Oregon v. Miller, 709 P.2d 225 (Or. Sup. Ct. 1985).

Parry, J. (1986). A unified theory of substitute consent: Incompetent patient's right to individualized health care decision-making. *Mental and Physical Disability Law Reporter, 11,* 378–385.

Parry, J. (1987). Psychiatric care and the law of substitute decisionmaking. *Mental and Physical Disability Law Reporter, 11,* 152–159.

Peck v. Counseling Service of Addison County, Inc., 449 A.2d 422 (Vt. 1985).

People v. Blasquez, 165 Cal. App. 3d 408, 211 Cal. Rptr. 335 (1985).

Pesce v. J. Sterling Morton High School, 830 F.2d 789 (1987).

Reynaud v. Superior Court, 138 Cal. App. 3d 1, 187 Cal. Rptr. 660 (1982).

Robinson, W. P. III (1974). Testimonial privilege and the school guidance counselor. *Syracuse Law Review, 25,* 911–952.

Rosen, C. E. (1977). Why clients relinquish their rights to privacy under sign-away pressures. *Professional Psychology, 8,* 17–24.

Roth, L. H., & Meisel, A. (1977). Dangerousness, confidentiality, and the duty to warn. *American Journal of Psychiatry, 134,* 508–511.

Rozovsky, F. A. (1984). *Consent to treatment: A practical guide.* Boston: Little, Brown and Company.

Scarmeas, C. J. (1982). Rape victim-rape crisis counselor communications: A testimonial privilege. *Dickerson Law Review, 86,* 539–564.

Schloendorff v. Society of New York Hospital, 211 N.Y.125, 105 N.E.92 (1914).

Schmid, D., Appelbaum, P. S., Roth, L. H., &

Lidz, C. (1983). Confidentiality in psychiatry: A study of the patient's view. *Hospital and Community Psychiatry, 34,* 353–355.

Schuster v. Attenberg, No. 87-0115, 12 *Mental and Physical Disability Law Reporter* 371 (Wis. Sup. Ct. June 1, 1988).

Seligman, B. X. (1977). Untangling Tarasoff: Tarasoff v. Regents of the University of California. *Hastings Law Journal, 29,* 179–210.

Shah, S. T. (1969). Privileged communications, confidentiality, and privacy: Privileged communications. *Professional Psychology, 1,* 56–59.

Shah, S. T. (1970). Privileged communications, confidentiality, and privacy: Confidentiality. *Professional Psychology, 1,* 159–166.

Shaw v. Glickman, 45 Md. App. 718, 415 A.2d 625 (1980).

Sherlock, R., & Murphy, W. (1984). Confidentiality and therapy: An agency perspective. *Comprehensive Psychiatry, 25,* 88–95.

Shuman, D. W., & Weiner, M. F. (1982). The privilege study: An empirical examination of the psychotherapist–patient privilege. *North Carolina Law Review, 60,* 893–942.

Shwed, H. J., Kuvin, S. F., & Baliga, R. K. (1979). Medical audit: Crises in confidentiality and the patient-psychiatrist relationship. *American Journal of Psychiatry, 136,* 447–450.

Siegal, M. (1979). Privacy, ethics, and confidentiality. *Professional Psychology, 10,* 249–258.

Simon, R. I. (1987). *Clinical psychiatry and the law.* Washington, DC: American Psychiatric Press.

Sims v. Georgia, 251 Ga. 877, 311 S.E.2d 161 (1984).

Sloan, J. B., & Klein, S. B. (1977). Psychotherapeutic disclosures: A conflict between right and duty. *University of Toledo Law Review, 9,* 57–72.

Slovenko, R. (1977). Group psychotherapy: Privileged communications and confidentiality. *Journal of Psychiatry and Law, 5,* 405–466.

Smith, S. R., & Meyer, R. G. (1984). Child abuse reporting laws and psychotherapy: A time for reconsideration. *International Journal of Law & Psychiatry, 7,* 351–366.

State v. Tsavaris, 382 So.2d 56 (Fla. App. 1980), 394 So.2d 418 (Fla. 1981).

State of N.J. in interest of D.G., 174 N.J. Super 243, 416 A.2d 77 (1980).

Stone, A. A. (1976). The Tarasoff decision: Suing psychotherapists to safeguard society. *Harvard Law Review, 90,* 358–378.

Stouder, B. (1982). Criminal law and procedure (evidence)—Pennsylvania establishes new privilege for communications made to a rape crisis center counselor—*In re Pittsburgh Action Against Rape,* 494 Pa. 15, 428 A.2d 126 (1981). *Temple Law Quarterly, 55,* 1124–1148.

Stroube, M. K. (1979). The psychotherapist-patient privilege: Are some patients more privileged than others? *Pacific Law Journal, 10,* 801–824.

Suarez, J. M., & Balcanoff, E. J. (1966). Massachusetts psychiatry and privileged communications. *Archives of General Psychiatry, 15,* 619–623.

Swoboda, J. W., Elwork, A., Sales, B. D., & Levine, D. (1978). Knowledge of and compliance with privileged communications and child-abuse-reporting laws. *Professional Psychology, 9,* 448–457.

Tarasoff v. Board of Regents, 13 Cal.3d 177, 529 P.2d 553, 118 Cal. Rptr. 129 (1974). Vac. 17 Cal.3d 425, 551 P.2d 334, 131 Cal. Rptr. 14 (1976).

Thompson v. County of Alameda, 37 Cal.3d 741, 167 Cal. Rptr. 70, 614 P.2d 728 (1980).

Thurman, R. F. (1984). Incest and ethics: Confidentiality's severest test. *Denver Law Journal, 61,* 619–653.

Trempor, C. (1988). Protection of minors' confidentiality in psychotherapy. In D. Weisstub (Ed.), *Law and mental health: International perspectives.* Elmsford, NY: Pergamon Press.

Turner, J. F., & Thomason, J. W. (1970). Physician-patient confidences: Legal effects of computerization of records. *Alabama Lawyer, 31,* 193–202.

United States v. Blackburn, 446 F.2d 1089 (5th Cir. 1971).

Vickery, A. B. (1982). Breach of confidence: An emerging tort. *Columbia Law Review, 82,* 1426–1468.

Wadlington, W. J. (1983). Consent to medical care for minors: The legal framework. In G. B. Melton, G. P. Koocher, & M. J. Saks (Eds.), *Children's competence to consent* (pp. 57–74). New York: Plenum Press.

Weinappel, M., & Perr, I. N. (1981). The right of a minor to confidentiality: An aftermath of Bartley v. Kremens. *Bulletin of the American Academy of Psychiatry and Law, 9,* 247–254.

Weisberg, R., & Wald, M. (1984). Confidentiality laws and state efforts to protect abused or neglected children: The need for statutory reform. *Family Law Quarterly, 18,* 143–212.

Wexler, D. B. (1979). Patients, therapists and third parties: The victimological virtues of *Tarasoff. International Journal of Law and Psychiatry, 2,* 1–28.

Wexler, D. B. (1981). *Mental health law: Major issues.* New York: Plenum Press.

Williamson, K. E. (1984). Confidentiality of sexual assault victim—counselor communication: A proposed model statute. *Arizona Law Review, 26,* 416–488.

Wilson v. Lehman, 379 S.W.2d 478 (Ky. 1964).

Winslade, W. J. (1982). Confidentiality of medical records: An overview of concepts and legal policies. *The Journal of Legal Medicine, 3,* 497–533.

Wise, T. P. (1978). Where the public peril begins: A survey of psychotherapists to determine the effects of *Tarasoff. Stanford Law Review, 31,* 165–190.

Zurcher v. Stanford Daily, 436 U.S. 547 (1978).

AUTHOR INDEX

SUBJECT INDEX

ABOUT THE EDITORS
AND CONTRIBUTORS

ABOUT THE EDITORS

Thomas R. Kratochwill (PhD, University of Wisconsin, 1973) is Professor of Educational Psychology and Director of the School Psychology Program and Psychoeducational Clinic at the University of Wisconsin—Madison. He has authored and edited several books including *Single-Subject Research: Strategies for Evaluating Change, Selective Mutism: Implications for Research and Treatment,* and *Treating Children's Fears and Phobias: A Behavioral Approach* (with Richard J. Morris); he also edits the *Advances in School Psychology,* an annual series. Dr. Kratochwill has published numerous journal articles and book chapters on behavior therapy in assessment and research methodology. In 1977 he received the Lightner Witmer Award from Division 16 of the American Psychological Association. He has served as Associate Editor for *Behavior Therapy, The Journal of Applied Behavior Analysis,* and *School Psychology Review.* In addition to being on numerous editorial boards, he has edited the American Psychological Association Division 16

journal, *Professional School Psychology,* now *School Psychology Quarterly.* He has also been a practitioner in several applied settings and a consultant to numerous schools and other applied clinical treatment settings.

Richard J. Morris (PhD, Arizona State University, 1970) is Professor of Educational Psychology and Director of the School Psychology Program, College of Education, The University of Arizona. Previous to this position he was Professor of Special Education, The University of Arizona; Assistant to Associate Professor of Psychology, Clinical Psychology Training Program, Syracuse University; and Clinical Assistant Professor of Pediatrics, Upstate Medical Center, State University of New York at Syracuse. He has authored and edited several books, including *Behavior Modification With Children: A Systematic Guide, Perspectives in Abnormal Behavior,* and *Behavior Modification With Exceptional Children: Principles and Practices,* has coauthored with Thomas R. Kratochwill *Treating Children's Fears and Phobias: A Behavioral Approach,* and has coedited with Burton Blatt *Perspectives in Special Education* and *Special Education: Research and Trends*. He has published numerous journal articles and book chapters on children's behavior disorders and on behavior therapy. He is a member of several professional associations, a Fellow of the American Psychological Association, and serves on the editorial boards of a number of professional journals. He has been President of the Division of Rehabilitation Psychology of the American Psychological Association and has been a consultant to a number of publishing companies, child mental health and developmental disabilities treatment facilities, and schools.

ABOUT THE CONTRIBUTORS

Russell A. Barkley, PhD, is Professor of Psychiatry and Neurology and Director of Psychology at the University of Massachusetts Medical Center in Worcester. He received his PhD in clinical psychology from Bowling Green State University. Dr. Barkley is a diplomate both in clinical psychology and in clinical neuropsychology. He has authored three books, 20 book chapters, and over 50 scientific papers on attention-deficit hyperactivity disorder, parent training, and child neuropsychology. He also serves on the editorial boards of several scientific journals.

Jeffrey Braden received his PhD from the University of California, Berkeley in 1985. Currently he is Assistant Professor of Psychology and coordinates the School Psychology Program at San Jose State University.

Marjorie H. Charlop received her BA from UCLA and her PhD from Claremont Graduate School in 1981. She is presently Associate Professor in the Psychology Department at Claremont McKenna College and Director of the Claremont Center for the Study of Autism. Her research interests in behavior modification with autistic children focus on speech and language, echolalia, aberrant behaviors, generalization, and social skills.

David A. Coe is a fourth year doctoral student in clinical psychology at Louisiana State University. His research interests include mental retardation, autism, sensory impairments, and schizophrenia.

Mark B. DeKraai, JD, is a planner and policy analyst for the Nebraska Department of Public Institutions, where he specializes in children's mental health, mental health law, and mental retardation policy development. He is a graduate of the University of Nebraska College of Law where he is currently pursuing a PhD in psychology. His primary area of academic interest is the impact of litigation on human services systems.

George J. DuPaul, PhD is Assistant Professor of Psychiatry at the University of Massachusetts Medical Center in Worcester. He received his PhD in school psychology from the University of Rhode Island in 1985. His research interests are in the assessment and treatment of attention-deficit hyperactivity disorder and related behavioral difficulties.

Kenneth D. Gadow received his PhD in special education from the University of Illinois in 1978. He is currently Professor of Special Education and Affiliate Professor of Child Psychiatry, State University of New York at Stony Brook. He is the author of *Children On Medication* (Vols. 1 & 2), numerous journal articles, and is the editor of the research annual, *Advances in Learning and Behavioral Disabilities*. His research interests are in pediatric psychopharmacology, hyperactivity, childhood aggression, and television violence.

David C. Guevremont, PhD, is Assistant Professor of Psychiatry at the University of Massachusetts Medical Center in Worcester. He received his PhD in clinical child psychology at West Virginia University in 1987. His clinical and research interests are in the areas of applied behavior analysis, hyperactivity, and behavior disorders in children.

Daniel P. Hallahan received his BA in psychology from the University of Michigan in 1967 and his PhD in education and psychology from the same institution in 1971. He is Professor of Education at the University of Virginia and editor of *Exceptionality*. His research interests include attentional problems of and interventions for children with learning disabilities.

A. Dirk Hightower received his PhD from the University of Tennessee at Knoxville in 1982. He is presently Senior Research Associate and

Associate Professor at the University of Rochester and the CoDirector of the Primary Mental Health Project. His interests include social emotional assessment and primary and secondary prevention programs in mental health.

Nadine J. Kaslow received her PhD in clinical psychology from the University of Houston in 1983. Currently she is Associate Professor in Psychiatry and Psychology, and Chief Psychologist at Emory University, Atlanta, Georgia. Her research and clinical interests include depression and suicide in children and their families, eating disorders, and family therapy.

James M. Kauffman has been a teacher of nonhandicapped students and students with behavioral disorders. He received his EdD degree in special education from the University of Kansas in 1969. He is Professor of Education at the University of Virginia, where he has served as Chair of the Department of Special Education and Associate Dean for Research. He is President Elect (1989–1990) and President (1990–1991) of the Council for Children with Behavioral Disorders.

Alan E. Kazdin received his PhD in psychology from Northwestern University in 1970. Currently, he is Professor of Psychology and Child Psychiatry at Yale University and Director of the Child Conduct Clinic, an outpatient treatment service for antisocial children.

Clayton E. Keller taught students with behavior disorders for 8 years prior to his doctoral work at the University of Virginia. Since completing his PhD in 1988, he has been Assistant Professor of Special Education at the University of Minnesota, Duluth. His research interests include learning disabilities in mathematics, effective instruction for mainstreamed special education students, and teachers with disabilities.

Patricia F. Kurtz has a master's degree in psychology. Currently she is a PhD candidate at Claremont Graduate School. Her research interests in the area of behavioral treatment for autistic children focus on functional uses of aberrant behaviors.

John Wills Lloyd is Associate Professor in the Department of Curriculum, Instruction, and Special Education at the University of Virginia. Lloyd completed his graduate degrees at the University of Oregon, earning a PhD in 1976. He taught and conducted research at Northern Illinois University from 1976 to 1978 and joined the faculty at Virginia in 1978.

Johnny L. Matson received his PhD in psychology from Indiana State University and completed an APA-approved internship in clinical psychology at Central Louisiana State Hospital. He has held the positions of Assistant Professor of Child Psychiatry and Clinical Psychology at the University of Pittsburgh, and Professor in the Department of Learning, Development and Special Education at Northern Illinois University. He is currently Professor and Director of Clinical Training in the Department of Psychology at Louisiana State University. He is the founder and Editor-in-Chief of the journal, *Research in Developmental Disabilities,* and is the author of over 270 journal articles and 20 books.

Jesse B. Milby, PhD, is Professor of Psychiatry and Psychology at the University of Alabama at Birmingham and Chief of the Psychology Service at the Birmingham VA Medical Center. He is Adjunct Professor of Psychology at the University of Alabama, Tuscaloosa, where he received his PhD in clinical psychology in 1968. His research has been on behavior therapy approaches to anxiety mediation, including obsessive compulsive disorders and addictive behavior. He is the author of numerous scientific papers in that area.

John C. Pomeroy received his medical degree from the University of London in 1973. He is currently Assistant Professor of Child Psychiatry and Director of the Child Psychiatry Outpatient Service, State University of New York at Stony Brook. The topics of his research publications include, childhood psychosis, pervasive developmental disorders, and the mental health problems of mentally retarded individuals.

Lynn P. Rehm, PhD, received his doctorate in 1970 from the University of Wisconsin—Madison. He is Professor of Psychology at the University of Houston and is Editor of *Behavior Therapy for Depression: Present Status and Future Directions.*

Bruce Sales, JD, PhD, is Professor of Psychology, Sociology, and Law, and Director of the Law-Psychology and Policy Program at The University of Arizona. He founded the Law-Psychology Program at the University of Nebraska prior to going to Arizona, and was Founding Editor of the journal, *Law and Human Behavior*. His research focuses on mental health policy, and on other questions in the law and social science interface.

Laura Schreibman received her PhD in 1972 from the University of California, Los Angeles. She is currently Professor of Psychology at the University of California, San Diego, where she is Director of the autism research program. Her research interests include the experimental analysis of childhood autism, parent training, generalization of behavioral treatment effects, stimulus control, and deviant language. She has served on the editorial boards of several journals and as Associate Editor for the *Journal of Applied Behavior Analysis*. She is also the author of *Autism*.

Lawrence J. Siegel, PhD, is currently Professor in the Ferkauf Graduate School of Psychology at Yeshiva University. Previously he was Director of the Division of Pediatric Psychology at the University of Texas Medical Branch at Galveston and a member of the clinical psychology faculty at the University of Florida and at the University of Missouri—Columbia. He received his PhD from Case Western Reserve University in 1975. Dr. Siegel is President of the Society of Pediatric Psychology (Section 5, Division 12) of the American Psychological Association. He is coauthor of *Behavioral Medicine: Practical Applications in Health Care* and *Approaches to Child Treatment: Introduction to Theory, Research, and Practice*.

Karen E. Smith received her PhD from the University of Alabama at Birmingham in 1987. Currently she is Assistant Professor of Pediatrics at the University of Texas Medical Branch, Galveston. Her clinical and research interests include child and family adjustment to chronic medical conditions.

Anna Weber is a PhD student in medical clinical psychology at the University of Alabama at Birmingham and a collaborator with Dr. Milby in research on obsessive compulsive disorders.

Thomas A. Wood is Associate Professor in the Department of Rehabilitation and Special Education at Auburn University. He is director of the program in mental retardation. Dr. Wood received his EdD at Peabody College of Vanderbilt University in 1978.

Pergamon General Psychology Series

Editors: **Arnold P. Goldstein,** Syracuse University
Leonard Krasner, Stanford University &
SUNY at Stony Brook

*Out of print in original format. Available in custom reprint edition.